LIVING LITURGY™

LIVING LITURGY™

SPIRITUALITY, CELEBRATION, AND CATECHESIS FOR SUNDAYS AND SOLEMNITIES

Year C • 2016

Joyce Ann Zimmerman, C.PP.S.
Kathleen Harmon, S.N.D. de N.
Rev. John W. Tonkin

LITURGICAL PRESS
Collegeville, Minnesota

www.litpress.org

Design by Ann Blattner. Art by Br. Martin Erspamer, OSB, a monk of Saint Meinrad Archabbey, Indiana.

ISSN 1547-089X

ISBN 978-0-8146-4974-9

CONTENTS

CONTRIBUTORS

Joyce Ann Zimmerman, C.PP.S., is the director of the Institute for Liturgical Ministry in Dayton, Ohio, and is an adjunct professor of liturgy, a liturgical consultant, and a frequent facilitator of workshops. She has published numerous scholarly and pastoral liturgical works. She holds civil and pontifical doctorates of theology.

Kathleen Harmon, S.N.D. de N., is the music director for programs of the Institute for Liturgical Ministry in Dayton, Ohio, and is the author of numerous publications. An educator and musician, she facilitates liturgical music workshops and cantor formation programs. She holds a graduate degree in music and a doctorate in liturgy.

John W. Tonkin is a priest of the Archdiocese of Cincinnati who was ordained in 2005. He is the pastor of Sacred Heart Parish in McCartyville, Ohio, has served on a number of archdiocesan and other boards and committees, and is a member of his local ministerial league. He has pursued graduate studies in Sacred Scripture.

USING THIS RESOURCE

Many a parent, on a long drive to visit family members, has heard little ones ask over and over again, "Are we there yet?" Maybe the being "there" is about the delight of seeing Nana and Papa or cousins with whom they can spend many happy play hours. Maybe the being "there" is simply about relief from being cooped up in the car. Maybe the being "there" is freedom from limited freeway scenery. Whatever the reason, once "there," the little ones burst forth with abandon and joy.

Each Sunday Mass raises for us the question, "Are we there yet?" As we gather for this most important time of the week for us, the "there" is not a matter of arriving, but of reaching. We reach for the God who forgives, loves, teaches, sustains, nourishes. We reach for an eschatological "there" where we meet the risen Christ in all his glory. We reach for the kind of transformation that shapes us into Body-of-Christ-travelers who know our destiny (eternal Life) and how to get there (Gospel living). The importance of the destiny urges us to prepare well for these few moments out of every week that help us reach for an eternity of joy.

During Ordinary Time of the 2016 liturgical year, we read from Luke's gospel where prominent themes include God's mercy and forgiveness, prayer, and concern for the poor. These themes are played out on a long trip by Jesus and his disciples: the journey to Jerusalem. Each day this year, then, we might ask, "Are we there yet?" and use the question to assess how we journey. Do we ponder and pray the gospels in order to learn better how to be faithful followers of Jesus? Do we reach with all our being for the amazing joy that is offered us through our baptism, sharing in Christ's risen Life? Do we raise grateful hearts to the God who calls us to an everlasting, heavenly journey of unequaled grace, of being enveloped in the God of mercy and forgiveness, love and joy, compassion and peace?

This seventeenth volume of *Living Liturgy*™ continues the original purpose: to help people prepare for liturgy and live a liturgical spirituality (that is, a way of living that is rooted in liturgy), opening their vision to their baptismal identity as the Body of Christ and shaping their living according to the rhythm of paschal mystery dying and rising. The paschal mystery is the central focus of liturgy, of the gospels, and of this volume. Paschal mystery is the core of our baptismal/liturgical journey.

A threefold dynamic of daily living, prayer, and study continues to determine the basic structure of *Living Liturgy*™, captured in the layout under the headings "Spirituality," "Celebration," and "Catechesis." This threefold dynamic is lived by the three authors; this is why each year the new volume is fresh with new material. The titles and subtitles don't change, but the content does.

The music suggestions made in *Living Liturgy*™ are not intended to be an exhaustive list of suggestions for every Sunday (these are readily available in other publications), but to offer a model and accompanying catechesis for making good liturgical and pastoral choices. The musical suggestions in this current volume were drawn from resources updated to accord with the changes in Mass texts implemented in November of 2011 (yes, that long ago already!) and in print at the time this volume was being prepared. This necessarily limits the number of resources cited, but the model for making musical choices presumes those responsible for music ministry will draw from whatever wider spectrum of resources they have on hand.

ARE WE THERE YET?

MASS IS A TIME TO REACH FOR "THERE"

WHAT AWAITS US IS AMAZING

PASCHAL MYSTERY STILL CENTRAL FOCUS

SPIRITUALITY, CELEBRATION, AND CATECHESIS

A NOTE ABOUT MUSIC SUGGESTIONS

✝ INTRODUCTION to the Gospel of Luke

Luke, who lived in Antioch, wrote his gospel for a Gentile community somewhere between 80 and 85 AD. The people for whom he wrote never saw Jesus and probably never even knew anyone who did. Consequently, a problem facing the community was maintaining faithful continuity with the teaching and spirit of Jesus. Luke's response to this problem was the postresurrection story on the road to Emmaus, where the two disciples realized that they had experienced the Presence of Jesus after they heard him explain what the Scriptures said and recognized him in the breaking of the bread.

The gospel begins in Galilee, from where Jesus sets about preaching and then "sets his face" toward Jerusalem, where he will meet suffering and death; the gospel, then, is structured around this resolute journey to Jerusalem. The Acts of the Apostles (considered to be the second part of Luke's gospel) picks up in Jerusalem after Jesus' death and tells of his ascension to heaven and the coming of the Spirit upon the disciples. Filled with this Spirit of the risen Jesus, the disciples go out to preach and live the Good News. Whereas Jesus began his preaching in Galilee and was crucified in Jerusalem, the disciples—filled with the Spirit of Jesus—began their preaching and healing in Jerusalem and went forth from there to the four corners of the world to preach the Good News. Moreover, the preaching of the Good News does not die with the martyrdom of great apostles like Peter and Paul (highlighted in Acts), but is taken up through the ages all over the world. Now, in our own day, we are also called to continue the preaching of the Good News by the way we live as followers of Jesus, filled with this same Spirit.

Jesus being born in a stable and placed in a manger, the shepherds who visited him, the elderly Simeon and Anna who recognized him in the temple, the Good Samaritan, the Prodigal Son, the Widow of Nain: these narratives, unique to the Gospel of Luke, are among the best known and loved stories in the whole New Testament. Because the poor, outcasts, and sinners figure so prominently in Luke, this third gospel is often referred to as the "gospel of mercy." A few more examples illustrate this further. Whereas in Matthew's gospel Jesus calls us to "be perfect, just as your heavenly Father is perfect" (Matt 5:48), Luke replaces "perfect" with "merciful" (Luke 6:36). Luke 15 contains three familiar parables of mercy (the Lost Sheep, Lost Coin, and Prodigal Son; the last two are unique to Luke) that reveal God to be the One who deeply cares for and seeks out the lost. Likewise, this gospel is also called the "gospel of prayer" because Luke shows Jesus often going off by himself to pray. It is also called the "gospel of women" because of the prominent role of women in it.

Together, all these themes highlight Luke's message: salvation is for all, God cares for the poor, God's care and mercy is wonderfully shown through the life and ministry of Jesus. Luke's gospel invites us on Jesus' paschal journey through death to new Life. Thus this gospel invites us to deepen our own prayer life so that our discipleship truly continues Jesus' saving ministry.

ABBREVIATIONS

LITURGICAL RESOURCES

BofB   *Book of Blessings.* International Commission on English in the Liturgy. Collegeville: Liturgical Press, 1989.

BLS   *Built of Living Stones: Art, Architecture, and Worship.* Guidelines of the National Conference of Catholic Bishops, 2000.

CCC   *Catechism of the Catholic Church.* Washington DC: USCCB, 2004.

GIRM   *General Instruction of the Roman Missal* (2002/2011).

GNLYC General Norms for the Liturgical Year and the Calendar (1969).

ILM   Introduction to the *Lectionary for Mass* (1981).

SC   *Sacrosanctum Concilium.* (The Constitution on the Sacred Liturgy; 1963).

ST   *Sing to the Lord: Music in Divine Worship.* Washington DC: USCCB, 2007.

MUSICAL RESOURCES

BB   *Breaking Bread.* Portland, OR: Oregon Catholic Press, annual.

G3   *Gather,* Third Edition. Chicago: GIA Publications, Inc., 2011.

HG   *Hymns for the Gospels.* Chicago: GIA Publications, Inc., 2001.

JS3   *Journeysongs,* Third Edition. Portland, OR: Oregon Catholic Press, 2012.

LMGM2 *Lead Me, Guide Me,* Second Edition. Chicago: GIA Publications, Inc., 2012.

OF   *One in Faith.* Schiller Park, IL: World Library Publications, 2014.

SS   *Sacred Song.* Collegeville: Liturgical Press, 2011.

W4   *Worship,* Fourth Edition. Chicago: GIA Publications, Inc., 2011.

WC   *We Celebrate.* Schiller Park, IL: World Library Publications, 2014.

WS   *Word and Song.* Schiller Park, IL: World Library Publications, annual.

GIA   GIA Publications, Inc.

OCP   Oregon Catholic Press

WLP   World Library Publications

NOTE: The music suggestions made in *Living Liturgy*™ are not intended to be an exhaustive list of suggestions for every Sunday (these are readily available in other publications), but to offer a model and accompanying catechesis for making fruitful liturgical and pastoral choices. This necessarily limits the number of suggestions made, but the model for making musical choices presumes those responsible for music ministry will draw from whatever wider spectrum of resources they have on hand.

SEASON OF ADVENT

SPIRITUALITY

GOSPEL ACCLAMATION
Ps 85:8

R̸. Alleluia, alleluia.
Show us, Lord, your love;
and grant us your salvation.
R̸. Alleluia, alleluia.

Gospel

Luke 21:25-28, 34-36; L3C

**Jesus said to his disciples:
"There will be signs in the sun, the
     moon, and the stars,
   and on earth nations will be in
     dismay,
   perplexed by the roaring of the
     sea and the waves.
People will die of fright
   in anticipation of what is coming
     upon the world,
   for the powers of the heavens
     will be shaken.
And then they will see the Son
     of Man
   coming in a cloud with power and
     great glory.
But when these signs begin to happen,
   stand erect and raise your heads
   because your redemption is at hand.**

**"Beware that your hearts do not
     become drowsy
   from carousing and drunkenness
   and the anxieties of daily life,
   and that day catch you by surprise
     like a trap.
For that day will assault everyone
   who lives on the face of the earth.
Be vigilant at all times
   and pray that you have the strength
   to escape the tribulations that are
     imminent
   and to stand before the Son of Man."**

Reflecting on the Gospel

One of the largest sections in bookstores features romance novels. Go to any e-book website and romance novels are a prominent category. Romance is a frequent theme of movies. Romance is all around us. And why not? Love is a beautiful thing! We human beings can hardly be emotionally and spiritually healthy without it. But with what kind of love do the various media bombard us? All too often, it is a very selfish love, a love that satisfies one person at the expense of others. Selfishness is diametrically opposed to what love is. Selfishness is diametrically opposed to what holiness is. At first glance the gospel for this Sunday does not seem to be about love—or about holiness. Yet, underneath Jesus' prediction of events at the end of time, he is telling us a special story—a love story.

At first reading, it seems as though the gospel is only about tribulations and calamities and fear. Yes, right now, today, tribulations, wars, natural calamities are upon us. We can cringe in fear or "stand erect" in hope. Jesus tells us not to fear what calamities might do to us, but to be "vigilant" for his coming. He comes with redemption not only in glory at the end of time, but right now, today. And here is where the love story is endlessly told—in Jesus' abiding Presence to us. We are redeemed—renewed and made whole in our relationship with God—by God's altogether new act on behalf of humankind: our "redemption is at hand." We are vigilant for Christ's coming not because of fear of the calamities that might assail us, but because our "redemption is at hand." God's love story narrated to us through the divine Son Jesus Christ is not about the kind of love we might read in romance novels, but is a holy love emanating from God's very being. Holy love is the opposite of selfish love. Holy love is possible when there is a right relationship between God and us, measured by our right relationship with each other. Holy love is the caring exchange between Person and person whose regard for the other is at the very center of the relationship. We are redeemed by God's holy love. We are "blameless in holiness" (second reading) when we love as God loves us.

One sign of the Son of Man's redeeming Presence is that we are growing in love. Despite appearances to the contrary (disaster and destruction generated both by natural forces and human choices), God's plan and purpose are directed toward redemption and life. We need to read the right signs—new life in the midst of seeming destruction, the glory of the Son of Man coming into the darkness, the love of Christ growing in our hearts. We need to be attentive to holy love. The vigilance to which Jesus calls is possible when we embrace his Presence with holy love.

Living the Paschal Mystery

Vigilance for the many ways Christ is present to us involves self-emptying for the sake of the other. This means that our focus is not on our own wants and needs, but on the Christ who chooses to be intimately present to us. It means that we are able to see the Christ who dwells in the other. Holy love is the giving of self that brings us to "stand erect." We stand tall and confident because we know that we are choosing to be in right relationship with others. We stand tall because Christ is present to help us grow in the holy love he came to reveal. We stand tall because we know our "redemption is at hand." Love abounds! It is a beautiful thing!

Focusing the Gospel

Key words and phrases: will be signs, dismay, fright, Son of Man coming, stand erect, redemption, vigilant

To the point: Right now, today, tribulations, wars, natural calamities are upon us. We can cringe in fear or "stand erect" in hope. Jesus tells us not to fear what calamities might do to us, but to be "vigilant" for his coming. He comes with redemption not only in glory at the end of time, but right now, today.

Connecting the Gospel

to the second reading: Jesus Christ comes right now, today, to make us "increase and abound in love" so that we may become "blameless in holiness." This holy love is *the* sign of our redemption.

to experience: It's easier to get caught up in signs of cosmic destruction and earthly disasters than it is to recognize our own growth in holiness as *the* sign of redemption, of Christ's loving Presence among us even now.

Connecting the Responsorial Psalm

to the readings: In these verses from Psalm 25 we beg God to teach us the way we should go. The word "way" refers not only to a path one is walking, but also to a habitual manner of acting. We pray in this psalm, then, to walk in the direction God is pointing by living and acting as God does. This means doing what is "right and just" (first reading), conducting ourselves as Christ has instructed (second reading), and staying vigilant for Christ's coming (gospel). As we walk this way, we know God will guide our steps and surround us with "friendship" (psalm). On this first Sunday of a new liturgical year, we "stand erect" (gospel), lifting our souls to the God who is leading us in love to the fullness of Life.

to psalmist preparation: In this psalm you ask God to teach you a way that is far more than a set of rules. You ask to be formed in "ways" of goodness, uprightness, constancy, and fidelity. In other words, you ask that your behavior become like God's. How might this prayer deepen your humility? How might it shape your living of Advent?

ASSEMBLY & FAITH-SHARING GROUPS
- I cringe in fear when . . . What helps me "stand erect" in hope is . . .
- The tribulations of my daily living are . . . These keep me from . . .
- What helps me love as Christ loves and grow in holiness is . . .

PRESIDERS
I am a sign for my parish of Christ's love when I . . .

DEACONS
My ministry of service is a sign of Christ's Presence and love when I . . .

HOSPITALITY MINISTERS
My greeting calls those gathering for liturgy to renewed hope when I . . .

MUSIC MINISTERS
The tribulations of music ministry are . . . I "stand erect" in face of them when . . .

ALTAR MINISTERS
My vigilant service at the altar reflects my growing in . . .

LECTORS
What I hope for as I prepare to proclaim the word is . . .

EXTRAORDINARY MINISTERS OF HOLY COMMUNION
My manner of distributing Holy Communion is a sign of vigilant openness to Christ's many comings when . . .

CELEBRATION

Model Penitential Act

Presider: On this First Sunday of Advent, we turn our hearts to the Christ who will come in glory, and who is present among us now. Let us meet this Christ with vigilant hearts as we seek mercy and forgiveness . . . [pause]

 Lord Jesus, you are the Son of Man who comes in great power and glory: Lord . . .

 Christ Jesus, you are the promise of our redemption and our peace: Christ . . .

 Lord Jesus, you are the love that strengthens our hearts: Lord . . .

Homily Points

• With Christmas coming, children tend to be very vigilant about their good behavior. If we live in a crime-ridden neighborhood, we are vigilant about our personal safety all the time. A diabetic is constantly vigilant about sugar levels. If we are so vigilant in these everyday situations, then how vigilant are we about Christ's comings?

• To "stand erect" in hope means that we are constantly vigilant for Christ's comings, both in future time and in the present moment. How do we make this vigilance real and concrete?

• We are vigilant for Christ's comings when we choose to grow in the holiness to which we are called. We do this, for example, by engaging in works of mercy, remaining faithful to personal prayer, maintaining hope in face of life's inevitable challenges. In other words, we are vigilant when we respond to Christ's Presence, when we "stand erect" to meet Christ right now, today.

Model Universal Prayer (Prayer of the Faithful)

Presider: Our loving God is ever present to us and vigilant for our needs. And so we make known these needs.

Response:

Cantor:

That all members of the church faithfully witness in their lives that Christ is already present among us . . . [pause]

That all peoples of the world open themselves to the redemption that God offers . . . [pause]

That the hopeless find hope, the frightened find courage, the anxious find peace . . . [pause]

That each of us here grow in discerning the signs of redeeming love within and among us . . . [pause]

Presider: O God, you sent your only-begotten Son to save us. Hear these our prayers of need that we might remain vigilant to meet him when he comes, who lives and reigns forever and ever. **Amen.**

COLLECT
Let us pray.

Pause for silent prayer

Grant your faithful, we pray, almighty God,
the resolve to run forth to meet your Christ
with righteous deeds at his coming,
so that, gathered at his right hand,
they may be worthy to possess the
 heavenly Kingdom.
Through our Lord Jesus Christ, your Son,
who lives and reigns with you in the unity
 of the Holy Spirit,
one God, for ever and ever. **Amen.**

FIRST READING
Jer 33:14-16

The days are coming, says the LORD,
 when I will fulfill the promise
 I made to the house of Israel and Judah.
In those days, in that time,
 I will raise up for David a just shoot;
 he shall do what is right and just in the
 land.
In those days Judah shall be safe
 and Jerusalem shall dwell secure;
 this is what they shall call her:
 "The LORD our justice."

RESPONSORIAL PSALM

Ps 25:4-5, 8-9, 10, 14

R̊. (1b) To you, O Lord, I lift my soul.

Your ways, O Lord, make known to me;
   teach me your paths,
guide me in your truth and teach me,
   for you are God my savior,
   and for you I wait all the day.

R̊. To you, O Lord, I lift my soul.

Good and upright is the Lord;
   thus he shows sinners the way.
He guides the humble to justice,
   and teaches the humble his way.

R̊. To you, O Lord, I lift my soul.

All the paths of the Lord are kindness and
     constancy
   toward those who keep his covenant
     and his decrees.
The friendship of the Lord is with those
     who fear him,
   and his covenant, for their instruction.

R̊. To you, O Lord, I lift my soul.

SECOND READING

1 Thess 3:12–4:2

Brothers and sisters:
May the Lord make you increase and
     abound in love
   for one another and for all,
   just as we have for you,
   so as to strengthen your hearts,
   to be blameless in holiness before our
     God and Father
   at the coming of our Lord Jesus with all
     his holy ones. Amen.

Finally, brothers and sisters,
   we earnestly ask and exhort you in the
     Lord Jesus that,
   as you received from us
   how you should conduct yourselves to
     please God
   —and as you are conducting
     yourselves—
   you do so even more.
For you know what instructions we gave
   you through the Lord Jesus.

About Liturgy

Advent and redemption: The future is in God's hands and God will bring it to fulfillment. What we do know is the outcome (God comes with redemption) and how it is achieved (through intimacy with Christ). Advent is a special liturgical season which begins with looking to the future, comes to a climax in looking to the past, and bears fruit in the present. Advent is a season when we bring to mind and celebrate the three comings of Christ and redemption.

Christ's first coming (which we celebrate on Christmas) *fulfilled* the Old Testament prophecies that God's Messiah would come to restore all things new. Christ's birth as the incarnate Son fulfilled these promises. Jesus' public ministry showed us how God's new reign would come about: by repenting and believing in the Gospel. His death and resurrection assured us that salvation is at hand, but it is only at Christ's Second Coming that God's glory and justice will be *fully* revealed. We find ourselves in an age straddling the first and second comings of Christ, at a time when we need to be *strengthened* now. The third coming of Christ is *right now*, when Christ comes, first and foremost, in sacraments but no less through each other. Our Advent vigilance and waiting does not just look back to the first coming or forward to the Second Coming. The first coming bears fruit and the Second Coming is not frightening to the extent that our vigilance and waiting is in the here and now, recognizing Christ in the many sacramental comings of our everyday lives, exchanging a holy love that makes us whole.

About Liturgical Music

The character of music for Advent: GIRM, no. 313 states: "In Advent the organ and other musical instruments should be used with a moderation that is consistent with the season's character and does not anticipate the full joy of the Nativity of the Lord." In other words, a certain restraint should mark the music we use during this season. This restraint does not have the penitential character of Lent. Instead, its intent is to express a kind of "fasting" before the "feasting" that will enable us to enter more deeply into the waiting of Advent. Songs expressing joy and expectation (as do many of the Advent readings) are certainly appropriate, but the music overall needs to be characterized by a sense of holding back until the time for full celebration arrives.

Seasonal service music for Advent: One of the functions of service music is to help us enter more consciously into the liturgical season we are celebrating. A Mass setting appropriate for Advent draws us into joyful expectation without spilling over into the fuller exuberance of Christmas, and expresses quiet waiting without the penitential somberness of Lent. Since Advent and Christmas form a unified festal season, a Mass setting that can be sung simply during Advent and then embellished with choral and instrumental parts during Christmas makes good liturgical sense.

SPIRITUALITY

GOSPEL ACCLAMATION
Luke 3:4, 6

R̸. Alleluia, alleluia.
Prepare the way of the Lord, make straight his
    paths:
all flesh shall see the salvation of God.
R̸. Alleluia, alleluia.

Gospel

Luke 3:1-6; L6C

**In the fifteenth year of the
    reign of Tiberius Caesar,
when Pontius Pilate was
    governor of Judea,
and Herod was tetrarch of
    Galilee,
and his brother Philip tetrarch
    of the region of Ituraea
    and Trachonitis,
and Lysanias was tetrarch of
    Abilene,
during the high priesthood of Annas
    and Caiaphas,
the word of God came to John the
    son of Zechariah in the desert.
John went throughout the whole region
    of the Jordan,
proclaiming a baptism of repentance
    for the forgiveness of sins,
as it is written in the book of the
    words of the prophet Isaiah:**
*A voice of one crying out in the
    desert:
"Prepare the way of the Lord,
    make straight his paths.
Every valley shall be filled
    and every mountain and hill
        shall be made low.
The winding roads shall be made
    straight,
    and the rough ways made
        smooth,
and all flesh shall see the salvation
    of God."*

Reflecting on the Gospel

Saved by the bell! The firefighter saved the baby from sure death. The relief pitcher saved the game. We hear the word "save" frequently in our everyday chatter, and know immediately what it means: to be rescued from a bad situation, from danger, from an unwanted outcome. This Sunday's gospel doesn't have the word "save," but instead "salvation." What does it mean to "see the salvation of God" that Isaiah the prophet foretold? Here the meaning of "save" is not quite so straightforward. Much more is promised than being rescued. In fact, what the gospel is about is not so much being saved *from* as being saved *by* and *for*.

John quite clearly tells us how we are saved: seek "repentance for the forgiveness of sins." We are to actively level out the mountains and valleys of our own lives. We are to "make straight" our relationship with God and others. We sometimes don't understand nor are aware of the critical importance of repentance and forgiveness in our relationships with each other, and how critical they are for our salvation. Baruch's prophecy of a glorious future was fulfilled when Israel returned from exile (first reading and psalm). Isaiah's prophecy of future glory quoted in the gospel ("all flesh shall see the salvation of God") is fulfilled when we return to God through repentance and forgiveness. "[R]epentance for the forgiveness of sins" is an essential requirement for us to "see the salvation of God." We are saved *by* the actions of God *for* putting on "the splendor of glory from God forever" (first reading).

The salvation of God is progressively revealed in repentance (our work) and forgiveness (God's work). The meandering paths and winding roads of our lives are straightened and the valleys filled and mountains brought low when our lives are characterized by attitudes of repentance. To repent means to change one's mind, one's life; this is how we reach the fullness that is promised and our true home: by increasing our love for one another, discerning "what is of [true] value," and by being "filled with the fruit of righteousness" (see second reading). Our work of repentance is a matter of turning ourselves toward the God who embraces us in mercy and forgiveness and welcomes us home. Our work of repentance is our response to the word-invitation to "see the salvation of God." We are to hear the "word of God" and act on it. Do we? How well?

Living the Paschal Mystery

Let's be honest: it's not just the busyness of Christmas preparations now in full December fury that distract us from our ongoing work of repentance and forgiveness. Every day of the year we tend to be distracted by mountains of work, paths of indecision, valleys of doubt and fear. Like John the Baptist, we are to hear "the word of God" that comes to us, that challenges us to embrace a more Godlike way of living, that not only promises salvation, but shows us the path to it.

Changing our lives to live more faithfully Gospel values is not easy. Nor do we ever get to a point in our daily living when we have arrived at the mountaintop and no longer need to act on God's word, change our minds about what is most important to us, open ourselves to God's forgiveness of our wrongdoing and learn how we in turn forgive others. This is the path to salvation. Not an easy one. But a rewarding one.

Focusing the Gospel

Key words and phrases: word of God, John . . . proclaiming, repentance, forgiveness of sins, make straight, see the salvation of God

To the point: What does it mean to "see the salvation of God" that Isaiah the prophet foretold? John quite clearly tells us: seek "repentance for the forgiveness of sins." We are to actively level out the mountains and valleys of our own lives. We are to "make straight" our relationship with God and others. We are to hear the "word of God" and act on it. Do we? How well?

Connecting the Gospel

to the first reading: Baruch shows us what "the salvation of God" is: a time of glory and righteousness, a time of splendor and peace, a time of holiness and rejoicing, a time of joy and light.

to experience: When we hear the words "repentance" and "forgiveness of sins," we can limit our thinking merely to celebrating the sacrament of penance. John and the gospel, however, call us to repentance and forgiveness as a way of life.

Connecting the Responsorial Psalm

to the readings: When God delivered Israel from their captivity in Babylon, they responded with the creation of Psalm 126. Over time they came to use this psalm as a song of confidence any time they were in danger of destruction. The text moves from memorial of past deliverance (strophes 1 and 2) to petition for new deliverance (strophes 3 and 4). Israel's confidence was based on real historical events, not dreamed imaginings. Of this they were certain: the God who *had* saved them *would* save them again.

This, too, is our confidence as we journey through the season of Advent. We hear of restoration to come (first reading) and of salvation to be completed (second reading). With the Israelites we know our hope is not an empty dream but a realistic vision of what God will accomplish when Christ comes at last. We stand in the desert of Advent, but we dance with hope and joy.

to psalmist preparation: In this responsorial psalm you call the community to the long view of history, telling them to imagine the future by remembering what God has done in the past. You remind them that the God who *has* saved *will* save again. Your singing expresses the messianic hope of the church. Who and what helps keep this hope alive in you? When your hope flags, who and what revives it for you?

**ASSEMBLY &
FAITH-SHARING GROUPS**
- The "word of God" comes to me and . . . As a result, I must . . .
- I need to respond to John's call to "repentance for the forgiveness of sins" in terms of my relationship with . . .
- For me, salvation looks like . . . feels like . . . sounds like . . .

PRESIDERS
I enable my people to "see the salvation of God" by . . . How this affects my ministry is . . .

DEACONS
My service ministry helps others hear the "word of God" and respond by . . .

HOSPITALITY MINISTERS
My manner of greeting those gathering for liturgy helps them "make straight" their way to God when I . . .

MUSIC MINISTERS
When my music making is informed by the "word of God," the assembly . . .

ALTAR MINISTERS
As I consider John's proclamation, the really important Advent preparations in my life are about straightening up and smoothing out . . .

LECTORS
The "word of God came to" me when . . . I am God's word coming to others when I . . .

**EXTRAORDINARY MINISTERS
OF HOLY COMMUNION**
One way the Eucharist reveals the "salvation of God" for me is . . . When I receive Holy Communion I am called to embody this same salvation for others by . . .

Model Penitential Act

Presider: Our lives are constantly filled with the twists and turns and the mountains and valleys of everyday living, challenging us to keep focused on the God who comes to save us. We pause now to recognize God's mercy and forgiveness whenever we lose our way . . . [pause]

Lord Jesus, you are the glory and righteousness of God: Lord . . .

Christ Jesus, you are the salvation of God: Christ . . .

Lord Jesus, you are the mercy and forgiveness of God: Lord . . .

Homily Points

• A moment in time. A cast of characters. A place in history. A voice crying out. A challenge issued. A way of life. A call to "see the salvation of God." Then, in John the Baptist's time. Now, in our time!

• Time unfolds in "age-old" (first reading) ways, in the counting of years (see gospel), in a future not yet come (see second reading)—each the right moment when God acts and we are called to respond. As John the Baptist proclaimed, our call is to "a baptism of repentance for the forgiveness of sins" and our response is to "make straight" our relationship with God and others. The story of our salvation is scripted by divine call and human response.

• Our responses to God's call to salvation are not merely verbal, but must also be expressed in our way of life. We must cross the valley of isolation by offering or accepting forgiveness. We must tear down the mountain of prejudice by opening our hearts to see the dignity of others. We must straighten paths of indifference by recommitting ourselves to engaging in Gospel values. The story of our salvation is scripted by how we respond to God's call. Right now, in our time!

Model Universal Prayer (Prayer of the Faithful)

Presider: Hearing God's call to salvation, we ask God now for the help we need to respond faithfully.

Response:

Lord, hear our prayer.

Cantor:

we pray to the Lord,

That all members of the church announce the salvation of God through actions of forgiveness and mercy . . . [pause]

That all peoples of the world hear the call to repentance and open themselves to the salvation of God . . . [pause]

That the rough ways of those in any need be made smooth by the mercy and compassion of this community . . . [pause]

That each of us here take sufficient time during this busy Advent season to be mindful of what God is asking of us . . . [pause]

Presider: Saving God, you are merciful and forgiving. Hear these our prayers that we might be faithful in responding to your call to salvation and one day dwell with you in everlasting glory. We ask this through Christ our Lord. **Amen.**

COLLECT

Let us pray.

Pause for silent prayer

Almighty and merciful God,
may no earthly undertaking hinder those
who set out in haste to meet your Son,
but may our learning of heavenly wisdom
gain us admittance to his company.
Who lives and reigns with you in the unity
    of the Holy Spirit,
one God, for ever and ever. **Amen.**

FIRST READING
Bar 5:1-9

Jerusalem, take off your robe of mourning
    and misery;
    put on the splendor of glory from God
        forever:
wrapped in the cloak of justice from God,
    bear on your head the mitre
    that displays the glory of the eternal
        name.
For God will show all the earth your
        splendor:
    you will be named by God forever
    the peace of justice, the glory of God's
        worship.

Up, Jerusalem! stand upon the heights;
    look to the east and see your children
gathered from the east and the west
    at the word of the Holy One,
    rejoicing that they are remembered by
        God.
Led away on foot by their enemies they
        left you:
    but God will bring them back to you
    borne aloft in glory as on royal thrones.
For God has commanded
    that every lofty mountain be made low,
and that the age-old depths and gorges
    be filled to level ground,
    that Israel may advance secure in the
        glory of God.
The forests and every fragrant kind of
        tree
    have overshadowed Israel at God's
        command;
for God is leading Israel in joy
    by the light of his glory,
    with his mercy and justice for company.

RESPONSORIAL PSALM

Ps 126:1-2, 2-3, 4-5, 6

℟. (3) The Lord has done great things for us; we are filled with joy.

When the LORD brought back the captives
    of Zion,
  we were like men dreaming.
Then our mouth was filled with laughter,
  and our tongue with rejoicing.

℟. The Lord has done great things for us; we are filled with joy.

Then they said among the nations,
  "The LORD has done great things for
    them."
The LORD has done great things for us;
  we are glad indeed.

℟. The Lord has done great things for us; we are filled with joy.

Restore our fortunes, O LORD,
  like the torrents in the southern desert.
Those who sow in tears
  shall reap rejoicing.

℟. The Lord has done great things for us; we are filled with joy.

Although they go forth weeping,
  carrying the seed to be sown,
they shall come back rejoicing,
  carrying their sheaves.

℟. The Lord has done great things for us; we are filled with joy.

SECOND READING

Phil 1:4-6, 8-11

Brothers and sisters:
I pray always with joy in my every prayer
    for all of you,
  because of your partnership for the
      gospel
  from the first day until now.
I am confident of this,
  that the one who began a good work
      in you
  will continue to complete it
  until the day of Christ Jesus.
God is my witness,
  how I long for all of you with the
      affection of Christ Jesus.
And this is my prayer:
  that your love may increase ever more
      and more
  in knowledge and every kind of
      perception,
  to discern what is of value,
  so that you may be pure and blameless
      for the day of Christ,
  filled with the fruit of righteousness
  that comes through Jesus Christ
  for the glory and praise of God.

About Liturgy

Advent penance service: Many parishes offer communal penance liturgies at least twice a year, during Advent and Lent. The readings this Sunday remind us that this sacrament is not primarily about lists of sins but about repentance, changing one's heart. Just as with all the sacraments, we celebrate the ritual as a way of appropriating the insight of the sacrament, namely, to "take off" the robes of sin and "put on the splendor" (first reading) of the gospel attitudes of repentance and forgiveness.

Penitential act: Sometimes people claim that they have no need for the sacrament of penance because every Sunday Mass begins with a penitential act. Two points by way of response might be made to such objections. First of all, the penitential act isn't the same as the sacrament of penance and so it doesn't replace in our Christian practice the need for this special sacrament that is a concrete sign of God's forgiveness and promised healing. Second, the "penitential act" really isn't primarily about the forgiveness of sins as such but is about celebrating God's mercy and offer of salvation that always leads us to praise and thanksgiving.

Although it is always good to acknowledge our sinfulness and beg for God's mercy, it is telling that *The Roman Missal* gives us other choices for the introductory rites and it is good pastoral practice to choose carefully among them according to the liturgical season and/or festival. For example, since Lent is a penitential season, on the Sundays of Lent the strongest option among the choices for the penitential act might be to use the *Confiteor* ("I confess to almighty God . . ."). On other Sundays of the year another choice might be more appropriate, especially since every Sunday is a celebration of resurrection.

About Liturgical Music

Music suggestions: Already on this Second Sunday of Advent we hear John the Baptist cry out from the desert for our repentance. The Lord is coming and we must prepare the way! Examples of energetic entrance songs reiterating John's challenge include Kenneth W. Louis's "Prepare Ye the Way of the Lord!" (LMGM2), James Moore's "Prepare Ye the Way of the Lord" (LMGM2), Stephen Pishner's "Prepare! Prepare!" (G3), and Dan Schutte's "Let the Valleys Be Raised" (BB, JS3). "Like a Bird" (G3, W4) with its fresh text by Delores Dufner and engaging tune by Joncas would work well during the preparation of the gifts. Examples of songs appropriate in style and content for Communion on this Sunday include "While We Are Waiting, Come" (LMGM2) and Gerard Chiusano's "Maranatha" (JS3). Curtis Stephen's "Ready the Way" (BB, JS3) would work well as a closing song, sending us forth to do the work to which John calls us.

✚ SPIRITUALITY

GOSPEL ACCLAMATION
cf. Luke 1:28

℟. Alleluia, alleluia.
Hail, Mary, full of grace, the Lord is with you;
blessed are you among women.
℟. Alleluia, alleluia.

Gospel   Luke 1:26-38; L689

The angel Gabriel was sent from God
  to a town of Galilee called Nazareth,
  to a virgin betrothed to a man named
      Joseph,
  of the house of David,
  and the virgin's name was Mary.
And coming to her, he said,
  "Hail, full of grace! The Lord is with
      you."
But she was greatly troubled at what was
    said
  and pondered what sort of greeting this
      might be.
Then the angel said to her,
  "Do not be afraid, Mary,
  for you have found favor with God.
Behold, you will conceive in your womb and
    bear a son,
  and you shall name him Jesus.
He will be great and will be called Son of
    the Most High,
  and the Lord God will give him the throne
      of David his father,
  and he will rule over the house of Jacob
      forever,
  and of his Kingdom there will be no end."

Continued in Appendix A, p. 263.

See Appendix A, p. 263, for the other readings.

Reflecting on the Gospel

On December 28, 1975, Dallas Cowboys quarterback Roger Staubach heaved a desperate, very long forward pass to a wide receiver who caught it and waltzed into the end zone for the winning touchdown. When asked later about the pass, Staubach remarked that he just closed his eyes and said a "Hail Mary." Thus was popularized the phrase "Hail Mary pass." Since then "a Hail Mary" has come to be understood as any desperate, long-shot attempt at something. This solemnity's gospel opens with Gabriel addressing the Virgin Mary with "Hail, full of grace!" Was God desperate for a new way to bring us to faithfulness? Was Gabriel's visit to Mary God's long-shot attempt to wake us up?

No, God's plan of salvation isn't desperate or a long shot. This solemnity suggests to us that God's plan from the very beginning was to send the Son as our Savior. The first reading reminds us of the original sin, of the first alienation from God brought about by Adam and Eve's selfish choice. God, however, did not forsake us who are created in the divine image. God sent judges and prophets and sages to the people of old to bring them back into a holy relationship with God and each other. In time God sent the only-begotten Son to show us divine love and mercy. God chose us "before the foundation of the world" (second reading) to receive "every spiritual blessing" and to be "holy and without blemish."

In the midst of striving for holiness, each of us sometimes fails. Each of us is less than blameless. One human being, nevertheless, is different from all the rest of us. The Virgin Mary, from the very moment of her conception in her mother's womb, was pure and free from sin. From the moment of her conception, "yes" was the word in her heart and on her lips. She was the perfect vessel to nurture and give a human form to the very Son of God.

Mary responded to God's call to salvation by saying yes to the mystery of being overshadowed by the Holy Spirit and giving birth to the Son of God. We, too, respond to God's call to salvation by listening to the Spirit who dwells within us, by bearing Christ in the world today, by speaking an ongoing yes to whatever God asks of us. The mystery we live by our faithful response to God's call to salvation is truly the same mystery announced by the angel Gabriel to Mary. It is the mystery of God's loving, saving, incarnate Presence.

Living the Paschal Mystery

We don't know how many children St. Anne, the mother of Mary, bore, but we do believe that from the moment of conception Mary was free from sin. This is a privilege accorded her because she bore the Son of God, but it no doubt is also a privilege because she was always open to God's word for her and the direction her life should take. In this Mary is our Mother, a model for us of openness to God and a lifelong practice of saying yes to this God who saves.

None of us live our lives without sin, but nonetheless we can say yes to God's plan of salvation as Mary did. In our own times of prayer we can listen for the annunciation of a divine word and we, too, can say, "May it be done to me according to your word." Living the paschal mystery simply means conforming our will to God's. It means saying yes. It means that we, like Mary, give ourselves over to God to be instruments of salvation.

Focusing the Gospel

Key words and phrases: Holy Spirit . . . overshadow you, child to be born . . . Son of God, May it be done to me

To the point: Mary responded to God's call to salvation by saying yes to the mystery of being overshadowed by the Holy Spirit and giving birth to the Son of God. We, too, respond to God's call to salvation by listening to the Spirit who dwells within us, by bearing Christ in the world today, by speaking an ongoing yes to whatever God asks of us. The mystery we live by our faithful response to God's call to salvation is truly the same mystery announced by the angel Gabriel to Mary. It is the mystery of God's loving, saving, incarnate Presence.

Model Penitential Act

Presider: On this feast day we rejoice that Mary herself was conceived without sin and faithfully said yes to God all her life. We pause at the beginning of this celebration to examine our own faithfulness in saying yes to God . . . [pause]

Lord Jesus, you are the holy One, the Son of God: Lord . . .

Christ Jesus, you are the incarnate One, the Son of Mary: Christ . . .

Lord Jesus, you are the Savior of the world: Lord . . .

Model Universal Prayer (Prayer of the Faithful)

Presider: As surely as God showed favor to Mary, God will favor us and respond to the needs we now name in our prayer.

Response:

Cantor:

That Mary's fidelity to God's will be a model for how all members of the church live their own yes to God . . . [pause]

That all peoples of the world be open to the salvation offered by God . . . [pause]

That those who struggle to say yes to God's will be inspired by the divine Word to respond with greater fidelity . . . [pause]

That we ourselves joyfully live the mystery of God's Presence to us and within us . . . [pause]

Presider: Saving God, Mary the sinless one conceived and bore your only-begotten Son. Hear these our prayers that we might imitate her faithfulness and one day share with her in your everlasting glory. We ask this through that same Son, Jesus Christ our Lord. **Amen**.

FOR REFLECTION
- Unlike Mary, the sinless one, I sometimes am unfaithful to what God asks of me and so I need to . . .
- What helps me respond to God with "May it be done to me" is . . .
- One way I bear Christ for the world is . . .

Homily Points

• A pastor asked the first communicants what Mary might have said when the angel Gabriel appeared to her to announce that she would conceive the Son of God by the Holy Spirit. One of the little ones eagerly jumped up and said, "I know! She said, what in the world are you doing here?" Good question! Do *we* know?

• Gabriel's announcement to Mary changed the whole world. Since that announcement, Christ is incarnated in our midst and salvation has dawned. What in the world is the Son of God doing here? A good question! What is our response?

✠ SPIRITUALITY

GOSPEL ACCLAMATION
Isa 61:1 (cited in Luke 4:18)

℟. Alleluia, alleluia.
The Spirit of the Lord is upon me,
because he has anointed me
    to bring glad tidings to the poor.
℟. Alleluia, alleluia.

Gospel

Luke 3:10-18; L9C

The crowds asked John the Baptist,
    "What should we do?"
He said to them in reply,
    "Whoever has two cloaks
    should share with the person
        who has none.
And whoever has food should do
    likewise."
Even tax collectors came to be baptized
    and they said to him,
    "Teacher, what should we do?"
He answered them,
    "Stop collecting more than what is
        prescribed."
Soldiers also asked him,
    "And what is it that we should do?"
He told them,
    "Do not practice extortion,
    do not falsely accuse anyone,
    and be satisfied with your wages."

Now the people were filled with
    expectation,
    and all were asking in their hearts
    whether John might be the Christ.
John answered them all, saying,
    "I am baptizing you with water,
    but one mightier than I is coming.
I am not worthy to loosen the thongs of
    his sandals.
He will baptize you with the Holy Spirit
    and fire.
His winnowing fan is in his hand to
    clear his threshing floor
    and to gather the wheat into his barn,
    but the chaff he will burn with
        unquenchable fire."
Exhorting them in many other ways,
    he preached good news to the people.

Reflecting on the Gospel

In terms of our everyday lives, most of us are too over-scheduled even to think about asking a question such as, "What should we do?" We rush from one thing to the next, just barely squeaking by. Choices seem nonexistent. We just want to get through our day being on time for work, getting the kids to soccer, getting something to eat for ourselves and our family, finding time to get the homework finished, answering emails, checking up on our social media sites, texting a few messages. We fall into bed, sleep a few hours, then get up the next day and start the hectic routine all over again. "What should we do?" Ah, to even have the luxury of time to ask the question! At this midpoint in Advent, the gospel calls us to stop, examine our lives and relationships, and perhaps prioritize in a different way how we spend our time.

John the Baptist challenged the people who asked him, "What should we do?" by admonishing them to far exceed their present way of acting toward others. When we are so rushed, or don't put others first, or don't have God as the center of our lives, it is very easy to fall into doing only what is minimally required. John is saying that minimum is not enough. Minimum responses in our relationships do not take us beyond ourselves to encounter the goodness that is present to us. Minimum responses surely don't fill us with an expectation that our anxieties can be diminished when we act out of the realization that the "Lord is near" (second reading).

Yet even such "good news" does not measure up to what the "one mightier" than John will ask of us. Christ, who baptizes us "with the Holy Spirit," will require no less of us than living the Gospel he came to reveal, a Gospel that exacts the gift of our very selves. If we ask, "What should we do?" we must be prepared for an answer that challenges us. Are we willing even to ask the question? Are we willing to reorganize our lives so that Christ is truly at the center, so that the magnanimity of our hearts is measured by something other than getting through another hectic day? Just like John, our lives are about others. Like John, we are to give our all—yes, our very lives—so that others can live better and love more deeply. By taking the time to ask the right questions, we define ourselves not in terms of what we do but who we are in relation to Other and others. The *relationship* to others is the key, not what we or they do.

Living the Paschal Mystery

When we go beyond ordering our lives around doing the minimal things—fulfilling the requirements of our state in life and job or ministry—then we can seek the greater things, the greater One. Our being baptized in the Holy Spirit means that we already share in divine Life. Relationships to others take on a whole new meaning because they give us the opportunity to live like Christ did: for others.

In our daily living we, like John, point to the One who is to come by doing well what is expected of us. Even more importantly, we point to the One who is to come by being who we have become in Christ: the Presence of Christ for others; we ourselves are to be the "mighty one" for others. Because of God's indwelling, doing for others and being like Christ collapse into one: whatever it is we do, we always do so as bearers of Christ because we are "in Christ Jesus" (second reading). For this reason—we are the presence of the risen Christ for each other—nothing we do is small or inconsequential. Everything we do brings the Lord near to those around us.

Focusing the Gospel

Key words and phrases: What should we do?, Christ, one mightier, baptize you with the Holy Spirit, good news to the people

To the point: John the Baptist challenged the people who asked him, "What should we do?" by admonishing them to far exceed their present way of acting toward others. Yet even such "good news" does not measure up to what the "one mightier" than John will ask of us. Christ, who baptizes us "with the Holy Spirit," will require no less of us than living the Gospel he came to reveal, a Gospel that exacts the gift of our very selves. If we ask, "What should we do?" we must be prepared for an answer that challenges us. Are we willing even to ask the question?

Connecting the Gospel

to the first and second readings: These two readings make clear for us what is at the basis of our relationships with each other and of the "good news" that John preached: because "the LORD, your God, is in your midst, / a mighty savior" (first reading), your "kindness should be known to all" (second reading).

to experience: We live each day with many choices about what we do and how we do it. There is only one real choice: living consistently with having been baptized in the Holy Spirit.

Connecting the Responsorial Psalm

to the readings: Instead of psalm verses this Sunday, we sing a hymn from Isaiah proclaiming that the Holy One we await is already in our midst. The first and second readings affirm God is already present among us. John the Baptist announces the imminent arrival of the "one mightier than I" (gospel). No wonder we shout, "Cry out with joy and gladness" (psalm refrain)!

All is not joy and gladness, however. The very nearness of the Holy One makes our own unholiness more evident. We must change our behavior, for the coming Messiah will sort the wheat from the chaff and burn what he does not want (gospel). John's audience hears the call to conversion and the imminence of judgment as "good news" that heralds the coming of the Holy One of Israel. They hear that God's promise to renew them as a chosen people (first reading) is about to be fulfilled. What do we hear in John the Baptist's challenge? What response do we make, both in sung word and in lived behavior?

to psalmist preparation: In these verses you are the prophet Isaiah announcing God's saving Presence in the midst of the people. Even more, you are the church proclaiming the Holy One in our midst to be Jesus who saves us through the paschal mystery of his death and resurrection. How can your singing lead the assembly to see and encounter this Presence?

ASSEMBLY & FAITH-SHARING GROUPS
- If I could ask John the Baptist, "What should I do?" he would say to me . . . If I ask Christ, "What should I do?" he would say to me . . .
- I am most willing to ask Christ the question, "What should I do?" when . . . I resist asking this question when . . .
- For me, being baptized in the Holy Spirit means . . . For the world, it means . . .

PRESIDERS
When I call to mind that I am baptized in the Holy Spirit, my presiding at liturgy looks like . . .

DEACONS
My witness while serving others inspires them to ask themselves, "What should we do?" when I . . .

HOSPITALITY MINISTERS
That my "kindness should be known to all" (second reading) shapes the way I minister when . . .

MUSIC MINISTERS
"What should we do?" More than simply singing, at liturgy I lead others to . . . when . . .

ALTAR MINISTERS
When I remember that at the altar and in my daily life I am serving "one mightier than I," my serving becomes . . .

LECTORS
I am as bold as John the Baptist in proclaiming "the good news to the people" when I . . .

EXTRAORDINARY MINISTERS OF HOLY COMMUNION
Knowing that I distribute the Body/Blood of the One whose sandals "I am not worthy to loosen" challenges me to . . .

Model Penitential Act

Presider: This Third Sunday of Advent is traditionally called "rejoice" Sunday. We pause to call to mind the times we have failed to rejoice in the salvation Jesus came to bring us and ask him for mercy and forgiveness . . . [pause]

Lord Jesus, you are the Christ, the Son of God: Lord . . .

Christ Jesus, you are the mighty One who dwells among us: Christ . . .

Lord Jesus, you are the Good News of salvation: Lord . . .

Homily Points

• No young couple entering into marriage can anticipate what their commitment will cost. No person beginning graduate studies can calculate the demands. No military recruit starting boot camp knows fully what service in the armed forces entails. No person baptized in the Holy Spirit can reckon fully the demands of following Christ.

• The followers of John the Baptist make the mistake of asking, "What should we do?" They could not have been prepared for his answer, which was life changing. John's response went beyond the expected: share what one has generously, don't take what belongs to others, don't make unjust demands, be honest, be satisfied. When we ask Jesus, "What should we do?" are we prepared to live the answer?

• In short, Jesus answers our question by calling us to live as he himself lived. Like him, we are to give our very lives for the sake of others. This, essentially, is the Gospel Jesus came to reveal: live unreservedly for others. Knowing the high personal cost of this answer, are we willing even to ask the question? Are we willing to live the answer?

Model Universal Prayer (Prayer of the Faithful)

Presider: As we rejoice in the coming of our Savior, we are emboldened to ask God for what we need.

Response:

Cantor:

That all members of the church, baptized with the Holy Spirit, live fully the demand of the Gospel to give oneself for the sake of others . . . [pause]

That all peoples of the world come to salvation and rejoice in God's love and mercy . . . [pause]

That those in any need receive generously from the community of the faithful . . . [pause]

That each of us listen intently and then act boldly when we ask Jesus, "What should we do?" . . . [pause]

Presider: Mighty God, you sent John to announce the coming of your Son into the world. Hear these our prayers that we might recognize his Presence among us and follow wherever he leads us. We ask this through that same Christ our Lord. **Amen.**

COLLECT
Let us pray.

Pause for silent prayer

O God, who see how your people
faithfully await the feast of the Lord's
    Nativity,
enable us, we pray,
to attain the joys of so great a salvation
and to celebrate them always
with solemn worship and glad rejoicing.
Through our Lord Jesus Christ, your Son,
who lives and reigns with you in the unity
    of the Holy Spirit,
one God, for ever and ever. **Amen.**

FIRST READING
Zeph 3:14-18a

Shout for joy, O daughter Zion!
    Sing joyfully, O Israel!
Be glad and exult with all your heart,
    O daughter Jerusalem!
The Lord has removed the judgment
    against you,
    he has turned away your enemies;
the King of Israel, the Lord, is in your
    midst,
    you have no further misfortune to fear.
On that day, it shall be said to Jerusalem:
    Fear not, O Zion, be not discouraged!
The Lord, your God, is in your midst,
    a mighty savior;
he will rejoice over you with gladness,
    and renew you in his love,
he will sing joyfully because of you,
    as one sings at festivals.

RESPONSORIAL PSALM
Isa 12:2-3, 4, 5-6

℟. (6) Cry out with joy and gladness: for among you is the great and Holy One of Israel.

God indeed is my savior;
   I am confident and unafraid.
My strength and my courage is the LORD,
   and he has been my savior.
With joy you will draw water
   at the fountain of salvation.

℟. Cry out with joy and gladness: for among you is the great and Holy One of Israel.

Give thanks to the LORD, acclaim his name;
   among the nations make known his
      deeds,
   proclaim how exalted is his name.

℟. Cry out with joy and gladness: for among you is the great and Holy One of Israel.

Sing praise to the LORD for his glorious
      achievement;
   let this be known throughout all the
      earth.
Shout with exultation, O city of Zion,
   for great in your midst
   is the Holy One of Israel!

℟. Cry out with joy and gladness: for among you is the great and Holy One of Israel.

SECOND READING
Phil 4:4-7

Brothers and sisters:
Rejoice in the Lord always.
I shall say it again: rejoice!
Your kindness should be known to all.
The Lord is near.
Have no anxiety at all, but in everything,
   by prayer and petition, with
      thanksgiving,
   make your requests known to God.
Then the peace of God that surpasses all
      understanding
   will guard your hearts and minds in
      Christ Jesus.

About Liturgy

Ministry of the assembly: We hear much these days about the visible liturgical ministries (hospitality ministers, music ministers, altar ministers, lectors, eucharistic ministers). We also know that these ministries require preparation and formation. Rarely do we hear, however, about the ministry of the assembly itself. All these visible ministers—the presiders and deacons, and all the others who are present at any liturgy—together make up the *assembly*. We might think that the assembly is just *there* to pray and the visible ministers have all the *doing*. This isn't a very accurate assessment of the role of the assembly. A most important ministry at any liturgy is the *ministry of the assembly*.

To be sure, there is a *doing* on the part of the assembly: standing, sitting, kneeling, singing, responding, acclaiming, professing, and so forth. Sometimes we might fall into the trap of presuming that this is all the assembly does and this is all there is to participation. The most fruitful role of the assembly *comes out of* the doing. First and foremost the liturgical assembly is the Body of Christ gathered around the Head. The assembly, then, makes visible the church, makes visible Christ. One fundamental role of the assembly is to be present to one another, to relate to each other as the presence of the risen Christ. This relational ministry of the assembly makes concrete and visible how we live our everyday lives: relating to each other as members of the Body of Christ. The ministry of the assembly is to be Body of Christ made visible. While the question, "What should we do?" is an important one with respect to liturgy, it must always lead to the questions, Who shall we be? How self-giving are we?

About Liturgical Music

Music suggestions: The past two Sundays of Advent have kept our eyes looking toward the Second Coming of Christ at the end of time. This Sunday turns our focus toward Christ whose birth as a babe we now begin preparing to commemorate on Christmas. This is the Sunday to begin singing, "O Come, O Come, Emmanuel." Since this is *Gaudete* (rejoice) Sunday, "Awake! Awake, and Greet the New Morn" (in most resources) would make an appropriate song either at the entrance or after Communion. "O Come, Divine Messiah" (in most resources) would be suitable at the preparation of the gifts or as the recessional song. Deanna Light and Paul Tate's "Come, Emmanuel" (WC, WS) with its call-response verses would work well for either the entrance or the Communion procession. Also suitable for Communion would be Marty Haugen's "My Soul in Stillness Waits" (G3, W4) and Kathy Powell's "Maranatha, Lord Messiah" (G3, W4). Other well-known Advent songs which prepare us for the coming of the Christ Child include "Come, O Long Expected [Long-Awaited] Jesus"; "Creator of the Stars of Night"; and "People, Look East."

✝ SPIRITUALITY

GOSPEL ACCLAMATION
Luke 1:38

R̸. Alleluia, alleluia.
Behold, I am the handmaid of the Lord.
May it be done to me according to your
    word.
R̸. Alleluia, alleluia.

Gospel

Luke 1:39-45; L12C

Mary set out
   and traveled to the hill country
       in haste
   to a town of Judah,
   where she entered the house
       of Zechariah
   and greeted Elizabeth.
When Elizabeth heard Mary's
       greeting,
   the infant leaped in her
       womb,
   and Elizabeth, filled with
       the Holy Spirit,
   cried out in a loud voice and said,
   "Blessed are you among women,
   and blessed is the fruit of your
       womb.
And how does this happen to me,
   that the mother of my Lord should
       come to me?
For at the moment the sound of your
       greeting reached my ears,
   the infant in my womb leaped for joy.
Blessed are you who believed
   that what was spoken to you by the
       Lord
   would be fulfilled."

Reflecting on the Gospel

The phrase "gone, but not forgotten" is associated with songs, movies, a TV show episode, a novel, a poem. It is different from another well-known phrase, "out of sight, out of mind." These sayings address a common enough human experience: absence and presence. When someone is not immediately at hand, do we forget or remember this person? The answer to this question rests largely on how important this person is for us. The more love we have, the more this individual is always present to us. Physical proximity is not the measure of presence; attentiveness (even in absence) and love are. This Sunday's gospel addresses absence and presence.

Mary visited her cousin Elizabeth and they were present to each other in a most extraordinary encounter. Clearly also present and active was the Holy Spirit who overshadowed Mary to conceive the Savior of the world, inspired Elizabeth to extol Mary and the "fruit of [her] womb," and prompted the unborn John to leap for joy. The Holy Spirit brought an intensity to each encounter that augured the singularity and significance of all these happenings. Mary didn't simply "set out" to visit Elizabeth; she went "in haste." Elizabeth didn't simply say "hello" to Mary, but "cried out in a loud voice" the blessings of Mary and her unborn infant. John didn't simply give a gentle kick in Elizabeth's womb at this encounter, but "leaped for joy."

On this Fourth Sunday of Advent, quickly approaching our celebration of the birth of the Son of God, we need to open ourselves to receive this same intensity from the Holy Spirit. This same Holy Spirit overshadows, inspires, and prompts those of us who believe to "set out" "in haste" to touch others with divine Presence. Elizabeth blesses Mary because she "believed" that God would fulfill in her all that the angel Gabriel had said to her. Now so must we believe that God fulfills in us all the goodness and love that is promised.

Absent from this account is any sense that either woman resisted God's invitation to cooperate in the work of salvation. Absent from this account is any sense that either woman said no to God's will, even when that will was surely not clear, not within the boundaries of normal expectations, not easy to accept. Salvation is the convergence of God's will and our own will. Like Mary and Elizabeth, we must make any no to what God asks of us absent from our lives. Mary and Elizabeth show us the way to *our* being overshadowed by the Spirit by their offering their own bodies in cooperating with God's plan of salvation. So must we offer ourselves with the same willingness, with the same love response, with the same eager desire for divine Presence within and among us. This divine Presence is never gone, never absent. We cannot ever forget that.

Living the Paschal Mystery

God's plan of salvation is fulfilled by Christ's obedience to the Father's will (see second reading). Think about this: doing God's will is an incarnation of divine Presence! The circumstances of our self-giving won't be as spectacular as Mary's and Elizabeth's, but our own giving ourselves over to God's will is no less fruitful. In our helping hand, God is present. In our visits to the sick and elderly, God is present. In our disciplining and forming our children, God is present. In all our daily dying to self, God is present. This is incarnation: God is present. This is the depth of the Christmas mystery: we, too, incarnate divine Presence!

Focusing the Gospel

Key words and phrases: set out . . . in haste, filled with the Holy Spirit, Blessed . . . blessed is the fruit of your womb, leaped for joy, you who believed

To the point: The Holy Spirit overshadowed Mary to conceive the Savior of the world, inspired Elizabeth to extol Mary and the "fruit of [her] womb," and prompted the unborn John to leap for joy. This same Holy Spirit overshadows, inspires, and prompts those who believe to "set out" "in haste" to touch others with divine Presence.

Connecting the Gospel

to the second reading: The gospel discloses Mary and Elizabeth's willingness to do God's will; the second reading affirms Christ's willingness to do the will of his Father.

to experience: When do we drop everything and go "in haste" to someone? Frequently we do so when a tragedy happens, such as a serious accident or sudden death. We also go "in haste" for joyful events, such as an imminent birth. Momentous events galvanize us. How momentous the event that brought Mary "in haste" to Elizabeth!

Connecting the Responsorial Psalm

to the readings: In the responsorial psalm for the Fourth Sunday of Advent we pray to God, "let us see your face and we shall be saved." And where does God direct our vision? Beyond the face of the newborn Jesus to the face of the grown Christ carrying out God's will (second reading). And through the face of Christ to the faces of one another who, "consecrated" through Christ's offering, are now the Body of Christ continuing to shine the face of salvation upon the world. In this Sunday's liturgy we celebrate God's incarnation in human flesh—Christ's, Mary's, and ours. Beyond all expectation, God has indeed heard our prayer; beyond all expectation, God has indeed shown us the divine face!

to psalmist preparation: In this responsorial psalm you express the assembly's desire to turn more fully toward God. You lead them in begging to see God's face. How during this last week of Advent might you turn more toward God? Where might you look to see God's face? How might you be God's face for someone else?

ASSEMBLY & FAITH-SHARING GROUPS
- I feel the Holy Spirit overshadowing me by . . . inspiring me when . . . prompting me to . . .
- My believing looks like Mary's when . . . like Elizabeth's when . . .
- I leap for joy because of the birth of Christ when . . .

PRESIDERS
When I open my presiding to the inspiration of the Holy Spirit, the assembly . . .

DEACONS
My serving others is an encounter that brings them joy when I . . .

HOSPITALITY MINISTERS
In my hospitality ministry I have witnessed *in* others and *to* others the Presence of the Savior when . . .

MUSIC MINISTERS
The joy of my music making leads others to encounter the Presence of the Savior when . . .

ALTAR MINISTERS
The simple act of my serving at the altar is indeed a momentous event because . . .

LECTORS
When I believe that the word spoken through me by the Lord will be fulfilled, my proclamation and living become . . .

EXTRAORDINARY MINISTERS OF HOLY COMMUNION
The encounter between communicants and me reflects the encounter between Mary and Elizabeth when . . .

Model Penitential Act

Presider: As we hasten to the celebration of the birth of the Savior, we call to mind the times we have been slow in responding to his Presence among us . . . [pause]

Lord Jesus, you are the Savior conceived by the power of the Holy Spirit: Lord . . .

Christ Jesus, you are the blessed Fruit of Mary's womb: Christ . . .

Lord Jesus, you are the Word fulfilled in our hearing: Lord . . .

Homily Points

• In the carol "The Twelve Days of Christmas," we sing about "ten lords a leaping." In this Sunday's gospel we hear about another "lord" a leaping—the unborn John who leaps with joy in Elizabeth's womb in the presence of the unborn Child in Mary's womb. John leaps in the Presence of *the* Lord: the Savior of the world.

• This gospel makes clear to us that the coming of the Savior is the work of the Holy Spirit—then in the time of Mary and Elizabeth, now in our own time. As with Mary and Elizabeth, we must believe and be open to how the Spirit overshadows, inspires, and prompts us to bring Christ to birth among those whom we encounter every day.

• The work of the Holy Spirit compels us to leap for joy in the Presence of *the* Lord. As with Mary, our every choice, every act, every encounter must disclose our heart's desire to carry the Presence of the Lord to others. And to do so with haste.

Model Universal Prayer (Prayer of the Faithful)

Presider: Because we believe that the Savior is among us, we joyfully make our needs known.

Response:

Lord,————— hear our prayer.

Cantor:

we pray to the Lord,

May all members of the church joyfully announce the Presence of the Savior by the goodness of their lives . . . [pause]

May all peoples of the world live in peace and justice, and thus announce the nearness of God . . . [pause]

May those in any need be lifted up by the generosity this season of giving inspires . . . [pause]

May each of us encounter the Christmas mystery of the Savior's Presence in joyful sharing among family and friends . . . [pause]

Presider: Gracious God, you visit your people in so many ways. Hear these our prayers for our needs as we announce your nearness to all those we meet. We ask this through Christ our Lord. **Amen.**

COLLECT

Let us pray.

Pause for silent prayer

Pour forth, we beseech you, O Lord,
your grace into our hearts,
that we, to whom the Incarnation of Christ
    your Son
was made known by the message of an
    Angel,
may by his Passion and Cross
be brought to the glory of his
    Resurrection.
Who lives and reigns with you in the unity
    of the Holy Spirit,
one God, for ever and ever. **Amen.**

FIRST READING

Mic 5:1-4a

Thus says the Lord:
You, Bethlehem-Ephrathah
    too small to be among the clans of
        Judah,
from you shall come forth for me
    one who is to be ruler in Israel;
whose origin is from of old,
    from ancient times.
Therefore the Lord will give them up, until
    the time
    when she who is to give birth has borne,
and the rest of his kindred shall return
    to the children of Israel.
He shall stand firm and shepherd his flock
    by the strength of the Lord,
    in the majestic name of the Lord, his
        God;
and they shall remain, for now his
    greatness
    shall reach to the ends of the earth;
    he shall be peace.

RESPONSORIAL PSALM
Ps 80:2-3, 15-16, 18-19

R/. (4) Lord, make us turn to you; let us see
your face and we shall be saved.

O shepherd of Israel, hearken,
    from your throne upon the cherubim,
        shine forth.
Rouse your power,
    and come to save us.

R/. Lord, make us turn to you; let us see
your face and we shall be saved.

Once again, O LORD of hosts,
    look down from heaven, and see;
take care of this vine,
    and protect what your right hand has
        planted,
    the son of man whom you yourself
        made strong.

R/. Lord, make us turn to you; let us see
your face and we shall be saved.

May your help be with the man of your
        right hand,
    with the son of man whom you yourself
        made strong.
Then we will no more withdraw from you;
    give us new life, and we will call upon
        your name.

R/. Lord, make us turn to you; let us see
your face and we shall be saved.

SECOND READING
Heb 10:5-10

Brothers and sisters:
When Christ came into the world, he said:
    "Sacrifice and offering you did not
        desire,
        but a body you prepared for me;
    in holocausts and sin offerings you took
        no delight.
    Then I said, 'As is written of me in the
        scroll,
    behold, I come to do your will, O God.'"

First he says, "Sacrifices and offerings,
    holocausts and sin offerings,
    you neither desired nor delighted in."
These are offered according to the law.
Then he says, "Behold, I come to do your
    will."
He takes away the first to establish the
    second.
By this "will," we have been consecrated
    through the offering of the body of
        Jesus Christ once for all.

About Liturgy

Announcing the Christmas mystery: Opportunities for us to announce the Christmas mystery abound. Here are two clusters of possibilities.

First, with respect to the ritual "tangibles." The way we enhance the sacred space for Christmas, the music we choose, the way people are greeted (especially those who have been away from church for a while) all beg us to think about how we want to announce the Christmas mystery. Is the focus almost entirely on a babe who was born long ago? If so, there is the real danger that Christmas will come and go without affecting us and the way we live. Our Christmas preparations and celebrations must lead us to the deeper mystery: Christmas is a salvation feast that reminds us this babe whose birth we celebrate was obedient even to death on a cross. The mystery of birth always enfolds the mystery of death. Our environment, music, hospitality, and so forth all must affect us in such a way that we are led to announce the Christmas mystery as God's Presence to humanity and make that Presence known in the goodness of our daily living.

Second, with respect to the liturgy itself. Liturgy always makes demands on us: the word proclaimed, the homily's challenge, the Creed's demands for deeper believing, the intercession's follow-through, Communion's unity. All preparation for liturgy must open the space for the Spirit to work within the community so that liturgy, truly, transforms us into being better and more fruitful presences of Christ. The deepest and most lasting joy of Christmas spills beyond the liturgy into making the world a better place to be, a place of peace and goodwill to all. The liturgy itself must be celebrated in such a way as to lead us to announce in our daily living that we believe with all our hearts that the Lord is come and dwells within each of us.

About Liturgical Music

Music suggestions: Songs about the mystery of Mary's involvement in the incarnation include "See How the Virgin Waits" (BB), "The Angel Gabriel from Heaven Came" (in many resources), and Vince Ambrosetti's "Emmanuel" (WC, WS). Particularly appropriate to the story of the visitation (see gospel), "When to Mary, the Word" (*Hymns for the Gospels*, GIA) calls us to reach out to our neighbor as did Mary, and to see the Christ hidden within the other as did the infant John in Elizabeth's womb.

A good choice during Communion or as a hymn of praise after Communion would be a setting of the *Magnificat*. Rory Cooney's "Canticle of the Turning" (G3, W4) with its energetic refrain, "My heart shall sing of the day you bring. Let the fires of your justice burn. Wipe away all tears, for the dawn draws near, and the world is about to turn," would be particularly uplifting. On a quieter note, Mary Louise Bringle's "Now the Heavens Start to Whisper" (W4) would make a lovely reflective song during the preparation of the gifts, as would Carey Landry's "Waiting in Silence" (BB) or Dan Schutte's "Christ, Circle Round Us" (BB, JS3) during Communion.

As we enter the last days of Advent, John A. Dalles's "We Blew No Trumpet Blasts to Sound" (*Swift Currents and Still Waters*, GIA) would be a thought-provoking hymn to sing either as a post-Communion song or a recessional. The song challenges with these words: "We blew no trumpet blasts. . . . We built no bonfire. . . . We spread no welc'ming canopy. . . . [instead] We hurried through another week, unheeding, and unmoved. . . . Dear God, how unprepared we were to welcome Jesus, then. We pray you, help us not to miss your priceless gift again."

SEASON OF CHRISTMAS

To fall in love with God
is the greatest romance;
to seek God
is the greatest adventure;
to find God
is the greatest human achievement.

—St. Augustine

SPIRITUALITY

The Vigil Mass

GOSPEL ACCLAMATION

R̷. Alleluia, alleluia.
Tomorrow the wickedness of the earth will be
    destroyed:
the Savior of the world will reign over us.
R̷. Alleluia, alleluia.

Gospel

Matt 1:1-25; L13ABC

The book of the genealogy
    of Jesus Christ,
    the son of David, the son
    of Abraham.

Abraham became the father
    of Isaac,
    Isaac the father of Jacob,
    Jacob the father of Judah
        and his brothers.
Judah became the father of
    Perez and Zerah,
    whose mother was Tamar.
Perez became the father of
    Hezron,
    Hezron the father of Ram,
    Ram the father of Amminadab.
Amminadab became the father of
    Nahshon,
    Nahshon the father of Salmon,
    Salmon the father of Boaz,
    whose mother was Rahab.
Boaz became the father of Obed,
    whose mother was Ruth.
Obed became the father of Jesse,
    Jesse the father of David the king.

Continued in Appendix A, p. 264

or Matt 1:18-25 in Appendix A, p. 264.

See Appendix A, p. 265, for the other readings.

Reflecting on the Gospel and Living the Paschal Mystery

Key words and phrases: the genealogy of Jesus Christ, Mary was betrothed to Joseph, took his wife into his home, God is with us

To the point: God's love is boundless. God's love is intimate. God's love is life-giving salvation. Christmas is truly a feast of love and espoused relationship. God espouses us, and we enter into an intimate relationship with our divine Creator and Lord. The marvelous mystery of the "birth of Jesus Christ came about" because of the marvelous mystery of God's love.

To ponder and pray: More than any other time of year, Christmas brings out the natural generosity of people. Many organizations sponsor food and gift drives for the less fortunate. A most heartwarming scene is that of a child who has little receiving unexpected gifts at Christmastime. Tight hugs are given to the volunteers—there are no strangers when it comes to giving and receiving. Faces of both volunteers and children and parents are radiant. Joy emanates from deep within. These scenes remind us that Christmas is about love and relationships. There are no strangers when it comes to giving and receiving.

Isaiah in the first reading describes how much *God loves us* by using espousal imagery to portray the intimate relationship God desires to have with us. God does not want to be a stranger to us, but offers us the deepest and most intimate and most life-giving love. Jesus is the very incarnation of God's love and Presence, for he is "*Emmanuel . . . 'God is with us.'*" The mystery of the incarnation reveals our creator God's intimate love for us creatures, shows us how God prepared for our salvation from the very beginning, and how God desires to be one with us creatures. This day we celebrate God's love for us and the divine Presence to us, a love and Presence that are boundless.

How much Joseph must have loved Mary, since he was "unwilling to expose her to shame"! How much Joseph must have loved God, since he did all that "the angel of the Lord commanded him"! Joseph (and Mary) model for us the depths of love and relationship to which we humans are really capable. They show us a love that is kind and merciful, gentle and compassionate, just and peaceful. How we long for this love! At the same time we celebrate Joseph and Mary's faithful love; the mystery of Christmas turns us toward the mighty deeds of God worked through them. Joseph and Mary were instruments of God's love borne anew for the world.

The genealogy that makes up most of this gospel reminds us of more than Jesus' roots in Jewish patriarchs and kings. It reminds us of the espousal love that brings forth life. It reminds us that Jesus is born of espousal love, while conceived by the Holy Spirit. It reminds us of a God who works through ordinary human beings to bring about extraordinary divine actions. It reminds us of a God whose boundless love reaches out to us finite human beings and stretches us beyond ourselves—stretches us to be God's delight, God's espoused. Such a mystery of love!

We celebrate Christmas each time we cooperate with the Spirit who dwells within each of us, who overshadows us, who enables us to say yes to God. Our own yes is an incarnation of God's love for us that was so lavishly portrayed on that first Christmas night. Our own yes is an announcement of the intimate, espousal relationship God desires with each of us. Christmas celebrates the love of God for us expressed in the mightiest deed of salvation: *Emmanuel—* "God is with us."

SPIRITUALITY

Mass at Midnight

GOSPEL ACCLAMATION
Luke 2:10-11

R?. Alleluia, alleluia.
I proclaim to you good news of
    great joy:
today a Savior is born for us,
Christ the Lord.
R?. Alleluia, alleluia.

Gospel

Luke 2:1-14; L14ABC

In those days a decree went out
    from Caesar Augustus
  that the whole world should be
    enrolled.
This was the first
    enrollment,
  when Quirinius was governor
    of Syria.
So all went to be enrolled, each
    to his own town.
And Joseph too went up from
    Galilee from the town of
    Nazareth
  to Judea, to the city of David that is
    called Bethlehem,
  because he was of the house and
    family of David,
  to be enrolled with Mary, his
    betrothed, who was with child.
While they were there,
  the time came for her to have her child,
  and she gave birth to her firstborn son.
She wrapped him in swaddling clothes
    and laid him in a manger,
  because there was no room for them
    in the inn.

Continued in Appendix A, p. 265.

See Appendix A, p. 266, for the other readings.

Reflecting on the Gospel and Living the Paschal Mystery

Key words and phrases: Joseph too went up; Mary, his betrothed; wrapped in swaddling clothes

To the point: Mary, the virgin, was about to give birth. But she was not alone, not without a loving husband. "Joseph too went up." In this moment of life ushering forth, they shared the intimate love of those who were betrothed. Their shared love would protect, nourish, and teach this divine-human Son.

To ponder and pray: Tight hugs are the order of the day at Christmastime. As families gather, often not having seen one another for a while, hugs and kisses abound. When Mary gave birth to Jesus on that first Christmas night, no doubt Joseph and Mary hugged and kissed their newborn babe. He was their precious gift of Life whom they would protect and nourish. Mary wrapped her newborn babe in swaddling clothes—wrapped him tightly so he would experience the warmth and security, the boundedness and protection of the womb that gave him life and growth since the angel Gabriel announced to Mary that she would conceive by the Holy Spirit. Mary swaddle-hugged her newborn babe with a mother's tenderness. This infant was conceived by God's love and born into the love of Joseph and Mary. Mary and Joseph went up to Bethlehem in obedience to an earthly king's decree. While there, Mary gave birth to a heavenly King, One to whom the angels sang, One whom the shepherds came to adore.

Mary gave birth "to her firstborn son." In this she also gave birth to a way of life—this birth is more than about one life; it is about the life of all. Mary gave birth to a God-Man who from the very beginning wishes to seek us, to encounter us, to love us. While contained in human flesh, this newborn babe is still the infinite God who is the "savior . . . born" for us. This newborn babe is still the One who loves beyond compare. This newborn babe is still the One to whom we sing "Glory to God." This newborn babe teaches us love and intimacy, forgiveness and mercy, justice and peace. This newborn babe is like no other.

The birth of this newborn babe ushered in a new way to hug and kiss one another. This birth opens up new life and relationship between God and us, and between us and each other. With this birth no relationship can be the same. Called to the same love as Mary and Joseph shared with Jesus, we learn that our salvation comes through loving one another. Peace comes through loving one another. This love is no abstract love, but is the concrete self-giving that Joseph and Mary modeled in their obedient yes, is the concrete self-giving that Jesus modeled in his self-emptying life given for us. The intimate love to which this birth calls us is an action-love that changes us and the world around us. Through this love we hug the world tightly, we swaddle the world in obedience, we break open the confines of "lawlessness" (second reading) to enter into a "great light" (first reading). This light guides us into the loving intimacy that is the very meaning of this feast.

Christmas is a time of joy, because it is a time of loving. Christmas calls us to be attentive to the in-breaking of Jesus as was Mary and Joseph, the angels and shepherds. Christmas calls us to fall in love all over again, fall in love with this human-divine babe who became one of us so that we might learn to love as he did, learn to give to others as he did, learn to achieve the best we are to be, as he did.

SPIRITUALITY

Mass at Dawn

GOSPEL ACCLAMATION
Luke 2:14

R7. Alleluia, alleluia.
Glory to God in the highest,
and on earth peace to those
on whom his favor rests.
R7. Alleluia, alleluia.

Gospel

Luke 2:15-20; L15ABC

When the angels went
    away from them to
    heaven,
  the shepherds said to
    one another,
  "Let us go, then, to
    Bethlehem
  to see this thing that has taken place,
  which the Lord has made known to
    us."
So they went in haste and found Mary
    and Joseph,
  and the infant lying in the manger.
When they saw this,
  they made known the message
  that had been told them about this
    child.
All who heard it were amazed
  by what had been told them by the
    shepherds.
And Mary kept all these things,
  reflecting on them in her heart.
Then the shepherds returned,
  glorifying and praising God
  for all they had heard and seen,
  just as it had been told to them.

See Appendix A, p. 266, for the other readings.

Reflecting on the Gospel and Living the Paschal Mystery

Key words and phrases: went in haste, infant lying in a manger, glorifying and praising God

To the point: Every love encounter changes both the lover and the beloved. Our love encounter with this "infant lying in a manger" changes us in the most profound way possible. It saves us. It makes us holy. It makes us heirs of eternal Life.

To ponder and pray: Ads for jewelry stores abound at Christmastime. Engagement rings are frequently featured. The "question" is popped, sometimes in crazy ways: while flying in an airplane or hot air balloon, after the ring is found hidden in a favorite dessert, while scuba diving. No matter when or how the question comes, it is the answer that is crucial: Yes. Love—deep, intimate love—elicits yes from us. To say no to the beloved is to deny giving the gift of self. The shepherds in this gospel do as the angels bid them. They say yes to seeking the "infant lying in a manger." Not only do the shepherds say yes, but they also "went in haste." Something—Someone—urged them on. This was no ordinary message of a birth, no ordinary seeking of a beloved, no ordinary amazement they experienced. They were about to meet their Savior.

When the shepherds arrived at the stable of Jesus' birth, they observed something familiar: a manger. Now this they understood. They knew about animals, about caring for them, about fodder and straw. Yet something more was happening here. They observed "the kindness and generous love / of God our savior" (second reading). They observed a newborn babe who communicated more than the familiar to them. This divine encounter stirred their hearts to be raised in glory and praise of God. This simple encounter with a humble "infant lying in a manger" changed the shepherds. This simple encounter changes us.

We, too, are changed by our encounters with this Savior born to us. We are now "called the holy people" (first reading), those "justified by his grace" and "heirs in hope of eternal life" (second reading). The issue, however, isn't that we are changed automatically by divine encounter; the issue is that we must recognize and respond to divine encounter. We must say yes. We must seek. We must make haste to find God our Savior, to learn his message, to say yes by "glorifying and praising God" for all that has been accomplished through divine love.

Unlike the shepherds who had angels appear to them, our invitations to divine encounters are much more modest—but no less real. We encounter the Savior in the sick and suffering to whom we extend a healing hand, in the child who needs moral guidance, in the beleaguered parent who needs an encouraging word, in a lonesome youth who needs a friend. The human beings we encounter each day change us, too. We need to reflect upon the mystery of divine Presence coming to us every day in human flesh. We must open ourselves to the many ways our Savior comes to us, often in most unexpected ways and places.

The manger was familiar to the shepherds. We must seek our Savior both in the midst of the familiar and in the midst of the unexpected. Our response? Yes. Our mission: learn the message and, like the shepherds, make it known. The message? That our Savior has come. And our lives are never the same: we are God's beloved.

✠ SPIRITUALITY

Mass during the Day

GOSPEL ACCLAMATION
℟. Alleluia, alleluia.
A holy day has dawned upon us.
Come, you nations, and adore the Lord.
For today a great light has come upon the earth.
℟. Alleluia, alleluia.

Gospel

John 1:1-18; L16ABC

In the beginning was the
    Word,
    and the Word was with
        God,
    and the Word was God.
He was in the beginning with
    God.
All things came to be through
    him,
    and without him nothing
        came to be.
What came to be through him
    was life,
    and this life was the light
        of the human race;
the light shines in the darkness,
    and the darkness has not
        overcome it.
A man named John was sent from God.
He came for testimony, to testify to the
    light,
    so that all might believe through him.
He was not the light,
    but came to testify to the light.

Continued in Appendix A, p. 267

or John 1:1-5, 9-14 in Appendix A, p. 267.

See Appendix A, pp. 267–268, for the other readings.

Reflecting on the Gospel and Living the Paschal Mystery

Key words and phrases: the Word was God, light shines in the darkness, become children of God, the Word became flesh, made his dwelling among us, From his fullness we have all received

To the point: In spite of our choosing sometimes to say no to God's overtures of love, of choosing to dwell in darkness instead of the light, the Son of God came to dwell among us, to bring us the fullness of Life, to teach us the kind of self-giving that truly is love made visible.

To ponder and pray: Oh, how parents hate to hear the pitter-patter of little feet bounding into their bedroom early, early on Christmas morn! Their sleep is shattered by the gleeful shout, "Santa came!" Probably exhausted from all the finishing up activity of the night before, the last thing the parents want to do is crawl out of bed at the crack of dawn. But get up, they do. This morning is too special. The excitement is palpable. To a casual onlooker, this morning is about gifts and Christmas trees and lights. To a discerning observer, this morning is about love. Family love. God's love.

The "Word became flesh." Love became flesh. Then, in the Son of God. Now, in us: in a yes response to the eagerness of the children; in a yes response to the extended family and friends who gather; in a yes response to caring for the elderly. We learn this yes response from the One whose birth we celebrate this day. Our beloved dwells here among us. In the flesh. One like us in all things except sin. The One who through his loving word dispels the darkness of our own sinfulness. The act of self-giving of this divine One comes full circle, for from "his fullness we have all received." Indeed, through him we "become children of God." Through this birth we ourselves are rebirthed into divine Life itself. The One who took on our human flesh and dwelled among us is the "Father's only Son," he who chooses to be present to us in such an intimate way that we ourselves are made more perfectly into his image and likeness through the "grace and truth" he brings. The "glad tidings" (first reading) this birth brings is the good news of salvation, the good news that God dwells among us and is present to us in a whole new way. Oh, how God loves to hear the pitter-patter of "the feet of him who brings glad tidings"!

The glad tidings this morn brings is the good news of our salvation—nothing less than an invitation to be open to the inpouring of God's divine love-Life within us, made possible by this birth. Our salvation is nothing less than the grace and truth of our own lives, lived by simple acts of care and love for each other. With the marriage of the divine and human that the incarnation is, God's love is made visible in a whole new way. It is made visible in a divine Being who lives like us, who knows what the darkness of our despair and loneliness and alienation is. God's love is made visible in the God-Man who embraced the darkness of our human world and by his light shines forth the "refulgence of his glory" (second reading).

Our yes to God's overtures of love draws us into a new relationship with God—we are at once children with simple traits of love and excitement, of abandon and glee; adolescents who struggle to come to "believe in his name"; adults who shine forth the "fullness" we have received, "grace and truth" overflowing in a shared love-Life that far surpasses anything we could imagine. This Word made flesh draws us into an unimaginably fecund love, an espousal love. This day calls us to fall in love with our God once again.

CELEBRATION and CATECHESIS

Model Penitential Act

Presider: Today we celebrate the birth of the incarnate Son of God, Jesus our Savior. May we open our hearts to God's loving Presence to us, and beg mercy and forgiveness for the times when we have not lived as God's beloved sons and daughters . . . [pause]

Lord Jesus, you were born of the Virgin Mary: Lord . . .

Christ Jesus, you are *Emmanuel*, God with us: Christ . . .

Lord Jesus, you are the Prince of Peace: Lord . . .

Model Universal Prayer (Prayer of the Faithful)

Presider: As we celebrate the God who gives *the* love-gift of the Son, we are emboldened to ask for what we need.

Response:

Lord,   hear   our prayer.

Cantor:

we pray to the Lord,

For the people of God, who are the continued Presence of divine Love in the world . . . [pause]

For all peoples of the world, who are called from darkness into the Light . . . [pause]

For the poor and the lonely, the sick and the suffering, who are the beloved children of God . . . [pause]

For each of us here, who are called to the self-giving love which generates new life . . . [pause]

Presider: O saving God, you sent your only-begotten Son into the world to be your loving Presence among us. Hear these our prayers and help us to respond faithfully to your love. We pray through the incarnate Son, Jesus Christ our Lord. **Amen**.

FOR REFLECTION
• I become profoundly aware of the mystery of the incarnation as a love encounter between God and me when . . .
• When I truly live the mystery of the incarnation, I am changed in these ways . . .
• Christmas challenges me to . . .

Homily Points

• In one of our most beloved Christmas hymns, we sing:

Silent night, Holy night
Son of God, love's pure light
Radiant beams from thy holy face
With the dawn of redeeming grace,
Jesus, Lord at thy birth,
Jesus, Lord at thy birth.

Christmas is a feast of love! God-in-human-flesh is a blinding love-light made radiant by divine Self-giving.

• God loves us so intensely that we cannot help but respond. Long ago St. Augustine said, "To fall in love with God is the greatest romance; to seek God is the greatest adventure; to find God is the greatest human achievement." How well Augustine describes the love-mystery of the incarnation! Our response to God's love is to seek and find God, to encounter and embrace God's Presence, to become God's blinding love-light in our own time and place. God's love knows no bounds. Neither can ours.

SPIRITUALITY

GOSPEL ACCLAMATION
Col 3:15a, 16a

R̸. Alleluia, alleluia.
Let the peace of Christ control your hearts;
let the word of Christ dwell in you richly.
R̸. Alleluia, alleluia.

Gospel   Luke 2:41-52; L17C

Each year Jesus' parents went to
    Jerusalem for the feast of Passover,
  and when he was twelve years old,
  they went up according to festival
        custom.
After they had completed its days, as
        they were returning,
  the boy Jesus remained behind in
        Jerusalem,
  but his parents did not know it.
Thinking that he was in the caravan,
    they journeyed for a day
  and looked for him among their
        relatives and acquaintances,
  but not finding him,
  they returned to Jerusalem to look for
        him.
After three days they found him in the
        temple,
  sitting in the midst of the teachers,
  listening to them and asking them
        questions,
  and all who heard him were astounded
  at his understanding and his answers.

Continued in Appendix A, p. 268.

Reflecting on the Gospel

One of the great joys of the Christmas season is to behold the utter joy, innocence, beauty that light up the faces of little children. They are filled with wonder, delight, excitement. Year after year they grow into surer expectation about what happens with family and friends during Christmas. They grow into the family holiday traditions. This feast and these readings remind us that being a "holy" family is a matter of valuing the memories and traditions that make us who we are—a holy family, a holy people.

So much tradition shapes the event in this gospel: Passover in Jerusalem, significance of being twelve years old, traveling in caravan, being in the temple, obedience to parents. A surprising interruption of tradition also shapes this event: "the boy Jesus" astounded the teachers "at his understanding and his answers." Each family—the Holy Family, our own families—must find a way to keep worthy traditions alive while at the same time remain open to something astoundingly new. Holiness consists in finding that way. We know whether to accept something new into our family tradition when that change in tradition deepens our holiness.

The Holy Family provides us the model we need. They were faithful and obedient to the traditions that formed who they were. They were also open to God's astoundingly new in-breaking and willing to undergo the change that divine in-breaking invited for their lives. They teach us what it means to be "in [our] Father's house," where we learn our religious traditions and form the memories that make us who we are as members of the larger family of God. They teach us that we really belong to God, and everything about our living must reflect that we are most at home "in [our] Father's house." The Holy Family also teaches us to be obedient to the unknown and un-understood things to which God might be calling us. They teach us that our lives are about always growing "in wisdom and age and favor."

It is in giving ourselves over to God's unexpected new invitations that we, too, advance in "wisdom and age and favor / before God" and all those who know us. Our families are schools of holiness, for there we learn the memories and traditions that make us who we are and who God wants us to be: holy, God's beloved children. Holiness is finding the way to be who we are in God's sight: people of a tradition and people open to God's new in-breaking.

Living the Paschal Mystery

The familiarity of family life can sometimes blind us to see the goodness in each other. This feast reminds us to open our eyes and be "astonished" at the goodness of each other rather than being anxious about our own concerns. Families grow in holiness when each person in the family—from parents to the smallest child and including anyone extended the hospitality of the family—is treated as a member of God's family and, therefore, holy.

This is challenging when sometimes all we can see is each other's faults. It takes a great deal of dying to self to get beyond the normal, everyday annoyances that are part of family life and see others as holy and deserving of our honor, love, and respect. Mary and Joseph were not free from family struggles; after all, they lost Jesus on a trip! And when they found him they had to struggle to understand who he was and who he was meant to become. In doing so, they were able to help Jesus (and themselves) grow in wisdom, age, and grace. In this same love and care for each other we also grow in holiness as a family.

Focusing the Gospel

Key words and phrases: Jerusalem, Passover, twelve years old, caravan, in the temple, in the midst of the teachers, astounded, his understanding and his answers

To the point: So much tradition shapes the event in this gospel: Passover in Jerusalem, significance of being twelve years old, traveling in caravan, being in the temple, obedience to parents. A surprising interruption of tradition also shapes this event: "the boy Jesus" astounded the teachers "at his understanding and his answers." Each family—the Holy Family, our own families—must find a way to keep worthy traditions alive while at the same time remain open to something astoundingly new. Holiness consists in finding that way.

Connecting the Gospel

to the second reading: The motivation for choosing to be a "holy" family is God's inviting us into the "family" of the Holy Trinity: "See what love the Father has bestowed on us / that we may be called the children of God." From all eternity we have belonged to a "holy family."

to experience: This holiday time is a natural "family" time. For some this is a harmonious time. For others the tensions and alienation within families are appallingly apparent. In either case, how we respond is or is not a mark of holiness.

Connecting the Responsorial Psalm

to the readings: For the Israelites God's dwelling place was the temple in Jerusalem. There they journeyed three times a year to keep festival. These annual pilgrimages were joyous occasions, expressing the community's sense of identity as God's chosen people and their longing to be with God forever. Psalm 84 communicates this joy and this hope.

Because she knew she was one of God's chosen people, Hannah willingly gave her son to God (first reading). Because he knew he was God's Son, Jesus recognized his "Father's house" as his true home (gospel). We, too, know who we are ("the children of God") and where we dwell ("in him"; second reading). Like Jesus, like Mary and Joseph, like Hannah, we give ourselves in obedience and trust to the God who has made us God's own. We sing Psalm 84 to celebrate *our* blessedness as God's chosen ones and to express our desire to dwell more fully in God's Presence.

to psalmist preparation: In this responsorial psalm you call the assembly to become conscious of who they are—a holy family who dwell in the house of the Lord. What would strengthen your own sense of yourself as a member of God's family? How might you live this week so that this identity be more evident to others?

ASSEMBLY & FAITH-SHARING GROUPS
- My most treasured family traditions are . . . They shape me in holiness in that . . .
- My family calls me to holiness by . . . My family models holiness when . . .
- To deepen my family's holiness, something astoundingly new we might embrace is . . .

PRESIDERS
I help families realize that "we are God's children now" (second reading) when I . . .

DEACONS
My ministry deepens the holiness of my family by . . .

HOSPITALITY MINISTERS
My hospitality—whether with my family or the parish family—helps others be comfortable in God's house when . . .

MUSIC MINISTERS
My music ministry leads the assembly to experience themselves as God's holy family when . . .

ALTAR MINISTERS
What my ministry of service has taught me about being a holy family is . . .

LECTORS
I model what it truly means to listen to and ponder God's word as did the Holy Family when . . .

EXTRAORDINARY MINISTERS OF HOLY COMMUNION
As the holy family of the church processes to receive Holy Communion, I see . . .

Model Penitential Act

Presider: Gathered together as God's holy family, let us call to mind the times we have not lived as children of God . . . [pause]

Lord Jesus, you show us the way to holiness: Lord . . .

Christ Jesus, you are seated at the right hand of your Father: Christ . . .

Lord Jesus, you call us to grow in wisdom and grace: Lord . . .

Homily Points

• How often are we confident—even complacent—about knowing where to find Jesus, only to be startled—even frightened—to discover that he is not there? Our response is to search frantically for him, but when we find him we are further stunned by where he is and what he has to say to us. How, we ask, are we to go from here in order truly to advance in "wisdom and age and favor"?

• Mary and Joseph's experience of losing Jesus in the temple stretched them to relate to and understand their Son Jesus in a deeper way. Jesus was not the only one who returned to Nazareth and grew in "wisdom and age and favor." So did Mary. So did Joseph. This openness to God's new in-breaking was a mark of their holiness.

• Our own openness to God's new in-breaking is a mark of our holiness. God's action in our lives is never stagnant, but dynamically leads us forward to newer insights, deeper understanding, and greater courage to change. This feast of the Holy Family pushes us to seek ever anew God's action in our lives and respond with newfound forms of fidelity.

Model Universal Prayer (Prayer of the Faithful)

Presider: The God who forms us into a family surely hears our prayers that we may grow in holiness.

Response:

Lord, hear our prayer.

Cantor:

we pray to the Lord,

For all members of the community of the church, the family of God . . . [pause]

For the peoples of the world, the family of humanity . . . [pause]

For families suffering loss, division, or hardship . . . [pause]

For ourselves gathered here, the parish family . . . [pause]

Presider: Gracious God, you gave us the Holy Family of Jesus, Mary, and Joseph. Hear these our prayers that our families may be strengthened in our dedication to you and one day be with you for ever and ever. **Amen**.

Let us pray.

Pause for silent prayer

O God, who were pleased to give us
the shining example of the Holy Family,
graciously grant that we may imitate them
in practicing the virtues of family life and
    in the bonds of charity,
and so, in the joy of your house,
delight one day in eternal rewards.
Through our Lord Jesus Christ, your Son,
who lives and reigns with you in the unity
    of the Holy Spirit,
one God, for ever and ever. **Amen**.

FIRST READING
1 Sam 1:20-22, 24-28

In those days Hannah conceived, and at
    the end of her term bore a son
    whom she called Samuel, since she had
        asked the Lord for him.
The next time her husband Elkanah was
    going up
    with the rest of his household
    to offer the customary sacrifice to the
        Lord and to fulfill his vows,
    Hannah did not go, explaining to her
        husband,
    "Once the child is weaned,
    I will take him to appear before the Lord
    and to remain there forever;
    I will offer him as a perpetual nazirite."

Once Samuel was weaned, Hannah
    brought him up with her,
    along with a three-year-old bull,
    an ephah of flour, and a skin of wine,
    and presented him at the temple of the
        Lord in Shiloh.
After the boy's father had sacrificed the
    young bull,
    Hannah, his mother, approached Eli and
        said:
    "Pardon, my lord!
As you live, my lord,
    I am the woman who stood near you
        here, praying to the Lord.
I prayed for this child, and the Lord
    granted my request.
Now I, in turn, give him to the Lord;
    as long as he lives, he shall be dedicated
        to the Lord."
Hannah left Samuel there.

RESPONSORIAL PSALM
Ps 84:2-3, 5-6, 9-10

℟. (cf. 5a) Blessed are they who dwell in
your house, O Lord.

How lovely is your dwelling place, O LORD
of hosts!
My soul yearns and pines for the courts
of the LORD.
My heart and my flesh cry out for the
living God.

R̸. Blessed are they who dwell in your
house, O Lord.

Happy they who dwell in your house!
Continually they praise you.
Happy the men whose strength you are!
Their hearts are set upon the
pilgrimage.

R̸. Blessed are they who dwell in your
house, O Lord.

O LORD of hosts, hear our prayer;
hearken, O God of Jacob!
O God, behold our shield,
and look upon the face of your
anointed.

R̸. Blessed are they who dwell in your
house, O Lord.

SECOND READING
1 John 3:1-2, 21-24

Beloved:
See what love the Father has bestowed
on us
that we may be called the children of
God.
And so we are.
The reason the world does not know us
is that it did not know him.
Beloved, we are God's children now;
what we shall be has not yet been
revealed.
We do know that when it is revealed we
shall be like him,
for we shall see him as he is.

Beloved, if our hearts do not condemn us,
we have confidence in God and receive
from him whatever we ask,
because we keep his commandments
and do what pleases him.
And his commandment is this:
we should believe in the name of his
Son, Jesus Christ,
and love one another just as he
commanded us.
Those who keep his commandments
remain in him, and he in them,
and the way we know that he remains
in us
is from the Spirit he gave us.

*See Appendix A, pp. 268–269, for
optional readings.*

✛ CATECHESIS

About Liturgy

Choice of readings: The revised Lectionary on some festivals has provided readings for all three years of the Lectionary cycle. The feast of the Holy Family is one such festival. In order to plumb the riches of the Lectionary the *Living Liturgy*™ team has chosen to go with the proper readings now given for each year; hence, our reflections are based on the readings that may be used for Year C.

Strengthening family life: Immediately following our celebration of Christmas, the church provides us with a number of related celebrations helpful for strengthening family life: December 26, the Feast of St. Stephen, the first martyr; December 27, the Feast of St. John the Evangelist; December 28, the Feast of the Holy Innocents (since these are weekday celebrations many may not be aware of them). All three of these feasts remind us that following Christ has its demands, even to the point of giving one's life in order to remain faithful to Christian discipleship. Naturally, family life has its demands but none of these exceed our strength if we remember that God has given us the gift of the divine Son who dwells within each of us because of our baptism.

The church also celebrates this feast of the Holy Family. Although the gospel passages about the Holy Family are scanty, we know that life wasn't easy for Jesus, Mary, and Joseph. They model for us a family life not beyond our reach, but one that is very real and built on caring for and loving each other, built upon openness to God's will, built on a reliance of God for guidance and assurance.

About Liturgical Music

Music suggestions: On the heels of Christmas, the feast of the Holy Family confronts us with the disappearance of the twelve-year-old Jesus in Jerusalem, and Mary and Joseph's struggle with who he is and what his life must be about. Appropriate song choices are ones which speak about who this Child will become. James Woodford's "Within the Father's House" (*Hymns for the Gospels*, GIA) retells the story of the gospel and asks God to reveal Jesus' hidden identity to us in "full epiphany." Alan Hommerding's "Come, Sing a Home and Family" (OF, WC, WS) makes vivid the influence of Mary and Joseph on the adult person Jesus was to become. The fourth-century text "Of the Father's Love Begotten" (in most resources) mystically unfolds the identity of who this wondrous Child begotten "Ere the worlds began to be" truly is. Delores Dufner's "What Feast of Love" (*Sing a New Church*, OCP) moves from the gift of Jesus in his birth at Bethlehem to his ongoing gift of self in the Eucharist. Sung to GREENSLEEVES ("What Child Is This"), this hymn enables us to reflect on the traditional text with deepened insight.

✠ SPIRITUALITY

GOSPEL ACCLAMATION

R⁊. Alleluia, alleluia.
In the past God spoke to our ancestors through
    the prophets;
in these last days, he has spoken to us through
    the Son.
R⁊. Alleluia, alleluia.

Gospel

Luke 2:16-21; L18ABC

**The shepherds went in haste to
    Bethlehem and found Mary and
    Joseph,
and the infant lying in the manger.
When they saw this,
    they made known the message
    that had been told them about this
    child.
All who heard it were amazed
    by what had been told them by
    the shepherds.
And Mary kept all these things,
    reflecting on them in her heart.
Then the shepherds returned,
    glorifying and praising God
    for all they had heard and seen,
    just as it had been told to them.**

**When eight days were completed for
    his circumcision,
he was named Jesus, the name given
    him by the angel
before he was conceived in the
    womb.**

See Appendix A, p. 269, for the other readings.

Reflecting on the Gospel

Other than celebrations honoring the divine Son, our liturgical year has more festivals celebrating the Blessed Virgin Mary than anyone else. We celebrate Mary's conception and birth, her presentation in the temple, and her being taken into heaven. We celebrate Mary under various titles, such as Our Lady of Lourdes, Fatima, Mount Carmel, Guadalupe, the Rosary. We celebrate her visitation to her cousin Elizabeth, her immaculate heart, her queenship, her sorrows. Almost every month of the year has at least one festival honoring Mary—the only exceptions being March and April. It ought to come as no surprise to us, then, that on the revised liturgical calendar of 1969, the octave day of Christmas was changed in title to honor Mary under the title "the Holy Mother of God."

The gospel assigned for this day describes the shepherds' actions after the birth of Jesus; their actions parallel Mary's actions before the birth. Angels made known to the shepherds the glad tidings of the birth of the Savior; the angel Gabriel made known to Mary that she would conceive and bear a Son who was to be "named Jesus." After receiving their divine message, the shepherds "went in haste" to see for themselves this Savior; Mary went in haste to visit her cousin Elizabeth. The shepherds glorified and praised God for God's mighty deeds; Mary sang the *Magnificat*, her great song of praise extolling God for mighty deeds. The shepherds and Mary reveal to us a pattern for our own engagement with the events of salvation: hear God's ongoing divine word of revelation, hasten to respond to this divine word, and give God glory and praise. How God related to the shepherds and Mary is how God relates to us.

The shepherds obeyed the angel's revelation and searched for the newborn babe, the Savior, the Messiah. Mary, the Mother of this wondrous Child, also had a message made known to her by an angel. She heard, accepted, and said yes to what God revealed to her. She gave birth to Jesus, the Savior, the Messiah. She is the Mother of God. She is our Mother who helps us hear this same message. When do we go "in haste" and tell everyone we meet what has been told to us?

Living the Paschal Mystery

The mystery of the incarnation and salvation is too big to celebrate during one week of the year and too deep for us to grasp easily. Like Mary, we must ponder these things in our hearts so that, as children of God (see second reading), we can continually glorify and praise God. Like Mary, we too must "give flesh" to the Savior, ponder his Presence within us, and then let that Presence guide us in the way we respond to the daily tasks and events we face.

Authentic Gospel living can only happen if we ponder God's words spoken to us, reflect on God's Presence and guidance, and then act according to God's will. This solemnity so closely following Christmas helps us realize that the joy of Christmas is ongoing only when we ourselves are the incarnation of Christ for others and are the bearers of his message of Good News. We "give flesh" to the Savior in the simple, ordinary demands of our daily living when they are done from our own yes to God. Our actions flow from Gospel values that first shape us and which we learn through pondering God's deeds on our behalf. Thus is the Word made flesh in our lives. This is what Mary our Mother models for us.

Focusing the Gospel

Key words and phrases: went in haste, made known the message, just as it had been told to them, Mary, Jesus

To the point: The shepherds obeyed the angel's revelation and searched for the newborn babe, the Savior, the Messiah. Mary, the Mother of this wondrous Child, also had a message made known to her by an angel. She heard, accepted, and said yes to what God revealed to her. She gave birth to Jesus, the Savior, the Messiah. She is the Mother of God. She is our Mother who helps us hear this same message. When do we go "in haste" and tell everyone we meet what has been told to us?

Model Penitential Act

Presider: Today we honor Mary the Mother of God who gave birth to Jesus, the Savior of the world and the Son of God. Let us pause a moment and ask God's mercy for the times we have not been open to the Presence of the Savior in our lives . . . [pause]

Lord Jesus, you are the Son of God and Son of Mary: Lord . . .

Christ Jesus, you are worthy of all glory and praise: Christ . . .

Lord Jesus, you are the Savior of the world: Lord . . .

Model Universal Prayer (Prayer of the Faithful)

Presider: God sent the divine Son to bring us salvation and peace. Let us pray that we and all peoples in our world may be blessed this year.

Response:

Cantor:

That all members of the church continually make known God's ongoing revelation of the message of salvation . . . [pause]

That all peoples of the world enjoy peace and receive justice during this new year . . . [pause]

That those who lack spiritually and materially receive from the generosity of this community what they need to grow in fullness of life . . . [pause]

That each of us during this coming year learn from Mary how to hear, accept, and say yes to God's word of salvation . . . [pause]

Presider: God of peace and justice, you bless us and are gracious to us beyond measure: hear these our prayers that we might live as faithful daughters and sons of Mary our Mother. We ask this through her Son, Jesus Christ our Lord. **Amen**.

COLLECT

Let us pray.

Pause for silent prayer

O God, who through the fruitful virginity of Blessed Mary
bestowed on the human race
the grace of eternal salvation,
grant, we pray,
that we may experience the intercession of her,
through whom we were found worthy
to receive the author of life,
our Lord Jesus Christ, your Son.
Who lives and reigns with you in the unity of the Holy Spirit,
one God, for ever and ever. **Amen**.

FOR REFLECTION

- I have heard the message of salvation from . . .
- My daily living—among family, neighbors, and coworkers—makes "known the message" about this mystery whenever I . . .
- From Mary, I learn . . .

Homily Points

- The technology revolution has made communication instant and constant. But this communication is often abbreviated and impersonal. By contrast, God's unbroken communication of the mystery of salvation is unabbreviated and personal. It is brought to fullness in the birth of the Savior; it is personal in the womb of Mary and the hearts of all who hear the message, encounter the Savior of the world, and make his Presence known.

- In the "fullness of time" (second reading) came fullness within the womb of Mary. The womb of Mary brought forth Jesus, the fullness of salvation for all peoples. This fullness is what the shepherds made known after they found the Child in the manger (see gospel). Mary pondered in her heart this fullness—the ongoing revelation of the mystery of salvation. Now the revelation is communicated to us. Now the "fullness of time" is for us. What do we ponder? What do we proclaim?

33

SPIRITUALITY

GOSPEL ACCLAMATION
Matt 2:2

℟. Alleluia, alleluia.
We saw his star at its rising
and have come to do him homage.
℟. Alleluia, alleluia.

Gospel   Matt 2:1-12; L20ABC

When Jesus was born in
    Bethlehem of Judea,
in the days of King
    Herod,
behold, magi from
    the east arrived
    in Jerusalem,
    saying,
"Where is the
    newborn king
    of the Jews?
We saw his star at
    its rising
and have come
    to do him
    homage."
When King Herod heard this,
    he was greatly troubled,
    and all Jerusalem with him.
Assembling all the chief priests and the
    scribes of the people,
    he inquired of them where the Christ was
    to be born.
They said to him, "In Bethlehem of Judea,
    for thus it has been written through the
    prophet:
And you, Bethlehem, land of Judah,
    are by no means least among the
    rulers of Judah;
since from you shall come a ruler,
    who is to shepherd my people Israel."
Then Herod called the magi secretly
    and ascertained from them the time of
    the star's appearance.
He sent them to Bethlehem and said,
    "Go and search diligently for the child.
When you have found him, bring me word,
    that I too may go and do him homage."
After their audience with the king they set
    out.

Continued in Appendix A, p. 269.

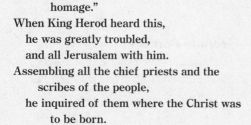

Reflecting on the Gospel

A TV commercial a while back sang the praises of the human eye. The commercial portrayed how our amazing eyes can see the light of a single candle in the darkness from one hundred football fields away. That's over thirty thousand feet! In the gospel, the "magi from the east" followed the light of a star. A light of heaven that guided them. A light of revelation that manifested "the newborn king of the Jews" to Gentile wise men. A light of warning that protected this Child from harm until his time had come. Like the magi, we must follow this light to *the* Light. Like the magi, we must offer "the child" homage—the gift of our very selves become the Light of his Presence. A Light that guides, reveals, warns.

The light of the glory of God's Presence is all around us. Unlike the magi, we don't have to undertake an arduous journey. We need only to open our eyes to see through the darkness. We need only to allow God to guide us by word, sacrament, grace. We need only to heed the warning signs of those who might lead us astray, those who refuse to see the light, those who choose not to give God the humble homage of which God is worthy. The real challenge of this gospel is that we do not seek the light outside of ourselves, as did the magi, but within ourselves. We do not need to look up to the heavens, to observe starlight, to go on a long journey. The light that guides, reveals, and warns us is right here among us. It is within us. We are the light that shines forth the Presence of God.

The mystery we celebrate this day is that this "newborn king of the Jews" is as present to us as he was present to the magi who came to do him homage and offer him gifts. Just as this "newborn king of the Jews" manifested himself to the "magi from the east," symbolizing the Gentiles, so does he now manifest himself to all peoples and all nations at all times. He manifests himself to us. His Light, however, does not emanate from a distant star, but from within each of us who is open to his divine Presence, open to his saving love, open to his gift of Life.

We ourselves are the guiding light; we ourselves reveal God's divine Presence through the goodness of who we are; we ourselves warn others by the way we live of the danger of closing our eyes to this Light. We ourselves are to be the gift offered to others, a gift that shines brightly for all to see because this "newborn king of the Jews" dwells within us and among us. Such a light we behold!

Living the Paschal Mystery

Because God's generosity in offering us divine Presence is so lavish, our response must be just as lavish. God has given us great treasures, two of which are mystery so deep: the gift of the only-begotten Son as the divine Presence which dwells among and within us, and the gift of our own selves being "members of the same body" (see second reading) with the power to manifest that divine Presence for others. Our response can be no less than the total gift of ourselves.

At baptism we become "coheirs" and "copartners" in Christ (see second reading). We are copartners, therefore, in Jesus' saving ministry. Clearly, seeing the revelation of Christ among us requires of us a unique kind of seeing. We do not "look at" the light; we become the Light. We do not simply "see" the glory of divine Presence; we become the glory of that divine Presence. Our gift for others is the Light that shines forth from the "newborn king" who dwells within us.

Focusing the Gospel

Key words and phrases: magi from the east, newborn king of the Jews, saw his star, did him homage, offered him gifts, warned in a dream

To the point: The "magi from the east" followed the light of a star. A light of heaven that guided them. A light of revelation that manifested "the newborn king of the Jews" to Gentile wise men. A light of warning that protected this Child from harm until his time had come. Like the magi, we must follow this light to *the* Light. Like the magi, we must offer "the child" homage—the gift of our very selves become the Light of his Presence. A Light that guides, reveals, warns.

Connecting the Gospel

to the first reading: The first reading announces to Jerusalem, "Your light has come." Upon Jerusalem "the LORD shines" and all nations "shall walk by your light." In the gospel, the light shines to lead the magi—all nations—to the Light of the world, the Christ Child.

to experience: All major occasions include some form of gift-giving: births, birthdays, anniversaries, weddings; even at funerals we send cards and flowers. It is not surprising that the magi bring gifts to the "newborn king"—gold, frankincense, and myrrh. Their greatest gift, however, was the gift of themselves, expressed in their humble homage.

Connecting the Responsorial Psalm

to the readings: Historically, Psalm 72 was a prayer for the king of Israel who represented God. The people asked God to endow the king with divine judgment so that justice might reign, the poor and afflicted be rescued, and peace blossom for all time. Then light would shine from Jerusalem and all nations would recognize and pay homage to the true King, the Lord God (first reading).

Liturgically, the Lectionary uses verses from Psalm 72 to identify Christ as the fulfillment of Israel's prayer: this newborn babe is the King *par excellence*, God's justice and mercy in the flesh, come to rescue the poor and bring peace to all nations. Those who "see" recognize who he is and come to adore him (gospel). In the second reading, Paul tells us the revelation made known in the coming of Christ is complete and universal. Nonetheless, leading all people to see and recognize Christ requires action on our part: we are "copartners in . . . Christ." And so our singing of this psalm is more than just a celebration of what God has done for salvation. It is also a commitment on our part to spread the Good News of God's saving work to all nations.

to psalmist preparation: When you sing this responsorial psalm, you reveal who Christ is: the justice, peace, and mercy of God in human flesh. You also participate in the church's prayer that all peoples recognize who Christ is and come to adore him. What might you do this week to be the justice of God in human flesh for someone? Who needs you to be the mercy of God made flesh?

ASSEMBLY & FAITH-SHARING GROUPS
- The light I follow is . . . It leads me to . . .
- I search for Christ when . . . I am the revelation of Christ for others when . . .
- Like the magi, I encounter the "newborn king" when . . . The gift I offer him is . . .

PRESIDERS
When Christ's light shines in and through my ministry, it looks like . . . It leads others to . . .

DEACONS
My servant ministry manifests the Light of Christ to others by . . .

HOSPITALITY MINISTERS
Through my hospitality ministry, I guide those gathering for liturgy to . . .

MUSIC MINISTERS
I offer the homage of my very self to the "newborn king" through my music making when I . . .

ALTAR MINISTERS
Through my servant ministering, I manifest the Light of Christ to . . .

LECTORS
My manner of proclamation gives light to those searching for the "newborn king" whenever I . . .

EXTRAORDINARY MINISTERS OF HOLY COMMUNION
I am radiant with the Light of Christ when I distribute Holy Communion because . . .

Model Penitential Act

Presider: The magi followed the star to the newborn King. Let us prepare ourselves to celebrate this liturgy by examining how well we have followed God's light in our own lives and ask for God's mercy when we have chosen to walk in darkness . . . [pause]

Lord Jesus, your Presence was revealed by the light of a star: Lord . . .

Christ Jesus, you are worthy of all homage and praise: Christ . . .

Lord Jesus, you are Light for all nations: Lord . . .

Homily Points

• Incandescent lightbulbs are being replaced by more energy efficient and longer lasting CFL, LED, and halogen lightbulbs. These are more expensive, but in the long run bring many cost-effective benefits. God's "light" is the most energy efficient, long lasting, benefit-giving Light there is. It is also the most expensive! The price is our very selves.

• The magi ask, "Where is the newborn king of the Jews?" They have committed themselves to follow the light of the star, searching until they find this King. Unfortunately, they ask the wrong person for the light of guidance along the way. Fortunately, they choose to follow God's light and they find the Treasure for which they have been searching. They offer "gifts of gold, frankincense, and myrrh," but much more: they offer the gifts of themselves in humble homage.

• How committed are we to finding Christ? What light guides us? Do we persevere in following the light? Do we ask the right persons for guidance and help? Do we listen to them? When we find Christ anew, are we willing to pay the cost of walking in his Light? Are we willing to pay with the gift of our very selves?

Model Universal Prayer (Prayer of the Faithful)

Presider: Through the light of a star, God guided the magi to find the Christ Child, the Savior of the world. This same God guides us and hears our prayers.

Response:

Lord, hear our prayer.

Cantor:

we pray to the Lord,

That all members of the church faithfully follow the light God shines upon us . . . [pause]

That all peoples walk in the light that leads to salvation . . . [pause]

That those walking in darkness search diligently for the light that leads to an encounter with Christ . . . [pause]

That each of us here may willingly follow the Light of Christ no matter what the personal cost . . . [pause]

Presider: Generous God, you manifest the light of salvation to all nations: hear these our prayers that we might one day receive the fullness of your light, Life everlasting. We ask this through Christ our Lord. **Amen.**

COLLECT

Let us pray.

Pause for silent prayer

O God, who on this day
revealed your Only Begotten Son to the
    nations
by the guidance of a star,
grant in your mercy
that we, who know you already by faith,
may be brought to behold the beauty of
    your sublime glory.
Through our Lord Jesus Christ, your Son,
who lives and reigns with you in the unity
    of the Holy Spirit,
one God, for ever and ever. **Amen.**

FIRST READING

Isa 60:1-6

Rise up in splendor, Jerusalem! Your light
    has come,
    the glory of the Lord shines upon you.
See, darkness covers the earth,
    and thick clouds cover the peoples;
but upon you the LORD shines,
    and over you appears his glory.
Nations shall walk by your light,
    and kings by your shining radiance.
Raise your eyes and look about;
    they all gather and come to you:
your sons come from afar,
    and your daughters in the arms of their
        nurses.

Then you shall be radiant at what you see,
    your heart shall throb and overflow,
for the riches of the sea shall be emptied
        out before you,
    the wealth of nations shall be brought
        to you.
Caravans of camels shall fill you,
    dromedaries from Midian and Ephah;
all from Sheba shall come
    bearing gold and frankincense,
    and proclaiming the praises of the LORD.

RESPONSORIAL PSALM
Ps 72:1-2, 7-8, 10-11, 12-13

R̸. (cf. 11) Lord, every nation on earth will adore you.

O God, with your judgment endow the
    king,
  and with your justice, the king's son;
he shall govern your people with justice
  and your afflicted ones with judgment.

R̸. Lord, every nation on earth will adore you.

Justice shall flower in his days,
  and profound peace, till the moon be no
    more.
May he rule from sea to sea,
  and from the River to the ends of the
    earth.

R̸. Lord, every nation on earth will adore you.

The kings of Tarshish and the Isles shall
    offer gifts;
  the kings of Arabia and Seba shall
    bring tribute.
All kings shall pay him homage,
  all nations shall serve him.

R̸. Lord, every nation on earth will adore you.

For he shall rescue the poor when he cries
    out,
  and the afflicted when he has no one to
    help him.
He shall have pity for the lowly and the
    poor;
  the lives of the poor he shall save.

R̸. Lord, every nation on earth will adore you.

SECOND READING
Eph 3:2-3a, 5-6

Brothers and sisters:
You have heard of the stewardship of
    God's grace
  that was given to me for your benefit,
  namely, that the mystery was made
    known to me by revelation.
It was not made known to people in other
    generations
  as it has now been revealed
to his holy apostles and prophets by the
    Spirit:
  that the Gentiles are coheirs, members
    of the same body,
  and copartners in the promise in Christ
    Jesus through the gospel.

About Liturgy

Gift of worship: Each Sunday when the Christian assembly gathers for liturgy, many gifts are given to God: the gift of time and talent shown in the various ministries; the gift of money and food goods for those in need and the upkeep of the parish; the gift of ourselves to each other by our presence and full, conscious, and active participation. All of this is good. At the same time we must never forget that we gather on Sunday *in response to* God's prior gifts to us summed up in the Son and our share in divine Life. Thus our Sunday celebration most of all ought to be characterized by thankfulness for all God has given us and praise (homage) for this God who chooses to be so intimately present to us.

It is all too easy for our Sunday celebrations to be subtly focused on ourselves. Although we can never be passive at Sunday Mass (and our greeting each other, hospitality, offerings are an important and indispensable part of the time spent in worship), we must never forget, however, that we are there first and foremost to give God praise and thanksgiving. The purpose of Sunday worship is just that: *worship.* Threaded through the speaking and singing, gestures and postures, relating and responding must be an attitude of awe, reverence, and deep-felt gratitude for God's lavish generosity to us in so many ways. In the end the only lasting gift we can really give God is ourselves in worship and self-emptying service of others.

About Liturgical Music

Music suggestions: An Epiphany hymn suitable for the entrance procession would be "What Star Is This" (in most resources). The song has been widely used since the early eighteenth century as a hymn for Vespers (Evening Prayer) on Epiphany. Its delightful dance-like quality expresses well the festive mood of this day. Delores Dufner's "Infant Wrapped in God's Own Light" (SS) would also work well for the entrance song, as would Francis Patrick O'Brien's "Epiphany Carol" (G3, SS). Because of its verse-refrain structure, Mary Louise Bringle's "The People Who Walked in Darkness" (G3, W4) would work well during Communion.

Ruth Duck's "O Radiant Christ, Incarnate Word," in *Dancing in the Universe* (GIA), captures both the confidence we feel in the revelation brought by Christ and the struggle we experience letting that revelation guide human affairs: "Our bartered, busy lives burn dim, too tired to care, too numb to feel . . . Come, shine upon our shadowed world . . . illumine all we say and do . . . lead the peoples to your peace, as stars once lead the way to you." The text is set to the tune RADIANT LIGHT in which the shifts between C major and C minor aptly express the light-darkness-light shifts in the text itself. The choir alone could sing the hymn during the preparation of the gifts. Or the entire assembly could sing it using a familiar tune such as WAREHAM.

SPIRITUALITY

GOSPEL ACCLAMATION
cf. Luke 3:16

R̸. Alleluia, alleluia.
John said: One mightier than I is coming;
he will baptize you with the Holy Spirit and with
fire.
R̸. Alleluia, alleluia.

Gospel   Luke 3:15-16, 21-22; L21C

The people were filled with
    expectation,
  and all were asking in their
    hearts
  whether John might be the
    Christ.
John answered them all, saying,
  "I am baptizing you with water,
  but one mightier than I is
    coming.
I am not worthy to loosen the
    thongs of his sandals.
He will baptize you with the Holy
    Spirit and fire."

After all the people had been
    baptized
  and Jesus also had been baptized and
    was praying,
  heaven was opened and the Holy
    Spirit descended upon him
  in bodily form like a dove.
And a voice came from heaven,
  "You are my beloved Son;
  with you I am well pleased."

Reflecting on the Gospel

Eighteenth-century English poet Alexander Pope once remarked that if we expect nothing, we shall never be disappointed. Such a low bar we might set for ourselves! Yes, great expectations might disappoint by blinding us to the good already in front of us, or leading us to future failure. Yet, it is better to risk disappointment than be stuck with nothing to look forward to, nothing to excite us, nothing to increase our hope. Expectations spur us on to remarkable achievement; urge us to seek excellence with greater diligence; push us to the kind of creativeness that opens the door for something new to happen, for discovering new possibilities, for embracing the unknown.

The people in the gospel looked to John the Baptist to be the long-awaited Messiah. It was precisely their expectation—misdirected though it was—that kept them looking for the Messiah. John redirected them from himself to the person of Jesus, the "beloved Son" of God. Our own baptism with "the Holy Spirit and fire" initiates us on a journey of discovery not only of who Jesus is, but also who we are in him. This gospel, then, teaches us something about John, Jesus, and ourselves.

Who was John the Baptist? He was set apart, prophetic, radical, clear about his message of repentance, sure about his identity as the herald of One who would be greater than he. Who is Jesus? He is the Messiah to whom John pointed, the "beloved Son" of God, the One who, because of his own prophetic, radical, and sure message, would be misunderstood, rejected, ridiculed, deserted, crucified.

Who are we? We are those who, through our baptism "with the Holy Spirit and fire," are conformed to Jesus and take up his saving mission. From his baptism by John to his crucifixion, the Messiah did not meet mere human expectations. Rather, he exceeded them with his Good News, his healing, his love. From our own baptism to our death, we also must not meet mere human expectations. Rather, we must achieve the full potential of our own graced identity as God's own people (see second reading) expressed through a Gospel way of living.

Living the Paschal Mystery

Being baptized by "the Holy Spirit and fire" means that we share in Jesus' mission, including the total gift of ourselves. Who we are manifests God's Presence in the very dying to self we do each day as we conform ourselves to God's will. We learn our mission from experiencing and encountering the Divine through others. Our Christian journey is about realizing that *we ourselves* are God's Presence for another. We must constantly redirect our own expectations so that we keep focused on the One "mightier than I" who comes to others, now, through us.

The gift of divine Life and its attendant call to self-giving discipleship does make demands on us. Taking our baptism seriously means that the ritual moment is just the beginning of a lifetime of openness to God's continuing grace "training" us (second reading) to be faithful to who God calls us to be. God's giving us a share in divinity is so gracious that the only response is self-giving in fidelity to our baptismal call. Further, while our baptismal living manifests dying for the sake of others, it also manifests a hope that is sure because God's ultimate gracious gift of everlasting Life is a promise already being fulfilled.

Focusing the Gospel

Key words and phrases: filled with expectation, John might be the Christ, one mightier than I is coming, the Holy Spirit and fire, beloved Son

To the point: The people in the gospel looked to John the Baptist to be the long-awaited Messiah. It was precisely their expectation—misdirected though it was—that kept them looking for the Messiah. John redirected them from himself to the person of Jesus, the "beloved Son" of God. Our own baptism with "the Holy Spirit and fire" initiates us on a journey of discovery not only of who Jesus is, but also who we are in him. What great expectations!

Connecting the Gospel

to the first and second readings: Both readings depict what happens to God's people when the Messiah comes. Both readings stress God's Presence to the people. Both readings describe the transformation the coming of the Messiah brings.

to experience: We all dream of a perfect world. Descriptions of messianic times unveil that perfect world, yet it is way beyond our present lived experience. Only faithful baptismal living hastens the fulfillment of messianic hopes.

Connecting the Responsorial Psalm

to the readings: In these verses from Psalm 104, we praise God who spreads out the heavens, rules the water and the wind, creates all that roams the earth and swims the seas, and gives all creatures their food in due season. The readings and gospel reveal that the fullness of God's power and glory has appeared in the person of Christ. He is God's "beloved Son" (gospel) who will shepherd us to fuller life (see first reading). He is the Son who will "baptize [us] with the Holy Spirit" (gospel), setting us on fire as a people "eager to do . . . good" (second reading). He is the Son through whom the Spirit will "renew the face of the earth" (psalm). Let us cry out at the top of our voices that in him salvation has come, and God is here (see first reading)!

to psalmist preparation: In these psalm verses, you bless God for giving the Spirit of life, for giving the "beloved Son" who leads us to fullness of Life, for giving the baptism that sets us on fire to "do good." In fact, you sing some of the same psalm verses you will sing later in the liturgical year for Pentecost Sunday. What is the connection between Christ's baptism and Pentecost? between your baptism and Pentecost?

ASSEMBLY & FAITH-SHARING GROUPS

- Each day, my expectations include . . . They become misdirected when . . . Jesus redirects them by . . .
- Having been baptized "with the Holy Spirit and fire" means to me . . .
- On my journey of discovering who Jesus is, I have learned . . . of discovering who I am, I have learned . . .

PRESIDERS

I remind the assembly of their baptismal dignity whenever I . . . and I call them to baptismal responsibility whenever I . . .

DEACONS

When I serve others, I discover this about myself . . .

HOSPITALITY MINISTERS

My hospitality ministry affirms the baptismal dignity of others when . . .

MUSIC MINISTERS

My manner of doing music ministry directs the assembly toward the person of Jesus when . . .

ALTAR MINISTERS

Serving at the altar brings out my expectations about who Jesus is for me when . . .

LECTORS

Like John the Baptist, in my proclamation I point to the Presence of the Messiah when I . . .

EXTRAORDINARY MINISTERS OF HOLY COMMUNION

When others come forward in procession to receive Holy Communion, I see Jesus in them when I . . . when they . . .

CELEBRATION

Model Rite for the Blessing and Sprinkling of Water

Presider: Today we celebrate the baptism of Jesus and God's revelation of him as the beloved Son. As we bless and sprinkle this water, we remember our own baptism when we became God's beloved children.

[*continue with* The Roman Missal, *Appendix II*]

Homily Points

• How easy it is to have great expectations, but how often can they be misdirected! For example, someone looking for "Mr. or Ms. Right" can miss the beauty of a person already reaching out in friendship and love. Our expectations must line up with who we are and who God is enabling us to become. Our expectations must be directed to the best for us and others. Our expectations must be consistent with what God wants for us.

• Who is the Messiah? Jesus, the beloved Son of God. What does the Messiah do? Baptize us with the Holy Spirit and fire. Who are we? The beloved of God. What are we to do? Embrace a journey of discovery about Jesus and ourselves that sets us on fire for God. When we are on fire for God, all our expectations are directed toward faithful baptismal living.

• Faithful baptismal living both fulfills expectations and generates new ones. This is why baptismal living is a journey of discovery. Baptism opens us to a Presence that continually transforms who we are and what we can do for others. Baptism offers us new Life in the Holy Spirit that is steadfast yet unpredictable, familiar yet surprising, restful yet energizing. Baptism sets us on fire.

Model Universal Prayer (Prayer of the Faithful)

Presider: In baptism we become beloved daughters and sons of God. Such an identity encourages us to make known our needs to God, fully expecting that God will respond.

Response:

Cantor:

May the church, the Body of Christ, be filled with the fire of the Holy Spirit . . . [pause]

May all peoples, the children of God, faithfully receive the offer of God's salvation . . . [pause]

May the poor, the beloved of God, share more justly in the gifts of this world . . . [pause]

May each of us, followers of Jesus, be faithful to our baptismal promises in our daily living . . . [pause]

Presider: Gracious God, you revealed our Savior Jesus as your beloved Son and through baptism call us to a share in his divine Life. Hear our prayers and bring us to the fullness of our baptismal living. We ask this through Christ our Lord. **Amen.**

Let us pray.

Pause for silent prayer

Almighty ever-living God,
who, when Christ had been baptized in the
    River Jordan
and as the Holy Spirit descended upon
    him,
solemnly declared him your beloved Son,
grant that your children by adoption,
reborn of water and the Holy Spirit,
may always be well pleasing to you.
Through our Lord Jesus Christ, your Son,
who lives and reigns with you in the unity
    of the Holy Spirit,
one God, for ever and ever. **Amen.**

FIRST READING
Isa 40:1-5, 9-11

Comfort, give comfort to my people,
    says your God.
Speak tenderly to Jerusalem, and proclaim
    to her
    that her service is at an end,
    her guilt is expiated;
indeed, she has received from the hand of
    the LORD
    double for all her sins.

    A voice cries out:
In the desert prepare the way of the LORD!
    Make straight in the wasteland a
        highway for our God!
Every valley shall be filled in,
    every mountain and hill shall be made
        low;
the rugged land shall be made a plain,
    the rough country, a broad valley.
Then the glory of the LORD shall be
        revealed,
    and all people shall see it together;
    for the mouth of the LORD has spoken.

Go up onto a high mountain,
    Zion, herald of glad tidings;
cry out at the top of your voice,
    Jerusalem, herald of good news!
Fear not to cry out
    and say to the cities of Judah:
    Here is your God!
Here comes with power
    the Lord GOD,
    who rules by a strong arm;
here is his reward with him,
    his recompense before him.
Like a shepherd he feeds his flock;
    in his arms he gathers the lambs,
carrying them in his bosom,
    and leading the ewes with care.

RESPONSORIAL PSALM

Ps 104:1b-2, 3-4, 24-25, 27-28, 29-30

℟. (1) O bless the Lord, my soul.

O Lord, my God, you are great indeed!
　You are clothed with majesty and glory,
robed in light as with a cloak.
　You have spread out the heavens like a
　　tent-cloth.

℟. O bless the Lord, my soul.

You have constructed your palace upon the
　　waters.
　You make the clouds your chariot;
you travel on the wings of the wind.
　You make the winds your messengers,
and flaming fire your ministers.

℟. O bless the Lord, my soul.

How manifold are your works, O Lord!
　In wisdom you have wrought them all—
　　the earth is full of your creatures;
the sea also, great and wide,
　in which are schools without number
　of living things both small and great.

℟. O bless the Lord, my soul.

They look to you to give them food in due
　　time.
When you give it to them, they gather it;
　when you open your hand, they are filled
　　with good things.

℟. O bless the Lord, my soul.

If you take away their breath, they perish
　　and return to the dust.
When you send forth your spirit, they are
　　created,
　and you renew the face of the earth.

℟. O bless the Lord, my soul.

SECOND READING

Titus 2:11-14; 3:4-7

Beloved:
The grace of God has appeared, saving all
　and training us to reject godless ways
　　and worldly desires
　and to live temperately, justly, and
　　devoutly in this age,
　as we await the blessed hope,
　the appearance of the glory of our great
　　God
　and savior Jesus Christ,
　who gave himself for us to deliver us
　　from all lawlessness
　and to cleanse for himself a people as
　　his own,
　eager to do what is good.

Continued in Appendix A, p. 270.

About Liturgy

Symbols of baptism: The symbols of the baptismal rite put into focus the primary gift of baptism—a share in divine Life which is for us a new identity:

Water—plunged into the baptismal waters, we are plunged into Christ's death; rising, we share in divine Life. Water brings both death (to our old selves) and a rebirth of life (new Life in God).

Chrism—anointed with chrism, we share in the threefold office of Christ—priest, prophet, ruler. Our being anointed with chrism is a consecration of ourselves to conform our life to Christ's.

White garment—clothed in a white garment, we are reminded of our new, holy, risen Life in Christ. We are to live unstained until we enjoy eternal Life with God.

Lighted candle—enlightened by Christ, we are also to be the light of Christ dispelling sin and darkness in the world. We ourselves are manifestations that in Christ the light of salvation has come into the world.

Although all of these symbols also imply the demands of discipleship (*water*—dying to self; *chrism*—conforming ourselves to Christ; *white garment*—living lives worthy of who we are; *lighted candle*—overcoming the darkness of evil), they primarily help us understand who we become in baptism—members of the Body of Christ sharing in divine identity. Moreover, greater awareness and appreciation of our identity enables us to be more faithful in our discipleship.

About Liturgical Music

Service music for Ordinary Time: The celebration of the Baptism of the Lord is the hinge Sunday marking the changeover from the Christmas season back to Ordinary Time. Because the solemnity stands as a turning point and faces both directions, it would be appropriate either to sing the service music used during Christmas season one last time or to begin using one of the Ordinary Time settings.

Music suggestions: A number of excellent songs celebrate the meaning of baptism, both for Jesus and for us. Examples include Alan Hommerding's "To Jordan Jesus Humbly Came" (W4, WC, WS) and his "Baptized in Living Waters" (WC, WS); Herman Stuempfle's "Jesus Christ, Your Footprints through the Desert" (HG); and "When Jesus Comes to Be Baptized" (BB, JS3).

Herman Stuempfle's "The Hills Are Still, the Darkness Deep" (in *The Word Goes Forth*, GIA) suits our return this Sunday to Ordinary Time. The text brings us down from the glories of Christmas and plants us firmly in the reality of ordinary life. The song of angels no longer fills the sky, but instead a "hungry cry"; shepherds once roused by glorious light have returned to "cold and lonely vigil"; the kings have departed leaving Mary to tend a Child in the night. The final verse captures well the challenge of Ordinary Time: "O God, when glory fades away And duties fill the night, the day: By grace unseen but present still, Give strength to heart and hand and will." This would make an excellent text for the assembly to sing after Communion as a quiet renewal of their baptism and its meaning for daily life.

ORDINARY TIME I

SPIRITUALITY

GOSPEL ACCLAMATION
See 2 Thess 2:14

R̸. Alleluia, alleluia.
God has called us through the Gospel
to possess the glory of our Lord Jesus Christ.
R̸. Alleluia, alleluia.

Gospel   John 2:1-11; L66C

There was a wedding at Cana in
    Galilee,
    and the mother of Jesus was there.
Jesus and his disciples were also
    invited to the wedding.
When the wine ran short,
    the mother of Jesus said to him,
    "They have no wine."
And Jesus said to her,
    "Woman, how does your concern
        affect me?
My hour has not yet come."
His mother said to the servers,
    "Do whatever he tells you."
Now there were six stone water jars there
    for Jewish ceremonial washings,
    each holding twenty to thirty gallons.
Jesus told them,
    "Fill the jars with water."
So they filled them to the brim.
Then he told them,
    "Draw some out now and take it to the
        headwaiter."
So they took it.
And when the headwaiter tasted the
    water that had become wine,
    without knowing where it came from
    —although the servers who had drawn
        the water knew—,
    the headwaiter called the bridegroom
        and said to him,
    "Everyone serves good wine first,
    and then when people have drunk
        freely, an inferior one;
    but you have kept the good wine until
        now."
Jesus did this as the beginning of his
    signs at Cana in Galilee
    and so revealed his glory,
    and his disciples began to believe in him.

Reflecting on the Gospel

No matter what is potentially inside gift-wrapped boxes, little children will invariably go for the biggest one. They want the largest piece of pie. They want the prettiest doll. They want the heaviest baseball bat. They want the most french fries. From earliest childhood we have an innate sense that more is better, and we carry that into adulthood. We shy away from scarcity and gravitate toward plenty. We avoid want and embrace having. We seek to have savings, reserves, supplies, extras, storage bins. Of course, we can go overboard on abundance. Yet, we all know that just enough isn't enough. This Sunday's gospel is about running out, not having enough. It is about a bride and groom potentially being embarrassed on their most important day. It becomes about abundance signifying that all is well, that love and life abound. It becomes about Jesus' "hour."

What is Jesus' "hour"? It is a time of the revelation of God's immense gift of abundance. In this gospel, not one jar of water became wine, but six. Not a little bit of wine, but over a hundred gallons. Not partially filled jars, but "to the brim." Not inferior wine, but "good wine." Not just one sign, but "the beginning of his signs." More is yet to come. In the "more" is God's glory revealed. In the "more" is God's abundance—a sign of the fullness of Life and love God offers us.

The epiphany of Jesus' glory is a sign of the persistence of God's overtures of love to us, a love so immense that it is not measurable, not able to be contained, not ever exhausted. There are signs of God's abundant love—God's most lavish gift to us—all around us. What are the signs? Obvious miracles, yes, in Jesus' time. But many miracles are still happening today: the gift of life at the birth of a baby, the peace of reconciliation, the warmth of faithful love, the satisfaction of success, the beauty of a sunrise or sunset. God's glory is revealed in many signs of abundance. Abundance, ultimately, is a sign of messianic times, of God's fullness of salvation offered to us. This is why Jesus came. In the abundance of who he is, Jesus reveals the fullness of who we might become. God's glory is God's Presence. Yes, God's glory is revealed in many signs of abundance. Most fully in Jesus himself. Most fully in us, the Body of Christ, as we come to deeper belief and continue his ministry.

Living the Paschal Mystery

Belief is directed to a *Who* rather than a *what*. Our own encounters with Jesus (in prayer, through others, in struggling with daily self-giving) are truly epiphanies of God's glory which also invite *us* to respond to abundance with belief. These epiphany signs might come in many ways—through others in a cry for help, in a lonely person's plea for companionship, in the spontaneous laughter of delight, in the beauty of nature. The challenge for us is to see these as revelations of God's glory, as epiphanies of God's love for us, and an opportunity to respond in belief.

Yes, these common, ordinary signs of God's abundance, love, and glory are all around us. By *responding* to other persons (recognizing them as revelations of God to us) we ourselves also become signs of God's abundance, God's fullness. We ourselves are the good wine kept until after Jesus' ascension when we take up Jesus' mission as disciples. Living the paschal mystery means that we empty ourselves in order to be filled with the goodness of God's glory.

Focusing the Gospel

Key words and phrases: My hour, Fill the jars, revealed his glory, believe in him

To the point: What is Jesus' "hour"? It is a time of the revelation of God's immense gift of abundance. In this gospel, not one jar of water became wine, but six. Not a little bit of wine, but over a hundred gallons. Not partially filled jars, but "to the brim." Not inferior wine, but "good wine." Not just one sign, but "the beginning of his signs." God's glory is revealed in many signs of abundance. Most fully in Jesus himself. Most fully in us, the Body of Christ, as we come to deeper belief and continue his ministry.

Connecting the Gospel

to the first reading: By using espousal imagery the first reading expresses God's abundant and intimate love for Israel. God's espousal love for all humanity is revealed through many signs, above all in Jesus—and in us who believe.

to experience: Is it time yet? Is the roast at the right temperature? Are the guests at the front door? Are the little ones rubbing their eyes indicating the need to go to bed? Jesus' time—his "hour"—arrives in response to a need and at the invitation of another. So does our time.

Connecting the Responsorial Psalm

to the readings: These verses from Psalm 96 begin by commanding us to sing to God, bless God's name, announce God's wondrous deeds to all the world. They conclude with us calling all nations to join in our praise and worship of God. The first reading and gospel reveal that what we praise God for is the superabundance of the gift of salvation. God surpasses the wants and dreams of the Israelites, transforming their identity (first reading). Jesus surpasses the expectations of the wedding guests, transforming ordinary water into extraordinary wine (gospel). Those who saw this sign came to believe in him. In this responsorial psalm we announce that we, too, see in the person of Jesus the superabundance of God's gift of salvation, and we want to tell all the world.

to psalmist preparation: Sometimes the saving acts of God come in extraordinary ways, but most often they come in the quiet events of ordinary, everyday living. The trick is to see these signs so that you can believe. How is Christ turning the ordinary water of your life into the wine of salvation?

**ASSEMBLY &
FAITH-SHARING GROUPS**
- God's abundance that surrounds me is . . . I notice this abundance best when . . .
- Jesus reveals his glory to me in . . . by . . . through . . .
- I reveal God's glory when . . .

PRESIDERS
I help others come to know God's abundance fills them to the brim when I . . .

DEACONS
When I experience God's abundance, my service ministry becomes . . .

HOSPITALITY MINISTERS
My manner of welcoming expresses God's "Delight" (first reading) in those who gather by . . .

MUSIC MINISTERS
In my music making I become a sign leading others to believe more deeply in Jesus when . . .

ALTAR MINISTERS
I fill "water jars" while serving at liturgy when I . . . while serving others when I . . .

LECTORS
My proclamation is a sign of God's abundance when . . .

**EXTRAORDINARY MINISTERS
OF HOLY COMMUNION**
Those who have been living signs (Eucharist) of Jesus' glory for me are . . .

Model Penitential Act

Presider: Jesus performed his first public sign at the wedding feast at Cana. We pause at the beginning of this celebration to reflect on Jesus' gift of abundance to us and ask for God's mercy for times when we have failed to share this abundance . . . [pause]

Lord Jesus, you are the fullness of God's gift to us: Lord . . .

Christ Jesus, you are the new wine that leads us to glory: Christ . . .

Lord Jesus, you are the One who calls us to belief and discipleship: Lord . . .

Homily Points

• An hour. Some hours fly by quickly. Some hours drag so slowly. But all hours are composed of sixty minutes, each minute composed of sixty seconds. So just what is this "hour" of which Jesus speaks? Not a clock hour! It is a time of ending and a time of beginning. A time of stepping out to fulfill why he came.

• Jesus came to bring us the abundance of salvation, the new "wine" of God's love and mercy, the glory of divine Presence. Jesus performed his first "sign" of this abundance during a wedding feast in response to an ordinary need. His "hour" had come.

• At what "hour" do we taste the water that has "become wine"? When, for example, holiness shines from the wrinkled face of an aging parent; unselfishness flows from the actions of a small child; reconciliation heals a broken relationship. Whenever the ordinariness of our lives has been transformed by the power of Christ, we experience an extraordinary gift of grace. The "hour" has come for us.

Model Universal Prayer (Prayer of the Faithful)

Presider: God lavishly shares abundance with us. Confident of God's gifts, we make known our needs.

Response:

Lord,— hear our prayer.

Cantor:

we pray to the Lord,

That all members of the church grow in their belief in Jesus, God's gift of abundance to us . . . [pause]

That world leaders always be attentive to the needs of those under their care . . . [pause]

That the poor share in the abundant wine of God's gifts through the generosity of this community . . . [pause]

That all of us gathered here open ourselves to the revelation of God's glory in the ordinariness of our daily lives . . . [pause]

Presider: O God, your love for us is a never-ending abundance. Hear these our prayers that one day we might share forever in the glory of your heavenly wedding banquet. We ask this through Christ our Lord. **Amen.**

COLLECT

Let us pray.

Pause for silent prayer

Almighty ever-living God,
who govern all things,
both in heaven and on earth,
mercifully hear the pleading of your
    people
and bestow your peace on our times.
Through our Lord Jesus Christ, your Son,
who lives and reigns with you in the unity
    of the Holy Spirit,
one God, for ever and ever. **Amen.**

FIRST READING

Isa 62:1-5

For Zion's sake I will not be silent,
    for Jerusalem's sake I will not be quiet,
until her vindication shines forth like the
    dawn
    and her victory like a burning torch.

Nations shall behold your vindication,
    and all the kings your glory;
you shall be called by a new name
    pronounced by the mouth of the LORD.
You shall be a glorious crown in the hand
    of the LORD,
    a royal diadem held by your God.
No more shall people call you "Forsaken,"
    or your land "Desolate,"
but you shall be called "My Delight,"
    and your land "Espoused."
For the LORD delights in you
    and makes your land his spouse.
As a young man marries a virgin,
    your Builder shall marry you;
and as a bridegroom rejoices in his bride
    so shall your God rejoice in you.

RESPONSORIAL PSALM
Ps 96:1-2, 2-3, 7-8, 9-10

R⁊. (3) Proclaim his marvelous deeds to all the nations.

Sing to the LORD a new song;
   sing to the LORD, all you lands.
Sing to the LORD; bless his name.

R⁊. Proclaim his marvelous deeds to all the nations.

Announce his salvation, day after day.
Tell his glory among the nations;
   among all peoples, his wondrous deeds.

R⁊. Proclaim his marvelous deeds to all the nations.

Give to the LORD, you families of nations,
   give to the LORD glory and praise;
   give to the LORD the glory due his name!

R⁊. Proclaim his marvelous deeds to all the nations.

Worship the LORD in holy attire.
   Tremble before him, all the earth;
say among the nations: The LORD is king.
   He governs the peoples with equity.

R⁊. Proclaim his marvelous deeds to all the nations.

SECOND READING
1 Cor 12:4-11

Brothers and sisters:
There are different kinds of spiritual gifts
      but the same Spirit;
   there are different forms of service but
      the same Lord;
   there are different workings but the
      same God
   who produces all of them in everyone.
To each individual the manifestation of
      the Spirit
   is given for some benefit.
To one is given through the Spirit the
      expression of wisdom;
   to another, the expression of knowledge
      according to the same Spirit;
   to another, faith by the same Spirit;
   to another, gifts of healing by the one
      Spirit;
   to another, mighty deeds;
   to another, prophecy;
   to another, discernment of spirits;
   to another, varieties of tongues;
   to another, interpretation of tongues.
But one and the same Spirit produces all
      of these,
   distributing them individually to each
      person as he wishes.

About Liturgy

Eucharist's epiphanies: Year C in the Lectionary cycle is the only one in which the three traditional themes of epiphany occur on three consecutive Sundays: epiphany to the magi, Jesus' baptism, and the sign at the wedding feast at Cana. Yet, each time we celebrate liturgy God manifests divine Self to us in a number of ways. For example, in the *introductory rites* we are given an opportunity to be aware that God calls us into divine Presence and asks us to be attentive to the times we have failed to respond to God in belief. In the *Liturgy of the Word* God speaks to us—sometimes in terms of promise and fulfillment, sometimes exhorting us to right living, sometimes assuring us with divine love, sometimes challenging us to change our ways—and in the epiphany of word invites a response of a renewed commitment to follow Jesus as disciples. In the *Liturgy of the Eucharist* Christ becomes substantially present to us in the consecrated bread and wine and gives his very Body and Blood for our food and drink. This epiphany shows us God's tremendous love for us and God's desire for intimacy; it also shows forth our own dignity as we ourselves are and are becoming the very Body of Christ. In the *concluding rite* we are sent forth to be the epiphany of God's Presence in our everyday living.

The Sunday Eucharist is a most sublime epiphany of God. Moreover, through our being transformed by the ritual action, we ourselves are reminded over and over again to be the Presence of Christ in our world. God loves us so much as to send the Son to be our savior; God trusts us so much as to send us to be the manifestation of God's Presence!

About Liturgical Music

Selecting seasonal service music: Just as vestments and environment relate to the liturgical season, so does well-chosen service music. Appropriately chosen service music helps us enter into the character of each season and into the unfolding rhythms of the liturgical year.

Selecting seasonal service music begins by considering the liturgical year, both as a whole and in its individual seasons. Why does the church follow a liturgical year? What relationship exists between the unfolding seasons and solemnities of the liturgical year and the identity and mission of the church? Why, in the midst of the busy commercialism of pre-Christmas, do we have the four Sundays of Advent? Why each year do we enter into the renewal period of Lent prior to the resurrection celebration of the weeks of Easter? What is the purpose of Ordinary Time and what formative influence does it bear on our growth in Christian living?

Answering questions such as these will lead to a roster of service music in keeping with the different seasons of the liturgical year, a roster that can be followed year after year and draw us more deeply into our celebration of each season.

SPIRITUALITY

R/. Alleluia, alleluia.
The Lord sent me to bring glad tidings to the
    poor,
and to proclaim liberty to captives.
R/. Alleluia, alleluia.

Gospel   Luke 1:1-4; 4:14-21;
L69C

Since many have undertaken to
    compile a narrative of the
    events
    that have been fulfilled among us,
just as those who were
    eyewitnesses from the
    beginning
and ministers of the word have
    handed them down to us,
I too have decided,
after investigating everything
    accurately anew,
to write it down in an orderly
    sequence for you,
most excellent Theophilus,
so that you may realize the certainty
    of the teachings
you have received.

Jesus returned to Galilee in the power
    of the Spirit,
and news of him spread throughout
    the whole region.
He taught in their synagogues and was
    praised by all.

He came to Nazareth, where he had
    grown up,
and went according to his custom
    into the synagogue on the sabbath day.
He stood up to read and was handed a
    scroll of the prophet Isaiah.
He unrolled the scroll and found the
    passage where it was written:
The Spirit of the Lord is upon me,
    because he has anointed me
    to bring glad tidings to the poor.

Continued in Appendix A, p. 270.

Reflecting on the Gospel

Writing an autobiography is not as easy as it sounds. We are immediately faced with choices: Do we strictly tell the facts of our lives, or do we help people get an insight into our likes and dislikes, emotions and feelings, ambitions and goals? How much of who we really are do we want to reveal? If the autobiography is meant for family legacy, both facts and self-revelation are important. If the autobiography is by a political figure, then facts are what count. If the autobiography is by an entertainment personality, then personal revelation is more interesting. How we write depends on what we want to convey. At the beginning of Luke's gospel he explicitly states that he sets out to "compile a narrative of the events" of Jesus' person and mission. He claims that he has "investigat[ed] everything accurately anew." Luke wants to get it right. He knows how important his writing is—its purpose is to "realize the certainty of the teachings" Jesus brought us. Luke's story of Jesus, however, is more than facts.

In this gospel Jesus clearly proclaims who he is and what he comes to bring. He is One who lives "in the power of the Spirit"; he comes to bring a new teaching. He is God's anointed; he comes to bring the human community glad tidings, liberty, sight, freedom, favor. He is the long-awaited Messiah; he comes to bring manifest signs of salvation. The "eyes of all . . . looked intently at him." Do our eyes look intently upon him? Why should we? Because in Jesus is fulfilled all our longings, all our hopes, all our expectations.

The same intensity with which the people of Nehemiah's time heard the Law proclaimed by Ezra is focused on Jesus in the synagogue. Their intense anticipation is met by Jesus' dramatic assertion that the Scripture passage from Isaiah "is fulfilled" in their hearing. In the first reading Ezra reads from the book of the Law; in the gospel Jesus *is* the book, the Good News, the Word made flesh. Ezra interprets what he read; in the gospel Jesus himself *is* the interpretation. Ezra's word was an inspiring word that had power and moved the people to worship and praise; Jesus' word is a creative word fulfilled *in him* and continues in the gospel in which *we ourselves* encounter Jesus and are moved to be disciples. The feasting, joy, and new strength on the holy day when Ezra read the Law are now fulfilled in a new order in which the feasting is on Jesus and the strength comes from our sharing in the same Spirit.

Living the Paschal Mystery

Jesus is enfleshed today in the lives of those who encounter him, the gospel's very fulfillment, throughout the ages. Now we—our own lives—announce the meaning of the Word proclaimed and enfleshed. We can do so because, like Jesus, in our baptism we also have been anointed with the Spirit. By our baptism we have received a share in Jesus' saving deeds. As his followers, we make present his saving mystery.

Living the paschal mystery means that we continually look for the poor, captive, blind, and oppressed among us. We don't have to look very far! "Today this Scripture passage is fulfilled" is now true only when we ourselves respond to those around us who need a nourishing, strengthening, joyful word. This means that God's word isn't something we only hear on Sunday, but becomes a living word in our hearts, inspiring us to be in our very selves living gospels. As we gradually grow into being anointed by the Spirit, we, like Jesus, are the fulfillment of the Scriptures.

Focusing the Gospel

Key words and phrases: compile a narrative . . . fulfilled

To the point: In this gospel Jesus clearly proclaims who he is and what he comes to bring. He is One who lives "in the power of the Spirit"; he comes to bring a new teaching. He is God's anointed; he comes to bring the human community glad tidings, liberty, sight, freedom, favor. He is the long-awaited Messiah; he comes to bring manifest signs of salvation. The "eyes of all . . . looked intently at him." Do our eyes look intently upon him?

Connecting the Gospel

to the first reading: It is not enough simply to hear God's word. As with the people of old—those hearing Ezra and those hearing Jesus—we must "look[ ] intently" (gospel) and "understand" (first reading). We must take God's word to heart and live it.

to experience: Text messaging often reduces words to mere information exchange. Word as proclamation does far more than swap information in abbreviated forms; proclamation is presence, power, invitation to action, fullness.

Connecting the Responsorial Psalm

to the readings: The responsorial psalm proclaims that the word of God is perfect, trustworthy, right, and clear. The word of God refreshes the soul, rejoices the heart, and enlightens the eye. In the first reading this word is the Law read by Ezra to the assembled people who weep at its hearing. In the gospel this word from the prophet Isaiah is announced by Jesus to the synagogue gathering who "looked intently at him" for its interpretation. His interpretation is a stunner: this word is his very person "fulfilled in your hearing."

The word of God given in the Law and the Prophets expresses God's will for human salvation. Jesus reveals that this will is himself, the Word-will of God in flesh and bone, bringing Good News to the poor, restoring sight to the blind, and granting freedom to the oppressed. The Word which is trustworthy and clear, which rejoices the heart and enlightens the eye is the very person of Christ. He is the Word/Law about which we sing in Psalm 19.

to psalmist preparation: The word of God about which you sing in this responsorial psalm is fulfilled in the person of Christ. As you pray the psalm in preparation this week, you might substitute the name of Christ for the words "law," "decree," "precept," and so on. How does this deepen your understanding of who Christ is? How will this affect your singing of the psalm?

**ASSEMBLY &
FAITH-SHARING GROUPS**
- I look intently upon Jesus when . . . What I see is . . . What I hear is . . .
- The power of the Spirit moves me to . . . drives me to . . .
- I continue Jesus' mission to the poor, captives, blind, and oppressed whenever I . . .

PRESIDERS
When I preach "in the power of the Spirit," I . . . the assembly . . .

DEACONS
My ministry to the poor, captives, blind, and oppressed changes me by . . .

HOSPITALITY MINISTERS
My manner of greeting people prepares them to look intently toward Jesus who is present when . . .

MUSIC MINISTERS
When I look intently upon Jesus—both during preparation and during liturgy—my music making becomes . . .

ALTAR MINISTERS
My serving at the altar helps me become more mindful of the needs of others when . . .

LECTORS
My prayerful hearing of God's word moves me to . . . It helps me proclaim better in that . . .

**EXTRAORDINARY MINISTERS
OF HOLY COMMUNION**
When I look intently upon the faces of those coming to receive Holy Communion, I see . . .

Model Penitential Act

Presider: Jesus announced that the word he proclaimed in the synagogue was being fulfilled in him. At the beginning of this celebration let us open ourselves to God's word and seek mercy for the times when we have not acted on this word . . . [pause]

Lord Jesus, you came in the power of the Spirit: Lord . . .

Christ Jesus, you are the fulfillment of God's word: Christ . . .

Lord Jesus, you are glad tidings for all those who hear: Lord . . .

Homily Points

• Children love to have stories read to them, and they listen intently. We never quite lose this fascination with stories, even as adults. We read mystery novels, romances, biographies. As captivating as these stories are, the greatest story ever told is the story of salvation.

• The beginning of Luke's "narrative of . . . events" is a continuation of the story begun in the Hebrew Scriptures. From the beginning, the "power of the Holy Spirit" has driven this story forward. From the beginning, this story has been about salvation: liberty for captives, sight for the blind, freedom for the oppressed, and glad tidings for the poor. From the beginning, this story has captured our attention, brought us to look intently, opened us to the mystery of God's Presence, mercy, and love. All this, fulfilled in Christ.

• "Today this Scripture passage is fulfilled in your hearing." What a claim by Jesus! What word is fulfilled? That the human condition—poverty, slavery, blindness, oppression—will give way to "a year acceptable to the Lord." What is acceptable to the Lord? That we be "eyewitnesses" to Jesus' saving deeds, that we faithfully hand them on to others, that we live out of the "certainty" of Jesus' words and Presence.

Model Universal Prayer (Prayer of the Faithful)

Presider: Let us pray that the glad tidings of God's love and care for those in need be brought to fulfillment.

Response:

Lord,—— hear our prayer.

Cantor:

we pray to the Lord,

That all members of the church proclaim by their way of living the glad tidings of God's favor . . . [pause]

That all peoples of the world intently look for the signs of salvation among them . . . [pause]

That there be liberty for captives, sight for the blind, freedom for the oppressed, and glad tidings for the poor . . . [pause]

That the word of God be fulfilled in each of us . . . [pause]

Presider: O God, you sent your Son in the power of the Holy Spirit to bring us the glad tidings of salvation. Hear our prayers that we may come to the fullness of life Jesus proclaimed. We ask this through that same Christ our Lord. **Amen.**

COLLECT

Let us pray.

Pause for silent prayer

Almighty ever-living God,
direct our actions according to your good
    pleasure,
that in the name of your beloved Son
we may abound in good works.
Through our Lord Jesus Christ, your Son,
who lives and reigns with you in the unity
    of the Holy Spirit,
one God, for ever and ever. **Amen.**

FIRST READING

Neh 8:2-4a, 5-6, 8-10

Ezra the priest brought the law before the
        assembly,
    which consisted of men, women,
    and those children old enough to
        understand.
Standing at one end of the open place that
        was before the Water Gate,
    he read out of the book from daybreak
        till midday,
    in the presence of the men, the women,
    and those children old enough to
        understand;
    and all the people listened attentively to
        the book of the law.
Ezra the scribe stood on a wooden
        platform
    that had been made for the occasion.
He opened the scroll
    so that all the people might see it
    —for he was standing higher up than
        any of the people—;
    and, as he opened it, all the people rose.
Ezra blessed the LORD, the great God,
    and all the people, their hands raised
        high, answered,
    "Amen, amen!"
Then they bowed down and prostrated
        themselves before the LORD,
    their faces to the ground.
Ezra read plainly from the book of the law
        of God,
    interpreting it so that all could
        understand what was read.
Then Nehemiah, that is, His Excellency,
        and Ezra the priest-scribe
    and the Levites who were instructing
        the people
    said to all the people:
    "Today is holy to the LORD your God.
Do not be sad, and do not weep"—
    for all the people were weeping as they
        heard the words of the law.

He said further: "Go, eat rich foods and
   drink sweet drinks,
   and allot portions to those who had
      nothing prepared;
   for today is holy to our LORD.
Do not be saddened this day,
   for rejoicing in the LORD must be your
      strength!"

RESPONSORIAL PSALM

Ps 19:8, 9, 10, 15

R℣. (cf. John 6:63c) Your words, Lord, are
Spirit and life.

The law of the LORD is perfect,
   refreshing the soul;
the decree of the LORD is trustworthy,
   giving wisdom to the simple.

R℣. Your words, Lord, are Spirit and life.

The precepts of the LORD are right,
   rejoicing the heart;
the command of the LORD is clear,
   enlightening the eye.

R℣. Your words, Lord, are Spirit and life.

The fear of the LORD is pure,
   enduring forever;
the ordinances of the LORD are true,
   all of them just.

R℣. Your words, Lord, are Spirit and life.

Let the words of my mouth and the
      thought of my heart
   find favor before you,
O LORD, my rock and my redeemer.

R℣. Your words, Lord, are Spirit and life.

SECOND READING

1 Cor 12:12-14, 27

Brothers and sisters:
As a body is one though it has many parts,
   and all the parts of the body, though
      many, are one body,
   so also Christ.
For in one Spirit we were all baptized into
      one body,
   whether Jews or Greeks, slaves or free
      persons,
   and we were all given to drink of one
      Spirit.
Now the body is not a single part, but
   many.
You are Christ's body, and individually
   parts of it.

or 1 Cor 12:12-30

See Appendix A, p. 271.

About Liturgy

Eucharistic word and its fulfillment: Each Sunday during the Liturgy of the
Word we hear God's word proclaimed. Would that this word so moved us that, like the
people of Ezra's time, we would prostrate ourselves before the Presence of God! Yet,
even when our hearing the word is less intent, God still fulfills it.

The Liturgy of the Word always opens onto the Liturgy of the Eucharist. There is
a very real pastoral danger that we focus during this part of the Mass only on receiving Holy Communion. Important as that moment is, we cannot neglect the eucharistic
prayer. In this prayer narrative we hear the story of God's faithful deeds in bringing
about our salvation. The eucharistic prayer is Jesus' "autobiography" writ small. Now,
with our twenty-twenty hindsight, we are hearing a narrative of salvation *already
fulfilled in Christ* and in this are encouraged and strengthened to respond to the word
that we have just heard. We come forward in the Communion procession, toward the
altar-table which is a symbol of the messianic banquet, to feast and have our fill at
God's table, knowing that God nourishes us to be ourselves the fulfillment of the word
in our daily lives.

Coming to Communion without paying due attention to the Liturgy of the Word
and the salvation narrative of the eucharistic prayer is like coming late for a banquet
meal and missing all the conversation that brings the joy and satisfaction to the meal.
This gospel challenges us to prepare well for Sunday liturgy—not just to reflect on the
readings but also occasionally to read prayerfully the eucharistic prayers so that they
are truly *prayers*. Eucharistic Prayer IV borrows words from this Sunday's gospel and
it would be a good choice to begin our prayerful reflection on these beautiful narratives
of salvation.

About Liturgical Music

The gospel acclamation: Both the first reading and the gospel this Sunday relate
occasions when the word of God is proclaimed in the midst of the community. This
offers a good opportunity to examine the meaning and importance of the gospel acclamation. While we remain seated during the proclamation of the first and second
readings, we stand for the proclamation of the gospel and we greet this proclamation
by singing the acclamation. Singing this acclamation announces our belief that the
person of Christ becomes present in our midst in the very proclamation of the gospel
(GIRM, no. 62). The accompanying verse sung by cantor or choir is usually taken from
the gospel text and acts as an invitation that we open our hearts to truly
hear what will be proclaimed and let ourselves be transformed by it
(like a "liturgical *hors d'oeuvre*" offered to whet our appetites for
the meal to come). The most suitable gesture dur-
ing the singing of the acclamation would be
to turn our bodies toward the *Book of the
Gospels* as it is carried to the ambo.

SPIRITUALITY

GOSPEL ACCLAMATION
Matt 4:18

℟. Alleluia, alleluia.
The Lord sent me to bring glad
    tidings to the poor,
to proclaim liberty to captives.
℟. Alleluia, alleluia.

Gospel   Luke 4:21-30; L72C

Jesus began speaking in the
    synagogue, saying:
    "Today this Scripture
        passage is fulfilled in
        your hearing."
And all spoke highly of him
    and were amazed at the
        gracious words that
        came from his mouth.
They also asked, "Isn't this the
    son of Joseph?"
He said to them, "Surely you will quote me
    this proverb,
    'Physician, cure yourself,' and say,
    'Do here in your native place
    the things that we heard were done in
        Capernaum.'"
And he said, "Amen, I say to you,
    no prophet is accepted in his own native
        place.
Indeed, I tell you,
    there were many widows in Israel in the
        days of Elijah
    when the sky was closed for three and a
        half years
    and a severe famine spread over the
        entire land.
It was to none of these that Elijah was sent,
    but only to a widow in Zarephath in the
        land of Sidon.
Again, there were many lepers in Israel
    during the time of Elisha the prophet;
    yet not one of them was cleansed, but
        only Naaman the Syrian."
When the people in the synagogue heard this,
    they were all filled with fury.
They rose up, drove him out of the town,
    and led him to the brow of the hill
    on which their town had been built,
    to hurl him down headlong.
But Jesus passed through the midst of them
    and went away.

Reflecting on the Gospel

Whose side do we want to be on? The winners, of course! But unwittingly the people in the gospel story choose to be on the wrong side! At first they "all spoke highly of" Jesus. But then they heard him say what they didn't like and turned on him. "Today this Scripture passage is fulfilled in your hearing." However, more than one Scripture passage is being fulfilled in this gospel. The words and deeds of Jesus fulfill the Scripture passage from Isaiah about the coming of salvation: glad tidings for the poor, liberty for captives, sight for the blind, freedom for the oppressed. The words and deeds of the people fulfill the Scripture passages about rejecting and killing God's prophets: they question Jesus' origins, become furious at his words, and act to destroy him. The people choose the wrong side! Which Scripture passages do we hear? Which do we fulfill?

When Jesus challenges the people's narrowness with the examples of Elijah's and Elisha's outreach to Gentiles (Sidon and Syria), they grow furious. Jesus challenged the crowd because the Good News is always broader than selective preferences or limited understanding—yes, salvation would be for Gentiles as well as Jews. While the gospel is always good news, it is not always comfortable because it ever stretches us beyond where we are now. Which Scripture passages do we hear? Which do we fulfill?

The demise of the prophets came about because they forced choices; the challenge of the gospel is also that it forces choices. The comforting thing about God's word is that we have always had the reassurance that God will protect and deliver us (see first reading). The disturbing thing is that the protection and deliverance don't always come as quickly as we might like or in the way we might like. Jeremiah ended up in a cistern and some of the prophets were killed; Jesus ended up on the cross. Prophets may be rejected and destroyed, but God's word is always enduring. One symbol of this is that Jesus does escape the crowd in this gospel, demonstrating that, like God's word, the gospel will prevail. And what is our response to the challenge of the gospel? Amazement or fury? Welcoming Jesus or expelling him from our midst? Growing in discipleship or stagnating in narrowness? Choosing the winning ways of the gospel or the losing ways of narrow-mindedness? Which Scripture passages do we hear? Which do we fulfill?

Living the Paschal Mystery

If we never meet doubt or opposition over values in our daily living, then we must examine how committed to the Gospel we are. Most of us aren't called "professionally" to preach the Good News. All of us, however, because of our baptism, are committed to living it. Living the Gospel is what must shape our everyday choices and responses. This means, for example, that if the chatter around the watercooler at work grows uncharitable or coarse, we have the courage to walk away. Another example: if prejudice exists among our friends and acquaintances, we have the courage to extol the dignity of the minority. Dying to oneself means that we place Gospel values before any others and are willing to stake our lives on them. We might not always concretely experience God's protection and deliverance in the given moment; but we know from Jesus' life that God is there when it really counts—leading us to Life everlasting.

Focusing the Gospel

Key words and phrases: Today this Scripture passage is fulfilled in your hearing

To the point: "Today this Scripture passage is fulfilled in your hearing." However, more than one Scripture passage is being fulfilled in this gospel. The words and deeds of Jesus fulfill the Scripture passage from Isaiah about the coming of salvation: glad tidings for the poor, liberty for captives, sight for the blind, freedom for the oppressed. The words and deeds of the people fulfill the Scripture passages about rejecting and killing God's prophets: they question Jesus' origins, become furious at his words, and act to destroy him. Which Scripture passages do we hear? Which do we fulfill?

Connecting the Gospel

to the first reading: There are at least two points of contact between the first reading and the gospel. The first is the presentation of Jeremiah and Jesus as prophets who are rejected. The second is God's promise of protection and deliverance.

to experience: We love to hear gracious words of praise and compliments. We hate to hear words that threaten us too much or words that challenge what we believe.

Connecting the Responsorial Psalm

to the readings: Like Jesus (gospel) and Jeremiah (first reading), we are sent to proclaim salvation to the world. Like Jesus and Jeremiah, we will meet opposition, persecution, even death as we fulfill this mission. But the psalm promises we shall be protected even as we are persecuted, for the God who has loved us since before our birth will be our salvation. The psalm invites us to fulfill our mission, fully conscious of the suffering it will bring, but equally conscious of the salvation God has promised beyond that suffering. This is not a psalm which we sing naively, but with hope-filled realism. And Jesus sings with us.

to psalmist preparation: The confidence expressed in this psalm counterbalances the reality of persecution faced by those who remain faithful to God's call (first reading, gospel). If you choose to be faithful to the mission you share with Christ, you will meet opposition and rejection. But you will also have the presence and protection of God who will be leading you to Life. Do you believe this? Are you willing to make the same choice as Jesus?

ASSEMBLY & FAITH-SHARING GROUPS
- Words that anger me are . . . I react by . . .
- Words of Jesus that are amazing and "gracious" to me are . . . Words of Jesus that I would rather not hear are . . .
- My words and deeds reveal that I listen to these Scripture passages . . .

PRESIDERS
I am most comfortable preaching and living Sacred Scripture when . . .

DEACONS
The views of God and salvation that have been stretched in me because of my experiences in ministry are . . .

HOSPITALITY MINISTERS
In my ministry, I bring glad tidings for the poor, liberty for captives, sight for the blind, freedom for the oppressed when I . . .

MUSIC MINISTERS
My music making fulfills in me . . . fulfills in the assembly . . .

ALTAR MINISTERS
The demands of my service amaze me when . . . infuriate me when . . .

LECTORS
I heed or dismiss a passage from Sacred Scripture based on . . .

EXTRAORDINARY MINISTERS OF HOLY COMMUNION
My manner of distributing Holy Communion bespeaks a gracious word to the communicants when I . . .

Model Penitential Act

Presider: In today's gospel, Jesus' gracious words are rejected by the very people he came to save. As we prepare to celebrate these saving mysteries, let us examine when we have rejected God's word . . . [pause]

Lord Jesus, you are the gracious Word of salvation spoken to all: Lord . . .

Christ Jesus, you are the prophetic Word that challenges us to come to fullness of Life: Christ . . .

Lord Jesus, you are the living Word that leads us to do God's will: Lord . . .

Homily Points

• We tend to limit who people can be and what they can become when they are very familiar to us, when they are close to home. In the gospel the people "were amazed at the gracious words that came from [Jesus'] mouth"—until they realized he was Joseph's son. How could the son of a Nazareth carpenter—how could one of their own—be the fulfillment of Scripture?

• In the beginning Jesus' hearers respond to his "gracious words" with amazement. In the end they become "filled with fury" at his words and attempt to destroy him. What has transpired in between? Jesus has confronted them with the truth about their resistance to who he really is.

• Who is Jesus? Not merely a Nazarene, not merely Joseph's son, not merely even a prophet. Jesus is the fulfillment of Scripture. The challenge of this gospel for us is to realize that our whole lives are spent learning who Jesus is and how to live the fullness of salvation he came to offer us. We do this in simple, everyday ways such as seeing the face of Christ in the person in need, accepting those who are not part of our inner circle, being transformed by words of challenge from unexpected people and events.

Model Universal Prayer (Prayer of the Faithful)

Presider: The God who has been faithful in all the story of Sacred Scripture will hear the prayers of those who cry out in need.

Response:

Lord, hear our prayer.

Cantor:

we pray to the Lord,

That all members of the church hear Jesus' gracious words and allow them to be fulfilled in their own words and deeds . . . [pause]

That all peoples of the world hear God's gracious words promising salvation . . . [pause]

That the poor and the suffering may have their burdens lifted by those who have heard and heeded God's word . . . [pause]

That each of us risk being prophets in our own native places . . . [pause]

Presider: Saving God, you sent your Son to speak to us words both gracious and challenging. Hear our prayers that we might heed what he speaks to us and live faithfully the life to which he calls us. We ask this through Christ our Lord. **Amen.**

COLLECT
Let us pray.

Pause for silent prayer

Grant us, Lord our God,
that we may honor you with all our mind,
and love everyone in truth of heart.
Through our Lord Jesus Christ, your Son,
who lives and reigns with you in the unity
    of the Holy Spirit,
one God, for ever and ever. **Amen.**

FIRST READING
Jer 1:4-5, 17-19

The word of the LORD came to me, saying:
  Before I formed you in the womb I knew
    you,
  before you were born I dedicated you,
  a prophet to the nations I appointed you.

  But do you gird your loins;
    stand up and tell them
    all that I command you.
  Be not crushed on their account,
    as though I would leave you crushed
      before them;
  for it is I this day
    who have made you a fortified city,
  a pillar of iron, a wall of brass,
    against the whole land:
  against Judah's kings and princes,
    against its priests and people.
  They will fight against you but not
    prevail over you,
    for I am with you to deliver you, says
      the LORD.

RESPONSORIAL PSALM
Ps 71:1-2, 3-4, 5-6, 15, 17

R̠. (cf. 15ab) I will sing of your salvation.

In you, O LORD, I take refuge;
  let me never be put to shame.
In your justice rescue me, and deliver me;
  incline your ear to me, and save me.

R̠. I will sing of your salvation.

Be my rock of refuge,
  a stronghold to give me safety,
  for you are my rock and my fortress.
O my God, rescue me from the hand of the
  wicked.

R̠. I will sing of your salvation.

For you are my hope, O Lord;
    my trust, O God, from my youth.
On you I depend from birth;
    from my mother's womb you are my
       strength.

R. I will sing of your salvation.

My mouth shall declare your justice,
    day by day your salvation.
O God, you have taught me from my
      youth,
    and till the present I proclaim your
      wondrous deeds.

R. I will sing of your salvation.

SECOND READING
1 Cor 13:4-13

Brothers and sisters:
Love is patient, love is kind.
It is not jealous, it is not pompous,
    it is not inflated, it is not rude,
    it does not seek its own interests,
    it is not quick-tempered, it does not
      brood over injury,
    it does not rejoice over wrongdoing but
      rejoices with the truth.
It bears all things, believes all things,
    hopes all things, endures all things.

Love never fails.
If there are prophecies, they will be
      brought to nothing;
    if tongues, they will cease;
    if knowledge, it will be brought to
      nothing.
For we know partially and we prophesy
      partially,
    but when the perfect comes, the partial
      will pass away.
When I was a child, I used to talk as a
      child,
    think as a child, reason as a child;
    when I became a man, I put aside
      childish things.
At present we see indistinctly, as in a
      mirror,
    but then face to face.
At present I know partially;
    then I shall know fully, as I am fully
      known.
So faith, hope, love remain, these three;
    but the greatest of these is love.

or 1 Cor 12:31–13:13

See Appendix A, p. 271.

About Liturgy

Liturgy of the Word: When we claim that God's word is enduring, we are saying more than the fact that it is proclaimed throughout the world every Saturday evening and Sunday (and weekdays, too!). The mere *saying* or *proclaiming* God's word isn't what makes it enduring; it is *receiving*, *internalizing*, and *living* God's word that makes it enduring. God's word endures as each of us is transformed, realizing ever more perfectly the spread of God's reign. God's word endures *in us*.

Almost always on Sundays the Lectionary selections include both a prophetic word and a comforting word. First challenge: we must truly hear God's word and not let it simply go over our heads. The best way to *hear* (receive) God's word is not to come to liturgy cold; if this is our first hearing, we probably won't get much out of the Liturgy of the Word. A good spiritual practice for all of us is to read the Scriptures well in advance of Sunday so that we can be thinking about them as we go through our normal everyday routines.

Second challenge: we must hear God's word in terms of how it challenges each of us *personally*. This means that almost every Sunday we will hear something in the word that calls us to change (internalize the word) some behavior or attitude. We must help ourselves get into the habit of truly *listening* for that personal word to us. Let our prayer during the rest of the Mass then be one in which we beg God's help to live this word.

Third challenge: we must let that internalized word help us see what in our personal lives and the world in which we live needs to be addressed (living the word). Sometimes our world is so complex that we don't even recognize the hurts and injustices around us. God's enduring word within us helps us see our world with new eyes— God's eyes. We will no longer be able to take things for granted; we will begin to understand that hearing God's word each Sunday makes demands on us.

About Liturgical Music

Music suggestions: A number of songs capture the conflict exemplified in this Sunday's gospel. Many hearers oppose Jesus and the words he speaks. "Good News" (G3) speaks of Jesus as the fulfillment of Isaiah's prophecy of good news for the needy, of the opposition Jesus met in his own native place, and of his refusal to flee his mission no matter what the cost. Its Ethiopian melody is both gentle and joyful, and would work well at preparation of the gifts. "You, Lord, Are Both Lamb and Shepherd" (HG, W4) expresses well our mixed reactions to Christ, the "peace-maker and sword-bringer" whom we "both scorn and crave," and would work well during the preparation of the gifts. The strong text and tune of "The Kingdom of God" (G3, OF, W4, WC) make this song suitable for the entrance procession. The text identifies the kingdom of God as both "challenge and choice" and calls us to "Believe the good news, repent and rejoice!" Another good choice for the entrance would be "Praise to You, O Christ, Our Savior" (BB, G3, JS3, W4), a hymn of praise to Christ the Word who calls, leads, and teaches us.

SPIRITUALITY

GOSPEL ACCLAMATION
Matt 4:19

℟. Alleluia, alleluia.
Come after me
and I will make you fishers of men.
℟. Alleluia, alleluia.

Gospel Luke 5:1-11; L75C

While the crowd was
pressing in on Jesus
and listening to the
word of God,
he was standing
by the Lake of
Gennesaret.
He saw two boats there
alongside the lake;
the fishermen had
disembarked and were
washing their nets.
Getting into one of the boats, the one
belonging to Simon,
he asked him to put out a short
distance from the shore.
Then he sat down and taught the
crowds from the boat.
After he had finished speaking, he said
to Simon,
"Put out into deep water and lower
your nets for a catch."
Simon said in reply,
"Master, we have worked hard all
night and have caught nothing,
but at your command I will lower the
nets."
When they had done this, they caught a
great number of fish
and their nets were tearing.
They signaled to their partners in the
other boat
to come to help them.
They came and filled both boats
so that the boats were in danger of
sinking.

Continued in Appendix A, p. 272.

Reflecting on the Gospel

We catch a ball. We catch a train. We catch a cold. We catch a meaning. We catch a sly glance. We catch a lot in our everyday living! And, yes, sometimes we "catch" people. A fiancée might be told she got a good "catch." "Catch" means to intercept and hold. Don't drop! Hang on! What a marvelous "catch" Jesus makes in this gospel! Jesus makes such a bigger catch than Peter! After fishing all night and catching nothing, Peter obeys Jesus, putting out his boat and nets once again. He makes a great catch of fish. Even more, he comes to a great insight about himself. Encounter with Jesus leads Peter to see himself as he really is ("I am a sinful man"), and to become what he is not yet: a follower of Jesus participating in his saving mission. Jesus "caught" Peter. He will "catch" us, too. All we need to do is heed Jesus' word.

What precipitated the radical response of the first disciples who "left everything and followed" Jesus? Clearly, Jesus' words and actions. To fishermen who had labored fruitlessly all night, Jesus says try again and leads them to a great catch. To a sinful Peter who considers himself unworthy of Jesus' company, Jesus says follow me and transforms his life's purpose. Jesus' words are powerful words that bind us to himself.

Jesus "taught the crowds." The miracle of the great catch makes concrete the good news of Jesus' teaching: God's intervention overturning the futility of mere human work, the superabundance of God's actions on our behalf, the invitation to follow in Jesus' footsteps. The miracle of the catch of fish is the bridge to another miracle: hearing the Good News and living it. The disciples' willingness to be caught enabled them to see more deeply into the truth of Jesus' teaching. It's the power of Jesus' good news that drew them to follow him. Today we are the "catch" that makes the Good News visible when we allow God to work in and through us.

Following Jesus can hardly be an impulse decision, although the gospel account might make it seem that way. Between the miracle of the great catch and the disciples leaving everything to follow Jesus stands Peter's recognition that he is "a sinful man." Their encounter with Jesus helped the disciples see themselves for who they were and opened up the willingness to change their life course. They would still be fishermen—but now their catch would be human beings to whom they would tell the good news of God's presence. Jesus is the net God lowers into the sea of humanity, knowing full well there will be a great catch.

Living the Paschal Mystery

For most of us, Jesus does not come in dramatic and miraculous ways and bid us to follow him, but in the ordinary events of daily living. The gospel invites us to look at the simple ways we live the Gospel to indicate the ways we have changed our purpose in life to follow Jesus. For example, in the generosity of so many volunteers, in the faithfulness of husbands and wives, in the unselfishness of pastoral workers, in the uncomplaining suffering of the sick, in the gracious wisdom of the elderly we see faithful followers of Jesus living his teachings. Our yes response is to imitate these good behaviors and by doing so we are faithful followers. Living the paschal mystery means we respond to God in these little, everyday things. The astonishing thing about this Good News is that we are all made worthy followers simply because God calls. We allow ourselves to be caught.

Focusing the Gospel

Key words and phrases: word of God, Put out . . . lower your nets, I will, caught a great number of fish, I am a sinful man, followed him

To the point: After fishing all night and catching nothing, Peter obeys Jesus, putting out his boat and nets once again. He makes a great catch of fish. Even more, he comes to a great insight about himself. Encounter with Jesus leads Peter to see himself as he really is ("I am a sinful man"), and to become what he is not yet: a follower of Jesus participating in his saving mission. Jesus "caught" Peter. He will "catch" us, too. All we need to do is heed Jesus' word.

Connecting the Gospel

to the first reading: In responding to God's call personal worthiness is not the issue, for all humanity is sinful as both Isaiah and Peter declare. All that matters is to hear God's word and respond with "I will."

to experience: So often when asked to volunteer, people respond with "I'm not good enough," "I don't know enough," "I'm not confident enough to do that." The good news is that God calls us as we are, and works through our humanity for the greater good.

Connecting the Responsorial Psalm

to the readings: Encounter with the Holy One, be it the "Lord of hosts" in heaven (first reading) or Jesus in an ordinary life situation (gospel), is a wake-up call. Individuals are shaken out of their complacency and change the direction of their lives. Both Isaiah and Peter acknowledge their own unholiness, and then find themselves sent on mission. The responsorial psalm reveals more beneath the surface, however. God heard the "words" uttered by Isaiah and Peter. God perceived the weakness each felt and replaced it with strength. Supported by such divine initiative, these two readily accept their mission, for they are confident that God "will complete what he has" begun in them.

The Holy One comes to us, too, sometimes in extraordinary ways, but most times in the ordinary circumstances of our daily lives. Each time, the Holy One shows us ourselves as we really are, strengthens us, then sends us to continue our baptismal mission. Like Isaiah and Peter, we can readily respond, "Send me!" for we know, as does the psalmist, who has begun and who will complete this work in us.

to psalmist preparation: What is the mission to which God calls you as psalmist? To what extent do you feel unworthy of this mission? How does God give you the confidence and strength you need? And how is this mission changing your life?

**ASSEMBLY &
FAITH-SHARING GROUPS**

- I recognize my sinfulness when . . . This leads me to . . .
- I find it easiest to hear Jesus' words of invitation when . . . I find it easiest to heed them when . . .
- Jesus "caught" me when . . . by . . . to . . .

PRESIDERS

I invite those in my pastoral care to participate in the saving mission of Jesus by . . .

DEACONS

I put out "nets" of service and catch . . . Jesus is with me when I cast my "nets" of service when . . .

HOSPITALITY MINISTERS

The manner of my welcome helps others to hear Jesus' word and respond when . . .

MUSIC MINISTERS

What I have to leave behind to do my music ministry as a follower of Jesus is . . .

ALTAR MINISTERS

The insights about myself I receive by serving faithfully at the altar are . . .

LECTORS

When I heed Jesus' word in my daily living, my proclamation sounds like . . .

**EXTRAORDINARY MINISTERS
OF HOLY COMMUNION**

My encounters with Jesus during Holy Communion bring me to . . .

Model Penitential Act

Presider: Jesus commands Peter to put out his boat and cast his nets in spite of Peter's having been out all night and catching nothing. As we prepare to celebrate these sacred mysteries, let us reflect on the times we have not heeded Jesus' commands and ask for God's mercy . . . [pause]

Lord Jesus, you are the Word of God calling us to confess who we are: Lord . . .

Christ Jesus, you are the fullness of Life transforming who we are: Christ . . .

Lord Jesus, you are the voice of God calling us to follow you: Lord . . .

Homily Points

• "I've had enough!" "I'm done with this!" "I've done all I can!" We often set limits on our perseverance, on our patience, on our willingness to keep trying in face of seeming failure. When we quit too soon, we miss opportunities to grow, to succeed, to encounter something or someone new and surprising. Peter did not quit.

• Had Peter, the experienced fisherman, not heard and obeyed Jesus' command to put out again and cast his nets, he would have missed the opportunity to know himself better and become more than he was. He would never have made the great catch of fish, nor would he himself have been "caught" by Jesus.

• "Put out into deep water . . ." How often we are in shallow water as Christians! How often we are reluctant to put into the deep water of following Christ! How often we let fear deter us from true discipleship! How often we hold back our talents, time, willingness to serve! Yet Jesus demands, desires, deserves our all. Will we leave everything and put out into the deep?

Model Universal Prayer (Prayer of the Faithful)

Presider: The God who calls us to follow the divine Son will give us what we need to be faithful. And so we pray.

Response:

Lord,——— hear our prayer.

Cantor:

we pray to the Lord,

That all members of the church heed Jesus' call to participate in his saving mission . . . [pause]

That all peoples of the world be truthful about who they are and grow in virtue and holiness . . . [pause]

That those who are hungering be fed by the bounty of those who follow Christ . . . [pause]

That each of us hear and obey whatever God asks of us . . . [pause]

Presider: O God, you sent your Son among us so we might follow him in bringing others to salvation. Hear these our prayers that we might be faithful in all we do and come one day to share the fullness of Life with you. We ask this through Christ our Lord. **Amen.**

COLLECT

Let us pray.

Pause for silent prayer

Keep your family safe, O Lord, with
    unfailing care,
that, relying solely on the hope of
    heavenly grace,
they may be defended always by your
    protection.
Through our Lord Jesus Christ, your Son,
who lives and reigns with you in the unity
    of the Holy Spirit,
one God, for ever and ever. **Amen.**

FIRST READING
Isa 6:1-2a, 3-8

In the year King Uzziah died,
    I saw the Lord seated on a high and
        lofty throne,
    with the train of his garment filling the
        temple.
Seraphim were stationed above.

They cried one to the other,
    "Holy, holy, holy is the LORD of hosts!
All the earth is filled with his glory!"
At the sound of that cry, the frame of the
        door shook
    and the house was filled with smoke.

Then I said, "Woe is me, I am doomed!
For I am a man of unclean lips,
    living among a people of unclean lips;
    yet my eyes have seen the King, the
        LORD of hosts!"
Then one of the seraphim flew to me,
    holding an ember that he had taken
        with tongs from the altar.

He touched my mouth with it, and said,
    "See, now that this has touched your
        lips,
    your wickedness is removed, your sin
        purged."

Then I heard the voice of the Lord saying,
    "Whom shall I send? Who will go for
        us?"
"Here I am," I said; "send me!"

RESPONSORIAL PSALM
Ps 138:1-2, 2-3, 4-5, 7-8

R̸. (1c) In the sight of the angels I will sing
your praises, Lord.

I will give thanks to you, O Lord, with all
my heart,
for you have heard the words of my
mouth;
in the presence of the angels I will sing
your praise;
I will worship at your holy temple
and give thanks to your name.

Ry. In the sight of the angels I will sing
your praises, Lord.

Because of your kindness and your truth;
for you have made great above all things
your name and your promise.
When I called, you answered me;
you built up strength within me.

Ry. In the sight of the angels I will sing
your praises, Lord.

All the kings of the earth shall give
thanks to you, O Lord,
when they hear the words of your mouth;
and they shall sing of the ways of the Lord:
"Great is the glory of the Lord."

Ry. In the sight of the angels I will sing
your praises, Lord.

Your right hand saves me.
The Lord will complete what he has
done for me;
your kindness, O Lord, endures forever;
forsake not the work of your hands.

Ry. In the sight of the angels I will sing
your praises, Lord.

SECOND READING
1 Cor 15:3-8, 11

Brothers and sisters,
I handed on to you as of first
importance what I also received:
that Christ died for our sins
in accordance with the Scriptures;
that he was buried;
that he was raised on the third day
in accordance with the Scriptures;
that he appeared to Cephas, then to the
Twelve.
After that, he appeared to more
than five hundred brothers at once,
most of whom are still living,
though some have fallen asleep.
After that he appeared to James,
then to all the apostles.
Last of all, as to one born abnormally,
he appeared to me.
Therefore, whether it be I or they,
so we preach and so you believed.

or 1 Cor 15:1-11

See Appendix A, p. 272.

✚ CATECHESIS

About Liturgy

"Lord, I am not worthy . . . " At Mass our response to the invitation to Holy Communion includes the words, "Lord, I am not worthy." This Sunday's gospel challenges us to utter these words not simply as a confession of sinfulness or a way to debase our own dignity as daughters and sons of God, but as a simple statement of recognizing our own status as creatures before God's all-powerful and divine holiness. The amazing generosity of Jesus' self-offering of his Body and Blood for our nourishment and drink is that God doesn't focus on our unworthiness but raises us up to share in divinity. Holy Communion should always be a kind of wake-up call in which we praise and thank God for the call to holiness, and also resolve to be faithful to God's call to continue Jesus' mission. Sharing in God's holiness is also sharing in God's mission.

About Liturgical Music

Music suggestions: In this Sunday's gospel Jesus meets Peter where and how he is, then calls him to "[p]ut out into deep water." This deep water is not only the sea where Peter experiences a miraculous catch of fish, but also a new way of life that will change everything Peter has understood about himself. In every celebration of liturgy, Jesus calls us to "[p]ut out into deep water" and undergo transformation.

"Pescador de Hombre/Lord, You Have Come" (in many resources) flows directly from the gospel story and would be a good choice for Communion. In Michael Ward's "Here I Am, Lord" (OF, WC, WS), we join sinful Peter in saying to Jesus, "What joy it is to stand amid your glory. Let me always stay in your presence, O God" (verse 2), and "Make of me what pleases you" (refrain). This verse-refrain song would be suitable for Communion. In "Lead Me, Guide Me" (in most resources), we speak to Jesus about our weakness and our need for his strength and power, praying to be led by him all along the way of discipleship. This hymn would make an excellent recessional song.

SEASON
OF LENT

SPIRITUALITY

GOSPEL ACCLAMATION
See Ps 95:8

If today you hear his voice,
harden not your hearts.

Gospel   Matt 6:1-6, 16-18; L219

Jesus said to his disciples:
"Take care not to perform righteous
        deeds
    in order that people may see them;
    otherwise, you will have no recompense
        from your heavenly Father.
When you give alms,
    do not blow a trumpet before you,
    as the hypocrites do in the synagogues and
        in the streets
    to win the praise of others.
Amen, I say to you,
    they have received their reward.
But when you give alms,
    do not let your left hand know
        what your right is doing,
    so that your almsgiving may be secret.
And your Father who sees in secret will
    repay you.

"When you pray,
    do not be like the hypocrites,
    who love to stand and pray in the
        synagogues and on street corners
    so that others may see them.
Amen, I say to you,
    they have received their reward.
But when you pray, go to your inner room,
    close the door, and pray to your Father in
        secret.
And your Father who sees in secret will
    repay you.

"When you fast,
    do not look gloomy like the hypocrites.
They neglect their appearance,
    so that they may appear to others to be
        fasting.
Amen, I say to you, they have received their
    reward.
But when you fast,
    anoint your head and wash your face,
    so that you may not appear to be fasting,
    except to your Father who is hidden.
And your Father who sees what is hidden
    will repay you."

See Appendix A, p. 273, for other readings.

Reflecting on the Gospel

The art of teaching and learning how to ride a bike is a balancing act on a grand, grand scale. The child must learn to balance a two-wheeler, pedal and steer, brake and get off—all at the same time. No one of these skills can stand alone; they must all work together or the little one will end up falling. The teacher must do a balancing act, too. He or she must know when to hang on and when to let go, when to push the child harder and when to back off, when to be lavish with encouragement and when to let the child go it alone. When we think about it, learning any new and worthwhile skill is a balancing act, often requiring another person to accompany one on the way. Sometimes the teaching and learning are effective quickly; sometimes they take a long, long time.

The gospel for this, the first day of Lent, presents a balancing act on a grand, grand scale. The gospel poses for us a number of contrasts: penance that is public or private, observable or unseen, directed to human praise or divine recompense, human reward or divine repayment. At the beginning of Lent, then, we must make two crucial choices: first, about the specific penance we want to undertake; second, about the motivation and manner of our doing penance. Yet, while we make these choices for our Lenten living, we don't go it alone. The Father in heaven "who sees in secret" is very much part of our decision, motivation, and action. Any spiritual growth during Lent is a cooperation between our resolve and God's mercy. Any conversion during Lent is a co-effort between our turning away from sin and God's invitation to a deeper relationship. Our Lenten penance is a grand balancing act between us and God.

Jesus admonishes his hearers not to seek human adulation or reward when performing penitential acts. The spirit in which we do penance—and, indeed, the purpose of all of Lent—is openness to *God's work* in us leading to conversion of heart. We can do nothing without God—not even penance. Lenten penance that transforms us and makes a difference in our ongoing daily living and deepens our relationship with God and each other is our response to God's overture of Presence and grace. The outward signs of Lenten penance are indications that God is at work in us. Even our choice to do penance is a response to God.

The reason for undertaking Lenten penance is conversion of heart that deepens our relationships. Lent directs us inward to self-transformation which opens us to new relationships with God and each other. Any transformation presupposes that we set right our relationships. In other words, our Lenten practices include the kind of inward renewal which changes how we relate to God and others. Changed behaviors and "righteous deeds" flow from our changed relationships.

Living the Paschal Mystery

Because our own transformation deepens our relationships, good choices for Lenten practices are those which really change us, really lead to conversion. Our Lenten practices "retrain" our way of living, our way of relating, our way of being. In other words, simply "giving up" something and forgetting about the practice when Lent is over doesn't really help us do what the gospel is asking of us. Our Lenten penance must be directed to *transformation* (conversion) of self that lasts beyond Lent. Transformed, we begin a new balancing act in our daily living, one that witnesses to our reliance on God and our renewed relationships.

Focusing the Gospel

Key words and phrases: Take care not to perform, Father who sees

To the point: Jesus admonishes his hearers not to seek human adulation or reward when performing penitential acts. The spirit in which we do penance—and, indeed, the purpose of all of Lent—is openness to *God's work* in us leading to conversion of heart. We can do nothing without God—not even penance.

Model Universal Prayer (Prayer of the Faithful)

Presider: As we begin this solemn time of discipline and conversion, let us pray that we will grow in our love for God and each other.

Response:

Cantor:

That all members of the church enter into this Lenten season with a spirit open to conversion and a heart open to God's mercy . . . [pause]

That all peoples of the world work for reconciliation and forgiveness . . . [pause]

That those trapped in self-adulation and reward-seeking be open to God leading them to conversion . . . [pause]

That each of us here gathered surrender ourselves to the work God will do in us this Lent . . . [pause]

Presider: Gracious and merciful God, you work in us for our good even when we are not aware. Hear these our prayers and during this Lenten season keep us faithful in the penance we undertake and lead us to conversion of heart. We ask this through Christ our Lord. **Amen.**

COLLECT
Let us pray.

Pause for silent prayer

Grant, O Lord, that we may begin with holy fasting
this campaign of Christian service,
so that, as we take up battle against spiritual evils,
we may be armed with weapons of self-restraint.
Through our Lord Jesus Christ, your Son,
who lives and reigns with you in the unity of the Holy Spirit,
one God, for ever and ever. **Amen.**

FOR REFLECTION

* I lose sight of God's work in me and seek human reward when . . .
* This Lent, the work God will be doing in me is . . .
* This Lent, I will respond to God by being faithful in my chosen penance, and what will happen is . . .

Homily Points

* "What's in it for me?" is a question that subtly underlies much of our motivation when choosing to do something. Even the penance we undertake during Lent can subtly be turned inward on ourselves. Is Lent just forty days of a self-help program, or is it a surrender to God's work in us leading to conversion?

* The Father takes the lead in who we are and who we are becoming. "In secret" the Father transforms us. And God's hidden work is made visible in our conversion of heart—our turning from self toward God and others. "What's in it for us?" A whole new way of being. A whole new way of relating. Ultimately, eternal Life.

SPIRITUALITY

GOSPEL ACCLAMATION
Matt 4:4b

One does not live on bread alone,
but on every word that comes forth
   from the mouth of God.

Gospel   Luke 4:1-13; L24C

Filled with the Holy Spirit, Jesus
   returned from the Jordan
and was led by the Spirit into the
   desert for forty days,
to be tempted by the devil.
He ate nothing during those days,
   and when they were over he was
   hungry.
The devil said to him,
   "If you are the Son of God,
   command this stone to become bread."
Jesus answered him,
   "It is written, *One does not live on bread
      alone.*"
Then he took him up and showed him
   all the kingdoms of the world in a single
      instant.
The devil said to him,
   "I shall give to you all this power and glory;
   for it has been handed over to me,
   and I may give it to whomever I wish.
All this will be yours, if you worship me."
Jesus said to him in reply,
   "It is written:
   *You shall worship the Lord, your God,
      and him alone shall you serve.*"
Then he led him to Jerusalem,
   made him stand on the parapet of the
      temple, and said to him,
   "If you are the Son of God,
   throw yourself down from here, for it is
      written:
   *He will command his angels
         concerning you, to guard you,*
   and:
   *With their hands they will support you,
      lest you dash your foot against a stone.*"
Jesus said to him in reply,
   "It also says,
   *You shall not put the Lord, your God, to
      the test.*"
When the devil had finished every
      temptation,
   he departed from him for a time.

Reflecting on the Gospel

It so happens that this year the First Sunday of Lent falls on Valentine's Day. What a contradiction! During the season when we practice self-discipline, this day promotes self-indulgence. At a time when we remember God's forgiveness and mercy for our wrongdoings, this day seems to forget about the challenge and hard work of growing in relationships. For six weeks we look to the God of love to teach us self-giving, while this day tends to extol a gooey kind of love fed by insipid platitudes. Lent reminds us of our failings and need for conversion; Valentine's Day overlooks human imperfection and glorifies any kind of relationship. On the other hand, the coincidence of this Sunday with Valentine's Day is a happy event, too. Both are about who we are, how we want to be in relation to others, and the importance of personal encounter for our very well-being.

In this gospel, the encounter of Jesus with "the devil" parallels our own encounters with "the devil." None of us—not even the God-Man—is exempt from temptation. By resisting the devil's temptations to act as "the Son of God," Jesus fully embraces his human identity. Jesus facing temptation witnesses to how fully he identifies with who we are as human beings. By resisting the devil's temptations to act against who God created us to be, we fully embrace our own human identity: graced beings created in the image of God. Jesus chooses not to misuse his divine power, taking up the mission for which he was sent. He was not sent to lord it over us, but to use his divine power to lead us to saving wholeness and well-being. We choose not to act against the divine Life God has bestowed upon us, taking up the mission on which we have been sent. We continue Jesus' saving ministry, reaching out to others with the Good News that God is forgiving and merciful, ever calling us to deeper relationship.

Temptation is an occasion for showing that our lives are turned to God, in whom we find our very identity and being. Like Jesus, temptations and our very resistance to them strengthen us in our choices for goodness and holiness. In making these choices we are continually choosing who we want to be: those who faithfully serve God by doing good for others—this is our life's mission. Temptations' lure to self-satisfaction is overcome by an even stronger lure: growth in holiness and transformation into being ever more beloved sons and daughters of God.

Living the Paschal Mystery

The ritual act of professing our faith during Sunday Mass is no substitution for *living* it in our daily lives. When we are tested by temptations, our faith is put to the test, too, and we are faced with a choice of who we are and how we want to live. Lent is a time to examine our choices. Lent is a time to grow in who we are.

Just as God led Israel to a "land flowing with milk and honey" (first reading), so will God lead us to salvation if each of us "calls on the name of the Lord" (second reading). For us, though, our desert is the demands of everyday living and our salvation is found on the cross. Each day we take up our cross and lay down our life for the sake of others, we are building strength to resist temptation and come to greater well-being. Our simple acts of kindness are helping us resist temptation. Our doing well whatever the task at hand helps us resist temptation. Our complimenting another or offering a word of encouragement helps us resist temptation.

We don't have to go out into a desert to find temptation! But we do need God's nearness to resist it. And that God has promised us.

Focusing the Gospel

Key words and phrases: tempted by the devil, If you are the Son of God, Jesus answered him

To the point: In this gospel, the encounter of Jesus with "the devil" parallels our own encounters with "the devil." By resisting the devil's temptations to act as "the Son of God," Jesus fully embraces his human identity. By resisting the devil's temptations to act against who God created us to be, we fully embrace our human identity. Jesus chooses not to misuse his divine power, taking up the mission for which he was sent. We choose not to act against the divine Life God has bestowed upon us, taking up the mission on which we have been sent.

Connecting the Gospel

to the first reading: The Israelites bowed down in worship before God, offering "the firstfruits" of the "land flowing with milk and honey" to which God had brought them. The devil offers Jesus much more than firstfruits if he would bow down and worship him. Jesus makes clear that we worship only our God.

to experience: All temptation faces us with a choice about who we want to be. Do we choose ourselves, making ourselves a god? Do we choose God, who fills us with divine Life?

Connecting the Responsorial Psalm

to the readings: As the psalm refrain indicates, Jesus is in "trouble." Hungry after forty days of fasting, he is accosted by Satan with every possible temptation. Yet he steadfastly "clings" to God (psalm). He chooses to "bow down" (first reading) only before God; he chooses to live not by bread, but by the word of God; he refuses to test God, but chooses to trust instead in a guarantee already given (psalm). Jesus' mission will lead to his death, but he knows God will "deliver him and glorify him" because this is what God has promised to do. Jesus remains true to who he is because he knows he can count on God remaining true to who God is. As we enter this new season of Lent, our forty-day testing period, we sing this psalm with Jesus, and stand with him on God's promise.

to psalmist preparation: As you enter this new Lenten season, this is a good time to examine how you may be tempted at times to misuse your power as psalmist. When are you tempted to focus the assembly's attention on yourself rather than on the psalm? When are you tempted to use your position to dominate the assembly rather than serve them? When you are so tempted, how does Christ keep you faithful to discipleship and service?

ASSEMBLY & FAITH-SHARING GROUPS
- The devil tempts me to . . . I am able to resist because . . .
- The misguided personal gain I am most tempted to pursue is . . . This makes me less human in that . . .
- I am most aware of God's gift of divine Life when . . .

PRESIDERS
I help people remain faithful to who God created them to be when I . . .

DEACONS
In my service ministry, I embrace what is most fully human in the other when I . . .

HOSPITALITY MINISTERS
My greeting of those gathering for liturgy opens the way for them to encounter God and the divine Life God gives when I . . .

MUSIC MINISTERS
Sometimes in my very music making I am tempted to turn from God by . . . What keeps me faithful to God is . . .

ALTAR MINISTERS
I respond to the reminders of Lent that surround me by . . .

LECTORS
When I have been faithful to my Lenten practices as I prepare to proclaim God's word, my ministry . . .

EXTRAORDINARY MINISTERS OF HOLY COMMUNION
My manner of distributing Holy Communion helps communicants realize that God is continually creating them to be more perfectly the Body of Christ when . . .

Model Penitential Act

Presider: In the gospel today the devil tempts Jesus to abuse his power as the Son of God. Jesus refuses to give in to the temptations. Let us ask God to pardon us for the times we have given in to temptation . . . [pause]

    Confiteor: I confess . . .

Homily Points

• Long ago, comedian Flip Wilson coined the now-famous phrase, "The devil made me do it!" When we are caught doing what we know is wrong, we often look for someone or something outside ourselves to blame. The devil is readily at hand! But *we* choose right or wrong; *we* choose to give in to or resist temptation. The devil can't make us do anything.

• In this gospel two competing powers, the Spirit and the devil, act on Jesus. The Spirit leads Jesus into the desert to be tempted. The devil tempts Jesus to act as the "Son of God" in a way that misuses his divine power. In his confrontation with the devil Jesus chooses to be fully human and not capitalize on his being divine—even to gain all "power and glory." Jesus chooses right; Jesus resists temptation.

• Temptation itself isn't wrongdoing; wrongdoing is the choice to do what we know we ought not, what we know will hurt us, what we know diminishes who we are. For example, when we tear down another in order to look good, we tarnish our identity. When we lie or cheat, we rob ourselves of integrity. When we refuse to respond to the need of another, we are unfaithful to the self-giving mission of Christ we have taken up. Growing in the divine Life God bestows on us means we choose right; we resist temptation. And the devil can't make us *not* do this!

Model Universal Prayer (Prayer of the Faithful)

Presider: God is with us at all times, helping us to resist temptation. We pray that during Lent we may grow in choosing what is right and good.

Response:

Cantor:

That during Lent all members of the church deepen their resolve to resist temptation and grow in God's Life . . . [pause]

That all peoples of the world resist temptation to wrongdoing and come to the salvation God offers . . . [pause]

That all those who are weak in face of temptations open themselves to the strength God unceasingly offers . . . [pause]

That those preparing for the initiation sacraments be led by the Spirit to new Life . . . [pause]

That each of us enter into Lent with seriousness of purpose and resolve of will to grow in our baptismal identity . . . [pause]

Presider: Merciful God, you send your Spirit to strengthen us when we are tempted to wrongdoing. May we remain always faithful to you in the choices we make, and come to fullness of Life. We ask this through Christ our Savior. **Amen.**

COLLECT

Let us pray.

Pause for silent prayer

Grant, almighty God,
through the yearly observances of holy
    Lent,
that we may grow in understanding
of the riches hidden in Christ
and by worthy conduct pursue their
    effects.
Through our Lord Jesus Christ, your Son,
who lives and reigns with you in the unity
    of the Holy Spirit,
one God, for ever and ever. **Amen.**

FIRST READING

Deut 26:4-10

Moses spoke to the people, saying:
    "The priest shall receive the basket from
        you
        and shall set it in front of the altar of
            the Lord, your God.
Then you shall declare before the Lord,
        your God,
    'My father was a wandering Aramean
        who went down to Egypt with a small
           household
        and lived there as an alien.
But there he became a nation
        great, strong, and numerous.
When the Egyptians maltreated and
        oppressed us,
        imposing hard labor upon us,
        we cried to the Lord, the God of our
           fathers,
        and he heard our cry
        and saw our affliction, our toil, and our
           oppression.
He brought us out of Egypt
        with his strong hand and outstretched
           arm,
        with terrifying power, with signs and
           wonders;
        and bringing us into this country,
        he gave us this land flowing with milk
           and honey.
Therefore, I have now brought you the
        firstfruits
    of the products of the soil
        which you, O Lord, have given me.'
And having set them before the Lord, your
        God,
    you shall bow down in his presence."

RESPONSORIAL PSALM

Ps 91:1-2, 10-11, 12-13, 14-15

℟. (cf. 15b) Be with me, Lord, when I am in trouble.

You who dwell in the shelter of the Most
    High,
  who abide in the shadow of the
    Almighty,
say to the LORD, "My refuge and fortress,
  my God in whom I trust."

℟. Be with me, Lord, when I am in trouble.

No evil shall befall you,
  nor shall affliction come near your tent,
for to his angels he has given command
    about you,
  that they guard you in all your ways.

℟. Be with me, Lord, when I am in trouble.

Upon their hands they shall bear you up,
  lest you dash your foot against a stone.
You shall tread upon the asp and the viper;
  you shall trample down the lion and the
    dragon.

℟. Be with me, Lord, when I am in trouble.

Because he clings to me, I will deliver him;
  I will set him on high because he
    acknowledges my name.
He shall call upon me, and I will answer
    him;
  I will be with him in distress;
I will deliver him and glorify him.

℟. Be with me, Lord, when I am in trouble.

SECOND READING

Rom 10:8-13

See Appendix A, p. 273.

About Liturgy

Creed, universal prayer, and baptism: The general intercessions we pray at Mass are a kind of practical continuation of the profession of faith already begun in the Creed. The name used now for this time of intense prayer that concludes the Liturgy of the Word is universal prayer (prayer of the faithful), and this name suggests that this prayer, then, is a "profession" of our faithful relationship to God that spills over to faithful relationship with each other. It is a priestly prayer uttered by all those who have been baptized.

The format used for the universal prayer in *Living Liturgy*™ involves the baptized assembly in two ways. First of all, they are short—only giving an *announcement* of a general intention that flows from the readings, particularly the gospel. The slight pause indicated by the ellipses is time for *each of us to pray with all our hearts*. Thus, the first involvement is in genuine prayer for the needs of the church, the world, the less fortunate, and our own parish or liturgical community. Second, the universal prayer isn't finished when we respond *Amen* to the presider's concluding collect. In fact, the prayer we pray during Mass is only the beginning of our responsibility to those for whom we pray. In this prayer we also make a commitment to actually die to self, that is, to get involved in helping God's reign become a reality in our world. This prayer is a commitment to fidelity to doing good for others, a commitment of fidelity to our baptismal promises.

During Lent, an intense time of preparation for the elect and candidates preparing for the initiation sacraments, it would be good to add a fifth intention for those whom we will receive into full communion with the church and who soon will be exercising their baptismal priesthood and praying the universal prayer with the whole parish community.

First readings during Lent: The Old Testament readings during Lent provide a thumbnail of salvation history and, because they have their own purpose, won't necessarily accord with the gospel. The Lectionary is instructing us in God's ways and mighty deeds in the first reading and asking for a faith response in the gospels.

About Liturgical Music

Music for the Lenten season: GIRM no. 313 provides us with directives concerning music during the seasons of Advent and Lent. During Advent, musical instruments should be used with moderation. During Lent, instruments should be used only to support the singing of the assembly. These directives are applications of the principle of progressive solemnity (STL, nos. 110–14). Some liturgical days and seasons call for musical exuberance, while other days and seasons call for musical restraint. Applying the principle of progressive solemnity allows the paschal mystery dynamic of the liturgical year—its built-in rhythm of not yet-already, of anticipation-celebration, of dying-rising—to have a formative effect upon us. This rhythm is no inconsequential thing, for it is the very rhythm which marks our identity as Body of Christ and our daily living as faithful members of the church.

SPIRITUALITY

Gospel   Luke 9:28b-36; L27C

Jesus took Peter, John, and James
and went up the mountain to
pray.
While he was praying his face
changed in appearance
and his clothing became
dazzling white.
And behold, two men were
conversing with him, Moses
and Elijah,
who appeared in glory and
spoke of his exodus
that he was going to accomplish in
Jerusalem.
Peter and his companions had been
overcome by sleep,
but becoming fully awake,
they saw his glory and the two men
standing with him.
As they were about to part from him,
Peter said to Jesus,
"Master, it is good that we are here;
let us make three tents,
one for you, one for Moses, and one
for Elijah."
But he did not know what he was
saying.
While he was still speaking,
a cloud came and cast a shadow over
them,
and they became frightened when
they entered the cloud.
Then from the cloud came a voice that
said,
"This is my chosen Son; listen to
him."
After the voice had spoken, Jesus was
found alone.
They fell silent and did not at that time
tell anyone what they had seen.

Reflecting on the Gospel

Shortsightedness limits potential, cuts off possibilities, diminishes growth.
Peter wakes from sleep to behold shining glory. His response is surely quite
shortsighted: he wants to pitch tents and stay put on the mountain. He "did
not know what he was saying." We can imagine he was flabbergasted so much
at the vision that he blabbered the first thing that came to mind. The gospel
doesn't directly tell us that Peter heard "Moses and Elijah" speak of Jesus'
"exodus." But maybe he did. Maybe this prompted his blabbering. Maybe
Peter chose shortsightedness rather than an unknown, seemingly
inglorious future. Only by disciples going through life with Jesus,
embracing his "exodus"—his passing through suffering and death
to risen Life—can they shatter the limits of potential, open up
new possibilities, and embrace flowering growth.

In this telling of the transfiguration event, Moses and Elijah
speak of exodus, of going forth to Jerusalem. By contrast, Peter
speaks of pitching tents, of staying on the mountain in the moment of glory. He chooses to stay with the beauty and wonder
of the glory he sees, but by doing so he would deny his own
share in this same glory. Are we to stay or to go? Both! Disciples
must stay in Jesus' Presence and "listen to him," *and* go to
their own Jerusalem to pass over from death to new Life.
Stay or go? Both! Our own transfiguration lies in both going
and staying. Only by choosing the longer vision of going to
Jerusalem with Jesus can we hope to share in his glory. Only by
staying close to Jesus can such a journey end in a share in his glory.

Jesus' transfiguration—in all its glory—cannot erase the stark reality of
the self-giving that traveling to Jerusalem with him requires. Simply put,
glory only comes through embracing the passion. This is the paradox of the
paschal mystery: that something as desirable as a share in Jesus' transfigured
glory only comes through our embracing something as demanding as dying
to self for the good of others. Even in this glorious moment of transfiguration—which gives us encouragement and hope on our Lenten journey—we are
reminded that the only way to remain in that glory is to die to self. We have to
come down off the mountain and go our own journey through death to glory.

Living the Paschal Mystery

Luke's allusions to Jesus' death in Jerusalem prompt us to consider our being
plunged into Jesus' dying and rising in the baptismal waters. We are invited
this Sunday to see our baptism in light of the transfiguration.

Baptism isn't simply a ritual we perform, but initiates a covenant with God
that we live out the rest of our lives. During Lent as we walk with the elect
through their final preparation for baptism we, too, prepare to renew our covenant with God at Easter. This means that we not only already share in God's
Life and look forward to that day when we will share eternal glory with God,
but we also embrace the suffering and death.

Let's face it: constant dying to self gets tiresome! This Sunday we are given
a glimpse of glory to help ease away the discouragement of a lifetime of self-
emptying. This tells us something about how we might keep Sundays. If each
Sunday is a day of rest, a time to be good to ourselves, to do something special
that is uplifting, to enter into a moment of glory, we would be better fortified to
continue dying to self. Sunday is a weekly opportunity for us to enter into the
glory of transfiguration.

Focusing the Gospel

Key words and phrases: spoke of his exodus, they saw his glory, let us make three tents, listen to him

To the point: In this telling of the transfiguration event, Moses and Elijah speak of exodus, of going forth to Jerusalem. By contrast, Peter speaks of pitching tents, of staying on the mountain in the moment of glory. Are we to stay or to go? Both! Disciples must stay in Jesus' Presence and "listen to him," *and* go to their own Jerusalem to pass over from death to new Life. Stay or go? Both!

Connecting the Gospel

to the second reading: Paul assures us Christ "will change our lowly body to conform with his glorified body." Like him, one day we will receive the fullness of glory, be transfigured.

to experience: We are often pulled in two different directions. Do we go out with our friends or stay at a family gathering? Do we go with a new investment or stay with what is secure? Discipleship merges two seemingly different directions into one: we stay with Jesus as we go to our own Jerusalem to die to self and rise to new Life.

Connecting the Responsorial Psalm

to the readings: Sung in a Lenten context, these verses from Psalm 27 remind us that the fearlessness which comes from knowing God is our salvation will not spare us from the reality of suffering and death. The transfigured Jesus glowed with the divine light (gospel) of God, our "light and [our] salvation" (psalm refrain). Jesus could face the "terrifying darkness" (first reading) of his passion and death because he counted on the covenant relationship God had established. In singing these psalm verses, we, like Jesus, make God the center and focus of our lives. Like Jesus we choose to undergo the "exodus" (gospel) required of us. And like him we, too, shall be transformed into glory by the light of God (second reading).

to psalmist preparation: As part of your preparation to sing this responsorial psalm, read and pray with the whole of Psalm 27. Filled with images of danger and death, the psalm nonetheless maintains its confidence in God's ultimate promise of life. For you as a baptized Christian, the danger is the struggle with evil, and the death is dying to self. How are you being called this Lent to this dying? How are you experiencing God's promise of resurrection?

ASSEMBLY & FAITH-SHARING GROUPS

- I am most attentive to listening to Jesus when . . . What helps me stay with him is . . .
- My own Jerusalem where I pass over from death to new Life is . . .
- I experience a share in Jesus' transfigured glory when . . .

PRESIDERS

The dying to self I must constantly choose in order to lead my people well is . . . The transfiguration I experience in this is . . .

DEACONS

My serving others becomes a revelation of Jesus' transfigured glory when . . .

HOSPITALITY MINISTERS

My greeting of those gathering for liturgy helps them listen to Jesus now and in their daily living when I . . .

MUSIC MINISTERS

I find my ministry transforming me more gloriously into the Body of Christ when . . . The dying to self that makes this transformation possible is . . .

ALTAR MINISTERS

The self-emptying of serving is . . . The glory of serving is . . .

LECTORS

My manner of proclaiming helps others listen to Jesus more fruitfully when . . .

EXTRAORDINARY MINISTERS OF HOLY COMMUNION

My manner of distributing Holy Communion helps others share more fully in Jesus' transfigured glory when . . .

Model Penitential Act

Presider: In today's gospel we hear about Jesus' transfigured glory. We pause to reflect on the times when we have closed our eyes to this glory because of sin and ask God's pardon and mercy . . . [pause]

    Confiteor: I confess . . .

Homily Points

• When we are enveloped in overwhelming peace, beauty, and silence, our tendency is to say, "I want to stay here forever." When we are immersed in pain and suffering, difficulties and trials, misunderstandings and hardships, our tendency is to say, "I want to go away from this." We live "stay" and "go" as opposites. In this gospel, stay and go come together in disciple living.

• Peter, James, and John are asleep when Jesus is transfigured, and become "fully awake" to the experience only for a moment. The event of Jesus' transfiguration, though fully revelatory of who he is, is frighteningly powerful, even if happening only momentarily. The disciples are left tongue-tied by what they have seen (the glory of Jesus) and what they have heard ("This is my chosen Son; listen to him."). Only by continuing on the journey of discipleship do they learn how to both stay in glory and go with Jesus to dying and rising.

• How do we learn on our journey of discipleship both to stay in glory and to go forward in our dying to self and rising to new Life? We learn, for example, by appreciating the silence and beauty around us and staying in God's Presence to be renewed in it. We learn by listening to Jesus—on Sunday in the Liturgy of the Word, in daily personal prayer, through words of other faithful disciples. We learn by experiencing in self-giving the joy and happiness we can bring to another. Stay or go? For faithful discipleship, both!

Model Universal Prayer (Prayer of the Faithful)

Presider: We pray to the God of glory that we might have the strength to die to self for the good of others.

Response:

Lord, hear our prayer.

Cantor:

we pray to the Lord,

That all members of the church embrace dying to self as necessary on our journey to eternal glory . . . [pause]

That all peoples of the world be open to the glory of salvation that God offers . . . [pause]

That those who cannot see through their suffering to the glory awaiting them be comforted by the nearness of God . . . [pause]

That those preparing for the Easter sacraments listen to the words Jesus speaks and go where he bids them go . . . [pause]

That we gathered here awaken to the glory of Christ and be strengthened in our Lenten practices . . . [pause]

Presider: Glorious God, you make known your salvation through the Presence of your transfigured Son. Grant our prayers of petition that one day we might share in your eternal glory. We ask this through that same Son, Jesus Christ our Lord. **Amen.**

COLLECT
Let us pray.

Pause for silent prayer

O God, who have commanded us
to listen to your beloved Son,
be pleased, we pray,
to nourish us inwardly by your word,
that, with spiritual sight made pure,
we may rejoice to behold your glory.
Through our Lord Jesus Christ, your Son,
who lives and reigns with you in the unity
    of the Holy Spirit,
one God, for ever and ever. **Amen.**

FIRST READING
Gen 15:5-12, 17-18

The Lord God took Abram outside and
    said,
    "Look up at the sky and count the stars,
        if you can.
Just so," he added, "shall your descendants
    be."
Abram put his faith in the LORD,
    who credited it to him as an act of
        righteousness.

He then said to him,
    "I am the LORD who brought you from Ur
        of the Chaldeans
    to give you this land as a possession."
"O Lord GOD," he asked,
    "how am I to know that I shall possess
        it?"
He answered him,
    "Bring me a three-year-old heifer, a
        three-year-old she-goat,
    a three-year-old ram, a turtledove, and a
        young pigeon."
Abram brought him all these, split them
    in two,
    and placed each half opposite the other;
    but the birds he did not cut up.
Birds of prey swooped down on the
    carcasses,
    but Abram stayed with them.
As the sun was about to set, a trance fell
    upon Abram,
    and a deep, terrifying darkness
        enveloped him.

When the sun had set and it was dark,
    there appeared a smoking fire pot and a
        flaming torch,
    which passed between those pieces.
It was on that occasion that the LORD made
    a covenant with Abram,
    saying: "To your descendants I give this
        land,
    from the Wadi of Egypt to the Great
        River, the Euphrates."

RESPONSORIAL PSALM

Ps 27:1, 7-8, 8-9, 13-14

R̸. (1a) The Lord is my light and my salvation.

The LORD is my light and my salvation;
   whom should I fear?
The LORD is my life's refuge;
   of whom should I be afraid?

R̸. The Lord is my light and my salvation.

Hear, O LORD, the sound of my call;
   have pity on me, and answer me.
Of you my heart speaks; you my glance
      seeks.

R̸. The Lord is my light and my salvation.

Your presence, O LORD, I seek.
   Hide not your face from me;
do not in anger repel your servant.
   You are my helper: cast me not off.

R̸. The Lord is my light and my salvation.

I believe that I shall see the bounty of the
      LORD
   in the land of the living.
Wait for the LORD with courage;
   be stouthearted, and wait for the LORD.

R̸. The Lord is my light and my salvation.

SECOND READING

Phil 3:17–4:1

Join with others in being imitators of me,
      brothers and sisters,
   and observe those who thus conduct
         themselves
   according to the model you have in us.
For many, as I have often told you
   and now tell you even in tears,
   conduct themselves as enemies of the
         cross of Christ.
Their end is destruction.
Their God is their stomach;
   their glory is in their "shame."
Their minds are occupied with earthly
      things.
But our citizenship is in heaven,
   and from it we also await a savior, the
         Lord Jesus Christ.
He will change our lowly body
   to conform with his glorified body
   by the power that enables him also
   to bring all things into subjection to
         himself.

Therefore, my brothers and sisters,
   whom I love and long for, my joy and
         crown,
   in this way stand firm in the Lord.

or Phil 3:20–4:1, see Appendix A, p. 273.

About Liturgy

Parish baptisms: Easter is the preferred time for baptisms, especially for those who have embraced the conversion process of the Rite of Christian Initiation of Adults (RCIA). In most parishes, however, it is not practical *only* to baptize during the season of Easter, especially the infants. Liturgical renewal has encouraged us to celebrate baptisms occasionally at Sunday Mass when the community is gathered. One reason for this is so that we understand that baptism is a *community* event, not some privatized ritual that is happening to this individual. Baptism is an initiation into the Body of Christ, the Christian community. When the parish gathers weekly to celebrate the Lord's resurrection, it is fitting that we share in the reception of an infant or young child into the church community.

Celebrating baptisms occasionally during Sunday Mass also reminds each of us that our own baptisms are ongoing—they are not finished and over with at the last prayer of the baptismal ritual, but continue in our daily dying and rising with Christ. These necessary reminders that we already share in Christ's glory encourage and strengthen us to continue with our daily dying to self.

This being said, there ought to not be so many baptisms at the Easter Vigil or during the year at Sunday Mass that we lose sight of the primary purpose of these liturgical celebrations, which is to *enact* the death and resurrection of Jesus. Although baptism, like all sacraments, does make present the paschal mystery in its very enactment, its immediate purpose is primarily initiation, a different emphasis from our weekly and yearly celebration of the paschal mystery. This poses some pastoral challenges that ought to be given careful consideration.

About Liturgical Music

Music suggestions: Well-known songs specific to the transfiguration event proclaimed every year on the Second Sunday of Lent include "'Tis Good, Lord, to Be Here"; "Transform Us"; and "From Ashes to the Living Font" (all found in many resources). Newly-appearing songs related to Jesus' and our transfiguration include Ricky Manalo's setting of the Brian Wren text "Transfiguration" (BB, JS3), appropriate for either the entrance or Communion, and Bob Hurd's "Transfigure Us, O Lord" (BB, JS3), suitable in style for Communion.

Particularly fitting this year would also be songs that explicitly relate the transfiguration to the mystery of the cross. Examples include Christoph Tietze's "Then Let Us Glory in the Cross" (OF, WC, WS), Tony Alonso's "We Should Glory in the Cross" (OF, WS), Francis Patrick O'Brien's "The Cross of Jesus" (G3, SS), and "Take Up Your Cross" (in most resources).

✠ SPIRITUALITY

GOSPEL ACCLAMATION
Matt 4:17

Repent, says the Lord;
the kingdom of heaven is at hand.

Gospel   Luke 13:1-9; L30C

Some people told Jesus about the
   Galileans
   whose blood Pilate had mingled with
      the blood of their sacrifices.
Jesus said to them in reply,
   "Do you think that because these
      Galileans suffered in this way
   they were greater sinners than all
      other Galileans?
By no means!
But I tell you, if you do not repent,
   you will all perish as they did!
Or those eighteen people who were
   killed
   when the tower at Siloam fell on
      them—
   do you think they were more guilty
      than everyone else who lived in
      Jerusalem?
By no means!
But I tell you, if you do not repent,
   you will all perish as they did!"

And he told them this parable:
   "There once was a person who had
      a fig tree planted in his orchard,
   and when he came in search of fruit
      on it but found none,
   he said to the gardener,
   'For three years now I have come in
      search of fruit on this fig tree
   but have found none.
So cut it down.
Why should it exhaust the soil?'
He said to him in reply,
   'Sir, leave it for this year also,
   and I shall cultivate the ground
      around it and fertilize it;
   it may bear fruit in the future.
If not you can cut it down.'"

*See Appendix A, pp. 274–276, for optional
readings.*

Reflecting on the Gospel

Question: What are five verbs beginning with "re" that capture this gospel's challenge to us? Answer: repent, retry, reconcile, renew, restore. We are to *repent* of our sinfulness; *retry* the cultivation God constantly does in order for us to be fruitful in our daily living; *reconcile* with whomever and whatever keeps us from growing; *renew* our resolve to avoid whatever might cut us off from God; and *restore* any broken relationships hindering our receiving the fullness of Life. Not to accept this challenge to personal transformation is to choose to perish. What is obvious in these statements is that *we* choose to perish or live. God gives us all we need and even more so that we bear fruit. Lent is a reminder that we are prone to sinfulness, but that we are given a chance over and over again to choose Life. Why would we choose to cut ourselves off from God and each other and perish? This is our work of *repenting*: that we turn from sinfulness toward God's transforming mercy, knowing full well this turning is our choice. This is our work of *retrying*: that we never give up on God's work of mercy, our God who takes what is almost dead and coaxes it back to new life. This is our work of *reconciling*: to heal the wounds that separate. This is our work of *renewing*: that we undertake the necessary steps to rebuild our relationships with God and each other. This is our work of *restoring*: that we allow God's new Life so freely given to us to redirect all our being to bear the good fruit of righteous living.

In this gospel, Jesus attacks a misconception his hearers held: tragic death—and illness or other misfortunes—is not the result of sinning. Sinning is always our own choice, not a consequence of some impersonal outside force. Jesus issues a clear warning: sinfulness is not to be ignored—we must repent and bear the good fruit of right living. If not, we will perish. We will die an eternal death. The work of Lent is to choose the eternal Life God continuously cultivates within us. Our encouragement is that God is ever patient, ever merciful. God never gives up on us.

Living the Paschal Mystery

Repentance is about changing one's mind, letting go of the narrowness of our own perception of how life should be to embrace the effusiveness of God's mercy and compassion. Repentance, in terms of changing one's mind, is really the same as conversion. The dying to self of repentance and coming to new Life through God's gracious mercy must characterize our Christian living and make real and concrete our baptismal commitment. If we wish to bear fruit, we must die to ourselves. Here is an interesting paradox: if we don't bear fruit, we die; but we must die to bear fruit. The choice before us is about dying: meaningless dying (selfishness) or fruitful dying (to self for the sake of others).

The gospel parable says for "three years" the owner of the fig tree had been waiting for good fruit. God waits more than three years for us to bear fruit— God waits each and every day of our lives for us to bear fruit. The good news is that God never gives up on us. God continually cultivates and fertilizes—especially by the ongoing proclamation of God's word and the invitation to God's table. All we need to do is repent, retry, reconcile, renew, restore. All we need to do is choose the new Life God offers those who turn from sinfulness to receive divine mercy and compassion.

Focusing the Gospel

Key words and phrases: suffered . . . sinners, By no means!, killed . . . guilty, By no means!, not repent . . . perish

To the point: In this gospel, Jesus attacks a misconception his hearers held: tragic death—and illness or other misfortunes—are not the result of sinning. Nonetheless, he issues a clear warning: sinfulness is not to be ignored—we must repent and bear the good fruit of right living. If not, we will perish. We will die an eternal death. The work of Lent is to choose the eternal Life God continuously cultivates within us.

Connecting the Gospel

to the second reading: Paul, like Jesus, warns us that our sinful actions will bear dire consequences. Further, since "the end of the ages has come," there is an urgency about repentance; we cannot put it off—the landowner only gave the fig tree one more year to bear fruit.

to experience: Tragedy survived (for example, a near-fatal auto accident, a serious heart attack) is often experienced as a "wake-up call." Lent is our "wake-up call" to reassess our lives and make choices turning us from sin and leading to fuller Life.

Connecting the Responsorial Psalm

to the readings: This Sunday's gospel and second reading require that we repent and do so immediately. The demand is unequivocal: if we do not repent we shall perish. Yet in the parable of the fig tree, Jesus seems to soften this demand when he reveals that God will always give us one more chance. The psalm tells us why: God is infinitely merciful, compassionate, kind, and forgiving. God is not vindictive, but "slow to anger" and quick to "pardon." The way to repentance, then, is to reach out and receive the gracious mercy God steadfastly offers us. Our task during Lent is to let our hearts be cultivated by One whose mercy and care will transform what is barren within us to new life. May our singing about this God whose mercy knows no bounds motivate our repentance and keep us faithful to the task at hand.

to psalmist preparation: While the gospel demands you repent and the second reading warns you not to take salvation for granted, the responsorial psalm reminds you of God's mercy and compassion. The message, however, is not "do what you will and know you'll be forgiven" but "let us be faithful to this God who loves us so much." How does this message motivate your own repentance? How does it keep you faithful to the Lenten task of conversion of heart?

**ASSEMBLY &
FAITH-SHARING GROUPS**

- Those who have helped me face my own sinfulness are . . .
- When I hear "repent [or] you will all perish," my first response is . . . What I hear Jesus asking of me is . . .
- This Lent God is cultivating and fertilizing my life by . . . The fruit I hope to bear through my repentance is . . .

PRESIDERS
In my ministry, I am like the gardener who coaxes fruit out of the barren fig tree when I . . .

DEACONS
Serving others cultivates in them a desire to turn more fully toward God when I . . .

HOSPITALITY MINISTERS
My welcoming the members of the assembly opens them to hear God's call to repentance when I . . .

MUSIC MINISTERS
The repentance I need to do in order that my music ministry bear fruit in Christ is . . .

ALTAR MINISTERS
My serving the liturgy cultivates in me a desire for sincere repentance when I . . .

LECTORS
My manner of proclamation reveals that I have heard the call to repentance and am responding by . . .

EXTRAORDINARY MINISTERS OF HOLY COMMUNION
The manner of my distributing Holy Communion witnesses to the eternal Life God is cultivating within . . .

CELEBRATION

Model Penitential Act

Presider: In today's gospel Jesus lays before us the choice to repent of our sinfulness or perish. We pause now to acknowledge our need for repentance and ask God to pardon and heal us . . . [pause]

   Confiteor: I confess . . .

Homily Points

• Just give me one more chance! Just let me try again! Just let me do that one more time! How often we are the fig tree in the parable, hoping another will coax out of us the fruit we have yet to bear! How utterly crucial it is that we be open to the help we are being offered to repent of our sins and bear the fruit of right living!

• The issue, Jesus tells us, is not that we sin (we inevitably do), but that we refuse to repent, to undergo conversion of heart. God will grant us the time we need to change and will carefully nurture us toward growth and fruitfulness. Nonetheless, the choice to change remains ours and if we refuse, we will perish. What, this Lent, will our choice be?

• We repent when we seek reconciliation with those we've hurt. We repent when we turn from dishonesty to integrity both in word and deed. We repent when we replace anger with empathy. Multiple times each day we are faced with choices about turning away from actions that diminish life toward actions that bear the fruit of goodness in ourselves and others. What, this Lent, will our choice be?

Model Universal Prayer (Prayer of the Faithful)

Presider: We pray to God for the grace we need to be faithful to the Lenten work of repentance.

Response:

Cantor:

That the leadership of the church lead those they shepherd to the new Life repentance promises . . . [pause]

That all peoples repent of sinfulness so God's reign of peace may be established . . . [pause]

That those broken by hurtful relationships be restored to wholeness through reconciliation . . . [pause]

That those preparing to receive the initiation sacraments at Easter continue to hear Christ calling them to conversion of heart . . . [pause]

That we here gathered bear the fruit of right living God is cultivating in each of us . . . [pause]

Presider: Merciful God, you call us to repent and to receive new Life. Hear these our prayers that we might turn from our sinful ways and bear fruit in our daily living. We ask this through Christ our Lord. **Amen.**

COLLECT
Let us pray.

Pause for silent prayer

O God, author of every mercy and of all goodness,
who in fasting, prayer and almsgiving have shown us a remedy for sin,
look graciously on this confession of our lowliness,
that we, who are bowed down by our conscience,
may always be lifted up by your mercy.
Through our Lord Jesus Christ, your Son,
who lives and reigns with you in the unity of the Holy Spirit,
one God, for ever and ever. **Amen.**

FIRST READING
Exod 3:1-8a, 13-15

Moses was tending the flock of his father-in-law Jethro,
   the priest of Midian.
Leading the flock across the desert, he came to Horeb,
   the mountain of God.
There an angel of the LORD appeared to Moses in fire
   flaming out of a bush.
As he looked on, he was surprised to see that the bush,
   though on fire, was not consumed.
So Moses decided,
   "I must go over to look at this remarkable sight,
   and see why the bush is not burned."

When the LORD saw him coming over to look at it more closely,
   God called out to him from the bush,
   "Moses! Moses!"
He answered, "Here I am."
God said, "Come no nearer!
Remove the sandals from your feet,
   for the place where you stand is holy ground.
I am the God of your fathers," he continued,
   "the God of Abraham, the God of Isaac, the God of Jacob."
Moses hid his face, for he was afraid to look at God.
But the LORD said,
   "I have witnessed the affliction of my people in Egypt
   and have heard their cry of complaint against their slave drivers,
   so I know well what they are suffering.
Therefore I have come down to rescue them
   from the hands of the Egyptians

and lead them out of that land into a
    good and spacious land,
a land flowing with milk and honey."

Moses said to God, "But when I go to the
    Israelites
and say to them, 'The God of your
    fathers has sent me to you,'
if they ask me, 'What is his name?'
    what am I to tell them?"
God replied, "I am who am."
Then he added, "This is what you shall tell
    the Israelites:
I AM sent me to you."

God spoke further to Moses, "Thus shall
    you say to the Israelites:
The LORD, the God of your fathers,
    the God of Abraham, the God of Isaac,
    the God of Jacob,
has sent me to you.

"This is my name forever;
    thus am I to be remembered through all
    generations."

RESPONSORIAL PSALM
Ps 103:1-2, 3-4, 6-7, 8, 11

R⁒. (8a) The Lord is kind and merciful.

Bless the LORD, O my soul;
    and all my being, bless his holy name.
Bless the LORD, O my soul,
    and forget not all his benefits.

R⁒. The Lord is kind and merciful.

He pardons all your iniquities,
    heals all your ills.
He redeems your life from destruction,
    crowns you with kindness and
        compassion.

R⁒. The Lord is kind and merciful.

The LORD secures justice
    and the rights of all the oppressed.
He has made known his ways to Moses,
    and his deeds to the children of Israel.

R⁒. The Lord is kind and merciful.

Merciful and gracious is the LORD,
    slow to anger and abounding in
        kindness.
For as the heavens are high above the
        earth,
    so surpassing is his kindness toward
        those who fear him.

R⁒. The Lord is kind and merciful.

SECOND READING
1 Cor 10:1-6, 10-12

See Appendix A, p. 274.

About Liturgy

Year C Lenten gospels: During Year C of the Lectionary three-year cycle, a common thread runs through the gospels from the third to the fifth Sundays of Lent—that of repentance. Not only is this an important Lenten theme, but it is an important theme in Luke's gospel as well.

The penitential act and confession of sins: During Lent we have been suggesting the use of the *Confiteor* (I confess to almighty God . . .) for the penitential act at the beginning of Mass. If we consider all the helpful choices we have for the introductory rites and use them well, we can establish a rhythm at the beginning of Mass that captures something of the rhythm of Christian living. Using the *Confiteor* during Lent (and on Fridays for daily Mass at other times of the year) reminds us that we still must overcome our sinful ways and are always in need of repentance and reconciliation. Acknowledging God's gifts to us in bringing us to salvation and our sometimes refusal (like Israel of old) of those gifts fosters a genuine humility in us and right relationships with God and others.

Using the Rite for the Blessing and Sprinkling of Water during Easter (and on a few other appropriate Sundays during the year, for example, the feast of the Baptism of the Lord) reminds us that we are the redeemed Body of Christ, plunged into baptismal waters that bring us a share in divine Life. Using the *Kyrie* invocations as a litany of praise during Ordinary Time reminds us that the Lord Jesus has walked the journey before us and showed us the way through death to new Life. The rhythm, then, flows among repentance and reconciliation, celebration of divine Life, and praise for Jesus' example of dying and rising.

About Liturgical Music

Music suggestions: This Sunday invites us to sing songs about human repentance and God's mercy. Examples appearing in a number of resources include "Return to God," a good choice for the entrance; "Our Father, We have Wandered," also fitting for the entrance or for the preparation of the gifts; "Draw Near, O Lord/Attende Domine" and "Spare Us, Lord/Parce Domine," both suitable for the Communion procession. Francis Patrick O'Brien's "The Cross of Jesus" (G3, SS) would work well for either the entrance or the preparation of the gifts. "Come, You Sinners, Poor and Needy" (W4) would also work well during the preparation of the gifts.

Reginald Heber's "Bread of the World" is a particularly appropriate text for Communion: "Bread of the world, in mercy broken, Wine of the soul in mercy shed, By whom the words of life were spoken, And in whose death our sins are dead. Look on the heart by sorrow broken, Look on the tears by sinners shed; And be your feast to us the token That by your grace our souls are fed." Paul Tate has set the text to an appealing pentatonic melody and added verses which can be sung either by cantor/choir or the whole assembly (OF, WC, WS). His SAB choral harmonization is simple yet rich, and satisfying to sing (WLP, 008844).

SPIRITUALITY

GOSPEL ACCLAMATION
Luke 15:18

I will get up and go to my Father and shall say to him:
Father, I have sinned against heaven and against you.

Gospel   Luke 15:1-3, 11-32; L33C

Tax collectors and sinners were
    all drawing near to listen to
    Jesus,
  but the Pharisees and scribes
      began to complain, saying,
  "This man welcomes sinners and
      eats with them."
So to them Jesus addressed this
    parable:
"A man had two sons, and the
    younger son said to his father,
  'Father give me the share of your
      estate that should come to me.'
So the father divided the property between
    them.
After a few days, the younger son collected
    all his belongings
  and set off to a distant country
  where he squandered his inheritance on
    a life of dissipation.
When he had freely spent everything,
  a severe famine struck that country,
  and he found himself in dire need.
So he hired himself out to one of the local
    citizens
  who sent him to his farm to tend the
    swine.
And he longed to eat his fill of the pods on
    which the swine fed,
  but nobody gave him any.
Coming to his senses he thought,
  'How many of my father's hired workers
  have more than enough food to eat,
  but here am I, dying from hunger.
I shall get up and go to my father and I
    shall say to him,
  "Father, I have sinned against heaven
      and against you.

Continued in Appendix A, p. 276.

See Appendix A, pp. 277–278, for optional readings.

Reflecting on the Gospel

This Fourth Sunday of Lent is traditionally called "*Laetare* Sunday," from the Latin meaning "to rejoice" or "to be joyful." This is a perfect Sunday on which to proclaim this gospel about the Prodigal Son. The father is so joyful at his son's return home that he forgives his wanderings and squanderings and orders a feast to be prepared and celebrated. Sinners though we are, just so does our merciful Father long to embrace and celebrate with us. We have only to return to him.

Expecting, hoping, anticipating minimal response from his father, the son returns home and receives lavishly from his father. The father doesn't answer the son's confession with words. Rather, he begins the concrete actions of showing lavish mercy and welcome. The point: Jesus' welcome of sinners makes visible the love and mercy of God our Father, a love and mercy we all need because we all are sinful and in need of forgiveness. Forgiveness brings us to accept others (and ourselves) as weak human beings who often hurt others and cause them anguish. Forgiveness helps us to not let the past determine our choices and actions.

Furthermore, the "ministry of reconciliation" (second reading) given to us by God places us in the role of the merciful father, reminding us of not only the value but the necessity of forgiveness. We are like the parable father when we are compassionate and forgiving toward those who have harmed us, when we are urged to celebrate a feast when someone (ourselves included, of course!) turns from wrongful ways. Sometimes we are like the two sons who act rashly and need forgiveness. Sometimes we are like the father who extends lavish forgiveness.

According to "the Pharisees and scribes" in this gospel, Jesus entertained all the wrong people! Who would want to associate with, let alone feast with, sinners? In the parable, the prodigal son entertained all the wrong desires! The elder son entertained anger and jealousy, pettiness and closed heartedness! On the other hand, the father tendered reconciliation leading to feasting. In our lives, God tenders mercy and forgiveness leading to new Life. What do we entertain in our hearts? What do we tender in our relationships? With whom do we feast?

Living the Paschal Mystery

Sometimes, like the two sons in the parable, we entertain all the wrong things. Repentance helps us entertain the right things. Our human tendency is to think we can make a go of life on our own. If we are happy to settle for minimums, some of us can muddle through life reasonably well. This parable reminds us that God offers us so much more.

The father is a model of mercy and reconciliation. It is the father who models for us paschal mystery living. It is the father in the parable who models for us the mercy of our heavenly Father—mercy that not only forgives and reconciles, but offers a feast. If we choose to die to self ("coming to [our] senses") and return to God, we are greeted with forgiveness and feasting. Even more, at our heavenly Father's feast we aren't simply welcomed back as the sons and daughters we were, but are transformed into more perfect sons and daughters sharing in divine Life. We feast on much more than a fattened calf; the feast to which we are invited is nothing less than the Body and Blood of the Son. Receiving God's forgiveness and mercy, and offering the same to one another, is how we pass from Wednesday ashes to Easter feasting. Let us rejoice!

Focusing the Gospel

Key words and phrases: welcomes sinners and eats with them, squandered his inheritance on a life of dissipation, father . . . filled with compassion, let us celebrate with a feast, he refused to enter the house, now we must celebrate and rejoice

To the point: According to "the Pharisees and scribes," Jesus entertained all the wrong people! In the parable, the prodigal son entertained all the wrong desires! The elder son entertained anger and jealousy, pettiness and closed heartedness! On the other hand, the father tendered reconciliation leading to feasting. In our lives, God tenders mercy and forgiveness leading to new Life. What do we entertain in our hearts? What do we tender in our relationships? With whom do we feast?

Connecting the Gospel

to the second reading: "Whoever is in Christ is a new creation." Our work now is that of making all things new through "the ministry of reconciliation" which has been given to us by God. We are to be like the father in the gospel parable who embraces his wayward son, leading him to new Life.

to experience: Like the two sons in the parable, we often entertain wrong desires, anger and jealousy, pettiness and closed heartedness. Like the two sons in the parable, we all need to come to repentance. Then our Father in heaven rejoices, clothes us with new dignity, gives us the feast of all feasts.

Connecting the Responsorial Psalm

to the readings: In praying these verses from Psalm 34, we proclaim that we have tasted the goodness of the Lord. We know what it means to be the lowly who cry out to God for help and receive salvation. We join the enslaved Israelites who survived the terrible desert journey and feasted in the land of God's deliverance (first reading). We become the distant and dissipated prodigal son who crossed the terrain of regret and repentance and feasted at his father's table (gospel). We become a new creation in Christ (second reading), made ambassadors of the message: repent, come home, the feast is ready and—oh, so good—it is God!

to psalmist preparation: The verses of this responsorial psalm arise from personal experience of the God who leads from famine to feast (first reading), from sin to reconciliation (gospel). What experience of God's goodness and mercy will shape your singing of this psalm? What radiance will shine on your face?

**ASSEMBLY &
FAITH-SHARING GROUPS**
- The thoughts and sentiments I entertain are . . .
- God tenders me reconciliation when . . . I need to tender reconciliation to . . .
- I need to feast when . . . I need to feast with . . .

PRESIDERS
What helps me minister as the forgiving and merciful father in the parable is . . .

DEACONS
My service ministry tenders the mercy of God to others when . . .

HOSPITALITY MINISTERS
My manner of welcoming people to liturgy helps ready them to enter into the feast when . . .

MUSIC MINISTERS
My music ministry helps the assembly "celebrate with a feast" when I . . .

ALTAR MINISTERS
As I serve at liturgy, I entertain in my heart . . .

LECTORS
My proclamation enables the assembly to hear and receive the words of a merciful God calling us to repentance when . . .

**EXTRAORDINARY MINISTERS
OF HOLY COMMUNION**
Imitating this compassionate father in the parable, someone I need to invite back to the feast is . . .

Model Penitential Act

Presider: In today's parable of the Prodigal Son, we encounter God as the merciful Father who always welcomes back repenting children with forgiveness and mercy. To prepare ourselves to celebrate this eucharistic feast, let us repent of our sinfulness . . . [pause]

> *Confiteor:* I confess . . .

Homily Points

• When we have a dinner party, we tend to invite and entertain those of like mind, those of similar values, those with whom we are comfortable. In this gospel, Jesus "welcomes sinners and eats with them," persons who hardly measure up to his level of holiness. The sheer reality of Jesus' all-embracing welcome invites us to repent, to enter into his holy life, and to feast with him with clean hearts.

• In this gospel, Jesus uses a parable to challenge the habitual mind-set of the Pharisees and scribes that sinners are to be excluded from the community. By contrast, the father in the parable welcomes home his repentant self-serving son with forgiveness and a feast. So, too, must we forgive the failings of one another and not act like the elder son. We are able to do so because our heavenly Father welcomes us, sinners that we are, with mercy and compassion. And invites us to *the* feast!

• What we habitually entertain in our hearts, is what we eventually tender to others. For example, brooding over how people have slighted us, we tend to lash out at them the next time we see them. Relishing the joy of hard work well done, we are more likely to notice the hard work of others and compliment them. Lent invites us to repent of our un-welcoming thoughts and behaviors and change them to a welcoming mind-set of mercy and compassion. This is the transformation that prepares us for the feast.

Model Universal Prayer (Prayer of the Faithful)

Presider: Aware of God's mercy and forgiveness, let us pray with confidence to this loving Father.

Response:

Lord, hear our prayer.

Cantor:

we pray to the Lord,

That all members of the church be quick to open their arms to repentant sinners, welcoming them back to the feast of the Lord . . . [pause]

That world leaders govern in such a way that all nations, through forgiveness and mercy, dwell in peace . . . [pause]

That those who are homeless, jobless, impoverished be welcomed by those around them . . . [pause]

That those preparing to receive the Easter sacraments continue to open themselves to the love and mercy of God . . . [pause]

That each of us be ambassadors of reconciliation in our families, among our friends, and in our places of work . . . [pause]

Presider: Merciful God, you forgive sinners who repent and welcome them back to your loving embrace. Hear these our prayers that we might one day be with you forever at your everlasting feast. We ask this through Christ our Lord. **Amen.**

COLLECT
Let us pray.

Pause for silent prayer

O God, who through your Word
reconcile the human race to yourself in a
    wonderful way,
grant, we pray,
that with prompt devotion and eager faith
the Christian people may hasten
toward the solemn celebrations to come.
Through our Lord Jesus Christ, your Son,
who lives and reigns with you in the unity
    of the Holy Spirit,
one God, for ever and ever. **Amen.**

FIRST READING
Josh 5:9a, 10-12

The Lord said to Joshua,
    "Today I have removed the reproach of
        Egypt from you."

While the Israelites were encamped at Gilgal
    on the plains of Jericho,
    they celebrated the Passover
    on the evening of the fourteenth of the
        month.
On the day after the Passover,
    they ate of the produce of the land
    in the form of unleavened cakes and
        parched grain.
On that same day after the Passover,
    on which they ate of the produce of the
        land, the manna ceased.
No longer was there manna for the
    Israelites,
    who that year ate of the yield of the
        land of Canaan.

CATECHESIS

RESPONSORIAL PSALM
Ps 34:2-3, 4-5, 6-7

R⁊. (9a) Taste and see the goodness of the Lord.

I will bless the LORD at all times;
  his praise shall be ever in my mouth.
Let my soul glory in the LORD;
  the lowly will hear me and be glad.

R⁊. Taste and see the goodness of the Lord.

Glorify the LORD with me,
  let us together extol his name.
I sought the LORD, and he answered me
  and delivered me from all my fears.

R⁊. Taste and see the goodness of the Lord.

Look to him that you may be radiant with
    joy,
  and your faces may not blush with
      shame.
When the poor one called out, the LORD
    heard,
  and from all his distress he saved him.

R⁊. Taste and see the goodness of the Lord.

SECOND READING
2 Cor 5:17-21

Brothers and sisters:
Whoever is in Christ is a new creation:
  the old things have passed away;
  behold, new things have come.
And all this is from God,
  who has reconciled us to himself
      through Christ
  and given us the ministry of
      reconciliation,
  namely, God was reconciling the world
      to himself in Christ,
  not counting their trespasses against
      them
  and entrusting to us the message of
      reconciliation.
So we are ambassadors for Christ,
  as if God were appealing through us.
We implore you on behalf of Christ,
  be reconciled to God.
For our sake he made him to be sin who
    did not know sin,
  so that we might become the
      righteousness of God in him.

About Liturgy

Sin affects the whole Body: As each of us grows in our awareness of being members of the Body of Christ, we also grow in our understanding that there is no such thing as a "private" sin. The prodigal son returned to his merciful father and declared that he had "sinned against heaven and against" his father. Each time we choose the death-dealing blow of sin, we have "sinned against heaven and against" all other members of the Body. In the Body we are one in Christ. When one member is built up, the whole Body is built up. When one member sins, the whole Body is weakened. There can be many motivations for repentance besides "dying from hunger" and the dire necessity faced by the prodigal son. One strong motivation might be our genuine Christian love for one another; if we sin, we weaken the Body. At the same time, when we repent and seek reconciliation, we make the Body stronger. Repentance and a worthy reception of the sacrament of penance help us pass from death to Life.

This is about the time in Lent when many parishes offer Lenten communal penance liturgies. Part of our preparation for this wonderful opportunity to repent and be forgiven ought to be a serious consideration of how our sin affects those with whom we live, work, and spend our leisure time. It is too easy simply to go to confession and list one's sins, being assured of God's forgiveness through the sacramental ministry of the ordained priest. Perhaps recognizing how we hurt others and reaching out to seek their forgiveness, too, might be the best deterrent for sin and the most fruitful motivation to repent.

About Liturgical Music

Music suggestions: As with last Sunday, the readings this week celebrate the God who embraces human repentance with divine mercy. Two particularly appropriate hymns based on the parable of the Prodigal Son are "Our Father, We Have Wandered" (in many resources) and Herman Stuempfle's "Far From Home We Run Rebellious" (HG). The first hymn is set to the PASSION CHORALE tune so strongly associated with the season of Lent, and could be used for either the entrance procession or the preparation of the gifts. The second song tells of returning home after having abandoned God's love for false treasures and empty, self-centered dreams. This hymn would be very effective during the preparation of the gifts. Also appropriate this Sunday would be "Hosea" (in many resources). In the refrain we hear how longingly God has waited for us to come home to "new life." This song would suit either the preparation of the gifts or Communion. In the refrain of Lucien Deiss's "Yes, I Shall Arise" (OF, WC, WS), we tell God we are returning home; in the verses we beg for God's mercy. This song would also be appropriate during Communion.

MARCH 6, 2016
FOURTH SUNDAY OF LENT

SPIRITUALITY

GOSPEL ACCLAMATION
Joel 2:12-13

Even now, says the Lord,
return to me with your whole heart;
for I am gracious and merciful.

Gospel   John 8:1-11; L36C

Jesus went to the Mount of Olives.
But early in the morning he arrived again
in the temple area,
and all the people started coming to
him,
and he sat down and taught them.
Then the scribes and the Pharisees
brought a woman
who had been caught in adultery
and made her stand in the middle.
They said to him,
"Teacher, this woman was caught
in the very act of committing adultery.
Now in the law, Moses commanded us to
stone such women.
So what do you say?"
They said this to test him,
so that they could have some charge to
bring against him.
Jesus bent down and began to write on
the ground with his finger.
But when they continued asking him,
he straightened up and said to them,
"Let the one among you who is without
sin
be the first to throw a stone at her."
Again he bent down and wrote on the
ground.
And in response, they went away one by
one,
beginning with the elders.
So he was left alone with the woman
before him.
Then Jesus straightened up and said to her,
"Woman, where are they?
Has no one condemned you?"
She replied, "No one, sir."
Then Jesus said, "Neither do I condemn
you.
Go, and from now on do not sin any more."

See Appendix A, pp. 279–281, for optional readings.

Reflecting on the Gospel

Most of us prefer comedies over tragedies, stories with happy endings over sad endings. This gospel account is a story that refuses to be so simply categorized. The gospel account begins with deadly accusation, and ends with divine mercy. It begins with condemnation that would have led the adulterous woman to death, and ends with Jesus' mercy leading her to new Life. The account begins with human testing of Jesus, and ends with divine invitation to repent. It begins with a narrow focus on application of a law as an excuse for testing the fidelity of Jesus to Jewish covenantal law, and ends with Jesus revealing a new order in which all are called to repentance and an experience of divine mercy. Jesus' desire for us is not death but new Life. This journey of moving from sinfulness to new Life is both tragic and comic. It is sad and happy. It is a choice. A critical choice.

The crowd brings before Jesus a woman caught in adultery, condemns her, and demands her life. Jesus doesn't condemn the woman. He does condemn her act ("do not sin any more"), then calls her to repent and choose a new way of living. Lent calls us to the same kind of encounter with Jesus so that we face our own sinfulness, hear his invitation to embrace a new way of living, and make right choices. Central to this gospel is not simply the adulterous woman nor even the crowd that comes to a realization of their own sinfulness. Taking a central place is encounter with Jesus who calls us to repentance and offers us divine mercy. We are quick to condemn each other; Jesus assures us, "Neither do I condemn you." We must acknowledge our sinfulness and turn toward God. This is repentance. It rests in divine encounter and results in truth: our sinfulness, God's mercy, the promise of new Life.

The "scribes and the Pharisees" use the proscription of the law in an attempt to entrap Jesus. He responds by confronting them with the reality of their own hard-heartedness and sinfulness. They slink away "one by one," leaving the adulterous woman alone to face Jesus. He extends mercy and compassion as well as judgment and a command to change her life. Do we dare to stand alone before Jesus, bare our own sinfulness, and hear him say to us, "Go, and from now on do not sin any more"?

Living the Paschal Mystery

The gospel reminds us that we encounter Jesus at our own risk: we will be confronted with the truth of our own sinfulness, with the tragedy of our own sinful living. But encounter with Jesus also brings hope: in the confrontation and invitation to repent Jesus offers the joy of new Life.

We begin the last third of the Lenten season. Even if we haven't been all that faithful to our chosen Lenten practices, it isn't too late now to resolve to open ourselves to encounters with Jesus so that we can approach Easter with a renewed spirit seeking new Life. Like the crowd in the gospel, it is often easier for us to focus on the sins of others than on our own weaknesses. Also like the crowd in the gospel, we can encounter Jesus and face the truth of ourselves. Lent is a time to encounter Jesus, turn from our sinfulness in repentance, and seek divine mercy. The remarkable good news of this gospel is that by facing and repenting of our own sinfulness we establish new relations with those around us. Acknowledgment of our own sins and how we have hurt others builds us into stronger members of Christ's Body.

Focusing the Gospel

Key words and phrases: woman . . . caught in adultery, test him, went away one by one, Neither do I condemn you, do not sin any more

To the point: The "scribes and the Pharisees" use the proscription of the law in an attempt to entrap Jesus. He responds by confronting them with the reality of their own hard-heartedness and sinfulness. They slink away "one by one," leaving the adulterous woman alone to face Jesus. He extends mercy and compassion as well as judgment and a command to change her life. Do we dare to stand alone before Jesus, bare our own sinfulness, and hear him say to us, "Go, and from now on do not sin any more"?

Connecting the Gospel

to the second reading: Paul reiterates the basic message of this gospel: that righteousness is not based on keeping the law, but on "the supreme good of knowing Christ Jesus" and being "taken possession of by" him.

to experience: "Who am I to judge?" How often have these five words of Pope Francis been quoted! Judgment is reserved for God and God alone, who never extends judgment without also extending compassion and mercy.

Connecting the Responsorial Psalm

to the readings: The first reading from Isaiah recounts God's mighty acts in restoring Israel as a nation after the Babylonian captivity. As Isaiah asserts, this restoration will make the exodus look as if it were nothing ("Remember not the events of the past . . . I am doing something new!"). The gospel reading recounts God's acting again to do something new in Jesus. Salvation becomes personalized in the adulterous woman whom Jesus does not condemn but grants new life, both physically and spiritually.

God constantly revolutionizes our expectations by saving us in newer, deeper ways. Psalm 126 is our "pinch me" response: we are not dreaming; this salvation is really happening. The readings remind us, however, that the challenge is not just to see but to believe. We must let this new righteousness take possession of us (second reading). We must change our ways and let go of our judgments (gospel). Only then can we "forget . . . what lies behind" and look toward the future (second reading). Only then can we realize the past about which we sing is just the beginning.

to psalmist preparation: As you sing this psalm you do not just retell past events; you establish hope for the future. The great things God has already done are as nothing compared to what God is yet to do for us in Christ. In what way this week might you let Christ take possession of you (second reading) so that you can sing of this hope with conviction?

ASSEMBLY & FAITH-SHARING GROUPS
- What is satisfying to me in pointing out the sins of others is . . . What helps me stop this and face my own sinfulness is . . .
- When Jesus has said to me, "Neither do I condemn you," I have felt . . .
- What helps me repent of my own sinfulness and change my way of living is . . .

PRESIDERS
When confronted with my own sinfulness, my way of ministering to others becomes . . .

DEACONS
Whenever I serve another, God's mercy and compassion are visible because . . .

HOSPITALITY MINISTERS
My hospitality enables the assembly to stand honestly before the Lord when I . . .

MUSIC MINISTERS
My music making helps the members of the assembly stand before the Lord with ears open to hear when . . .

ALTAR MINISTERS
The judgments I make while serving at the liturgy form me in the right judgments I must make in my daily living when . . .

LECTORS
When I proclaim the word out of the humility of knowing myself to be in need of God's mercy and compassion, it sounds like . . .

EXTRAORDINARY MINISTERS OF HOLY COMMUNION
Looking on the faces of communicants draws me to extend greater compassion and mercy toward others by . . .

Model Penitential Act

Presider: Jesus does not condemn the adulterous woman in today's gospel, but commands her to sin no more. As we begin this liturgy, let us acknowledge our own sinfulness and open ourselves to God's mercy and compassion . . . [pause]

> *Confiteor:* I confess . . .

Homily Points

• Does anyone in this room understand what I'm trying to say? Does anyone else see what needs to be done? Does anyone realize how serious this situation is? We get frustrated when people are not on the same wavelength as we are, especially when the occasion is serious. How frustrated Jesus must have been with the scribes and Pharisees in the gospel! They certainly were not on his wavelength. They are concerned with the proscription of the law and testing Jesus; he is concerned with repentance, with conversion and newness of life.

• But does anyone in this gospel repent? The gospel doesn't explicitly tell us if even the adulterous woman repented. Yet both "the scribes and the Pharisees" and the adulterous woman were faced with the truth of their sinful condition as they stood before Jesus. The scribes and Pharisees "went away one by one"; Jesus tells the adulterous woman to "Go, and from now on do not sin any more." Do we ourselves dare to stand alone before Jesus, bare our own sinfulness, and choose repentance?

• Lent is the classic time for even the most hardened of sinners to repent. Repentance is how we get on the same wavelength as Jesus.

Model Universal Prayer (Prayer of the Faithful)

Presider: God continually calls us to repentance and new life. Let us pray for what we need to be faithful.

Response:

Lord, hear our prayer.

Cantor:

we pray to the Lord,

That all members of the church stand before Jesus, turn from their sinfulness, and embrace new life . . . [pause]

That all peoples of the world share in the salvation that our merciful and compassionate God offers . . . [pause]

That those in need of mercy and forgiveness be met with compassion . . . [pause]

That those about to receive the Easter sacraments stand before God with repentant hearts, eager to receive newness of Life . . . [pause]

That each of us gathered here in faith share with others the mercy and compassion with which God has blessed us . . . [pause]

Presider: Merciful God, hear these our prayers that we might more fully share in the new Life of your Son Jesus Christ our Lord. **Amen.**

COLLECT

Let us pray.

Pause for silent prayer

By your help, we beseech you, Lord our
    God,
may we walk eagerly in that same charity
with which, out of love for the world,
your Son handed himself over to death.
Through our Lord Jesus Christ, your Son,
who lives and reigns with you in the unity
    of the Holy Spirit,
one God, for ever and ever. **Amen.**

FIRST READING

Isa 43:16-21

Thus says the Lord,
    who opens a way in the sea
    and a path in the mighty waters,
who leads out chariots and horsemen,
    a powerful army,
till they lie prostrate together, never to rise,
    snuffed out and quenched like a wick.
Remember not the events of the past,
    the things of long ago consider not;
see, I am doing something new!
    Now it springs forth, do you not
        perceive it?
In the desert I make a way,
    in the wasteland, rivers.
Wild beasts honor me,
    jackals and ostriches,
for I put water in the desert
    and rivers in the wasteland
    for my chosen people to drink,
the people whom I formed for myself,
    that they might announce my praise.

RESPONSORIAL PSALM

Ps 126:1-2, 2-3, 4-5, 6

R℣. (3) The Lord has done great things for
us; we are filled with joy.

When the Lord brought back the captives
    of Zion,
    we were like men dreaming.
Then our mouth was filled with laughter,
    and our tongue with rejoicing.

R℣. The Lord has done great things for us;
we are filled with joy.

Then they said among the nations,
    "The Lord has done great things for
        them."
The Lord has done great things for us;
    we are glad indeed.

R℣. The Lord has done great things for us;
we are filled with joy.

Restore our fortunes, O Lord,
  like the torrents in the southern desert.
Those that sow in tears
  shall reap rejoicing.

R⃒. The Lord has done great things for us;
we are filled with joy.

Although they go forth weeping,
  carrying the seed to be sown,
they shall come back rejoicing,
  carrying their sheaves.

R⃒. The Lord has done great things for us;
we are filled with joy.

SECOND READING
Phil 3:8-14

Brothers and sisters:
I consider everything as a loss
  because of the supreme good of
    knowing Christ Jesus my Lord.
For his sake I have accepted the loss of all
    things
  and I consider them so much rubbish,
  that I may gain Christ and be found in
    him,
  not having any righteousness of my
    own based on the law
  but that which comes through faith in
    Christ,
  the righteousness from God,
  depending on faith to know him and the
    power of his resurrection
  and the sharing of his sufferings by being
    conformed to his death,
  if somehow I may attain the
    resurrection from the dead.

It is not that I have already taken hold of it
  or have already attained perfect maturity,
  but I continue my pursuit in hope that I
    may possess it,
  since I have indeed been taken
    possession of by Christ Jesus.
Brothers and sisters, I for my part
  do not consider myself to have taken
    possession.
Just one thing: forgetting what lies behind
  but straining forward to what lies
    ahead,
  I continue my pursuit toward the goal,
  the prize of God's upward calling, in
    Christ Jesus.

About Liturgy

Why communal dimension of sin and repentance?: One of the major challenges of the liturgical renewal of the last five decades has been to shift from approaching liturgy as private prayer to liturgy as a communal celebration of the paschal mystery. Although some still lament the demise of liturgy as private devotional time, most in the church today appreciate the communal dimension of liturgy.

One challenge is to see this communal dimension as resting in a common identity that runs far deeper than our doing the same things together. Not since the early period of the church has there been such an emphasis on our baptismal identity as the Body of Christ. Herein rests the communal dimension of liturgy: through baptism we are plunged into the saving death/resurrection mystery of Christ; as the Body of Christ we are called to embrace that same death and resurrection. Because we share a common identity, everything we do affects the other members of the Body. When we do good, we build up the Body. Conversely, when we sin, we weaken the Body. For this reason sin and repentance can never be mere individual acts; our own sinfulness and repentance affect all others in the Body.

This communal dimension of sin and repentance requires that we constantly nurture our bonds in the Body of Christ in order for us to come to greater realization of how our actions affect others. In other words, our common identity as Body of Christ must become so real for us that we not only believe it in our heads but live it every day. One practical way to bring this home to ourselves is that each time we receive Communion and hear "The Body of Christ," we hear this acclamation as a statement of our own identity, too, in addition to acknowledging the real presence of Christ in the Eucharist; let our "Amen" be an affirmation of who we are and a promise that we grow in our awareness of solidarity with each other—in both grace and repentance.

About Liturgical Music

Music suggestions: Appropriate this Sunday would be Lenten hymns acknowledging our need for God's mercy and forgiveness, as would songs challenging us to give up condemning one another. Set to ICH GLAUB AN GOTT, "The Master Came to Bring Good News" (G3, W4) would make a strong entrance song, as would "Help Us Accept Each Other" (W4) set to ELLACOMBE. Set to a gentler tune, "Help Us Forgive, Forgiving Lord" (HG, W4) would work well during the preparation of the gifts. The song variously titled "Forgive Our Sins" (G3, SS, W4) and "Forgive Our Sins As We Forgive" (OF, WC, WS) acknowledges our need for God's grace to put into practice challenging words we pray in the Our Father. The style and tempo of this hymn make it suitable for the preparation of the gifts. James Marchionda's "As We Forgive" (OF, WC) draws even more of its text from the Our Father, adding at verse 3, "Our Father in heaven, heal our jealous hearts. May we not judge, lest we be judged; help us to practice mercy." This refrain-verse song can be led by cantor or choir and would be suitable during the preparation of the gifts. "With the Lord," Michael Joncas's setting of Psalm 130 (BB), would be a good choice for the Communion procession.

SPIRITUALITY

GOSPEL ACCLAMATION
Ps 84:5

Blessed are those who dwell in your house, O Lord;
they never cease to praise you.

Gospel   Luke 2:41-51a; L543

Each year Jesus' parents went to
    Jerusalem for the feast of
    Passover,
    and when he was twelve years
    old,
    they went up according to festival
    custom.
After they had completed its days,
    as they were returning,
    the boy Jesus remained behind in
    Jerusalem,
    but his parents did not know it.
Thinking that he was in the caravan,
    they journeyed for a day
    and looked for him among their relatives
    and acquaintances,
    but not finding him,
    they returned to Jerusalem to look for
    him.
After three days they found him in the
    temple,
    sitting in the midst of the teachers,
    listening to them and asking them
    questions,
    and all who heard him were astounded
    at his understanding and his answers.
When his parents saw him,
    they were astonished,
    and his mother said to him,
    "Son, why have you done this to us?
Your father and I have been looking for you
    with great anxiety."
And he said to them,
    "Why were you looking for me?
Did you not know that I must be in my
    Father's house?"
But they did not understand what he said to
    them.
He went down with them and came to
    Nazareth,
    and was obedient to them.

or Matt 1:16, 18-21, 24a in Appendix A, p. 282.

See Appendix A, p. 282, for the other readings.

Reflecting on the Gospel

Sometimes when the role of parent and child is reversed, it is because the parent needs care. For example, if a parent has a debilitating chronic illness, even rather young children step up to give care and comfort, becoming the "parent." Children in this situation grow up quite quickly, often at the expense of having any childhood at all. At other times when the role of parent and child are reversed, it is because of an unhealthy relationship. For example, a child might assume authority in the family because a parent wants to be "friend" to the child rather than parent. Children in this situation tend to become overbearing and spoiled. Parents should be parents, and children ought to be able to be children. In this gospel parent-child roles are reversed at the same time that Mary and Joseph remain parents and Jesus remains subject to them. However, he is no longer a child. He is growing into his own identity and mission. Mary and Joseph are learning about who Jesus is—they are growing into a new relationship with their divine Son.

By choosing to "remain[ ] behind" in the temple, Jesus reversed the role of parent and child. Sitting with "the teachers," Jesus demonstrated his "understanding" about being in his "Father's house," while Mary and Joseph "did not understand what he said to them." Jesus was no longer "the boy," but the "Son." Nonetheless, he returned home with them and was "obedient to them." On their part, Mary and Joseph resumed their role as parents in a new way and with new understanding. Jesus revealed to them where his true home is—in his "Father's house"—and that his life would be about astounding his hearers with his understanding of the human condition, with his demonstrating his great love for his heavenly Father, with his single-mindedness about his saving mission. Their love for Jesus and daily living with him help Mary and Joseph to discover more about who their divine Son is, and to grow in the kind of holiness for which we honor St. Joseph on this feast.

Living the Paschal Mystery

Joseph shows us a new way of living in relation to the divine Son. His whole life was one of obedient self-giving. Each time he is mentioned in the gospels, Joseph is doing something out of the ordinary. Yet he also models that the ordinary way we live our baptismal commitment to enter into the dying and rising of Jesus is through fulfilling faithfully the regular demands of Christian living. Living the paschal mystery means nothing less than being faithful to an everyday yes to God, as Joseph was faithful. It doesn't mean we have to do big, heroic things. It does mean that we are faithful to accepting God's will, even when we don't understand fully what God is asking of us.

The quiet strength of Joseph reminds us that our Christian living is most profound when our choices—our yes to whatever God asks of us—leave us open to understanding Jesus and his ways with more depth. Joseph-like Christian living is a matter of searching diligently for Jesus in our own lives. This might mean renewing our efforts to be faithful to daily prayer. It might mean seeing Jesus in the person who annoys us by recalling that the other is a member of the Body of Christ, too. Coming to understand Jesus doesn't come in some sudden dream or revelation. It comes by doing the everyday things well, by discerning what God is asking of us, by letting Jesus draw us into his "Father's house."

Focusing the Gospel

Key words and phrases: the boy, remained behind, found him in the temple, astounded / at his understanding, Son, they did not understand, obedient to them

To the point: By choosing to "remain[ ] behind" in the temple, Jesus reversed the role of parent and child. Sitting with "the teachers," Jesus demonstrated his "understanding" about being in his "Father's house," while Mary and Joseph "did not understand what he said to them." Jesus was no longer "the boy," but the "Son." Nonetheless, he returned home with them and was "obedient to them." On their part, Mary and Joseph resumed their role as parents in a new way and with new understanding.

Model Penitential Act

Presider: We take a day during our Lenten penance to honor St. Joseph, one who was ever faithful to God's plan of salvation. As we prepare to celebrate this liturgy, let us reflect on how our own lives imitate Joseph's faithfulness . . . [pause]

Lord Jesus, you are the foster Son of Joseph to whom you were obedient: Lord . . .

Christ Jesus, you astounded the teachers in the temple with your understanding: Christ . . .

Lord Jesus, you teach us obedience to your Father in heaven: Lord . . .

Model Universal Prayer (Prayer of the Faithful)

Presider: Let us ask St. Joseph to intercede for us as we make our needs known before God.

Response:

Lord, hear our prayer.

Cantor:

we pray to the Lord,

Through the intercession of St. Joseph, may all members of the church be obedient to God's will and come to salvation . . . [pause]

Through the intercession of St. Joseph, may world leaders be obedient to God's laws of righteousness and justice . . . [pause]

Through the intercession of St. Joseph, may those who are dying find strength and peace . . . [pause]

Through the intercession of St. Joseph, may each of us continue to grow in our understanding of who Jesus is for us and our role in his saving mission . . . [pause]

Presider: Heavenly Father, you are ever attentive to the needs of your faithful children. Through the intercession of St. Joseph hear our prayers that one day we might enjoy everlasting Life with you. We ask this through Christ our Lord. **Amen**.

FOR REFLECTION

• What I understand about Jesus is . . . What I have yet to understand is . . .

• Like Jesus, I remain in my "Father's house" to . . .

• What Joseph teaches me about my role of participating in Jesus' work of salvation is . . .

Homily Points

• The gospels tell us that Joseph was a good foster father. He accepted Jesus from the very beginning when the angel explained in a dream about how Mary had conceived; he acted on another dream to take his little family to Egypt out of harm's way; he returned "with great anxiety" to Jerusalem to search for Jesus whom he thought was lost. What the gospels do not tell us is how Joseph continually came to know and appreciate Jesus in new ways and with new understanding.

• Joseph came to know Jesus not as a mere "boy" but as the Father's "Son" embarking on his mission to move God's people toward a fuller understanding of God's plan of salvation. From the beginning, Joseph didn't fully grasp the divine plan, but grew into understanding it—and Jesus himself. Like Joseph, living with and encountering Jesus every day brings *us* to greater understanding of Joseph's foster Son and his saving mission. For this, Joseph is our model.

SPIRITUALITY

GOSPEL ACCLAMATION
Phil 2:8-9

Christ became obedient to the point of death,
even death on a cross.
Because of this, God greatly exalted him
and bestowed on him the name which is above
    every name.

Gospel at the Procession with Palms
Luke 19:28-40; L37C

Jesus proceeded on his journey up to
    Jerusalem.
As he drew near to Bethphage and
    Bethany
  at the place called the Mount of
    Olives,
  he sent two of his disciples.
He said, "Go into the village opposite
    you,
  and as you enter it you will find a colt
    tethered
  on which no one has ever sat.
Untie it and bring it here.
And if anyone should ask you,
  'Why are you untying it?'
  you will answer,
  'The Master has need of it.'"
So those who had been sent went off
  and found everything just as he had
    told them.
And as they were untying the colt, its
    owners said to them,
  "Why are you untying this colt?"
They answered,
  "The Master has need of it."
So they brought it to Jesus,
  threw their cloaks over the colt,
  and helped Jesus to mount.
As he rode along,
  the people were spreading their cloaks
    on the road;
  and now as he was approaching the
    slope of the Mount of Olives,
  the whole multitude of his disciples
  began to praise God aloud with joy
  for all the mighty deeds they had seen.

Continued in Appendix A, p. 283.

Gospel at Mass   Luke 22:14–23:56;
L38ABC
or Luke 23:1-49 in Appendix A, pp. 283–286.

Reflecting on the Gospel

If we were given one wish, and guaranteed that it would come true, what would that wish be? For many of us, the wish probably would be about an everyday life different from the one we presently live. We might want power, wealth, and fame. Or we might wish for good health free from advancing age and any suffering. Or we might hope for passionate love, caring friends, steadfast relationships. No matter what our wish, it would point to an underlying dissatisfaction with our present condition and a desire for a better life. In our future-looking, however, it is possible to miss the fact that what we long for is already present to us. We only need to see with different eyes, hear with different ears, expect with different hearts.

Jesus suffers, dies, and is buried. All because neither the Jewish leadership, the Roman leadership, nor the apostles understand. Throughout Luke's passion account, Jesus is trying to turn his accusers and hearers away from their understanding of kingdom to embracing "the kingdom of God." He is trying to show them that what they really want is upon them, just in a way different from what they expect. Even on the cross, he continues to show how different his kingdom is, for he forgives the very ones who cause him suffering and death. The "kingdom of God" that Jesus proclaims is so different. What reigns in his kingdom is not power, wealth, or fame; not freedom from misunderstanding and suffering or even death; not betrayal, denial, and abandonment. What reigns in "the kingdom of God" is patience and caring, forgiveness and reconciliation, promise full of life and dying full of promise. All this is what Luke's passion account sets before us.

The "kingdom of God" is not a place we can enclose, not a space we can occupy. It is a face we encounter—the very face of God, the very Presence of God. This kingdom is present whenever we wholeheartedly join ourselves with Jesus' utterance in the Garden: "not my will but yours be done." This kingdom is present whenever we speak the truth about who we know and follow, shower compassion upon those sorrowing or in need, forgive those who harm us, bring hope to the despairing, commend ourselves to God with conviction and purpose.

Jesus suffers, dies, and is buried. The gift of his death? He confers on us his kingdom and invites us to be with him in Paradise. Two kingdoms: the one of this world, the one of Jesus. Which kingdom do we choose?

Living the Paschal Mystery

For most of us Holy Week unfolds like many other weeks; we still contend with work, school, preparing meals, doing laundry, cranky folks, the usual triumphs and setbacks. Palm Sunday begins an extraordinary week—a week that concentrates in a few days the ultimate meaning of our whole Christian life. We must slow ourselves down and make choices so that this week doesn't go by without our taking the time to enter into its meaning. We celebrate in the liturgies what we live every day—all the dying to self that characterizes truly faithful disciples of Jesus, all the dying to self that proclaims our choice to live in God's kingdom. This choice is our way of continuing Jesus' saving mission, our way of making visible our ultimate desire: to live forever with God, united with this Jesus who suffered, died, and was buried. This Jesus who was raised. Living in this kingdom is possible when we, too, commend ourselves into God's hands.

Focusing the Gospel

Key words and phrases: fulfillment in the kingdom of God, until the kingdom of God comes, I confer a kingdom on you, seated at the right hand of the power of God, forgive them, be with me in Paradise

To the point: Jesus suffers, dies, and is buried. All because neither the Jewish leadership, the Roman leadership, nor the apostles understand. Throughout Luke's passion account, Jesus is trying to turn his accusers and hearers away from their understanding of kingdom to embracing "the kingdom of God." Even on the cross, he continues to show how different his kingdom is, for he forgives the very ones who cause him suffering and death. The gift of his death? He confers on us his kingdom and invites us to be with him in paradise. Which kingdom do we choose?

Connecting the Gospel

to the first reading: Isaiah is a type for Jesus Christ in two ways. He was a prophet whose words were not understood and for this, he was rejected and persecuted. He was a prophet whose words challenged the kingdom of Israel to a new and just way of living.

to experience: When another confronts us with something we don't want to hear, our immediate response is resistance, anger, and self-defense. Only persistent confrontation with the truth opens us to hear and accept what is being said. Without this openness, transformation does not happen.

Connecting the Responsorial Psalm

to the readings: The whole of Psalm 22 is a masterpiece of poetry and theology. The psalmist struggles with an increasing sense of being abandoned (from "My God, my God, why have you abandoned me" to "All who see me scoff at me" to violent imagery of destruction and death) while also experiencing deepening intimacy with God (the one who is far away and does not answer is also the one who has been present "from [my mother's] womb"; v. 10). The psalmist begs to be saved from suffering and violence, then offers God lengthy praise. Most lament psalms end with one or two short verses of praise, but here the praise continues for nearly one-third of the text. Furthermore, the psalmist invites an ever-widening circle to join in the praise: first the psalmist's immediate family, then all of Israel, then all nations, then generations yet unborn, and, finally, even the dead.

Psalm 22 helps us understand the passion, both Christ's and ours. God is not distant from the suffering, but very near. And the depth of the suffering becomes the wellspring of the most profound praise. May our singing of these verses from Psalm 22 give us the courage we need to enter Holy Week aware of both the pain and the praise, the loss and the glory, to which it will lead.

to psalmist preparation: To sing this psalm well, you must take some time to pray the full text of Psalm 22. You sing not only about Christ's suffering, but about his transformation into risen Life through his suffering and death. You sing about your own transformation as well, for through baptism you have been incorporated into Jesus' death and resurrection. How willing are you to undergo this transformation? How willing are you to invite the assembly to do so?

ASSEMBLY & FAITH-SHARING GROUPS

- What blocks me from hearing and understanding the words of Jesus to me is . . . What opens me to hear and understand is . . .
- When I seek the kingdom of God, I . . . When I live in the kingdom of God, my life looks like . . .
- The cost to me of choosing to live in the kingdom of God is . . .

PRESIDERS

The manner of my preaching God's word challenges those hearing to accept and change their way of living when . . .

DEACONS

When my ministry brings me face-to-face with the suffering of others, what enables me to extend the love and mercy of the kingdom of God is . . .

HOSPITALITY MINISTERS

My manner of greeting those gathering for liturgy encourages them to choose being in the kingdom of God in that . . .

MUSIC MINISTERS

My manner of doing music ministry reveals my openness to the demands of living in the kingdom of God in that . . .

ALTAR MINISTERS

Serving at the altar has changed my perception of the kingdom of God in these ways . . .

LECTORS

What opens me to hear and understand the many and rich readings during this Holy Week is . . .

EXTRAORDINARY MINISTERS OF HOLY COMMUNION

The Communion procession is a journey into the kingdom of God in that . . .

Model Penitential Act *(used only with the Simple Entrance)*

Presider: Let us begin this solemn Holy Week by resolving to enter into liturgy with fervor, admitting our sinfulness, and asking for God's strength and mercy . . . [pause]

 Confiteor: I confess . . .

Homily Points

• Which kingdoms do we acclaim by our choices and manner of living? The kingdoms of entertainment, sports, wealth, popularity, power? How and when do we acclaim the kingdom of God? When there are clashes between the kingdoms of this world and the kingdom of God, which do we choose?

• In the gospel before the procession with palms, the people hail Jesus with "Blessed is the king who comes / in the name of the Lord." What king and kingdom were they hailing? To acclaim the kingdom of God and live in it with integrity and fidelity, we must hear and understand what Jesus teaches us.

• Jesus teaches that God's kingdom is not about self-adulation, power over others, or getting ahead. Living in God's kingdom requires that we speak the truth about the Gospel, shower compassion upon those sorrowing or in need, forgive those who harm us, bring hope to the despairing, commend ourselves to God with conviction and purpose. This is the kingdom Jesus chose. Which kingdom do we choose? What does it cost us?

Model Universal Prayer (Prayer of the Faithful)

Presider: Let us pray that we enter into this Holy Week with fervor, uniting ourselves with Christ's suffering and death so that we might share more fully in Easter joy.

Response:

Lord, hear our prayer.

Cantor:

we pray to the Lord,

That all members of the church faithfully choose the self-giving required to live in the kingdom of God . . . [pause]

That all peoples in the world may live according to the values and virtues of the kingdom of God . . . [pause]

That those who are scorned and those who suffer might be comforted by the love and compassion of those who live in the kingdom of God . . . [pause]

That all those preparing to receive the Easter sacraments fully embrace the special graces of this Holy Week . . . [pause]

That each of us enter fervently into the mystery of salvation we celebrate this week and grow in faithfully following Jesus . . . [pause]

Presider: Saving God, you sent your only-begotten Son to save us from our sins. Strengthen our resolve to surrender ourselves to your will and come to salvation. We ask this through that same Son, Jesus Christ our Lord. **Amen.**

COLLECT
Let us pray.

Pause for silent prayer

Almighty ever-living God,
who as an example of humility for the
 human race to follow
caused our Savior to take flesh and submit
 to the Cross,
graciously grant that we may heed his
 lesson of patient suffering
and so merit a share in his Resurrection.
Who lives and reigns with you in the unity
 of the Holy Spirit,
one God, for ever and ever. **Amen.**

FIRST READING
Isa 50:4-7

The Lord GOD has given me
 a well-trained tongue,
that I might know how to speak to the
 weary
 a word that will rouse them.
Morning after morning
 he opens my ear that I may hear;
and I have not rebelled,
 have not turned back.
I gave my back to those who beat me,
 my cheeks to those who plucked my
 beard;
my face I did not shield
 from buffets and spitting.

The Lord GOD is my help,
 therefore I am not disgraced;
I have set my face like flint,
 knowing that I shall not be put to
 shame.

RESPONSORIAL PSALM
Ps 22:8-9, 17-18, 19-20, 23-24

℟. (2a) My God, my God, why have you
abandoned me?

All who see me scoff at me;
 they mock me with parted lips, they
 wag their heads:
"He relied on the LORD; let him deliver him,
 let him rescue him, if he loves him."

℟. My God, my God, why have you
abandoned me?

Indeed, many dogs surround me,
  a pack of evildoers closes in upon me;
they have pierced my hands and my feet;
  I can count all my bones.

R⁊. My God, my God, why have you
abandoned me?

They divide my garments among them,
  and for my vesture they cast lots.
But you, O LORD, be not far from me;
  O my help, hasten to aid me.

R⁊. My God, my God, why have you
abandoned me?

I will proclaim your name to my brethren;
  in the midst of the assembly I will
      praise you:
"You who fear the LORD, praise him;
  all you descendants of Jacob, give glory
      to him;
  revere him, all you descendants of
      Israel!"

R⁊. My God, my God, why have you
abandoned me?

SECOND READING
Phil 2:6-11

Christ Jesus, though he was in the form
      of God,
  did not regard equality with God
      something to be grasped.
Rather, he emptied himself,
  taking the form of a slave,
  coming in human likeness;
  and found human in appearance,
  he humbled himself,
  becoming obedient to the point of
      death,
      even death on a cross.
Because of this, God greatly exalted him
  and bestowed on him the name
  which is above every name,
  that at the name of Jesus
  every knee should bend,
  of those in heaven and on earth and
      under the earth,
  and every tongue confess that
  Jesus Christ is Lord,
  to the glory of God the Father.

About Liturgy

"*. . . sweat became like drops of blood . . . ":* The only time we hear the story of Jesus' struggle when praying on the Mount of Olives is on Palm Sunday in one of the three synoptic passion accounts. This year, in the account from Luke, there is included a provocative detail: "He was in such agony and he prayed so fervently / that his sweat became like drops of blood / falling on the ground." It is tempting to think that because Jesus was the divine Son of God that the decision to be faithful to God's will even to suffering and death was easy. This scene tells us otherwise. Because it is only one tiny part of the whole passion account, Jesus' agony in the Garden can easily be overlooked.

For Jews blood is the seat of life, and we see how in the very decision to be faithful to his Father's will, Jesus' life already was ebbing out. Decision-making is not easy, either in daily living or in making decisions about liturgical celebrations. Decision-making that demands the very self-emptying the passion proclaims is even more difficult. Just as an angel strengthened Jesus to say, "not my will but yours be done," so will we be strengthened to make the same commitment of self to God.

Participation in the passion gospels: The passion accounts proclaimed on Palm Sunday and Good Friday are very lengthy and call for effort to pay attention and enter into the accounts. We participate best not by reading along ourselves but by being roused by the word of the proclamation to live the self-emptying and fidelity of Jesus. In this way these accounts are not just long gospels we hear twice a year during Holy Week, but become the very meaning of our lives.

Some assembly members claim that they feel more engaged in the gospel reading when they use both senses of hearing and sight, and prefer to read along with the passion account. The issue here isn't more active involvement as it is surrender to the word of God being proclaimed. An example might help: when a young man proposes marriage to his lady love, he doesn't give her a text to read while he speaks his proposal to make sure she pays attention. The quality of his voice, intensity of his eye contact, eagerness of his body language all convey that something important is happening. This is the kind of engagement demanded by the proclamation of the gospel. It is entirely relational—between lector and assembly and between Christ and Christian—rather than an exercise in hearing and reading.

About Liturgical Music

Music suggestions: Palm Sunday opens Holy Week with the first of our yearly proclamations of the passion. This proclamation is different from the passion account according to the Gospel of John which we will hear on Good Friday. Good Friday celebrates the glory into which Jesus has already entered even as he enters his passion, and the glory of the cross which leads to victory over sin and death. By contrast, Palm Sunday focuses clearly on Jesus' suffering and death. The liturgy moves from loud shouts of "Hosanna!" in Jesus' favor (gospel before the procession) to angry demands for his crucifixion. From Jesus' lips we hear his words of forgiveness, his words of welcome to the repentant thief, and his words of surrender as he gives his spirit over to his Father. This is the Sunday to sing songs such as "Were You There," "O Sacred Head Surrounded," "When I Survey the Wondrous Cross," and "When Jesus Wept." A quiet, repetitive singing of "Jesus, Remember Me" would be particularly appropriate at the close of Mass, as all leave ready to enter the liturgies and meaning of Holy Week.

EASTER TRIDUUM

If you have not understood, said I,
believe.
For understanding is the
reward of faith.
Therefore do not seek to understand
in order to believe,
but believe
that you may understand.

—St. Augustine, *Tractates on the Gospel of John*, Tractate 29 (John 7:14-18): 6

Reflecting on the Triduum

The "faithing" mystery: How often do the gospels speak of faith! How often does Jesus recognize the faith of another, extol faith, teach about faith, address the power of faith! How often does Jesus heal because of the faith of the other! During these high holy days of the Easter Triduum, we celebrate the "saving" mystery of Jesus Christ. We might coin a word and phrase here: we celebrate the "faithing" mystery of Jesus Christ. What might we mean by this?

During healing encounters, Jesus often expressly acknowledges the person's faith. Gospel examples abound. When the woman "afflicted with hemorrhages for twelve years" (Mark 5:25) reaches out to touch "his cloak" (v. 27), Jesus says to her, "Daughter, your faith has saved you" (v. 34; see also Matt 9:22 and Luke 8:48). He says the same thing to the blind Bartimaeus: "your faith has saved you" (Mark 10:52; see also Luke 18:42). And yet again the same thing to the leper who came back to Jesus to give thanks: "your faith has saved you" (Luke 17:19). Another example, this one of spiritual healing: while dining in the home of a Pharisee, a "sinful" woman washes Jesus' feet with her tears and dries them with her hair; Jesus forgives her sins, saying, "Your faith has saved you" (Luke 7:50). In all these encounters faith is linked to health, wholeness, well-being, which is the Hebrew root meaning for the word "salvation." To be saved means to be made whole, and Jesus indicates that there is a clear connection between our physical and spiritual wholeness. Jesus attends to both our physical and spiritual needs. Jesus responds to our need; we but need to come to him.

In each of these healing instances, the person comes to Jesus, reaches out to him. Faith is expressed as *action*, as reaching out to Jesus, as *encounter*. Without the effort to encounter Jesus, these healings would not have happened. Our very pursuit of the risen Christ—what we are truly about during this Easter Triduum—and our desire for encounter with him is an act of faith. We must actively seek encounters with Jesus Christ in prayer, in good works, in our holy relationships with each other.

Encounter with Christ draws forth from us an "obedience of faith" (Rom 1:5). Encounter means emulating Jesus, living like Jesus. Preeminently, Jesus was ever faithful to his Father's will. In the Our Father—that prayer Jesus himself taught us—we pray, "thy will be done." Augustine makes clear that to believe means that we understand, and understanding is more than an assent of the mind. It is a commitment of heart to do God's will. Triduum is the "faithing" mystery because these days draw us into encounter and surrender.

Living the Paschal Mystery

Faith frees us from the limits of the kingdoms of this world. Faith frees us for living in the spaciousness of God's kingdom. This divine kingdom is not a place, but an orientation of the heart and an attitude of the will. God's reign is identified by forgiveness, compassion, encounter, healing, transformation. Our faith is a response to God's goodness and Life, to Jesus' saving mystery—a response that commits us to live and act as God does toward us, and as Jesus showed us during his public ministry.

St. Paul tells us that the only thing that counts is "faith working through love" (Gal 5:6). Our faith, then, is made visible by our acts of love and care for one another. Our faith is the Beatitudes made visible. Our faith is Jesus' saving mystery made visible. Our "faithing" is a matter of doing God's will, of living as Jesus did, of being visible presences of the Presence of the risen Christ who, through the power of the Holy Spirit, dwells within and among us. Faith is our surrender to that divine indwelling.

TRIDUUM

"Triduum" comes from two Latin words (*tres* and *dies*) which mean "a space of three days." But since we have four days with special names—Holy Thursday, Good Friday, Holy Saturday, and Easter Sunday— the "three" may be confusing to some.

The confusion is cleared up when we understand how the days are reckoned. On all high festival days the church counts a day in the same way as Jewish people count days and festivals; that is, from sundown to sundown. Thus, the Triduum consists of *three* twenty-four-hour periods that stretch over four calendar days.

Therefore, the Easter Triduum begins at sundown on Holy Thursday with the Mass of the Lord's Supper and concludes with Easter evening prayer at sundown on Easter Sunday; its high point is the celebration of the Easter Vigil (GNLYC no. 19).

SOLEMN PASCHAL FAST

According to the above calculation, Lent ends at sundown on Holy Thursday; thus, Holy Thursday itself is the last day of Lent. This doesn't mean that our fasting concludes on Holy Thursday, however; the church has traditionally kept a solemn forty-hour fast from the beginning of the Triduum (Holy Thursday evening, thus the solemn fast is contiguous with the Lenten fast) until the fast is broken at Communion during the Easter Vigil.

✚ SPIRITUALITY

GOSPEL ACCLAMATION
John 13:34

I give you a new commandment, says the Lord:
love one another as I have loved you.

Gospel John 13:1-15; L39ABC

Before the feast of Passover, Jesus knew
    that his hour had come
    to pass from this world to the Father.
He loved his own in the world and he loved
    them to the end.
The devil had already induced Judas, son of
    Simon the Iscariot, to hand him over.
So, during supper,
    fully aware that the Father had put
        everything into his power
    and that he had come from God and was
        returning to God,
    he rose from supper and took off his
        outer garments.
He took a towel and tied it around his waist.
Then he poured water into a basin
    and began to wash the disciples' feet
    and dry them with the towel around his
        waist.
He came to Simon Peter, who said to him,
    "Master, are you going to wash my feet?"
Jesus answered and said to him,
    "What I am doing, you do not understand
        now,
    but you will understand later."
Peter said to him, "You will never wash my
    feet."
Jesus answered him,
    "Unless I wash you, you will have no
        inheritance with me."

Continued in Appendix A, p. 287.
See Appendix A, p. 287, for the other readings.

Reflecting on the Gospel and Living the Paschal Mystery

Key words and phrases: Jesus knew that his hour had come, he loved, washed their feet, given you a model, you should also do

To the point: On this night when we commemorate Jesus' gift of his Body and Blood, his gift of the Eucharist to us, this gospel is a wondrous commentary on his faith and love. He doesn't *talk* faith to his disciples; he makes it visible by embracing "his hour." He doesn't *talk* love; he makes it visible by washing feet. Yes, actions speak louder than words!

To ponder and pray: St. Francis of Assisi supposedly admonished, "Preach the gospel often and, if necessary, use words." We have other similar sayings, such as "Walk the talk." And we have sayings that admonish just the opposite, too, such as "Do as I say, not as I do." With the latter we have an innate sense that there is a disconnect, a lack of integrity in the speaker. With all the former sayings, there is great integrity: the speaker commits to actions that convey inner conviction, truth of self, integration of being and doing. Faith is an integration of being and doing. This is what Jesus teaches us this night.

In a most startling and profound action, Jesus sums up in the simple action of washing feet what his whole life and ministry have been about. The profound message Jesus proclaimed by his faith-in-action is the extent of his love—"he loved them to the end." Jesus' self-sacrificing love is not simply a word, but is deeds for the sake of others. Loving is serving; loving is spilling out our very body and blood for others. Pouring forth one's body and blood is indeed an act of Eucharist—it is giving oneself for another's life. Serving others, Eucharist, and love all meld into one action—an action Jesus profoundly modeled so perfectly for us. Jesus' loving and serving is faith-in-action. It is *the* manifestation of our "faithing" mystery.

This sacred night, with its ritual of footwashing, sums up what Christian living is. Jesus invites each of us to be washed and, indeed, we have been washed in the waters of baptism. This plunges us deeply into Jesus' saving—"faithing"—mystery. This demands of us that we, too, become servants to all. It demands that we make our faith visible. It demands that our actions speak louder than our words. It demands that our preaching the Gospel carries the truth of our daily living. In this gospel Jesus shows us that love—giving self unreservedly for the good of others—is down-to-earth practical. It is faith-in-action.

Jesus raises serving others to a new level—it is a sign of faith and love in action. Jesus reminds us that love knows no bounds, excludes no one, is self-giving. We come to the table worthily when we do as the Master has done: empty ourselves in self-giving love for the good of others. Jesus loved us to the end. But the end wasn't the cross. The end is feasting at the messianic table, being nourished by the Body and Blood of Christ—now and in eternity.

Jesus' "hour" is the time for him to make visible the depths of his love, the fidelity of his will to that of his Father, the totality of his faith that leads him to embrace even those who betray and deny. In Jesus' Body there is no room for less than total self-giving, nor is there room for less than absolute integrity between word and deed. He showed us the way. Do we follow?

Model Penitential Act

Presider: Each time that we gather to celebrate Eucharist, we experience Jesus' self-giving love for us. Tonight we ritualize Jesus' love in the washing of feet. Let us prepare for this liturgy by opening our hearts to hear God's word and ask for God's mercy for the times we have not given our love to others . . . [pause]

Lord Jesus, you give us an example of serving others: Lord . . .

Christ Jesus, you give us new Life: Christ . . .

Lord Jesus, you give us your Body and Blood as our nourishment: Lord . . .

Homily Points

• Incessant talkers can tire us. Incessant doers can tire us. In this gospel Jesus both talks ("you should also do") and does ("washed their feet"). His talking and his doing sum up who he is—the One who came to give us himself. This he does incessantly. However, his talking and doing never tire us. Or do they?

• On this day we celebrate Jesus' self-giving—the giving of his Body and Blood as our heavenly food. We also celebrate Jesus' model of what his self-giving does for us—transforms us into those who willingly, generously, and incessantly serve others.

• Most of us are not going to literally wash feet. But all of us are called to feed the hungry, clothe the naked, shelter the homeless, embrace the stranger, set aright injustices. We are also called to give our children a listening ear, our neighbor a friendly smile, an elderly parent a helping hand. This is the model Jesus gave us. In all this serving, Jesus nourishes us with his very Body and Blood. Do we sometimes tire? Yes, from the actions. But never from the faith and love that feed the actions.

Model Universal Prayer (Prayer of the Faithful)

Presider: We lift grateful hearts in thanksgiving to God for the wondrous gift of the Eucharist and for Jesus' model of serving others. Let us pray that we always be faithful to what Jesus gives us and asks of us.

Response:

Lord, hear our prayer.

Cantor:

we pray to the Lord,

That all members of the church eagerly come with faith and love to receive Jesus' Body and Blood in the Eucharist . . . [pause]

That all people of the world encounter God's gift of Self and come to salvation . . . [pause]

That all who hunger be fed physically, emotionally, and spiritually . . . [pause]

That all of us faithfully serve others as Jesus has commanded at the Last Supper . . . [pause]

Presider: Loving God, you sent your Son to model for us self-giving love. Hear these our prayers that we might follow his example of serving others, and one day enjoy life with you forever at the messianic banquet of love. We ask this through that same Son, Jesus Christ our Lord. **Amen.**

COLLECT
Let us pray.

Pause for silent prayer

O God, who have called us to participate
in this most sacred Supper,
in which your Only Begotten Son,
when about to hand himself over to death,
entrusted to the Church a sacrifice new for
    all eternity,
the banquet of his love,
grant, we pray,
that we may draw from so great a mystery,
the fullness of charity and of life.
Through our Lord Jesus Christ, your Son,
who lives and reigns with you in the unity
    of the Holy Spirit,
one God, for ever and ever. **Amen.**

FOR REFLECTION

• My actions say to others . . . Jesus' actions toward me say . . .

• The way serving others (footwashing) and being nourished at the eucharistic table are connected for me is . . .

• My faith and daily living make love visible by . . .

SPIRITUALITY

GOSPEL ACCLAMATION
Phil 2:8-9

Christ became obedient to the point of death,
even death on a cross.
Because of this, God greatly exalted him
and bestowed on him the name which is above
    every other name.

Gospel   John 18:1–19:42; L40ABC

Jesus went out with his disciples across
    the Kidron valley
    to where there was a garden,
    into which he and his disciples
        entered.
Judas his betrayer also knew the place,
    because Jesus had often met there with
        his disciples.
So Judas got a band of soldiers and guards
    from the chief priests and the Pharisees
    and went there with lanterns, torches,
        and weapons.
Jesus, knowing everything that was going to
        happen to him,
    went out and said to them, "Whom are
        you looking for?"
They answered him, "Jesus the Nazorean."
He said to them, "I AM."
Judas his betrayer was also with them.
When he said to them, "I AM,"
    they turned away and fell to the ground.
So he again asked them,
    "Whom are you looking for?"
They said, "Jesus the Nazorean."
Jesus answered,
    "I told you that I AM.
So if you are looking for me, let these men
        go."
This was to fulfill what he had said,
    "I have not lost any of those you gave me."
Then Simon Peter, who had a sword, drew
        it,
    struck the high priest's slave, and cut off
        his right ear.
The slave's name was Malchus.
Jesus said to Peter,
    "Put your sword into its scabbard.
Shall I not drink the cup that the Father
        gave me?"

Continued in Appendix A, pp. 288–289.
See Appendix A, p. 290, for the other readings.

Reflecting on the Gospel and Living the Paschal Mystery
Key words and phrases: I AM, drink the cup that the Father gave me, What is truth?, Standing by the cross, It is finished, he handed over the spirit

To the point: Duplicity reigns in this passion account. Judas betrays; Peter denies; the Jewish leaders claim criminality of someone they know is innocent; soldiers mock; Pilate tries to release Jesus, but doesn't. However, integrity also reigns. Jesus' mother, other women, and the Beloved Disciple stand by the cross; Joseph of Arimathea gives Jesus a worthy burial. The greatest integrity, the greatest act of faith, however, is made visible by Jesus himself: "he handed over the spirit."

To ponder and pray: It is tempting in the passion accounts to focus primarily on the heinous betrayal, bogus trial, meanness of some of the people, terrific suffering, and terrible death. While all this is included in the passion accounts, the real import of the accounts is that what Jesus came to do "is finished." He drank fully of the cup the Father gave him. This cup is not one of a sadistic father who exacts suffering and death to compensate for the waywardness of children, but instead a cup of blessing, a cup of grace, a cup of salvation. The Father willed that Jesus become incarnate and identify with humanity so much that we could be lifted up to a new relationship with God, the divine "I AM." The Father willed that we be saved from ourselves for everlasting glory. This cup Jesus drinks is a cup of obedience, a cup of willingness to do whatever it takes to coax us humans into opening ourselves to receive the gifts the Father offers.

The cross of Jesus is not so much an instrument of suffering as it is an opportunity to make visible unwavering faith and self-giving love—again and again. Even on Good Friday—the day we commemorate Jesus' passion and death and seeming end—we cannot lose sight of what God has in store: giving us the overwhelming love that leads to everlasting exaltation.

Good Friday is more than a step to resurrection; it is a day on which we celebrate Jesus' obedience, his kingship, the everlasting establishment of his reign, his side being opened and himself being poured out so that we can be washed in his very blood and water. The real scandal of the cross isn't suffering and death; the real scandal of the cross is that death is vanquished by Jesus' self-giving, visible love. Death has no power over God. Jesus, our high priest, has offered himself obediently and willingly and "became the source of salvation for all" (second reading).

Even so great a gift as Jesus' faithful obedience and absolute love cannot erase the fact that some of us choose to be duplicitous. We choose to act without integrity. This day, Good Friday, reminds us that the One who acted in perfect integrity was willing to undergo anything so that we might have Life. He suffered and died because he lived the faith and obedience of integrity. This day, Good Friday, calls us to embrace the same faith and obedience of integrity, no matter how much ours falls short of the model Jesus gave us. What is finished is any doubt that God loves us to eternal Life. What is finished is a death that has no meaning. What is finished is any sense that this life is all there is. When we hand over our spirit to live as Jesus did, we enter into the fulfillment of who we are: the beloved of God, saved through the cross.

Homily Points

• Crosses abound. They are hung on walls, worn around necks, tattooed on bodies, found on key rings, etched on tombstones. They have become so common, so familiar that *the* cross may have lost its impact and deepest meaning. The cross of Jesus is a sign of fidelity, obedience, integrity, trust, love. It empowers us to embrace the life Jesus took up, handed over, and took up again.

• Good Friday is not just a day—it is a way of living. We are to live Jesus' integrity, his faith. We do so by handing over our spirit every day so that others might live more happily, more freely, more fully. When we do so, the cross is more than a devotional object. It is a sign of the power of Jesus' death and resurrection, our dying to self, and the new Life God gives.

Music Suggestions

The Good Friday liturgy does not *historicize* or reenact the past event of Jesus' crucifixion, but *ritualizes* our participation here-and-now in the mystery that the cross of Christ is the tree of life. The songs we sing this day need to lead us into this liturgical meaning rather than engage us in a devotional experience centered on details of Jesus' suffering and death.

Singing the solemn intercessions: Just as the Easter Vigil is the mother of all vigils, so the Good Friday intercessions are the mother and model of all general intercessions. Because of their solemnity, they are meant to be sung, using the simple chant given in *The Roman Missal*, and to include short periods of silent prayer after each statement of intention. If it is not possible that these intercessions be sung, they should be spoken with solemnity, with time allowed for the appropriate silent pauses.

Music during the adoration of the Holy Cross: Three times before we begin the adoration of the Holy Cross, the assigned minister sings, "Behold the wood of the cross, on which hung the salvation of the world" and we all respond, "Come, let us adore." What we sing reminds us that what we honor is not the One crucified, but the cross itself which embodies the mystery of Jesus'—and our—redemptive triumph over sin and death. We kiss the cross not in sorrow or expiation, but in gratitude and in confident acceptance (the very sentiments expressed in the closing verses of the responsorial psalm). The songs we sing during this procession, then, need to speak about the mystery and triumph of the cross rather than about the details of Jesus' suffering and death. Appropriate examples include Marty Haugen's "In the Cross of Christ" (G3, SS); Jerome Siwek's "We Acclaim the Cross of Jesus" (OF, WC, WS); Delores Dufner's "We Glory in the Cross" (SS, W4); "O Cross of Christ, Immortal Tree" (OF, WC); and Tony Alonso's "We Should Glory in the Cross" (OF).

Music during Holy Communion: The verses of Dan Schutte's "Glory in the Cross" (BB, JS3) assigned for Holy Thursday would be very appropriate for Communion on Good Friday (more appropriate to the liturgical meaning of this day, in fact, than the verses he gives for Good Friday). Verses 3 and 4 connect the mystery of the cross to the mystery of the Eucharist. Also appropriate for Communion is Schutte's "Only This I Want" (BB, G3, JS3) in which we sing of our willingness to "bear his cross, so to wear the crown he wore."

COLLECT

Let us pray.

Pause for silent prayer

Remember your mercies, O Lord,
and with your eternal protection sanctify
　　your servants,
for whom Christ your Son,
by the shedding of his Blood,
established the Paschal Mystery.
Who lives and reigns for ever and ever.
　　Amen.

or

O God, who by the Passion of Christ your
　　Son, our Lord,
abolished the death inherited from ancient
　　sin
by every succeeding generation,
grant that just as, being conformed to him,
we have borne by the law of nature
the image of the man of earth,
so by the sanctification of grace
we may bear the image of the Man of
　　heaven.
Through Christ our Lord. **Amen.**

FOR REFLECTION

• I tend to be duplicitous when . . . I have experienced duplicity when . . .

• The integrity of faith reigns in me most when . . . least when . . .

• I hand over my spirit to God when . . . God gives back to me . . .

SPIRITUALITY

Gospel   Luke 24:1-12; L41ABC

At daybreak on the first day of the week
     the women who had come from
          Galilee with Jesus
     took the spices they had
          prepared
     and went to the tomb.
They found the stone rolled away
     from the tomb;
     but when they entered,
     they did not find the body of the
          Lord Jesus.
While they were puzzling over
     this, behold,
     two men in dazzling garments
          appeared to them.
They were terrified and bowed their
     faces to the ground.
They said to them,
     "Why do you seek the living one
          among the dead?
He is not here, but he has been raised.
Remember what he said to you while
     he was still in Galilee,
     that the Son of Man must be handed
          over to sinners
     and be crucified, and rise on the
          third day."
And they remembered his words.
Then they returned from the tomb
     and announced all these things to the
          eleven
     and to all the others.
The women were Mary Magdalene,
     Joanna, and Mary the mother of
          James;
     the others who accompanied them
          also told this to the apostles,
     but their story seemed like nonsense
     and they did not believe them.
But Peter got up and ran to the tomb,
     bent down, and saw the burial cloths
          alone;
     then he went home amazed at what
          had happened.

Readings continued in Appendix A, pp. 291–296.

Reflecting on the Gospel and Living the Paschal Mystery

Key words and phrases: two men in dazzling garments appeared to them, he has been raised, announced all these things, did not believe them, got up . . . ran . . . and saw

To the point: The women arose early on the first day of the week, three days after Jesus' death and burial, to do him the homage of caring for his lifeless body. They were greeted with an empty tomb, with "two men in dazzling garments." Perhaps they were Moses and Elijah who had appeared with Jesus at his transfiguration? Perhaps they were the ones who helped the women remember Jesus' words? Perhaps they were the ones who encouraged the women to go to the other disciples and announce "all these things"? This announcement had never before been made, even from the beginning of creation: He is risen!

To ponder and pray: How little it takes for us to move from belief to unbelief! While Jesus was with them, full of life and promise and love, his followers believed. Once Jesus was dead and buried, their belief was shaken and they forgot about his words and deeds.

This is the night when the stones of our Lenten penance are rolled away and we are invited to peer into the empty space and see ourselves in "dazzling garments." This is the night when we announce all these things to anyone who will hear. This is the night when our words of belief spill over into the mighty deed of announcing, He is risen!

This is the night when Jesus passes from death to risen Life. This is the night when we remember that we, too, "were indeed buried with him through baptism into death" (epistle). This is the night when we celebrate that we, too, "live in newness of life." This is the night when our own being and doing collapse into a living faith that is full, robust, eager to announce the Good News that death is overcome, that our belief is not in vain, that Jesus lives on in us who are baptized. This is the night—just this one night—when we can ignore the sting of death because life is so abundant.

This is the night when we celebrate our own becoming the Life and Presence of the risen One. This is the night to celebrate God's invitation to be transfigured into being more perfectly the Body of Christ.

This is the night when the announcement of salvation cannot be contained. And so this night has its challenge: the new Life isn't simply for our own gain, but so that God can renew creation. "Let there be light," God creatively spoke so long ago. This is the night when God speaks again and now that light is the risen Son. And so the challenge of this night is that we, too, bring light to a world still darkened by disbelief and "slavery to sin" (epistle). In the simple smile, helping hand, listening ear we bring risen Life. In the kind word, the self-giving love and care of another, the daily dying to self we bring risen Life to all those we encounter. In these and many other simple ways of living, our belief becomes visible in the good we are and do.

The utter amazement of this night is that while we celebrate Jesus' resurrection, we also celebrate our own new life. Jesus' resurrection is a pledge of our own transfiguration, an invitation to us to keep our own "dazzling garments" that we received at baptism pure and spotless. Our belief gives us a share in Jesus' risen Life. No wonder our alleluias cannot be contained. He is risen!

Homily Points

• What kinds of things are formally announced? Births, engagements, marriages, deaths, graduations, promotions, election results. All of these events have great import for the lives of individuals and the community. The "two men in dazzling garments" make an amazing announcement to the women gone to the burial place of Jesus: "He is not here, but he has been raised." This announcement has import not only for Jesus, who now lives, but for the community of disciples, the community of nations, the entire cosmos. Then and now.

• The disciples do not believe the women who return from the empty tomb with a message to announce. Peter and John must run and see the empty tomb for themselves. This gospel story relates that they were "amazed." What amazed them? That they "saw the burial cloths alone"? What the "two men in dazzling garments" had said to the women: that "he has been raised"? That they were brought from unbelief to belief?

• Do we believe the message announced to us in the words of this gospel? Do we need to run and see for ourselves? And, if so, where do we run? Where do we look? What do we believe? What do we announce?

Model Universal Prayer (Prayer of the Faithful)

Presider: On this joyous night when we celebrate the new Life of the risen Christ, let us ask God to deepen our belief and increase the risen Life in which we already share.

Response:

Lord, hear our prayer.

Cantor:

we pray to the Lord,

That all members of the church faithfully announce the Good News for which Jesus lived, died, and rose . . . [pause]

That our broken world be led to the peace and new life made possible by the death and resurrection of Jesus . . . [pause]

That anyone in need be raised to a share in the abundance with which God blesses us . . . [pause]

That the newly baptized radiate Christ's new Life within them and remain faithful to their promises . . . [pause]

That all of us gathered here grow in our Easter joy and amazement at all the good God does for us . . . [pause]

Presider: Redeeming God, you raised your Son to new Life that we might share in his glory. Hear these our prayers that all of us may be brought to everlasting Life. Through that same risen Son, Jesus Christ our Lord. **Amen.**

COLLECT

Let us pray.

Pause for silent prayer

O God, who make this most sacred night radiant
with the glory of the Lord's Resurrection,
stir up in your Church a spirit of adoption,
so that, renewed in body and mind,
we may render you undivided service.
Through our Lord Jesus Christ, your Son,
who lives and reigns with you in the unity
     of the Holy Spirit,
one God, for ever and ever. **Amen.**

FOR REFLECTION

• I am prompted to remember Jesus' words about being handed over, crucified, and raised up when . . . My remembering challenges the way I live in that . . .

• "He is risen" has been announced to me when . . . by . . . because . . .

• I announce "He is risen" to . . . when . . . by . . .

SPIRITUALITY

GOSPEL ACCLAMATION
cf. 1 Cor 5:7b-8a

℟. Alleluia, alleluia.
Christ, our paschal lamb, has been sacrificed;
let us then feast with joy in the Lord.
℟. Alleluia, alleluia.

Gospel

John 20:1-9; L42ABC

On the first day of the week,
   Mary of Magdala came to the tomb
      early in the morning,
  while it was still dark,
  and saw the stone removed from
      the tomb.
So she ran and went to Simon Peter
  and to the other disciple whom
      Jesus loved, and told them,
  "They have taken the Lord from the
      tomb,
  and we don't know where they put him."
So Peter and the other disciple went out
  and came to the tomb.
They both ran, but the other disciple ran
    faster than Peter
  and arrived at the tomb first;
  he bent down and saw the burial cloths
    there, but did not go in.
When Simon Peter arrived after him,
  he went into the tomb and saw the
    burial cloths there,
  and the cloth that had covered his head,
  not with the burial cloths but rolled up
    in a separate place.
Then the other disciple also went in,
  the one who had arrived at the tomb
    first,
  and he saw and believed.
For they did not yet understand the
    Scripture
  that he had to rise from the dead.

or

Luke 24:1-12; L41C *in Appendix A, p. 297*

or, at an afternoon or evening Mass

Luke 24:13-35; L46 *in Appendix A, p. 297.*

See Appendix A, p. 298, for the other readings.

Reflecting on the Gospel and Living the Paschal Mystery

Key words and phrases: we don't know, saw and believed, did not yet understand, rise from the dead

To the point: On this day when the gospel announces an empty tomb, we feel the contradictory reactions that the resurrection mystery arouses—seeing and believing on the one hand, misunderstanding and confusion on the other. This mystery defies all human understanding. The Easter stories tell us that the resurrection isn't something we fully understand, but believe and live.

To ponder and pray: The act of seeing with the eye is a physical, complicated process. It begins with light rays bouncing off an object and being captured by the eye. It is impossible to see in darkness. It was "early in the morning, / while it was still dark" that Mary Magdalene went to the tomb. How did she see? How did she know? She ran to Peter and John and they ran to the tomb. They, too, saw. More than saw. Their seeing was more than light refraction. Their seeing could penetrate the darkness of not understanding. Their seeing was a response of the heart that led to their believing. The mystery of the resurrection cannot be seen with a physical process, no matter how complicated. The mystery is able to be seen because God gives us eyes of faith.

The gospel identifies only three characters: Mary of Magdala, Peter, and the "disciple whom Jesus loved." By not being named, John can function symbolically—all of us are the "disciple whom Jesus loved." Instead of trying to understand, we simply "run" to the mystery and embrace it so that we, like John, can enter into it and see and believe. In John's gospel seeing and believing aren't mental exercises but actions that express one's inner disposition. Our belief in the resurrection is a matter of a willingness to encounter the risen One, surrender ourselves to him, and give ourselves over for the good of others.

Even on this Easter day when we rejoice in the risen Life of Jesus, we are reminded that resurrection has its cost: self-giving for the sake of others. The only way to open ourselves and receive the new Life that God promises through the resurrection of Jesus Christ is to open ourselves to the needs of others in self-giving. If we try to *understand* this resurrection mystery we will miss it. The readings today invite us to *live* the mystery by believing, an action. Believing is risen Life made visible when we live and act as Jesus did. Paramount in the life of those who follow Jesus is taking up his love, care, and empathy for others. The paradox of Christianity is that dying to self isn't something to avoid, but is the way we remove the stone that blocks our own hearts from receiving new Life. We have the next fifty days of Easter to help us grasp in our hearts and daily living that when we reach out to others we ourselves are actually living Jesus' risen Life. We only need to take the time to contemplate this mystery and recognize the good with which God blesses us. We need to see beyond the obvious—an empty tomb and the demands of self-giving—to the glory that God has bestowed through Christ Jesus. Our seeing must become believing.

The alleluia that bursts forth with the news of resurrection expresses a heartfelt cry that we be willing to identify ourselves with the dying and rising Christ. Our knowing gives way to an alleluia-believing.

Model Penitential Act

Presider: On this day when we celebrate with joy the resurrection of Jesus from the dead, we also renew our baptismal promises. Let us prepare ourselves to renew this commitment by surrendering ourselves to living as the risen Christ calls us . . . [pause]

Lord Jesus, you are the resurrection and the Life: Lord . . .

Christ Jesus, you are the Paschal Lamb sacrificed for us: Christ . . .

Lord Jesus, you are the feast of love poured forth for us: Lord . . .

Homily Points

• Sometimes confusion results from not knowing all the facts, from twisting the facts, from denying the facts. Sometimes seeing and believing result from clarity of facts, personal experience, testimony of an eyewitness. In this Easter Sunday gospel, there is no clear announcement of Jesus' resurrection; there is only an empty tomb. Without all the facts, the disciples "did not yet understand."

• On this Sunday when the church celebrates the resurrection, this gospel passage includes the word "tomb" seven times. "Tomb" speaks to us of death and finality, end and loss. No wonder Mary and the disciples "did not yet understand" when they found the tomb empty. They had no experience of someone rising from the dead, to die no more. Before they could see, believe, and announce the risen Lord, they needed an encounter with him.

• Our encounters with the risen Christ come in many and varied ways and times. We encounter him in the personal holiness that shines in the face of faithful disciples, in the good deeds done in Jesus' name, in the community of the faithful who seek to live the Gospel. Like the early disciples, these encounters lead us to believe what we don't always fully see or understand: that Christ has risen, that he is present within and among us, that his resurrection is a pledge of our own share in his glory.

Model Universal Prayer (Prayer of the Faithful)

Presider: On this Easter day when we celebrate Jesus' resurrection, let us pray that the power of his risen Life become evident in our lives.

Response:

Lord, hear our prayer.

Cantor:

we pray to the Lord,

May all members of the church express their seeing and believing in the resurrection by self-giving love for others . . . [pause]

May all peoples in the world come to salvation through seeing and believing in God's Presence to them . . . [pause]

May all those entombed by sin be freed by an encounter with the risen Christ . . . [pause]

May those who celebrate the Easter sacraments this weekend shine forth with the joy of risen Life . . . [pause]

May we here who feast at the Easter table of the Lord be emboldened to lead others to see and believe in risen Life . . . [pause]

Presider: God of glory, you raised your Son from death to new Life. Hear these our prayers that we may grow in our Easter joy and share more deeply in Jesus' risen Life. We ask this through that same Son, Jesus Christ our Lord. **Amen**.

COLLECT

Let us pray.

Pause for silent prayer

O God, who on this day,
through your Only Begotten Son,
have conquered death
and unlocked for us the path to eternity,
grant, we pray, that we who keep
the solemnity of the Lord's Resurrection
may, through the renewal brought by your
    Spirit,
rise up in the light of life.
Through our Lord Jesus Christ, your Son,
who lives and reigns with you in the unity
    of the Holy Spirit,
one God, for ever and ever. **Amen.**

FOR REFLECTION

• Like Mary Magdalene, I have been compelled to tell another what I find when I go looking for Jesus when . . .

• The times in my life when I have run to find the risen Christ (like Peter and the other disciple did) are . . . The times I have run away are . . .

• "Seeing" and "believing" in Jesus' resurrection means to me . . . The way I try to live this mystery is . . .

SEASON
OF EASTER

SPIRITUALITY

GOSPEL ACCLAMATION
John 20:29

R⁊. Alleluia, alleluia.
You believe in me, Thomas, because you have
    seen me, says the Lord;
blessed are those who have not seen me, but
    still believe!
R⁊. Alleluia, alleluia.

Gospel   John 20:19-31; L45C

On the evening of that first day of
    the week,
  when the doors were locked,
      where the disciples
      were,
  for fear of the Jews,
  Jesus came and stood in their
      midst
  and said to them, "Peace be with you."
When he had said this, he showed them
    his hands and his side.
The disciples rejoiced when they saw the
    Lord.
Jesus said to them again, "Peace be with
    you.
As the Father has sent me, so I send you."
And when he had said this, he breathed on
    them and said to them,
  "Receive the Holy Spirit.
Whose sins you forgive are forgiven them,
    and whose sins you retain are retained."

Thomas, called Didymus, one of the
    Twelve,
  was not with them when Jesus came.
So the other disciples said to him, "We
    have seen the Lord."
But he said to them,
  "Unless I see the mark of the nails in
      his hands
  and put my finger into the nailmarks
  and put my hand into his side, I will not
      believe."

Now a week later his disciples were again
    inside
  and Thomas was with them.
Jesus came, although the doors were locked,
  and stood in their midst and said,
      "Peace be with you."

Continued in Appendix A, p. 298.

Reflecting on the Gospel

Lent is a practical time, a season we can easily understand, embrace, use to progress in our spiritual lives. We choose to undertake penitential practices. They are concrete: give up something we enjoy; do something that will help us grow. These penitential practices come from and are directed to our everyday living. Now we are in the Easter season. This season is not so easily understood; risen Life is not something practical deriving from certain spiritual practices. We know Jesus rose from the dead; we cannot so easily grasp how this has an immediate effect on us. The resurrection is a mystery. Risen Life is different, a new happening, a fresh experience. Most surely, risen Life is of God. It instills Easter joy. Like the penance of Lent, it ought to make a difference in our everyday living.

This gospel shows us why the resurrection makes all the difference in the world. When the risen Lord appears to the disciples locked away behind closed doors, fear is allayed by peace, sin is allayed by forgiveness, doubt is allayed by Presence, unbelieving is allayed by seeing-believing. The Lord comes to the disciples a first time on that first Easter Sunday evening when Thomas is not present. Thomas makes known quite clearly to the other disciples what he needs in order to believe that Jesus is alive. He must encounter, see, touch—put his finger and hand in the wounds that he expects to see on Jesus' body.

A week later, when Thomas is present, Jesus appears to the disciples again, and responds to Thomas's unbelief. Jesus is not angry with Thomas for not believing; he does not judge him. He simply invites: here, see, touch, and believe. Seeing-believing—for Thomas and for us—is not merely an exercise in intellectual assent, but a practical encounter played out through our acceptance of the risen Life that is offered us. We know *to whom and what* our belief is directed: to Jesus and the gift of risen Life. We know *how* we receive risen Life: through Jesus' gift of the breath of the Holy Spirit dwelling within us. Jesus' resurrection is a divine pledge of "life in his name." Risen Life is God's divine Life transforming who and how we are. Resurrection makes all the difference—for us, for all of creation.

Living the Paschal Mystery

Perhaps we unfairly fault Thomas. Perhaps he is a good model for us of authentic seeing-believing. Our believing cannot stand on hearsay, on blind acceptance of what others have seen and believe. Rather, our believing must be grounded in personal encounter with the risen Christ, in ongoing conversation with him that leads to conscious choice, and in expressing our belief in him by the way we reach out to others. Here is where the resurrection and the Life it brings becomes very concrete and practical for our daily living. Christ's risen Life within us enables us to choose to live the Gospel he preached. His risen Life within us prompts us to set aside fear and doubt and embrace forgiveness and peace.

Jesus allays our fears and offers us a whole new relationship with him—not one where we need to touch his wounds, but one in which we utter with joyful conviction, "My Lord and my God!" We enter into a whole new relationship with each other as we continue the works of Jesus that lead others to seeing-believing. Resurrection makes all the difference—for us, for all of creation.

Focusing the Gospel

Key words and phrases: fear, peace, sin, forgiven, Unless I see, Jesus . . . stood in their midst, come to believe, life in his name

To the point: The resurrection makes all the difference in the world! Fear is allayed by peace. Sin is allayed by forgiveness. Doubt is allayed by Presence. Unbelieving is allayed by seeing-believing. Jesus' resurrection is a divine pledge of "life in his name." Risen Life is God's divine Life transforming who and how we are. Resurrection makes all the difference—for us, for all of creation.

Connecting the Gospel

to the second reading: Moved by the Spirit, John describes his encounter with the risen Christ, while the gospel describes Thomas's encounter with the same risen Christ. In John's vision, Jesus reaches out and touches him; in the gospel, Jesus invites Thomas to reach out and touch him. What happened to John and Thomas "will happen afterwards" to us.

to experience: When someone exclaims, "Let me see that," the person often really wants to reach out and touch, hold, experience. Our heart's desire to "see" the risen Christ expresses a desire also to touch, to hold, to experience. Seeing-believing is touching, holding, experiencing.

Connecting the Responsorial Psalm

to the readings: In these verses from Psalm 118, we invite an ever-widening circle to join in praising God for mercy and deliverance. We do so as the community of believers commissioned to "[w]rite down . . . what [we] have seen, / and what is happening, and what will happen afterwards" (second reading). What has happened and will continue to happen is God's victory over death (second reading), disease (first reading), and sin (gospel). God takes what is flawed, useless, and inconsequential—the rejected stone (psalm), our failing lives (psalm), our diseased bodies (first reading), our doubting hearts (gospel)—and makes them the cornerstone of faith and forgiveness. This is resurrection, done "by the Lord" and "wonderful in our eyes." And it happens every day in "signs and wonders" (first reading) both great and small. For this we "[g]ive thanks to the Lord" (psalm refrain).

to psalmist preparation: In singing Psalm 118 you call the church to recognize and give thanks for the enduring mercy of God. You can only give a "joyful shout" because you have had personal experience of God's saving intervention, because you have been "hard pressed" and "falling" and known God's help. What story will you be telling when you sing?

ASSEMBLY & FAITH-SHARING GROUPS
- What makes enough of a difference to me that I transform my life is . . .
- My experience of the resurrection transforms my life when . . .
- My seeing-believing looks like . . .

PRESIDERS
I help others turn fear to peace, sin to forgiveness, doubt to seeing-believing when I . . .

DEACONS
The peace of Christ I invite the assembly to share with one another at liturgy calls me to . . .

HOSPITALITY MINISTERS
My hospitality unlocks doubting hearts to believe in the Presence and peace of the risen Lord by . . .

MUSIC MINISTERS
My music making embodies the joy and peace the risen Lord gives me when I . . .

ALTAR MINISTERS
Easter joy shows in my serving when I . . .

LECTORS
My manner of proclaiming the word announces that I have encountered the risen Christ and believe when I . . .

EXTRAORDINARY MINISTERS OF HOLY COMMUNION
Distributing Holy Communion is a sign of forgiveness given and received in that . . .

Model Rite for the Blessing and Sprinkling of Water

Presider: Dear friends, as we ask God to bless this water which reminds us of our baptism, let us pray for deeper faith in the risen Lord . . . [pause]

[*continue with* The Roman Missal, *Appendix II*]

Homily Points

• A number of historical events have significantly transformed our world. Positively, the invention of the printing press, the discovery of penicillin, landing on the moon. Negatively, plagues, wars, repressive leaders. The most transforming event ever is the resurrection of Christ.

• Jesus' resurrection ushers in the new Life that transforms: sin is forgiven, fear is overcome, doubt is conquered by seeing-believing. Jesus' appearance to the disciples in the Upper Room is only the beginning, however. The end has not yet come. In our response to the risen Christ today, we are hastening the end. And the end is . . . ?

• We live risen Life and hasten its fulfillment when we, like Thomas, see and believe. Seeing *is* believing. What do we see? People in need. How do we believe? Reach out and touch them with transforming presence. What do we see? Unjust situations. How do we believe? Act to transform systems and relationships. What do we see? Holiness in others who follow Christ. How do we believe? Choose to be transformed with them as Body of Christ. And the end is . . .

Model Universal Prayer (Prayer of the Faithful)

Presider: Having just professed our faith, let us confidently lift our needs to God.

Response:

Lord, hear our prayer.

Cantor:

we pray to the Lord,

That the church may always be a font of the forgiveness and peace of the risen Christ . . . [pause]

That all peoples of the world may come to salvation through encounters with a loving and life-giving God . . . [pause]

That those facing struggle, tension, or suffering may be transformed by the peace of the risen Christ . . . [pause]

That those newly received into the church may continue to encounter the risen Christ and grow in their believing . . . [pause]

That each of us gathered here may touch others with Christ's risen Presence by the manner of our living the Good News . . . [pause]

Presider: Ever-living God, through your risen Son you breathe upon us the Spirit of new Life. Hear these our prayers that one day we might share that Life with you for ever and ever. **Amen**.

Let us pray.

Pause for silent prayer

God of everlasting mercy,
who in the very recurrence of the paschal feast
kindle the faith of the people you have made your own,
increase, we pray, the grace you have bestowed,
that all may grasp and rightly understand
in what font they have been washed,
by whose Spirit they have been reborn,
by whose Blood they have been redeemed.
Through our Lord Jesus Christ, your Son,
who lives and reigns with you in the unity of the Holy Spirit,
one God, for ever and ever. **Amen.**

FIRST READING
Acts 5:12-16

Many signs and wonders were done
among the people
at the hands of the apostles.
They were all together in Solomon's portico.
None of the others dared to join them, but the people esteemed them.
Yet more than ever, believers in the Lord,
great numbers of men and women, were added to them.
Thus they even carried the sick out into the streets
and laid them on cots and mats
so that when Peter came by,
at least his shadow might fall on one or another of them.
A large number of people from the towns
in the vicinity of Jerusalem also gathered,
bringing the sick and those disturbed by unclean spirits,
and they were all cured.

RESPONSORIAL PSALM
Ps 118:2-4, 13-15, 22-24

R/. (1) Give thanks to the Lord for he is good, his love is everlasting.
or
R/. Alleluia.

Let the house of Israel say,
"His mercy endures forever."
Let the house of Aaron say,
"His mercy endures forever."
Let those who fear the LORD say,
"His mercy endures forever."

R/. Give thanks to the Lord for he is good, his love is everlasting.
or
R/. Alleluia.

I was hard pressed and was falling,
    but the LORD helped me.
My strength and my courage is the LORD,
    and he has been my savior.
The joyful shout of victory
    in the tents of the just:

R̸. Give thanks to the Lord for he is good,
his love is everlasting.
    or
R̸. Alleluia.

The stone which the builders rejected
    has become the cornerstone.
By the LORD has this been done;
    it is wonderful in our eyes.
This is the day the LORD has made;
    let us be glad and rejoice in it.

R̸. Give thanks to the Lord for he is good,
his love is everlasting.
    or
R̸. Alleluia.

SECOND READING
Rev 1:9-11a, 12-13, 17-19

I, John, your brother, who share with you
    the distress, the kingdom, and the
        endurance we have in Jesus,
    found myself on the island called
        Patmos
    because I proclaimed God's word and
        gave testimony to Jesus.
I was caught up in spirit on the Lord's day
    and heard behind me a voice as loud as
        a trumpet, which said,
    "Write on a scroll what you see."
Then I turned to see whose voice it was
    that spoke to me,
    and when I turned, I saw seven gold
        lampstands
    and in the midst of the lampstands one
        like a son of man,
    wearing an ankle-length robe, with a
        gold sash around his chest.

When I caught sight of him, I fell down at
    his feet as though dead.
He touched me with his right hand and
    said, "Do not be afraid.
I am the first and the last, the one who
    lives.
Once I was dead, but now I am alive
    forever and ever.
I hold the keys to death and the
    netherworld.
Write down, therefore, what you have
    seen,
    and what is happening, and what will
        happen afterwards."

✝ CATECHESIS

About Liturgy

First reading from Acts and the Easter Lectionary: During these eight Sundays of Easter the first reading deviates from the norm: rather than selected from Old Testament books, it is always taken from the Acts of the Apostles. This first book of the New Testament after the four gospels records for us the reception of Easter faith in the early Christian community. Although these first readings don't accord with the gospels for these Sundays in the usual way—either by a parallel theme or account, a promise-fulfillment motif, or a contrast—they do in one sense accord with the gospels.

The Easter Lectionary presents eight gospels that form a marvelous progression and whole: the first three Sundays of Easter all present appearance accounts of the risen Jesus; the Fourth Sunday of Easter is Good Shepherd Sunday when we are assured of Jesus' continued care and love; the fifth through seventh Sundays of Easter prepare us to be disciples who receive the Holy Spirit and carry on the saving ministry of Jesus; the eighth Sunday is Pentecost when we celebrate the giving and receiving of the Holy Spirit. We move in these eight gospels from celebrating the risen Lord to being given the power (the Holy Spirit) to continue the works of Jesus.

The selections from the Acts of the Apostles simply record for us how those first Christians received the Spirit and carried forward Jesus' mission. We see in this "mini history" how the new Life of Jesus' resurrection re-created these people. These accounts from Acts, then, make concrete what the gospels promise and help us see how we make risen Life real in our own lives.

About Liturgical Music

Music suggestions: The hymns we sing over the course of the Sundays of Easter are an effective means of reinforcing the thematic progression which unfolds in the Lectionary readings (see above). The first three Sundays call for hymns which allow us simply to exult over Christ's resurrection (most Easter hymns fall into this category). On the fourth Sunday we need to sing songs which assure us of Christ's ongoing presence, of his tender nurturance, of his active support as we strive to live out our discipleship, hymns such as, for example, "The King of Love My Shepherd Is" and "Sing of One Who Walks Beside Us." For the final Sundays we need to sing texts that call us to our mission of bringing Christ's risen life to all people, such as, for example, "We Know That Christ Is Raised," "Christ Is Alive," "Now We Remain," and "Go to the World."

APRIL 3, 2016
SECOND SUNDAY OF EASTER
or OF DIVINE MERCY

SPIRITUALITY

John 1:14ab

The Word became flesh and made his dwelling
among us
and we saw his glory.

Gospel Luke 1:26-38; L545

The angel Gabriel was sent from God
  to a town of Galilee called Nazareth,
  to a virgin betrothed to a man named
    Joseph,
  of the house of David,
  and the virgin's name was Mary.
And coming to her, he said,
  "Hail, full of grace! The Lord is with
    you."
But she was greatly troubled at what
    was said
  and pondered what sort of greeting
    this might be.
Then the angel said to her,
  "Do not be afraid, Mary,
  for you have found favor with God.
Behold, you will conceive in your womb and
    bear a son,
  and you shall name him Jesus.
He will be great and will be called Son of
    the Most High,
  and the Lord God will give him the throne
    of David his father,
  and he will rule over the house of Jacob
    forever,
  and of his Kingdom there will be no end."
But Mary said to the angel,
  "How can this be,
  since I have no relations with a man?"
And the angel said to her in reply,
  "The Holy Spirit will come upon you,
  and the power of the Most High will over-
    shadow you.
Therefore the child to be born
  will be called holy, the Son of God.
And behold, Elizabeth, your relative,
  has also conceived a son in her old age,
  and this is the sixth month for her who
    was called barren;
  for nothing will be impossible for God."
Mary said, "Behold, I am the handmaid of
    the Lord.
May it be done to me according to your word."
Then the angel departed from her.

See Appendix A, p. 299, for the other readings.

Reflecting on the Gospel

More than two hundred years ago Ben Franklin coined the familiar witticism that the only thing we have to do in life is die and pay taxes. While he states only this one certitude, we know there are really many more "givens" for us than dying and paying taxes. For example, we learn quite young that life isn't always fair. We also learn that pain is a part of life, as well as change and disruptions. We learn to live with the givens as we grow in experience. We learn to be stronger because of them. This is no less true of Mary, whose life had a number of givens: she would marry and live with Joseph, she would have children, she would grow old in a loving family. Nothing could have prepared Mary for Gabriel's appearance, greeting, and annunciation. Nothing could have prepared Mary for a new given in her life: that she would be the mother of God.

Gabriel greeted Mary with "Hail, full of grace! The Lord is with you." Mary's holiness was a given. Her holiness made her yes response to Gabriel a given. And because of Mary's yes to God's plan of salvation, because of her Son's yes and his resurrection, *we* also share in God's fullness of grace and the risen Lord is *with us*. All this grace and Life is a given for us, if we but imitate Mary's yes. All this grace and Life we welcome into our lives and hope and pray that this grace of goodness never leaves us, never changes, never is disrupted.

What is not a given is our yes. What is not a given is that we choose to live our "name" as the Body of Christ, as those baptized in the risen Son. What is not a given is that we accept "nothing will be impossible for God," even knowing that sometimes we do say no to God and put in jeopardy all the grace and goodness, Life and holiness given to us. For sure, what is a given is that we must make choices every day. We must continually say yes to whatever God asks of us and sometimes, like Mary, say that yes as a leap in the dark. When we are faced with the given of our own holiness, like Mary we must do everything we can to reinforce the yes we choose to make to God by the way we live every day. Givens still require choices. What choices do we make?

This is the unthinkable of this solemnity: God brought forth the Life of the divine Son through the willing yes of Mary and God continues to bring forth the Life of the divine Son through the willing yes of each of us. The amazingly Good News of this solemnity is that God offers us the same Life that God offered Mary. Like Mary, we too must surrender our plans, our lives, and our bodies so that Jesus Christ can become incarnate in the world through us. May it be done to all of us "according to [God's] word." May our choice to say yes to God be the most constant given in our life.

Living the Paschal Mystery

Mary probably had no idea at any point in her life that two thousand years later people would be celebrating the surrender of herself to God's plans. Mary was a simple maiden who, without understanding fully how or why, gave herself over to God. She was overshadowed by "the power of the Most High." The challenge in our own lives is to let God take over our lives, to let God do the work, to let "the power of the Most High" overshadow us. We don't have to have all the answers to God's plan for us; we just need to say yes, like Mary. Only by dying can we come to new Life and help bring that Life to the whole world.

Focusing the Gospel

Key words and phrases: Hail, full of grace! The Lord is with you; you shall name; nothing will be impossible for God; May it be done to me

To the point: Gabriel greeted Mary with "Hail, full of grace! The Lord is with you." Because of Mary's yes to God's plan of salvation, because of her Son's yes and his resurrection, *we* also share in God's fullness of grace and the risen Lord is *with us.* All this is a given. What is not a given is our yes. What is not a given is that we live our "name" as those baptized in the risen Son. What is not a given is that we accept "nothing will be impossible for God." What is a given is that we must make choices every day. What choices do we make?

Model Penitential Act

Presider: Gabriel appears to Mary and hails her as one "full of grace" and chosen to conceive the "Son of God." As we prepare to celebrate this liturgy, let us ask God for the strength to say yes in our own lives as Mary said yes . . . [pause]

Lord Jesus, you were conceived by the power of the Holy Spirit: Lord . . .

Christ Jesus, you are holy, the Son of God: Christ . . .

Lord Jesus, you are the Savior who brings Life to all: Lord . . .

Model Universal Prayer (Prayer of the Faithful)

Presider: Our loving God hears our prayers and grants us our needs.

Response:

Lord, hear our prayer.

Cantor:

we pray to the Lord,

That all members of the church may say yes to God and participate in God's plan of salvation . . . [pause]

That all people in the world come to know that they are graced by God . . . [pause]

That those who are poor and in need may receive strength through the intercession of Mary . . . [pause]

That each of us here may live more faithfully our baptismal promises and our identity as members of the Body of Christ . . . [pause]

Presider: O saving God, you grace us with risen Life in your Son. Hear these our prayers that one day we might enjoy the fullness of that Life with you. We pray through your risen Son, Jesus Christ our Lord. **Amen.**

FOR REFLECTION

• Mary is full of grace because . . . I am full of grace when . . .

• Mary's yes cost her . . . My yes to God costs me . . .

• The most difficult choice I face each day is . . . The easiest choice I make is . . .

Homily Points

• Mary was confronted by Gabriel with these startling announcements: she is "full of grace"; the "Lord is with" her; she has "found favor with God"; she "will conceive . . . and bear a son"; the Child "will be called Son of the Most High"; her relative Elizabeth has "conceived a son in her old age." In humility and trust, Mary utters, "May it be done to me." She made her choice.

• The disciples were also confronted with startling events, and their response at first was, "How can this be"? How often in his resurrection appearances Jesus told the disciples not to be afraid, just as Gabriel told Mary not to be afraid. At the annunciation Mary put aside any fear and any lack of understanding when she said yes to a personal future that would chart the future of all humankind. By opening her womb she opened the way for the opening of a tomb that should leave us forever unafraid. And "full of grace." And having the risen Lord with us. Mary made her choice. Now we must make ours.

SPIRITUALITY

GOSPEL ACCLAMATION

R̸. Alleluia, alleluia.
Christ is risen, creator of all;
he has shown pity on all people.
R̸. Alleluia, alleluia.

Gospel   John 21:1-19; L48C

At that time, Jesus revealed himself
    again to his disciples at the Sea of
    Tiberias.
He revealed himself in this way.
Together were Simon Peter,
    Thomas called Didymus,
    Nathanael from Cana in Galilee,
    Zebedee's sons, and two
        others of his disciples.
Simon Peter said to them,
    "I am going fishing."
They said to him, "We also
    will come with you."
So they went out and got into the
    boat,
    but that night they caught
        nothing.
When it was already dawn, Jesus was
    standing on the shore;
    but the disciples did not realize that it
        was Jesus.
Jesus said to them, "Children, have you
    caught anything to eat?"
They answered him, "No."
So he said to them, "Cast the net over the
    right side of the boat
    and you will find something."
So they cast it, and were not able to pull
    it in
    because of the number of fish.
So the disciple whom Jesus loved said to
    Peter, "It is the Lord."
When Simon Peter heard that it was the
    Lord,
    he tucked in his garment, for he was
        lightly clad,
    and jumped into the sea.
The other disciples came in the boat,
    for they were not far from shore, only
        about a hundred yards,
    dragging the net with the fish.

Continued in Appendix A, pp. 299–300.

Reflecting on the Gospel

Sometimes people on diets figure that a good way to cut calories and lose weight is to begin early in the morning and skip breakfast. However, nutritionists tell us that breakfast is the most important meal of the day. Breakfast gives us the personal jolt we need to get ourselves going with school or work or whatever; a balanced, nutritious breakfast also jolts our metabolism and gives us energy. After the resurrection, the disciples need a jolt. They cannot return to their former way of living. They have encountered Jesus during his earthly ministry. Now they encounter the risen Christ and are invited to share in his ongoing ministry.

This Sunday's gospel is one in which the word "breakfast" occurs (twice). This is the only occurrence of the word in all of Scripture! It is early in the morning—"already dawn." The right time for breakfast with all its advantages. The disciples have been out fishing and, upon returning to shore, Jesus asks them, "have you caught anything to eat?" Their answer was a simple, unqualified "No." No fish, no breakfast. Not so! Jesus invites them, "Come, have breakfast." It is as though Jesus knows the disciples need a jolt—they need to be tugged out of their familiar routine and transformed. They need the spiritual nutrition of encounter and belief for them to declare their love and follow with fidelity.

This gospel details the transformation made possible by the risen Christ. Disciples net a great number of fish after a catch-less night. Peter jumps impetuously into the sea instead of staying in the boat. Peter thrice declares his love, supplanting his triple denial—a love that is declared "[w]hen they had finished breakfast," after Peter is fortified by the gift of breakfast bread and fish, but even more so by the gift of encounter with the risen Christ. The Resurrection transforms the way things are. The risen Christ transforms the way we are, enabling us to obey his ongoing invitation, "Follow me." We are fortified by Jesus' risen Presence, by his invitation to follow, by his own love for us that transforms our love into faithfulness and fruitfulness. Risen Life fortifies us for the transformation needed on our discipleship journey of seeing-believing. Risen Life is given to us by Christ, but we must also seek it. Risen Life is a gift, but we must also grasp it.

Living the Paschal Mystery

Risen Life has its demand—we must eat breakfast with the risen Christ! That is, we must open ourselves to be fortified by all the gifts given to us so that our follow-response is energetic, sustained, and fruitful. Jesus gives us all the nourishment we need in order to meet the demands of daily discipleship. Accepting the nourishment that Jesus offers means that by following him we ourselves become his risen Presence, those who lead others to him. Every day we must take care that our actions announce Jesus' gift of nourishment at the same time that they speak of his goodness and care.

Leading others to Jesus doesn't mean doing big things; it means doing the little things well and so reflect the risen Life dwelling within us. It might mean once a week sitting down and having breakfast with our family. It might mean serving in a soup kitchen once a month. It might mean regularly contributing food gifts for the poor to be brought up during the presentation of gifts at Mass. No matter what our act of love, or when, it always means saying yes to Jesus and to risen Life.

Focusing the Gospel

Key words and phrases: Jesus revealed himself, It is the Lord, do you love me, I love you, Follow me

To the point: This gospel depicts the transformation made possible by the risen Christ. Disciples net a great number of fish after a catch-less night. Peter jumps impetuously into the sea instead of staying in the boat. Peter thrice declares his love, supplanting his triple denial. The resurrection transforms the way things are. The risen Christ transforms the way we are, enabling us to obey his ongoing invitation, "Follow me."

Connecting the Gospel

to the first reading: In face of the Sanhedrin's opposition, Peter boldly declares, "We must obey God rather than men." There is no doubt in his mind or hesitation in his behavior what it means to fulfill faithfully the invitation Jesus extends in the gospel, "Follow me."

to experience: Human beings tend to resist change and often need an outside stimulus to move forward. This is even more true about discipleship. Fortunately, Jesus stands ever on the seashore of life beckoning us to embrace the new Life he offers.

Connecting the Responsorial Psalm

to the readings: Although probably written before the Babylonian exile, the superscription or "title" given to Psalm 30—"A song for the dedication of the Temple" (NABRE)—indicates that it came to be used at Chanukah, the annual festival commemorating the reconsecration of the temple after it had been desecrated by the Seleucid army. The psalm is a song of thanksgiving to God for restoration after destruction.

What is the restoration we celebrate this Sunday? Most obviously Jesus' resurrection from death. But also Peter's restoration to loving relationship with Jesus after his denial of him before the passion (gospel). Once fearful of speaking up in Jesus' name, Peter now rejoices in the very suffering which doing so will bring him (first reading). With joy he joins the crowds in heaven who cry out in praise of the "Lamb that was slain" (second reading). In singing Psalm 30 we make Peter's restoration our restoration. We celebrate that we, too, have been "brought . . . up from the netherworld" of sin, infidelity, and fear of death to a new life of courageous witness to the power of Jesus' resurrection.

to psalmist preparation: In singing this responsorial psalm you not only celebrate deliverance from death, but also accept the mission of proclaiming what God has done. The apostles accepted this mission knowing full well what it would cost (first reading). What is the cost to you? What is the reward?

**ASSEMBLY &
FAITH-SHARING GROUPS**

- What in me needs to be transformed by risen Life is . . .
- I encounter the risen Lord when . . . This encounter means . . .
- At this point in my life following Jesus is leading me to . . .

PRESIDERS

I lead others to encounter the risen Lord and embrace transformation when I . . .

DEACONS

When I tend Jesus' flock out of genuine love my service is like . . .

HOSPITALITY MINISTERS

My manner of greeting those coming to liturgy helps them be open to the transformation liturgy invites when I . . .

MUSIC MINISTERS

I show forth in my music making how I am choosing to follow the risen Lord by . . .

ALTAR MINISTERS

My serving at the altar is an encounter with the risen Lord when . . . He transforms me by . . .

LECTORS

The manner of my proclamation calls the assembly to follow the risen Lord more faithfully when I . . .

**EXTRAORDINARY MINISTERS
OF HOLY COMMUNION**

The ways I feed and tend to the risen Lord's flock in my family are . . . in my parish are . . .

✠ CELEBRATION

Model Rite for the Blessing and Sprinkling of Water

Presider: Dear friends, as we ask God to bless this water, may it remind us of our baptismal commitment to follow the risen Lord faithfully as his disciples . . . [pause]

[*continue with* The Roman Missal, *Appendix II*]

Homily Points

• There were the Twelve. Seven went fishing. Judas was dead. Where were the others? Where are we? What transformation must happen in order to hear Jesus' call to follow him and remain faithful as his disciples?

• The risen Lord stands on the shore, invites the disciples who had gone fishing to breakfast with him, and challenges them to follow him. He invites them to be transformed from feeling separated from him to encountering him, from confusion to understanding, from being fishermen to becoming shepherds. How does the risen Lord now call us to transformation? to follow him?

• The risen Lord stands on the shore of all our activity waiting to reveal to us the depths of what we cannot find on our own, the depths of who we can become. Risen Life is not found by going back to who we used to be and where we were. Risen Life is only found by continuing to follow the risen Lord in new directions, wherever he leads us. Even where we might "not want to go."

Model Universal Prayer (Prayer of the Faithful)

Presider: Jesus tells the fishermen disciples to cast their nets again, and they catch a great number of fish. Trusting in God's abundant providence, we lift up our prayers.

Response:

Lord, hear our prayer.

Cantor:

we pray to the Lord,

That all members of the church might love the risen Lord with all their hearts and follow him faithfully to abundant Life . . . [pause]

That world leaders shepherd their people to freedom, justice, and peace . . . [pause]

That all those in any need share in the abundance the resurrection offers . . . [pause]

That the newly baptized continue to be faithful to their call to follow the risen Lord . . . [pause]

That each of us here daily live the joy that the gift of Easter Life brings . . . [pause]

Presider: Saving God, you give us new Life through the resurrection of your Son. Through our prayers may we all share more abundantly in this risen Life and live the Gospel more faithfully. We ask this through this same risen Son, Jesus Christ our Lord. **Amen.**

COLLECT

Let us pray.

Pause for silent prayer

May your people exult for ever, O God,
in renewed youthfulness of spirit,
so that, rejoicing now in the restored glory
    of our adoption,
we may look forward in confident hope
to the rejoicing of the day of resurrection.
Through our Lord Jesus Christ, your Son,
who lives and reigns with you in the unity
    of the Holy Spirit,
one God, for ever and ever. **Amen.**

FIRST READING

Acts 5:27-32, 40b-41

When the captain and the court officers had
        brought the apostles in
    and made them stand before the
        Sanhedrin,
    the high priest questioned them,
    "We gave you strict orders, did we not,
    to stop teaching in that name?
Yet you have filled Jerusalem with your
        teaching
    and want to bring this man's blood
        upon us."
But Peter and the apostles said in reply,
    "We must obey God rather than men.
The God of our ancestors raised Jesus,
    though you had him killed by hanging
        him on a tree.
God exalted him at his right hand as
        leader and savior
    to grant Israel repentance and
        forgiveness of sins.
We are witnesses of these things,
    as is the Holy Spirit whom God has given
        to those who obey him."

The Sanhedrin ordered the apostles
    to stop speaking in the name of Jesus,
    and dismissed them.
So they left the presence of the Sanhedrin,
    rejoicing that they had been found
        worthy
    to suffer dishonor for the sake of the
        name.

RESPONSORIAL PSALM

Ps 30:2, 4, 5-6, 11-12, 13

℟. (2a) I will praise you, Lord, for you have rescued me.

or

℟. Alleluia.

I will extol you, O Lord, for you drew me
    clear
    and did not let my enemies rejoice over
    me.
O Lord, you brought me up from the
    netherworld;
    you preserved me from among those
    going down into the pit.

R̶̸. I will praise you, Lord, for you have
rescued me.
    or
R̶̸. Alleluia.

Sing praise to the Lord, you his faithful
    ones,
    and give thanks to his holy name.
For his anger lasts but a moment;
    a lifetime, his good will.
At nightfall, weeping enters in,
    but with the dawn, rejoicing.

R̶̸. I will praise you, Lord, for you have
rescued me.
    or
R̶̸. Alleluia.

Hear, O Lord, and have pity on me;
    O Lord, be my helper.
You changed my mourning into dancing;
    O Lord, my God, forever will I give you
    thanks.

R̶̸. I will praise you, Lord, for you have
rescued me.
    or
R̶̸. Alleluia.

SECOND READING
Rev 5:11-14

I, John, looked and heard the voices of
    many angels
    who surrounded the throne
    and the living creatures and the elders.
They were countless in number, and they
    cried out in a loud voice:
        "Worthy is the Lamb that was slain
        to receive power and riches,
            wisdom and strength,
        honor and glory and blessing."
Then I heard every creature in heaven and
    on earth
    and under the earth and in the sea,
    everything in the universe, cry out:
        "To the one who sits on the throne and
        to the Lamb
            be blessing and honor, glory and
            might,
            forever and ever."
The four living creatures answered,
    "Amen,"
    and the elders fell down and worshiped.

✠ CATECHESIS

About Liturgy

Eucharist is God's gift asking for a response: Each time we share in the eucharistic banquet we are invited to be aware of God's gracious gifts to us. The gift of Eucharist is already a share in Christ's risen Life. By eating and drinking Christ's very Body and Blood we are transformed into being more perfect members of the Body of Christ. This means that we follow Christ more perfectly since we are more identified with him—follow him even to "where [we] do not want to go." Thus, the gift of Eucharist requires of us a response in kind. Jesus' gift of self to us means that we respond with the gift of self to others.

Far from a privatized action, Eucharist is the action of the whole church through which we share in God's abundant Life and are called to bring that Life to others. Integral to Eucharist is a call to love and just actions on behalf of the whole world. One way to evaluate the quality of our eucharistic celebrations is not by simply focusing on the elements of the rite itself (as important as that task is!), but by focusing on how Christ's Life is lived in the community. If the liturgical assembly doesn't become more loving, more charitable, more just by receiving Jesus' self-gift of heavenly food, then clearly those celebrations are not doing what they are supposed to do. Suitable questions to ask by way of evaluation: How do we visibly love one another more? How are we making a difference in our neighborhoods, city, nation, world? Do we relate to the general intercessions as universal prayers (prayers of the faithful) that extend beyond the celebration of Eucharist and demand a commitment of life from us?

About Liturgical Music

Music suggestions: Bob Hurd's "Two Were Bound for Emmaus" (BB, JS3) retells the stories of the risen Jesus coming to both the disheartened disciples on the way to Emmaus and the discouraged Peter and his companions in this Sunday's gospel. Verse 4 is particularly expressive of the weariness and weakness we often feel in discipleship and the need to keep our eyes turned toward the risen Jesus who will support us: "When the road makes us weary, when our labor seems but loss, when the fire of faith weakens and too high seems the cost, let the Church turn to its risen Lord, who for us bore the cross, and we'll find our hearts burning at the sound of his voice." This hymn would work well during the preparation of the gifts. A good choice for Communion would be Martin Willett's "Behold the Lamb" (G3, BB, JS3), which integrates our sharing in the glory of the Lamb (see second reading) with our participation in eating and drinking his Body and Blood.

SPIRITUALITY

GOSPEL ACCLAMATION
John 10:14

R̸. Alleluia, alleluia.
I am the good shepherd, says the Lord;
I know my sheep, and mine know me.
R̸. Alleluia, alleluia.

Gospel

John 10:27-30; L51C

Jesus said:
"My sheep hear my voice;
   I know them, and they follow me.
I give them eternal life, and they shall
      never perish.
No one can take them out of my hand.
My Father, who has given them to me,
      is greater than all,
   and no one can take them out of the
         Father's hand.
The Father and I are one."

Reflecting on the Gospel

We sometimes hear it said that to give is already to receive. In the very gift-giving, the giver receives intangible but very real benefits in return. Nor do the benefits depend on the size or worth of the gift. Generous, loving gift-giving deepens relationships, strengthens commitment, promotes mutual action. Gift-giving creates memories of goodness, establishes a habit of self-giving, assures the gift-giver of sharing in the dignity of the receiver. The focus of this gospel is giving, giving, giving. The Father gives us to Jesus as his flock. We give Jesus our attentive listening and faithful following. Jesus gives us eternal Life. There are no qualifying words in this gospel at all, no "ifs" about the giving. This is simply the way living risen Life is. Jesus gives us the gift of risen Life; we give Jesus the gift of ourselves.

The gospel conveys Jesus' great, tender care and concern for his "sheep." This care does not keep his followers from "violent abuse" (first reading) or "great distress" (second reading). It does assure them of protection in the midst of persecution ("No one can take them out of my hand") and of eternal Life ("they shall never perish"). But this assurance only comes when we followers of Jesus "hear [his] voice" and live out of the personal relationship God offers us. It comes when we give the gift of ourselves in hearing and following.

We follow first by listening. The call to follow is a call to faithful obedience (the root word for obedience means "to hear"). In other words, hearing Jesus—heeding his voice—is already an act of following. Heeding Jesus' voice is already our own participation in proclaiming the Gospel. But probably most importantly, hearing Jesus' voice is already our participation in risen Life. Ultimately this promise of risen Life is the reassurance and care that Jesus offers: by hearing Jesus' voice and following him we will not perish. No better care than this could the Good Shepherd give us as gift!

Living the Paschal Mystery

Most of our reflections on the paschal mystery revolve around reminders that being plunged into the dying and rising mystery of Christ through our baptism means we must die to self if we wish to share in eternal Life. We look for ordinary opportunities in our daily living to die to self and thus transform what appears to be ordinary, human actions into extensions of the ministry of the Good Shepherd himself. For example, comforting the sick and dying isn't simply a caring human action; in the context of our baptismal commitment it is an expression of Jesus' love for us and the dignity of the other as member of the Body of Christ.

This is true and surely the heart of the mystery. This Sunday, however, we might turn this around and rest a bit in what the Good Shepherd offers us when we live the paschal mystery: eternal Life, the gift of the assurance that we will never perish. For all our efforts to die to self for the good of others, they do not equal the gift of self that Jesus gives us. Sometimes we are so caught up in the effort of dying that we do forget that risen Life is already within us and among us. This is a good Sunday to bask in Jesus' care and protection; listen to his voice calling us to his loving, embracing hands; and rejoice in the gift of goodness showered upon us who are faithful to his call. This, too, is living the paschal mystery. Giving the gift of ourselves to others, to Jesus is living the paschal mystery.

Focusing the Gospel

Key words and phrases: hear, follow, give them eternal life, given them to me

To the point: The focus of this gospel is giving, giving, giving. The Father gives us to Jesus as his flock. We give Jesus our attentive listening and faithful following. Jesus gives us eternal Life. There are no qualifying words in this gospel at all, no "ifs" about the giving. This is simply the way living risen Life is.

Connecting the Gospel

to the first reading: While the gospel presumes that all who are part of the Good Shepherd's flock listen to his word and follow him, this is not so in the first reading. Paul and Barnabas are faithfully preaching the Gospel, but some who hear reject the word. The verdict? They are "unworthy of eternal life."

to experience: Often, what is given in human relationships is qualified, explicitly or implicitly. For example, we might say to an unruly child, "If you settle down, I'll give you a cookie." Another example: giving a birthday gift to a casual friend might convey the unspoken expectation that a gift be offered in return. The giving happening in the gospel, by contrast, is free, unconditional, and ongoing.

Connecting the Responsorial Psalm

to the readings: Psalm 100 is part of a set of psalms (Pss 93; 95–100) which celebrate God's sovereignty over all things. Peoples of the ancient Near East acclaimed a god powerful because of specific acts, the greatest of which was creation. The Israelites believed that God acted not only to create the world but also to create them as a people. All forces inimical to Israel as a community—from natural disasters to human enemies—quelled before the power of God, who arranged all events in the cosmos to support their coming together as a people.

In Christ God showed the ultimate creative power by overcoming death with resurrection. Out of this act God formed a new people beyond the boundaries of the community of Israel (first reading), a people "which no one could count, / from every nation, race, people, and tongue" (second reading). No powers of hell or destruction will prevail against this people, for it is God who leads and shepherds them (second reading, gospel). In singing Psalm 100 we proclaim who we are because of Christ's death and resurrection: a people created by God, protected by God, and called by God to eternal Life.

to psalmist preparation: The Israelites understood that God created them as a people and continually shepherded them. So, too, does the church recognize that she is created and shepherded by God. How have you experienced God's shepherding love for the church? How has God shepherded you as an individual disciple? In what way(s) does the church particularly need God's shepherding care today? In what way(s) do you?

ASSEMBLY & FAITH-SHARING GROUPS

- When I realize that the Father has given me to the risen Christ, I . . .
- I hear Jesus say to me . . . His words call me to . . .
- God unconditionally gives me . . . I unconditionally give to God . . . to others . . .

PRESIDERS

The risen Lord shepherds me to . . . I shepherd my parishioners to . . .

DEACONS

My service ministry is an unconditional giving when . . .

HOSPITALITY MINISTERS

My hospitality communicates to the assembly that the Good Shepherd "know[s] them" when . . .

MUSIC MINISTERS

My music making is a shepherding activity that opens the assembly to listen to Jesus' voice when . . .

ALTAR MINISTERS

My service is a giving of myself to the risen Christ in that . . . to my parishioners in that . . .

LECTORS

My manner of proclamation helps the assembly to hear and heed the voice of the Shepherd when . . .

EXTRAORDINARY MINISTERS OF HOLY COMMUNION

My manner of distributing Holy Communion helps others experience the care and concern of the Good Shepherd when . . .

CELEBRATION

Model Rite for the Blessing and Sprinkling of Water

Presider: Dear friends, this water we ask God to bless reminds us of our baptism when we became members of the Good Shepherd's flock. Let us open our hearts to the Good Shepherd and prepare ourselves to hear his voice and follow him more faithfully . . . [pause]

[*continue with* The Roman Missal, *Appendix II*]

Homily Points

• Charismatic leaders can sometimes be dangerous and destructive. For example, in 1978 Jim Jones led nine hundred people to commit mass suicide in Jonestown, Guyana. On the contrary, our Good Shepherd is a charismatic leader who is always life-giving, always trustworthy, always true to his promises.

• What a reassuring, hope-filled gospel! Every line engenders confidence because the Father has given us into the care of Jesus our Good Shepherd. Jesus affirms that we, his sheep, "hear [his] voice" and follow him. He gives us "eternal life" and gives the promise that no one can snatch us out of his hand. All this giving—no wonder we call him our Good Shepherd! To be possessed by the risen Christ is our greatest joy, our greatest hope, our greatest promise.

• Since nothing qualifies the Good Shepherd's commitment to and care of us, nothing ought to qualify our response. But being weak human beings, sometimes our response is far from perfect. Even then our Good Shepherd remains steadfast, caring for us and gently calling us back to him. Our source of confidence and hope is this Good Shepherd who never abandons his flock, who shares his risen Life with us, who never tires of loving us. This is *the* charismatic leader we can hear trustingly and follow confidently.

Model Universal Prayer (Prayer of the Faithful)

Presider: Our loving God shepherds us with care and protection and so we are confident that these needs we place before God will be heard.

Response:

Cantor:

That all members of the church hear the voice of the Good Shepherd and follow him with confidence and trust that he is leading us to eternal Life . . . [pause]

That leaders of nations shepherd their people with the justice and care that lead to peace and well-being . . . [pause]

That those who are perishing through sickness, depression, or hopelessness might be strengthened by the care and nearness of the Good Shepherd . . . [pause]

That each one of us here might shepherd others to hear and follow more faithfully the voice of the Good Shepherd . . . [pause]

Presider: Loving God, you shepherd your people with unfailing care. Hear these our prayers that one day we might all enjoy eternal Life with you. We ask this through our Good Shepherd and Savior, Jesus Christ our Lord. **Amen.**

COLLECT
Let us pray.

Pause for silent prayer

Almighty ever-living God,
lead us to a share in the joys of heaven,
so that the humble flock may reach
where the brave Shepherd has gone before.
Who lives and reigns with you in the unity
    of the Holy Spirit,
one God, for ever and ever. **Amen.**

FIRST READING
Acts 13:14, 43-52

Paul and Barnabas continued on from
    Perga
    and reached Antioch in Pisidia.
On the sabbath they entered the
    synagogue and took their seats.
Many Jews and worshipers who were
    converts to Judaism
    followed Paul and Barnabas, who spoke
      to them
    and urged them to remain faithful to the
      grace of God.

On the following sabbath almost the whole
    city gathered
    to hear the word of the Lord.
When the Jews saw the crowds, they were
    filled with jealousy
    and with violent abuse contradicted
      what Paul said.
Both Paul and Barnabas spoke out boldly
    and said,
    "It was necessary that the word of God
      be spoken to you first,
    but since you reject it
    and condemn yourselves as unworthy
      of eternal life,
    we now turn to the Gentiles.
For so the Lord has commanded us,
    I have made you a light to the Gentiles,
    that you may be an instrument of
      salvation
    to the ends of the earth."

The Gentiles were delighted when they
    heard this
    and glorified the word of the Lord.
All who were destined for eternal life came
    to believe,
    and the word of the Lord continued to
      spread
    through the whole region.

The Jews, however, incited the women of
    prominence who were worshipers
and the leading men of the city,
    stirred up a persecution against Paul
    and Barnabas,
and expelled them from their territory.
So they shook the dust from their feet in
    protest against them,
    and went to Iconium.
The disciples were filled with joy and the
    Holy Spirit.

RESPONSORIAL PSALM
Ps 100:1-2, 3, 5

R̸. (3c) We are his people, the sheep of his
flock.
    or
R̸. Alleluia.

Sing joyfully to the LORD, all you lands;
    serve the LORD with gladness;
    come before him with joyful song.

R̸. We are his people, the sheep of his
flock.
    or
R̸. Alleluia.

Know that the LORD is God;
    he made us, his we are;
    his people, the flock he tends.

R̸. We are his people, the sheep of his
flock.
    or
R̸. Alleluia.

The LORD is good:
    his kindness endures forever,
    and his faithfulness, to all generations.

R̸. We are his people, the sheep of his
flock.
    or
R̸. Alleluia.

SECOND READING
Rev 7:9, 14b-17

See Appendix A, p. 300.

About Liturgy

Hinge Sunday in Easter Lectionary: Traditionally known as "Good Shepherd Sunday," this Fourth Sunday of Easter is something of a hinge Sunday. On the one hand, the image of a loving, caring shepherd bids us look back to the first three Sundays of Easter on which the gospels all record appearance accounts of the risen Jesus; these Sundays assure us that Jesus is alive and continues to be present to us, teach us, and care for us. On the other hand, the image of a loving, caring shepherd bids us look forward to the next three Sundays and Pentecost; Jesus prepares us to be disciples by "knowing" us. No matter what demands our discipleship make on us (at least the demand of dying to self), we are assured on this Sunday (as on all Sundays) that Jesus will never let us "perish." Such reassurance gives the hope and courage we need to be faithful to Jesus' call to follow.

Hands as sacramental symbol: Jesus reassures us in this gospel that "[n]o one can take [us] out of [his] hand." Because using the hands is often such a powerful gesture, it ought to come as no surprise to us that hands are used as a symbol in all of our Catholic sacraments. Four of the sacraments (baptism, confirmation, sacrament of the sick, holy orders) expressly call for an imposition of the hands that includes actual physical touch. The other three sacraments (Eucharist, penance, marriage) use extended hands (and, sometimes, in face-to-face confession the confessor might actually touch the head of the penitent during absolution). This latter gesture of extended hands usually signifies an *epiclesis*, which means calling down the Holy Spirit in blessing and/or consecration. In all cases the symbolic gesture with hands conveys the intimacy with which God chooses to be connected with us.

About Liturgical Music

Music suggestions: In last Sunday's gospel Jesus already began calling us, the church, to ministry ("Feed my lambs"). In the coming Sundays his call to take up his mission will become even more explicit. This Sunday's gospel places the call to discipleship and mission within the Good Shepherd's promise of his Presence, his protection, and his gift of eternal Life. Good Shepherd songs abound (for example, "My Shepherd Will Supply My Need"; "Shepherd of Souls, Refresh and Bless"; "The King of Love My Shepherd Is"; "Shepherd Me, O God"; "With a Shepherd's Care"; "Shepherd of My Heart"). Most would be suitable for either the preparation of the gifts or Communion. With so much repertoire available, however, it is important not to overload the liturgy with too many Good Shepherd songs. One is sufficient; two would be appropriate only if their texts complement rather than repeat one another.

SPIRITUALITY

GOSPEL ACCLAMATION
John 13:34

R̸. Alleluia, alleluia.
I give you a new commandment, says the Lord:
love one another as I have loved you.
R̸. Alleluia, alleluia.

Gospel

John 13:31-33a, 34-35; L54C

**When Judas had left them, Jesus said,
"Now is the Son of Man glorified, and
God is glorified in him.
If God is glorified in him,
God will also glorify him in himself,
and God will glorify him at once.
My children, I will be with you only a
little while longer.
I give you a new commandment: love
one another.
As I have loved you, so you also should
love one another.
This is how all will know that you are
my disciples,
if you have love for one another."**

Reflecting on the Gospel

When we love someone very much, any leave-taking always brings sadness. When the absence is prolonged or feared permanent, leave-taking can be mighty heartrending. Children and spouse with tears streaming down their faces cling to a soldier leaving for a tour of duty. Family members move slowly, looking back over their shoulders at the hospital bed when leaving the room of someone who has been critically injured in an accident. Graduations include leave-takings, and possibly never seeing friends again. Leave-taking is part of everyone's life. It reminds us that we human beings are fragile, that our earthly life is transitory, that the only sure and permanent reality is the abiding love of the risen Lord and the glory that is the outcome of our living his commandment of love. This gospel is about leave-taking—one leads to betrayal and despair; the other leads to an invitation to participate in the love-Life of the One who willingly embraces death and in that embrace conquers it for himself and for us.

Two departures are noted in this gospel: that of Judas ("When Judas had left") and that of Jesus ("I will be with you only a little while longer"). Judas's departure initiates the events of Jesus' passion, death, and resurrection. Jesus' imminent departure initiates his giving the disciples the commandment to love as he has loved. Jesus' passion and death is the full revelation to us of what it means to love as Jesus loved. Love means giving one's life for others. It is the full revelation of how we are to love: not counting the cost, but always looking to the glory that is the outcome of deep and abiding love. This is God's glory. This is Jesus' glory. This is our glory. Jesus' resurrection is the full revelation of this glory.

Jesus doesn't ask of us anything that he himself hasn't already undertaken to the fullest: the Good Friday-Easter events make clear the extent of Jesus' love for us—he will lay down his very life so that we might have a share in his risen Life and glory. As disciples we are commanded to love as the risen Lord loved. If our love is to imitate his, then our love must also include the willingness to lay down our lives for others. The kind of love that Jesus commands leads to self-emptying dying to self.

Glory and love are promised to us—but we share in them only if we imitate Jesus' self-giving way of living. As the gospel says, Jesus was with the disciples "only a little while longer"; Jesus departed. However, he remains with us. Through our own self-giving love we continue his mission of loving others unto salvation whereby God is glorified. Loving one another, then, isn't just a nice idea. Loving one another is the very way we participate in Jesus' saving mission and make him present. Our loving others as Jesus loves us assures us that this love leads not to leave-taking, but to the glory of the fullness of Presence and Life.

Living the Paschal Mystery

In so many ways we already act out of the love that Jesus commands in this gospel. We need only to do the everyday things we are already doing with new meaning: we share in Jesus' mission when we love others as he loves us. If, however, an examination of our lives suggests that perhaps we are not so self-giving and loving as Jesus, then this gospel is an invitation to love more completely. What is at stake is a share in Jesus' everlasting Life and glory. This Life and glory is so worth loving for!

Focusing the Gospel

Key words and phrases: When Judas had left, glorified, glorify, I will be with you only a little while longer, As I have loved you, love one another

To the point: Two departures are noted in this gospel: that of Judas ("When Judas had left") and that of Jesus ("I will be with you only a little while longer"). Judas's departure initiates the events of Jesus' passion, death, and resurrection. Jesus' imminent departure initiates his giving the disciples the commandment to love as he has loved. Jesus' passion and death is the full revelation to us of what it means to love as Jesus loved. His resurrection is the full revelation of God's glory. Love means giving one's life for others. This is God's glory. This is Jesus' glory. This is our glory.

Connecting the Gospel

to the second reading: We cooperate with God to bring about a "new heaven and a new earth" when we fulfill Jesus' new commandment to love in the measure that Jesus loved—by giving our all.

to experience: It is so easy to misunderstand both "glory" and "love." Misdirected glory is self-aggrandizement; misdirected love is self-serving. Jesus teaches us that true glory shines forth God's Presence, evidence of self-giving love.

Connecting the Responsorial Psalm

to the readings: In this responsorial psalm we call God to let divine works reveal the splendor of God's kingdom "for all ages." This kingdom is governed by God with graciousness, mercy, kindness, and compassion (psalm). This kingdom is the Good News Paul and Barnabas successfully preached to the Gentiles (first reading). This kingdom is the new heaven and new earth envisioned by John (second reading). In this kingdom we love one another as Jesus has loved us (gospel). We are capable of loving in this way because of the work of God in us, who has re-created us and chooses to dwell with us (second reading). When we let God do this work in us, we praise God's name, we reveal the glory of God's kingdom, we become God's greatest work.

to psalmist preparation: Your singing of this responsorial psalm needs to invite the assembly to see themselves as a work of God, a new creation, giving praise. What might you do this week to help yourself see them in this way? to see yourself in this way? How is this way of seeing a living out of Jesus' commandment to love one another as he has loved us?

ASSEMBLY & FAITH-SHARING GROUPS

- I depart from Jesus when . . . What draws me back to him is . . .
- Love is . . .
- Loving one another as Jesus loved glorifies God because . . . My love glorifies God . . . others . . . myself . . .

PRESIDERS

My ministry reveals my love for Jesus whenever I . . . It reveals my love for the people I serve when . . .

DEACONS

My serving ministry glorifies . . . because . . .

HOSPITALITY MINISTERS

My hospitality reveals that I love as Jesus loves when I . . .

MUSIC MINISTERS

My music making reveals the beauty of God's glory when . . .

ALTAR MINISTERS

When my service is an expression of love it looks like . . . When it is not done in love it looks like . . .

LECTORS

When I take to heart Jesus' command to love as he loves, my proclamation becomes . . .

EXTRAORDINARY MINISTERS OF HOLY COMMUNION

Holy Communion is Jesus' self-giving love and glory made visible in that . . .

Model Rite for the Blessing and Sprinkling of Water

Presider: Dear sisters and brothers, this water reminds us of our baptism and the full measure of love and Life God offers us. May our sprinkling of this water call us to self-giving love for which Jesus is the model . . . [pause]

[*continue with* The Roman Missal, *Appendix II*]

Homily Points

• Departures often indicate an end, a finality, a closure. Judas's departure presaged his end, his finality, his closure. In contrast, Jesus' imminent departure presaged a beginning, an opening, a new creation. His death and resurrection opens us to a new way of being: to love as he has loved; to glorify God as he glorified God. Self-giving love begets glory.

• In the gospel Jesus calls the disciples to obey his new commandment to love one another as he has loved. It is only this kind of self-giving love that makes visible the glory of God. It is only this kind of self-giving love that makes death not a finality, but a tomb opening to risen Life.

• Jesus loves us to death, through death, beyond death. To receive Jesus' love, we must open the many tombs that imprison us and cut off our life: the tombs of fear, anxiety, selfishness, doubt, pride, greed, hatred, anger, deceit. What opens these tombs is our acceptance of Jesus' self-giving love. Self-giving love means giving our own life for others. This is God's glory. This is Jesus' glory. This is our glory. Will we love this way?

Model Universal Prayer (Prayer of the Faithful)

Presider: Jesus commands us to love as he has loved. Let us pray to be faithful to this command.

Response:

Cantor:

That all members of the church live faithfully Jesus' command to love one another as he loves us . . . [pause]

That all peoples glorify God by selfless caring for one another . . . [pause]

That those lacking love or deprived of dignity be embraced and lifted up by the love of the faithful followers of the risen Christ . . . [pause]

That those received into the church during this Easter season shine with the glory of the risen Life in which they share . . . [pause]

That each of us grow in faithful discipleship by encountering more fully the risen Christ in our daily living . . . [pause]

Presider: Loving God, you always hear our prayers and grant our needs. Help us to take up your Son's command to love so that our world might reflect more fully your glory. We ask this through that same Son, Jesus Christ our Lord. **Amen.**

COLLECT
Let us pray.
Pause for silent prayer

Almighty ever-living God,
constantly accomplish the Paschal Mystery within us,
that those you were pleased to make new in Holy Baptism
may, under your protective care, bear much fruit
and come to the joys of life eternal.
Through our Lord Jesus Christ, your Son,
who lives and reigns with you in the unity of the Holy Spirit,
one God, for ever and ever. **Amen.**

FIRST READING
Acts 14:21-27

After Paul and Barnabas had proclaimed the good news to that city
and made a considerable number of disciples,
they returned to Lystra and to Iconium and to Antioch.
They strengthened the spirits of the disciples
and exhorted them to persevere in the faith, saying,
"It is necessary for us to undergo many hardships
to enter the kingdom of God."
They appointed elders for them in each church and,
with prayer and fasting, commended them to the Lord
in whom they had put their faith.
Then they traveled through Pisidia and reached Pamphylia.
After proclaiming the word at Perga they went down to Attalia.
From there they sailed to Antioch,
where they had been commended to the grace of God
for the work they had now accomplished.
And when they arrived, they called the church together
and reported what God had done with them
and how he had opened the door of faith to the Gentiles.

RESPONSORIAL PSALM
Ps 145:8-9, 10-11, 12-13

R̸. (cf. 1) I will praise your name forever, my king and my God.
or
R̸. Alleluia.

The LORD is gracious and merciful,
   slow to anger and of great kindness.
The LORD is good to all
   and compassionate toward all his
      works.
R⁊. I will praise your name forever, my
king and my God.
   or
R⁊. Alleluia.

Let all your works give you thanks,
   O LORD,
   and let your faithful ones bless you.
Let them discourse of the glory of your
      kingdom
   and speak of your might.
R⁊. I will praise your name forever, my
king and my God.
   or
R⁊. Alleluia.

Let them make known your might to the
      children of Adam,
   and the glorious splendor of your
      kingdom.
Your kingdom is a kingdom for all ages,
   and your dominion endures through all
      generations.
R⁊. I will praise your name forever, my
king and my God.
   or
R⁊. Alleluia.

SECOND READING
Rev 21:1-5a

Then I, John, saw a new heaven and a new
      earth.
The former heaven and the former earth
      had passed away,
   and the sea was no more.
I also saw the holy city, a new Jerusalem,
   coming down out of heaven from God,
   prepared as a bride adorned for her
      husband.
I heard a loud voice from the throne
      saying,
   "Behold, God's dwelling is with the
      human race.
He will dwell with them and they will be
      his people
   and God himself will always be with
      them as their God.
He will wipe every tear from their eyes,
   and there shall be no more death or
      mourning, wailing or pain,
   for the old order has passed away."

The One who sat on the throne said,
   "Behold, I make all things new."

CATECHESIS

About Liturgy

The dismissal at the end of Mass: At the end of every Mass we are blessed, then sent forth to live what we have celebrated. It is too easy to be eager to leave church and get on with the rest of our day; we can readily miss the real import of this very short but important rite. One of the dismissal formulae in *The Roman Missal* is, "Go in peace, glorifying the Lord by your life." This speaks directly to this Sunday's gospel. We glorify the Lord when we follow through on his new commandment of love. This love is not the fleeting and shallow love projected so often by the entertainment industry, but is the life-giving love that Jesus himself modeled for us. Our daily living must be characterized by the kind of self-giving love that brings us to put the good of others before our own self-interests. It is the kind of love that prompts us to empty ourselves for the sake of others, no matter what the cost. When we love as Jesus loves us, then every moment of every day glorifies God.

About Liturgical Music

Music suggestions: An excellent hymn speaking of the new creation ushered in by Christ's resurrection is "We Know That Christ Is Raised and Dies No More" (OF, WC, SS). The text speaks of sharing by water in Jesus' death and new Life. Especially apropos is verse 4, "A new creation comes to life and grows As Christ's new body takes on flesh and blood. The universe restored and whole will sing." This hymn would be appropriate for the entrance procession or for the sprinkling rite. Another hymn relating to the new creation is Brian Wren's "Christ Is Risen! Shout Hosanna!" (G3, OF, SS, W4, WC, WS). The catchy, upbeat tune would make the hymn work well either for the entrance procession or as a song of praise after Communion.

The gospel reveals that a central part of the new creation in Christ is his command that we love one another as he has loved us. A setting of *Ubi Caritas* would be most appropriate for Communion, as would "Christians, Let Us Love One Another" (BB, JS3) and Michael Joncas's "No Greater Love" (G3, SS, W4). A good choice during the preparation of the gifts would be Herman Stuempfle's "Lord, Help Us Walk Your Servant Way" (HG, SS, W4), which makes specific from the life of Jesus what loving as he loved entails.

SPIRITUALITY

GOSPEL ACCLAMATION
John 14:23

Ry. Alleluia, alleluia.
Whoever loves me will keep my word, says the
      Lord,
and my Father will love him and we will
      come to him.
Ry. Alleluia, alleluia.

Gospel

John 14:23-29; L57C

Jesus said to his
      disciples:
   "Whoever loves me
      will keep my word,
   and my Father will love
      him,
   and we will come to him and
      make our dwelling with him.
Whoever does not love me does not
      keep my words;
   yet the word you hear is not mine
   but that of the Father who sent me.

"I have told you this while I am with
      you.
The Advocate, the Holy Spirit,
   whom the Father will send in my
      name,
   will teach you everything
   and remind you of all that I told you.
Peace I leave with you; my peace I give
      to you.
Not as the world gives do I give it to
      you.
Do not let your hearts be troubled or
      afraid.
You heard me tell you,
   'I am going away and I will come
      back to you.'
If you loved me,
   you would rejoice that I am going to
      the Father;
   for the Father is greater than I.
And now I have told you this before it
      happens,
   so that when it happens you may
      believe."

Reflecting on the Gospel

"Why?" the child asks when a parent gives an ultimatum about doing some-thing. "Because I said so," the parent answers. This has never been a very satisfactory answer for a child; we can imagine a teenager rolling the eyes in response. This answer doesn't give any explanation for doing what is asked, but simply states a chain of command, a line of authority. In this gospel Jesus' desire that we keep his words functions something like a "Because I said so."

Extraordinary gifts are given to us if we keep his words. His words rest on the authority of himself, his Father, and the Holy Spirit. This is about as high that a chain of command, a line of authority can get. It all rests on "If you love[ ] me."

To enable us to keep his word, Jesus promises us the gift of a divine indwelling—the Holy Spirit—through whom we are re-created as persons able to live and love as Jesus himself did. We are a new creation empowered to continue the mission of Jesus in peace and with fearlessness. To be created anew means that we share in the Life of the risen Lord—in a very real way, we share in Jesus' very identity. Indeed, this is the gift of baptism: that we are made members of the Body of Christ. Only because we share in Jesus' identity as members of his Body can we love as he does, truly keep his word, and carry on his saving mission.

Jesus' word is a promise of a new relationship with him and his Father, where God comes and dwells within us through the power of the Holy Spirit. We keep his word, therefore, when we embody in our living the fearlessness and peace of Jesus that are evidence of the Presence of the Spirit. We keep his word when we respond to indwelling divine Love with self-giving as modeled by Jesus. The truth and power of the word come from within, and it is the truth and power of the Holy Spirit. We are fearless not because of our own power, but because of the Spirit dwelling within us.

The word of Jesus we are to keep is his command to love as he loves us. Jesus' word, however, is not simply spoken—"Because I said so"—but is love-in-action. His love-in-action is the gift of the Spirit of peace, of untroubled hearts, of rejoicing, of believing. His love-in-action is ultimately the gift of the resurrection, of new Life and relationship with him. Our love-in-action flows from the gift of the Holy Spirit dwelling in us and teaching us to keep Jesus' word-command to love. Our love-in-action is risen Life-made-visible. Jesus' "Because I said so" is so much more than simply words. It is his own obedience to his Father, his own handing over his spirit, his own love-in-action. So must it be ours.

Living the Paschal Mystery

Living the paschal mystery is as demanding as loving with the same self-giving as Jesus, and as easy as responding to God's indwelling as an intimate Friend who is always with us, never forsakes us, and at all times is there for us giving care and strength. These Sundays before Pentecost when we cele-brate the gift of the Spirit are so important for our daily Christian living: they remind us that as disciples we never have to feel like the whole task of living the Gospel falls on our shoulders alone. God is always present, dwelling within us, to give us the strength we need to be faithful to Jesus' commands. Only in this way can our everyday lives be fruitful, can we keep Jesus' word as our own word, can we show forth Jesus' love-in-action.

Focusing the Gospel

Key words and phrases: keep my word, love, Holy Spirit, teach you everything, rejoice, believe

To the point: The word of Jesus we are to keep is his command to love as he loves us. Jesus' word, however, is not simply spoken, but is love-in-action. His love-in-action is the gift of the Spirit of peace, of untroubled hearts, of rejoicing, of believing. His love-in-action is ultimately the gift of the resurrection. Our love-in-action flows from the gift of the Holy Spirit dwelling in us and teaching us to keep Jesus' word-command to love. Our love-in-action is risen Life-made-visible.

Connecting the Gospel

to the second reading: The radiant vision of God's dwelling among us (see second reading) is realized when disciples take up the practical way of life Jesus commands in the gospel: keep his word-command to love. To take up this daunting way of life Jesus sends his Spirit.

to experience: Some word-commands coming from parents, employers, governments leave us resistant, resentful, and recalcitrant. The word-command of love coming from Jesus calls us to receptiveness, contentment, and obedience. Our positive response leads us to peace, untroubled hearts, rejoicing, believing.

Connecting the Responsorial Psalm

to the readings: Psalm 67 was a hymn of thanksgiving for a fruitful harvest. The Israelites prayed that God would extend these abundant blessings to all the earth. In this way all nations would know God's saving care and offer joyful praise. In the context of this Sunday's readings, Psalm 67 invites us to make our very way of living the abundant harvest God offers the world. When we love Jesus and keep his word, we move beyond the temptation to limit God's Presence and power to specific practices (first reading) and places (second reading). We become the very dwelling place of God on earth (gospel). Let us pray together that our manner of living and relating will make God's way "known upon earth" (psalm) and that through us all nations will come to know salvation.

to psalmist preparation: The harvest for which you praise God in this responsorial psalm is the salvation wrought through the death and resurrection of Christ. You pray that all nations will come to know this salvation. Who has helped you come to know and believe in it? To whom are you making it known?

ASSEMBLY & FAITH-SHARING GROUPS

- This Easter the word of Jesus that I am being called to keep is . . .
- The Holy Spirit is teaching me to . . .
- My love-in-action looks like . . .

PRESIDERS

When my spoken words are in line with Jesus' love-in-action, those who hear are moved to . . .

DEACONS

I embody the word of Jesus in my servant ministry when . . .

HOSPITALITY MINISTERS

Through my hospitality, I help people realize that God dwells within them by . . .

MUSIC MINISTERS

When my music making is love-in-action, it sounds like . . . the assembly hears . . . the assembly responds by . . .

ALTAR MINISTERS

My serving others makes visible my desire to live Jesus' word-command to love when I . . .

LECTORS

When I remember that Sacred Scripture is the Father's word given to us, my proclamation becomes . . . the assembly hears . . .

EXTRAORDINARY MINISTERS OF HOLY COMMUNION

When I live in the peace of the eucharistic Presence, my manner of distributing Holy Communion becomes . . .

CELEBRATION

Model Rite for the Blessing and Sprinkling of Water

Presider: Dear sisters and brothers, as we ask God to bless this water about to be sprinkled, may it help us to keep Jesus' word-command to love each other as he has loved us . . . [pause]

[*continue with* The Roman Missal, *Appendix II*]

Homily Points

• Whose words do we keep? Those who are beloved to us, those who inspire us, those who lead us in right paths, those whom we trust, those who challenge us to a better life. In this gospel Jesus invites us to keep his word. We do so because he is beloved, inspiring, leading us rightly, trustworthy, challenging.

• Every word Jesus spoke during his preaching and teaching, every action he undertook of healing and forgiving, he did so with love. He did so because he loved his Father. He did so because he loves us continually and unconditionally. Jesus' love is the model for our own lives. As Jesus loves, so are we to love. Totally.

• We are able to fulfill Jesus' word-command to love as he loves because the Holy Spirit dwelling within prompts us to total self-giving. The Holy Spirit prompts us, for example, to embrace the sick and the suffering, to be present to those in need, to ease the troubled heart, to bring peace in the midst of anxiety, to rejoice at the success of others, to believe in the goodness of others. As Jesus loves, so are we to love. Totally. This is what discipleship demands.

Model Universal Prayer (Prayer of the Faithful)

Presider: Living the word of Jesus makes demands on us. Let us pray to be faithful followers of Jesus.

Response:

Lord, hear our prayer.

Cantor:

we pray to the Lord,

That all members of the church continually grow in loving one another as Jesus loves us . . . [pause]

That government leaders faithfully keep God's word, building peace and justice for all . . . [pause]

That those whose hearts are frightened or troubled be granted the peace of the Holy Spirit . . . [pause]

That those who have been received into the church this Easter season respond ever faithfully to their baptismal call . . . [pause]

That each of us here live more perfectly the self-giving prompted by the indwelling of the Holy Spirit . . . [pause]

Presider: Loving God, your Spirit dwells within us and enables us to keep the word of your divine Son. Grant these our prayers that we might always be his faithful and loving disciples. We pray through that same Son, Jesus Christ our Lord. **Amen.**

So we are sending Judas and Silas
  who will also convey this same message
    by word of mouth:
  'It is the decision of the Holy Spirit and
    of us
  not to place on you any burden beyond
    these necessities,
  namely, to abstain from meat sacrificed
    to idols,
  from blood, from meats of strangled
    animals,
  and from unlawful marriage.
If you keep free of these,
  you will be doing what is right. Farewell.'"

RESPONSORIAL PSALM

Ps 67:2-3, 5, 6, 8

R⃰. (4) O God, let all the nations praise you!
or
R⃰. Alleluia.

May God have pity on us and bless us;
  may he let his face shine upon us.
So may your way be known upon earth;
  among all nations, your salvation.

R⃰. O God, let all the nations praise you!
or
R⃰. Alleluia.

May the nations be glad and exult
  because you rule the peoples in equity;
  the nations on the earth you guide.

R⃰. O God, let all the nations praise you!
or
R⃰. Alleluia.

May the peoples praise you, O God;
  may all the peoples praise you!
May God bless us,
  and may all the ends of the earth fear
    him!

R⃰. O God, let all the nations praise you!
or
R⃰. Alleluia.

SECOND READING

Rev 21:10-14, 22-23

See Appendix A, p. 300.

Or, where the Ascension is celebrated on
Sunday, the second reading and gospel for
the Seventh Sunday of Easter may be used
on this Sunday.

Rev 22:12-14, 16-17, 20, p. 133.

John 17:20-26, p. 130.

✝ CATECHESIS

About Liturgy

God's indwelling: Divine indwelling has been part of our Catholic doctrine from the
very beginning. In particular, the sacraments of initiation celebrate a divine love that
is so great that God chooses to live within us and among us. In baptism we are plunged
into the paschal mystery of Christ, dying to self so that we might rise to new life in
Christ. We are sealed in baptism with the gift of the Holy Spirit and strengthened in
confirmation to live this new life. In Eucharist we are nourished by Christ's Body and
Blood and by eating and drinking so sublime a food we become what we eat—the
Body of Christ in whom God dwells in glory.

The challenge, of course, is that these sacraments remain not simply actions we
go through but become dynamic ways of living. This is one reason why we celebrate
liturgy each Sunday—so that we remember Jesus' words and deeds. One practice that
might help us make this practical in our daily living—and over the years see real spiritual growth in ourselves—is to make sure we take one thought that leads to particular
action in our daily living from each Sunday celebration. A question to ask might be,
How, this week, might I express to others that God dwells within me; how does this
week's gospel challenge me to live?

About Liturgical Music

Hymn suggestions: We have available to us many songs related to the coming of
the Holy Spirit, many more than we will need for the celebration of Pentecost. In this
Sunday's gospel the words of Jesus already anticipate the sending of the Spirit on Pentecost, and so we can draw upon our treasury of Holy Spirit songs already this week.
For example, Delores Dufner's "O Spirit All-embracing" (G3, W4), a strong text set to a
strong tune (THAXTED), would work as an after-Communion hymn. The more meditative "Come Down, O Love Divine" (G3, JS3, OF, W4, WC) would fit the preparation of
the gifts, as would "O Breathe on Me, O Breath of God" (in most resources). The lyrical
refrain of Ricky Manalo's "By the Waking of Our Hearts" (BB, JS3) would make this
piece work well during the Communion procession. Other suitable choices for Communion would be David Haas's "Send Us Your Spirit" (BB, G3, SS) and Paul F. Page's
verse-refrain piece "Come, Spirit, Come" (SS). "Into Our Hearts, O Spirit, Come" (OF,
WC) would work well as a recessional.

SPIRITUALITY

℞. Alleluia, alleluia.
Go and teach all nations, says the Lord;
I am with you always, until the end of
the world.
℞. Alleluia, alleluia.

Gospel

Luke 24:46-53; L58C

**Jesus said to his disciples:
"Thus it is written that
the Christ would
suffer
and rise from the dead
on the third day
and that repentance,
for the forgiveness
of sins,
would be preached in his
name
to all the nations, beginning from
Jerusalem.
You are witnesses of these things.
And behold I am sending the promise
of my Father upon you;
but stay in the city
until you are clothed with power
from on high."**

**Then he led them out as far as
Bethany,
raised his hands, and blessed them.
As he blessed them he parted from
them
and was taken up to heaven.
They did him homage
and then returned to Jerusalem with
great joy,
and they were continually in the
temple praising God.**

Reflecting on the Gospel

Human beings began wearing clothes around 100,000 or so years ago. Other members of the animal kingdom have "natural" clothes: their hides, scales, or shells. Human beings, however, are the only animals that fashion clothes, and this for various purposes. Among utilitarian uses, we put on clothes to keep warm, to protect us from rain and other elements, to insulate us from heat or danger, to mark us as having a particular job, purpose, or rank. Among the aesthetic uses of clothes, we wear clothes to enhance our skin color, body shape, or hide imperfections. Clothes can adorn us with status, mark a special occasion, and differentiate genders or cultures. Clothes can make us look more attractive and more powerful looking. All these differing uses of clothes, however, have one thing in common: clothes are always something added to us, apart from our being, and can be put on or taken off.

In this gospel Jesus speaks to his disciples about being "clothed with power from on high." We can reject Jesus' offer of a unique clothing, not pay attention to it, not use it rightly. Or we can wear this clothing with dignity and gratitude. The clothing Jesus offers us is not something made from plant fibers or animal skins. This clothing is a power that is the Holy Spirit who takes up divine abode within us.

Jesus' ascension is inseparable from Pentecost. The disciples continue Jesus' ministry of preaching the Good News of death leading to risen Life only after they have been "clothed with power from on high." This is a "clothing" worn on the inside, a personal Presence—the Holy Spirit who empowers them to be a new Presence of Christ in the world after his ascension. Jesus' blessing before he was "taken up to heaven" was his last action-word in their midst. His blessing was his affirmation of the action-word they were to become on Pentecost. We disciples become for our world, through the power of the Holy Spirit, who Jesus was for his world: the visible promise of salvation unfolding through action-words that pack the power of the Holy Spirit. Our being clothed in the power of the Holy Spirit is neither merely utilitarian nor simply aesthetic. This clothing changes us into those who become members of the very Body of Christ. This clothing becomes a habit of Life.

Jesus' ascension, for us, is a gift and commissioning. We receive the gift of the Holy Spirit. We preach and teach in his name. We don't do this on our own, as Jesus promised. We can't set out to take up Jesus' mission to preach the Good News until we open ourselves to the Holy Spirit's Presence with and among us. This ensures us that our work isn't ours but Christ's. Ultimately our mission is to preach not simply events but a Person—Jesus Christ, the risen One. Even more: with the Spirit, we *are* the Presence of the risen Lord. This clothing is unequaled.

Living the Paschal Mystery

We are all familiar with the Catholic doctrine that the Holy Scriptures are the inspired word of God. Through the indwelling of the Holy Spirit, each of us is an inspired action-word of God when we are faithful to Jesus. This means, as the gospel suggests, that we are to preach and live as Jesus commanded. Repentance and forgiveness require that we first are willing to do as Jesus did—give ourselves over to the Spirit of God who heals and gives Life. Having first experienced God's saving action, we can be that saving action for others.

Focusing the Gospel

Key words and phrases: rise from the dead, preached in his name, clothed with power from on high, blessed them

To the point: Jesus' ascension is inseparable from Pentecost. The disciples continue Jesus' ministry of preaching the Good News of death leading to risen Life only after they have been "clothed with power from on high." This is a "clothing" worn on the inside, a personal Presence—the Holy Spirit who empowers them to be a new Presence of Christ in the world after his ascension. Jesus' blessing before he was "taken up to heaven" was his last action-word in their midst. His blessing was his affirmation of the action-word they were to become on Pentecost.

Connecting the Gospel

to the first reading: The ascension account in the first reading makes clear who is the "power from on high" that will be given to us: the Holy Spirit who instructs us, in whom we are baptized, and who empowers us to continue Jesus' mission on earth.

to experience: A caress speaks volumes about love and care. A parent's gentle push speaks volumes about "let's get moving." Jesus' blessing was an action-word speaking volumes about his love and care, pushing us to "get moving" with his saving ministry.

Connecting the Responsorial Psalm

to the readings: Psalm 47 was an enthronement psalm used when the ark of the covenant was carried in procession into the temple. It celebrated God's sovereignty over all heaven and earth. The song contains verses (omitted from this responsorial psalm) which express Israel's belief that God chose them to play a special role in establishing God's kingship over all nations.

Knowing the full text of this psalm brings its use on this solemnity into fuller perspective. The psalm is not just about the historical ascension of Jesus to the throne of God, but includes our participation in his ascendancy. We, too, "have confidence of entrance into the sanctuary" (second reading). Though we do not know the time of the kingdom's coming, we do witness to its presence (first reading). We have been blessed by Christ to tell of it (gospel). By Jesus' ascension all humanity is raised to the glory of God. When we sing Psalm 47 on this solemnity, this is what we witness to, celebrate, and proclaim.

to psalmist preparation: On the surface you can interpret this psalm as a celebration of the historical event of Jesus' ascension. But it is about far more than that. The psalm is about the complete victory of the whole Body of Christ over the forces of sin and death. Who sits on the "holy throne"? You do. The assembly does. The church does. As you prepare to sing this psalm, you need to reflect on this fuller understanding so that you can move the assembly, and yourself, from historicizing about Jesus' life and mission to personally participating in it.

**ASSEMBLY &
FAITH-SHARING GROUPS**

- I know that I am "clothed with power from on high" when I . . .
- I am a new Presence of Christ to my family, friends, coworkers in these ways . . .
- I feel Jesus' blessing upon me when . . . It affirms me by . . .

PRESIDERS
My preaching becomes an action-word when I . . .

DEACONS
My service ministry is an action-word that says . . .

HOSPITALITY MINISTERS
My hospitality is a blessing affirming who the assembly members are when I . . .

MUSIC MINISTERS
The assembly experiences the risen Presence of Christ through my music ministry when . . .

ALTAR MINISTERS
My service is action-word that . . .

LECTORS
When I prepare and fulfill my ministry aware that I am "clothed with power from on high," what happens is . . .

**EXTRAORDINARY MINISTERS
OF HOLY COMMUNION**
My daily living "distributes" the risen Presence of Christ when I . . .

127

Model Rite for the Blessing and Sprinkling of Water

Presider: Dear friends, this water will be blessed and sprinkled to remind us of our baptism through which we receive the Holy Spirit. As we begin this liturgy, let us open ourselves to God's Presence so that we can be this Presence for others . . . [pause]

   [*continue with* The Roman Missal, *Appendix II*]

Homily Points

• Wearing a new outfit that fits well, is the right color and style for us, and is of fine quality makes us feel good about ourselves and stand a little taller. In this gospel Jesus promises that we will be "clothed with power from on high." This "clothing" which fits us well, is eminently right for us, and is of unsurpassable quality makes us stand so tall that we are lifted "up to heaven." This "clothing" is the Holy Spirit who dresses us from within and empowers us to continue Jesus' saving ministry.

• On Easter Jesus rose from the tomb; on the ascension he rose from earth "up to heaven." Before he left them, Jesus blessed his disciples, a gesture affirming that those who are clothed with the Holy Spirit continue Jesus' saving ministry. The Holy Spirit raises disciples from the tomb of inaction and lifts disciples "up to heaven" with the Gift of indwelling divine Presence.

• Being clothed with the Holy Spirit is pure Gift. Being faithful to this Gift is pure choice. We choose to be faithful when we continue the saving work of Jesus by repenting when we have hurt another, by forgiving those who hurt us, by clothing others with dignity and honor, by doing daily tasks joyfully, by acknowledging the Presence of God in the compliment of another. Continuing Jesus' saving ministry happens in big ways and little ways. We do not always have to buy a complete new outfit. The Holy Spirit has already provided one for us. We just have to wear it well.

Model Universal Prayer (Prayer of the Faithful)

Presider: Let us pray that we might be faithful in taking up Jesus' saving ministry.

Response:

Lord, hear our prayer.

Cantor:

we pray to the Lord,

Clothed with power from on high, may all members of the church continue the saving mission of Jesus through the good works they do . . . [pause]

Clothed with power from on high, may the peoples of all nations build a world of forgiveness, peace, and justice . . . [pause]

Clothed with power from on high, may those in any need stand up with dignity and honor . . . [pause]

Clothed with power from on high, may those newly received into the church remain faithful to their baptismal promises . . . [pause]

Clothed with power from on high, may each of us put into action the Good News that has been preached to us . . . [pause]

Presider: Good and gracious God, the risen Christ blessed his disciples before he ascended into heaven. Grant our prayers and help us to be faithful to the Gift of the Holy Spirit dwelling within us. We ask this through Jesus Christ our Lord. **Amen.**

COLLECT

Let us pray.

Pause for silent prayer

Gladden us with holy joys, almighty God,
and make us rejoice with devout
   thanksgiving,
for the Ascension of Christ your Son
is our exaltation,
and, where the Head has gone before in
   glory,
the Body is called to follow in hope.
Through our Lord Jesus Christ, your Son,
who lives and reigns with you in the unity
   of the Holy Spirit,
one God, for ever and ever. **Amen.**

or

Grant, we pray, almighty God,
that we, who believe that your Only
   Begotten Son, our Redeemer,
ascended this day to the heavens,
may in spirit dwell already in heavenly
   realms.
Who lives and reigns with you in the unity
   of the Holy Spirit,
one God, for ever and ever. **Amen.**

FIRST READING
Acts 1:1-11

In the first book, Theophilus,
   I dealt with all that Jesus did and taught
      until the day he was taken up,
      after giving instructions through the
         Holy Spirit
   to the apostles whom he had chosen.
He presented himself alive to them
   by many proofs after he had suffered,
   appearing to them during forty days
   and speaking about the kingdom of
      God.
While meeting with them,
   he enjoined them not to depart from
      Jerusalem,
   but to wait for "the promise of the
      Father
   about which you have heard me speak;
   for John baptized with water,
   but in a few days you will be baptized
      with the Holy Spirit."

When they had gathered together they
      asked him,
   "Lord, are you at this time going to
      restore the kingdom to Israel?"
He answered them, "It is not for you to
      know the times or seasons
   that the Father has established by his
      own authority.
But you will receive power when the Holy
      Spirit comes upon you,

and you will be my witnesses in
    Jerusalem,
throughout Judea and Samaria,
    and to the ends of the earth."
When he had said this, as they were
    looking on,
    he was lifted up, and a cloud took him
        from their sight.
While they were looking intently at the
    sky as he was going,
    suddenly two men dressed in white
        garments stood beside them.
They said, "Men of Galilee,
    why are you standing there looking at
        the sky?
This Jesus who has been taken up from
    you into heaven
    will return in the same way as you have
        seen him going into heaven."

RESPONSORIAL PSALM
Ps 47:2-3, 6-7, 8-9

R̸. (6) God mounts his throne to shouts of
joy: a blare of trumpets for the Lord.
    or:
R̸. Alleluia.

All you peoples, clap your hands,
    shout to God with cries of gladness,
for the LORD, the Most High, the awesome,
    is the great king over all the earth.

R̸. God mounts his throne to shouts of joy:
a blare of trumpets for the Lord.
    or:
R̸. Alleluia.

God mounts his throne amid shouts of joy;
    the LORD, amid trumpet blasts.
Sing praise to God, sing praise;
    sing praise to our king, sing praise.

R̸. God mounts his throne to shouts of joy:
a blare of trumpets for the Lord.
    or:
R̸. Alleluia.

For king of all the earth is God;
    sing hymns of praise.
God reigns over the nations,
    God sits upon his holy throne.

R̸. God mounts his throne to shouts of joy:
a blare of trumpets for the Lord.
    or:
R̸. Alleluia.

SECOND READING
Eph 1:17-23

or

Heb 9:24-28; 10:19-23

See Appendix A, p. 301.

About Liturgy

Choice of second reading for Ascension: Since the second reading from Ephesians is the only option given for Year A, we suggest that reading be reserved for Year A and the reading from the Letter to the Hebrews be chosen for this Year C. Making these Lectionary reading choices exposes us to a larger number of Scripture selections in the course of a liturgical year.

Silences during Mass: Several times during Mass it is appropriate to pause in silence. These silent times enable us to surrender ourselves to God's Presence, to remember that the Spirit dwells within us and enables us to reverse the "absence" of the Ascension: through the power of the Spirit within us the risen Christ is present.

First, both the Rite for the Blessing and Sprinkling of Water and the Penitential Act call for a brief period of silence and reflection. This time allows us to make the transition from our busy lives into God's Presence, consciously surrender ourselves to God's word-action within us, and call to mind anything that we have done that keeps us from giving ourselves over to taking up Jesus' saving mission as his faithful disciples "clothed with power from on high." Although this time is brief (and in some cases so brief as to be nonexistent!) it is mightily important; this opens the door for our participation in the rest of Mass. We take much time to prepare for important events in our lives; surely this brief time is no less important!

Second, after Communion there may be a brief period of silence. Since we have just shared in eating and drinking the Body and Blood of Christ, this is time afforded us to appreciate more fully what we have shared and think about how we might be a better presence of the Body and Blood of Christ to others in our daily living. We might consider one specific way during the coming week when we will consciously be the presence of the risen Christ for someone else.

Mother's Day: If the Ascension is celebrated on Sunday, May 8, it is celebrated on Mother's Day; see the comments under Catechesis: About Liturgy given on the Seventh Sunday of Easter.

About Liturgical Music

Music suggestions: Hymns celebrating the ascension of Jesus into heaven are readily marked in every hymn resource. Particularly appropriate are texts which connect Jesus' ascension with the elevation of all humanity to glory. Other good choices this day are hymns for Christ the King, such as "To Jesus Christ Our Sovereign King" and "Rejoice, the Lord Is King." A very good contemporary text for the recessional would be Sylvia Dunstan's ascension hymn "Lift Up Your Hearts, Believers" (*Hymns for the Gospels*, GIA).

This solemnity is another good day to consider singing a song after Communion calling the Spirit to come. For example, quietly singing the Taizé *Veni, Sancte Spiritus* with its suggested shifts in dynamic levels and harmonizations would be an effective way to enter into the prayer and expectancy of the church as she awaits the day of Pentecost. A similar lovely piece with ostinato refrain is Paul F. Page's "Come, Spirit, Come" (SS, and *Mantras for the Seasons*, WLP). Although in general it is appropriate for the assembly to stand for the hymn after Communion, the meditative nature and purpose of either of these songs suggest it would be better to be seated, then to stand for the prayer after Communion. And, as always when singing a post-Communion hymn, it is preferable to omit a recessional hymn and go immediately to an instrumental postlude.

MAY 5, 2016 (Thursday) or MAY 8, 2016
THE ASCENSION OF THE LORD

SPIRITUALITY

GOSPEL ACCLAMATION
cf. John 14:18

℟. Alleluia, alleluia.
I will not leave you orphans, says the Lord.
I will come back to you, and your hearts will
    rejoice.
℟. Alleluia, alleluia.

Gospel

John 17:20-26; L61C

Lifting up his eyes to heaven,
    Jesus prayed, saying:
  "Holy Father, I pray not
      only for them,
  but also for those who
      will believe in me
      through their word,
  so that they may all be one,
  as you, Father, are in me and I in you,
  that they also may be in us,
  that the world may believe that you
      sent me.
And I have given them the glory you
    gave me,
  so that they may be one, as we are
      one,
  I in them and you in me,
  that they may be brought to
      perfection as one,
  that the world may know that you
      sent me,
  and that you loved them even as you
      loved me.
Father, they are your gift to me.
I wish that where I am they also may be
    with me,
  that they may see my glory that you
      gave me,
  because you loved me before the
      foundation of the world.
Righteous Father, the world also does
    not know you,
  but I know you, and they know that
      you sent me.
I made known to them your name and I
    will make it known,
  that the love with which you loved me
      may be in them and I in them."

Reflecting on the Gospel

The saying "Blood is thicker than water" goes back at least to the twelfth century. In different languages and various literary works there are multiple ways of putting it, but the message is essentially the same: our family ties and heritage are stronger and more enduring than other relationships we form. In wholesome, loving families, the shared unity is based not only on a common gene pool ascribing similar physical traits, characteristics, and mannerisms, but on a bond of tradition, habits, and beliefs. The shared unity is an alliance of persons that time, distance, or even death cannot completely erase. In this gospel Jesus prays that we "may all be one" as Jesus and his Father are one. This is no casual relationship that Jesus is desiring. It is a unity of persons with Persons, grounded in divine Love, that goes back much farther than the twelfth century—this unity reaches back into eternity itself.

Jesus' prayer for his disciples at the Last Supper is not only for them, "but also for those who will believe in" him because they have heard the disciples' word. This includes each one of us, here and now. His prayer for us? First and foremost, that we "be one" in him. This oneness is a communion of Jesus' disciples with himself and his Father that knows no limits and knows no time restrictions, enduring into eternity itself. Jesus' loving prayer for unity spills over into his desire that we share in his risen glory, that we "be brought to perfection," that we be loved, that we know he was sent by the Father. This prayer equips us with all we need to be faithful disciples and makes clear our work as his followers: help "the world" come to unity, glory, perfection, love. Our work, ultimately, is to transform the world.

In this intimate prayer of Jesus before his suffering and death, we see clearly how much Jesus sustains us in our discipleship. Our peek into what is deepest in Jesus' heart encourages us. The gift of the Spirit that we receive helps us see who we are to be as the one Body of Christ: those whose lives are spent in self-giving surrender for the sake of others. Truly, Jesus' prayer at the Last Supper is not only for the disciples who were present with him so many years ago at the Last Supper, but is also his prayer for us today. In this very heartfelt prayer, Jesus reveals the intimacy he enjoys with his Father—the same intimacy he desires with and for us. Such a love! Such a unity! Such a gift! Such a Life!

Living the Paschal Mystery

Most often when we think of living the paschal mystery we think in terms of the concrete self-surrendering acts we undertake in order to live the dying and rising mystery of Christ. The gospel for this Sunday affords us an opportunity to reflect on a completely different kind of self-surrender—that of giving ourselves over to God in the intimacy of prayer.

Just as Jesus' prayer reveals us as sharing in Jesus' love for and unity with his Father, so will our own prayer reveal both our love and union with God and our love and union with each other. As Jesus was prompted in his prayer to look not to himself but to the well-being of his disciples, so does our prayer draw us out of ourselves toward God and concern for others. Thus, prayer itself is a kind of self-giving surrender for others. Our intimate prayer leads to a stronger bond of communion with God. This bond unites us with each other in the same love, intimacy, and oneness that Jesus shares with his Father.

Focusing the Gospel

Key words and phrases: Jesus prayed, also for those who will believe, through their word

To the point: Jesus' prayer for his disciples at the Last Supper is not only for them, "but also for those who will believe in" him because they have heard the disciples' word. This includes each one of us, here and now. His prayer for us? That we "be one" in him, that we share in Jesus' risen glory, that we "be brought to perfection," that we be loved, that we know Jesus was sent by the Father. This prayer makes clear our work as his disciples: help "the world" come to unity, glory, perfection, love. Our work: to transform the world.

Connecting the Gospel

to the first reading: Stephen was able to be faithful even to death because he had heard the word of those who preached "the Son of Man." Stephen truly received all the gifts Jesus prayed at the Last Supper his disciples would be given.

to experience: Most of our intercessory prayer is for real persons whom we know and love. Jesus' prayer at the Last Supper is also for real persons he knows and loves, then and now.

Connecting the Responsorial Psalm

to the readings: Psalm 97 is a hymn celebrating God's sovereignty over all that exists. The verses used here retell the vision which strengthens Stephen to remain steadfast in discipleship to the point of death (first reading). Stephen sees the glory of God in heaven and Jesus standing at God's right hand and proclaims what he sees to the people surrounding him. Even more, he dies as Jesus did, giving himself over to God and forgiving those who murdered him. In return he is raised to the glory of eternal Life (second reading). We sing these psalm verses because we have been granted the same vision as Stephen, and we have been called to the same discipleship. In singing this psalm we acclaim that we, too, have seen the glory of Jesus and that we, too, will stake our lives on it.

to psalmist preparation: Because Psalm 97 is a generic text about the glory of God, it would be easy to sing it in a perfunctory way. But the context of Stephen's martyrdom (first reading) and Jesus' prayer that his disciples be one with him and the Father (gospel) invite a much deeper interpretation. To see the glory of God means to discover the mystery of your own glory. To become one with Christ means to accept that such glorification can come only through death. To sing these verses means to lay down your life in surrender and belief as did Stephen. This, then, is no simple song. Are you willing to sing it?

ASSEMBLY & FAITH-SHARING GROUPS

- As I listen to Jesus' prayer for me, what is most comforting is . . . what is most challenging is . . .
- As I listen to Jesus' prayer for me, I am drawn to pray for . . .
- I am transforming the world of my family, my neighborhood, my nation by . . .

PRESIDERS

My prayer for my parishioners is . . . The prayer I need them to raise for me is . . .

DEACONS

My love for others is visible through my service ministry when . . .

HOSPITALITY MINISTERS

Where I could bring about love and unity among those who are alienated (in my family or parish) is . . .

MUSIC MINISTERS

My music making leads me—and the assembly—to union with Christ and one another when . . . What gets in the way of this union is . . .

ALTAR MINISTERS

My service helps bring to perfection in me the risen Life of Christ in that . . .

LECTORS

Through my proclamation of God's word, my life becomes a word leading others to . . .

EXTRAORDINARY MINISTERS OF HOLY COMMUNION

Jesus' prayer that we "may all be one" expresses a fruit of Holy Communion in that . . .

Model Rite for the Blessing and Sprinkling of Water

Presider: Dear friends, we ask God to bless this water and we sprinkle it as a reminder of our baptism into the unity of the Body of Christ. As we celebrate this liturgy, may we hear the risen Christ's prayer that we be one with him and with one another . . . [pause]

  [*continue with* The Roman Missal, *Appendix II*]

Homily Points

• Whenever we see someone at devout prayer, we are touched deeply and inspired by their belief in, love for, and oneness with God. In this gospel we are privileged to hear Jesus' prayer for us. How does his prayer touch and inspire us? What does his prayer move us to do?

• Jesus came into the world so that the fractured human community might be drawn back into the unity God intended from the beginning of creation. This unity flows from God: "may all be one, as you, Father, are in me and I in you." This unity flows from a love "made known" to us by the words and deeds of Jesus. This unity flows from the glory Jesus was sent to reveal. Now we, through our words and deeds, are to make this same unity, love, and glory known.

• We make known our oneness in the risen Christ when we embrace all—even strangers and enemies—with care and compassion. We make known God's love when we give ourselves unstintingly for those in any need. We make known God's glory when our passion and resolve to be faithful followers of Jesus shines forth from us into the world. This is our work which transforms the world. This is our prayer, too.

Model Universal Prayer (Prayer of the Faithful)

Presider: Let us unite our prayer with Jesus' prayer for us, asking God to help us to be faithful followers of the risen Christ.

Response:

Cantor:

For all members of the church to witness in their daily living to the love with which God has first loved us . . . [pause]

For all peoples of the world to build a bond of unity that brings peace and justice for all . . . [pause]

For those most in need of our prayer . . . [pause]

For those newly received into the church to shine forth the glory of their commitment to the risen Christ . . . [pause]

For all of us here gathered to pray with the same intimacy and fervor as Jesus . . . [pause]

Presider: Glorious God, you invite us to share in your divine love and unity. Hear these our prayers that we might one day share in your everlasting glory. We ask this through Christ our risen Savior. **Amen.**

COLLECT
Let us pray.

Pause for silent prayer

Graciously hear our supplications, O Lord,
so that we, who believe that the Savior of
    the human race
is with you in your glory,
may experience, as he promised,
until the end of the world,
his abiding presence among us.
Who lives and reigns with you in the unity
    of the Holy Spirit,
one God, for ever and ever. **Amen.**

FIRST READING
Acts 7:55-60

Stephen, filled with the Holy Spirit,
    looked up intently to heaven and saw
        the glory of God
    and Jesus standing at the right hand of
        God,
    and Stephen said, "Behold, I see the
        heavens opened
    and the Son of Man standing at the
        right hand of God."
But they cried out in a loud voice,
    covered their ears, and rushed upon him
        together.
They threw him out of the city, and began
    to stone him.
The witnesses laid down their cloaks
    at the feet of a young man named Saul.
As they were stoning Stephen, he called
    out,
    "Lord Jesus, receive my spirit."
Then he fell to his knees and cried out in a
    loud voice,
    "Lord, do not hold this sin against
        them";
    and when he said this, he fell asleep.

RESPONSORIAL PSALM

Ps 97:1-2, 6-7, 9

R̸. (1a and 9a) The Lord is king, the most
high over all the earth.
or
R̸. Alleluia.

The Lᴏʀᴅ is king; let the earth rejoice;
   let the many islands be glad.
Justice and judgment are the foundation of
   his throne.

R̸. The Lord is king, the most high over all
the earth.
or
R̸. Alleluia.

The heavens proclaim his justice,
   and all peoples see his glory.
All gods are prostrate before him.

R̸. The Lord is king, the most high over all
the earth.
or
R̸. Alleluia.

You, O Lᴏʀᴅ, are the Most High over all
   the earth,
   exalted far above all gods.

R̸. The Lord is king, the most high over all
the earth.
or
R̸. Alleluia.

SECOND READING

Rev 22:12-14, 16-17, 20

I, John, heard a voice saying to me:
   "Behold, I am coming soon.
I bring with me the recompense I will give
      to each
   according to his deeds.
I am the Alpha and the Omega, the first
      and the last,
   the beginning and the end."

Blessed are they who wash their robes
   so as to have the right to the tree of life
   and enter the city through its gates.

"I, Jesus, sent my angel to give you this
      testimony for the churches.
I am the root and offspring of David,
   the bright morning star."

The Spirit and the bride say, "Come."
Let the hearer say, "Come."
Let the one who thirsts come forward,
   and the one who wants it receive the gift
      of life-giving water.

The one who gives this testimony says,
   "Yes, I am coming soon."
Amen! Come, Lord Jesus!

✚ CATECHESIS

About Liturgy

The intimacy of prayer: We are comfortable praying together the traditional prayers such as the rosary or novenas, but it is seldom that we are comfortable praying aloud spontaneously when others can hear us. Even people who belong to shared prayer groups and have much practice in this kind of prayer can find it unsettling. It makes us quite vulnerable! Yet one of the most precious gifts we can give to each other is a share in our prayer life.

This kind of shared prayer—when we pour out our hearts to God and allow others to witness it—is a wonderful gift of love to others. It says that we trust them and desire the same kind of unity with them that we have with God. Shared prayer together between husband and wife and among family members, among parish staff, at parish meetings, and so forth, can all promote a new kind of tolerance for one another so the differences we naturally have with each other seem less divisive.

Prayer as the gift of the elder members of the community: One of the most priceless gifts the elder members of our parish or liturgical communities can give to others is the gift of prayer. Generally when we retire we have a bit more time on our hands. What better way to spend this time for the good of others than to pray for those in need! In a real way elder parish members can make up what is "lacking" in the prayer life of the busier members of the parish. This is another way we can witness to the unity of the one Body of Christ: all our prayers together help build up the Body.

Mother's Day: This second Sunday of May is traditionally observed as Mother's Day. Although it would be very inappropriate to focus the liturgy on mothers, two ritual elements are always appropriate.

1) The following model intercession based on the gospel might be used as an intercession during the universal prayer (prayer of the faithful): That all mothers' self-giving love enable them to shine with the glory of God and receive strength from it . . . [pause]. Three other model intercessions are given in BofB, chapter 55, no. 1727.

2) In BofB, chapter 55, no. 1728 a prayer over the people is given and may replace the prayer over the people given in *The Roman Missal* for the Seventh Sunday of Easter.

About Liturgical Music

Music suggestions: A very appropriate hymn for Communion this Sunday would be "At That First Eucharist" with its refrain, "Thus may we all one Bread, one Body be, Through this blessed Sacrament of Unity." A good choice for the preparation of the gifts would be "Eternal Christ, Who, Kneeling" (in *Hymns for the Gospels*, GIA). Its opening verse reads, "Eternal Christ, who, kneeling When earthly tasks were done, Turned unto God appealing, 'That they may all be one,' We thank you for your vision of unity un-torn, Of faith without division With which your church was born."

A good choice for choral prelude would be Owen Alstott's "We Have No Glory" (OCP 8971). The refrain reads, "We have no glory, we have no name. We are as grains of sand upon the shore. Our only glory, our only name, is Jesus Christ." The verses speak of Christ as the source of all our life and being, and of our mission to "become the name of Christ upon the earth."

MAY 8, 2016

SEVENTH SUNDAY OF EASTER
or CELEBRATION OF ASCENSION

SPIRITUALITY

GOSPEL ACCLAMATION

R̹. Alleluia, alleluia.
Come, Holy Spirit, fill the hearts of your faithful
and kindle in them the fire of your love.
R̹. Alleluia, alleluia.

Gospel   John 14:15-16, 23b-26; L63C

Jesus said to his disciples:
  "If you love me, you will keep
      my commandments.
And I will ask the Father,
  and he will give you another
      Advocate to be with you always.

"Whoever loves me will keep my
      word,
  and my Father will love him,
  and we will come to him and make
      our dwelling with him.
Those who do not love me do not keep
      my words;
  yet the word you hear is not mine
  but that of the Father who sent me.

"I have told you this while I am with you.
The Advocate, the Holy Spirit whom the
      Father will send in my name,
  will teach you everything
  and remind you of all that I told you."

or John 20:19-23

On the evening of that first day of the
      week,
  when the doors were locked, where the
      disciples were,
  for fear of the Jews,
  Jesus came and stood in their midst
  and said to them, "Peace be with you."
When he had said this, he showed them
      his hands and his side.
The disciples rejoiced when they saw the
      Lord.
Jesus said to them again, "Peace be with
      you.
As the Father has sent me, so I send you."
And when he had said this, he breathed
      on them and said to them,
  "Receive the Holy Spirit.
Whose sins you forgive are forgiven them,
  and whose sins you retain are retained."

Reflecting on the Gospel

As the saying goes, "You can lead a horse to water, but you can't make it drink." Horses can have a mind of their own and be stubborn. So can humans! We often need prodding—motivation—to do something, especially if it's something we don't enjoy. When it comes to us humans, motivation plays a huge role in why we do anything and how we do everything. Need is a strong motivator, as is love. Another's enthusiasm and passion can prod us into action. Admiration for someone's goodness can move us to follow in his or her footsteps. We tend to do more and be more when we act in union with others. There is strength in numbers, not only to ease the load any one person carries, but also to increase creative insight and ideas, encourage and support each other, and to fill up what is lacking in any individual. We will drink the proverbial water to which we are led when we are thirsty enough or motivated enough.

This solemnity is really about motivation, the reason why we listen to Jesus and choose to follow him. We followers of Jesus never stand alone. We have each other to motivate ourselves toward faithful action. But even more: we always have the Spirit who dwells within and among us and binds us into one. Through the Holy Spirit we all share in the same risen Life, the same saving mission, the same love. There is strength in numbers. There is motivation in numbers. Our strength is the gift of the Spirit who binds us in love and unity as the one Body of Christ. Our motivation is that with the gift of the Holy Spirit we become one with God's love in a unique way. We become bigger than ourselves.

In this gospel Jesus reminds us that our love binds us together and to him. Our love motivates us to keep his commandments and word, the measure of our being together in community. Love is a strong motivator. The strength of our love for Jesus is the measure of how well we keep his commandments and word, how well we care for each other. Why and how we keep Jesus' commandments and word is, in the end, keeping *him*—the divine Word who was sent by the Father. Pentecost is a celebration of both the gift of the Spirit and the effects of that gift—we are sharers in the one Body of Christ who take up Jesus' mission to preach the Good News of salvation.

The Father sent the "Advocate, the Holy Spirit" to teach us "everything." What is this "everything" we need the Spirit to teach us? Why and how keeping Jesus' commandments and word is the unconditional condition of loving him. Why and how this love is the wellspring of our relationship to Jesus and his Father in their Spirit. What the Spirit teaches us, in the end, is why we do anything and how we do everything. Oh, how we need Pentecost!

Living the Paschal Mystery

The gift of the Holy Spirit motivates us to live as faithful followers of Jesus who share in his risen Life. This way of living might be so simple as a reassuring touch or helping hand. It might be so great as making a sacrifice of time to join the parish choir or volunteering for some task that needs to be done for the good of all. Living the Gospel means that we bask in the good gift of God's Life that the Spirit brings. Living the paschal mystery means that this good gift has its cost—we still must die to ourselves in order to be the true Presence of Christ for others.

Focusing the Gospel

Key words and phrases: If you love me; keep my commandments; keep my word; Advocate, the Holy Spirit; teach you everything

To the point: The Father sent the "Advocate, the Holy Spirit" to teach us "everything." What is this "everything" we need the Spirit to teach us? Why and how keeping Jesus' commandments and word is the unconditional condition of loving him. Why and how this love is the wellspring of our relationship to Jesus and his Father in their Spirit. What the Spirit teaches us, in the end, is why we do anything and how we do everything. Oh, how we need Pentecost!

Connecting the Gospel

to the second reading (from Romans): The Spirit of our God who teaches us everything chooses to dwell within *us*, raising us to the dignity of being "children of God" and "joint heirs with Christ."

to experience: We never forget a favorite teacher from whom we learned not just the basics of the three Rs, but also the basics of human relating and loving. In our foundational years, this mentor taught us what is of lasting value. The Holy Spirit is the teacher who, from our birth, has been teaching us everything: the kind of loving and relating that have everlasting value.

Connecting the Responsorial Psalm

to the readings: Psalm 104 is a masterful hymn praising God for the creation of the cosmos. It unfolds in a seven-part structure paralleling the creation account in Genesis 1. The Hebrews believed the cause of creation to be God's breath or spirit (*ruach*). Take breath away and creatures would die; give them breath/spirit and they would live (vv. 29-30).

In the first reading this breath of God comes like a "strong driving wind" which enables the disciples to witness to "the mighty acts of God." In the second reading this breath comes as a "Spirit of adoption" making us sons and daughters of God. In the gospel this breath comes as Advocate sent in Jesus' name to teach us all things. This is the Spirit we ask God to send us in the responsorial psalm: the power pushing us forward in mission, the love which is God's very Life within us, and the spokesperson reminding us of all that Jesus has taught—truly a Breath that will re-create the universe!

to psalmist preparation: You pray in this responsorial psalm for the renewal of the church—the renewal of her knowledge of Christ (gospel), the renewal of her sense of identity as one Body (second reading), and the renewal of her commitment to mission (first reading). How have these weeks of Easter renewed you as a member of the church?

ASSEMBLY & FAITH-SHARING GROUPS

- Right now in my life, the Holy Spirit is teaching me . . .
- When I keep Jesus' commandments and word, I learn that love is . . .
- The wellspring of my relationship to my family and friends is . . . to my enemies is . . . to God is . . .

PRESIDERS
My presiding, preaching, presence teaches my parishioners . . .

DEACONS
My service ministry makes visible my love for the risen Christ and his Spirit dwelling within me and those I serve when I . . .

HOSPITALITY MINISTERS
When I show unconditional love to others in my daily living, my hospitality ministry becomes . . .

MUSIC MINISTERS
Some things the Spirit has taught me through my music ministry have been . . . Some things which the Spirit needs to remind me of are . . .

ALTAR MINISTERS
Serving makes visible my love, and it looks like . . .

LECTORS
One way I need the Holy Spirit to teach me to *live* more fully the word I proclaim is . . .

EXTRAORDINARY MINISTERS OF HOLY COMMUNION
In love, the Holy Spirit teaches me to look upon the face of every communicant with . . .

Model Rite for the Blessing and Sprinkling of Water

Presider: Dear friends, on this Pentecost Sunday we celebrate the gift of the Holy Spirit who teaches us everything. As we ask God to bless this water and we sprinkle it, may we open our hearts to this Spirit who dwells within us . . . [pause]

[*continue with* The Roman Missal, *Appendix II*]

Homily Points

• In our relationships we human beings do few things without conditions. We give a favor and presume the favor will be returned. We commit ourselves to a friendship and presume it will be held sacred. We give others advice and presume they will do as we suggest. Our relationship with God also has a condition, but a very different one: that we respond to the indwelling Spirit teaching us the why and how of the love Jesus himself lived and taught us.

• Our love for Jesus has a clear and concrete condition: that we keep his commandments and word. Jesus' commandments and word guide us to live in a way that overflows with God's very love. Why and how we live this way is taught to us by the Holy Spirit whom the Father sends to dwell within us.

• The Holy Spirit teaches us the ways of love. Out of this wellspring, for example, we become more aware of the need of others and respond with compassion, we live the Gospel in deed as well as word, we do all that is necessary to deepen our relationships with others. The Spirit who dwells within us teaches us how and why to love and live in this way. Come, O Holy Spirit!

Model Universal Prayer (Prayer of the Faithful)

Presider: Today we celebrate receiving the gift of the Holy Spirit who dwells within us. Let us pray fervently that we be a fitting dwelling place for God's Love.

Response:

Lord, hear our prayer.

Cantor:

we pray to the Lord,

That all members of the church continually learn from the Spirit how to keep Jesus' commandments and word . . . [pause]

That all world leaders learn the ways of peace and justice . . . [pause]

That those struggling to love selflessly listen to the prompting of the Spirit within their hearts . . . [pause]

That those recently initiated into the church continue to learn what the Spirit is teaching them . . . [pause]

That each one of us here grow in our love for God and each other . . . [pause]

Presider: Loving God, you send your Spirit to dwell within us and teach us everything we need to know to come to salvation. Hear these our prayers that we might come to the fullness of Life in the Spirit. We ask this through your Son, Jesus Christ the risen Lord. **Amen.**

COLLECT

Let us pray.

Pause for silent prayer

O God, who by the mystery of today's
    great feast
sanctify your whole Church in every people
    and nation,
pour out, we pray, the gifts of the Holy Spirit
    across the face of the earth
and, with the divine grace that was at work
    when the Gospel was first proclaimed,
fill now once more the hearts of believers.
Through our Lord Jesus Christ, your Son,
who lives and reigns with you in the unity
    of the Holy Spirit,
one God, for ever and ever. **Amen.**

FIRST READING

Acts 2:1-11

When the time for Pentecost was fulfilled,
    they were all in one place together.
And suddenly there came from the sky
    a noise like a strong driving wind,
    and it filled the entire house in which
        they were.
Then there appeared to them tongues as
    of fire,
    which parted and came to rest on each
        one of them.
And they were all filled with the Holy Spirit
    and began to speak in different tongues,
    as the Spirit enabled them to proclaim.

Now there were devout Jews from every
    nation under heaven
        staying in Jerusalem.
At this sound, they gathered in a large
    crowd,
    but they were confused
    because each one heard them speaking
        in his own language.
They were astounded, and in amazement
    they asked,
    "Are not all these people who are
        speaking Galileans?
Then how does each of us hear them in his
    native language?
We are Parthians, Medes, and Elamites,
    inhabitants of Mesopotamia, Judea and
        Cappadocia,
    Pontus and Asia, Phrygia and Pamphylia,
Egypt and the districts of Libya near
    Cyrene,
    as well as travelers from Rome,
    both Jews and converts to Judaism,
        Cretans and Arabs,
    yet we hear them speaking in our own
        tongues
    of the mighty acts of God."

RESPONSORIAL PSALM
Ps 104:1, 24, 29-30, 31, 34

R̸. (cf. 30) Lord, send out your Spirit, and renew the face of the earth.
or
R̸. Alleluia.

Bless the LORD, O my soul!
  O LORD, my God, you are great indeed!
How manifold are your works, O LORD!
  The earth is full of your creatures.

R̸. Lord, send out your Spirit, and renew the face of the earth.
or
R̸. Alleluia.

If you take away their breath, they perish
  and return to their dust.
When you send forth your spirit, they are created,
  and you renew the face of the earth.

R̸. Lord, send out your Spirit, and renew the face of the earth.
or
R̸. Alleluia.

May the glory of the LORD endure forever;
  may the LORD be glad in his works!
Pleasing to him be my theme;
  I will be glad in the LORD.

R̸. Lord, send out your Spirit, and renew the face of the earth.
or
R̸. Alleluia.

SECOND READING
Rom 8:8-17

or

1 Cor 12:3b-7, 12-13

See Appendix A, p. 301.

SEQUENCE

See Appendix A, p. 302.

About Liturgy

Pentecost readings: For all three years given in the Lectionary, the first reading from Acts relating the Pentecost account and the responsorial psalm are the same. For Years B and C two choices are given for the second reading and gospel, with the first of those choices proper for Year A. Therefore, we suggest that the second reading and gospel proper for the respective year be used. This maximizes the use of Sacred Scripture on these great feasts.

The gospel given for Year C is similar to the gospel proclaimed just two weeks ago on the Sixth Sunday of Easter, but with different verses. These different verses and the Pentecost context suggest that our interpretation be different from that of two weeks ago. On the Sixth Sunday of Easter we stressed Jesus' word as love-in-action. This Pentecost Sunday we stress that the primary motivation for love-in-action is the indwelling of the Holy Spirit.

Pentecost—birthday of the church?: We have customarily interpreted Pentecost as the birthday of the church. We must take care that we don't trivialize this (for example, using birthday cakes, singing happy birthday). The more demanding effect of the birth of the church through the coming of the Holy Spirit who dwells in us and makes us one is that through the indwelling of the Spirit we become the missionary Presence of the risen Christ—*we ourselves* continue God's plan of salvation. Any "birthing" that happens is our openness to have the Spirit work through us and motivate us to make present for others God's Life and saving grace.

About Liturgical Music

Singing the sequence: In the Middle Ages myriads of sequences were added to the liturgy to expand on and explain the meaning of certain feasts and celebrations. Today only four remain: the obligatory ones on Easter and Pentecost and optional ones on The Body and Blood of Christ and Our Lady of Sorrows. Most often the sequences were attached to the gospel acclamation (hence, why the Easter one concludes with "Amen. Alleluia"). One can conjecture, then, that the sequences accompanied extended gospel processions.

To honor its original purpose as well as to demonstrate the centrality of the gospel in the life of the church, the Pentecost sequence could be sung as part of an extended gospel procession using incense and moving among the people. Musical settings already exist in which cantor(s) or choir sing the verses and the assembly joins in an alleluia refrain. "Come, Holy Spirit, on Us Shine" (WC, WS) uses the familiar tune O FILII ET FILIAE. "Come, Holy Spirit" (JS3) includes a refrain with alleluia; the verses could be split between women and men in the choir, with the assembly singing the refrain. "Come, O Holy Spirit" (BB, JS3) is set to HYMN TO JOY. This setting could be framed beginning and end with the Mode VI Easter Alleluia. The choir could sing the first half of each verse, the assembly the second half, and everyone the concluding "Come, O Holy Spirit, come!"

Appropriate posture during the procession is to stand just as we do for the gospel acclamation every Sunday.

ORDINARY
TIME II

SPIRITUALITY

GOSPEL ACCLAMATION
Cf. Rev 1:8

R⁊. Alleluia, alleluia.
Glory to the Father, the Son, and the Holy Spirit;
to God who is, who was, and who is to come.
R⁊. Alleluia, alleluia.

Gospel

John 16:12-15; L166C

**Jesus said to his disciples:
"I have much more to tell you, but
you cannot bear it now.
But when he comes, the Spirit
of truth,
he will guide you to all truth.
He will not speak on his own,
but he will speak what he hears,
and will declare to you the things that
are coming.
He will glorify me,
because he will take from what is
mine and declare it to you.
Everything that the Father has is mine;
for this reason I told you that he will
take from what is mine
and declare it to you."**

Reflecting on the Gospel

At first reading this gospel sounds like a mysterious riddle Jesus is sharing with his disciples at the Last Supper to befuddle them. What is the "more" that Jesus has to tell his disciples that they cannot bear? Clearly Jesus is speaking of a pretty weighty issue. So weighty that he promises to send his Spirit to guide them "to all truth." Ultimately, Jesus is speaking of life and death—his own and ours—which are probably the most weighty issues any of us ever faces. We human beings cling to life like a dog with a bone—we fight for it, we do all we can to preserve and prolong it. Jesus is facing his own imminent death; he is faced with the decision to give over his life. He is preparing his disciples for the same choice. We cling to our life like it is ours, but it really is not. Life is a gift from God.

On this Sunday when we celebrate the mystery of the Holy Trinity, when we celebrate the Life the Trinity shares among the three Persons and also shares with us, we cannot help but be like a dog with a bone. More even than our human life, we who have come to know Jesus and commit ourselves to him cling to the fullness of divine Life he offers us. We choose to receive this Life and, like Jesus, hand it over for the sake of others.

Surely this mystery of our God giving Life is so great that we "cannot bear it now" fully. Revelation is always gradual. The fullness of "all truth" would be overwhelming if we heard it in its full power, for the revelation of "all truth" is the gift of the Trinity's very Life dwelling within and among us. This festival celebrates the mystery that the Life and love of the Trinity "has been poured out into our hearts" (second reading). Like the Holy Trinity itself, we must let go, give that gift to others by surrendering our own selves for their good. Jesus showed us the way. He prepared his disciples for his suffering and death; he prepared his disciples to receive the Holy Spirit who enables Jesus' followers to share in his suffering and death in such a way as to also share in his risen Life, the very Life of the Holy Trinity itself. Life is a gift. We take that gift from God so that we can give that gift to others. All relationships are about give-and-take. This is no less true of the relationships of the divine Persons in the Holy Trinity. This is no less true of the relationships that bind us together in the Life of the one Body of Christ.

The Father gives everything to Jesus—all Life, all love, all truth. The Spirit takes from Jesus to "declare to [us] the things that are coming." Give and take. Such is the dynamic of the inner Life of the Trinity. Such is the dynamic of how the Father, Jesus, and the Spirit engage us in their Life. Give and take. We can "bear" the "much more" the Spirit has to tell us when we surrender more fully to the trinitarian Life within us. What is coming? Full entry into the glory of trinitarian Life. All give and take. It is ours to choose.

Living the Paschal Mystery

As difficult as it is to grasp the mystery of God's triune majesty, it is even more difficult to grasp that God loves us enough to share divine Life and glory with us. God chooses to dwell within and among us. Living the dying and rising of the paschal mystery means that we are faithful witnesses to the God within. The give-and-take necessary for growing in God's Life is the dynamic rhythm of the give-and-take, dying-and-rising of the paschal mystery. We give ourselves over for the good of others so that we can take the risen Life God gives us in the Holy Spirit.

Focusing the gospel

Key words and phrases: Jesus said, much more to tell you, bear it, Spirit, things that are coming, take, Everything that the Father has

To the point: The Father gives everything to Jesus; the Spirit takes from Jesus to "declare to [us] the things that are coming." Give and take. Such is the dynamic of the inner Life of the Trinity. Such is the dynamic of how the Father, Jesus, and the Spirit engage us in their Life. Give and take. We can "bear" the "much more" the Spirit has to tell us when we surrender more fully to the trinitarian Life within us. What is coming? Full entry into the glory of trinitarian Life. All give and take.

Connecting the Gospel

to the first reading: The first reading describes "the beginning" when God "poured forth" wisdom who "found delight in the human race." Jesus came to reveal that this wisdom is the Holy Spirit, and our God is a Trinity of Persons who "delight in the human race" in a new way. The Father shares with us through Jesus and the Spirit the very Life of the Trinity.

to experience: Good mysteries capture us in a way that we want to delve more and more into them and simply can't let go. This is no less true of our trying to grasp the mystery of the Holy Trinity. The Trinity can be as abstract as the seeming impossibility of Three-in-One, yet as concrete as divine Love-Life poured out in give-and-take.

Connecting the Responsorial Psalm

to the readings: The responsorial psalm for this solemnity of the Most Holy Trinity asks who we are in the eyes of God. The readings for this Sunday reveal the high value God places on us human beings. In the first reading the wisdom of God "play[s] on the surface of his earth" and "[finds] delight in the human race." In the second reading God pours God's own love into our hearts through the gift of the Holy Spirit. In the gospel Jesus promises that the Spirit will give to us everything that belongs to him and the Father. Truly God has "made [us] little less than the angels" and has "crowned [us] with glory and honor" (psalm). In singing this psalm we acknowledge the greatness of the Trinity who gives all so that we might become more.

to psalmist preparation: This responsorial psalm is not so much about our greatness as human beings as about the beneficence of God who treats us with unimaginable dignity and grace. How this week might you treat those whom you meet with this same dignity and grace—at home? at work? on the street?

**ASSEMBLY &
FAITH-SHARING GROUPS**
- The Trinity's inner dynamic Life of give-and-take urges me to . . .
- The give-and-take of my own life looks like . . .
- The "much more" I hear the Spirit telling me is . . . I can "bear" the "things that are coming" because . . .

PRESIDERS
In my preaching I do not speak on my own but with the voice of the Spirit when I . . .

DEACONS
The give-and-take of my service ministry reveals . . .

HOSPITALITY MINISTERS
I give to those gathering "Everything that the Father has" when I . . .

MUSIC MINISTERS
My collaboration with others in the ministry of music embodies the give-and-take of the trinitarian Life within me when I . . .

ALTAR MINISTERS
What I give by doing my ministry is . . . What I take is . . .

LECTORS
When I am aware of God's Life within me, my proclamation becomes . . .

EXTRAORDINARY MINISTERS OF HOLY COMMUNION
I am aware that Holy Communion is a foretaste of the fullness of the glory of the trinitarian Life when . . .

Model Penitential Act

Presider: This Sunday we celebrate the glory of the Life of our trinitarian God. Let us open ourselves to the mystery of divine Life within us and ask mercy for the times we have fallen short of what God's Life demands of us . . . [pause]

Lord Jesus, you are the glory of the Father: Lord . . .

Christ Jesus, you are the Son sent to save us: Christ . . .

Lord Jesus, your Spirit guides us in all truth: Lord . . .

Homily Points

• Children naturally take. They must be taught to give. Give-and-take is essential not only when we are young, but every day of our lives. As we grow in our Christian self-understanding, we realize more and more that our giving and taking flow from the very Life of the Trinity dwelling within us.

• Everything we do and are flows from the trinitarian God who dwells within and is pure Gift. The Spirit guides us to a fuller and fuller understanding of the truth of God's Life within. To be guided is to first admit that we don't know the way. God knows, and leads us rightly.

• To be led by the Spirit rightly, we must hear God's word and follow it. We hear God's word declared at Mass, but also through the words and deeds of others, through events in our own lives, through the graces and challenges that come our way each day. We follow God's word when our daily giving and taking draw us and those we encounter more deeply into God's abiding Presence. When others see the glory of God shining through us, we know we are surrendering to being led rightly.

Model Universal Prayer (Prayer of the Faithful)

Presider: In confidence we pray for our needs to the triune God who chooses to share divine Life with us.

Response:
Lord, hear our prayer.

Cantor:
we pray to the Lord,

That all members of the church follow faithfully the Spirit who guides us in right ways . . . [pause]

That all people grow in God's Life by acts of charity and justice that bring peace to our world . . . [pause]

That those struggling to find their way in life be led to wholeness and happiness . . . [pause]

That each of us reflect the glory of God's Presence dwelling within us by the way we give and receive in our relationships with one another . . . [pause]

Presider: Triune God, you fill us with your grace and Presence. Hear these our prayers that one day we might share the fullness of your glory for ever and ever. **Amen.**

COLLECT
Let us pray.

Pause for silent prayer

God our Father, who by sending into the
 world
the Word of truth and the Spirit of
 sanctification
made known to the human race your
 wondrous mystery,
grant us, we pray, that in professing the
 true faith,
we may acknowledge the Trinity of
 eternal glory
and adore your Unity, powerful in majesty.
Through our Lord Jesus Christ, your Son,
who lives and reigns with you in the unity
 of the Holy Spirit,
one God, for ever and ever. **Amen.**

FIRST READING
Prov 8:22-31

Thus says the wisdom of God:
"The Lᴏʀᴅ possessed me, the beginning of
 his ways,
 the forerunner of his prodigies of long
 ago;
from of old I was poured forth,
 at the first, before the earth.
When there were no depths I was brought
 forth,
 when there were no fountains or springs
 of water;
before the mountains were settled into
 place,
 before the hills, I was brought forth;
while as yet the earth and fields were not
 made,
 nor the first clods of the world.

"When the Lord established the heavens
 I was there,
 when he marked out the vault over the
 face of the deep;
when he made firm the skies above,
 when he fixed fast the foundations of
 the earth;
when he set for the sea its limit,
 so that the waters should not transgress
 his command;
then was I beside him as his craftsman,
 and I was his delight day by day,
playing before him all the while,
 playing on the surface of his earth;
 and I found delight in the human race."

RESPONSORIAL PSALM
Ps 8:4-5, 6-7, 8-9

R̸. (2a) O Lord, our God, how wonderful your name in all the earth!

When I behold your heavens, the work of
    your fingers,
  the moon and the stars which you set in
    place—
what is man that you should be mindful
    of him,
  or the son of man that you should care
    for him?

R̸. O Lord, our God, how wonderful your name in all the earth!

You have made him little less than the
    angels,
  and crowned him with glory and honor.
You have given him rule over the works of
    your hands,
  putting all things under his feet.

R̸. O Lord, our God, how wonderful your name in all the earth!

All sheep and oxen,
  yes, and the beasts of the field,
the birds of the air, the fishes of the sea,
  and whatever swims the paths of the
    seas.

R̸. O Lord, our God, how wonderful your name in all the earth!

SECOND READING
Rom 5:1-5

Brothers and sisters:
Therefore, since we have been justified by
    faith,
  we have peace with God through our
    Lord Jesus Christ,
  through whom we have gained access
    by faith
  to this grace in which we stand,
  and we boast in hope of the glory of God.
Not only that, but we even boast of our
    afflictions,
  knowing that affliction produces
    endurance,
  and endurance, proven character,
  and proven character, hope,
  and hope does not disappoint,
  because the love of God has been
    poured out into our hearts
  through the Holy Spirit that has been
    given to us.

About Liturgy
Making the sign of the cross: Because we sign ourselves in the form of a cross, this traditional Catholic gesture is probably more readily connected with Christ and his paschal mystery than with the mystery of the Holy Trinity. Yet the words of the gesture—"In the name of the Father, and of the Son, and of the Holy Spirit"—clearly connect this gesture with the whole triune majesty and mystery of God.

We begin and end each Mass with the sign of the cross. When we make it at the beginning of Mass, we are prompted to remember that this celebration is God's invitation to be in God's triune Presence. Mass isn't primarily *our* celebration, but God's gift of Self to us by which we are transformed into being more perfect members of the Body of Christ. It is well that we make this sign slowly and deliberately at the beginning of Mass and ask God to help us to surrender ourselves to this great mystery of God's Presence to us.

When we are blessed and sent forth at the end of Mass, we are prompted to remember that we are dismissed to be God's Presence to all those we meet in the ordinary circumstances of our daily lives. By signing ourselves with the cross in blessing, we also make a commitment to live in such a way that others might see the goodness in us that is God's Presence. Further, this signing and blessing remind us that in our ordinary actions we are to carry on the work of our triune God; that is, to re-create our world in newness of Life, to redeem our world from the evil that besets it, and to bring God's glory and holiness to all we meet. Through the indwelling God we participate in God's loving work on behalf of all.

About Liturgical Music
Music suggestions: A number of hymns connect well with this year's Trinity Sunday readings. Verses 1 and 2 of Brian Wren's "How Wonderful the Three-in-One" (in many resources) capture especially well the content of the first reading: "How wonderful the Three-in-One, Whose energies of dancing light Are undivided, pure and good, Communing love in shared delight. Before the flow of dawn and dark, Creation's lover dreamed of earth, And with a caring deep and wise, All things conceived and brought to birth." Mary Louise Bringle's "The Play of the Godhead" (*Joy and Wonder, Love and Longing*, GIA) begins with the phrase, "The play of the Godhead, the Trinity's dance, Embraces the earth in a sacred romance . . ." This hymn would work well during the preparation of the gifts. Bernadette Farrell's "God beyond All Names" (BB) proclaims that the God beyond "our dreams . . . all names . . . all words . . . all time . . ." is also the "God of tender care" who has "cradled us in goodness" and "mothered us in wholeness" and "loved us into birth." This hymn would fit either the preparation of the gifts or the Communion procession. "May God's Love Be Fixed above You" (HG) is an extended blessing asking that God's love be "fixed above you . . . advance before you . . . be close beside you . . . remain upon you." The suggested tune (LAUDA ANIMA) is well-known and perfect for the text. This hymn would make an excellent song after Communion through which the assembly could express their prayer for one another as they reenter Ordinary Time in the grace of the Trinity.

SPIRITUALITY

John 6:51

R⁊. Alleluia, alleluia.
I am the living bread that came down from heaven,
says the Lord; / whoever eats this bread will live
    forever.
R⁊. Alleluia, alleluia.

Gospel   Luke 9:11b-17; L169C

Jesus spoke to the crowds
    about the kingdom of
    God,
  and he healed those who
    needed to be cured.
As the day was drawing to a
    close,
  the Twelve approached him
    and said,
  "Dismiss the crowd
  so that they can go to the
    surrounding villages and farms
  and find lodging and provisions;
  for we are in a deserted place here."
He said to them, "Give them some food
    yourselves."
They replied, "Five loaves and two fish
    are all we have,
  unless we ourselves go and buy food
    for all these people."
Now the men there numbered about
    five thousand.
Then he said to his disciples,
  "Have them sit down in groups of
    about fifty."
They did so and made them all sit down.
Then taking the five loaves and the two
    fish,
  and looking up to heaven,
  he said the blessing over them, broke
    them,
  and gave them to the disciples to set
    before the crowd.
They all ate and were satisfied.
And when the leftover fragments were
    picked up,
  they filled twelve wicker baskets.

Reflecting on the Gospel

What do we usually do with leftovers? They become tomorrow's lunch or next week's garbage. Sometimes leftovers are even better the second time around—the flavors have had more time to blend together for an even more pleasing eating experience. In this gospel story about multiplication of loaves and fish to feed the hungry crowd—about food and leftovers—Jesus does far more than satisfy physical hunger and provide tomorrow's lunch for the disciples. He foreshadows the gift of his very self as the Bread of Life.

Jesus taught the crowds and "healed those who needed to be cured." Our need for Jesus and what he gives us, however, goes beyond teaching and healing. Even more, we need the food Jesus gives in unfathomable abundance. This food sublimely satisfies us. Yet even more: it transforms us into being the "leftover fragments"—the Body of Christ—continuing Jesus' ministry of giving self over for others.

Jesus' gospel command is clear: we are to feed others. We give to others not from the "deserted place" of our own hearts, but from the "leftover fragments" of God's blessings (see first reading). God's abundant nourishment is most startlingly given in the handing over of Jesus' life (see second reading)—on the cross, in the bread and wine. As Jesus' followers we are to be God's abundant nourishment for others by our own self-gift of life. God's abundant giving continues in our own self-giving lives.

The Twelve are taught by Jesus' word-deed that they themselves are to be the "leftover fragments" that nourish others. Jesus makes clear God's intention for us: "Give them some food yourselves." He is really saying, "Give them the good that is yourselves." Perhaps the amazement of this gospel and festival is that God so willingly chooses us humans to make known divine superabundance and blessing.

The gospel moves from the practical, tangible level of feeding hungry people to the mystery of God's abundance and excess; the gospel moves from the disciples' concern about feeding the crowd to their becoming the "leftover fragments" that nourish God's hungry people. This solemnity celebrates God's graciousness to us—a gift of superabundance. We are invited to participate in God's graciousness by our passing on this abundance. Our lives, then, must witness to the intersection of need and generosity. Our lives must witness to the intersection of Jesus' Life and our lives, given for others in a superabundance that just keeps getting better.

Living the Paschal Mystery

The first reading relates the priest Melchizedek's bringing out gifts of bread and wine and blessing Abram. The last line of the reading records Abram's response: "Then Abram gave him a tenth of everything." Like Abram, we've been given many gifts, surely not least being the Eucharist. Our response, like Abram, must be to "tithe" ourselves, to share those gifts with others, to share our very selves with others. We proclaim the death of the Lord when we are the "body that is for [others]" (second reading). Death leading to new Life lies in giving of ourselves, of being willing "leftover fragments" that bring God's Life and nourishment to others. If we dare to share in the sublime gift of Jesus' Body and Blood, then we must also dare to die to ourselves and share our own selves with others. Gift demands response. Sublime gift demands ultimate response—dying to ourselves so that we might share eucharistic Life with the world.

Focusing the Gospel

Key words and phrases: Jesus spoke, healed, Give them some food your-selves, gave them to his disciples, ate and were satisfied, leftover fragments

To the point: Jesus taught the crowds and "healed those who needed to be cured." Our need for Jesus and what he gives us, however, goes beyond teach-ing and healing. Even more, we need the Food Jesus gives in unfathomable abundance. This Food sublimely satisfies us. Yet even more: it transforms us into being the "leftover fragments"—the Body of Christ—continuing Jesus' ministry of giving self over for others.

Connecting the Gospel

to the second reading: Paul reiterates what Jesus taught at the Last Supper: in remembrance of him we are to eat his Body and drink his Blood. Our remem-brance of Jesus also entails *being* his Body, the "leftover fragments" who give ourselves for others.

to experience: We tend to narrow our consideration of the Eucharist to eat-ing and drinking the sacramental elements of bread and wine. Eucharist de-mands more—our own commitment to give ourselves to others as Jesus gives himself to us.

Connecting the Responsorial Psalm

to the readings: Psalm 110 was a royal psalm used at the coronation cere-mony of a king descended from the line of David. The text promised the king a place of honor next to God, victory over enemies, and a priestly role before the people. In the first reading Melchizedek, "a priest of God Most High," gives food, drink, and blessing to Abram. In the gospel Jesus heals those in need and feeds the starving crowd, creating an amazing abundance out of a meager sup-ply. In the second reading Paul reminds us that the food and drink Jesus gives us is his very Body and Blood. In singing this psalm we recognize what Jesus does and who Jesus is. He is the One victorious over all that impedes fullness of Life. He is the One who feeds us with his very self. He is the completion of the Davidic line and a "priest forever, in the line of Melchizedek."

to psalmist preparation: The psalm you sing this Sunday acclaims the power and priesthood of Christ, both most evident to us in the gift of his Body and Blood for food. What might you do this week to affirm your per-sonal faith in Jesus and express your gratitude for what he does in giving us the Eucharist?

ASSEMBLY & FAITH-SHARING GROUPS

- When Jesus says, "Give them some food yourselves," he is telling me . . .
- Jesus satisfies me with unfathomable abundance when . . . My response is . . .
- I know myself to be the "leftover frag-ments," the Body of Christ, most surely when . . .

PRESIDERS
I help others grow in their self-awareness as the Body of Christ when I . . .

DEACONS
A time when I was abundantly satisfied through serving others was . . .

HOSPITALITY MINISTERS
I help those gathering for liturgy more deeply hunger for the food only Jesus can give when I . . .

MUSIC MINISTERS
My ministry of music is a gift of self that feeds others when . . .

ALTAR MINISTERS
My ministry satisfies me when . . . It leaves me hungering when . . .

LECTORS
My manner of proclamation satisfies the hunger of the assembly when I . . .

EXTRAORDINARY MINISTERS OF HOLY COMMUNION
My ministry of distributing Holy Commun-ion at Mass urges me to "distribute" my self to others by . . .

✠ CELEBRATION

Model Penitential Act

Presider: Today we celebrate Jesus' gracious gift of abundance to us in giving us his Body and Blood for nourishment on our journey of discipleship. We pause to ask God's mercy for the times we have not lived the fullness of the gift of the Eucharist . . . [pause]

Lord Jesus, you nourish us with your Body and Blood: Lord . . .

Christ Jesus, your gift of self leads us to the fullness of Life: Christ . . .

Lord Jesus, your abundant love is revealed in the gift of your Body and Blood: Lord . . .

Homily Points

• In today's usage, a baker's dozen indicates generosity on the part of the giver. For example, the customer pays for twelve donuts and receives thirteen. In this gospel Jesus gives the hungry crowd far more than a baker's dozen. He satisfies their hunger, with a dozen "wicker baskets" over and above.

• Jesus isn't merely a generous baker who gives an extra loaf of bread, and he doesn't just feed the crowd until they are satisfied. He provides an astonishing abundance that ushers in "the kingdom of God" and a new way of living. We are to be the "leftover fragments"—the Body of Christ—continuing his ministry of giving self for others.

• We are the baker's dozen—the extra "food" given in generosity and joy from the One who desires to provide salvation for all people. We are food for others when we satisfy their hunger for deeper relationships, their hunger for appreciation, their hunger for meaning in life. In these and many other ways we are truly the Body of Christ making present his love, his graciousness, and his nourishment.

Model Universal Prayer (Prayer of the Faithful)

Presider: Our God is gracious and abundantly gives us all we need and so we pray.

Response:
Lord, hear our prayer.

Cantor:
we pray to the Lord,

That all members of the church be satisfied and transformed by the gift of Jesus' Body and Blood in the Eucharist . . . [pause]

That all peoples live in the kingdom of God where all hungers are satisfied . . . [pause]

That all those in any need be satisfied by the generosity of those who feast at God's table . . . [pause]

That each of us here generously give ourselves to others as Jesus gives himself to us . . . [pause]

Presider: Gracious God, you give us all good things in unsurpassed abundance and generosity. Grant these our prayers and through your gift of Eucharist transform us into being ever more perfect members of the Body of Christ. Who lives and reigns for ever and ever. **Amen.**

COLLECT

Let us pray.

Pause for silent prayer

O God, who in this wonderful Sacrament have left us a memorial of your Passion, grant us, we pray, so to revere the sacred mysteries of your Body and Blood that we may always experience in ourselves the fruits of your redemption. Who live and reign with God the Father in the unity of the Holy Spirit, one God, for ever and ever. **Amen.**

FIRST READING

Gen 14:18-20

In those days, Melchizedek, king of Salem, brought out bread and wine, and being a priest of God Most High, he blessed Abram with these words: "Blessed be Abram by God Most High, the creator of heaven and earth; and blessed be God Most High, who delivered your foes into your hand."
Then Abram gave him a tenth of everything.

RESPONSORIAL PSALM

Ps 110:1, 2, 3, 4

R̸. (4b) You are a priest forever, in the line of Melchizedek.

The LORD said to my Lord: "Sit at my right hand
  till I make your enemies your footstool."

R̸. You are a priest forever, in the line of Melchizedek.

The scepter of your power the LORD will stretch forth from Zion:
  "Rule in the midst of your enemies."

R̸. You are a priest forever, in the line of Melchizedek.

"Yours is princely power in the day of your birth, in holy splendor;
  before the daystar, like the dew, I have begotten you."

R̸. You are a priest forever, in the line of Melchizedek.

The LORD has sworn, and he will not repent:
  "You are a priest forever, according to the order of Melchizedek."

R̸. You are a priest forever, in the line of Melchizedek.

SECOND READING

1 Cor 11:23-26

Brothers and sisters:
I received from the Lord what I also
  handed on to you,
  that the Lord Jesus, on the night he was handed over,
  took bread, and, after he had given thanks,
  broke it and said, "This is my body that is for you.
Do this in remembrance of me."
In the same way also the cup, after supper, saying,
  "This cup is the new covenant in my blood.
Do this, as often as you drink it, in remembrance of me."
For as often as you eat this bread and drink the cup,
  you proclaim the death of the Lord until he comes.

OPTIONAL SEQUENCE

See Appendix A, p. 302.

About Liturgy

Breadth of the eucharistic mystery: We rightly think of the Eucharist as God's gift of nourishment for us when we share in the Body and Blood of the Lord and recognize this as a sublime gift that Jesus has left us. The readings for this solemnity also help us think of the eucharistic mystery in even broader terms.

First, by sharing in the Body and Blood of Christ we are *transformed* into being more perfect members of the Body of Christ. Thus, sharing in Eucharist is our way of growing more deeply into our own baptismal identity. Second, the eucharistic mystery includes continually establishing God's reign which is evidenced by healing, reconciling, and feeding others. Third, the eucharistic mystery calls forth from us practical, everyday actions by which we ourselves help establish God's reign by dying to ourselves for the sake of others. Fourth, the eucharistic mystery demands a response and so we "tithe" the gifts given to us for the sake of others less fortunate. In a real sense the eucharistic mystery begins at Mass, reaches a high point during Communion, and then extends beyond the ritual moment to our everyday lives when we live its self-giving demand-response.

About Liturgical Music

Music suggestions: Both Steven Janco's "Draw Near" (G3, OF, W4, WC, WS) and James Chepponis's "Come to the Banquet" (G3, SS, W4) are verse-refrain settings of the seventh-century hymn *Sancti, venite, Christi corpus sumite.* The text invites us to draw near and receive Christ's gift of himself to us in the Eucharist.

Also appropriate for Communion on this solemnity would be songs which express our participation in Christ's feeding of the hungry. David Haas's "Now We Remain" (in most resources) comes to mind, not only because of its refrain but also because of its final verse, "We are the presence of God; this is our call. Now to become bread and wine: food for the hungry, life for the weary, for to live with the Lord, we must die with the Lord." Tom Porter's "Let Us Be Bread" (G3) offers this refrain, "Let us be bread, blessed by the Lord, broken and shared, life for the world. Let us be wine, love freely poured. Let us be one in the Lord." Rory Cooney's "Bread of Life" (BB, JS3) uses the refrain, "I myself am the bread of life. You and I are the bread of life, taken and blessed, broken and shared by Christ that the world might live." Delores Dufner's "Amen to the Body of Christ" (W4) reminds us that in our Amen to the Body of Christ we become "bread for the life of the world." Dufner's "We Come with Joy" (HG, SS) combines narration of the story of Jesus' feeding the crowd with the call that we do likewise, "For Christ will bless our bit of bread, The loaves our hands provide, Till empty baskets overflow And all are satisfied." This hymn could be sung during the preparation of the gifts, during the Communion procession, or after Communion as a song of praise.

SPIRITUALITY

GOSPEL ACCLAMATION
Matt 11:29ab

R̸. Alleluia, alleluia.
Take my yoke upon you, says the Lord;
and learn from me, for I am meek and humble
    of heart.
R̸. Alleluia, alleluia.

or

John 10:14

R̸. Alleluia, alleluia.
I am the good shepherd says the Lord,
I know my sheep, and mine know me.
R̸. Alleluia, alleluia.

Gospel

Luke 15:3-7; L172C

Jesus addressed this parable to the
    Pharisees and scribes:
"What man among you having a
    hundred sheep and losing one of
    them
would not leave the ninety-nine in the
    desert
and go after the lost one until
    he finds it?
And when he does find it,
he sets it on his shoulders with great
    joy
and, upon his arrival home,
he calls together his friends and
    neighbors and says to them,
'Rejoice with me because I have
    found my lost sheep.'
I tell you, in just the same way
there will be more joy in heaven over
    one sinner who repents
than over ninety-nine righteous
    people
who have no need of repentance."

See Appendix A, p. 303, for other readings.

Reflecting on the Gospel

Very often there is safety in numbers. When youngsters go out at night, parents warn them to stay in a group. When swimming, children are taught the buddy system. Animals flock and school and herd together. In this gospel, the sheep who remain in the fold are relatively safe in their numbers. The lone sheep who wanders from the fold is in grave danger. Even the shepherd who leaves the flock to search for the lost sheep places himself in the same danger; he himself could be attacked and killed. To bring us back to his fold, our Shepherd placed himself in danger—ultimately being attacked and killed for our eternal safety. How good is our Shepherd!

In the gospel parable, instead of punishing the errant sheep when found, the Good Shepherd puts it on his shoulders and tenderly carries it back to the fold. The single sheep is treated with inestimable worth. Our Good Shepherd searches for us diligently when we are lost and carries each of us with the same solicitude and care when we are found, granting us the same inestimable worth. It is such tenderness, love, and joy flowing from the Sacred Heart that we celebrate this day. This festival reminds us that the Good Shepherd's heart is large enough to welcome the stranger and tender enough to search out the lost and straying. This festival reminds us that we ourselves are still to be counted among the lost, among those whom Jesus is persistent to search after, caring enough to forgive, and loving enough to embrace with joy.

Whenever we wander, the Good Shepherd seeks us with persistence and love. There is always gentle invitation to repent (see the first reading: "The lost I will seek out . . . shepherding them rightly"), always ample reminders of God's desire to be in relationship with us (see the second reading: we are "reconciled . . . through the death of his Son"), always joy (see gospel: in heaven, no less!) when we allow the Good Shepherd to carry us toward wholeness and new Life. The Sacred Heart is a powerful image for us because it captures so completely the loving sacrifice of the Son, God's regard for our worth, and the persistence of God's saving mission.

Living the Paschal Mystery

Jesus' image of the persistent sheep owner who leaves ninety-nine to find the one lost sheep is a model for paschal mystery living. We often speak of dying to self. One way to die to self is to search out the "one" among the "ninety-nine." Who among us is lonely? Reach out to that person. Is someone being neglected because of age, religion, social status, economic status? Reach out to that person. Do the physically or mentally challenged leave us uncomfortable? Find out enough about them that we can be comfortable reaching out with a friendly word or gesture.

If we open our eyes and look, we will no doubt discover many among us who seem isolated and alone. Emulating the sacred, tender heart of Jesus means that we make room in our own hearts for everyone, not just those who are naturally close to us or with whom we are most comfortable. This doesn't mean that we don't have a justified predilection for our family and friends. It does mean that we are willing to break out of our usual family, work, and social groups to be present to those who seem alone or lost. Dying to self can mean caring enough to have room in our own hearts for all who come.

Focusing the Gospel

Key words and phrases: hundred sheep, losing one of them, go after the lost one, found

To the point: The sheep who remain in the fold are relatively safe in their numbers. The lone sheep who wanders from the fold is in grave danger. Even the shepherd who leaves the flock to search for the lost sheep places himself in the same danger; he himself could be attacked and killed. To bring us back to his fold, our Shepherd placed himself in danger—ultimately being attacked and killed for our eternal safety. How good is our Shepherd!

Model Penitential Act

Presider: Jesus is persistent in searching out the lost and tenderly gathers them close to his Sacred Heart. We pause at the beginning of this liturgy to see how we have strayed from Jesus' embrace and open ourselves to his loving Presence . . . [pause]

Lord Jesus, you are the Good Shepherd who seeks the lost: Lord . . .

Christ Jesus, you lead us to the fullness of Life: Christ . . .

Lord Jesus, you rejoice when the lost repent: Lord . . .

Model Universal Prayer (Prayer of the Faithful)

Presider: The Good Shepherd intercedes for us before his gracious Father. Let us make known our needs.

Response:

Cantor:

That the leaders of the church shepherd God's people with tenderness and compassion . . . [pause]

That civil authorities lead justly and bring their peoples together in unity and joy . . . [pause]

That the lost and forsaken find comfort in Jesus' Sacred Heart . . . [pause]

That each one of us search for the lost, embrace the found, and rejoice in those who repent . . . [pause]

Presider: Loving and caring God, the Sacred Heart of your Son Jesus seeks those who have strayed from your fold. Hear these our prayers that one day all who are lost will rest forever in your loving embrace. We make our prayer through the Good Shepherd, your Son, Jesus Christ our Lord. **Amen.**

COLLECT

Let us pray.

Pause for silent prayer

Grant, we pray, almighty God,
that we, who glory in the Heart of your
  beloved Son
and recall the wonders of his love for us,
may be made worthy to receive
an overflowing measure of grace
from that fount of heavenly gifts.
Through our Lord Jesus Christ, your Son,
who lives and reigns with you in the unity
  of the Holy Spirit,
one God, for ever and ever. **Amen.**

or

O God, who in the Heart of your Son,
wounded by our sins,
bestow on us in mercy
the boundless treasures of your love,
grant, we pray,
that, in paying him the homage of our devotion,
we may also offer worthy reparation.
Through our Lord Jesus Christ, your Son,
who lives and reigns with you in the unity
  of the Holy Spirit,
one God, for ever and ever. **Amen.**

FOR REFLECTION

- What this parable teaches me about the Sacred Heart of Jesus is . . . What it teaches me about my heart is . . .
- I need the Good Shepherd to find me when . . . to carry me when . . .
- In order to imitate the Sacred Heart of Jesus, what I must do is . . .

Homily Points

- The heart of the Good Shepherd is different from that of so many of us. Who would leave ninety-nine for one? The Good Shepherd. When any one of us is lost, he goes after us, finds us, carries us back to the safety of the fold, and celebrates our return with "great joy."

- It is such tenderness, love, and joy flowing from the Sacred Heart that we celebrate this day. The Good Shepherd goes to any length to bring back a lost heart—even to the point of suffering and death. We must have this same Heart—even to daily dying to self for others.

TENTH SUNDAY IN ORDINARY TIME

SPIRITUALITY

GOSPEL ACCLAMATION
Luke 7:16

℞. Alleluia, alleluia.
A great prophet has risen in our midst,
God has visited his people.
℞. Alleluia, alleluia.

Gospel

Luke 7:11-17; L90C

Jesus journeyed to a
city called Nain,
and his disciples and
a large crowd
accompanied him.
As he drew near to the
gate of the city,
a man who had died was
being carried out,
the only son of his mother, and she
was a widow.
A large crowd from the city was with
her.
When the Lord saw her,
he was moved with pity for her and
said to her,
"Do not weep."
He stepped forward and touched the
coffin;
at this the bearers halted,
and he said, "Young man, I tell you,
arise!"
The dead man sat up and began to
speak,
and Jesus gave him to his mother.
Fear seized them all, and they glorified
God, exclaiming,
"A great prophet has arisen in our
midst,"
and "God has visited his people."
This report about him spread through
the whole of Judea
and in all the surrounding region.

Reflecting on the Gospel

Limericks are five-line, rhyming poems that became popular during social gatherings in the eighteenth century. They were a way for the partygoers to engage in creative poetry-making whereby individuals would make up a limerick followed by a group response. Often sung, they had a cadence and rhythm accompanying movement. This Sunday's gospel has all the makings of a limerick: crowd, special occasion, group interaction. We might come up with a five-liner like this, for example:

There once was a widow from Nain
whose life had become a great pain.
Her son was dead
from the city she fled.
But her life was not to wane.

But the seriousness of the situation draws us far beyond the whimsical. Many details reveal the power and depth of Jesus' words and deeds. Jesus has power over life and death; he clearly chooses life for this widow. Her life was not to wane upon losing her "only son." His death became the occasion for Jesus to take the initiative in proclaiming God's desire that we share life to the fullest. The cadence and rhythm of his words and deeds move us toward the celebration of life and hope.

The widow of Nain had lost everything dear to her: her husband and her only son. By losing her husband, she had lost her life support; at that time most women were totally dependent upon their husbands for livelihood. She had a son, and he no doubt supported her after his father's death. Then he dies and any hope of posterity ceases. She is utterly alone; she is now the last in her ancestral line. The widow and a "large crowd from the city" were processing to bury her son. Without even being asked, Jesus with great compassion comforts her, touches the son's coffin, raises her son from the dead, and gives him back to his mother. By word and deed Jesus restores the widow's life and hope. She is no longer alone in this world without support and hope of posterity.

In Jesus "God has visited his people." He brings gifts that are only God's to give: life and hope. No wonder news of Jesus' words and deeds spread rapidly! In him something new is happening. Death is not an end, but a sign of God's power and saving grace. In Jesus God continues to visit us, offering hope and life, even without our asking. Do we accept?

Living the Paschal Mystery

Life and death are great mysteries. We know we are born to die. We know that we live in gradual diminishment. With the coming of Jesus, we also are people of hope in Life beyond this life. We need not even ask for what will enhance our life; Jesus comes with all we need. We accept the Life and hope he offers us when we in turn give this to others. A smile showered on an overly exhausted parent towing a youngster along in the supermarket can bring Life and hope. A word of encouragement to the insecure can bring Life and hope. A touch of comfort for the sick can bring Life and hope. None of these simple gestures needs to be requested. Like Jesus, our compassion spills over without asking. Like Jesus, we die to self for the good of the other. The cadence and rhythm of our daily living is the paschal mystery where self-giving and Life-receiving are a defining rhythm of all our words and deeds.

Focusing the Gospel

Key words and phrases: man who had died, only son, widow, moved with pity, arise, gave him to his mother, "God has visited his people"

To the point: The widow of Nain had lost everything dear to her: her husband and her only son. In them she had lost her life support and any hope of posterity. Without even being asked, Jesus with great compassion raises her son from the dead and gives him back to her. By word and deed Jesus restores the widow's life and hope. In Jesus "God has visited his people." In Jesus God continues to visit us, offering hope and life, even without our asking. Do we accept?

Connecting the Gospel

to the first reading: In the first reading we hear of a child who dies and is raised to life through Elijah's prayer to God. In the gospel Jesus himself raises the widow's son to life. It is God who gives life.

to experience: Life is both fragile and precious. It is a gift from God that we sometimes take all too much for granted. We are brought face-to-face with how much we cling to life and God when life is taken away.

Connecting the Responsorial Psalm

to the readings: The Sunday Lectionary uses Psalm 30 four times (Easter Vigil 4, Third Sunday of Easter C, Tenth Sunday in Ordinary Time C, and Thirteenth Sunday in Ordinary Time B), and every time the readings deal with our need to be delivered from death. Even though God has made all things for life, we nonetheless experience death coming toward us over and over, bringing pain, grief, and even guilt (first reading). The stories of two grieving widows, however, show us God acting to change our weeping into rejoicing, our mourning into dancing (psalm). In the first reading God restores life through the prayer of a faithful prophet. In the gospel God restores life through the words and actions of Christ who holds power over death. These verses from Psalm 30 acknowledge what oftentimes only our faith can see: that death with its contingent weeping and mourning is not the end of the story—life is.

to psalmist preparation: When you sing this psalm, you embody the confidence of the entire Body of Christ that God saves from death, even when the whole world groans under its threat. Pray this week for those who are facing death in any form—physical, mental, emotional. Pray that your singing may be a song of hope for them.

ASSEMBLY & FAITH-SHARING GROUPS

- Without even asking, Jesus gives me . . .
- God visits me when . . . I respond with . . .
- That for which I hope most dearly is . . . The life I seek with all my being is . . .

PRESIDERS

Without even their asking me, I respond to people's need for renewed hope when . . .

DEACONS

By word and deed, what I restore to those I serve is . . .

HOSPITALITY MINISTERS

I prepare those gathering for liturgy to encounter the "God [who] has visited his people" when I . . .

MUSIC MINISTERS

My music making supports the Life-seeking of the members of the assembly when I . . .

ALTAR MINISTERS

What is dear to me that I bring to my service at the altar is . . .

LECTORS

My proclaimed words become inspiring deeds when I . . .

EXTRAORDINARY MINISTERS OF HOLY COMMUNION

When I say to a communicant, "The Body [Blood] of Christ," in effect I am saying "arise!" in that . . .

Model Penitential Act

Presider: In today's gospel Jesus raises the dead son of the widow of Nain to life. Let us ask for God's mercy when we have been dead to the Life God has given us . . . [pause]

> Lord Jesus, you are the resurrection and the Life: Lord . . .
> Christ Jesus, you raise us to the fullness of Life: Christ . . .
> Lord Jesus, you show us compassion and mercy: Lord . . .

Homily Points

• It is an unwritten "rule" that parents should die before their children. The death of a child is a most painful event that a parent never quite gets over. It is easy for us, then, to identify with the pain of the widow in the gospel who lost her only son. And yet Jesus says to her, "Do not weep." How can he say that?

• Jesus knows the plan: "God has visited his people." God desires not death, but life. Not despair, but hope. As the Son of God, Jesus has the power and authority to restore life, and so he does. Jesus has the compassion to bring hope, and so he does. Then, in Nain, and now for us.

• God visits us in Jesus with new life and hope, for example, when the pain of a child's death is eased through prayer and faith in God's promise of eternal Life, and the support of family and friends; when an addict successfully enters recovery and returns to healthy family relationships; when painful illness is mitigated by the joy of laughter. In each of these visitations, Jesus is saying to us, "Do not weep," I am here with compassion, healing, love, and Life.

Model Universal Prayer (Prayer of the Faithful)

Presider: God is the author of Life and giver of hope. We confidently place our needs in the hands of this God.

Response:

Lord, hear our prayer.

Cantor:

we pray to the Lord,

That all members of the church bring life and hope to all those they encounter in everyday living . . . [pause]

That the peoples of the world come in hope to the fullness of Life God offers . . . [pause]

That those who are without hope, without quality of life, without healing be visited by our compassionate God . . . [pause]

That all of us here gathered faithfully respond whenever God visits us with saving Presence . . . [pause]

Presider: God of Life and hope, you sent your Son Jesus to bring us compassion and love. Grant our prayers that one day we might come to enjoy the fullness of Life with you forever. Through Christ our Lord. **Amen.**

COLLECT

Let us pray.

Pause for silent prayer

O God, from whom all good things come,
grant that we, who call on you in our need,
may at your prompting discern what is
 right,
and by your guidance do it.
Through our Lord Jesus Christ, your Son,
who lives and reigns with you in the unity
 of the Holy Spirit,
one God, for ever and ever. **Amen.**

FIRST READING

1 Kgs 17:17-24

Elijah went to Zarephath of Sidon to the
 house of a widow.
The son of the mistress of the house fell
 sick,
 and his sickness grew more severe until
 he stopped breathing.
So she said to Elijah,
 "Why have you done this to me, O man
 of God?
Have you come to me to call attention to
 my guilt
 and to kill my son?"
Elijah said to her, "Give me your son."
Taking him from her lap, he carried the
 son to the upper room
 where he was staying, and put him on
 his bed.
Elijah called out to the LORD:
 "O LORD, my God,
 will you afflict even the widow with
 whom I am staying
 by killing her son?"
Then he stretched himself out upon the
 child three times
 and called out to the LORD:
 "O LORD, my God,
 let the life breath return to the body of
 this child."
The LORD heard the prayer of Elijah;
 the life breath returned to the child's
 body and he revived.
Taking the child, Elijah brought him down
 into the house
 from the upper room and gave him to
 his mother.
Elijah said to her, "See! Your son is alive."
The woman replied to Elijah,
 "Now indeed I know that you are a man
 of God.
The word of the LORD comes truly from
 your mouth."

RESPONSORIAL PSALM
Ps 30:2, 4, 5-6, 11, 12, 13

R̅. (2a) I will praise you, Lord, for you have rescued me.

I will extol you, O Lord, for you drew me
    clear
    and did not let my enemies rejoice over
    me.
O Lord, you brought me up from the
    nether world;
    you preserved me from among those
    going down into the pit.

R̅. I will praise you, Lord, for you have rescued me.

Sing praise to the Lord, you his faithful
    ones,
    and give thanks to his holy name.
For his anger lasts but a moment;
    a lifetime, his good will.
At nightfall, weeping enters in,
    but with the dawn, rejoicing.

R̅. I will praise you, Lord, for you have rescued me.

Hear, O Lord, and have pity on me;
    O Lord, be my helper.
You changed my mourning into dancing;
    O Lord, my God, forever will I give you
    thanks.

R̅. I will praise you, Lord, for you have rescued me.

SECOND READING
Gal 1:11-19

I want you to know, brothers and sisters,
    that the gospel preached by me is not of
    human origin.
For I did not receive it from a human
    being, nor was I taught it,
    but it came through a revelation of
    Jesus Christ.

For you heard of my former way of life in
    Judaism,
    how I persecuted the church of God
    beyond measure
    and tried to destroy it, and progressed
    in Judaism
    beyond many of my contemporaries
    among my race,
    since I was even more a zealot for my
    ancestral traditions.

Continued in Appendix A, p. 303.

About Liturgy
Bury the dead: We probably rarely think that when we attend a funeral we are undertaking a corporal work of mercy: bury the dead. This act is far more than disposing of a dead body. It is the final rite of the Order of Christian Funerals. Called the "Rite of Committal," it is preceded by a procession, usually from the place of the funeral Mass to a cemetery. Processions are always symbolic: they physically take us from one place to another. This procession takes us from a celebration of the joy of the funeral Mass and the new Life the deceased entered into to a final celebration of the respect and dignity we accord the human body, which was once a temple of the Holy Spirit. There are prayers for both the deceased and the loved ones who bring the body for burial.

In the prayer over the place of committal, we call to mind Jesus' three days in the tomb, the hope and promise of resurrection, and the anticipation of eternal glory. The rite acknowledges the sadness of taking a final leave of the deceased person, at the same time it continues its prayer for peace and consolation. The coffin may be sprinkled with holy water, reminding us again of our baptism and incorporation into the Body of Christ. The prayer over the people begs for strength before the assembled people are blessed and sent forth with the peace of Christ.

The funeral Mass focuses on the joy of the resurrection. The Rite of Committal recognizes the sadness of this final act of leave-taking. The church walks with us through the rhythm of joy and sorrow, life and death. This walk is always with the risen Christ, who has died and risen, and shows us the way to eternal Life.

About Liturgical Music
Music suggestions: Using the verses specific to this Sunday's gospel, Herman Stuempfle's "O Christ, Who Shared Our Mortal Life" (W4) would make an excellent reflection on the gospel reading during the preparation of the gifts. A delightfully appropriate song for Communion this Sunday would be Sydney Carter's "I Danced in the Morning [Lord of the Dance]" (in most resources). In it, we tell the world, and one another, the story of Christ's birth, life, death, and resurrection, and join him in his eternal dance of Life. Another good choice for Communion would be Stephen Pishner's "God Will Wipe Away the Tears" (G3). Verses 5 and 6 of M. D. Ridge's "In the Day of the Lord" (BB, JS3) would make a fitting recessional song.

SPIRITUALITY

GOSPEL ACCLAMATION
1 John 4:10b

R℣. Alleluia, alleluia.
God loved us and sent his Son
as expiation for our sins.
R℣. Alleluia, alleluia.

Gospel

Luke 7:36—8:3; L93C

A Pharisee invited Jesus to dine with
 him,
 and he entered the Pharisee's house
 and reclined at table.
Now there was a sinful woman in
 the city
who learned that he was at
 table in the house of the
 Pharisee.
Bringing an alabaster flask of
 ointment,
 she stood behind him at his feet
 weeping
and began to bathe his feet with her
 tears.
Then she wiped them with her hair,
 kissed them, and anointed them with
 the ointment.
When the Pharisee who had invited
 him saw this he said to
 himself,
 "If this man were a prophet,
he would know who and what sort of
 woman this is who is touching
 him,
 that she is a sinner."
Jesus said to him in reply,
 "Simon, I have something to say to
 you."
"Tell me, teacher," he said.
"Two people were in debt to a certain
 creditor;
 one owed five hundred days' wages
 and the other owed fifty.
Since they were unable to repay the
 debt, he forgave it for both.
Which of them will love him more?"

Continued in Appendix A, p. 304.

Continued in Appendix A, p. 304.

Reflecting on the Gospel

How many tears would need to be shed in order to have enough to wash feet? A bucketful! What would precipitate such an overflowing amount of tears? Extraordinary loss, sadness, sorrow. In the case of the "sinful woman" in this Sunday's gospel, her tears were precipitated by her great sense of unworthiness and her profound repentance. All the woman's gestures toward Jesus were *very personal*—weeping, wiping his feet with her hair, kissing his feet. Her gestures of touching him were ones of connectedness, of closing the distance between alienation and communion, of desiring a new relationship with someone who heals.

The Pharisee's response of indignation indicated how distant he really was from a life-changing relationship with Jesus. Contrary to what the Pharisee was thinking in response to the sinful woman's actions, Jesus was indeed a prophet, for he was able to see into the woman's heart and forgive her. He looked into the heart of the Pharisee, and saw there a lack of love. He saw distance. He saw one who did not wish to change.

Thus this gospel depicts two very different ways of relating to Jesus. Simon the Pharisee related to Jesus as a one-time visitor, maintaining only a surface relationship having no power to transform him; he kept Jesus at a safe distance from him. The "sinful woman," on the other hand, related to Jesus as an intimate, avowing an underlying relationship that transformed her. Jesus revealed the depth of her transformation: "Your faith has saved you." What is our relationship to Jesus? What does he say to us? Do we wish to be intimate and close to Jesus, or do we keep a protective distance?

The last part of the long form of this gospel shows us how effectively Jesus draws to himself sinners and those weakened by infirmities. Repentant sinners and those healed by Jesus stay near him. The women who followed Jesus were weak and sinful people who had been touched by Jesus. Their encounter with this Healer, this Prophet bound them to him and each other with new bonds of freedom. No longer turned in on themselves, they were free to provide for others "out of their resources." Loved by Jesus, they were freed to embrace self-giving that was a personal transformation setting them firmly on their own saving journey. Of such is our discipleship: to be touched by Jesus, to draw near to him, to stay with him. Jesus' journey is one of healing body and spirit. Our journey is one of being transformed by his touch, his nearness, his saving Presence.

Living the Paschal Mystery

The Pharisee neglected to see Jesus' need for hospitality and the sinful woman's need for forgiveness and salvation. It is so easy to miss seeing the needs of others! Part of that seeing is to forget self so that we can truly encounter the other. Forgetfulness of self is freeing, allowing new ways to reach out to others with personal touch and healing.

If we are wrapped up in our own needs, it is impossible to see the needs of others. One way to live this gospel is to practice every day reaching out to another with a simple gesture of kindness or hospitality. This can be so simple as saying hello to someone we pass in a hallway, smiling at someone who seems depressed, or lending a helping hand to someone who seems burdened. What happens in our reaching out to others is that distances in relationships are closed, we discover in others unforeseen goodness and worth, and both they and we are transformed by this self-giving way of relating.

Focusing the Gospel

Key words and phrases: Pharisee invited Jesus, sinful woman, bathe his feet with her tears, wiped them with her hair, kissed them, Your faith has saved you

To the point: This gospel depicts two very different ways of relating to Jesus. Simon the Pharisee relates to Jesus as a one-time visitor, maintaining only a surface relationship having no power to change him. The "sinful woman" relates to Jesus as an intimate, avowing an underlying relationship that transforms her. Jesus reveals the depth of her transformation: "Your faith has saved you." What is our relationship to Jesus? What does he say to us?

Connecting the Gospel

to the first reading: In the gospel, the woman openly admits her sinfulness by her actions when encountering Jesus. In the first reading, David openly admits his sinfulness when confronted by Nathan the prophet. Both the woman and David receive God's forgiveness and favor.

to experience: Tears are an overflow of great emotion, whether of sorrow or joy. The sinful woman in the gospel expresses deep sorrow through her tears. What tears of joy must she have shed upon hearing Jesus' words of forgiveness and salvation!

Connecting the Responsorial Psalm

to the readings: In this responsorial psalm the one praying relates a personal experience of having confessed sin and received divine mercy. The Lectionary omits verses 3-4 of Psalm 32 in which the person praying admits to having initially refused to accept his or her guilt, choosing instead to resist self-examination and honest confession. When the psalmist finally relents and confesses, God grants overwhelming forgiveness. The story of Psalm 32 is told dramatically in the confrontation between Nathan and David (first reading) and in the encounter between the sinful woman and Jesus (gospel). Moreover, it is told dramatically in our own lives every time we confess our wrongdoing. God forgives us and replaces our guilt with newfound freedom and joy (psalm).

to psalmist preparation: Spend some time this week reflecting on the overwhelming mercy of God who longs to forgive no matter what the sin. What moves you to ask for this forgiveness? What moves you to resist it?

ASSEMBLY & FAITH-SHARING GROUPS

- Words and images that best capture my relationship to Jesus are . . .
- As my relationship to Jesus grows, I am being transformed in these ways . . .
- Jesus is saying to me . . .

PRESIDERS

My relationship with Jesus grows through . . . As this relationship grows, my ministry is transformed to . . .

DEACONS

When my service ministry flows from my relationship with Jesus, it looks like . . .

HOSPITALITY MINISTERS

My welcome of those gathering for liturgy helps them encounter Jesus in a new way when I . . .

MUSIC MINISTERS

The manner of my music making reveals the nature of my relationship to Jesus in that . . .

ALTAR MINISTERS

My attending to the needs of liturgy looks like the humble sinful woman's attending to Jesus when I . . .

LECTORS

As I prepare for proclamation, I hear God say to *me* . . .

EXTRAORDINARY MINISTERS OF HOLY COMMUNION

My encounters with communicants transform my relationship with Jesus in that . . .

Model Penitential Act

Presider: In today's gospel we hear the story of a sinful woman who washes Jesus' feet with her tears of sorrow. Let us open ourselves to the God who washes away our sins . . . [pause]

Lord Jesus, you forgive those who come to you in sorrow: Lord . . .

Christ Jesus, you are the salvation of all who repent: Christ . . .

Lord Jesus, you came to give us God's mercy and compassion: Lord . . .

Homily Points

• Tears often relieve us of great internal burden. Our weeping releases the grip we are trying to hold on ourselves by remaining "strong," not letting ourselves feel some pain, not admitting our powerlessness and brokenness in face of some terrible loss or suffering. The weeping of the sinful woman in this gospel reveals that she has come to a grace-filled turning point in her life's journey.

• The sinful woman's tears express an extraordinary breaking-open of herself that allows Jesus and his mercy to enter her heart and bathe her in forgiveness. She comes to Jesus to express her sorrow. In response Jesus not only forgives her sinfulness, but also affirms her faith and assures her of salvation.

• We relate to Jesus in a way that breaks us open to his transforming Presence when we, for example, reach out to each other with forgiveness, or reach out to someone weeping in sorrow. We are transformed when we truly listen to his voice both in Sacred Scripture and in the words of one another. We are transformed when we go out of our way to do some good for another in need. In each grace-filled turning point in our life's journey, what is Jesus saying to us?

Model Universal Prayer (Prayer of the Faithful)

Presider: Let us now pray to the God of forgiveness, whose Son came to bring us mercy and salvation.

Response:

Lord, hear our prayer.

Cantor:

we pray to the Lord,

That all members of the church may deepen their relationship with Jesus through honest confession of sinfulness . . . [pause]

That all peoples of the world may come to salvation through forgiveness of one another . . . [pause]

That outcasts and sinners might be embraced by the love and mercy of others . . . [pause]

That all of us gathered here may be transformed by our loving encounters with Jesus and each other . . . [pause]

Presider: Merciful God, you sent your Son to speak to us words of forgiveness and salvation. Grant our prayers that we hear the words of your Son and one day rejoice with you in everlasting joy. We ask this through that same Son, Jesus Christ our Lord. **Amen.**

COLLECT
Let us pray.

Pause for silent prayer

O God, strength of those who hope in you,
graciously hear our pleas,
and, since without you mortal frailty can
    do nothing,
grant us always the help of your grace,
that in following your commands
we may please you by our resolve and our
    deeds.
Through our Lord Jesus Christ, your Son,
who lives and reigns with you in the unity
    of the Holy Spirit,
one God, for ever and ever. **Amen.**

FIRST READING
2 Sam 12:7-10, 13

Nathan said to David:
"Thus says the Lord God of Israel:
    'I anointed you king of Israel.
I rescued you from the hand of Saul.
I gave you your lord's house and your
    lord's wives for your own.
I gave you the house of Israel and of
    Judah.
And if this were not enough, I could count
    up for you still more.
Why have you spurned the Lord and done
    evil in his sight?
You have cut down Uriah the Hittite with
    the sword;
    you took his wife as your own,
    and him you killed with the sword of
        the Ammonites.
Now, therefore, the sword shall never
    depart from your house,
    because you have despised me
    and have taken the wife of Uriah to be
        your wife.'"
Then David said to Nathan,
    "I have sinned against the Lord."
Nathan answered David:
    "The Lord on his part has forgiven your
        sin:
    you shall not die."

RESPONSORIAL PSALM
Ps 32:1-2, 5, 7, 11

R⁊. (cf. 5c) Lord, forgive the wrong I have done.

Blessed is the one whose fault is taken
    away,
  whose sin is covered.
Blessed the man to whom the LORD
    imputes not guilt,
  in whose spirit there is no guile.

R⁊. Lord, forgive the wrong I have done.

I acknowledged my sin to you,
  my guilt I covered not.
I said, "I confess my faults to the LORD,"
  and you took away the guilt of my sin.

R⁊. Lord, forgive the wrong I have done.

You are my shelter; from distress you will
    preserve me;
  with glad cries of freedom you will ring
    me round.

R⁊. Lord, forgive the wrong I have done.

Be glad in the LORD and rejoice, you just;
  exult, all you upright of heart.

R⁊. Lord, forgive the wrong I have done.

SECOND READING
Gal 2:16, 19-21

Brothers and sisters:
 We who know that a person is not
    justified by works of the law
  but through faith in Jesus Christ,
  even we have believed in Christ Jesus
  that we may be justified by faith in
    Christ
  and not by works of the law,
  because by works of the law no one will
    be justified.
For through the law I died to the law,
  that I might live for God.
I have been crucified with Christ;
  yet I live, no longer I, but Christ lives
    in me;
  insofar as I now live in the flesh,
  I live by faith in the Son of God
  who has loved me and given himself up
    for me.
I do not nullify the grace of God;
  for if justification comes through the
    law,
  then Christ died for nothing.

About Liturgy

Hospitality at liturgy: We usually think of liturgy and hospitality in terms of the obvious liturgical ministry. Greeters welcome us and help us feel at home. Ushers take care of making sure the space is well prepared and comfortable, and seat us if the church is crowded. Hospitality ministers help us find restrooms, get help if we are ill, direct us to where the coffee and donuts are after Mass. All of this ministry is important. It helps us become a caring community. It takes care of our needs.

There is another dimension of liturgical hospitality, however. And this approach is much less tangible than what we mentioned above, yet even so much more important. Liturgical hospitality includes all assembly members opening themselves to encounter God and each other, becoming transparent enough so that others can see us as wanting to be part of this community, letting go of any expectations we might have with regard to how we want the liturgy to be celebrated. Liturgical hospitality is about closing distances so that we all might draw near to God. Liturgical hospitality might mean that we must quiet ourselves when we come to liturgy agitated over the pressures and demands of life. It might mean that we are willing to encounter the stranger—to greet someone we don't know, to help someone who is disabled, to volunteer when the parish needs additional liturgical ministers or workers for social events or justice actions. Above all, liturgical hospitality means that we see in the face of others the Christ whom we have come to liturgy to encounter.

About Liturgical Music

Music suggestions: Appropriate this Sunday would be songs celebrating God's life-giving mercy and our need to admit sinfulness and seek forgiveness. Examples include "Amazing Grace"; "Grant to Us, O Lord"; "There's a Wideness in God's Mercy"; "With the Lord"; "Hosea"; "Softly and Tenderly Jesus Is Calling"; "Come, You Sinners, Poor and Needy." Also appropriate would be songs which call us to offer the same forgiving mercy to one another, such as "The Master Came to Bring Good News" and "Forgive Our Sins [as We Forgive]."

Mary Louise Bringle's "In Boldness, Look to God" (*Joy and Wonder, Love and Longing*, GIA) speaks of many women in Scripture who dared address God with boldness. Verse 1 uses the story of the Canaanite woman who begged Jesus to cure her ailing child. Verse 2 draws on the courage of the woman who sought healing by reaching out to touch Jesus' hem. Verse 3 tells of Mary who risked censure to sit at Jesus' feet and listen to his teaching. Verse 4 honors the sinful woman who, despite "the world's harsh stare," washed Jesus' feet and wiped them with her hair. Sung during the preparation of the gifts, this hymn would make an excellent reflection on the gospel.

SPIRITUALITY

GOSPEL ACCLAMATION
John 10:27

R⁊. Alleluia, alleluia.
My sheep hear my voice, says the Lord;
I know them, and they follow
    me.
R⁊. Alleluia, alleluia.

Gospel

Luke 9:18-24; L96C

Once when Jesus
    was praying in
    solitude,
and the disciples were
    with him,
he asked them, "Who
    do the crowds say that I am?"
They said in reply, "John the Baptist;
    others, Elijah;
    still others, 'One of the ancient
    prophets has arisen.'"
Then he said to them, "But who do you
    say that I am?"
Peter said in reply, "The Christ of
    God."
He rebuked them
    and directed them not to tell this to
    anyone.

He said, "The Son of Man must suffer
    greatly
    and be rejected by the elders, the
    chief priests, and the scribes,
    and be killed and on the third day be
    raised."

Then he said to all,
    "If anyone wishes to come after me,
    he must deny himself
    and take up his cross daily and
    follow me.
For whoever wishes to save his life will
    lose it,
    but whoever loses his life for my
    sake will save it."

Reflecting on the Gospel

We often say things, the implications of which only become clear as time passes. We might promise to help someone move to a new home, only later to find out how much stuff they have, how much packing still needs to be done, how much more time-consuming our offer is than we originally thought. We might say that we will stick by a friend no matter what, only later to discover that to do so might entail jeopardizing our values. When Peter in this gospel said to Jesus that he is "The Christ of God," did Peter really understand the implications of what he was saying?

The exchange between Jesus and his disciples took place within a very significant context: "Jesus was praying in solitude." It was out of this prayer that he asked his disciples, "who do you say that I am?" and revealed that his very identity entailed suffering, rejection, death, and resurrection. Our own prayer is to lead us to clearer understanding of who we are, and to the revelation that our very identity as disciples entails denying self, taking up our daily cross, and losing our life for the sake of others. Dare we pray? Dare we ask Jesus, "who do *you* say that *I* am?" Dare we accept the identity Jesus offers us and the implications of being faithful to that identity?

Prayer—a personal encounter with God—helps us come to a clearer understanding of who we are and enables us to say yes to following Jesus, no matter what the implications. Jesus' mission is an extension of who Jesus is—Savior. We usually think of Jesus' mission as teaching and preaching, healing and working miracles and so it was. But underlying these activities is the ultimate one—his suffering, death, and resurrection. So it is with us. When we say yes to our identity as the Body of Christ, we spend our whole lives grasping the implications: with Jesus, we must take up our cross daily. This means that our life is marked by the same self-giving love as Jesus' life.

Living the Paschal Mystery

The first reading from the prophet Zechariah mentions "a fountain to purify from sin and uncleanness." For us Christians we naturally think of the baptismal font that purifies and cleanses us. Through baptism we share in Jesus' identity and mission—we are plunged into the waters of baptism, dying to self and rising to new life in Christ and thus are made members of the Body of Christ. Our own identity and mission is that of Jesus: to die to self so that we are raised to new Life. Following Jesus has its cost.

These waters of baptism don't flow just once. The ritual is an action that aptly describes an ongoing sacramental reality in our lives: we are constantly being washed clean. One way to do this, of course, is through confessing our sins either in prayer itself or in sacramental confession. We sometimes forget, though, that good works also cleanse us of our sins! So, the denying self and carrying our daily cross mentioned in the gospel are cleansing activities that lead us to forgiveness and new Life.

Baptismal purification is also tied into our Christian identity. We are not only freed from sin, but are made members of Christ's Body. As such, we might expect to happen to us the same things that happened to Jesus. To be practical, that means that when we live our baptismal promises we can expect to be misunderstood, ridiculed, shunned, and so on. Paschal mystery living has its demands (dying to self) and rewards (new Life). Self-giving is always life-giving. Self-giving is always love-giving.

Focusing the Gospel

Key words and phrases: Jesus was praying, who do you say that I am, suffer, rejected, killed, raised, anyone wishes to come after me, deny himself, take up his cross, loses his life

To the point: The exchange between Jesus and his disciples took place within a very significant context: "Jesus was praying in solitude." It was out of this prayer that he asked his disciples, "who do you say that I am?" and revealed that his very identity entailed suffering, rejection, death, and resurrection. Our own prayer is to lead us to clearer understanding of who we are, and to the revelation that our very identity as disciples entails denying self, taking up our daily cross, and losing our life for the sake of others. Dare we pray? Dare we ask Jesus, "who do *you* say that *I* am?"

Connecting the Gospel

to the first reading: The prophecy of Zechariah referring to the fate of Israel's king can be applied to Jesus the Messiah King whose side is pierced on the cross and for whom we all mourn.

to experience: We naturally recoil from unpleasantness: suffering, hard conversations, giving up something we love. Yet, to follow Jesus means embracing more than unpleasantness; it means taking up his cross daily.

Connecting the Responsorial Psalm

to the readings: In the first reading God pours onto the people a "spirit of grace and petition." Their prayer moves them to acknowledge their sinfulness, mourn what they have done, and receive purification. The gospel also relates a moment of prayer out of which Jesus leads the disciples to acknowledge who he is and to accept the suffering that he, and they with him, must undergo.

The responsorial psalm reminds us that prayer—thirsting for God—is the fountainhead of redemption. On the one hand, prayer is a gift from God (first reading). On the other, it is a choice on our part. Always it is a relationship that reveals both who God is and who we are. Prayer teaches us that we are souls in need of divine nourishment (psalm), sinners in need of repentance and purification (first reading), and disciples called to acknowledge Christ and carry the cross (gospel). Prayer also teaches us that God is our greatest good and ultimate satisfaction, that God acts to bring us to repentance, and that God in Christ takes up the cross ahead of us. May we know for whom we thirst, and may we drink deeply and be transformed.

to psalmist preparation: In the context of this Sunday's readings, this responsorial psalm is a courageous prayer to make. Jesus pours out his thirst for God in his own prayer (gospel). You join Jesus in this prayer and in the choice it implies to accept suffering and death in order to follow Jesus. Are you willing to accept where thirsting for God will ultimately lead you?

**ASSEMBLY &
FAITH-SHARING GROUPS**

- My prayer is an encounter with God that reveals to me that I am . . .
- I find it most difficult to shoulder my daily cross when . . . to deny self when . . . to give my life for another when . . .
- My prayer is most fruitful and life-sustaining for my discipleship when . . .

PRESIDERS
My prayer in solitude leads me to . . .

DEACONS
When I serve others, what I "lose" is . . . What God saves is . . .

HOSPITALITY MINISTERS
My greeting helps those gathering for liturgy to enter more fully into prayer when I . . .

MUSIC MINISTERS
In order for my music ministry to lead the assembly to Christ, I must die to myself by . . .

ALTAR MINISTERS
My serving identifies who I know myself to be for my family . . . for my parish . . . for God . . .

LECTORS
Engaging with God's word in a prayerful way entails . . .

**EXTRAORDINARY MINISTERS
OF HOLY COMMUNION**
My ministry of distributing Holy Communion is itself prayer when . . .

Model Penitential Act

Presider: In today's gospel Jesus tells his disciples that they must take up their daily cross in following him. As we prepare to celebrate this liturgy, let us seek God's mercy for the times we have failed to carry our daily cross in following Jesus . . . [pause]

Lord Jesus, you suffered greatly, were rejected, killed, and raised on the third day: Lord . . .

Christ Jesus, you are the Christ of God: Christ . . .

Lord Jesus, you call us to take up our daily cross and follow you: Lord . . .

Homily Points

• When a youngster says, "I dare you," there is pressure to accept the dare. When the youngster says, "I double dare you," the dare simply cannot be refused. If we wish to be saved, we must hear Jesus' teaching in this gospel as a double dare: we simply must, as disciples, deny self, take up our daily cross, lose our life for the sake of others.

• No doubt, Jesus prayed "in solitude" many more times than just "once." No doubt, he also raised the reality of the cross to his disciples more than just "once." No doubt, he told his disciples more than just "once" that to follow him faithfully they, too, must deny themselves, lose their lives, and take up their daily cross. What is the relationship between prayer, discipleship, and the reality of suffering, dying, and rising?

• In honest prayer we stand before God, stripped of false self-images and misleading life goals. In prayer we come to know who we are as Jesus' disciples and accept the demands of following him faithfully. In prayer we encounter the God who never forsakes us, who strengthens us to face our daily crosses, and who encourages us to be faithful. Dare we pray? How can we not? Dare we ask Jesus, "who do *you* say that *I* am?" Why would we not?

Model Universal Prayer (Prayer of the Faithful)

Presider: Discipleship is demanding and costly, and so we pray to the God who gives us the strength to be faithful.

Response:

Lord, hear our prayer.

Cantor:

we pray to the Lord,

For all members of the church, the Body of Christ, called to deny themselves, take up their cross, and follow Jesus . . . [pause]

For all peoples of the world, called to lose their lives for the sake of others . . . [pause]

For all those in need, saved by Jesus' life, death, and resurrection . . . [pause]

For ourselves, strengthened by the bonds of community with one another to be faithful disciples of Jesus . . . [pause]

Presider: Loving God, you strengthen us to be faithful disciples. Grant our prayers, help us to accept our daily crosses, and bring us one day to fullness of Life with you. We ask this through your Son, Jesus Christ our Lord. **Amen.**

Let us pray.

Pause for silent prayer

Grant, O Lord,
that we may always revere and love your
holy name,
for you never deprive of your guidance,
those you set firm on the foundation of
your love.
Through our Lord Jesus Christ, your Son,
who lives and reigns with you in the unity
of the Holy Spirit,
one God, for ever and ever. **Amen.**

FIRST READING
Zech 12:10-11; 13:1

Thus says the LORD:
I will pour out on the house of David
and on the inhabitants of Jerusalem
a spirit of grace and petition;
and they shall look on him whom they
have pierced,
and they shall mourn for him as one
mourns for an only son,
and they shall grieve over him as one
grieves over a firstborn.

On that day the mourning in Jerusalem
shall be as great
as the mourning of Hadadrimmon in
the plain of Megiddo.

On that day there shall be open to the
house of David
and to the inhabitants of Jerusalem,
a fountain to purify from sin and
uncleanness.

RESPONSORIAL PSALM
Ps 63:2, 3-4, 5-6, 8-9

R̸. (2b) My soul is thirsting for you,
O Lord my God.

O God, you are my God whom I seek;
for you my flesh pines and my soul
thirsts
like the earth, parched, lifeless and
without water.

R̸. My soul is thirsting for you, O Lord my
God.

Thus have I gazed toward you in the
sanctuary
to see your power and your glory,
for your kindness is a greater good than
life;
my lips shall glorify you.

R̸. My soul is thirsting for you, O Lord my
God.

Thus will I bless you while I live;
    lifting up my hands, I will call upon
        your name.
As with the riches of a banquet shall my
    soul be satisfied,
    and with exultant lips my mouth shall
        praise you.

℟. My soul is thirsting for you, O Lord my
God.

You are my help,
    and in the shadow of your wings I
        shout for joy.
My soul clings fast to you;
    your right hand upholds me.

℟. My soul is thirsting for you, O Lord my
God.

SECOND READING
Gal 3:26-29

Brothers and sisters:
Through faith you are all children of God
        in Christ Jesus.
For all of you who were baptized into
        Christ
    have clothed yourselves with Christ.
There is neither Jew nor Greek,
    there is neither slave nor free person,
    there is not male and female;
    for you are all one in Christ Jesus.
And if you belong to Christ,
    then you are Abraham's descendant,
    heirs according to the promise.

✠ CATECHESIS

About Liturgy

The cross: The cross has been a Christian symbol of self-denial, self-sacrifice, redemption, and identity with Christ from at least the fourth century. It has become the primary symbol of Christianity. The cross leads processions (GIRM 117, 119, and 122) and is venerated with incense (GIRM 49 and 277) as are the altar and paschal candle. A cross with a corpus is to be on or near the altar during Mass (GIRM 117 and 308) which helps us relate the sacrifice of the Mass to the sacrifice of Calvary.

In the Eastern Church the custom has been to use a cross rather than a crucifix (a cross with a corpus), often studded with jewels or richly decorated. Sometimes an image of Christ the High Priest may be used. The cross in this context celebrates Christ's victory over death and sin and is a symbol of triumph. In the Western Church the custom has been to use a crucifix with an image of the dying or dead Jesus. The cross in this context reminds us of Jesus' self-sacrificing love demonstrated through his passion and death.

Father's Day: The Mass of the Sunday is to be respected even if this Sunday is Father's Day. A fifth intercession might be added to the general intercessions at the universal prayer (prayer of the faithful; see BofB 1732) and a blessing for the fathers may be given in place of the prayer over the people for the Sunday (see BofB 1733).

About Liturgical Music

Music suggestions: In this Sunday's gospel the disciples grow in their awareness of who Jesus is and are confronted with the challenge of the cross. "Let Kings and Prophets Yield Their Name" (*Hymns for the Gospels*, GIA) was composed specifically for this gospel reading and would make an excellent text to sing during the preparation of the gifts. Dan Schutte's "Only This I Want" (BB, G3, JS3) would also be a good choice for the preparation of the gifts, as would Roc O'Connor's "Jesus, the Lord" (BB, G3, JS3). Suitable choices for Communion include Bernadette Farrell's "Unless a Grain of Wheat" (BB, G3, JS3, W4) and Lucien Deiss's "Keep in Mind" (in most resources). "Take Up Your Cross" (in most resources) would make a fitting and challenging recessional song.

SPIRITUALITY

GOSPEL ACCLAMATION
cf. Luke 1:76

℞. Alleluia, alleluia.
You, child, will be called prophet of the Most High,
for you will go before the Lord to prepare his way.
℞. Alleluia, alleluia.

Gospel   Luke 1:57-66, 80; L587

When the time arrived for
    Elizabeth to have her child
  she gave birth to a son.
Her neighbors and relatives heard
  that the Lord had shown his
    great mercy toward her,
  and they rejoiced with her.
When they came on the eighth
    day to circumcise the child,
  they were going to call him
    Zechariah after his
    father,
  but his mother said in reply,
"No. He will be called John."
But they answered her,
  "There is no one among your relatives
    who has this name."
So they made signs, asking his father what
    he wished him to be called.
He asked for a tablet and wrote, "John is his
    name,"
  and all were amazed.
Immediately his mouth was opened, his
    tongue freed,
  and he spoke blessing God.
Then fear came upon all their neighbors,
  and all these matters were discussed
    throughout the hill country of Judea.
All who heard these things took them to
    heart, saying,
  "What, then, will this child be?"
For surely the hand of the Lord was with him.

The child grew and became strong in spirit,
  and he was in the desert until the day
  of his manifestation to Israel.

See Appendix A, pp. 304–305, for the other readings.

Reflecting on the Gospel

Medical science research is teaching us more and more about the gene pool and its implications for predicting and treating potential diseases. The first thing a doctor does during a new patient visit is go over family medical history: Is heart disease, cancer, or diabetes in the family? Who has had it? One of the reasons adopted children might search for birth parents is to know their medical history and what actions to take in face of it. Family lineage is important to us for many reasons. As we celebrate the birth of John the Baptist, we are drawn by this gospel to consider family lineage.

Zechariah and Elizabeth had been barren and now they have a newborn son. God has blessed them and "shown his great mercy" toward them. How much joy they must have felt when their boy was born! The "neighbors and relatives" were rejoicing too, and they already had a name picked out for this new blessing and life: "they were going to call him Zechariah after his father." How startled they were when Elizabeth announced his name would be John!

Had Elizabeth and Zechariah named their son after his father, he would have belonged only to their family lineage. But in obedience to the angel, they named him "John," for he was not just their son. He was the precursor of a whole new family of the God who is gracious. Now we are the continuation of that family lineage, passing on the heritage of obedience and fidelity to God's saving plan of "great mercy" in Jesus Christ.

The centerpiece of the gospel, then, is not so much rejoicing at the blessing of a newborn, but the obedience of Elizabeth and Zechariah to God's word in naming their newborn son John. The name John was cause for great amazement among the people who wondered, "What, then, will this child be?" We know that John became the forerunner of the One who would come to save us. John was not born simply to bring joy to barren parents. He was born to point to a whole new in-breaking of God.

Something new is happening—God continues Jesus' saving work through us when we, too, obediently listen for and act upon God's word, when we recognize ourselves in the divine lineage that makes us members of God's family and invests us with a name, too. We are Christians, those who belong to the Body of Christ. In this way we ourselves are both precursor and the Presence of Christ in the world. Never before has this happened, even in John's time. We announce Jesus and *are* the Presence of the risen Christ. No wonder we are amazed. No wonder we rejoice. And no wonder we, too, are just a bit fearful. Such an awesome task God entrusts to us: to cooperate in fulfilling the divine plan of salvation. Such an awesome privilege it is to be a member of God's family, doing our part to pass on the heritage of God's saving grace.

Living the Paschal Mystery

John could point his disciples to Jesus as the Savior. We, too, point to the Presence of the risen Christ among us. More than by words, we do so by our obedience to God. We do so by living the paschal mystery in such a way that our own actions and way of living is so filled with love, so radically new—so radically different—that people are moved to ask of us, "What, then, is this person?" This doesn't mean that we leave all and go out into a desert. It does mean that we allow ourselves to grow "strong in the spirit" and live as those who have been baptized into Christ the Savior. It means that we live as members of God's family.

Focusing the Gospel

Key words and phrases: great mercy, John is his name, manifestation to Israel

To the point: Had Elizabeth and Zechariah named their son after his father, he would have belonged only to their family lineage. But in obedience to the angel, they named him "John," for he was not just their son. He was the precursor of a whole new family of the God who is gracious. Now we are the continuation of that family lineage, passing on the heritage of obedience and fidelity to God's saving plan of "great mercy" in Jesus Christ.

Model Penitential Act

Presider: We celebrate this day the birth of John the Baptist; we also celebrate our own birth into the family of our gracious God. We pause to call to mind the times we have not been faithful family members and ask for God's great mercy . . . [pause]

Lord Jesus, you are the One whose coming John announced: Lord . . .

Christ Jesus, you are the Savior of the world: Christ . . .

Lord Jesus, you are the Word of our gracious God: Lord . . .

Model Universal Prayer (Prayer of the Faithful)

Presider: As God showed great mercy to Elizabeth and Zechariah, so does God show us great mercy when we ask. And so we pray.

Response:

Lord, hear our prayer.

Cantor:

we pray to the Lord,

That each member of the church be obedient and faithful in continuing God's saving plan . . . [pause]

That leaders of nations lead their people to be faithful members of God's family . . . [pause]

That those who are hungering be fed from the table of God's great mercy . . . [pause]

That each one of us rejoice in the birth of John the Baptist and announce by the way we live that Jesus is among us . . . [pause]

Presider: Saving God, you hear the prayers of your faithful and obedient people. Grant us what we need so that one day we might join the saints in heaven and share everlasting Life with you. We ask this through Christ our Lord. **Amen.**

COLLECT

Let us pray.

Pause for silent prayer

O God, who raised up Saint John the Baptist
to make ready a nation fit for Christ the
    Lord,
give your people, we pray,
the grace of spiritual joys
and direct the hearts of all the faithful
into the way of salvation and peace.
Through our Lord Jesus Christ, your Son,
who lives and reigns with you in the unity
    of the Holy Spirit,
one God, for ever and ever. **Amen.**

FOR REFLECTION

* Because of my family lineage, I . . . Because I belong to the family of God, I . . .

* My obedience to God's saving plan calls me to . . . My fidelity to God's plan costs me . . .

* God is gracious to me by . . . when . . . In turn, I am gracious to . . . by . . . when . . .

Homily Points

* Family lineage is important. Knowing where we come from has implications for health issues, values, inheritance. Lineage also shapes our sense of identity and our mode of behavior. Knowing our history in God's "family" has the same implications—for our spiritual health, values, and eternal inheritance.

* We remain in and continue the lineage of God's family when we are obedient and faithful to God's saving plan as were Elizabeth, Zechariah, and John. Parents are obedient and faithful when, for example, they teach their children to have faith, to pray, to treat others with respect. Employees are obedient and faithful when, for example, they put in an honest day's work and are honest in their dealings with their employer. All of us are obedient and faithful when we live Gospel values.

THIRTEENTH SUNDAY IN ORDINARY TIME

SPIRITUALITY

GOSPEL ACCLAMATION
1 Sam 3:9; John 6:68c

℟. Alleluia, alleluia.
Speak, Lord, your servant is listening;
you have he words of everlasting life.
℟. Alleluia, alleluia.

Gospel   Luke 9:51-62; L99C

When the days for Jesus' being
    taken up were fulfilled,
  he resolutely determined to
    journey to Jerusalem,
  and he sent messengers ahead of
    him.
On the way they entered a Samaritan
    village
  to prepare for his reception there,
  but they would not welcome him
  because the destination of his journey
    was Jerusalem.
When the disciples James and John saw this
    they asked,
  "Lord, do you want us to call down fire
    from heaven
  to consume them?"
Jesus turned and rebuked them, and they
    journeyed to another village.

As they were proceeding on their journey
    someone said to him,
  "I will follow you wherever you go."
Jesus answered him,
  "Foxes have dens and birds of the sky
    have nests,
  but the Son of Man has nowhere to rest
    his head."

And to another he said, "Follow me."
But he replied, "Lord, let me go first and
    bury my father."
But he answered him, "Let the dead bury
    their dead.
  But you, go and proclaim the kingdom of
    God."
And another said, "I will follow you, Lord,
  but first let me say farewell to my family
    at home."
To him Jesus said, "No one who sets a hand
    to the plow
  and looks to what was left behind is fit
    for the kingdom of God."

Reflecting on the Gospel

Some people can be so bullheaded. They choose to stay the course at any cost. These folks are not simply stubborn; they are obstinate in a foolish or stupid way. Children can be bullheaded about who can or cannot play with them, based on whom they like or not. An employer might be bullheaded about who can use a conference room and for how long. A student might be bullheaded about choosing to do homework sloppily. In this gospel, when we hear that Jesus was "resolutely determined to journey to Jerusalem," we might be tempted to think he was really bullheaded. After all, "Jerusalem" represents death, the end of life's journey. Traveling to Jerusalem to meet suffering and death seems to be a stupid move. Peter, and presumably the other disciples, certainly did not want Jesus to embark on this journey (see Matt 16:21). They did not understand that Jerusalem represents more than the end of a journey, more than death. Jerusalem symbolizes the new Life beyond death.

The journey Jesus invites us to take is the journey through death to new Life. We know the cost, even better than the disciples knew, even as we also know the new Life that awaits beyond. We need to get started on this journey, and stay on an unswerving path. We must be single-minded, but not bullheaded. We must travel this journey with full understanding of that to which we commit ourselves. We also take this journey with full understanding of what is "beyond" Jerusalem.

Following Jesus requires much more than simply walking with him from village to village. Following Jesus calls for being "resolutely determined" to journey with him all the way to Jerusalem—and beyond. Any excuses, no matter how seemingly legitimate, keep us from letting go of where we are and embracing where we must go. To be on this journey requires total self-surrender to what Jerusalem holds as well as to "being taken up" into what is "beyond" Jerusalem: the new Jerusalem, "the kingdom of God" fulfilled.

The challenge of this gospel is for us to be as resolutely determined to accept the dying to self that is necessary to follow Jesus and cooperate with him in establishing God's reign as Jesus was resolutely determined to go to his own suffering and death. We can be neither naive, stupid, nor self-excusing. To be "fit for the kingdom of God" we must keep our eyes on Jesus and our destiny. We must let him be our motivation to stay the course. The course: Jerusalem. The price: dying. The stakes: new Life.

Living the Paschal Mystery

The context for this Sunday's gospel is that Jesus is "resolutely determined" to go to Jerusalem and this sets the tone for the next months of Ordinary Time for us. On our own journey to the end of the liturgical year in November (hardly on our minds at this point in June!) we, too, must be resolute about hearing the gospel faithfully and following Jesus, even when that means we, too, are going to "Jerusalem," which symbolizes the ongoing dying to self that is what living the paschal mystery really is.

We hear the gospel faithfully when that gospel is lived in our everyday circumstances. Hearing is more than words going into our ears; it demands of us resolute action. The gospels often are challenging. This one challenges us to go to Jerusalem with Jesus, and be his faithful followers by proclaiming that "the kingdom of God" is at hand.

164

Focusing the Gospel

Key words and phrases: being taken up, fulfilled, resolutely determined, journey to Jerusalem, Follow me, kingdom of God

To the point: Following Jesus requires much more than simply walking with him from village to village. Following Jesus calls for being "resolutely determined" to journey all the way with him to Jerusalem—and beyond. Any excuses, no matter how seemingly legitimate, keep us from letting go of where we are and embracing where we must go. To be on this journey requires total self-surrender to what Jerusalem holds as well as to "being taken up" into what is "beyond" Jerusalem: the new Jerusalem, "the kingdom of God" fulfilled.

Connecting the Gospel

to the first reading: There is a dramatic contrast between Elijah's response to Elisha and Jesus' response to those who wish to follow him. Elijah permits Elisha to bid farewell to his parents and settle his affairs. Jesus calls his disciples to let go of everything immediately and follow him.

to experience: Any journey we undertake can have multiple purposes; for example, a business trip might include recreational time for sightseeing. The Christian journey, on the other hand, has a single purpose—to make present "the kingdom of God." About this single purpose we must be resolute.

Connecting the Responsorial Psalm

to the readings: Confronted with the urgency of God's call, Elisha abandoned everything and followed Elijah without hesitation, leaving no possessions intact, not stopping even to bid his parents good-bye (first reading). Similarly, the gospel reveals how radically pressing the journey to Jerusalem is for Jesus. Jesus waits for nothing and no one, wastes no time on those unable to receive him, and cuts no slack for those who hesitate to follow him. For Jesus the urgency of the kingdom overrides everything else.

The responsorial psalm reveals what it is that enables Jesus and Elisha to so radically abandon all for the sake of the kingdom. They can relinquish everything, even what seems necessary for a safe and happy life (home and homeland, family and possessions), because they know they possess the very person of God (psalm refrain). They abandon all because they have been given even more. In this gospel Jesus asks us to make the same choice. Full of divine promise and Presence, the psalm gives us the courage to say yes. May it become our journey-to-Jerusalem song.

to psalmist preparation: Your singing of this psalm testifies that you have come to know that the reward of discipleship is far more valuable than its cost. Because you have chosen to follow Jesus, you have been given God's very self as your "portion" and "lot." How have you come to know this? Who has shown you? Whom might you show?

ASSEMBLY & FAITH-SHARING GROUPS

• Being "resolutely determined to journey to Jerusalem" with Jesus entails for me . . .

• One thing I must let go of in order to journey to Jerusalem with Jesus more faithfully is . . .

• Beyond "Jerusalem," God promises me . . .

PRESIDERS

What I need to let go of in order to preside well is . . . to lead my people to the new Jerusalem is . . .

DEACONS

The kind of service I must render on my journey to the new Jerusalem is . . . What helps me journey faithfully is . . .

HOSPITALITY MINISTERS

Hospitality is not a haven *from* the journey to "Jerusalem," but support for those *on* the journey, and so I must . . .

MUSIC MINISTERS

In order to follow Jesus to Jerusalem through my music ministry, some things I have to let go of are . . .

ALTAR MINISTERS

The way I am assisting others on their journey to Jerusalem is . . .

LECTORS

My daily living proclaims "the kingdom of God" when . . . This helps me when I proclaim Scripture because . . .

EXTRAORDINARY MINISTERS OF HOLY COMMUNION

Participation in the eucharistic banquet is already a share in the new Jerusalem in that . . .

CELEBRATION

Model Penitential Act

Presider: Today's gospel calls us to follow Jesus on his journey to Jerusalem where he will suffer, die, and be raised to new Life. As we prepare ourselves to hear this call, let us ask for mercy for those times when we have not been faithful . . . [pause]

Lord Jesus, you lead us on the journey to the fullness of Life: Lord . . .

Christ Jesus, you suffered, died, and were raised to new Life: Christ . . .

Lord Jesus, you call us to proclaim the kingdom of God: Lord . . .

Homily Points

• An anonymous saying dating from at least mid-nineteenth century states that "Life is not a destination, but a journey." In other words, life is not about staying put, but about moving forward. This gospel suggests that even more than moving forward, life is about moving "beyond."

• Jesus "resolutely determined to journey to Jerusalem," where he would face suffering and death. But this journey's destination and his death were not the end. Rather, they were a beginning leading to resurrection, ascension, eternal Life. Now we journey with Jesus to "Jerusalem." Is our life-journey taking us to our Life-beyond?

• We often generate excuses to stay where we are instead of journeying with Jesus to "Jerusalem." For example, we don't reach out to our neighbor in need because we won't let go of our own concerns. Or we don't move toward healing a relationship because we won't let go of a past hurt. To be on the life-journey to our Life-beyond, however, requires letting go of everything that keeps us from moving forward with Jesus, both to "Jerusalem" and beyond to the new Jerusalem.

Model Universal Prayer (Prayer of the Faithful)

Presider: We ask God for strength to be faithful and resolute on our Christian journey.

Response:

Lord, hear our prayer.

Cantor:

we pray to the Lord,

That all members of the church resolutely follow Jesus on the journey through death to new Life . . . [pause]

That leaders of nations resolutely lead their people to justice and peace . . . [pause]

That those who falter on the journey of life might be guided in God's ways . . . [pause]

That each of us wholeheartedly surrender to the daily demands of being faithful on our journey of discipleship . . . [pause]

Presider: Gracious God, your Son Jesus walks with us on our life's journey as his followers. Grant our prayers that one day we may enjoy the fullness of Life you offer us. We ask this through that same Son, Jesus Christ our Lord. **Amen.**

COLLECT

Let us pray.

Pause for silent prayer

O God, who through the grace of adoption
chose us to be children of light,
grant, we pray,
that we may not be wrapped in the
    darkness of error
but always be seen to stand in the bright
    light of truth.
Through our Lord Jesus Christ, your Son,
who lives and reigns with you in the unity
    of the Holy Spirit,
one God, for ever and ever. **Amen.**

FIRST READING
1 Kgs 19:16b, 19-21

The LORD said to Elijah:
    "You shall anoint Elisha, son of Shaphat
        of Abel-meholah,
    as prophet to succeed you."

Elijah set out and came upon Elisha, son
        of Shaphat,
    as he was plowing with twelve yoke of
        oxen;
    he was following the twelfth.
Elijah went over to him and threw his
        cloak over him.
Elisha left the oxen, ran after Elijah,
        and said,
    "Please, let me kiss my father and
        mother goodbye,
    and I will follow you."
Elijah answered, "Go back!
Have I done anything to you?"
Elisha left him and, taking the yoke of
        oxen, slaughtered them;
    he used the plowing equipment for fuel
        to boil their flesh,
    and gave it to his people to eat.
Then Elisha left and followed Elijah as his
        attendant.

RESPONSORIAL PSALM
Ps 16:1-2, 5, 7-8, 9-10, 11

R℟. (cf. 5a) You are my inheritance, O Lord.

Keep me, O God, for in you I take refuge;
    I say to the LORD, "My Lord are you.
O LORD, my allotted portion and my cup,
    you it is who hold fast my lot."

R℟. You are my inheritance, O Lord.

I bless the LORD who counsels me;
    even in the night my heart exhorts me.
I set the LORD ever before me;
    with him at my right hand I shall not be
      disturbed.

R℟. You are my inheritance, O Lord.

Therefore my heart is glad and my soul
    rejoices,
    my body, too, abides in confidence
because you will not abandon my soul to
    the netherworld,
    nor will you suffer your faithful one to
      undergo corruption.

R℟. You are my inheritance, O Lord.

You will show me the path to life,
    fullness of joys in your presence,
    the delights at your right hand forever.

R℟. You are my inheritance, O Lord.

SECOND READING
Gal 5:1, 13-18

Brothers and sisters:
For freedom Christ set us free;
    so stand firm and do not submit again
      to the yoke of slavery.

For you were called for freedom, brothers
    and sisters.
But do not use this freedom
    as an opportunity for the flesh;
    rather, serve one another through love.
For the whole law is fulfilled in one
    statement,
    namely, *You shall love your neighbor as*
      yourself.
But if you go on biting and devouring one
    another,
    beware that you are not consumed by
      one another.

I say, then: live by the Spirit
    and you will certainly not gratify the
      desire of the flesh.
For the flesh has desires against the Spirit,
    and the Spirit against the flesh;
    these are opposed to each other,
    so that you may not do what you want.
But if you are guided by the Spirit, you are
    not under the law.

About Liturgy

Processions at Mass: Processions are like mini journeys—they lead us from one place to another. They always have a goal. During Mass there are actually four processions, each with its own goal. Although the General Instruction of the Roman Missal refers to the four processions (see GIRM 44, 47, 73, 86, 119, 133), it gives no explanation or theology for them. The following comments may help fill in this lacuna.

    1. Entrance procession. This procession at the beginning of Mass is symbolic of the gathering of all the people into a unity for a common purpose of worship and transformation. The entrance procession symbolizes our journey from being individual *members* of the Body of Christ to *being* the Body of Christ gathered around the one Head, Christ made visible in his church.

    2. Gospel procession. The procession with the gospel book (usually from the altar to the ambo) is an opportunity for the assembly to acclaim the Presence of Christ in the proclaimed word. It also is a symbolic expression of their journey from *hearing* God's word to putting it into practice. We are now invited to turn toward the gospel book and follow its journey to the place of proclamation (see GIRM 133) as a sign of respect.

    3. Procession with the gifts. The procession and presentation of the gifts symbolize the gift of ourselves presented to God for transformation into being more perfect members of the Body of Christ, just as the bread and wine are transformed into being the Real Presence of Christ. As the gifts are placed on the altar we place ourselves on the altar and offer ourselves with Christ in sacrifice. It is symbolic of the ongoing journey of self-sacrifice that characterizes Christian living.

    4. Communion procession. The Communion procession symbolizes our journey to the messianic table, that heavenly banquet in which we already share by partaking in Jesus' Body and Blood at Holy Communion, and also in which we will forever share when we die and go to heaven. This procession most clearly proclaims what it means when the Communion lines actually move forward toward the altar.

About Liturgical Music

Music suggestions: In the song "Come and Journey with a Savior" (G3), we call one another to follow Jesus wherever he leads and whatever the cost, knowing he will always be present with us, leading the way. The song would be an appropriate entrance hymn for this Sunday. More meditative in tone, "Jesus, Lead the Way" (G3, W4) asks Jesus to be our light in darkness, our strength in grief, our source of "redeeming graces," even when leading us "through rough places." This would be an effective reflection on the gospel during the preparation of the gifts.

A good choice for Communion would be "The Love of the Lord" (G3, W4) in which we declare that sharing in Jesus' suffering and death matters more to us than all the riches of the earth. A good choice for the preparation of the gifts, or the recessional, would be "Jerusalem, My Destiny" (G3, SS) in which we sing that we have "fixed [our] eyes" and "set our hearts," like Jesus, on the journey to Jerusalem.

JUNE 26, 2016
THIRTEENTH SUNDAY
IN ORDINARY TIME

SS. PETER AND PAUL, APOSTLES

SPIRITUALITY

GOSPEL ACCLAMATION
Matt 16:18

R⁊. Alleluia, alleluia.
You are Peter and upon this rock I will build my
church,
and the gates of the netherworld shall not
prevail against it.
R⁊. Alleluia, alleluia.

Gospel   Matt 16:13-19; L591

When Jesus went into the region of
    Caesarea Philippi
  he asked his disciples,
  "Who do people say that the Son
      of Man is?"
They replied, "Some say John the
    Baptist, others Elijah,
  still others Jeremiah or one of
      the prophets."
He said to them, "But who do you
    say that I am?"
Simon Peter said in reply,
  "You are the Christ, the Son of the
      living God."
Jesus said to him in reply, "Blessed are
    you, Simon son of Jonah.
For flesh and blood has not revealed this
    to you, but my heavenly Father.
And so I say to you, you are Peter,
  and upon this rock I will build my
      Church,
  and the gates of the netherworld shall
      not prevail against it.
I will give you the keys to the Kingdom of
    heaven.
Whatever you bind on earth shall be
    bound in heaven;
  and whatever you loose on earth shall
      be loosed in heaven."

*See Appendix A, pp. 305–306, for the other
readings.*

Reflecting on the Gospel

Jesus' question to his disciples seems a bit unfair! He asks them, "who do you say that I am?" Does he really think the disciples know? Peter answers correctly: "You are the Christ, the Son of the living God." But it is this same Peter who denies him. Does he really know who Jesus is? The disciples abandon him. Do they know Jesus? One disciple betrays him. Does he know Jesus? Coming to know who Jesus is, confessing his identity, remaining faithful to him is not easy, is not something that happens once and is done, is not simply a matter of a momentary insight. Confessing "You are the Christ" is a lifelong adventure during which we, like the disciples, take a few steps forward and then a few steps backward. Jesus is very patient with us as we learn who he is and what are the costs and joys of discipleship. Peter and Paul learned. So must we.

While this festival is about two great apostles of Jesus, the readings direct us to God's actions on behalf of the church which Jesus founds. In the gospel it is God who reveals to Peter who Jesus really is. In the first and second readings it is God who rescues both Peter and Paul from death. Nothing can "prevail against" God's plan for the growth and endurance of the community of the church. These two apostles were not without their faults. Both, however, were open to encounter Jesus, grow in their knowledge and response to him, and were faithful in the end to all that was asked of them.

We have been given the same faith in Christ Jesus as Peter and Paul. Because of this we can be as extraordinary as they were. All we need to do is surrender ourselves like they did to the mystery of God's actions on behalf of the church. We honor Peter and Paul as the two apostles upon whom the universal mission of the church rests; this feast challenges us to accept that this same mission is continued in our own efforts to be faithful to Jesus' Gospel. Yes, Peter and Paul are amazing and cause for wonder. Because we share in their same mission to make known Christ in the world, so can our efforts be amazing and cause for wonder. Like these apostles, we need only to acknowledge that Jesus is the Christ and resolve to follow him wherever he leads. We are the church. We are the manifestation of God's mighty acts of salvation. We are the new pillars upon which this church continues to be built.

Jesus asks the disciples, "who do you say that I am?" Peter unveils Jesus' deepest identity in his response and so Jesus builds his church on Peter, the rock. After his conversion, Paul also proclaimed Jesus' identity. Jesus builds the Gentile church on Paul, the missionary. The work of building up the church now belongs to us. Are we rock solid missionaries in the mold of Peter and Paul?

Living the Paschal Mystery

Jesus' question about who he is might seem a bit unfair. Its very boldness presents a challenge to us. Being great apostles of Christ isn't a matter of doing great things; it is a matter of encountering and keeping faith in Christ Jesus. By recognizing ourselves as church—the Body of Christ—all of our actions are truly God's actions on behalf of the church. It is through us that the proclamation of the Good News of Jesus' death and resurrection is being completed. And, like these two great apostles, the Lord will give us strength to carry on the mission, will rescue us from evil, and bring us safely "to his heavenly kingdom."

Focusing the Gospel

Key words and phrases: who do you say that I am, Peter said in reply, upon this rock I will build my Church

To the point: Jesus asks the disciples, "who do you say that I am?" Peter unveils Jesus' deepest identity in his response and so Jesus builds his church on Peter, the rock. After his conversion, Paul also proclaimed Jesus' identity. Jesus builds the Gentile church on Paul, the missionary. The work of building up the church now belongs to us. Are we rock solid missionaries in the mold of Peter and Paul?

Model Penitential Act

Presider: We honor today Saints Peter and Paul because they were faithful to preaching the Gospel and cooperating with Christ in establishing his church. Let us prepare ourselves to celebrate this liturgy by surrendering ourselves to God's action within us so that we, too, can be faithful disciples . . . [pause]

Lord Jesus, you are the Christ: Lord . . .

Christ Jesus, you are the Son of the living God: Christ . . .

Lord Jesus, you build your church upon your faithful disciples: Lord . . .

Model Universal Prayer (Prayer of the Faithful)

Presider: Let us pray that Christ's church will continue to be built up and lead all people to fullness of Life.

Response:

Lord, hear our prayer.

Cantor:

we pray to the Lord,

That all members of the church, like Peter and Paul, be strong in their faith and steadfast in their discipleship . . . [pause]

That all leaders of the world's nations, like Peter and Paul, guide their people in truth and goodness . . . [pause]

That those wavering in faith or courage be strengthened by the community of Christ's church . . . [pause]

That each of us, like Peter and Paul, deepen our understanding of who Jesus is and our own self-understanding as his followers . . . [pause]

Presider: Almighty God, you strengthen all Jesus' disciples to be rocks upon which he continually builds up his church. Grant our prayers through the intercession of Saints Peter and Paul. Through Christ our Lord. **Amen.**

COLLECT
Let us pray.

Pause for silent prayer

O God, who on the Solemnity of the
    Apostles Peter and Paul
give us the noble and holy joy of this day,
grant, we pray, that your Church
may in all things follow the teaching
of those through whom she received
the beginnings of right religion.
Through our Lord Jesus Christ, your Son,
who lives and reigns with you in the unity
    of the Holy Spirit,
one God, for ever and ever. **Amen.**

FOR REFLECTION

• When Jesus asks me, "who do you say that I am?" I answer . . .

• As with Peter, Christ is building his church on me by . . .

• Like Paul, I am called to be a rock solid missionary to . . .

Homily Points

• We might say, derogatorily, to someone who isn't thinking straight, "What do you have, rocks in your head?" We might say, impatiently, to someone lollygagging on a job, "What do you have, rocks in your shoes?" This solemnity honoring Peter and Paul shows us two disciples who think straight about who Jesus is and his mission, and who do everything but lollygag about following him.

• Instead of rocks in our head or rocks in our shoes, we need rocks in our heart: solid faith, steadfast discipleship, firm commitment, immovable courage, unshakable sense of both who Jesus is and who we are in relation to him. Upon these rocks Jesus builds his church. Peter and Paul show us the way.

† SPIRITUALITY

GOSPEL ACCLAMATION
Col 3:15a, 16a

R7. Alleluia, alleluia.
Let the peace of Christ control your hearts;
let the word of Christ dwell in you richly.
R7. Alleluia, alleluia.

Gospel Luke 10:1-12, 17-20; L102C

At that time the Lord appointed
    seventy-two others
  whom he sent ahead of him in
      pairs
  to every town and place he
      intended to visit.
He said to them,
  "The harvest is abundant but
      the laborers are few;
  so ask the master of the
      harvest
  to send out laborers for his harvest.
Go on your way;
  behold, I am sending you like lambs
      among wolves.
Carry no money bag, no sack, no
      sandals;
  and greet no one along the way.
Into whatever house you enter, first say,
  'Peace to this household.'
If a peaceful person lives there,
  your peace will rest on him;
  but if not, it will return to you.
Stay in the same house and eat and
      drink what is offered to you,
  for the laborer deserves his payment.
Do not move about from one house to
      another.
Whatever town you enter and they
      welcome you,
  eat what is set before you,
  cure the sick in it and say to them,
  'The kingdom of God is at hand for
      you.'
Whatever town you enter and they do
      not receive you,
  go out into the streets and say,
  'The dust of your town that clings to
      our feet,
  even that we shake off against you.'

Continued in Appendix A, p. 306.

Reflecting on the Gospel

A really good spiritual director, a really good listener, a really good counselor all have at least one thing in common: they quietly take in words, body language, eye movement and then respond appropriately. They read people and situations quickly and accurately. Being in a conversation with those who are glancing at their cell phone every other second sends an important message to us: they are not giving full attention to the conversation and the phone is more important than the conversation. Even worse, the phone is more important than we are. This situation usually draws a rather negative response from us. We might roll our eyes, stop the conversation, or even walk away from the phone-bound person. Interactions and responses are part of our everyday living. Often they are inconsequential enough. Sometimes, however, interaction and response have long-lasting consequences. This gospel is about Jesus' disciples reading people and responses. The interaction-response has long-lasting and life-changing consequences.

When Jesus sends disciples forth as "laborers for his harvest," he predicts two responses to their presence. Either disciples will be welcomed and will be able to minister fruitfully, or they will be rejected and their ministry becomes judgment against the unwelcoming town. In either case, however, the "kingdom of God is at hand." In either case, the acceptance or rejection of the disciples makes clear that the "kingdom of God" is not dependent upon any one response, but upon God's gracious gift of Presence. How so? Whether accepted or rejected, disciples "harvest" the "kingdom of God" by their very presence, by their very proclamation of Jesus' name, by their very fidelity to Jesus' mission. No wonder disciples rejoice! Their rejoicing is an acknowledgment that God is present and working through them. The "kingdom of God" is present in the very persons of those who take up Jesus' invitation to be laborers in bringing about an abundant harvest.

The abundance of the harvest is guaranteed in two ways. If Jesus' disciples are not welcomed, they are not to quit the journey but continue it. Part of the ministry of laborer-disciples is the very "going"—the disciples' faithfulness to Jesus' sending them forth to proclaim that the "kingdom of God is at hand." While response to Gospel proclamation is obviously important, there can be no response at all unless disciples go forth on the journey, proclaim the Gospel faithfully, and rely on God's gift of divine Presence through them. We must respond to God's gift of Presence to us before we can call forth response from others. This divine Presence is the source of disciples' rejoicing.

Living the Paschal Mystery

The establishment of God's reign is already an in-breaking of the final glory that will be ours—our "names are [already] written in heaven." References to the abundance of the end times are captured in the "harvest" metaphor Jesus uses. Jesus looks at the harvest and sees abundance, fulfillment. Some of this abundance and fulfillment is surely realized in our own taking up of Jesus' mission to bring peace, to heal, and to dispel evil. The challenge of the gospel is that we don't get so lost in doing Jesus' mission that we forget being faithful disciples is in itself already an in-breaking of God's kingdom. Living the paschal mystery means that we let go of even the responses others might give to our Gospel living and surrender ourselves to be laborers for the harvest of peace and Presence.

Focusing the Gospel

Key words and phrases: he sent, laborers for his harvest, welcome you, kingdom of God is at hand, do not receive you, kingdom of God is at hand, because of your name, rejoice

To the point: When Jesus sends disciples forth as "laborers for his harvest," he predicts two responses to their presence. Either disciples will be welcomed and able to minister fruitfully, or they will be rejected and their ministry becomes judgment against the unwelcoming town. In either case, however, the "kingdom of God is at hand." How so? Whether accepted or rejected, disciples "harvest" the "kingdom of God" by their very presence, by their very proclamation of Jesus' name, by their very fidelity to Jesus' mission. No wonder disciples rejoice!

Connecting the Gospel

to the first reading: Isaiah prophesied that God's kingdom would be restored after the Babylonian exile as a land of comfort, abundance, and prosperity where the people would rejoice. Through the ministry of Jesus and his disciples the "kingdom of God is at hand" where peace, healing, and rejoicing are brought to a new fullness in Jesus' name.

to experience: We respond to any experience of rejection with sadness, pain, and discouragement. Yet Jesus reveals that rejection experienced in service of his mission to bring to fullness the "kingdom of God" actually leads to rejoicing.

Connecting the Responsorial Psalm

to the readings: In these verses from Psalm 66, the psalmist calls the entire earth to come and see the marvelous works of the Lord and to shout praises for God who has wrought such "tremendous . . . deeds!" In the first reading it is the Lord who calls the people to rejoice over marvelous deeds done on behalf of Jerusalem. In her arms the people will be fed and comforted and will discover how God has acted to save and restore. In the gospel Jesus sends his disciples out to proclaim the same message: God is acting to save, the kingdom is at hand. Some will welcome this message, others will reject it. But regardless of the response, the kingdom of God will not be thwarted: evil will be destroyed, healing will come, and peace will prevail.

Like the disciples, we, too, face failure as well as success as we go about the mission of announcing the Good News of the kingdom. Nonetheless, we "cry out . . . with joy" (psalm refrain) for we know that the indomitable power of God will make the kingdom prevail, and that our names are already "written there" (gospel).

to psalmist preparation: In this Sunday's gospel Jesus sends the disciples on mission to announce his coming. Your singing of the responsorial psalm is part of that mission, for it is a hymn of praise telling of God's saving deeds. Where have you experienced these deeds in your own life? in the lives of others? How have you announced them to the world?

ASSEMBLY & FAITH-SHARING GROUPS
- For me, the "kingdom of God" is . . .
- I experience being sent forth as a laborer for Jesus' harvest of the "kingdom of God" when . . . My response is . . .
- As Jesus' disciple, I am welcomed when . . . I am rejected when . . . In either case, Jesus says to me . . .

PRESIDERS
My very presence, my very proclamation of Jesus' name, my very fidelity to my ordained ministry brings forth a harvest of . . .

DEACONS
My daily life and my service ministry reveal that "the kingdom of God is at hand" when . . .

HOSPITALITY MINISTERS
My hospitality manifests that God's kingdom is at hand when I . . .

MUSIC MINISTERS
What helps my music ministry announce the presence of God's kingdom within the assembly is . . .

ALTAR MINISTERS
The harvest my service ministry makes visible is . . .

LECTORS
I proclaim that "the kingdom of God is at hand" in my daily living when . . .

EXTRAORDINARY MINISTERS OF HOLY COMMUNION
My very ministry of distributing Holy Communion harvests the fullness of God's kingdom in that . . .

CELEBRATION

Model Penitential Act

Presider: In today's gospel Jesus sends forth the seventy-two disciples who are sometimes accepted and sometimes rejected. As we prepare for this liturgy, let us open ourselves to God's Presence and mercy . . . [pause]

Lord Jesus, your Presence brings peace and healing: Lord . . .

Christ Jesus, you now live in the fullness of God's kingdom: Christ . . .

Lord Jesus, you send us forth to reap an abundant harvest: Lord . . .

Homily Points

• The harvesting of much of our fresh produce is very labor intensive. So is harvesting the "kingdom of God" labor intensive. The fruitfulness of this labor is not measured by bushel baskets, boxes, or bottom line—or by being accepted or rejected. It is measured by presence, proclamation, and perseverance in pursuit of Jesus' mission which brings about the "kingdom of God."

• Jesus tells his laborer-disciples what to do when they are not received: shake the town's dust off their feet. They are not to waste time, but to get on with the harvest elsewhere. Their labor will always produce fruit, for the "kingdom of God" cannot be shaken off—it is here, at hand, to stay.

• We are the laborer-disciples who must shake off the dust of the temptation to quit when facing difficulties or opposition, the dust of discouragement when there seemingly is no fruit for our efforts, the dust of indifference or ignorance. However, what keeps us present and faithful is a growing awareness that we do not labor alone or in vain. Whether facing rejection or receiving acceptance, our labor for the "kingdom of God" is guaranteed success, for the guarantor is Jesus. The harvest will always be great.

Model Universal Prayer (Prayer of the Faithful)

Presider: Jesus sends us forth as disciples to make present God's kingdom. Let us pray for what we need to be faithful to this mission.

Response:

Lord, hear our prayer.

Cantor:

we pray to the Lord,

That all members of the church be faithful laborers for the kingdom of God . . . [pause]

That all peoples come to salvation by welcoming the kingdom of God into their lives . . . [pause]

That the sick and those in need of healing be touched by those faithfully laboring for the kingdom of God . . . [pause]

That each of us here gathered rejoice in our call to follow Jesus and produce an abundant harvest for our country, for our world . . . [pause]

Presider: God of abundance, you give us all good things in order that your kingdom may be firmly established. Hear these our prayers that one day we might share in the fullness of your kingdom. We pray through Jesus Christ our Lord. **Amen.**

Let us pray.

Pause for silent prayer

O God, who in the abasement of your Son
have raised up a fallen world,
fill your faithful with holy joy,
for on those you have rescued from slavery
  to sin
you bestow eternal gladness.
Through our Lord Jesus Christ, your Son,
who lives and reigns with you in the unity
  of the Holy Spirit,
one God, for ever and ever. **Amen.**

FIRST READING
Isa 66:10-14c

Thus says the LORD:
Rejoice with Jerusalem and be glad
    because of her,
  all you who love her;
exult, exult with her,
  all you who were mourning over her!
Oh, that you may suck fully
  of the milk of her comfort,
that you may nurse with delight
  at her abundant breasts!
  For thus says the LORD:
Lo, I will spread prosperity over Jerusalem
    like a river,
  and the wealth of the nations like an
    overflowing torrent.
As nurslings, you shall be carried in her
    arms,
  and fondled in her lap;
as a mother comforts her child,
  so will I comfort you;
  in Jerusalem you shall find your
    comfort.

When you see this, your heart shall rejoice
  and your bodies flourish like the grass;
the LORD's power shall be known to his
    servants.

RESPONSORIAL PSALM

Ps 66:1-3, 4-5, 6-7, 16, 20

℟. (1) Let all the earth cry out to God with joy.

Shout joyfully to God, all the earth,
  sing praise to the glory of his name;
  proclaim his glorious praise.
Say to God, "How tremendous are your
  deeds!"

℟. Let all the earth cry out to God with joy.

"Let all on earth worship and sing praise
  to you,
  sing praise to your name!"
Come and see the works of God,
  his tremendous deeds among the
  children of Adam.

℟. Let all the earth cry out to God with joy.

He has changed the sea into dry land;
  through the river they passed on foot.
Therefore let us rejoice in him.
  He rules by his might forever.

℟. Let all the earth cry out to God with joy.

Hear now, all you who fear God,
  while I declare what he has done for me.
Blessed be God who refused me not
  my prayer or his kindness!

℟. Let all the earth cry out to God with joy.

SECOND READING

Gal 6:14-18

Brothers and sisters:
May I never boast except in the cross of
  our Lord Jesus Christ,
  through which the world has been
  crucified to me,
  and I to the world.
For neither does circumcision mean
  anything, nor does uncircumcision,
  but only a new creation.
Peace and mercy be to all who follow this
  rule
  and to the Israel of God.

From now on, let no one make troubles
  for me;
  for I bear the marks of Jesus on my
  body.

The grace of our Lord Jesus Christ be
  with your spirit,
  brothers and sisters. Amen.

About Liturgy

Choosing the longer or shorter form of a reading: Sometimes the Lectionary offers a longer or shorter form of a reading and which to use is left to the pastoral discretion of liturgy planners. It is not good to assume that the shorter reading is always best; often it is the longer reading which fills out and completes an important message of the Liturgy of the Word.

In the case of the gospel for this Sunday, for example, the longer form adds that as disciples sent on mission we act in Jesus' name (not our own), with Jesus' power (not our own), and are given eschatological reward (our names are "written in heaven").

When would one use the shorter form? Some pastoral situations (for example, in a children's Liturgy of the Word) might demand simpler readings. Or when the specific point that is being developed in the homily and carried through the universal prayer (prayer of the faithful) does not benefit from the extra Scripture verses. The point is, choices must be made deliberately, carefully, and with good reason.

July 4th: Monday is July 4th and there is always a pastoral temptation on such days to blend the Sunday liturgy with the national holiday. Good liturgical planning would enable the Sunday liturgy to take precedence, but still acknowledge the holiday. For example, the last petition in the model universal prayer (prayer of the faithful) takes into consideration the holiday. Some comments might be made in the presider's introduction. There is a proper Mass for July 4th given in the US edition of *The Roman Missal*, but it may not replace the proper Mass for this Sunday.

About Liturgical Music

Music suggestions: Verse 1 of Carl Daw's "Not Alone, but Two by Two" (W4) tells the story of this Sunday's gospel. Verse 2 applies the story to us: "Have we still such daring hearts? Can we claim their faith and nerve? Do we truly love the world Jesus calls for us to serve? Can we plant again the seed Sown in mutual ministry, Patterned on a life of faith Rooted in community?" Verse 3 is a prayer to the Holy Spirit to bind us in the unity we need to carry out the mission given to us. This hymn would make an excellent reflection on the gospel reading during the preparation of the gifts or an excellent recessional song. Suitable for either the entrance procession or the preparation of the gifts would be "God Is Working His Purpose Out" (W4). Good choices for the recessional would be "City of God" (BB, JS3, OF, WC, WS), "Go to the World" (SS, W4, WC, WS), and "God's Blessing Sends Us Forth" (OF, WC, WS).

Because of its origins, "Battle Hymn of the Republic"/"Mine Eyes Have Seen the Glory" is generally considered more a patriotic song than a religious hymn. But its text heralds more than national victory over enemies (in this case the Union army over the Confederacy). On a deeper, eschatological level the text celebrates the ultimate victory of the kingdom of God over all opposing forces. Furthermore, the fourth verse lays down the ultimate challenge of discipleship: that we give our lives that this kingdom come. In light of its theology, this hymn connects well, then, with this Sunday's gospel and would make an appropriate recessional song. The hymn needs to be used cautiously, however. An assembly that does not grasp its eschatological meaning will sing it only as a patriotic hymn celebrating July 4. It is important that they understand this hymn is not a battle cry for national victory in war, but a testimony that the kingdom of God will triumph no matter what forces vie against it. To this end it might be wise to run a blurb in the bulletin explaining the hymn's deeper religious meaning and its connection with this Sunday's gospel.

SPIRITUALITY

GOSPEL ACCLAMATION
cf. John 6:63c, 68c

R. Alleluia, alleluia.
Your words, Lord, are Spirit and life;
you have the words of everlasting life.
R. Alleluia, alleluia.

Gospel
Luke 10:25-37; L105C

There was a scholar of
    the law who stood up
    to test Jesus and said,
"Teacher, what must I
    do to inherit eternal
    life?"
Jesus said to him, "What is
    written in the law?
How do you read it?"
He said in reply,
    "You shall love the Lord, your God,
    with all your heart,
    with all your being,
    with all your strength,
    and with all your mind,
    and your neighbor as
        yourself."
He replied to him, "You have
    answered correctly;
    do this and you will live."

But because he wished to justify
    himself, he said to Jesus,
"And who is my neighbor?"
Jesus replied,
"A man fell victim to robbers
as he went down from Jerusalem to
    Jericho.
They stripped and beat him and went
    off leaving him half-dead.
A priest happened to be going down
    that road,
    but when he saw him, he passed by
        on the opposite side.
Likewise a Levite came to the place,
    and when he saw him, he passed by
        on the opposite side.

Continued in Appendix A, p. 306.

Reflecting on the Gospel
Many countries and US states have Good Samaritan laws. These laws protect from legal prosecution for wrongdoing anyone who helps or tends to someone who is ill or injured. In a litigation-prone society, these laws are a necessary complement to the charity with which many of us naturally respond when we encounter another in distress. In a sense, these laws protect charity, protect our acting with compassion, mercy, and love toward those in need. These laws take their name from this Sunday's gospel. This gospel not only expands the notion of neighbor, but also describes how, ultimately, we are to love as God loves us. Neighbor is not simply a victim, someone in need. Neighbor is anyone who deserves our love. And that is everyone!

The generosity of the Good Samaritan goes way beyond expected neighborliness and simple human compassion. He personally cares for the victim: tending to his wounds, carrying him on his own animal, caring for him at the inn. Yet even this is not enough: he leaves money for his continued care. By this parable Jesus teaches that to inherit "eternal life" we must go beyond who we love and how we love them. We must love as God loves: personally, extravagantly, continually.

Jesus' commandment of love is not impossibly far beyond us because his own life manifests here and now how to live loving relationships with others. Jesus teaches us how far we must go in loving others. Love has no limits, as Jesus himself illustrated by his own life. He loved even to dying for us. Our own loving one another must go this far, too. This kind of boundless love redefines who our neighbor is (everyone) and sets no limits on our time or care for others. Further, we show our love for God "with all [our] heart[s]" precisely when we love our neighbor.

Ironically, the way we inherit eternal Life is by dying to self for the sake of another. The Samaritan in the parable isn't moved to help the stricken traveler because of a commandment, but because he was a person of loving compassion and mercy—he illustrates unbounded love. This is the law written within our hearts (see first reading)—not details about keeping specific commandments, but a positive regard for the other that arises out of genuine love. Our love must be as wide as our universe and embrace all of God's beloved. Only by loving in this way can we truly be neighbor. Only by loving in this way can we, like God, be defined as love.

Living the Paschal Mystery
Probably in our society and church today we need to become more aware of the value of keeping laws. Our reflection, however, alerts us to the fact that simply keeping laws and commandments isn't enough. All our actions must be directed to the good of others. Keeping laws promotes good order in any community; doing good for others promotes right relationships in those same communities. Love is the glue that binds us to each other, that helps us make sense out of just laws, that expands our notion of neighbor to include everyone. Love is of God. It must be of us.

Law is something external to us, rather easily measured. Mercy and compassion, love and care are internal to us and can be measured only in terms of the good we actually do for others. Laws are internalized—written in our hearts—when they are kept for the sake of others. We are to do as the Good Samaritan in the parable: let the law of love and compassion guide us and gain for us eternal Life.

Focusing the Gospel

Key words and phrases: "Teacher, what must I do to inherit eternal life?"; love . . . God . . . neighbor; "And who is my neighbor?"; Samaritan . . . moved with compassion . . . approached the victim; cared for him

To the point: The generosity of the Good Samaritan goes way beyond expected neighborliness and simple human compassion. He personally cares for the victim: tending to his wounds, carrying him on his own animal, caring for him at the inn. Yet even this is not enough: he leaves money for his continued care. By this parable Jesus teaches that to inherit "eternal life" we must go beyond who we love and how we love them. We must love as God loves: personally, extravagantly, continually.

Connecting the Gospel

to the first reading: God's law "is not too mysterious and remote"—it is "already in your mouths and in your hearts; / you have only to carry it out." In the gospel the Good Samaritan shows what carrying out this law written in our hearts requires.

to experience: We usually think of "neighbor" as the other—the person next door, down the street, in our neighborhood. This parable reveals that we ourselves are the "neighbor" called to reach out with mercy and compassion to everyone.

Connecting the Responsorial Psalm

to the readings: At first glance Psalm 69 (the first of two choices given in the Lectionary for this Sunday) seems unrelated to either the first reading or the gospel, but deeper reflection reveals the connection. In the first reading Moses counsels the people that the commandments are not beyond them, but within them. In the gospel Jesus teaches that the commandments to love God and neighbor are not hazy, but clear and applicable: to love God means to love the immediate neighbor in need. The verses from Psalm 69 remind us that whenever *we* have been in need, God has responded unhesitatingly. We know God's law of love because we have experienced God loving us, directly and personally. And we know who is the neighbor in need because we have been that neighbor. It is this knowledge which fills our hearts and inspires us to act compassionately toward others. Psalm 69 grounds our loving in the One who has first, and always, loved us.

to psalmist preparation: To love one's neighbor as oneself is a tall order, and even more so when that neighbor is a stranger or an enemy. But you have only to turn to God for the strength you need to love in this way (see psalm refrain). When has the grace of God helped you love a neighbor in need?

ASSEMBLY & FAITH-SHARING GROUPS

- What I find challenging about Jesus' reply to "who is my neighbor?" is . . .
- To "inherit eternal life," I must love . . . by . . .
- I know God loves me personally, extravagantly, and continually because . . .

PRESIDERS

I tend to the wounds of my parishioners most lovingly when . . .

DEACONS

Just as the Samaritan was "moved" not by the law but by compassion, in my ministry I am moved by compassion when I . . .

HOSPITALITY MINISTERS

Times when my hospitality was merely a formality are . . . When I minister with compassion, my ministry becomes . . .

MUSIC MINISTERS

My music ministry is personal in that . . . It is extravagant when . . . It is continual because . . .

ALTAR MINISTERS

Serving others is continually forming me as a "good Samaritan" because . . .

LECTORS

The word that is "very near" to me and already in my heart (first reading) is . . . To "carry it out," I must . . .

EXTRAORDINARY MINISTERS OF HOLY COMMUNION

In my distributing Holy Communion, I am being a good "neighbor" in that . . .

CELEBRATION

Model Penitential Act

Presider: The Good Samaritan is a familiar parable reminding us to love and care for each other as God loves and cares for us. As we prepare for this liturgy, let us pause to ask God's mercy for the times we have not been a Good Samaritan for others . . . [pause]

Lord Jesus, you are compassionate and merciful to all: Lord . . .

Christ Jesus, you show us the way to eternal Life: Christ . . .

Lord Jesus, you loved us even to death on a cross: Lord . . .

Homily Points

• The parable of the Good Samaritan is so well known that its meaning has become part of our everyday vocabulary. For example, many Catholic hospitals in the United States carry the name Good Samaritan. When someone does a compassionate and merciful deed, we often say the person is a good Samaritan. Jesus teaches that a good Samaritan is, in fact, a good neighbor.

• The most important question raised by this gospel, however, is not "who is my neighbor," but how we should love our neighbor. Our love must be like that of the Good Samaritan: personal, extravagant, and continual. Indeed, this is how God loves us.

• Jesus' view of neighbor is someone in need—a person who needs help, a person who needs *my* help. In our global society, who is *not* my neighbor? In our global society, how can any of us not *be* neighbor—loving personally, extravagantly, continually? This is how God loves us. "Go and do likewise."

Model Universal Prayer (Prayer of the Faithful)

Presider: Our God is compassionate and merciful and so surely hears the prayers of those who cry out in need.

Response:

Lord, hear our prayer.

Cantor:

we pray to the Lord,

That each member of the church be a good Samaritan to all neighbors as Jesus teaches us: personally, extravagantly, continually . . . [pause]

That all nations live as neighbors in peace and love, compassion and mercy . . . [pause]

That those in any need be cared for by those who are faithful good Samaritans . . . [pause]

That all of us here continue to love with the extravagant compassion and mercy that God bestows on us . . . [pause]

Presider: Loving God, you hear the prayers of those who cry out to you. Grant our prayers, strengthen us in our love, and lead us to enjoy eternal Life with you. We ask this through Christ our Lord. **Amen.**

COLLECT

Let us pray.

Pause for silent prayer

O God, who show the light of your truth
to those who go astray,
so that they may return to the right path,
give all who for the faith they profess
are accounted Christians
the grace to reject whatever is contrary to
    the name of Christ
and to strive after all that does it honor.
Through our Lord Jesus Christ, your Son,
who lives and reigns with you in the unity
    of the Holy Spirit,
one God, for ever and ever. **Amen.**

FIRST READING
Deut 30:10-14

Moses said to the people:
    "If only you would heed the voice of the
        Lord, your God,
    and keep his commandments and statutes
    that are written in this book of the law,
    when you return to the Lord, your God,
    with all your heart and all your soul.

"For this command that I enjoin on you
        today
    is not too mysterious and remote for you.
It is not up in the sky, that you should say,
    'Who will go up in the sky to get it for us
    and tell us of it, that we may carry it out?'
Nor is it across the sea, that you should
        say,
    'Who will cross the sea to get it for us
    and tell us of it, that we may carry it out?'
No, it is something very near to you,
    already in your mouths and in your
        hearts;
    you have only to carry it out."

RESPONSORIAL PSALM
Ps 69:14, 17, 30-31, 33-34, 36, 37

℞. (cf. 33) Turn to the Lord in your need,
and you will live.

I pray to you, O Lord,
    for the time of your favor, O God!
In your great kindness answer me
    with your constant help.
Answer me, O Lord, for bounteous is your
        kindness:
    in your great mercy turn toward me.

℞. Turn to the Lord in your need, and you
will live.

I am afflicted and in pain;
    let your saving help, O God, protect me.
I will praise the name of God in song,
    and I will glorify him with
        thanksgiving.

R7. Turn to the Lord in your need, and you
will live.

"See, you lowly ones, and be glad;
    you who seek God, may your hearts
        revive!
For the LORD hears the poor,
    and his own who are in bonds he spurns
        not."

R7. Turn to the Lord in your need, and you
will live.

For God will save Zion
    and rebuild the cities of Judah.
The descendants of his servants shall
        inherit it,
    and those who love his name shall
        inhabit it.

R7. Turn to the Lord in your need, and you
will live.

or

RESPONSORIAL PSALM
Ps 19:8, 9, 10, 11

See Appendix A, p. 306.

SECOND READING
Col 1:15-20

Christ Jesus is the image of the invisible
    God,
    the firstborn of all creation.
For in him were created all things in
        heaven and on earth,
    the visible and the invisible,
    whether thrones or dominions or
        principalities or powers;
    all things were created through him and
        for him.
He is before all things,
    and in him all things hold together.
He is the head of the body, the church.
He is the beginning, the firstborn from the
        dead,
    that in all things he himself might be
        preeminent.
For in him all the fullness was pleased to
        dwell,
    and through him to reconcile all things
        for him,
    making peace by the blood of his cross
    through him, whether those on earth or
        those in heaven.

✠ CATECHESIS

About Liturgy
Liturgical law—enslavement or freedom?: Some liturgists, liturgy committees or commissions, and segments of the church get so caught up in keeping every detail of liturgical law that the celebration of liturgy is robbed of any focus on our love and worship of God and concern for others. We are careful to pay attention to liturgical laws, but we must be equally careful that our liturgies unfold as prayer and worship, as making present the paschal mystery, as celebrations of God's word and sacrament that transform us into being better members of Christ's Body living with love, compassion, and mercy toward all. If our adherence to liturgical law does not aid in this transformation, then we have missed its point. We have made the law external rubrics to be followed for their own sake rather than something written in our hearts. This skews the real purpose of liturgical law—to ensure that liturgy remains the liturgy of the whole church making present Christ's mystery, and not just an idiosyncratic ritual of a few.

Choice of responsorial psalm: This Sunday the Lectionary gives us two choices for a responsorial psalm and which one is chosen for use will depend upon the approach taken to the readings and gospel. The verses selected from Psalm 69 are a better choice for the approach we have taken in these reflections because they focus on God's mercy as a model for our own mercy. The verses selected from Psalm 19 focus more on the preciousness of the law itself and how the law brings life.

About Liturgical Music
Preludes and postludes: The principle of progressive solemnity suggests that the Sunday Eucharist should be celebrated in such a way that it emerges as clearly more important than weekday eucharistic celebrations. One way of marking this significance is to frame the celebration with a musical prelude and postlude. These musical elements unify the celebration as a whole. The prelude helps the gathering assembly ready themselves for the liturgy. The postlude adds a festive note to their leave-taking. Ideally the prelude connects thematically with the liturgical season or is musically related to the entrance hymn. Likewise the postlude relates to the liturgical season; it can be based on the hymn of praise after Communion or the recessional hymn, or can simply be a generic piece appropriate to the conclusion of Mass.

    Preludes and postludes can be instrumental or choral. The minutes right before Mass begins are often the best time for the choir to sing a piece related to the season or day. When the assembly sings a hymn of praise after Communion and the recessional hymn is then omitted, the choir can sing a festive postlude. For instrumental preludes and postludes, numerous resources for organ and piano pieces based on hymn tunes and related to liturgical seasons can be found in every major music publishing catalogue.

✛ SPIRITUALITY

GOSPEL ACCLAMATION
cf. Luke 8:15

℟. Alleluia, alleluia.
Blessed are they who have kept the word with a
  generous heart
and yield a harvest through perseverance.
℟. Alleluia, alleluia.

Gospel

Luke 10:38-42; L108C

Jesus entered a village
  where a woman whose name was
    Martha welcomed him.
She had a sister named Mary
  who sat beside the Lord at his feet
    listening to him speak.
Martha, burdened with much serving,
  came to him and said,
    "Lord, do you not care
  that my sister has left me by myself
    to do the serving?
Tell her to help me."
The Lord said to her in reply,
  "Martha, Martha, you are anxious
    and worried about many things.
There is need of only one thing.
Mary has chosen the better part
  and it will not be taken from her."

Reflecting on the Gospel

Attentiveness can be challenging sometimes. An older sister is trying to finish a term paper while her little brother keeps pestering her to play. Friends are out for a nice dinner together to catch up on news and one keeps answering her cell phone. The dog keeps barking to be let out while the owner is riveted to the ball game on TV. To be attentive—especially to be attentive to another person—means that we focus, that we eliminate distractions, that we allow one thing to command our full attention. This gospel is about attentiveness. Martha is attentive about getting food prepared and serving; Mary is attentive about listening to her Guest. Both are doing good things. However, one is choosing the "better part."

Jesus tells Martha in this gospel that there "is need of only one thing." What is it? On the surface, the answer would seem to be "listening to him speak," as Mary is doing. Even this is not enough, however. We must also heed how Jesus judges Martha: "you are anxious and worried about many things." The "one thing" is to be single-minded, single-hearted, open-minded, open-hearted. The "one thing" is to surrender ourselves to Jesus' Presence, whether sitting or standing, resting or working, receiving or giving.

The gospel is about hosts and guest and hospitality, but Jesus puts an unparalleled twist on the notion of hospitality. Martha's "hospitality" was made edgy because of her becoming burdened with the cooking and serving and only focusing on that, losing sight of Jesus. Martha settles for being only a servant (and complaining about it at that!) while Jesus is looking for disciples. Mary's hospitality was more gracious than Martha's because she focused her attention on Jesus: "sat beside the Lord at his feet listening to him." The surprise is that Jesus affirms that the "better part" is to be attentive to his Presence. The "better part" is to be a disciple, attuned to the Master!

A welcoming hospitality implies an "at-homeness" and belonging that parallels the unique relationship of disciple to Jesus. A welcoming hospitality does not mean choosing either serving or listening. It means that whatever we are doing, we are attentive to Jesus' Presence. Sometimes listening and learning about discipleship, as Mary is doing, is what we must choose. Sometimes being about the everyday tasks of life and serving others, as Martha is doing, is what we must choose. Jesus judges us not so much for choosing either listening or serving, but for choosing to be attentive to his Presence.

Living the Paschal Mystery

There are many ways that Jesus is present to us if we take the time to be attentive to his Presence. We usually address living the paschal mystery in terms of how we die to ourselves in our everyday living. This gospel suggests a radically different—and complementary—way of living the paschal mystery: being attentive to Jesus' abiding Presence. Practically speaking, this means being attentive to the proclamation of the Scriptures (especially the gospel) during Mass. It means taking the time to be with Jesus in prayer—not just saying prayers, but being quiet and listening to how Jesus speaks to our hearts. It means hearing Jesus in the cry of another for help. There is truly a great deal of self-sacrificing in letting go of our busyness in order to be attentive to Jesus' Presence and see him in all circumstances of our daily living!

I thank my God **whenever** I think of you; **and** every time I pray for **all of** you, I pray with joy..."
[Ph. 1:3].

Focusing the Gospel

Key words and phrases: listening to him speak, burdened with much serving, anxious and worried, need of only one thing

To the point: Jesus tells Martha in this gospel that there "is need of only one thing." What is it? On the surface, the answer would seem to be "listening to him speak," as Mary is doing. Even this is not enough, however. We must also heed how Jesus judges Martha: "you are anxious and worried about many things." The "one thing" is to be single-minded, single-hearted, open-minded, open-hearted. The "one thing" is to surrender ourselves to Jesus' Presence, whether sitting or standing, resting or working, receiving or giving.

Connecting the Gospel

to the first reading: Both Abraham and Martha are busy about many things. Abraham, however, remains attentive to the presence of his guests. Martha, on the other hand, is burdened by her tasks and loses sight of true hospitality: focus on the presence of guests.

to experience: We tend to be "either-or" in our thinking. This is also how we tend to interpret this gospel. Jesus is not saying hospitality and serving are unimportant; he is inviting us to reflect on how and when we are attentive to his Presence.

Connecting the Responsorial Psalm

to the readings: Psalm 15 was part of a ritual followed when a person wished to gain admittance to the temple. Because the temple was God's dwelling, no one could enter without permission. The individual was questioned at the gate by a priest who would ask, "LORD, who may abide in your tent?" (v. 1 of Psalm 15, omitted in the Lectionary). The person then answered by reciting subsequent verses of the psalm: one who does justice, thinks truth, slanders not, and so forth. This ritual expressed Israel's understanding that entrance into God's dwelling place required right living.

In the first reading Abraham stands as a type of the right living which grants entrance into the divine Presence. He receives strangers with hospitality and is blessed for it. That he responds so immediately to their needs, however, indicates he was already living "in the presence of the Lord" (psalm refrain). Such was the consistent orientation of his life. This is the orientation to which the psalm calls us and to which Jesus calls us when he praises Mary's choice of the "better part" in the gospel. May our abiding desire be to live in the Presence of God and may that Presence shape our manner of living.

to psalmist preparation: In preparing to sing this responsorial psalm, spend some time reflecting on how you choose to live in the Presence of God and how that choice shapes your manner of living. When and how do you take time to be with God? How, in concrete ways, do you let God's Presence challenge your living?

ASSEMBLY & FAITH-SHARING GROUPS

- When being present to Jesus, I am more like Martha when . . . like Mary when . . .
- Jesus judges me "anxious and worried about many things" when I . . .
- The "one thing" I need is . . . To receive it, I must surrender . . .

PRESIDERS

My homilies are most effective when I surrender to . . . The "one thing" that Jesus is asking of me is . . .

DEACONS

When I feel "burdened with much serving," my ministry becomes . . . The "one thing" that Jesus is asking of me is . . .

HOSPITALITY MINISTERS

My manner of being present to those gathering for liturgy enables them to be fully present because . . . The "one thing" that Jesus is asking of me is . . .

MUSIC MINISTERS

The "better part" of my music ministry is . . . The "one thing" that Jesus is asking of me is . . .

ALTAR MINISTERS

When I am "anxious and worried" about my ministry, what happens is . . . The "one thing" that Jesus is asking of me is . . .

LECTORS

I listen to God's word in my daily life in these ways . . . The "one thing" that Jesus is asking of me is . . .

EXTRAORDINARY MINISTERS OF HOLY COMMUNION

In my actively distributing Holy Communion, I receive . . . The "one thing" that Jesus is asking of me is . . .

Model Penitential Act

Presider: Jesus tells Martha in today's gospel that there "is need of only one thing": to be truly present to Jesus, whether sitting at his feet listening to him or serving him in others. As we prepare to listen to Jesus and receive him during this Eucharist, let us ask God's mercy for the times we have failed to be attentive to the Presence of Jesus in our lives . . . [pause]

Lord Jesus, you are present to us in word and deed: Lord . . .

Christ Jesus, you are the eternal Guest abiding in our hearts: Christ . . .

Lord Jesus, you are the promise of eternal Life: Lord . . .

Homily Points

• Needing only one thing is well beyond our normal longings and experience. We tend to want many things well beyond even our needs. This gospel calls us to examine what we truly need, and consider the "one thing" we must pursue or we will lose everything else we have.

• The gospel is full of seeming contrasts: sitting or standing, resting or working, receiving or giving. The "one thing" necessary in face of all life's contrasts is to be single-minded, single-hearted, open-minded, open-hearted to Jesus' Presence—no matter what we are doing.

• Jesus says in this gospel, "There is need of only one thing." What is it? To welcome Jesus into our home? To be taught by Jesus? To listen to Jesus? To give undivided attention to Jesus? To be in the Presence of Jesus? To serve Jesus? To be judged by Jesus? To be encouraged and affirmed by Jesus? To be unburdened by Jesus? Yes! Pursue this "one thing," and we will be given everything.

Model Universal Prayer (Prayer of the Faithful)

Presider: Jesus tells Martha that there is need of only one thing. As we make our many needs known to God, let us be confident that God gives us the "one thing."

Response:

Lord, hear our prayer.

Cantor:

we pray to the Lord,

That all members of the church pursue attentiveness to Jesus' Presence as the one thing always needed . . . [pause]

That all peoples of the world pursue the salvation that only God offers . . . [pause]

That those who are burdened with the cares of life pursue what will bring them God's Presence and healing . . . [pause]

That each of us here pursue the kind of hospitality that is at the heart of Jesus' saving mission . . . [pause]

Presider: Gracious God, you give us all we need to come to fullness of Life. Grant our prayers that we may pursue the "one thing" that leads us steadfastly to your Presence. We ask this through Christ our Lord. **Amen.**

COLLECT

Let us pray.

Pause for silent prayer

Show favor, O Lord, to your servants
and mercifully increase the gifts of your grace,
that, made fervent in hope, faith and charity,
they may be ever watchful in keeping your commands.
Through our Lord Jesus Christ, your Son,
who lives and reigns with you in the unity of the Holy Spirit,
one God, for ever and ever. **Amen.**

FIRST READING

Gen 18:1-10a

The LORD appeared to Abraham by the terebinth of Mamre,
as he sat in the entrance of his tent,
while the day was growing hot.
Looking up, Abraham saw three men standing nearby.
When he saw them, he ran from the entrance of the tent to greet them;
and bowing to the ground, he said:
"Sir, if I may ask you this favor,
please do not go on past your servant.
Let some water be brought, that you may bathe your feet,
and then rest yourselves under the tree.
Now that you have come this close to your servant,
let me bring you a little food, that you may refresh yourselves;
and afterward you may go on your way."
The men replied, "Very well, do as you have said."

Abraham hastened into the tent and told Sarah,
"Quick, three measures of fine flour! Knead it and make rolls."
He ran to the herd, picked out a tender, choice steer,
and gave it to a servant, who quickly prepared it.
Then Abraham got some curds and milk,
as well as the steer that had been prepared,
and set these before the three men;
and he waited on them under the tree while they ate.

They asked Abraham, "Where is your wife Sarah?"
He replied, "There in the tent."
One of them said, "I will surely return to you about this time next year,
and Sarah will then have a son."

RESPONSORIAL PSALM

Ps 15:2-3, 3-4, 5

R⁒. (1a) He who does justice will live in the presence of the Lord.

One who walks blamelessly and does justice;
  who thinks the truth in his heart
  and slanders not with his tongue.

R⁒. He who does justice will live in the presence of the Lord.

Who harms not his fellow man,
  nor takes up a reproach against his neighbor;
by whom the reprobate is despised,
  while he honors those who fear the Lord.

R⁒. He who does justice will live in the presence of the Lord.

Who lends not his money at usury
  and accepts no bribe against the innocent.
One who does these things
  shall never be disturbed.

R⁒. He who does justice will live in the presence of the Lord.

SECOND READING

Col 1:24-28

Brothers and sisters:
Now I rejoice in my sufferings for your sake,
  and in my flesh I am filling up
  what is lacking in the afflictions of Christ
  on behalf of his body, which is the church,
  of which I am a minister
  in accordance with God's stewardship given to me
  to bring to completion for you the word of God,
  the mystery hidden from ages and from generations past.
But now it has been manifested to his holy ones,
  to whom God chose to make known the riches of the glory
  of this mystery among the Gentiles;
  it is Christ in you, the hope for glory.
It is he whom we proclaim,
  admonishing everyone and teaching everyone with all wisdom,
  that we may present everyone perfect in Christ.

About Liturgy

Hospitality ministers: Most parishes and liturgical communities have hospitality ministers—whether they are called that or greeters or ushers or some combination of all these. Although we Catholics could certainly take some lessons in church hospitality from our Protestant brothers and sisters (it is only in recent church renovations that we are providing for such simple human necessities as bathrooms and cloakrooms!), we must also take care that our hospitality ministry doesn't limit what the gospel for this Sunday implies.

Hospitality at church is far more than a pleasant greeting and welcome (although surely these are important aspects of the ministry). Hospitality ministers must understand themselves first of all as disciples and, like Mary in the gospel, must assume in their lives and ministry a listening stance toward Jesus and a practiced attentiveness to his abiding Presence. The ministry points to Christ's Presence in the community, emphasizes all are welcome because all are members of the Body of Christ, and helps the assembling church members to prepare to *listen* to Jesus speak to their hearts during the liturgy. Hospitality ministry is more than a practical convenience or a social nicety; it is an expression of Jesus' own ministry that recognizes the other's dignity as a member of the Body of Christ.

About Liturgical Music

Role of the responsorial psalm, part 1: One way to look at the role of the responsorial psalm is to see it as a bridge between the first reading and the gospel. The image of a bridge conveys both movement forward and connectedness, and accords with the principle that the climax of the Liturgy of the Word is the gospel for which the preceding elements prepare us (see the Introduction to the Lectionary for Mass no. 13).

The movement forward aspect of the bridge metaphor implies that we begin the Liturgy of the Word in one place and cross over to another. There is a journey here. The connectedness aspect of the metaphor indicates that the beginning and ending of this journey are related. The starting point and the ending point form opposing shorelines. What we cross over in between varies; sometimes it is moving water, sometimes it is a valley bursting with grain, and sometimes it is a dry gulch or even a frighteningly deep canyon.

The crossing-over is not a journey through time from the Old Testament to the New Testament, but a journey of transformation. We begin the Liturgy of the Word standing on the threshold of a new moment of encounter with the word of God and we cross over to a new level of self-understanding as Body of Christ. The structural element that carries us from one way of being to another is the responsorial psalm.

✠ SPIRITUALITY

GOSPEL ACCLAMATION
Rom 8:15bc

℟. Alleluia, alleluia.
You have received a Spirit of adoption,
through which we cry, Abba, Father.
℟. Alleluia, alleluia.

Gospel
Luke 11:1-13; L111C

Jesus was praying in a certain
    place, and when he had
    finished,
one of his disciples said to
    him,
"Lord, teach us to pray
    just as John taught his
    disciples."
He said to them, "When you pray, say:
Father, hallowed be your name,
    your kingdom come.
    Give us each day our daily bread
    and forgive us our sins
    for we ourselves forgive everyone
        in debt to us,
    and do not subject us to the final
        test."

And he said to them, "Suppose one of
    you has a friend
to whom he goes at midnight and says,
'Friend, lend me three loaves of bread,
for a friend of mine has arrived at
    my house from a journey
and I have nothing to offer him,'
and he says in reply from within,
'Do not bother me; the door has
    already been locked
and my children and I are already in
    bed.
I cannot get up to give you anything.'
I tell you,
    if he does not get up to give the
        visitor the loaves
    because of their friendship,
    he will get up to give him whatever
        he needs
    because of his persistence.

Continued in Appendix A, p. 307.

Reflecting on the Gospel

In an early church writing called the *Didache* (The Teaching of the Twelve Apostles; probably second century), we have the first "commandment" about prayer: to pray the Our Father "as the Lord bid us in his gospel . . . pray in this way three times a day" (8:2, 3). The *Didache* doesn't say *when* the three times a day are to be, but presumably at traditional prayer times: upon rising, at midday, upon retiring. This prayer has been in the hearts of Christians since the early disciples asked Jesus to teach them to pray. He gave them words. But he also gave them much more. Jesus, in this gospel, gives us a way to address God (as "Father"), how we ought to pray (with perseverance), and why we pray (because God gives us all "good gifts"). Jesus teaches us that prayer is and must be from oneself, very personal. Prayer is a gift of self.

Jesus' disciples want him to teach them to pray "just as John taught his disciples." Jesus couldn't teach them the prayer of John, however, because he was not John. He was himself, and would teach a prayer that is the very gift of himself to us. Jesus' prayer to his Father flows from who he is—the One who praises, intercedes, forgives, reconciles, and protects. In this he gives us a pattern for our prayer, even if we do not use these very words. Our prayer flows from our physical needs, our emotional attachments and relationships, our spiritual desires. In the end, however, Jesus' prayer is for his Father to "give the Holy Spirit." Then, no request is too great, no seeking is unrewarded, no door is locked. The Holy Spirit transforms our prayer—and us—into turning ourselves toward God, into allowing the prayer to change us into those who seek only what God desires for us.

The two examples that Jesus uses (neighborly friendship and father-son kinship) reveal that what is always granted through prayer is deeper relationship with God and others. Jesus teaches us that the One to whom we pray is our "Father" whose love and care for us is unlimited. This deeply intimate and personal relationship with God inspires in us the confidence ("how much more . . .") to pray with "persistence" and the realization that what we pray for is not so important as the fact that we address God in such intimate terms. The prayer always deepens our relationship with God and this is already an answer to what we need. The prayer transforms our relationship with each other—opening us to forgiveness and reconciliation—and this is surely an answer to who we are and wish to become.

Living the Paschal Mystery

There is nothing wrong with praying for specific needs; after all, we do it every Mass at the universal prayer (prayer of the faithful) and during the eucharistic prayer, not to mention our own personal and daily prayers of petition. This gospel challenges us to go beyond specific needs and get to the larger picture: a focus on the gifts God offers us always in prayer, and often in surprising and unexpected ways. What inspires confidence in us is not whether God gives us what we specifically ask for in prayer; our confidence comes from the Spirit who dwells within and establishes a most intimate relationship between God and us—shared Life.

Unlike small children who seem to have a capacity to stay endlessly with some tasks, most of us need to develop a habit of daily prayer. With such busy schedules, this can be difficult. Choosing a specific time and being persistent about honoring that time for prayer helps.

Focusing the Gospel

Key words and phrases: teach us to pray, hallowed be your name, Give us each day, forgive us, forgive everyone, do not subject us, give the Holy Spirit

To the point: Jesus' disciples want him to teach them to pray "just as John taught his disciples." Jesus couldn't teach them the prayer of John, however, because he was not John. Jesus' prayer to his Father flows from who he is—the One who praises, intercedes, forgives, reconciles, and protects. In the end, his prayer is for his Father to "give the Holy Spirit." Then, no request is too great, no seeking is unrewarded, no door is locked.

Connecting the Gospel

to the first reading: How bold Abraham is when he approaches God—not once, but many times—to save Sodom and Gomorrah for the sake of those who are innocent of evil! How bold the disciples are to demand Jesus to teach them to pray! How bold a prayer Jesus does teach them.

to experience: How often have we prayed the Our Father? How often have we stopped to realize for whom or what really we are praying? Since the Our Father flows from who Jesus is, then truly praying it must transform us into being more fully like Jesus and who he is.

Connecting the Responsorial Psalm

to the readings: In the gospel Jesus responds on several levels to the disciples' request that he show them how to pray: he teaches them the Our Father; he encourages them to be persistent; he subtly suggests what it is they are to pray for (the gift of the Holy Spirit); and he calls them to ground their prayer in the goodness of God who is their Father. The first reading gives us a dramatic example of such prayer. Abraham persists in his petition. He remains humble yet audacious, speaking to God directly and forcefully. Finally, what he prays for is righteous judgment and protection of the innocent. On the divine side the story reveals that God waits for such prayer. God stands directly in front of Abraham and invites the conversation. God listens each time Abraham speaks and grants his request. Clearly this is a God who desires our salvation and who seeks human collaboration in bringing it about.

The responsorial psalm confirms that what grounds confidence in prayer is the nature of God who is great in kindness and true to every promise. God will answer when we call; God will complete the work of salvation begun in us. We need have no hesitation to petition such a God. We need only to carefully discern for what it is we ask.

to psalmist preparation: When you sing the responsorial psalm, what the assembly hears more than the beauty of your voice is the sound of your praying. Ask Christ this week to teach you how to pray the psalm.

ASSEMBLY & FAITH-SHARING GROUPS

- Jesus' prayer reveals him to be . . . When I pray his prayer, I become . . .
- I need the Holy Spirit when . . . I pray for the Holy Spirit to . . .
- In my prayer, I ask God for . . . God gives me . . .

PRESIDERS

I boldly stand before God and ask . . .

DEACONS

My ministry manifests the "how much more will the Father in heaven give" by . . .

HOSPITALITY MINISTERS

My hospitality invites the assembly to be bold during prayer when I . . .

MUSIC MINISTERS

My music ministry helps me pray by . . . My music ministry is prayer when . . .

ALTAR MINISTERS

My serving others becomes prayer when . . . My service aids the prayer of others by . . .

LECTORS

When my proclamation flows from God's gift of the Holy Spirit, the assembly . . .

EXTRAORDINARY MINISTERS OF HOLY COMMUNION

The ways I am "daily bread" for my family, neighbors, coworkers, those who are infirm, etc. are . . .

CELEBRATION

Model Penitential Act

Presider: In today's gospel the disciples ask Jesus to teach them to pray. Let us ask God's mercy for the times when we have not been faithful to daily prayer . . . [pause]

Lord Jesus, you teach us how to pray: Lord . . .

Christ Jesus, you sit at the right hand of your Father and offer eternal praise: Christ . . .

Lord Jesus, you intercede for us before the Father and give us all we need: Lord . . .

Homily Points

• We ask parents to teach us how to tie our shoes, how to ride a bike, how to drive a car, how to open a bank account, how to interview for a job. Life skills once learned are mastered. How often do we ask parents, teachers, ministers how to pray? Prayer skill is *the* life skill that is never mastered—we are always learning how to pray more boldly, persistently, authentically.

• When Jesus' disciples asked him to teach them how to pray, did they really know what they were asking? Jesus taught them not simply words, but an orientation of heart: in prayer how they are to relate to God and each other, to be persistent, to ask for the gift of the Holy Spirit. Then, no request would be too great, no seeking would be unrewarded, no door would be locked.

• Jesus in this gospel gives us words for prayer, orientation of heart for prayer, models for persistence in prayer. Every prayer is answered by God, but according to God's will and orientation of the divine heart. Our prayer does not change God; it changes us. As we surrender to our prayer, we become more like our Teacher, Jesus, who prays boldly, persistently, and authentically. We never master prayer; we let the prayer of Jesus master us.

Model Universal Prayer (Prayer of the Faithful)

Presider: Jesus taught us to pray persistently to our loving Father for our needs. Let us boldly ask God for what we need.

Response:

Lord, hear our prayer.

Cantor:

we pray to the Lord,

That all members of the church grow through prayer in their relationship with God and each other . . . [pause]

That all peoples of the world boldly lift their hearts to God in making their needs known . . . [pause]

That those who struggle with praying listen to the prompting of the Holy Spirit in their heart who gives them the words they need . . . [pause]

That each one of us learn by our praying how to become more like Jesus . . . [pause]

Presider: Gracious God, you hear the prayers of those who turn to you in boldness and persistence. Grant what we ask and bring us to your heavenly dwelling place where prayer is unceasing. We ask this through Christ our Lord. **Amen.**

184

COLLECT

Let us pray.

Pause for silent prayer

O God, protector of those who hope in you,
without whom nothing has firm
foundation, nothing is holy,
bestow in abundance your mercy upon us
and grant that, with you as our ruler and
guide,
we may use the good things that pass
in such a way as to hold fast even now
to those that ever endure.
Through our Lord Jesus Christ, your Son,
who lives and reigns with you in the unity
of the Holy Spirit,
one God, for ever and ever. **Amen.**

FIRST READING

Gen 18:20-32

In those days, the LORD said: "The outcry
against Sodom and Gomorrah is so
great,
and their sin so grave,
that I must go down and see whether or
not their actions
fully correspond to the cry against them
that comes to me.
I mean to find out."

While Abraham's visitors walked on
farther toward Sodom,
the LORD remained standing before
Abraham.
Then Abraham drew nearer and said:
"Will you sweep away the innocent with
the guilty?
Suppose there were fifty innocent people in
the city;
would you wipe out the place, rather
than spare it
for the sake of the fifty innocent people
within it?
Far be it from you to do such a thing,
to make the innocent die with the guilty
so that the innocent and the guilty would
be treated alike!
Should not the judge of all the world act
with justice?"
The LORD replied,
"If I find fifty innocent people in the city
of Sodom,
I will spare the whole place for their sake."
Abraham spoke up again:
"See how I am presuming to speak to
my Lord,
though I am but dust and ashes!
What if there are five less than fifty
innocent people?
Will you destroy the whole city because of
those five?"
He answered, "I will not destroy it, if I find
forty-five there."
But Abraham persisted, saying, "What if
only forty are found there?"

He replied, "I will forbear doing it for the
    sake of the forty."
Then Abraham said, "Let not my Lord
    grow impatient if I go on.
What if only thirty are found there?"
He replied, "I will forbear doing it if I can
    find but thirty there."
Still Abraham went on,
    "Since I have thus dared to speak to my
        Lord,
    what if there are no more than twenty?"
The LORD answered, "I will not destroy it,
    for the sake of the twenty."
But he still persisted:
    "Please, let not my Lord grow angry if I
        speak up this last time.
What if there are at least ten there?"
He replied, "For the sake of those ten, I will
    not destroy it."

RESPONSORIAL PSALM
Ps 138:1-2, 2-3, 6-7, 7-8

R⍰. (3a) Lord, on the day I called for help,
you answered me.

I will give thanks to you, O LORD, with all
        my heart,
    for you have heard the words of my
        mouth;
    in the presence of the angels I will sing
        your praise;
I will worship at your holy temple
    and give thanks to your name.

R⍰. Lord, on the day I called for help, you
answered me.

Because of your kindness and your truth;
    for you have made great above all things
        your name and your promise.
When I called you answered me;
    you built up strength within me.

R⍰. Lord, on the day I called for help, you
answered me.

The LORD is exalted, yet the lowly he sees,
    and the proud he knows from afar.
Though I walk amid distress, you preserve
        me;
    against the anger of my enemies you
        raise your hand.

R⍰. Lord, on the day I called for help, you
answered me.

Your right hand saves me.
    The LORD will complete what he has
        done for me;
your kindness, O LORD, endures forever;
    forsake not the work of your hands.

R⍰. Lord, on the day I called for help, you
answered me.

SECOND READING
Col 2:12-14

See Appendix A, p. 307.

✠ CATECHESIS

About Liturgy

Liturgy as prayer: We call liturgy a celebration, a ritual act, the communal worship of the people. We process during liturgy, sing, acclaim, proclaim. Liturgy is filled
with many different kinds of activities. This Sunday's gospel challenges us to consider
whether we approach liturgy as *prayer*. True, we pray the Our Father just before Holy
Communion, the prayer that Jesus taught us and we hear about in this Sunday's gospel.
Since this is the prayer that Jesus taught, we rightly think of its preeminence. At the
same time we cannot forget that *all* of liturgy is prayer from the beginning sign of the
cross to the concluding blessing and dismissal. A prayerful attitude should mark how
we celebrate liturgy.

Why is it important to insist that liturgy is prayer? An attitude of prayer keeps us
focused on the relationship with God that we share. It helps us realize that we don't
celebrate liturgy because of any power we have, but because God invites us and gives
us the Holy Spirit who enables us to respond with praise and thanksgiving.

True, different kinds of prayer mark our liturgies. Sometimes we pray aloud together, such as during the responsorial psalm and the Our Father. Sometimes we are
given silent time during which to pour our hearts out to God very personally in prayer,
such as in the quiet time after the readings and after receiving Holy Communion.
Sometimes we actively listen as another voices our prayer, such as during the presiden-
tial prayers (collect, prayer over the gifts, prayer after Communion) and the eucharistic
prayer. Surely our acclaiming and hymn singing is also prayer. But for all these (and
other) types of prayer during Mass, the real challenge is to make the *whole Mass* the
one prayer of the one Body of Christ.

About Liturgical Music

Role of the responsorial psalm, part 2: How does the responsorial psalm act as
bridge between the first reading and the gospel? How does the psalm help us surrender
to the transformation the gospel calls for? Part of what happens is that the movement
within the psalm text itself—its internal changes of mood, focus, content, and metaphor—parallel the movement meant to take place within us as we respond to the word
of God. There is an integral relationship between the process of transformation and
conversion within the heart, mind, and behavior of the original psalmist as he or she was
responding to the actions of God, and the change which takes place within us as we pray
that psalm within the context of this Liturgy of the Word. One of the implications here
is that the role of the psalmist is very important. The psalmist must personally embody
the transformation unfolding in the psalm and call us to that transformation. This is no small task, and certainly one that
involves far more than singing with a nice voice.

Each week "Connecting the Responsorial
Psalm" (found on the second page for each
Sunday) explores the relationship between the
psalm and the readings of the day. Sometimes
the connection is obvious, other times it is not
so clear, but it is always there. Identifying this
connection and reflecting on it deepens our
appreciation of the role of the psalm. Only
then can we sing it with understanding and
surrender to its transformative power.

✝ SPIRITUALITY

GOSPEL ACCLAMATION
Matt 5:3

℟. Alleluia, alleluia.
Blessed are the poor in spirit,
for theirs is the kingdom of heaven.
℟. Alleluia, alleluia.

Gospel

Luke 12:13-21; L114C

Someone in the crowd said to
    Jesus,
    "Teacher, tell my brother to
        share the inheritance
        with me."
He replied to him,
    "Friend, who appointed
        me as your judge and
        arbitrator?"
Then he said to the crowd,
    "Take care to guard against all greed,
    for though one may be rich,
    one's life does not consist of
        possessions."

Then he told them a parable.
"There was a rich man whose land
        produced a bountiful harvest.
He asked himself, 'What shall I do,
    for I do not have space to store my
        harvest?'
And he said, 'This is what I shall do:
    I shall tear down my barns and build
        larger ones.
There I shall store all my grain and
        other goods
    and I shall say to myself, "Now as for
        you,
    you have so many good things stored
        up for many years,
    rest, eat, drink, be merry!"'
But God said to him,
    'You fool, this night your life will be
        demanded of you;
    and the things you have prepared, to
        whom will they belong?'
Thus will it be for all who store up
        treasure for themselves
    but are not rich in what matters to
        God."

Reflecting on the Gospel

Linus is the Peanuts character who is always drawn holding a blanket to his head and sucking his thumb. Linus is a beloved character who reminds us that we all need a hug, a security blanket once in a while. Borrowing his name and image, Project Linus is a national organization that provides free security blankets for critically ill or traumatized children. Some of the blankets donated are larger, intended for older children. Pain, fear, and insecurity know no age limits.

Whenever we face any life-threatening occasion, we naturally reach out for whatever relieves us, whatever wraps us in hugs, love, security. We can readily identify, then, with the rich man in the gospel who has a "bountiful harvest" and doesn't want to waste a single grain. Although he is rich and probably already has plenty, he portrays what each of us harbors in the depth of our hearts: we can never have enough. We always want to increase whatever we think gives us security in face of life's inevitable exigencies. How mistaken we are!

The rich man in the gospel thinks building bigger barns to hold a boon of "grain and other goods" will give him enough security that he can "rest, eat, drink, be merry." When his life is "demanded" of him, however, his store of "grain and other goods" proves not to be the ultimate security—an eternal inheritance. He is misguided about the bigger barn he really needs to build. In the end, what "matters to God" is a "barn" full of what only God can give: life, love, holiness, fidelity, generosity, compassion, Life. No barn can ever be big enough to hold these. No barn we build can hold the security that is God alone. The only security we truly possess is a loving relationship with God—and this is surely what matters most to God. It should matter most to us.

Even with all our Christian living and reflection, we still struggle with what God graciously offers us—not more possessions, but fullness of Life. The gospel challenges us to direct all of our work toward a quality of life based on growing in our relationship with God and each other. Even our possessions and how we use them have this end—to bring us into right relationship with God and each other so that ultimately we possess what really counts: God's eternal Life. God offers us what matters most—fullness of Life and the secure happiness that only God can give. God alone is our sure security blanket.

Living the Paschal Mystery

If most of us take some time to think about the way we live, we would have to admit that the pressures of everyday life tend to be our main focus. We are all concerned about calendars and schedules, bills and getting ahead, sickness and health. Our lives tend to be so busy that our immediate goal is simply to get through another day. What would happen if we would truly take some time to think about what we possess (and where we store it all!) and what possesses us?

It takes conscious effort to ask the question, To whom do *we* belong? In some sense this is a question about priorities and putting God truly at the center of our lives. The answer must be more than an intellectual commitment to grow in our relationship with God and have God as our center. We must stop building (using) larger storage barns and begin changing the way we live so that our priorities are evident. Practically speaking, this probably means settling for fewer possessions. But with God at center, we really gain everything—fullness of Life.

Focusing the Gospel

Key words and phrases: inheritance; build larger ones; grain and other goods; rest, eat, drink, be merry; life will be demanded of you; what matters to God

To the point: The rich man in the gospel thinks building bigger barns to hold a boon of "grain and other goods" will give him enough security that he can "rest, eat, drink, be merry." When his life is "demanded" of him, however, his store of "grain and other goods" proves not to be the ultimate security—an eternal inheritance. He is misguided about the bigger barn he really needs to build. In the end, what "matters to God" is a "barn" full of what only God can give: life, love, holiness, fidelity, generosity, compassion, Life. No barn can ever be big enough to hold these. No barn we build can hold the security that is God alone.

Connecting the Gospel

to the first reading: Qoheleth teaches that it is a great "sorrow and grief" only to focus on the things of this world, which vanish like vapor ("vanity"). The gospel illustrates this poignantly.

to experience: The rich man's reality is everyone's desire: to have enough so that we don't have to worry about tomorrow's needs. Prudently providing for our future is responsible planning. Nevertheless, Jesus challenges us in this gospel not to place our security in possessions, but in God alone.

Connecting the Responsorial Psalm

to the readings: Psalm 90, from which this responsorial psalm is taken, contrasts the stability and steadfastness of God with the uncertainty and transience of human life. The verses used in the Lectionary express Israel's prayer that God teach them true assessment of their life and work. As the reading from Ecclesiastes indicates, they already realize hard work and physical possessions give no sure value. What is worth possessing is the kind and "gracious care" of God (psalm). Jesus affirms this stance when he challenges his hearers to turn from evaluating their worth based on physical possessions to evaluating it based on being "rich in what matters to God" (gospel).

It is significant that the psalm refrain is taken not from Psalm 90 but from Psalm 95, a psalm which refers to the infidelity of Israel's ancestors during their desert exodus from slavery to the Promised Land. No matter how much God gave them (water, manna), they constantly whined that they did not have enough. The Lectionary's choice of this refrain is acknowledgment that reckoning our days and assessing our worth in God's terms is a challenging task. May this be the work God prospers in us (psalm).

to psalmist preparation: The refrain for this responsorial psalm is particularly challenging. Sometimes when you hear God's voice, your heart hardens. When do you experience this happening for yourself? How does God help you hear in spite of your resistance?

ASSEMBLY & FAITH-SHARING GROUPS

- I need to build a bigger barn to hold . . . What my "barn" lacks is . . .
- If I knew that "this night [my] life will be demanded of [me]," I would . . .
- For me being "rich in what matters to God" means . . . My richness (or poverty) in what matters to God is revealed by . . .

PRESIDERS

My manner of presiding helps the assembly rest in the Lord, eat and drink more worthily, be merry in God's security when I . . .

DEACONS

My serving others helps me to be "rich in what matters to God" when . . .

HOSPITALITY MINISTERS

The way I greet and welcome those gathering for liturgy helps them to be more ready for the life God demands of them when I . . .

MUSIC MINISTERS

My music making helps the assembly build bigger and more appropriate "barns" when . . .

ALTAR MINISTERS

Serving is "toil and anxiety of heart" (first reading) when I . . . Serving embodies what it means to be "rich in what matters to God" when I . . .

LECTORS

My proclamation bespeaks God's desire that I already share in a rich inheritance when . . . That inheritance is . . .

EXTRAORDINARY MINISTERS OF HOLY COMMUNION

The way I distribute Holy Communion helps others see the fullness of Life God wishes for them by . . .

Model Penitential Act

Presider: In today's gospel Jesus tells the parable of the rich man who builds bigger barns to hold his "grain and other goods" so he can "rest, eat, drink, be merry." Let us ask God's mercy for the times we have built bigger barns to hold what is not of God . . . [pause]

Lord Jesus, you give us all good things: Lord . . .

Christ Jesus, you are the fullness of God's love and Life: Christ . . .

Lord Jesus, you call us to be rich in what matters to God: Lord . . .

Homily Points

• In this life, what do we need? Food, clothing, and shelter readily come to mind. But how much of these necessities of life do we *really* need? It is easy to confuse wants with needs, greed with security. This gospel challenges us to evaluate possessions, pursuits, priorities.

• This parable reminds us how fleeting are the things of this world and how easy it is to have a false sense of security in ourselves and our possessions. In both this world and the next, our ultimate security can be found only in God.

• What do we need to clean out of our "barn" to make more room for God? Perhaps we need to stop asking Jesus to correct the behavior of someone else ("tell my brother") and start letting him transform *our* values and behavior. Perhaps we need to take inventory of our possessions, attitudes, relationships in order to make more room for "what matters to God." The more room in our "barn" for the things of God, the more secure we become in God alone, the more surely we secure our eternal inheritance—eternal Life.

Model Universal Prayer (Prayer of the Faithful)

Presider: What matters most to God is that our hearts be turned toward the divine will. And so we pray.

Response:

Lord, hear our prayer.

Cantor:

we pray to the Lord,

That all members of the church witness to the world what it means to seek what matters most to God . . . [pause]

That all leaders of nations focus in their deliberations on what matters most to God . . . [pause]

That those who struggle with any need find their security in the God who gives all good things . . . [pause]

That each of us gathered here store up in our hearts the love and compassion that lead to an eternal inheritance . . . [pause]

Presider: Loving God, life is your most precious gift and in your Life is our lasting security. Grant these our prayers that one day we might all enjoy the inheritance of everlasting Life. We ask this through Jesus Christ our Lord. **Amen.**

COLLECT

Let us pray.

Pause for silent prayer

Draw near to your servants, O Lord,
and answer their prayers with unceasing
    kindness,
that, for those who glory in you as their
    Creator and guide,
you may restore what you have created
and keep safe what you have restored.
Through our Lord Jesus Christ, your Son,
who lives and reigns with you in the unity
    of the Holy Spirit,
one God, for ever and ever. **Amen.**

FIRST READING

Eccl 1:2; 2:21-23

Vanity of vanities, says Qoheleth,
    vanity of vanities! All things are vanity!

Here is one who has labored with wisdom
    and knowledge and skill,
    and yet to another who has not labored
        over it,
    he must leave property.
This also is vanity and a great misfortune.
For what profit comes to man from all the
        toil and anxiety of heart
    with which he has labored under the
        sun?
All his days sorrow and grief are his
        occupation;
    even at night his mind is not at rest.
This also is vanity.

RESPONSORIAL PSALM

Ps 90:3-4, 5-6, 12-13, 14 and 17

℟. (8) If today you hear his voice, harden
not your hearts.

You turn man back to dust,
    saying, "Return, O children of men."
For a thousand years in your sight
    are as yesterday, now that it is past,
    or as a watch of the night.

℟. If today you hear his voice, harden not
your hearts.

You make an end of them in their sleep;
    the next morning they are like the
        changing grass,
which at dawn springs up anew,
    but by evening wilts and fades.

℟. If today you hear his voice, harden not
your hearts.

Teach us to number our days aright,
that we may gain wisdom of heart.
Return, O Lord! How long?
Have pity on your servants!

R̂. If today you hear his voice, harden not
your hearts.

Fill us at daybreak with your kindness,
that we may shout for joy and gladness
all our days.
And may the gracious care of the Lord
our God be ours;
prosper the work of our hands for us!
Prosper the work of our hands!

R̂. If today you hear his voice, harden not
your hearts.

SECOND READING
Col 3:1-5, 9-11

Brothers and sisters:
If you were raised with Christ, seek what
is above,
where Christ is seated at the right hand
of God.
Think of what is above, not of what is on
earth.
For you have died,
and your life is hidden with Christ in
God.
When Christ your life appears,
then you too will appear with him in
glory.

Put to death, then, the parts of you that
are earthly:
immorality, impurity, passion, evil
desire,
and the greed that is idolatry.
Stop lying to one another,
since you have taken off the old self
with its practices
and have put on the new self,
which is being renewed, for knowledge,
in the image of its creator.
Here there is not Greek and Jew,
circumcision and uncircumcision,
barbarian, Scythian, slave, free;
but Christ is all and in all.

✝ CATECHESIS

About Liturgy

Liturgy's true focus: Just as with our everyday lives and all the possessions we have, it is also easy to lose sight of the true focus of liturgy itself. Without realizing it we can get so completely caught up in the *doing* of liturgy that subtly we put ourselves at the center. For example, we can be so concerned about hospitality that we forget this isn't a simple gathering of the folks, but an assembly gathered to hear God's call to be in divine Presence. Or we can be so caught up in doing good music that we forget the music's purpose is to draw us into the ritual action to be transformed into being more perfect members of Christ's Body, the church. Or we can be so caught up in our own need for private prayer time that we can easily forget that at liturgy we surrender ourselves and our own personal needs in order to be the church called into God's Presence.

Each Sunday it would be a good practice if each assembly member examined *why* he or she comes to celebrate liturgy. Ultimately we come to respond to God's call and to give praise and thanks for God's tremendous gifts of life and Godself to us. At each liturgy committee/commission meeting it would be a good practice to ask, what exactly is the parish's focus of liturgy? What are the liturgical priorities? Are we filling our liturgical "barns" with all the wrong things? What are the subtle ways we place ourselves and our own needs at the center? How faithful are we to the church's practice of liturgy that draws us into God's Presence for transformation?

About Liturgical Music

Role of the responsorial psalm, part 3: The primary transformation taking place in us as we respond to the Liturgy of the Word is deeper surrender to the paschal mystery. The word issues a prophetic challenge that we be true to the ideal which stands before us in the gospel, the person of Christ. The word reminds us that we are the Body of Christ and our mission is to heal the sick, feed the hungry, clothe the naked, and forgive those who injure us. The word confronts us with how far we fall short of that ideal and reassures us that God forgives this failure and continues to call us forward. What we hear in the proclamation of Scripture, then, is a continuously fresh presentation of the reality of God's faithfulness and of the ideal of faithfulness to which we are summoned in response.

When we sing the responsorial psalm, we express our surrender to the paschal mystery in song and voice. The psalmist leads the surrender, embodying it in breath and melody and mirroring through gesture the dialogue which is taking place between Christ and his assembled church. When we the assembly respond, we sacramentalize our assent, that is, we make our surrender audibly, visibly, physically apparent. In other words, we are doing far more in the responsorial psalm than merely singing a song. We are saying yes to the ideal being placed before us. Moreover, that ideal is not a set of directives but a living Person calling us to die to self so that we might have new and fuller life.

SPIRITUALITY

GOSPEL ACCLAMATION
Matt 24:42a, 44

℟. Alleluia, alleluia.
Stay awake and be ready!
For you do not know on what day the Son of
    Man will come.
℟. Alleluia, alleluia.

Gospel
Luke 12:32-48; L117C

Jesus said to his disciples:
    "Do not be afraid any longer,
        little flock,
    for your Father is pleased to
        give you the kingdom.
Sell your belongings and give
    alms.
Provide money bags for
    yourselves that do not wear out,
    an inexhaustible treasure in heaven
    that no thief can reach nor moth
        destroy.
For where your treasure is, there also
    will your heart be.

"Gird your loins and light your lamps
    and be like servants who await their
        master's return from a wedding,
    ready to open immediately when he
        comes and knocks.
Blessed are those servants
    whom the master finds vigilant on his
        arrival.
Amen, I say to you, he will gird
    himself,
    have them recline at table, and
        proceed to wait on them.
And should he come in the second or
    third watch
    and find them prepared in this way,
    blessed are those servants.
Be sure of this:
    if the master of the house had
        known the hour
    when the thief was coming,
    he would not have let his house be
        broken into.

Continued in Appendix A, p. 307.

Reflecting on the Gospel

Being busy is a good thing. It gets things done. It endears us to our employers. It fills time. Nonetheless, being busy can also have a negative side. We can keep ourselves so busy that we make ourselves sick, become depressed from lack of rest, don't take time to look at a broader vision of life. We can get so wrapped up in what we are doing that who we are, our being, gets lost. Values, virtues, and vision are all associated with *being*. In this gospel, Jesus tells parables about what servants *do* while the master is absent. Beneath the obvious application of the parables, Jesus is teaching us a lesson about how we are to *be*. He is teaching us about *who* we are to *be*.

In both of these parables about a master's absence, the critical issue is what the servants do while the master is away. They must be vigilant for the "master's return" and faithful in doing "the master's will." But this faithful doing does not necessarily make the servants good servants. They might be vigilant and faithful in doing the master's will out of fear of punishment. What the servants do must flow from who they are, their very being. They must be connected with their master in such a way that their doing is indicative of more than duty. Their doing is indicative of their desire for a wholesome, healthy relationship that is beneficial to both master and servant. When this relationship is in place, then even when the master is absent, servants who have appropriated his way of life will act as if the master were present. To belong to Jesus' household—God's kingdom—we must appropriate Jesus' way of life. We are to be his living, saving Presence. In us, he is never absent.

Living the Paschal Mystery

The final line of this gospel is most demanding and directly applicable to our daily paschal mystery living: "Much will be required of the person entrusted with much, / and still more will be demanded of the person entrusted with more." We've been entrusted with much: furthering Jesus' mission of bringing the Good News of salvation to all as his disciples. We have been entrusted with *even more*: we are not simply servants, but because of our baptism and being plunged into the paschal mystery we become members of the Body of Christ. We followers of Jesus are most vigilant for the *master*, that is, Jesus himself, when we are *being* who the Master is because his Life has been given to us. We are to be the presence of the Master himself, continuing his gracious ministry on behalf of others. Our faithfulness is measured by even more than doing God's will; it is measured by our *being* the presence of the risen Christ for all those we meet. Any doing must flow from our being. Only then do we truly continue Jesus' ministry.

The real surprise of the gospel is that we ourselves, in our daily paschal mystery living of dying to ourselves for the sake of others, become more perfectly that presence of the very Master for whom we are vigilant. In a sense our vigilance is less about looking for Someone and more about being Someone. Our vigilance is for our own faithfulness. If we are preoccupied by possessions, schedules, work, sports, entertainment, and so forth, our hearts are already filled with exhaustible, insecure, and corruptible matters. The challenge of this gospel is to redirect our hearts to what is our true treasure, Jesus, and then be faithful disciples. The gift is great. Our Treasure is Jesus.

Focusing the Gospel

Key words and phrases: kingdom, servants, master's return, vigilant, master's will

To the point: In both of these parables about a master's absence, the critical issue is what the servants do while the master is away. They must be vigilant for the "master's return" and faithful in doing "the master's will." Even when the master is absent, servants who have appropriated his way of life will act as if the master were present. To belong to Jesus' household—God's kingdom— we must appropriate Jesus' way of life. We are to be his living, saving Presence. In us, he is never absent.

Connecting the Gospel

to the first reading: As the "people awaited the salvation of the just" (first reading), so do faithful servants await the master's return (gospel). Today we are those servants who not only await Jesus' return, but who make him present now.

to experience: Children often carry on the traits and values of their parents, even after they are deceased. Those who faithfully follow Jesus carry on his way of life after his death, resurrection, and ascension.

Connecting the Responsorial Psalm

to the readings: Jesus tells us in this Sunday's gospel that where our treasure is, there our heart will be. Along this very line the responsorial psalm says something remarkable about God: we are God's treasure, chosen as "his own inheritance." And where God's treasure is, God's heart will be.

This is the reason why we can wait with hope and "sure knowledge" for the deliverance promised us, whether we know the hour of its arrival (first reading) or not (gospel). God has chosen us and already given us the kingdom (gospel). Our response is to keep our eyes turned toward the God whose eyes are fixed upon us (psalm), remaining faithful servants who fulfill the Lord's will in season and out (gospel).

to psalmist preparation: Preparing to sing the responsorial psalm means more than learning new words and music. Far more, it means preparing yourself for the coming of Christ in the Liturgy of the Word. No matter how many times you have sung a particular psalm, no matter how many times you have heard the proclamation of a particular gospel, there is always a new coming of Christ. May you be a vigilant and faithful servant!

**ASSEMBLY &
FAITH-SHARING GROUPS**

- Those who have taught me Jesus' way of life are . . . Those whom I teach Jesus' way of life are . . .
- In the Master's absence, I continue his saving mission by . . .
- What encourages me to remain faithful in the Master's absence is . . . What impedes my faithfulness is . . .

PRESIDERS
Instead of the "master," I am the "prudent steward" in my ministry when I . . .

DEACONS
What my serving others teaches me about *vigilance* is . . .

HOSPITALITY MINISTERS
When I am truly vigilant, those who have assembled for liturgy can be more attentive to the Master's Presence in that . . .

MUSIC MINISTERS
What encourages me to be faithful to the requirements of my music ministry is . . .

ALTAR MINISTERS
By serving others I am becoming a "faithful and prudent steward" because . . .

LECTORS
My proclamation reveals how I am faithful to the Master—whether absent or present— in that . . .

**EXTRAORDINARY MINISTERS
OF HOLY COMMUNION**
My ministering Holy Communion draws me to a more faithful way of Gospel living in that . . .

Model Penitential Act

Presider: Today's gospel calls us to be vigilant for the Master's Presence and faithful in doing his will. As we prepare to celebrate this liturgy, let us ask God's mercy for the times we have failed to live out this call . . . [pause]

Lord Jesus, you faithfully carried out your Father's will: Lord . . .

Christ Jesus, you will return in glory: Christ . . .

Lord Jesus, you entrust us to be your saving Presence: Lord . . .

Homily Points

• We appropriate the way of life of those whom we love and respect. Children continue the legacy of their parents' values. Students continue the legacy of a beloved teacher's wisdom. Franciscans continue the legacy of St. Francis of Assisi. All the baptized are called to continue the way of life of Jesus.

• The gospel is about absent masters and the actions of servants who are left in charge. Faithful servants are those who are vigilant about the master's return and who do his will even in his absence. The longer a servant has attended the master, the better this servant will know what is expected. The servant who appropriates the very rhythm and way of life of the household is the faithful one. Jesus is our Master who has left us in charge of his household, the "kingdom."

• We never finish being vigilant for the Master's Presence. We never finish doing the Master's will. We learn by doing. The more faithful we are in the doing, the more faithful we become in the living. The closer we are to Jesus and the more we appropriate his way of life, the more clearly we become his saving Presence. In us who are faithful, he is never absent.

Model Universal Prayer (Prayer of the Faithful)

Presider: We are called to be vigilant and faithful servants. And so we pray.

Response:

Lord, hear our prayer.

Cantor:

we pray to the Lord,

That all members of the church be vigilant in doing God's will and always remain faithful followers of Jesus . . . [pause]

That leaders of the world's nations be faithful in fulfilling the responsibilities entrusted to them . . . [pause]

That all employees be vigilant in doing their job and faithful to Gospel values . . . [pause]

That each of us carry forward Jesus' saving mission with vigilance and fidelity . . . [pause]

Presider: O God, you are a gentle Master who gives us all good things. Grant our prayers that we may be vigilant and faithful servants in your kingdom. We ask this through Jesus Christ our Lord. **Amen.**

COLLECT

Let us pray.

Pause for silent prayer

Almighty ever-living God,
whom, taught by the Holy Spirit,
we dare to call our Father,
bring, we pray, to perfection in our hearts
the spirit of adoption as your sons and
      daughters,
that we may merit to enter into the
      inheritance
which you have promised.
Through our Lord Jesus Christ, your Son,
who lives and reigns with you in the unity
      of the Holy Spirit,
one God, for ever and ever. **Amen.**

FIRST READING
Wis 18:6-9

The night of the passover was known
      beforehand to our fathers,
   that, with sure knowledge of the oaths
      in which they put their faith,
   they might have courage.
Your people awaited the salvation of the
      just
   and the destruction of their foes.
For when you punished our adversaries,
   in this you glorified us whom you had
      summoned.
For in secret the holy children of the good
      were offering sacrifice
   and putting into effect with one accord
      the divine institution.

RESPONSORIAL PSALM

Ps 33:1, 12, 18-19, 20-22

℞. (12b) Blessed the people the Lord has chosen to be his own.

Exult, you just, in the LORD;
    praise from the upright is fitting.
Blessed the nation whose God is the LORD,
    the people he has chosen for his own
        inheritance.

℞. Blessed the people the Lord has chosen to be his own.

See, the eyes of the LORD are upon those
        who fear him,
    upon those who hope for his kindness,
to deliver them from death
    and preserve them in spite of famine.

℞. Blessed the people the Lord has chosen to be his own.

Our soul waits for the LORD,
    who is our help and our shield.
May your kindness, O LORD, be upon us
    who have put our hope in you.

℞. Blessed the people the Lord has chosen to be his own.

SECOND READING

Heb 11:1-2, 8-19

Brothers and sisters:
Faith is the realization of what is hoped for
    and evidence of things not seen.
Because of it the ancients were well attested.

By faith Abraham obeyed when he was
        called to go out to a place
    that he was to receive as an inheritance;
he went out, not knowing where he was
        to go.
By faith he sojourned in the promised land
        as in a foreign country,
    dwelling in tents with Isaac and Jacob,
        heirs of the same promise;
    for he was looking forward to the city
        with foundations,
    whose architect and maker is God.
By faith he received power to generate,
    even though he was past the normal age
    —and Sarah herself was sterile—
    for he thought that the one who had
        made the promise was trustworthy.

Continued in Appendix A, p. 308.

✝ *CATECHESIS*

About Liturgy

Stewardship, faithfulness, and liturgy: Many parishes next month (September) undertake various stewardship activities. Often this includes filling out a form indicating monetary gifts to the parish as well as how one will contribute time and expertise during the next year. Our reflections on the gospel for this Sunday raise some issues about stewardship. Our hearts can be distracted in many ways, and if our hearts are distracted then we may lose sight of our true Treasure, Jesus.

For the good management of a parish, of course there must be monetary and time donations. This is part of the "faithfulness" of good disciples. At the same time we must always caution ourselves that we don't become so involved in *doing* that we neglect the way we encounter our Treasure in good celebration of liturgy. Our hearts must always be tuned into the praise and thanksgiving that is liturgy.

It is easy to be distracted during liturgy by the demands of *doing* ministry. Vigilance for our truest Treasure means that we always must bring ourselves back to full, conscious, and active participation in the liturgy that makes present the greatest gift God has given us—Jesus. Celebration of good liturgy makes demands on our energy (it takes more energy to make sure that our minds remain focused on the celebration) and calls us to vigilance (how God is transforming each of us into being richer members of the Body of Christ). Ultimately the most important stewardship is not the money or time we donate, but surrendering ourselves to being transformed. Our ultimate stewardship is how faithful we are to *being* Jesus' disciples.

About Liturgical Music

Text of the responsorial psalm: The text of the responsorial psalm is related to the readings of the day. Because of this correspondence, GIRM 61 directs that the responsorial psalm we sing should usually be the one given in the Lectionary for the day. In practical terms, this means that the Lectionary text is preferable to a paraphrased version. No matter how poetically beautiful and musically uplifting, a psalm that has been highly paraphrased can actually interfere with the responsorial psalm's role of leading us from the first reading to a paschal mystery encounter with Christ in the gospel. Such paraphrased psalms are more appropriately sung at other moments in the liturgy, such as during Communion.

Furthermore, the text of the psalm needs to predominate over the musical setting. A setting that is so complex, or chorally intricate, or instrumentally elaborate that the text cannot be understood interferes with the functioning of the psalm. The musical setting should always enhance the text, but never overshadow it; always draw us into the text, but never away from the text into itself.

AUGUST 7, 2016
NINETEENTH SUNDAY IN ORDINARY TIME

✦ SPIRITUALITY

GOSPEL ACCLAMATION
John 10:27

℟. Alleluia, alleluia.
My sheep hear my voice, says the Lord;
I know them, and they follow me.
℟. Alleluia, alleluia.

Gospel

Luke 12:49-53; L120C

Jesus said to his disciples:
 "I have come to set the earth
  on fire,
 and how I wish it were
  already blazing!
There is a baptism with
  which I must be baptized,
 and how great is my
  anguish until it is
  accomplished!
Do you think that I have come to
  establish peace on the earth?
No, I tell you, but rather division.
From now on a household of five will
  be divided,
 three against two and two against
  three;
 a father will be divided against his
  son
 and a son against his father,
 a mother against her daughter
 and a daughter against her mother,
 a mother-in-law against her
  daughter-in-law
 and a daughter-in-law against her
  mother-in-law."

Reflecting on the Gospel

For whatever reason, we human beings seem to enjoy whatever has shock value. The greater the shock, the more attractive the incident. Media keep a story running so long as its shock value attracts viewers or readers. So much of TV fare has high ratings because it has high shock value. Crime dramas are more and more grisly. Sci-fi is more and more strangely bizarre. Comedies are more and more gross. Reality shows are more and more flagrant. Newscasts are more and more sensationalistic. Each season a show must top the previous season in its shock value. Eventually we become immune to the shock. It is merely entertainment. This Sunday's gospel has a definite shock value about it. It speaks of things we tend to avoid in our lives: fire, anguish, division. What Jesus is teaching, however, is that to be faithful followers we must face some consequences of witnessing to the Good News we would naturally avoid. What we must learn in our faithful discipleship is that the Good News is as much in the fire, anguish, division as it is in the peace we ardently desire.

This is surely a bad news, good news gospel. The bad news is that Jesus' coming throws the world headlong into fire, anguish, division. The good news is that, in spite of Jesus speaking to the contrary, he does grant peace—to his disciples after his resurrection. His appearance after his resurrection to the fearful disciples includes the comforting gift, "Peace be with you." Faithful discipleship, faithful witnessing to the Good News of salvation, includes both the peace and the suffering, misunderstanding, and anger that sometimes come from radically living the call to be faithful to God's will, to be single-minded about continuing Jesus' saving ministry, to live counter to what our world is trying to shock us into accepting.

No, Jesus' gift of peace does not eliminate the fire, anguish, and division that come from faithful discipleship. Their absence from our daily living might be something of a judgment that we are not living up to Gospel demands. But good comes out of the negative aftermath of our saying yes to God. These painful consequences of faithful living sharpen the choice each of us must make: to be "baptized" with Jesus into his suffering and death. And this choice is not made once and for all. It is a choice we make every day. It is a choice about how we wish to live. Bad news. Good news. We live with both. We make our life choice in face of both. We do not make our life choice for shock value. We make it for Gospel value.

Living the Paschal Mystery

None of us chooses to live our discipleship for its shock value! We are, however, always faced with such consequential choices. We are hardly called like Jeremiah to announce to the Israelites that their beloved Jerusalem will fall into the hands of the Babylonians—nor are we thrown into a cistern to die! Nor like Jesus will we be nailed to a cross because of our preaching. Nevertheless, we are called to be faithful to God's word in the small, everyday things as well as at times when the more serious challenges come along. We do not seek division, but we do seek consistency in living Gospel values. We do not seek anguish, but we do suffer with Christ when it comes. The closer we come to Christ, the hotter the fire becomes! The very way we live our lives is Gospel fire. Sometimes strife and division are a sign of our faithful commitment. Gospel living is not always easy! The real shock is that we choose it and are faithful.

Focusing the Gospel

Key words and phrases: I have come, fire, baptism, anguish, peace, division

To the point: This is a bad news, good news gospel. The bad news is that Jesus' coming throws the world headlong into fire, anguish, division. The good news is that, in spite of Jesus speaking to the contrary, he does grant peace—to his disciples after his resurrection. His gift of peace, however, does not eliminate the fire, anguish, and division. These painful consequences of faithful living sharpen the choice each of us must make: to be "baptized" with Jesus into his suffering and death. Bad news. Good news. We live with both. We make our life choice in face of both.

Connecting the Gospel

to the first reading: The prophet Jeremiah brought to the people of his time the same fire, anguish, and division of which Jesus speaks in the gospel. As Jeremiah's prophecy was met with violence to him, so was Jesus' message of salvation met with violence.

to experience: Fire, anguish, and division in relationships are all life-negatives we want to avoid. They all destroy something outside or within us. To follow Jesus, we must accept these negatives as an inherent part of our decision to be faithful.

Connecting the Responsorial Psalm

to the readings: In the first reading Jeremiah is thrown into a muddy cistern because he challenged the leaders of Israel. Jesus tells us in the gospel that we, too, will face extreme opposition if we follow him. Discipleship demands a willingness to stand alone, to be cut off even from those close to us when the call of Christ requires it. But the responsorial psalm reminds us that we are not, in fact, left alone. When human persons turn away from or against us because of our fidelity to discipleship, God will stoop close. Nothing can eradicate the cost of discipleship, but neither can anything destroy God's care for and protection of us. Though we may die, as did Jesus, God will not abandon us to death, but will raise us to new life. This psalm expresses our absolute trust that God will "hold . . . back" nothing in our support.

to psalmist preparation: In this psalm you call upon God to "come to my aid." In the context of the readings, this is a cry raised in face of persecution experienced because you are being faithful to discipleship. When have you found yourself meeting such opposition? What helped you remain faithful? How did God come to your aid?

ASSEMBLY & FAITH-SHARING GROUPS

- I have experienced fire, anguish, division because of my faithful discipleship when . . .
- I have experienced Jesus' gift of peace because of my faithful discipleship when . . .
- The choice to be a faithful follower of Jesus is easiest when . . . most difficult when . . .

PRESIDERS

My preaching brings fire, anguish, division when . . . I need to preach in this way when . . .

DEACONS

My serving others brings peace to them when . . .

HOSPITALITY MINISTERS

My greeting is one of fire, anguish, division when . . . It is one of peace when . . .

MUSIC MINISTERS

My music making is a choice to . . .

ALTAR MINISTERS

The good news about my serving ministry is . . . The bad news about my serving ministry is . . .

LECTORS

When I must proclaim a particularly challenging Scripture passage, it demands of me . . .

EXTRAORDINARY MINISTERS OF HOLY COMMUNION

My distributing Holy Communion is good news that heals all bad news in that . . .

✦ CELEBRATION

Model Penitential Act

Presider: In today's gospel Jesus tells us that he has come "to set the earth on fire." As we begin this liturgy, let us ask God's mercy for the times we have not offered the wood of our life for this fire . . . [pause]

Lord Jesus, you bring the fire of God's love and mercy: Lord . . .

Christ Jesus, you are the resurrection and the Life: Christ . . .

Lord Jesus, you call us to reconciliation and peace: Lord . . .

Homily Points

• When someone approaches us with "I've got both good news and bad news, which do you want first," how do we answer? Either with "bad news" to get it out of the way, or with "good news" to soften the blow of the bad news. When Jesus in this gospel speaks of bad news, he doesn't soften it with good news. Instead, he clearly spells out the cost of his Good News.

• In this gospel Jesus doesn't mince words. His coming brings fire. His "baptism" causes him anguish. His preaching creates divisions. But this is not all his coming brings. His coming brings a clarity about the choice we must make to follow him faithfully.

• How ironic that the more faithfully we follow Jesus, the clearer the divisions among us become! Circumstances in our relationships with one another, most notably those closest to us, will clarify who Jesus is for us and force us to make choices we might prefer to avoid. Yet Jesus himself did not avoid the most difficult, divisive choice: he anguished over the "baptism" he had to face—his passion and death. We followers must also face this same most difficult, divisive choice. If we are not facing fire, anguish, division, are we being faithful in our discipleship?

Model Universal Prayer (Prayer of the Faithful)

Presider: Just as Jesus made the difficult choice to be faithful to his passion and death, so must we as his followers. Let us pray for strength and faithfulness.

Response:

Lord, hear our prayer.

Cantor:

we pray to the Lord,

That all members of the church choose faithful discipleship no matter what its cost . . . [pause]

That world leaders have the courage to make the difficult choices necessary to lead their people to unity and lasting peace . . . [pause]

That those suffering anguish or division because of their fidelity to Christ receive Christ's peace . . . [pause]

That each of us overcome anguish with joy, and division by reconciliation . . . [pause]

Presider: Merciful God, your Son is our salvation and our peace. Grant these prayers that we might be faithful disciples and come to the fullness of the Life he gained for us. We ask this through that same Son, Jesus Christ our Lord. **Amen.**

COLLECT

Let us pray.

Pause for silent prayer

O God, who have prepared for those who
    love you
good things which no eye can see,
fill our hearts, we pray, with the warmth
    of your love,
so that, loving you in all things and above
    all things,
we may attain your promises,
which surpass every human desire.
Through our Lord Jesus Christ, your Son,
who lives and reigns with you in the unity
    of the Holy Spirit,
one God, for ever and ever. **Amen.**

FIRST READING

Jer 38:4-6, 8-10

In those days, the princes said to the king:
    "Jeremiah ought to be put to death;
    he is demoralizing the soldiers who are
        left in this city,
    and all the people, by speaking such
        things to them;
    he is not interested in the welfare of our
        people,
    but in their ruin."
King Zedekiah answered: "He is in your
        power";
    for the king could do nothing with them.
And so they took Jeremiah
    and threw him into the cistern of Prince
        Malchiah,
    which was in the quarters of the guard,
    letting him down with ropes.
There was no water in the cistern, only
        mud,
    and Jeremiah sank into the mud.

Ebed-melech, a court official,
    went there from the palace and said to
        him:
    "My lord king,
    these men have been at fault
    in all they have done to the prophet
        Jeremiah,
    casting him into the cistern.
He will die of famine on the spot,
    for there is no more food in the city."
Then the king ordered Ebed-melech the
        Cushite
    to take three men along with him,
    and draw the prophet Jeremiah out of
        the cistern before he should die.

RESPONSORIAL PSALM
Ps 40:2, 3, 4, 18

℟. (14b) Lord, come to my aid!

I have waited, waited for the LORD,
    and he stooped toward me.

℟. Lord, come to my aid!

The LORD heard my cry.
He drew me out of the pit of destruction,
    out of the mud of the swamp;
he set my feet upon a crag;
    he made firm my steps.

℟. Lord, come to my aid!

And he put a new song into my mouth,
    a hymn to our God.
Many shall look on in awe
    and trust in the LORD.

℟. Lord, come to my aid!

Though I am afflicted and poor,
    yet the LORD thinks of me.
You are my help and my deliverer;
    O my God, hold not back!

℟. Lord, come to my aid!

SECOND READING
Heb 12:1-4

Brothers and sisters:
Since we are surrounded by so great a
        cloud of witnesses,
    let us rid ourselves of every burden and
            sin that clings to us
    and persevere in running the race that
            lies before us
    while keeping our eyes fixed on Jesus,
        the leader and perfecter of faith.
For the sake of the joy that lay before him
    he endured the cross, despising its
        shame,
    and has taken his seat at the right of
        the throne of God.
Consider how he endured such opposition
        from sinners,
    in order that you may not grow weary
        and lose heart.
In your struggle against sin
    you have not yet resisted to the point of
        shedding blood.

About Liturgy

Liturgy and strife: Strife and divisions are not located only within family households; they can also be evidenced on liturgy committees and in parishes! There are probably few things in parish life which cause divisions the way the decisions about the celebration of liturgy can. Is it not ironic that the very celebration whereby we express our unity in the Body of Christ can be the cause for so much anger, anguish, and divisiveness?

Sometimes a parish can be radically split about how to celebrate liturgy because "good" liturgy is judged in terms of what individuals or groups want, desire, or find satisfying. Ideally, everyone would come to Mass each Sunday and go home satisfied, filled, and spiritually and emotionally fed. In reality, this does not happen to everyone in the same way and the same time. One way to deal with this issue is to remember that the purpose of liturgy is not primarily to satisfy our personal needs; the purpose of liturgy is to give God praise and thanksgiving by offering ourselves with Christ on the altar. Only by such self-giving, and by keeping this the focus, can we hope to overcome divisions and improve our celebration of liturgy. Celebrating good liturgy means that we surrender our own desires to the larger good of the whole community.

About Liturgical Music

Musical setting of the responsorial psalm: The responsorial psalm plays an important role in the Liturgy of the Word, but nonetheless a secondary one. Practically speaking, this means that the musical setting of the psalm ought not to overshadow the rest of the Liturgy of the Word. If we find ourselves mentally humming the psalm refrain during proclamation of the second reading and gospel, then the musical setting (or how it was rendered) has overshot its mark. We must keep in mind that the psalm is meant to lead to the readings, not to itself. (Often the problem, however, is not that the setting of the psalm is too elaborate, but that the proclamation of the readings is too weak. The need here, then, is to improve the proclamation.)

This is not to say that we never use an elaborate musical setting of a responsorial psalm. This is more than appropriate, for example, on solemnities such as Christmas, Easter, and Pentecost. For these celebrations a highly embellished musical setting, with perhaps more than one cantor or the choir as a whole singing the verses in harmony, and with solo instrument(s) added, communicates the high festivity of the day in contrast with the less festive days of the year. Such solemnities call for more elaborate music. But using highly ornamented psalm settings on a regular basis, Sunday after Sunday, ignores the progressive solemnity built into the flow of the liturgical year.

SPIRITUALITY

R7. Alleluia, alleluia.
Mary is taken up to heaven;
a chorus of angels exults.
R7. Alleluia, alleluia.

Gospel   Luke 1:39-56; L622

Mary set out
  and traveled to the hill country in haste
  to a town of Judah,
  where she entered the house of
      Zechariah
  and greeted Elizabeth.
When Elizabeth heard Mary's
      greeting,
  the infant leaped in her womb,
  and Elizabeth, filled with the Holy
      Spirit,
  cried out in a loud voice and said,
  "Blessed are you among women,
  and blessed is the fruit of your womb.
And how does this happen to me,
  that the mother of my Lord should
      come to me?
For at the moment the sound of your
      greeting reached my ears,
  the infant in my womb leaped for joy.
Blessed are you who believed
  that what was spoken to you by the
      Lord
  would be fulfilled."

And Mary said:
  "My soul proclaims the greatness of
      the Lord;
  my spirit rejoices in God my Savior
  for he has looked with favor on his
      lowly servant.
From this day all generations will call
      me blessed:
  the Almighty has done great things
      for me,
  and holy is his Name.
He has mercy on those who fear him
  in every generation.

Continued in Appendix A, p. 308.

For other readings, see Appendix A, p. 309.

Reflecting on the Gospel

What a greeting Mary gave Elizabeth that the infant in her womb "leaped for joy"! This could not have been any ordinary greeting. Perhaps Mary's greeting flowed from Gabriel's greeting to her at the annunciation: "Hail, full of grace!" Mary is the pure vessel carrying the One to be born Savior of the world. Mary was a willing vessel. Hers was a greeting begotten by belief, by yes, by encounter. This, over her whole lifetime. Hers was a greeting that proclaimed God's mighty deeds then and now. Hers was a greeting that announced the Presence of the dawning of salvation. Hers is a greeting still spoken and being fulfilled today. Hers is a greeting we must hear. Do we hear the greeting? Are we leaping for joy?

This solemnity celebrates the "great things" God has done for Mary. But for others than Mary. Mary is a type for all of Israel, for all peoples at all times. Mary's assumption of body and soul into heaven celebrates the salvation of God and the promise to us of a share in the saving deeds of God. It is God who does great things because God has promised to be with us at all times. The great thing Mary does is say *yes* to being an instrument of God's promise. Her continual yes greets us and challenges us to say yes, too. The joy that this gospel notes is a deep delight in knowing that God's will is being done. This joy was known by Mary and Elizabeth, by Jesus and John, and by each of us. We only need to hear Mary's greeting of yes and then make that our own greeting.

In her *Magnificat* Mary already announces the new age to come which is established through faithful discipleship, grounded in faithful, daily yes responses to God. God's kingdom of the new age is brought to completion when all are gathered into a share in eternal Life. Mary's assumption—this festival—is a sign of the completion already coming about. This is why we might think of Mary's assumption as a festival of joyful yes-greeting. The assumption is a sign of God's salvation given and Mary's faithful yes. It is also a sign that our true home is with God. It is a sign that our yes-greeting must be as faithful as was Mary's.

Living the Paschal Mystery

Mary remained with Elizabeth "about three months." Mary remains with the church (with us) always, to be a sign of the "great things" God continues to do. Her discipleship continues in that she is a sign of hope flowing from her yes. So it is with us. One way our own discipleship is expressed is through our being a sign of hope through our yes to whatever God asks of us.

One important aspect of discipleship is to live in such a way as to witness to God's promise of salvation offered through the ongoing yes of those who are faithful to the divine Son. Practically speaking, this means that we hear God's word and respond with a resounding and joyful yes. In this we carry ourselves with dignity and bestow that same dignity on others. No one is beneath us or too "lowly" or insignificant to deserve our attention and respect. This is easier said than done!

Dying to self means treating others as those saved by God. First of all, this means that we don't judge others. Our judgments of each other are usually much more unkind than God's merciful judgment of us! This also means that we are careful never to speak negatively of others. Diminishing others surely doesn't raise them up and ultimately diminishes even ourselves. Finally, paschal mystery living means that we treat others as those blessed by God because of their own yes.

Focusing the Gospel

Key words and phrases: greeted Elizabeth, Mary's greeting, sound of your greeting, leaped for joy, Almighty has done great things

To the point: What a greeting Mary gave Elizabeth that the infant in her womb "leaped for joy"! It was a greeting begotten by belief, by yes, by encounter. It was a greeting that proclaimed God's mighty deeds then and now. It is a greeting still spoken and being fulfilled today. Do we hear the greeting? Are we leaping for joy?

Model Penitential Act

Presider: Today we celebrate the assumption of Mary body and soul into heaven. All the heavenly choir greet her as she greets her risen Son. Let us pause and prepare ourselves to celebrate this glorious day and ask God's help in being faithful as Mary was faithful . . . [pause]

Lord Jesus, your mother Mary is blessed through all generations: Lord . . .

Christ Jesus, you came with mighty deeds bringing salvation: Christ . . .

Lord Jesus, you are the Blessed Fruit of Mary's womb: Lord . . .

Model Universal Prayer (Prayer of the Faithful)

Presider: Let us place our needs before God through the intercession of Mary our mother.

Response:

Lord, hear our prayer.

Cantor:

we pray to the Lord,

That the church, like Mary, remain a faithful witness to God's promise of salvation for all . . . [pause]

That all peoples of the world respond to the mighty deeds of God with sincerity and truth . . . [pause]

That the lowly be lifted up, the hungry be fed, and the poor be regarded with dignity . . . [pause]

That each one of us, like Mary, respond to God's invitation to participate in the mighty deeds of salvation through acts of service and hospitality . . . [pause]

Presider: Almighty God, you assumed Mary body and soul into heaven. Grant these our prayers that through her intercession we might one day also live in glory with you. We ask this through the divine Son, Jesus Christ our Lord. **Amen.**

FOR REFLECTION

• Mary greets me by . . . when . . . Her greeting leads me to . . .

• The "great things" God did for Mary are . . . God does for me are . . .

• I proclaim God's mighty deeds to . . . by . . . when . . .

Homily Points

• Every day we greet and are greeted by others. But not all greetings are alike. A perfunctory "Hi" might not even elicit a response. A sincere "Hello, how are you?" might open up a heartfelt conversation. This latter greeting is the kind that leads to personal encounter.

• Mary greets Elizabeth in such a powerful way that encounter and revelation happen—not just between the two women, but also between the infants in their wombs. God's mighty deeds become evident through the mutual exchange of believing, of saying yes. On this Solemnity of the Assumption of the Blessed Virgin Mary, God's mighty deeds resound in the perpetual greeting Mary gives to her divine Son in heaven. And the perpetual greeting she gives us. Do we hear? Do we respond? Do we leap for joy?

✝ SPIRITUALITY

GOSPEL ACCLAMATION
John 14:6

℟. Alleluia, alleluia.
I am the way, the truth and the life, says the
    Lord;
no one comes to the Father, except through
    me.
℟. Alleluia, alleluia.

Gospel
Luke 13:22-30; L123C

Jesus passed through towns and
        villages,
    teaching as he went and making
        his way to Jerusalem.
Someone asked him,
    "Lord, will only a few people be
        saved?"
He answered them,
    "Strive to enter through the narrow
        gate,
    for many, I tell you, will attempt to
        enter
    but will not be strong enough.
After the master of the house has arisen
        and locked the door,
    then will you stand outside knocking
        and saying,
    'Lord, open the door for us.'
He will say to you in reply,
    'I do not know where you are from.'
And you will say,
    'We ate and drank in your company
        and you taught in our streets.'
Then he will say to you,
    'I do not know where you are from.
Depart from me, all you evildoers!'
And there will be wailing and grinding of
        teeth
    when you see Abraham, Isaac, and Jacob
    and all the prophets in the kingdom of
        God
    and you yourselves cast out.
And people will come from the east and
        the west
    and from the north and the south
    and will recline at table in the kingdom
        of God.
For behold, some are last who will be first,
    and some are first who will be last."

Reflecting on the Gospel

God has promised salvation from that first fateful fall of humanity. God has never forsaken us. While salvation is a gift freely given by God, we must choose it, work at it, desire it with all our hearts. This Sunday's gospel uses two images that indicate to us that we have work cut out for us: a "narrow gate" and locked door. We must squeeze and push our way through life if we wish to be saved. We must squeeze out any weakness that leads us astray; we must push aside anything that gets between God and us. To squeeze and push our way to salvation, we must be strong.

What strength is needed to enter "through the narrow gate," the locked door? The strength that comes from living so that the "master of the house" knows us and opens to us. The strength that comes from faithfully living "in the kingdom of God." The strength of conviction in following Jesus and seeking his way over our own way. This strength only comes from God who offers it to everyone, those "from the east and the west / and from the north and the south." Because of this strength we choose to journey "to Jerusalem," we choose to pass through death to Life, we choose salvation. Only this strength is truly "strong enough," for it is God's very Self, God's very Life. Yes, God desires that we be saved. The door of salvation is open to all those who have chosen to pass through the "narrow gate" of self-surrender and the locked door of curbed passions and false desires. So, why would we choose this journey? Because the immediate destination (Jerusalem, with its promised death) is the way to a greater destination (new and eternal Life).

By "making his way to Jerusalem" Jesus is being faithful to his own mission; by going to Jerusalem he fulfills his Father's will even when that means he must suffer and die. Jesus walks the journey with us and shows us the way to what we desire most for our lives—salvation. Our salvation is a great gift from God, but it is not without cost. We must pass through the "narrow gate" of conforming ourselves to Jesus and participating in his dying and rising. Being disciples of Jesus, then, demands more than being in Jesus' company (for example, being faithful to personal prayer and celebrating liturgy); it means we must take up the mission of Jesus to die and rise, that is, we must be on the way to Jerusalem.

What limits the scope of salvation is not God's reach (which is to east, west, north, and south—that is, salvation is offered to all people) but *our response*. We gain eternal salvation by the difficult and demanding path of following Jesus on his way to Jerusalem; we do this by dying to self and being faithful disciples.

Living the Paschal Mystery

We all claim to know Jesus; after all, we are for the most part faithful churchgoers who weekly eat and drink in his company. This gospel warns us that this isn't enough. There is an urgency about our paschal mystery living; we don't have forever to make up our minds to respond to God's offer of salvation. Each day we must take up our own cross, die to self, and live for the sake of others. This is how we enter through the narrow gate and how we get to know Jesus intimately enough to receive salvation: we must *live and act like Jesus*. Becoming least is a metaphor for dying to self; this is what Jesus asks: that the first become the last. What limits the scope of salvation is not God's reach but our weak response. We must beg God for the strength to respond fully. Our strength comes from God.

Focusing the Gospel

Key words and phrases: to Jerusalem, narrow gate, strong enough, open the door for us, know . . . you, people will come, kingdom of God

To the point: What strength is needed to enter "through the narrow gate," the locked door? The strength that comes from living so that the "master of the house" knows us and opens to us. The strength that comes from faithfully living "in the kingdom of God." This strength only comes from God who offers it to everyone, those "from the east and the west / and from the north and the south." Because of this strength we choose to journey "to Jerusalem," we choose to pass through death to Life. Only this strength is truly "strong enough," for it is God's very Self, God's very Life.

Connecting the Gospel

to the first reading: Both the first reading and gospel reinforce salvation's wide reach: "from all the nations" and "from the east and the west / and from the north and the south." All anyone needs to do is follow Jesus to Jerusalem, through death to Life.

to experience: Athletic coaches train us to have physical strength. Mental health counselors train us to have emotional strength. Spiritual directors train us to have spiritual strength. Jesus trains us to have the greatest strength possible—God's very Self, God's very Life.

Connecting the Responsorial Psalm

to the readings: Jesus challenges us in this Sunday gospel with the harsh reality that not everyone will be admitted to the kingdom of God. His message, however, is for those who have heard the Good News of salvation, not for those who have "never heard of [God's] fame, or seen [God's] glory" (first reading). To these God will send messengers to tell them the Good News and gather them to the holy dwelling, Jerusalem. For those who have already heard, radical demands are in place (Jesus has been spelling these out in previous Sundays' gospels). And the responsorial psalm gives yet another command: we are to be the messengers who spread the Good News of God's salvation to all the world. The psalm reminds us that we are a necessary part of God's plan of salvation for all. It also suggests that we cannot recline at God's table if we have not invited everyone else to be there with us.

to psalmist preparation: In singing this psalm you command the assembly to tell the world the Good News of salvation. Who in your life is especially in need of hearing this news? How do you tell them?

**ASSEMBLY &
FAITH-SHARING GROUPS**

- To be like Jesus and make my "way to Jerusalem," I must . . .
- The "narrow gate" and locked door I encounter on my daily journey are . . .
- The strength of God's very Self, God's very Life sustains me most clearly when . . .

PRESIDERS
I am aware of God's strength giving direction to the way I minister when . . . It brings me to . . .

DEACONS
My serving ministry takes me beyond mere familiarity with Jesus ("we ate and drank in your company") to following him to Jerusalem when . . .

HOSPITALITY MINISTERS
My hospitality communicates God's all-inclusive invitation to enter God's kingdom by . . .

MUSIC MINISTERS
My music ministry opens these doors for me . . . for the assembly . . .

ALTAR MINISTERS
The way my service goes beyond attending to vessels and rubrics to supporting others on their journey to Jerusalem is . . .

LECTORS
My proclamation of the word is encouragement and hope on the journey to salvation when . . .

**EXTRAORDINARY MINISTERS
OF HOLY COMMUNION**
The way I am God's "food" aiding and encouraging others to enter through the narrow gate is . . .

Model Penitential Act

Presider: In today's gospel Jesus admonishes us that the journey to salvation passes through a narrow gate. As we prepare to celebrate this liturgy, let us ask God to have mercy on us for the times we have not been faithful on our journey . . . [pause]

Lord Jesus, you are the strength on our journey to salvation: Lord . . .

Christ Jesus, you call all people into the kingdom of God: Christ . . .

Lord Jesus, you are the Way, the Truth, and the Life: Lord . . .

Homily Points

• Health care personnel constantly remind us of the necessity of exercise and strength training for physical well-being. None of us denies the validity of what they are saying, but how many of us follow their advice? Strength training is also necessary for our spiritual well-being and journey. How many of us follow Jesus' advice about this?

• Following Jesus on the journey to Jerusalem is arduous. The gate is narrow; the door is locked. We must undertake the spiritual training that makes us "strong enough" for this journey. To be "strong enough," we need God's strength—God's very Self, God's very Life. We must encounter Jesus and change our lives accordingly. We must constantly strive to know him more deeply and live more perfectly his word of salvation.

• People can be *in* Jesus' company, but not *of* his company. In the gospel, apparently some people ate and drank with Jesus without letting this change their lives. What assures us that we are *of* the company of Jesus? Transforming encounters with him that change how we know him, how we see ourselves, and how we live. This is the spiritual strength training we need. Again. And again. And again . . .

Model Universal Prayer (Prayer of the Faithful)

Presider: Let us ask God for the strength to walk faithfully with Jesus on the journey of salvation.

Response:

Lord, hear our prayer.

Cantor:

we pray to the Lord,

That all members of the church grow in the strength needed to follow Jesus faithfully through death to new Life . . . [pause]

That world leaders may have the strength to open the doors of justice and peace . . . [pause]

That those in need may find strength in the promise that Jesus will open the door of Life to them . . . [pause]

That all of us here strengthen each other by seeking encounters with Jesus that transform how we live . . . [pause]

Presider: Loving God, you offer salvation to all who come to you. Hear these our prayers that we have strength to enter through the narrow gate into your everlasting glory. We ask this through Jesus Christ our Lord. **Amen.**

COLLECT

Let us pray.

Pause for silent prayer

O God, who cause the minds of the faithful to unite in a single purpose,
grant your people to love what you command
and to desire what you promise,
that, amid the uncertainties of this world,
our hearts may be fixed on that place
where true gladness is found.
Through our Lord Jesus Christ, your Son,
who lives and reigns with you in the unity of the Holy Spirit,
one God, for ever and ever. **Amen.**

FIRST READING
Isa 66:18-21

Thus says the LORD:
I know their works and their thoughts,
and I come to gather nations of every language;
they shall come and see my glory.
I will set a sign among them;
from them I will send fugitives to the nations:
to Tarshish, Put and Lud, Mosoch, Tubal and Javan,
to the distant coastlands
that have never heard of my fame, or seen my glory;
and they shall proclaim my glory among the nations.
They shall bring all your brothers and sisters from all the nations
as an offering to the LORD,
on horses and in chariots, in carts, upon mules and dromedaries,
to Jerusalem, my holy mountain, says the LORD,
just as the Israelites bring their offering to the house of the LORD in clean vessels.
Some of these I will take as priests and Levites, says the LORD.

RESPONSORIAL PSALM

Ps 117:1, 2

℟. (Mark 16:15) Go out to all the world and tell the Good News.
or
℟. Alleluia.

Praise the LORD, all you nations;
    glorify him, all you peoples!

℟. Go out to all the world and tell the Good News.
or
℟. Alleluia.

For steadfast is his kindness toward us,
    and the fidelity of the LORD endures
        forever.

℟. Go out to all the world and tell the Good News.
or
℟. Alleluia.

SECOND READING

Heb 12:5-7, 11-13

Brothers and sisters,
You have forgotten the exhortation
        addressed to you as children:
    "My son, do not disdain the discipline
        of the Lord
        or lose heart when reproved by him;
    for whom the Lord loves, he disciplines;
        he scourges every son he
            acknowledges."
Endure your trials as "discipline";
    God treats you as sons.
For what "son" is there whom his father
        does not discipline?
At the time,
    all discipline seems a cause not for joy
        but for pain,
    yet later it brings the peaceful fruit of
        righteousness
    to those who are trained by it.

So strengthen your drooping hands and
        your weak knees.
Make straight paths for your feet,
    that what is lame may not be disjointed
        but healed.

About Liturgy

Prefaces: During Ordinary Time there are eight prefaces given in *The Roman Missal* for Sundays. Because these prefaces are used with a wide variety of Sunday Lectionary readings, they tend to be "generic," speaking more generally of the mystery of salvation. On festivals the prefaces always open up for us the mystery being celebrated.

The dialogue before the preface proper begins is one of the oldest of all liturgical texts. The dialogue invites the assembly to prayer, but much more elaborately than the usual "Let us pray" that begins the collect and prayer after Communion. First of all, the invitation to pray the eucharistic prayer is truly a dialogue between presider and assembly. The dialogue unfolds in three parts: greeting ("The Lord be with you"), command to a specific prayer sentiment or stance ("Lift up your hearts"), and an invitation to pray in a particular way ("Let us give thanks to the Lord our God"). The eucharistic prayer is our great thanksgiving to God for the work of salvation.

The body of the preface then unfolds as an act of thanksgiving and praise and includes reasons why we have these sentiments toward God. Often the preface includes a reference to God as Creator, to Jesus as Redeemer, and to the Holy Spirit as sanctifier.

Originally the Latin word which we translate as preface (*praefatio*) meant "proclamation" and was sometimes ascribed to the whole eucharistic prayer. Our English translation can get in the way here; rather than being merely "preliminary" (like the preface in a book) which can be skipped over or discarded, the preface to the eucharistic prayer is the first invitation to give God praise and thanks. It sets the tone for the whole prayer.

About Liturgical Music

Changing service music: At this point in Luke's gospel Jesus begins making his way intentionally toward Jerusalem, where he will face his death and resurrection. When asked who will be saved, he responds that the gate is narrow and great strength will be required to pass through it. It will not be enough merely to have eaten with him and listened to him speak. To enter into risen life we must journey with him to Jerusalem; we must join him in his self-emptying on the cross.

Jesus' turn toward Jerusalem in the gospel passage makes this Sunday an ideal one to change the service music that has been sung for Mass (note, for example, the change in music for the universal prayer in this resource). This shift in service music is not arbitrary, but liturgy-driven: the change of musical direction expresses our willingness to turn with Jesus and walk with him toward Jerusalem. Some catechesis would be important to help the people realize why the change in the service music has been initiated on this particular Sunday. One way to do this would be to run a short blurb in the bulletin explaining the liturgical reason for the change. It would be good to run this blurb both this Sunday and next to give people time to grasp it.

AUGUST 21, 2016
TWENTY-FIRST SUNDAY
IN ORDINARY TIME

SPIRITUALITY

GOSPEL ACCLAMATION
Matt 11:29ab

R⁄. Alleluia, alleluia.
Take my yoke upon you, says the Lord;
and learn from me, for I am meek and humble
    of heart.
R⁄. Alleluia, alleluia.

Gospel   Luke 14:1, 7-14; L126C

On a sabbath Jesus went to dine
    at the home of one of the
        leading Pharisees,
    and the people there were
        observing him carefully.

He told a parable to those who had
    been invited,
    noticing how they were choosing the
        places of honor at the table.
"When you are invited by someone to a
    wedding banquet,
    do not recline at table in the place of
        honor.
A more distinguished guest than you
    may have been invited by him,
    and the host who invited both of you
        may approach you and say,
    'Give your place to this man,'
    and then you would proceed with
        embarrassment
    to take the lowest place.
Rather, when you are invited,
    go and take the lowest place
    so that when the host comes to you
        he may say,
    'My friend, move up to a higher
        position.'
Then you will enjoy the esteem of your
    companions at the table.
For everyone who exalts himself will
    be humbled,
    but the one who humbles himself will
        be exalted."

Continued in Appendix A, p. 309.

Reflecting on the Gospel

This Sunday's gospel includes two related parables, one directed to banquet guests and the other to banquet hosts. However, the banquets in the parables are more than fine meals. At stake in these banquets is relationships and inclusivity. All are invited. All share in the one place of honor. All receive of the generosity of the divine Host who lavishes us with all good things.

The first parable about wedding guests invites us to reflect on knowing ourselves in relation to others. The "wedding banquet" imagery of the gospel is eschatological imagery; that is, we might think of God as the host and the wedding banquet as the Lord's heavenly banquet. We are all invited to the banquet (offered salvation); but we must remember that it is *God who invites.* Our own relation to God is as those who are poor; we cannot "buy" our own place in heaven. God invites us to this exalted position. God raises us up! By God's choosing us we are raised up to share in divine riches and bestowed the great dignity of sharing in God's very Life. If this is how God relates to us, then this is how the disciple relates to others. As God has bestowed dignity on us, so do we shower others with dignity. As God invites all of us, so do we invite all others into relationship with us that enlarges who we are and how we live.

The second parable about hosts invites us to reflect on how we wish God to relate to us. We know we are poor (a metaphor for sinners). God doesn't extend an invitation to the banquet only to those who seem worthy, but extends the invitation to all who would respond. No one is excluded from the banquet. Neither should we exclude others from our own attention and ministrations. If we wish God to invite us who are poor to the divine banquet, then we also extend ourselves to all others regardless of social, economic, religious, sexual status or orientation.

At Jesus' "wedding banquet" *all* who hear and heed Jesus' admonition to humility, inclusivity, and generosity sit in the *one* "place of honor." There is *one* "place of honor" because we are all one Body in Christ. There needs to be only *one* place near our Host, symbolizing our unity and strength in his one Body. Further, we can never exhaust the gift of this "place of honor." It is a share in the very Life and ministry of our Host. This "place of honor," therefore, is not a limited space, a single seat, a physical arrangement of host and guests one to another. It is a spacious relationship of all of us to the risen Jesus that is a share in his divine Life. This "place of honor" is given to "the righteous," all of us who have chosen to live and act as Jesus the Host. How blessed are we!

Living the Paschal Mystery

To be invited to the *one* "place of honor" means that we must let go of anything that limits our relationship to our Host and to each other. If we wish God to raise us up ("repaid at the resurrection of the righteous"), then we must live our lives raising others up. We must build strong relationships of unity. We must forget about seeking our own paltry honor and instead give ourselves over to the "place of honor" to which our Host invites us.

Each Sunday we are invited to God's banquet table. We ourselves are nourished at the same time that we are called to share the abundance of God's Life by reaching out to others in need. We eat and drink in order to be gracious to others. This is the most profound blessedness!

Focusing the Gospel

Key words and phrases: wedding banquet, place of honor, host, humbles himself, invite the . . . , blessed

To the point: At Jesus' "wedding banquet" *all* who hear and heed Jesus' admonition to humility, inclusivity, and generosity sit in the *one* "place of honor." This "place of honor" is not a limited space, a single seat, a physical arrangement of host and guests one to another. It is a spacious relationship to the risen Jesus that is a share in his divine Life. It is given to "the righteous," all those who have chosen to live and act as Jesus the Host. How blessed are they!

Connecting the Gospel

to the first reading: The first reading from the book of Sirach describes the manner of living of the righteous ones mentioned in the gospel: living with humility, not seeking what is beyond one's strength, being wise, giving alms.

to experience: At wedding banquets today, places at table are usually assigned according to the guests' relationship to the bridal couple. At Jesus' "wedding banquet," our place is assigned according to our relationship to him.

Connecting the Responsorial Psalm

to the readings: In this Sunday's gospel the people were "observing [Jesus] carefully." In the responsorial psalm we observe God carefully. What we see is a God who makes "a home for the poor" and provides "for the needy." When Jesus in the gospel advises us to invite to our table "the poor, the crippled, the lame, the blind," he is challenging us to model what we see God doing. And when we do so we experience a remarkable reversal in our own position. Choosing to give up the first place so that room be made for the poor and needy exalts us. Our humility "find[s] favor with God" (first reading). Even more, we become like God. When we sing this psalm, then, we are praying to become like the God we praise.

to psalmist preparation: This psalm praises God for goodness to the poor and needy. Only those who recognize themselves among the poor and needy can see what God is doing to lift them up. How are you poor and needy? How does God lift you up by inviting you to the banquet of Jesus' Body and Blood? How do you invite others to join you at this banquet?

ASSEMBLY & FAITH-SHARING GROUPS
- I would describe my relationship to Jesus as . . .
- I hear and heed Jesus' admonition to humility, inclusivity, and generosity by . . .
- I find it easiest to choose to live and act as Jesus did when . . . I find it most difficult when . . .

PRESIDERS
Jesus, the Host of the "wedding banquet," is visible in my presiding when I . . .

DEACONS
The blessing I receive (even now) whenever I minister to those who are unable to repay me is . . .

HOSPITALITY MINISTERS
My manner of greeting those assembling for liturgy opens them to a deeper relationship to the risen Jesus when I . . . to each other when I . . .

MUSIC MINISTERS
My music ministry is most humble, inclusive, and generous when I . . .

ALTAR MINISTERS
My serving ministry witnesses to how I have chosen to act as Jesus in my daily living when I . . .

LECTORS
I could better "conduct [my] affairs with humility" and wisdom (first reading) if I were to . . . This would enhance my proclamation by . . .

EXTRAORDINARY MINISTERS OF HOLY COMMUNION
Being more aware that I am a minister at Jesus' "wedding banquet" helps me to . . .

CELEBRATION

Model Penitential Act

Presider: The gospel speaks of taking a place of honor at a wedding banquet. As we prepare to participate in this heavenly banquet, let us ask for God's mercy for the times we have not taken our rightful place before God and one another . . . [pause]

Lord Jesus, you are the divine Host who nourishes us: Lord . . .

Christ Jesus, you invite us to share in "the resurrection of the righteous": Christ . . .

Lord Jesus, you call us to be guests at your eternal banquet: Lord . . .

Homily Points

• Little children beg to sit next to Grandma and Grandpa at holiday meals. Why? Because they want to be near those who love them and who shower them with attention and gifts. At Jesus' "wedding banquet," should we not all be clamoring to sit next to Jesus who loves us more than anyone and showers us with attention and gifts beyond imagining?

• Jesus uses the occasion of a dinner to teach us something about the true "place of honor" at his "wedding banquet." This is not a limited place reserved for a select few. We are all called to live and act as Jesus, the Host who invites us to deepen our relationship with him and each other. We are all called to be near him who showers us with the most unimaginable Gift of all: a share in his divine Life. Every time we respond to his invitation to nearness, he seats us at his "place of honor." How blessed are we!

• We live and act like Jesus our Host when we make him the most important guest in our heart. With him as guest in our heart, the space within us expands to include everyone— "the poor, the crippled, the lame, the blind." Many sit with us in the "place of honor" as we, like Jesus, make more and more room. How blessed are we, indeed!

Model Universal Prayer (Prayer of the Faithful)

Presider: God invites us to the heavenly banquet where we are nourished for our journey of life. Let us make known our needs to such a generous God.

Response:

Lord, hear our prayer.

Cantor:

we pray to the Lord,

For all members of the church, invited to sit at God's heavenly banquet . . . [pause]

For all people of the world, called to a saving relationship with God and each other . . . [pause]

For the poor and disadvantaged, denied a place at the table of abundance . . . [pause]

For each of us gathered here, gifted with God's love and Life . . . [pause]

Presider: Gracious God, you are the divine Host who invites us to a place of honor near you. Grant our needs that all of us may feast forever at your heavenly banquet. We ask this through Christ our Lord. **Amen.**

COLLECT

Let us pray.

Pause for silent prayer

God of might, giver of every good gift, put into our hearts the love of your name, so that, by deepening our sense of reverence, you may nurture in us what is good and, by your watchful care, keep safe what you have nurtured. Through our Lord Jesus Christ, your Son, who lives and reigns with you in the unity of the Holy Spirit, one God, for ever and ever. **Amen.**

FIRST READING
Sir 3:17-18, 20, 28-29

My child, conduct your affairs with humility,
and you will be loved more than a giver of gifts.
Humble yourself the more, the greater you are,
and you will find favor with God.
What is too sublime for you, seek not,
into things beyond your strength search not.
The mind of a sage appreciates proverbs,
and an attentive ear is the joy of the wise.
Water quenches a flaming fire,
and alms atone for sins.

CATECHESIS

RESPONSORIAL PSALM
Ps 68:4-5, 6-7, 10-11

R⁊. (cf. 11b) God, in your goodness, you
have made a home for the poor.

The just rejoice and exult before God;
   they are glad and rejoice.
Sing to God, chant praise to his name;
   whose name is the LORD.

R⁊. God, in your goodness, you have made
a home for the poor.

The father of orphans and the defender of
   widows
   is God in his holy dwelling.
God gives a home to the forsaken;
   he leads forth prisoners to prosperity.

R⁊. God, in your goodness, you have made
a home for the poor.

A bountiful rain you showered down, O
   God, upon your inheritance;
   you restored the land when it
     languished;
your flock settled in it;
   in your goodness, O God, you provided
     it for the needy.

R⁊. God, in your goodness, you have made
a home for the poor.

SECOND READING
Heb 12:18-19, 22-24a

Brothers and sisters:
You have not approached that which could
   be touched
   and a blazing fire and gloomy darkness
   and storm and a trumpet blast
   and a voice speaking words such that
     those who heard
   begged that no message be further
     addressed to them.
No, you have approached Mount Zion
   and the city of the living God, the
     heavenly Jerusalem,
   and countless angels in festal gathering,
   and the assembly of the firstborn
     enrolled in heaven,
   and God the judge of all,
   and the spirits of the just made perfect,
   and Jesus, the mediator of a new
     covenant,
   and the sprinkled blood that speaks
     more eloquently than that of Abel.

About Liturgy
Eschatological turning point in Luke's gospel: Toward the end of the liturgical year—as our sequential reading of a Synoptic Gospel brings events closer to Jerusalem and Jesus' passion and death—we begin to pick up Parousia (referring to Jesus' Second Coming) and eschatological themes. Often this begins toward the end of October or early November and culminates in the great eschatological festival, the Solemnity of Our Lord Jesus Christ the King. This year, however, themes that we would ordinarily be dealing with later in the liturgical year already show up now in late August. This is because of the structure of Luke's gospel, about one-third of which focuses on Jesus' journey to Jerusalem. Luke's gospel is structured as one long journey of preaching and teaching, healing and forgiving, relentlessly treading to Jerusalem. The prevailing journey theme in Luke's gospel is a reminder that our whole Christian life is a journey to our final union with Jesus in eschatological glory. May we be sure-footed on our journey, resolute in following Jesus, and strong in our constant growth in our relationship to Jesus and each other.

About Liturgical Music
Singing the acclamations, part 1: The acclamations we sing as part of Mass (i.e., the Gospel Acclamation; the Holy, Holy, Holy; the Mystery of Faith; and the Great Amen) are all acts of direct address to God. Despite their brevity, the acclamations have significant impact on our self-understanding and our manner of living out our baptismal identity. Singing the acclamations is a way we take ownership of ourselves and our relationship with God. The acclamations teach us that beneath all prayer, whether cries for help, or prayers for healing, or confessions of sin, or words of thanksgiving, stands the empowerment of our baptismal right to address God face-to-face. When we sing the acclamations we dare the one gesture forbidden mere mortals—to look directly upon the face of God—and discover in that act not death but dignity.

Once we understand what we are doing ritually in the acclamations we can never again look upon self or others in a demeaning way, nor can we ever again approach life's challenges with a sense of disempowerment. Instead we see in self and others the dignity bestowed by God, and act toward both with reverence and appreciation. And we interpret events, both personal and social, both close at hand and worldwide, not as interventions or judgments of a distant God, but as invitations to engage our power with God's in the mutual work of redemption. In short, we grow to full stature before God and take on our share of responsibility for the coming of the kingdom. To sing the acclamations, then, is to engage fully, consciously, and actively both in liturgical celebration and in all of Christian living.

AUGUST 28, 2016
TWENTY-SECOND SUNDAY
IN ORDINARY TIME

SPIRITUALITY

GOSPEL ACCLAMATION
Ps 119:135

℟. Alleluia, alleluia.
Let your face shine upon your servant;
and teach me your laws.
℟. Alleluia, alleluia.

Gospel Luke 14:25-33; L129C

Great crowds were traveling with
    Jesus,
    and he turned and addressed
        them,
    "If anyone comes to me without
        hating his father and mother,
    wife and children, brothers and sisters,
    and even his own life,
    he cannot be my disciple.
Whoever does not carry his
    own cross and come after me
    cannot be my disciple.
Which of you wishing to construct a
        tower
    does not first sit down and calculate
        the cost
    to see if there is enough for its
        completion?
Otherwise, after laying the foundation
    and finding himself unable to finish the
        work
    the onlookers should laugh at him and
        say,
    'This one began to build but did not
        have the resources to finish.'
Or what king marching into battle would
        not first sit down
    and decide whether with ten thousand
        troops
    he can successfully oppose another
        king
    advancing upon him with twenty
        thousand troops?
But if not, while he is still far away,
    he will send a delegation to ask for
        peace terms.
In the same way,
    anyone of you who does not renounce
        all his possessions
    cannot be my disciple."

Reflecting on the Gospel

We are always told to read the fine print before signing a contract. We want no surprises. We want to make sure that all parties of the contract receive their agreed share. As much as possible we want to be assured that the cost of whatever we are signing—whether in money, time, or work—is worth every ounce of ourselves we put into fulfilling the contract. This Sunday's gospel begins with the statement that "[g]reat crowds were traveling with Jesus." Interesting: they didn't know the fine print yet! Jesus bluntly challenges the crowd to take up the demands of discipleship with eyes wide open. He clearly spells out the fine print in large, large letters: disciples must put Jesus ahead of their families and even their own lives, carry their cross, and renounce all they have. Discipleship is total and unconditional. By the time Jesus arrives in Jerusalem, is tried and condemned, is nailed to the cross, the crowd had diminished greatly. Few were left. Most of his disciples abandoned him. The people turned on him. Fine print can be costly.

Jesus intends no surprises for those who choose discipleship. Here's the fine print: we have to die if we wish to follow Jesus. The cost of discipleship seems disproportionately high compared to anything we could want or value as humans. This doesn't seem like a very fair or advantageous contract. And this is the point: following Jesus to Jerusalem leads us beyond human calculations, beyond a signed deal. Following Jesus leads to death, to be sure, but to a death that grants us a share in God's very Life, an outcome worth any price.

Jesus forewarns the "[g]reat crowds" traveling with him that they must "calculate the cost" and the risk of journeying with him to Jerusalem. Even family relationships cannot come before the demands of following him. However, we really cannot calculate the cost of discipleship. Yes, we must follow Jesus with eyes wide open. We must read the fine print of the cost of following him. The cost of discipleship? Everything we have and are. The reward of discipleship? Everything God has and is.

Living the Paschal Mystery

The amazing thing is that we *know* the cost of discipleship, yet we spend our whole lives trying to figure it out! Or trying to avoid expending the cost. There is no easy road for disciples. We must follow Jesus wherever he leads. We know that we must hand our lives over to Jesus. At the same time, we know we are not traveling this journey alone. We know that we are given wisdom and the Holy Spirit to be faithful (see the first reading), even when we aren't quite sure what the cost will be. We just follow.

It would be nice to say that we shouldn't start what we can't finish. If we calculated the cost of our faithfulness, or had undue concern for what others think, or weighed the risks involved in living the Gospel faithfully, we might never begin the journey of discipleship. But we have in fact already begun this journey at baptism. The challenge, then, is not to look at the cost, but to keep our eyes on Jesus who is walking ahead of us showing us the way. In Jesus death always leads to new Life. This is the promise and it is worth the cost. This is the promising fine print upon which we keep our eyes. While the cost of discipleship is everything we have and are, the rewards of discipleship are so much greater. God gives us a share in divine Life. God promises an eternal share in glory. That's fine print we are pleased to read!

Focusing the Gospel

Key words and phrases: Great crowds, traveling with Jesus, calculate the cost

To the point: Jesus forewarns the "[g]reat crowds" traveling with him that they must "calculate the cost" and the risk of journeying with him to Jerusalem. Even family relationships cannot come before the demands of following him. The cost of discipleship? Everything we have and are. The reward of discipleship? Everything God has and is.

Connecting the Gospel

to the first reading: Disciples willing to accept the cost of following Jesus need God's help, for our "deliberations . . . are timid, / and unsure are our plans." Through the indwelling of the Holy Spirit, God gives us the wisdom, strength, and courage we need.

to experience: Before making any big decision that changes where we live, what we do, and who we are with, we calculate the cost in time, money, and emotional expenditure. Discipleship is the biggest decision of our life. And yet we never really know all the costs that will be required of us.

Connecting the Responsorial Psalm

to the readings: The first reading reminds us of a truth we already know: "the deliberations of mortals are timid, / and unsure." But Jesus challenges us in the gospel to be neither timid nor unsure when deliberating the cost of discipleship. It is total. Relationships must be abandoned, possessions must be renounced, the cross must be carried. The responsorial psalm promises, however, that we will not be left with only our own meager strength. God will grant us "wisdom" and will "prosper the work of our hands." God will give us both the wisdom to calculate the cost and the courage to pay it (first reading). God knows the all-encompassing cost of discipleship and will be with us when we need strength, support, encouragement, and mercy. In singing this psalm we profess our confidence in God who knows even better than we do what will be exacted of us and who has promised to see us through.

to psalmist preparation: The cost of following Christ is radical, but in this psalm you remind the assembly they have more than themselves to depend upon: their discipleship will prosper because God underwrites it. You sing realistically of both the tenuousness of human strength and the steadfastness of God. May your singing give the assembly courage.

ASSEMBLY & FAITH-SHARING GROUPS

- When I hear Jesus demanding that I place him ahead of family and my own self, I understand Jesus is asking me to . . .
- An example of when I placed someone or something ahead of my discipleship was . . . This choice cost me . . .
- I am willing to pay the high cost of discipleship when . . . I am unwilling when . . .

PRESIDERS

My preaching helps others hear and accept the cost of discipleship when I . . .

DEACONS

My ministry is a living witness to the cost of discipleship in that . . .

HOSPITALITY MINISTERS

My hospitality (at church, at home, at work) helps others embrace the cost of discipleship when . . .

MUSIC MINISTERS

The unexpected cost of my choosing to be a music minister has been . . .

ALTAR MINISTERS

What I must renounce in order to serve faithfully is . . .

LECTORS

When I embrace the cost of discipleship, my proclamation sounds like . . .

EXTRAORDINARY MINISTERS OF HOLY COMMUNION

Eucharist reveals the cost of discipleship by . . . Eucharist inspires and nourishes me to pay the cost when I . . .

Model Penitential Act

Presider: The cost of discipleship is high, as Jesus forewarns us in today's gospel: we must lose our lives, carry our crosses, and renounce our possessions. Let us prepare to celebrate Jesus' self-giving at this Mass by calling to mind the times we have not been willing to embrace the cost of following him . . . [pause]

Lord Jesus, you are the Savior of the world: Lord . . .

Christ Jesus, you conquered death and rose to new Life: Christ . . .

Lord Jesus, you strengthen us to bear the cross of discipleship: Lord . . .

Homily Points

• Big life decisions require calculated thought. We calculate the gains and losses of selling our home. We calculate the positives and negatives of accepting a new job. We calculate the strengths and weaknesses of each candidate when voting. "Great crowds" were following Jesus. Did they have any inkling of the cost? Did they remain a *great* crowd or become drifters?

• Jesus clearly forewarns us about the cost of journeying with him to Jerusalem: a priority relationship with him that demands total self-giving. Discipleship compels *total*: total self-renunciation, total commitment, total identity with Jesus. The cost of discipleship lies in the "total": it is *everything* we have and are.

• Faced with calculating the cost of discipleship, do we choose to be part of Jesus' faithful companions on the journey, or do we choose to become drifters? We are Jesus' faithful companions when, for example, we take the necessary steps to forgive someone who has seriously hurt us or stay the course of living with less so those with little can have what they need. We drift away from Jesus when, for example, we follow the path of least resistance in face of an unjust situation or we insist on our own way despite the needs of others in our family or workplace. The cost of discipleship is this choice: to be Jesus' companions—or drifters.

Model Universal Prayer (Prayer of the Faithful)

Presider: Confident that God hears our prayers, let us lift up our needs.

Response:

Lord, hear our prayer.

Cantor:

we pray to the Lord,

That all members of the church willingly remain faithful disciples of Jesus, regardless of the cost . . . [pause]

That all people of the world journey resolutely toward salvation . . . [pause]

That those in any need be served and supported by faithful disciples of Jesus . . . [pause]

That each of us give ourselves totally to Jesus and receive joyfully his total gift of Self to us in return . . . [pause]

Presider: O God, your divine Son calls us to faithful discipleship in spite of the great cost. Hear these our prayers that we remain faithful to Jesus and one day enjoy the promise of eternal glory with you. We ask this through that same Son, Jesus Christ our Lord. **Amen.**

COLLECT

Let us pray.

Pause for silent prayer

O God, by whom we are redeemed and
    receive adoption,
look graciously upon your beloved sons
    and daughters,
that those who believe in Christ
may receive true freedom
and an everlasting inheritance.
Through our Lord Jesus Christ, your Son,
who lives and reigns with you in the unity
    of the Holy Spirit,
one God, for ever and ever. **Amen.**

FIRST READING

Wis 9:13-18b

Who can know God's counsel,
    or who can conceive what the LORD
        intends?
For the deliberations of mortals are timid,
    and unsure are our plans.
For the corruptible body burdens the soul
    and the earthen shelter weighs down the
        mind that has many concerns.
And scarce do we guess the things on
        earth,
    and what is within our grasp we find
        with difficulty;
    but when things are in heaven, who can
        search them out?
Or who ever knew your counsel, except
        you had given wisdom
    and sent your holy spirit from on high?
And thus were the paths of those on earth
        made straight.

RESPONSORIAL PSALM

Ps 90:3-4, 5-6, 12-13, 14, 17

℟. (1) In every age, O Lord, you have been our refuge.

You turn man back to dust,
    saying, "Return, O children of men."
For a thousand years in your sight
    are as yesterday, now that it is past,
    or as a watch of the night.

℟. In every age, O Lord, you have been our refuge.

You make an end of them in their sleep;
    the next morning they are like the
        changing grass,
which at dawn springs up anew,
    but by evening wilts and fades.

R⁊. In every age, O Lord, you have been
our refuge.

Teach us to number our days aright,
    that we may gain wisdom of heart.
Return, O Lord! How long?
    Have pity on your servants!

R⁊. In every age, O Lord, you have been
our refuge.

Fill us at daybreak with your kindness,
    that we may shout for joy and gladness
        all our days.
And may the gracious care of the Lord
    our God be ours;
    prosper the work of our hands for us!
    Prosper the work of our hands!

R⁊. In every age, O Lord, you have been
our refuge.

SECOND READING
Phlm 9-10, 12-17

I, Paul, an old man,
    and now also a prisoner for Christ Jesus,
    urge you on behalf of my child
        Onesimus,
    whose father I have become in my
        imprisonment;
    I am sending him, that is, my own heart,
        back to you.
I should have liked to retain him for
        myself,
    so that he might serve me on your
        behalf
    in my imprisonment for the gospel,
    but I did not want to do anything
        without your consent,
    so that the good you do might not be
        forced but voluntary.
Perhaps this is why he was away from you
        for a while,
    that you might have him back forever,
    no longer as a slave
    but more than a slave, a brother,
    beloved especially to me, but even more
        so to you,
    as a man and in the Lord.
So if you regard me as a partner, welcome
        him as you would me.

About Liturgy

Intercessory prayer: When we read gospels such as this Sunday's we could easily become discouraged at the demands of faithful discipleship. Although Jesus speaks in metaphors, he also is making clear to us that following him will cost us dearly. One way we gain the strength to be faithful is through prayer—for ourselves and for other disciples.

Usually when we think of intercessory or petitionary prayer we think of the specific prayer requests of our own that we send to God or for which others have asked us to pray—perhaps for a sick family member, or success in the search for employment, or a friend who is suffering from depression. This kind of prayer is good and helps us connect with the everyday concerns of all of us. In the liturgy, however, most often the intercessory prayer is more general—both in intention and for the persons we pray. This more general intercessory prayer (the universal prayer or prayer of the faithful) helps us realize that we are all disciples together on the road to Jerusalem and one strength we receive is the prayer we have for each other. None of us is ever forgotten in our need.

After the universal prayer (prayer of the faithful) which concludes the Liturgy of the Word, intercessory prayer continues within the very heart of our great prayer of praise and thanksgiving, the eucharistic prayer. By continuing our intercessory prayer during the eucharistic prayer we are reminded that the ultimate praise and thanksgiving we can give God is the gift of our very lives in discipleship. Furthermore, when we are faithful disciples the church is fruitful in its mission. As we pray for the pope, bishops, ministers, and all God's people, we ought to be mindful of the seriousness of the task at hand. Our prayer is that we might not count the cost, but look to the fruits of our faithfulness.

Labor Day: This is Labor Day weekend, and it would be appropriate to add a fifth intention at the universal prayer (prayer of the faithful). For example, "That all laborers, by the quality of their work, proclaim God's care and love for all people."

About Liturgical Music

Singing the acclamations, part 2: The acclamations developed as a result of Vatican II's recovery of the priesthood of all the baptized and the essential nature of the liturgy as the celebration of all the people. They are *actions* in the form of song. As the ancient adage states, to sing is to pray twice. When we sing, we become more present, more attentive, more participative, and more powerful. When we sing, we enfold all the other members of the assembly with our voice, and communicate our choice to participate fully in the liturgical action, and vice versa. We sing the acclamations, then, not only to address God but also to direct personal support to one another in living out our identity and mission as Body of Christ. The singing of the acclamations is neither neutral nor inconsequential, for it expresses in an intense way the triple directedness of the liturgy toward God, toward other members in Christ, and toward the world. Our singing of the acclamations amplifies their energy and intent: their sound moves out from each of us as individual source, encircles all of us in mutual support, and sends us as community on mission. The more we understand their importance and the more intentionally we sing them, the more we will both deepen our participation in liturgy and our living out of the mission of the church.

SPIRITUALITY

GOSPEL ACCLAMATION
2 Cor 5:19

R∕. Alleluia, alleluia.
God was reconciling the world to himself in Christ
and entrusting to us the message of reconciliation.
R∕. Alleluia, alleluia.

Gospel
Luke 15:1-32; L132C

Tax collectors and sinners were all drawing near to listen to Jesus,
  but the Pharisees and scribes began to complain, saying,
"This man welcomes sinners and eats with them."
So to them he addressed this parable.
"What man among you having a hundred sheep and losing one of them
  would not leave the ninety-nine in the desert
  and go after the lost one until he finds it?
And when he does find it,
  he sets it on his shoulders with great joy
  and, upon his arrival home,
  he calls together his friends and neighbors and says to them,
  'Rejoice with me because I have found my lost sheep.'
I tell you, in just the same way
  there will be more joy in heaven over one sinner who repents
  than over ninety-nine righteous people who have no need of repentance.

"Or what woman having ten coins and losing one
  would not light a lamp and sweep the house,
  searching carefully until she finds it?

Continued in Appendix A, p. 310.

Reflecting on the Gospel
This Sunday's gospel unravels for us the movement of repentance, from overture through to coda. Repentance begins with being lost, moves through a sonata of straying and wandering and dissolution, and ends (hopefully!) with being found and feasting. Jesus uses not one but three parables to sound for us the mighty music of how much God seeks us when we are lost, how much God (and all of heaven!) rejoices when we are found. The shepherd man, housekeeper woman, and prodigal father have in common losing, searching and finding, and feasting. This is a glorious feast—the only one that brings us from death to Life. This is the feast of repentance, the only source of everlasting joy. This feast only happens through encounter with Jesus who knows when we are lost, ever seeks us and greatly desires that we be found, and offers the lavish feast of himself for our celebrating and rejoicing.

Jesus uses three situations (a lost sheep, a lost coin, a lost son) to dramatize that whenever we stray from God's steadfast compassion and love (become lost), God always seeks to find us and show us divine mercy. For our part, we must realize we are lost, recognize our need for God, and begin the journey home to be embraced by divine mercy. When God's offer of mercy is met by our repentance, all in heaven rejoice. God's feast is about rejoicing over us humans who stray from God, but repent and are welcomed back.

Tax collectors and sinners are "drawing near to listen to Jesus." Pharisees and scribes, on the other hand, observe what is happening and complain to Jesus. He answers their complaint with three parables that turn the table on their belief about who is really saved. Not those Pharisees and scribes who are self-righteous and unrelenting, but those sinners who are self-aware and repent. Jesus invites everyone to his table—his feast of mercy. But not everyone chooses to come. Only those come who recognize their need to be found. God always knows when we are lost and gives us every means to be found. God desires that no one be lost, that we repent and return to the Source of our Life. For this we rejoice and feast.

Living the Paschal Mystery
If God is so compassionate and loving with us, then as faithful followers of Jesus we must risk being so compassionate and loving with others. First of all, this means that we don't judge whether the other is worth our mercy and love. God shows us that all are—even outcasts and sinners. Second, we ourselves don't earn mercy and love. Since they are free gifts of God to us, they are gifts we freely give to others. We don't wait until someone wrongs us to show mercy and love—we offer these gifts simply because the other is a beloved of God.

It's much easier for us to be merciful and loving when the end situation is better for us. For example, we might forgive a family member some wrongdoing because we want peace in the family. It is far more risky to be merciful when there is no immediate gain for us in sight. As those who follow Jesus, we are called to be merciful simply because this is the way Jesus was. Living the paschal mystery means that we feast well and often because we realize that God unfailingly extends mercy and love without calculating whether we deserve it or not. All we need to do is repent. All we need to do is be willing to be found.

Focusing the Gospel

Key words and phrases: Tax collectors and sinners, drawing near to listen, Pharisees and scribes, complain, righteous people, sinner who repents, celebrate with a feast, found

To the point: In this gospel tax collectors and sinners are "drawing near to listen to Jesus." Pharisees and scribes, on the other hand, observe what is happening and complain to Jesus. He answers their complaint with three parables that turn the table on their belief about who is really saved. Not those Pharisees and scribes who are self-righteous and unrelenting, but those sinners who are self-aware and repent. Jesus invites everyone to his table—his feast of mercy. But not everyone chooses to come. Only those come who recognize their need to be found.

Connecting the Gospel

to the first reading: Israel has, indeed, strayed from God, as has the younger son strayed from his father in the gospel parable. As God relented in the punishment Israel deserved, so does the father in the parable refrain from punishing his younger son. God's mercy reigns!

to experience: We naturally avoid self-righteous and unrelenting people, and are easily drawn to those who are compassionate, open-minded, and open-hearted. In which group do we find ourselves? When?

Connecting the Responsorial Psalm

to the readings: In the first reading Moses talks God into relenting of the punishment unfaithful Israel deserves. In the gospel the prodigal son relents of his sinfulness and is embraced by his father. The Pharisees and scribes, on the other hand, refuse to relent in their judgment against Jesus for eating with sinners. The elder son refuses to relent of his resentment at his prodigal brother and his anger at his forgiving father.

The responsorial psalm for this Sunday, taken from Psalm 51, is our song of relenting. Through it we align ourselves with the tax collectors and sinners, with the lost sheep, and with the prodigal son. Such alignment is part of the radical gift of self which discipleship demands, for through it we give up any vestige of false self-image. We can be found because we admit that we are lost. We can receive God's unrestricted and limitless mercy because we confess we are in need of it.

to psalmist preparation: Your singing these verses from Psalm 51 is a public act of confession, for you stand before the assembly and admit sinfulness. But even more importantly, you confess the mercy of God who never spurns a contrite and humbled heart. As you prepare to sing this psalm, what forgiveness might you ask of God? What relenting of sin and pride might you need to do?

ASSEMBLY & FAITH-SHARING GROUPS

- When, like the tax collectors and sinners, I draw "near to listen to Jesus," what I hear is . . .
- Like the Pharisees and scribes, I have been self-righteous and unrelenting in these circumstances . . .
- I am most self-aware and repentant when . . . God's mercy . . .

PRESIDERS
When my ministry is one of helping the assembly draw near and listen to Jesus, it looks like . . .

DEACONS
My service ministry draws others to God's feast of mercy when I . . .

HOSPITALITY MINISTERS
My hospitality is a sign of God's steadfast mercy and love when . . .

MUSIC MINISTERS
Whenever I find myself straying from the real purpose of music ministry, Jesus seeks me out and brings me back by . . .

ALTAR MINISTERS
My ministry is about setting the table for the feast, and this brings me to . . .

LECTORS
When I draw near to listen to Jesus in my daily living, my proclamation becomes . . .

EXTRAORDINARY MINISTERS OF HOLY COMMUNION
Those to whom I minister as they come to the table of the Lord to feast bring me great joy in that . . . I bring them great joy when I . . .

Model Penitential Act

Presider: Whenever we are straying or lost on our Christian journey, God is there with divine mercy and love. As we prepare ourselves to celebrate this liturgy, let us open our hearts to such a merciful God . . . [pause]

Lord Jesus, you are merciful and loving: Lord . . .

Christ Jesus, you call us to your feast of love: Christ . . .

Lord Jesus, you seek those who are lost: Lord . . .

Homily Points

• It took a long time and many prayers by his mother before St. Augustine came to his senses and turned to God. His *Confessions* divulge the sinful life he led before he allowed himself to be found by Christ. His repentance brought him to a life of holiness, theological scholarship, and church leadership. He is a good model for growing in self-awareness, choosing repentance and God's mercy, and coming to God's feast. He models for us what it means to be saved—to be lost and then found.

• These three gospel parables are metaphors describing God's all-merciful deeds in bringing us to salvation. God never gives up on us when we are lost and feasts with us when we are found. On our part, we must admit that we are lost, come to our senses and be found, and feast on God's unfailing mercy. God is always ready to set the table. Are we ready to be found? Are we ready to come to the feast?

• Catholic tradition has tended to stress sinfulness over holiness, making salvation seem like an almost unattainable goal. Jesus assures us that, sinners though we are, God is always merciful, seeks us when we stray, and calls us to a feast of joy when we choose to come near him. Let the feast begin!

Model Universal Prayer (Prayer of the Faithful)

Presider: God is full of mercy and compassion, and seeks us when we are lost. And so we pray.

Response:

Lord, hear our prayer.

Cantor:

we pray to the Lord,

That all members of the church be quick to search out the lost with mercy and compassion . . . [pause]

That all peoples of the world be brought to the feast of God's table of mercy . . . [pause]

That those hungering for justice and mercy be fed at God's lavish table . . . [pause]

That each of us grow in our nearness to Jesus and heed his call to salvation . . . [pause]

Presider: Merciful God, you are ever faithful to your promise of salvation. Hear these our prayers that one day we might joyfully feast at your everlasting banquet table. We ask this through Christ our Lord. **Amen.**

COLLECT

Let us pray.

Pause for silent prayer

Look upon us, O God,
Creator and ruler of all things,
and, that we may feel the working of your mercy,
grant that we may serve you with all our heart.
Through our Lord Jesus Christ, your Son,
who lives and reigns with you in the unity of the Holy Spirit,
one God, for ever and ever. **Amen.**

FIRST READING
Exod 32:7-11, 13-14

The LORD said to Moses,
   "Go down at once to your people,
      whom you brought out of the land of Egypt,
   for they have become depraved.
They have soon turned aside from the way
      I pointed out to them,
   making for themselves a molten calf
      and worshiping it,
   sacrificing to it and crying out,
   'This is your God, O Israel,
   who brought you out of the land of Egypt!'
I see how stiff-necked this people is,"
      continued the LORD to Moses.
"Let me alone, then,
   that my wrath may blaze up against them to consume them.
Then I will make of you a great nation."

But Moses implored the LORD, his God, saying,
   "Why, O LORD, should your wrath blaze up against your own people,
   whom you brought out of the land of Egypt
   with such great power and with so strong a hand?
Remember your servants Abraham, Isaac, and Israel,
   and how you swore to them by your own self, saying,
   'I will make your descendants as numerous as the stars in the sky;
   and all this land that I promised,
   I will give your descendants as their perpetual heritage.'"
So the LORD relented in the punishment he had threatened to inflict on his people.

RESPONSORIAL PSALM

Ps 51:3-4, 12-13, 17, 19

R℟. (Luke 15:18) I will rise and go to my father.

Have mercy on me, O God, in your
    goodness;
  in the greatness of your compassion
      wipe out my offense.
Thoroughly wash me from my guilt
  and of my sin cleanse me.

R℟. I will rise and go to my father.

A clean heart create for me, O God,
  and a steadfast spirit renew within me.
Cast me not out from your presence,
  and your Holy Spirit take not from me.

R℟. I will rise and go to my father.

O LORD, open my lips,
  and my mouth shall proclaim your
      praise.
My sacrifice, O God, is a contrite spirit;
  a heart contrite and humbled, O God,
      you will not spurn.

R℟. I will rise and go to my father.

SECOND READING

1 Tim 1:12-17

Beloved:
I am grateful to him who has strengthened
    me, Christ Jesus our Lord,
  because he considered me trustworthy
    in appointing me to the ministry.
I was once a blasphemer and a persecutor
    and arrogant,
  but I have been mercifully treated
  because I acted out of ignorance in my
      unbelief.
Indeed, the grace of our Lord has been
    abundant,
  along with the faith and love that are in
      Christ Jesus.
This saying is trustworthy and deserves
    full acceptance:
  Christ Jesus came into the world to save
      sinners.
Of these I am the foremost.
But for that reason I was mercifully
    treated,
  so that in me, as the foremost,
  Christ Jesus might display all his
      patience as an example
  for those who would come to believe in
      him for everlasting life.
To the king of ages, incorruptible,
    invisible, the only God,
  honor and glory forever and ever. Amen.

About Liturgy

God's prodigality in liturgy: There can be no more concrete expression of God's lavish mercy and love for us than in the celebration of liturgy's sacred mysteries, especially the Eucharist. God's prodigality takes many special symbolic forms during Mass. Here are some examples.

1. *Gifts for the poor.* It is always acceptable and to be encouraged to bring gifts for the poor to be offered along with the bread and wine. These food staples and monetary gifts are concrete expressions of the solidarity we have in the Body of Christ with all others as well as a concrete way that we can share God's lavish gifts to us with others who are less fortunate.

2. *Intercessions.* Always at Mass there are a number of instances where we are invited to pray for others—after the "Let us pray" invitations, during the universal prayer (prayer of the faithful), at the prayers for the living and dead during the eucharistic prayer, during the Our Father, in the quiet meditation time after Communion (just to name a few of the obvious and communal times for intercessory prayer). Our prayer for each other is an aspect of discipleship and one way we express the worth of all others.

3. *Sign of peace.* The sign of peace is an embrace given in compassion and love. GIRM 82 specifies that the sign of peace is offered to those nearby. It doesn't say to family members and friends, but to those nearby. We don't judge whether the person is sinner or saint, wealthy or poor, lost or found—we simply offer this gift of peace because God has first given it to us. The dignity of the sign indicates the dignity of both the giver and receiver.

4. *Communion.* God invites us to the messianic banquet where we rejoice and feast on the very Body and Blood of God's only-begotten Son. There is no discrimination in how the line is formed and who may come; indeed, ministers are not to judge who may receive Holy Communion but simply offer it to all those who come. Especially important is the sign of the one bread and the one cup, for in the Body of Christ we are all beloved in God's eyes.

About Liturgical Music

Music suggestions: Many songs sing of God's infinite mercy toward us in our human wanderings from grace. In "All Who Hunger, Gather Gladly" we call all who "once were lost and scattered" to come to the table of the Lord as "welcome guest[s]." The HOLY MANNA setting (G3, SS, W4) would work well for the entrance procession, while Bob Moore's verse-refrain setting (G3, W4) would be excellent at Communion with choir or cantor singing the verses and the assembly the refrain. Lucien Deiss's classic verse-refrain piece "Yes, I Shall Arise" (OF, WS) would also be a good choice for Communion, as would "Amazing Grace" (in most resources). A good choice for the preparation of the gifts would be "Our Father, We Have Wandered" (in most resources).

Herman Stuempfle's "Shepherd, Do You Tramp the Hills" (HG, W4) retells all three of this Sunday's gospel parables in question and answer format. In verse 1 we ask, "Shepherd, do you tramp the hills, Tracking down one straying sheep . . . ?" In verse 2 we ask, "Woman, do you scour the house Just to find one coin that's lost . . . ?" In verse 3 we ask the father, "Father, does your heart still bleed For a child who chose to roam . . . ?" Verse 4 sums up the whole, "Shepherd, searcher, parent's care—By what image can we name Spendthrift love, impassioned grace, Incandescent as a flame? Christ, beyond all words you spoke, Stories that with wonder glow, You have shown us on a cross Love that will not let us go!" Sung in antiphonal fashion between the assembly and various soloists, this hymn would be a perfect response to the gospel reading during the preparation of the gifts.

SEPTEMBER 11, 2016
TWENTY-FOURTH SUNDAY IN ORDINARY TIME

SPIRITUALITY

GOSPEL ACCLAMATION
2 Cor 8:9

R⁊. Alleluia, alleluia.
Though our Lord Jesus Christ was rich, he
    became poor,
so that by his poverty you might become
    rich.
R⁊. Alleluia, alleluia.

Gospel
Luke 16:1-13; L135C

Jesus said to his disciples,
    "A rich man had a steward
    who was reported to him for
        squandering his property.
He summoned him and said,
    'What is this I hear about you?
Prepare a full account of your
        stewardship,
    because you can no longer be
        my steward.'
The steward said to himself,
    'What shall I do,
    now that my master is taking
        the position of steward away
        from me?
I am not strong enough to dig and I am
        ashamed to beg.
I know what I shall do so that,
    when I am removed from the
        stewardship,
    they may welcome me into their
        homes.'
He called in his master's debtors one
        by one.
To the first he said,
    'How much do you owe my master?'
He replied, 'One hundred measures of
        olive oil.'
He said to him, 'Here is your
        promissory note.
Sit down and quickly write one for
        fifty.'
Then to another the steward said, 'And
        you, how much do you owe?'
He replied, 'One hundred kors of wheat.'

Continued in Appendix A, p. 311.

Reflecting on the Gospel
This gospel puts to us a familiar and basic question: Whom do we serve? We have heard all our lives that we "cannot serve both God and mammon." This is such a common gospel saying; we are very familiar with it. We interpret the "mammon" as money, wealth, possessions. The basic question nudges us to think of serving "mammon" in another way, in terms of serving self. We are our own greatest wealth, our greatest possession. But even we ourselves can get in the way of Gospel living. The challenge is to pay attention to how we are living and sincerely ask the basic question, Whom do we serve? Our answer might surprise us at times.

The wily steward is clearly self-serving and decisive in doing what he thinks necessary for his own immediate well-being. But by acting in this way, he risks squandering his eternal well-being ("eternal dwellings"). To secure this, he needed to choose to serve God rather than self. Serving self keeps us mired in our immediate concerns, wants, needs. Serving God frees us to be decisive in doing what is necessary to secure the best for both this life and the next. The irony is that had the wily steward chosen to serve God and God alone, he would have, in fact, chosen to serve himself in the best way possible. By serving God and God alone he would have secured the only future worth having—eternal Life. So, the question for us remains, Whom do we serve? It is a critical and ongoing question for us.

Only by serving God alone can we ever secure for ourselves a sure future: being "welcomed into eternal dwellings." We must handle the things of this world and our daily actions in relation to what is eternal and with prudent decisiveness. Prudent decisiveness about our future means that we grow in our relationship to God, and that relationship is witnessed by the simple choices of our daily living. To put it simply, prudent decisiveness about our future means that God is truly at the center of our lives. Truly, we serve God and God alone.

Living the Paschal Mystery
When it comes to paschal mystery living, we often squander opportunities to gain "true wealth." The thrust of the gospel is that we act prudently in this life in order to "be welcomed into eternal dwellings." Prudence demands that we not squander opportunities to be charitable and just toward others. Prudence demands that we not squander opportunities to die to self. Prudence demands that we not squander opportunities to be trustworthy with the ministry of discipleship which we take on each time we say yes to our baptismal commitment.

Most of us are serious about our paschal mystery living. We honestly try to live good lives. When opportunities present themselves to act in a Christian way, most of us respond appropriately most of the time. This gospel challenges us to take this one step further. Paschal mystery living isn't simply a matter of *surrendering* to the self-sacrificing possibilities that come our way simply in the normal course of daily living. With an eye to the future, we must also *surrender* ourselves to actually *searching out* opportunities to live the paschal mystery. There is such an urgency about discipleship and proclaiming the Good News of salvation that we cannot be passive in any way. Ultimately, any kind of passivity is self-serving. This gospel calls us to be God-serving. Only by serving God do we gain everything for this life, and assure our place in "eternal dwellings."

Focusing the Gospel

Key words and phrases: What shall I do, dishonest steward, welcomed into eternal dwellings, cannot serve both God and mammon

To the point: This gospel puts to us a basic question: Whom do we serve? The wily steward is clearly self-serving and decisive in doing what he thinks necessary for his own immediate well-being. But by acting in this way, he risks squandering his eternal well-being ("eternal dwellings"). To secure this, he needed to choose to serve God rather than self. The irony is that had he chosen to serve God and God alone, he would have, in fact, chosen to serve himself in the best way possible. So, the question for us remains, Whom do we serve?

Connecting the Gospel

to the first reading: This reading from Amos makes clear that God does not forget the human choices made for selfish personal gain. The gospel makes clear that God remembers the human choices made to serve God and God alone. We are "welcomed into eternal dwellings."

to experience: To protect ourselves and our families and to have enough to get ahead in this life, we must be shrewd about many things. To win eternal Life, shrewdness, however, is not enough. We must be single-mindedly focused on God and honest and trustworthy in all things.

Connecting the Responsorial Psalm

to the readings: It is easy to see a connection between the responsorial psalm and the first reading. In the reading God swears never to forget an injustice done to the poor. In the psalm God redresses such wrongs and raises the poor from dust to nobility.

It is not so easy, however, to detect a connection between the psalm and the gospel. The first reading and the gospel both relate incidences of unjust and dishonest behavior pursued for the sake of personal gain. Jesus condemns the dishonest behavior, yet he commends the dishonest steward for pursuing it. What Jesus invites, however, is not imitation of the behavior but imitation of the shrewdness which motivates it. We must know what we want and act decisively to obtain it. We must desire what is just and true and act in its service. The psalm offers us the model of God who seeks what is just and true and acts decisively to redress wrongs and raise up the poor. To praise this God is to choose our Master.

to psalmist preparation: In singing this psalm you invite the assembly to praise God for acting on behalf of the poor and oppressed. In the context of the first reading and gospel, you also invite them to imitate God in their own manner of acting. In what ways do you choose God as your Master and guide? In what ways do you struggle with this choice? How might Christ help you?

ASSEMBLY & FAITH-SHARING GROUPS
- If Jesus were to say to me, "Prepare a full account of your stewardship," my response would be . . .
- I make shortsighted choices about my immediate well-being at the cost of my eternal well-being when . . .
- Who and what support me to serve God and God alone are . . .

PRESIDERS
I am self-serving when I . . . I am serving God and God alone when I . . . The impact each has on my ministry is . . .

DEACONS
I enhance my own well-being as I serve the well-being of others in that . . .

HOSPITALITY MINISTERS
In my ministry, putting others' needs ahead of my personal gain is a challenge when . . . is a grace when . . .

MUSIC MINISTERS
In my music ministry I know I am serving God when . . . I know I am serving another master when . . .

ALTAR MINISTERS
My ministering at the altar witnesses to my choice to serve God and God alone in my daily living when I . . .

LECTORS
When I serve God faithfully in my daily living, my proclamation becomes . . . When I am self-serving in my daily living, my proclamation becomes . . .

EXTRAORDINARY MINISTERS OF HOLY COMMUNION
My manner of distributing Holy Communion reveals that God is the center of my life when . . .

CELEBRATION

Model Penitential Act

Presider: In today's gospel Jesus reminds us that we cannot serve two masters. We must make a choice. Let us open our hearts to encounter Jesus in this liturgy and ask for his mercy for the times we have chosen to serve a master other than God . . . [pause]

Lord Jesus, you served your Father with undivided heart: Lord . . .

Christ Jesus, you call us to be with you in your eternal dwelling: Christ . . .

Lord Jesus, you show us how to serve God and God alone: Lord . . .

Homily Points

• We are normally very wary of wily people. We don't trust them because we know they are after their own gain, even sometimes at the expense of our well-being. Instead we choose to befriend trustworthy and other-centered people who increase our well-being rather than diminish it. We can have no better friend than Jesus who made the ultimate choice to serve God and God alone and thus gained everything—risen Life—for himself and for us.

• To share in what Jesus gained for us, we must make the same choice he made. We must choose to serve God and God alone. To serve effectively we must be shrewd and decisive, honest and trustworthy, faithful and resolute. Throughout all our life, in all our choices, in all our serving, the basic question always remains, Whom do we serve?

• Jesus does not commend the steward's dishonesty; he does commend his shrewdness in cleverly ensuring his immediate well-being. Disciples must be equally shrewd, but make very different choices: choosing trustworthy service over dishonesty for personal gain; choosing concern for others over personal needs; choosing eternal happiness over security in this world at any cost. In these very choices, disciples serve God and God alone. They also serve their own ultimate well-being.

Model Universal Prayer (Prayer of the Faithful)

Presider: We turn now to the God whom we serve and make known our needs.

Response:

Cantor:

That all members of the church deepen their choice to serve God and God alone . . . [pause]

That leaders of the world's nations faithfully serve the needs of their people . . . [pause]

That those threatened by an insecure future find support in the care of others . . . [pause]

That each of us remain trustworthy and faithful in following Jesus . . . [pause]

Presider: Dear God, you hear the prayers of those who call out to you. Help us to be prudent about the affairs of this life so that we serve you and you alone and one day come to enjoy the richness of your eternal glory. We ask this through Christ our Lord. **Amen.**

COLLECT

Let us pray.

Pause for silent prayer

O God, who founded all the commands of
   your sacred Law
upon love of you and of our neighbor,
grant that, by keeping your precepts,
we may merit to attain eternal life.
Through our Lord Jesus Christ, your Son,
who lives and reigns with you in the unity
   of the Holy Spirit,
one God, for ever and ever. **Amen.**

FIRST READING
Amos 8:4-7

Hear this, you who trample upon the
   needy
   and destroy the poor of the land!
"When will the new moon be over," you
   ask,
   "that we may sell our grain,
   and the sabbath, that we may display
      the wheat?
We will diminish the ephah,
   add to the shekel,
   and fix our scales for cheating!
We will buy the lowly for silver,
   and the poor for a pair of sandals;
   even the refuse of the wheat we will
      sell!"
The Lord has sworn by the pride of Jacob:
   Never will I forget a thing they have
      done!

RESPONSORIAL PSALM
Ps 113:1-2, 4-6, 7-8

R̂. (cf. 1a, 7b) Praise the Lord, who lifts up
the poor.
   or
R̂. Alleluia.

Praise, you servants of the Lord,
   praise the name of the Lord.
Blessed be the name of the Lord
   both now and forever.

R̂. Praise the Lord, who lifts up the poor.
   or
R̂. Alleluia.

High above all nations is the LORD;
  above the heavens is his glory.
Who is like the LORD, our God, who is
    enthroned on high
  and looks upon the heavens and the
    earth below?

R⁊. Praise the Lord, who lifts up the poor.
  or
R⁊. Alleluia.

He raises up the lowly from the dust;
  from the dunghill he lifts up the poor
to seat them with princes,
  with the princes of his own people.

R⁊. Praise the Lord, who lifts up the poor.
  or
R⁊. Alleluia.

SECOND READING
1 Tim 2:1-8

Beloved:
First of all, I ask that supplications,
    prayers,
  petitions, and thanksgivings be offered
    for everyone,
  for kings and for all in authority,
  that we may lead a quiet and tranquil
    life
  in all devotion and dignity.
This is good and pleasing to God our
    savior,
  who wills everyone to be saved
  and to come to knowledge of the truth.
    For there is one God.
    There is also one mediator between God
      and men,
    the man Christ Jesus,
    who gave himself as ransom for all.
This was the testimony at the proper time.
For this I was appointed preacher and
    apostle
  —I am speaking the truth, I am not
    lying—,
  teacher of the Gentiles in faith and
    truth.

It is my wish, then, that in every place the
    men should pray,
  lifting up holy hands, without anger
    or argument.

About Liturgy

Praying always: One way to thwart the temptation to be self-serving is to develop a habit of praying always (see, for example, 1 Thess 5:17). Even if our liturgical prayer is very rich and satisfying—and this is the goal of every parish—we also need our own personal, devotional prayer to complement liturgical prayer. If the only time of the week we think about God is during Sunday Mass, it will be quite difficult, if not impossible, to grasp that our daily decisions are really expressions of our commitment to be followers of Jesus who serve God alone.

Since Vatican II there has been something of a negative attitude about devotional prayer. Some of this derives from the historical fact that in the past not all devotions were good ones. The Constitution on the Sacred Liturgy gives criteria for good devotional prayer: it should help to draw us into the various liturgical seasons, lead us to a better celebration of liturgy, help us to live liturgy in our daily lives (SC 13). One sure way to accomplish this is to prepare for liturgy ahead of Sunday, especially by reflecting on the readings. Perhaps we might take the response to the psalm and make that a kind of mantra that is recited throughout the week, especially when difficult decisions come our way. If we are singers we might even sing it when we are driving somewhere or while we are doing work at home. It might begin and end our meals.

Meals—these could be another way of praying always. Families might have to make a concerted effort to eat at least one or two meals together during the week. Then during the meal there might be conscious sharing about each person's successes and failures, about how members of the family are trying to live the Gospel, about the good each one sees in the other. At first this might seem awkward and uncomfortable, especially if family members haven't shared in this way before. With time, each family will find what works best for them. Over time, members will see how more and more of their daily lives are lived with an eye to God.

About Liturgical Music

Music suggestions: Songs which express being decisive and faithful in our choice to serve God above all would connect well with this Sunday's celebration, as would songs which sing of Christ as the center and foundation of our discipleship. Examples include "Rise Up, O Saints of God" (OF, WC) and Bernadette Farrell's "Praise to You, O Christ Our Savior" (BB, G3, JS3, W4), for the entrance procession; the traditional Irish hymn "Be Thou My Vision" (BB, JS3, SS) for the preparation of the gifts; Michael Joncas's "The Love of the Lord" (G3, W4) and Paul Inwood's "Center of My Life" (G3, JS3, W4) for Communion. Taken from his collection *Communion Chants for the Church Year* (WLP), Charles Thatcher's "Seek First the Kingdom of God" (OF, WC, WS) is a setting of Psalm 37 that would be particularly fitting on this Sunday. In verse 3, for example, the cantor or choir sings, "Commit your way to the Lord; that God will act And make your integrity shine like the dawn, your vindication like noonday." In the refrain the assembly responds with "Seek first the kingdom of God, his justice and righteousness, and all these things will be given to you, alleluia."

✠ SPIRITUALITY

GOSPEL ACCLAMATION
2 Cor 8:9

℟. Alleluia, alleluia.
Though our Lord Jesus Christ was rich, he became poor,
so that by his poverty you might become rich.
℟. Alleluia, alleluia.

Gospel
Luke 16:19-31; L138C

Jesus said to the Pharisees:
  "There was a rich man who
      dressed in purple garments
      and fine linen
    and dined sumptuously each
      day.
  And lying at his door was a poor
      man named Lazarus, covered
      with sores,
    who would gladly have eaten his
      fill of the scraps
    that fell from the rich man's table.
  Dogs even used to come and lick his
      sores.
  When the poor man died,
    he was carried away by angels to the
      bosom of Abraham.
  The rich man also died and was buried,
    and from the netherworld, where he
      was in torment,
    he raised his eyes and saw Abraham
      far off
    and Lazarus at his side.
  And he cried out, 'Father Abraham, have
      pity on me.
  Send Lazarus to dip the tip of his finger
      in water and cool my tongue,
    for I am suffering torment in these
      flames.'
  Abraham replied,
    'My child, remember that you received
    what was good during your lifetime
    while Lazarus likewise received what
      was bad;
    but now he is comforted here, whereas
      you are tormented.

Continued in Appendix A, p. 311.

Reflecting on the Gospel

Someone who is "in our face" is bold and aggressive toward us about something, won't let go, keeps pushing. Sometimes our response is to shout at them to get out of our "personal space," meaning the person is too close, invading us, pushing us too far. Sometimes it takes someone who is in our face to get us to see something important. Sometimes someone has to invade our personal space in order for us to see that person. And, sometimes, even someone being in our face or invading our personal space doesn't capture our attention enough to make us notice. In this Sunday's gospel, the poor man Lazarus is invading the rich man's personal space—he is "lying at his door." He is right there. He is in the rich man's face. We can well imagine the rich man literally stepping over Lazarus. The rich man is so busy, so self-absorbed that Lazarus did not affect him. Until the rich man died and was tormented by his punishment for not responding to Lazarus. Only in torment does he notice Lazarus. He begs that the very man whom he ignored during his life should come to alleviate his torment, should bring him some cool water to ease him. Yet, he offered nothing to Lazarus while he was living.

The rich man in torment also begs Abraham to send "someone from the dead" to warn his five brothers to repent and change their way of living. In fact, during his earthly life, the rich man *had* "someone from the dead" warning him to repent and change—the sick, suffering, starving Lazarus "lying at his door" who was as good as "dead" to the rich man. The message of "Moses and the prophets" about how we are to live comes not only in the word of Scripture, but also through those lying at *our* door. And, unlike the rich man in the parable, we *do* have Someone among us who has "rise[n] from the dead." We need only to listen. This is how we gain the insight to see those in need at our own door and choose how to respond.

There is a great "chasm" between selfishness and self-surrender, between evil and good, between the lost and the saved. This chasm is a metaphor for *listening* to God's word and allowing ourselves to be guided by its demands. The time to respond decisively to God and others is *now*; after death it is too late. Indeed, "someone from the dead" *has* come to warn us. Who? Do we listen?

Living the Paschal Mystery

There is no need to be frightened about eternal Life if we allow God's word to guide us in our responses to others in need. Thus do we prepare for eternal Life. This is what is amazing about choosing to help others, no matter how insignificant the help might seem: whatever we do for others is a preparation for eternal Life.

God's word comes to us in more ways than the proclamations at Sunday Mass or taking time to read the Bible—as important as both of those are. God's word also comes to us through others. It can be presented as someone in need. God's word might come in some challenge to our self-centeredness or values. It might come through another's encouragement. It might come by someone being in our face about a behavior we need to change. In all these ways and countless others we are invited to *listen*. Listening is guidance for how to respond with compassion and care for those who are lying at our door.

Focusing the Gospel

Key words and phrases: rich man, lying at his door, poor man named Lazarus, died, torment, warn them, someone from the dead, repent, listen

To the point: The rich man in torment begs Abraham to send "someone from the dead" to warn his five brothers to repent and change their way of living. In fact, during his earthly life, the rich man *had* "someone from the dead" warning him to repent and change—the sick, suffering, starving Lazarus "lying at his door" who was as good as "dead" to the rich man. The message of "Moses and the prophets" about how we are to live comes not only in the word of Scripture, but also through those lying at *our* door. Indeed, "someone from the dead" *has* come to warn us. Who? Do we listen?

Connecting the Gospel

to the first reading: The first reading parallels the gospel teaching. The prophet Amos warns "the complacent in Zion" who, in their "wanton revelry," ignore the sufferings of the Hebrew people.

to experience: Oftentimes we are blind and ignore the needs of others, even those who are suffering greatly. What opens our eyes is an encounter with Jesus, the One raised from the dead, who moves us to repent and change our lives.

Connecting the Responsorial Psalm

to the readings: Those who are suffering and in need are beloved by God (gospel, psalm). If we separate ourselves from the poor and needy, as do the complacent in the first reading and the rich man in the gospel, we separate ourselves from God and from the possibility of blessed Life in eternity. Had they heeded Moses and the prophets (gospel), these individuals would have lived differently and secured a different future for themselves. By praising God who is never indifferent to human suffering, Psalm 146 is a message from Moses and the prophets to us. We must do more than merely sing this message, however. We must hear it and heed.

to psalmist preparation: As with last Sunday's psalm, this psalm holds God up as the model of behavior for faithful disciples. Disciples of Jesus are called to act on behalf of the poor and suffering just as God does. In singing this psalm you invite the assembly to respond to this call. In what ways are you responding? In what ways do you need to grow in your response?

**ASSEMBLY &
FAITH-SHARING GROUPS**
- The Lazarus lying at my door is . . . I respond by . . . with . . .
- I need to listen to . . . What I hear is . . .
- Considering my eternal Life, I . . .

PRESIDERS
Both my preaching and my manner of ministering calls my parishioners to repent and change their life in that . . .

DEACONS
I find myself listening to "Moses and the prophets" when . . . This helps me respond to those in need lying at my door by . . .

HOSPITALITY MINISTERS
My hospitality must include listening to others because . . . seeing others' needs when . . . responding by . . .

MUSIC MINISTERS
In my music ministry I must listen to . . . I hear . . . I act on . . .

ALTAR MINISTERS
My manner of serving witnesses that I have listened to "Moses and the prophets" in that . . . My listening helps me serve better when . . .

LECTORS
God's word has challenged my complacency about the needs of others when . . . This challenge has affected my proclamation by . . .

**EXTRAORDINARY MINISTERS
OF HOLY COMMUNION**
When I look into the eyes of each communicant, I see . . . I hear . . . I respond . . .

Model Penitential Act

Presider: In today's gospel Jesus tells the parable of the rich man and Lazarus, challenging us to recognize and respond to those in need. We ask for God's grace to repent for the times we have not responded to others with mercy . . . [pause]

    Lord Jesus, you are the Word teaching us to respond to those in need: Lord . . .

    Christ Jesus, you are the risen One speaking to us of new Life: Christ . . .

    Lord Jesus, you are the Prophet calling us to repentance: Lord . . .

Homily Points

• Who doesn't dream of hitting the lottery? of being so wealthy that life would have no worries? of being able to retire young with complete security? Given the choice, who of us would not choose to be rich? The real issue of the gospel, however, is not about riches or poverty. It is about how we respond to the person lying at our door.

• This gospel contrasts two life circumstances: rich or poor, basking in abundance or living in misery. It also contrasts two choices about how we relate to others: self-centered or other-centered. We often have little control over our life circumstances. But we have complete control over how we choose to relate to others.

• It is not only self-absorbed rich people who walk by those in need. How do *we* respond to the cashier in the grocery store? the wait staff in a restaurant? the housekeeping staff who cleans our hotel room? Sometimes we might be surprised by who is lying at our door. Like the rich man in the gospel, our response determines how we will spend eternity.

Model Universal Prayer (Prayer of the Faithful)

Presider: Let us pray that we might see and respond to those in need.

Response:

Lord, hear our prayer.

Cantor:

we pray to the Lord,

That all members of the church reach out to the Lazarus lying at their doorstep . . . [pause]

That all peoples of the world come to the salvation God offers by responding to the needs of one another . . . [pause]

That the sick, the poor, and the hungry have their needs filled through the generosity of those who hear and heed the word of God . . . [pause]

That all gathered here die to self-absorption and rise with Christ to newness of Life . . . [pause]

Presider: Merciful God, you hear the cries of the poor. May your Son's life and example teach us to respond with compassion and generosity to those around us in need. We ask this through that same Son, Jesus Christ our Lord. **Amen.**

COLLECT

Let us pray.

Pause for silent prayer

O God, who manifest your almighty power
above all by pardoning and showing
    mercy,
bestow, we pray, your grace abundantly
    upon us
and make those hastening to attain your
    promises
heirs to the treasures of heaven.
Through our Lord Jesus Christ, your Son,
who lives and reigns with you in the unity
    of the Holy Spirit,
one God, for ever and ever. **Amen.**

FIRST READING

Amos 6:1a, 4-7

Thus says the Lᴏʀᴅ, the God of hosts:
Woe to the complacent in Zion!
Lying upon beds of ivory,
    stretched comfortably on their couches,
they eat lambs taken from the flock,
    and calves from the stall!
Improvising to the music of the harp,
    like David, they devise their own
        accompaniment.
They drink wine from bowls
    and anoint themselves with the best oils;
    yet they are not made ill by the collapse
        of Joseph!
Therefore, now they shall be the first to go
    into exile,
    and their wanton revelry shall be done
        away with.

RESPONSIONAL PSALM

Ps 146:7, 8-9, 9-10

R⁒. (1b) Praise the Lord, my soul!
or
R⁒. Alleluia.

Blessed is he who keeps faith forever,
secures justice for the oppressed,
gives food to the hungry.
The Lord sets captives free.

R⁒. Praise the Lord, my soul!
or
R⁒. Alleluia.

The Lord gives sight to the blind.
The Lord raises up those who were
bowed down.
The Lord loves the just.
The Lord protects strangers.

R⁒. Praise the Lord, my soul!
or
R⁒. Alleluia.

The fatherless and the widow he sustains,
but the way of the wicked he thwarts.
The Lord shall reign forever;
your God, O Zion, through all
generations. Alleluia.

R⁒. Praise the Lord, my soul!
or
R⁒. Alleluia.

SECOND READING

1 Tim 6:11-16

But you, man of God, pursue righteousness,
devotion, faith, love, patience, and
gentleness.
Compete well for the faith.
Lay hold of eternal life, to which you were
called
when you made the noble confession in
the presence of many witnesses.
I charge you before God, who gives life to
all things,
and before Christ Jesus,
who gave testimony under Pontius
Pilate for the noble confession,
to keep the commandment without stain
or reproach
until the appearance of our Lord Jesus
Christ
that the blessed and only ruler
will make manifest at the proper time,
the King of kings and Lord of lords,
who alone has immortality, who dwells
in unapproachable light,
and whom no human being has seen or
can see.
To him be honor and eternal power. Amen.

✛ CATECHESIS

About Liturgy

Purple and Advent: This gospel's description of the rich man has him "dressed in purple garments and fine linen." The mention of the color isn't simply a nice detail about a man whose favorite color was purple. Purple dye was very expensive at that time when there were no inexpensive substitutes for natural dyes and so only the wealthy could afford clothes dyed purple. Purple clothing, then, proclaimed a status in society. Because purple was also frequently associated with emperors and kings, it also became a color associated with Jesus (see Mark 15:17 and John 19:2, where Jesus is clothed in a purple cloak during his scourging in mockery). When we celebrate Jesus as King (which we will do on the Thirty-Fourth Sunday in Ordinary Time, the Solemnity of Our Lord Jesus Christ, King of the Universe) we recall Jesus' victory and reign of glory. Purple, then, is a liturgical color that reminds us of eschatological glory and the end times when Jesus will come again to reign forever.

We make the distinction between royal purple (blue-purple) and violet purple (red-purple). We use the royal purple during Advent because it is a season that celebrates Jesus' victory and eternal reign. Already in late September the liturgy turns our attention toward the end times and Jesus' eschatological victory.

About Liturgical Music

Music suggestions: The rich man who ignored the poor man dying on his doorstep finds himself condemned to eternal torment after his own death, when it is too late to change the choices he made in life. There are a number of songs available which call us to act now on behalf of the poor and needy in our midst. "God of Day and God of Darkness" (in most resources) offers an excellent text; its length indicates it might work best during the preparation of the gifts. "Abundant Life" (G3) calls us to live in such a way "that all may have abundant life"; its gentle melody and tempo would be best suited for the preparation of the gifts. A superb choice for either the entrance or the recessional would be "God Whose Purpose Is to Kindle" (G3, W4), in which we ask God to "overcome our sinful calmness" and "disturb" the "complacency" we feel in face of "our neighbor's misery." Other good choices for the recessional include "We Are Called" (in most resources); "What Does the Lord Require" (W4); "The Church of Christ in Every Age" (in most resources); and "Go, Be Justice" (OF, WC, WS).

SEPTEMBER 25, 2016
TWENTY-SIXTH SUNDAY IN ORDINARY TIME

SPIRITUALITY

GOSPEL ACCLAMATION
1 Pet 1:25

R̶/. Alleluia, alleluia.
The word of the Lord remains forever.
This is the word that has been proclaimed to
  you.
R̶/. Alleluia, alleluia.

Gospel

Luke 17:5-10; L141C

The apostles said to the Lord,
  "Increase our faith."
The Lord replied,
  "If you have faith the size of a
    mustard seed,
  you would say to this mulberry
    tree,
  'Be uprooted and planted in the
    sea,' and it would obey you.

"Who among you would say to
    your servant
  who has just come in from plowing or
    tending sheep in the field,
  'Come here immediately and take
    your place at table'?
Would he not rather say to him,
  'Prepare something for me to eat.
Put on your apron and wait on me
    while I eat and drink.
You may eat and drink when I am
    finished'?
Is he grateful to that servant because
    he did what was commanded?
So should it be with you.
When you have done all you have been
    commanded,
  say, 'We are unprofitable servants;
  we have done what we were obliged
    to do.'"

Reflecting on the Gospel

We have great respect for people who are conscientious, fulfill their duties, do all that is expected of them. More than even respect, we have great awe for those who walk the extra mile, who reach out to others when this is not required, who go beyond normal expectations. Going beyond expectations is an enlargement of self that enables us to transcend boundaries and limits, and achieve the seemingly impossible. People who do this can move mountains, can shake foundations, can uproot a mulberry tree. These people inspire us, move us to greater heroics, challenge us to stretch ourselves so that we become even larger than life. These are people of great faith.

The apostles demand that Jesus increase their faith. Jesus responds that even faith "the size of a mustard seed" is enough to do great things. The "unprofitable servants" of Jesus' gospel teaching simply do what they are commanded—they do not go beyond normal expectations; they cannot uproot a mulberry tree. To go beyond expectations, we must risk doing the impossible and thereby become profitable servants. In this we align ourselves with God, become able to do as God does. Being aligned with God: this is faith.

Faith-filled persons take what they have—whether little or great—and *act*. If we wait until we think we have enough faith, we will never act. In the first example about the mulberry tree, Jesus is saying that even a little faith is enough to move this tree. The point about faith that Jesus makes is not that it be measured; active and fruitful faith is not a matter of "how much." But we must use what we do have, because even a little bit gives us great power to accomplish God's work. We have this power not on our own, but because we give ourselves over to God's will and God's ways. Faith is aligning ourselves with God so that we can act with God's power—then we can do the seemingly impossible.

Faith is more than faithfulness, is more than doing all we have been commanded. "Faith-filledness" is *acting* decisively as God would do. The faithful and faith-filled disciple is the one who doesn't wait for enough faith, but continues to respond to the everyday and never-ending demands of discipleship. The Master demands our service. And then gives us the faith to perform it well.

Living the Paschal Mystery

When we think of people of great faith, we often mention people like Gandhi or Mother Teresa. These were great religious leaders who obviously had great faith and accomplished great things. We make a mistake, however, if we identify faith only with doing great things. Or if we identify faith only with beliefs. Or if we identify faith with a religious system. Jesus reminds us in this gospel that our everyday actions, performed in loving service, are expressions of our faith because they align us with God.

The faith-filled person puts in an honest day's work and more. That person is gracious to those whom he or she comes in contact. That person is ready to reach out and help another, even beyond one's own workload. The faith-filled person sees Jesus in the other and responds to the situation with Jesus' love and care. Faith is obedience to responsibility. It is obedience to discipleship. It is obedience to our Master who encourages us, helps us, never abandons us. It is obedience to the "more" that aligns us with God.

Focusing the Gospel

Key words and phrases: Increase our faith, faith the size of a mustard seed, mulberry tree, did what was commanded, unprofitable servants

To the point: The apostles demand that Jesus increase their faith. Jesus responds that even faith "the size of a mustard seed" is enough to do great things. The "unprofitable servants" of Jesus' gospel teaching simply do what they are commanded—they do not go beyond normal expectations; they cannot uproot a mulberry tree. To go beyond expectations, we must risk doing the impossible and thereby become profitable servants. In this we align ourselves with God, become able to do as God does. Being aligned with God: this is faith.

Connecting the Gospel

to the first reading: Habakkuk laments the violence and destruction the Hebrew people are experiencing because they have not aligned themselves with God. On the other hand, the "just one, because of his faith, shall live."

to experience: We tend to think of "faith" as a quantity that can be increased. Faith is, rather, a relationship, a way of life, an active aligning ourselves with God and God's will.

Connecting the Responsorial Psalm

to the readings: Psalm 95, like other psalms such as Psalm 15, includes a ritual for entrance into the temple for worship. Before being admitted the people were asked if they had been faithful to God who created and shepherded them. The question was no idle one, for many of Israel's first ancestors had not been permitted entrance into the Promised Land because of their infidelity. This is the story behind verses 8-9, and the reason for the harsh words in the refrain, "harden not your hearts." Faith means following the vision God lays before us (first reading). Faith means doing what God expects of us (gospel). Faith means acting according to who we are, God's chosen people (psalm). Faith means aligning ourselves with God in a way that transforms our hearts and our behavior.

to psalmist preparation: The harsh shift between the beginning of this responsorial psalm and its conclusion only makes sense when you know the story behind the psalm. The psalm reminds you, and the assembly, that true worship includes fidelity to God's commands. When are you tempted to turn away from the demands of fidelity? What helps your heart hear God's voice and remain faithful?

ASSEMBLY & FAITH-SHARING GROUPS

- The "impossible" I have done because of my faith is . . .
- I have gone beyond what is expected or commanded of me when . . . What happened as a result is . . .
- I am most aligned with God when . . . I can tell I am not aligned with God when . . .

PRESIDERS

In my presiding ministry I help others do the impossible for God by . . .

DEACONS

My serving ministry requires risk on my part when . . . I respond by . . .

HOSPITALITY MINISTERS

My manner of greeting those gathering for liturgy helps them become more aligned with God when I . . .

MUSIC MINISTERS

In order for my music ministry to be aligned with God, the "mulberry tree" I must uproot is . . .

ALTAR MINISTERS

My service is, indeed, an expression of great faith in that . . .

LECTORS

When I remain aligned with God, my proclamation sounds like . . .

EXTRAORDINARY MINISTERS OF HOLY COMMUNION

My ministry helps communicants understand that receiving Holy Communion is an expression of faith when I . . .

225

✝ CELEBRATION

Model Penitential Act

Presider: Jesus tells us in today's gospel that even a little faith will enable us to move a mulberry tree. As we prepare to hear God's word and receive from God's table, let us ask God's mercy for the times we have doubted the power of faith . . . [pause]

Lord Jesus, you are the One in whom we have faith: Lord . . .

Christ Jesus, you invite us to a place at your table: Christ . . .

Lord Jesus, you call us to be faithful disciples: Lord . . .

Homily Points

• Aligning ourselves with the wrong people can take us down life paths that lead to violence and destruction. Aligning ourselves with good people can open up life-giving possibilities. Faith is aligning ourselves with God in such a way that we can even do the impossible, do what God can do: move mulberry trees. This faith brings the fulfillment of God's vision for our salvation.

• What really were the apostles demanding when they said to Jesus, "Increase our faith"? They misunderstood the nature and power of faith. Faith cannot be quantified, but its power can be impeded. Jesus teaches that with even a little bit of faith, we can achieve great and seemingly impossible things. We can do so because faith aligns us with God, the Almighty, who works through us with divine power to save.

• Aligned with God, we can do the seemingly impossible because we can do as God does. We can forgive someone who has broken our trust, love someone who rubs us the wrong way, relieve hunger even by simple acts of generosity, bring justice to situations where the powerful exploit the weak, remain faithful to prayer even when God seems absent. All these are acts of faith. All these go beyond normal expectations. All these reveal how powerful our God is, and how deep our faith can be.

Model Universal Prayer (Prayer of the Faithful)

Presider: Jesus teaches us that by our faith we can ask the seemingly impossible of God, even moving mulberry trees. So, in faith let us make our needs known.

Response:

Cantor:

That all members of the church face difficult life challenges with deep faith . . . [pause]

That leaders of nations collaborate to overcome the destruction and violence so evident in our world . . . [pause]

That those doubting the strength of their faith be encouraged by Jesus' words that even little faith can accomplish great things . . . [pause]

That each of us here gathered, by our faith, do more than is expected or demanded of us . . . [pause]

Presider: Gracious God, you give us the faith we need to be diligent followers of your divine Son. Grant these our prayers that one day we might live with you forever. We ask this through that same Son, Jesus Christ our Lord. **Amen.**

COLLECT
Let us pray.

Pause for silent prayer

Almighty ever-living God,
who in the abundance of your kindness
surpass the merits and the desires of those
    who entreat you,
pour out your mercy upon us
to pardon what conscience dreads
and to give what prayer does not dare to
    ask.
Through our Lord Jesus Christ, your Son,
who lives and reigns with you in the unity
    of the Holy Spirit,
one God, for ever and ever. **Amen.**

FIRST READING
Hab 1:2-3; 2:2-4

How long, O LORD? I cry for help
    but you do not listen!
I cry out to you, "Violence!"
    but you do not intervene.
Why do you let me see ruin;
    why must I look at misery?
Destruction and violence are before me;
    there is strife, and clamorous discord.
Then the LORD answered me and said:
    Write down the vision clearly upon the
        tablets,
    so that one can read it readily.
For the vision still has its time,
    presses on to fulfillment, and will not
        disappoint;
if it delays, wait for it,
    it will surely come, it will not be late.
The rash one has no integrity;
    but the just one, because of his faith,
        shall live.

CATECHESIS

RESPONSORIAL PSALM

Ps 95:1-2, 6-7, 8-9

℟. (8) If today you hear his voice, harden not your hearts.

Come, let us sing joyfully to the LORD;
    let us acclaim the Rock of our salvation.
Let us come into his presence with
        thanksgiving;
    let us joyfully sing psalms to him.

℟. If today you hear his voice, harden not your hearts.

Come, let us bow down in worship;
    let us kneel before the LORD who made
        us.
For he is our God,
    and we are the people he shepherds, the
        flock he guides.

℟. If today you hear his voice, harden not your hearts.

Oh, that today you would hear his voice:
    "Harden not your hearts as at Meribah,
    as in the day of Massah in the desert,
where your fathers tempted me;
    they tested me though they had seen my
        works."

℟. If today you hear his voice, harden not your hearts.

SECOND READING

2 Tim 1:6-8, 13-14

Beloved:
I remind you to stir into flame
    the gift of God that you have through the
        imposition of my hands.
For God did not give us a spirit of
        cowardice
    but rather of power and love and
        self-control.
So do not be ashamed of your testimony
        to our Lord,
    nor of me, a prisoner for his sake;
    but bear your share of hardship for the
        gospel
    with the strength that comes from God.

Take as your norm the sound words that
        you heard from me,
    in the faith and love that are in Christ
        Jesus.
Guard this rich trust with the help of the
        Holy Spirit
    that dwells within us.

About Liturgy

Ministry as service: We usually think of service in terms of doing for others. A very special kind of "doing for others" is the ministry each of us undertakes at any given liturgy. The General Instruction of the Roman Missal states in no. 95: "In the celebration of Mass the faithful form a holy people, a people of God's own possession and a royal Priesthood, so that they may give thanks to God and offer the unblemished sacrificial Victim not only by means of the hands of the Priest but also together with him and so that they may learn to offer their very selves. They should, moreover, take care to show this by their deep religious sense and their charity toward brothers and sisters who participate with them in the same celebration." There is a direct link between our ministry at liturgy and our service of each other, between doing what is expected of us and doing the "more" that aligns us with God.

The most important ministry at Mass is that of the assembly. This means, first, that each member of the assembly has an active, decisive ministry. To be assembly means to surrender ourselves to God's Presence and in that surrender we become church made visible. Our very act of surrender, then, is an expression of faith because it takes us beyond ourselves. This is made concrete in the common responses, gestures, postures, and singing we do at liturgy. Faith is also made concrete in the active listening to God's word proclaimed, in heartfelt giving of praise and thanks during the eucharistic prayer, in genuine gift of self to others in the sign of peace, and in walking together in procession to God's banquet table where we are nourished for the demands of discipleship.

Each of the specific, visible ministries at liturgy (presider, deacon, hospitality ministers, altar ministers, musicians, lectors, extraordinary ministers of Holy Communion) is, of course, also an opportunity to express faith through service. But we must never forget that the most important ministry is to surrender to being church made visible. This is the most demanding service because it requires us to lose ourselves in something bigger than ourselves. This is how faith the size of the mustard seed can move mulberry trees—we are not alone, but our service is always with the other members of the Body of Christ.

About Liturgical Music

Music suggestions: Delores Dufner's "Jesus Christ, by Faith Revealed" (OF, WC, WS) is a well-written hymn for the entrance song at any Mass, but particularly appropriate on this Sunday when we ask Jesus to increase our faith (gospel). In another well-crafted hymn, "Faith Begins by Letting Go" (W4), Dufner opens our understanding to the many dimensions of faith: "Faith begins by letting go, Giving up what had seemed sure . . ." (verse 1); "Faith endures by holding on, Keeping mem'ry's roots alive . . ." (verse 2); "Faith matures by reaching out, Stretching minds, enlarging hearts . . ." (verse 3). This hymn would work well during the preparation of the gifts. "A Living Faith" (G3, W4), the altered text of Frederick Faber's "Faith of Our Fathers," speaks of the faith of our fathers, the faith of our mothers, and the faith of our brothers and sisters. The final verse addresses our faith: "Faith born of God, O call us yet; Bind us with all who follow you, Sharing the struggle of your cross Until the world is made anew, Faith born of God, O living faith, we will be true to you till death." This hymn would be effective sung either during the preparation of the gifts or as the recessional song. Randall DeBruyn's "Jesus, Lord" (BB, JS3), with its refrain "Jesus, Lord, strengthen us with faith in you . . . Lift our hearts, fill us with new trust in your love," would be a good choice for Communion.

OCTOBER 2, 2016
TWENTY-SEVENTH SUNDAY
IN ORDINARY TIME

SPIRITUALITY

GOSPEL ACCLAMATION
1 Thess 5:18

℟. Alleluia, alleluia.
In all circumstances, give thanks,
for this is the will of God for you in Christ
    Jesus.
℟. Alleluia, alleluia.

Gospel Luke 17:11-19; L144C

As Jesus continued his journey to
    Jerusalem,
  he traveled through Samaria
    and Galilee.
As he was entering a village, ten
    lepers met him.
They stood at a distance from
    him and raised their voices,
    saying,
"Jesus, Master! Have pity on
    us!"
And when he saw them, he said,
  "Go show yourselves to the priests."
As they were going they were cleansed.
And one of them, realizing he had been
    healed,
  returned, glorifying God in a loud
    voice;
  and he fell at the feet of Jesus and
    thanked him.
He was a Samaritan.
Jesus said in reply,
  "Ten were cleansed, were they not?
Where are the other nine?
Has none but this foreigner returned to
    give thanks to God?"
Then he said to him, "Stand up and go;
    your faith has saved you."

Reflecting on the Gospel

In this gospel Jesus tells the one leper who returns to give him thanks for being healed that "your faith has saved you." What amazing words to speak to a leper, one who is removed from family and community, one who is an outcast! The ten lepers were all outcasts. Jesus, on his journey to Jerusalem which would end in salvation for all, healed them all. For Jesus, there are no outcasts. Yet only one of the ten demonstrates that being saved is being healed, is returning to the Healer, is glorifying God, is falling at the feet of Jesus, is giving thanks. Only one shows us *how* faith saves. Faith is not static; it is dynamic, unfolding in various movements.

Being healed: In our woundedness we must cry out, "Jesus, Master! Have pity on us!" Our crying out establishes a relationship with Jesus. We must admit our need for him, our need for healing. We must trust that he will respond. We must surrender ourselves into Jesus' care, risk overturning our outcast status to become a vital member of family and community.

Returning to the Healer: After receiving Jesus' healing touch, our returning to him to encounter him in a new way expresses that we have a new relationship with him. We are indebted to him, not just for healing, but for the restoration that enables us to see life through different lenses, live life through different experiences, appreciate life through different postures. Returning to the Healer helps us "Stand up and go," helps us go forth as a new Presence.

Glorifying God: More than in the quiet of our hearts, after a healing encounter with Jesus we are "glorifying God in a loud voice." We cannot contain our joy, our enthusiasm, our relief at breaking free from limiting wounds. Our freedom brings us to a new expression of our relationship with Jesus whereby we exalt God for mercy and care and proclaim God's power to save.

Falling at the feet of Jesus: A healing relationship brings us to our knees in the deepest humility. On our knees we acknowledge our need, our dependence, our creatureliness. On our own we are unable to sustain life's journey. In humble relationship to Jesus, we are able to grow into an intimate relationship with Jesus, one that raises us up to new Life.

Giving thanks: Thankfulness can only happen when two are present, can only happen in relationship. Giving thanks binds two together in an experience of self-giving. Healer and healed become one.

The grateful leper, through his actions, teaches us much. We learn that salvation is not freedom from disease, but a new relationship with Jesus. We learn *how* faith saves: by being in intimate relationship with Jesus, our Healer.

Living the Paschal Mystery

The leper was healed while "Jesus continued his journey to Jerusalem." This is what happens to us when by paschal mystery living we walk with Jesus to Jerusalem: on the way we are healed of our infirmities. Gratitude is an expression of paschal mystery living because by giving thanks we acknowledge our own indebtedness—we are poor and everything we are and are becoming is because God has raised us up.

By living Jesus' dying and rising in our own simple everyday tasks, we render God the greatest thanks and worship because our lives become like that of the divine Son. Our thanks is manifestation of God's salvation.

Focusing the Gospel

Key words and phrases: journey to Jerusalem, ten lepers, realizing he had been healed, returned, glorifying God, fell at the feet of Jesus, thanked him, your faith has saved you

To the point: The ten lepers were outcasts. Jesus, on his journey to Jerusalem which would end in salvation for all, healed them all. For Jesus, there are no outcasts. Yet only one of the ten demonstrates that being saved is being healed, is returning to the Healer, is glorifying God, is falling at the feet of Jesus, is giving thanks. Only one shows us *how* faith saves.

Connecting the Gospel

to the first reading: Upon being healed Naaman, like the one leper in the gospel who returns to Jesus, shows his faith, gratitude, and desire to worship God alone.

to experience: We all too often limit our understanding of faith to pietistic practices and doctrinal adherence. This gospel shows us how broad our expressions of faith can be: encountering Jesus, worshiping, having a sense of gratitude for all God's gifts to us.

Connecting the Responsorial Psalm

to the readings: Psalm 98, from which this Sunday's responsorial psalm is taken, sings about the completion of God's saving plan for Israel. All the forces which threaten God's chosen people—depicted in various psalms as enemy nations, roaring seas, evildoers, famine, disease—have been put to rout by God. God's "wondrous deeds" of salvation have been revealed, and the whole world rejoices. The healing stories in the first reading and gospel are concrete dramatizations of God's saving deeds. By singing Psalm 98 we join Naaman and the grateful leper in offering thanks to God for saving us from disease and death. We express our faith in God and are granted salvation.

to psalmist preparation: Reflect this week on where you have seen God's salvation unfold—in your own life, in the church, in the world. Let your singing of this responsorial psalm be both a proclamation of God's deeds and a thanksgiving for them.

ASSEMBLY & FAITH-SHARING GROUPS

- I feel like an outcast when . . . because . . . Jesus heals me by . . .
- The one leper who returns to Jesus teaches me that . . .
- My faith leads me to . . .

PRESIDERS
My faith leads those to whom I minister to encounter Jesus when . . . by . . .

DEACONS
Like Jesus, my healing ministry brings others to . . .

HOSPITALITY MINISTERS
My hospitality expresses Jesus' vision of there being no outcasts by . . .

MUSIC MINISTERS
Faith undergirds all my music making because . . . when . . .

ALTAR MINISTERS
My serving is a public act of faith because . . .

LECTORS
My manner of proclaiming is another way of showing how faith saves when . . .

EXTRAORDINARY MINISTERS OF HOLY COMMUNION
While distributing Holy Communion, I am moved to gratitude by . . .

CELEBRATION

Model Penitential Act

Presider: In today's gospel one leper returns to Jesus to give thanks for being healed. As we prepare to celebrate this liturgy, let us open our hearts in gratitude for God's Presence and healing power . . . [pause]

Lord Jesus, you heal us of all alienation: Lord . . .
Christ Jesus, you show us the fullness of Life: Christ . . .
Lord Jesus, you give us hope and save us: Lord . . .

Homily Points

• The drive to preserve our life leads us to stop at nothing to be healed when life and health are at stake. We undergo painful surgeries, tolerate devastating side effects of medications, travel great distances to receive the best care. We can well identify with the ten lepers in this gospel story who cry out, "Have pity on us!" Do we identify as well with the one leper who returns to give thanks?

• Of what were the lepers cleansed? A disfiguring and debilitating disease, for sure. But for only one did something happen in his heart that went beyond what had happened in his body. In his heart trust led to healing, healing led to gratitude, gratitude led to salvation. This is the dynamic of *how* faith saves.

• What are our diseases that make us cry out, "Jesus, Master! Have pity on us!"? We may suffer the "diseases" of racism, indifference, arrogance, lust, self-centeredness, self-indulgence, self-righteousness. The dynamic that saves us is awareness that we are unhealthy, desire for healing, trust that God will heal us, gratitude for the grace God works in us, faith in the divine Healer. To what lengths will we go for this kind of healing?

Model Universal Prayer (Prayer of the Faithful)

Presider: Let us make our needs known to our caring and loving God who heals us and grants us salvation.

Response:

Lord, hear our prayer.

Cantor:

we pray to the Lord,

That all members of the church give thanks always and everywhere for the good God bestows upon us . . . [pause]

That all peoples of the world be open to God's offer of salvation . . . [pause]

That those who are alienated from themselves or others be healed by the saving touch of Jesus . . . [pause]

That we here gathered seek the healing we need through the trust that faith gives us . . . [pause]

Presider: Gracious God, we glorify you and give you thanks. Grant our prayers that one day our faith may lead us to the fullness of Life with you. We ask this through Christ our Lord. **Amen.**

COLLECT
Let us pray.

Pause for silent prayer

May your grace, O Lord, we pray,
at all times go before us and follow after
and make us always determined
to carry out good works.
Through our Lord Jesus Christ, your Son,
who lives and reigns with you in the unity
    of the Holy Spirit,
one God, for ever and ever. **Amen.**

FIRST READING
2 Kgs 5:14-17

Naaman went down and plunged into the Jordan seven times
    at the word of Elisha, the man of God.
His flesh became again like the flesh of a little child,
    and he was clean of his leprosy.

Naaman returned with his whole retinue to the man of God.
On his arrival he stood before Elisha and said,
    "Now I know that there is no God in all the earth,
    except in Israel.
Please accept a gift from your servant."

Elisha replied, "As the LORD lives whom I serve, I will not take it";
    and despite Naaman's urging, he still refused.
Naaman said: "If you will not accept,
    please let me, your servant, have two mule-loads of earth,
    for I will no longer offer holocaust or sacrifice
    to any other god except to the LORD."

RESPONSORIAL PSALM
Ps 98:1, 2-3, 3-4

R. (cf. 2b) The Lord has revealed to the nations his saving power.

Sing to the LORD a new song,
    for he has done wondrous deeds;
his right hand has won victory for him,
    his holy arm.

R. The Lord has revealed to the nations his saving power.

The LORD has made his salvation known:
    in the sight of the nations he has
        revealed his justice.
He has remembered his kindness and his
    faithfulness
    toward the house of Israel.

R. The Lord has revealed to the nations his saving power.

All the ends of the earth have seen
    the salvation by our God.
Sing joyfully to the LORD, all you lands:
    break into song; sing praise.

R. The Lord has revealed to the nations his saving power.

SECOND READING
2 Tim 2:8-13

Beloved:
Remember Jesus Christ, raised from the
    dead, a descendant of David:
    such is my gospel, for which I am
        suffering,
    even to the point of chains, like a
        criminal.
But the word of God is not chained.
Therefore, I bear with everything for the
    sake of those who are chosen,
    so that they too may obtain the
        salvation that is in Christ Jesus,
    together with eternal glory.
This saying is trustworthy:
    If we have died with him
        we shall also live with him;
    if we persevere
        we shall also reign with him.
    But if we deny him
        he will deny us.
    If we are unfaithful
        he remains faithful,
        for he cannot deny himself.

About Liturgy

Eucharist—faithfulness and thankfulness: Eucharist defines Catholic worship and even Christians themselves because in Christ God has given us the most profound gift of sharing in divine Life. Our only response can be faithfulness and thankfulness.

Faithfulness: The divine gift of Eucharist calls us to be faithful in its celebration. Faithfulness means that we rejoice in God's most gracious gift and make every effort to participate fully, actively, and consciously. Faithful celebration, in turn, strengthens us for faithful discipleship. The Word and food of Eucharist is a continual renewal of God's Presence that invites us to an encounter with the One who heals and saves.

Thankfulness: Gratitude in face of God's great gifts to us is a recognition of indebtedness that can only be adequately expressed in worship. Each celebration of Eucharist is a profound acknowledgment that all we have is from God and that God still gives us even more. Without an attitude of thankfulness we cannot continually open up the capacity within ourselves to receive God's gifts. Thankfulness, then, is more than saying "thanks." It is opening ourselves to God by worship and self-surrender. Ultimately, gratitude also includes encounter.

Eucharist defines Catholic worship and Christian living because this is the only way we can adequately express what God desires of us—salvation in Christ. Eucharist not only changes the bread and wine into the Body and Blood of Christ, it changes us into being more perfect members of the Body of Christ. This is how we are saved—by encountering Christ and being transformed.

About Liturgical Music

Music suggestions: Songs about Jesus' healing response to those like the ten lepers who suffer include "Your Hands, O Lord, in Days of Old" (OF, W4, WC, WS); "Jesus Heard with Deep Compassion" (OF); and "Healer of Our Every Ill" (G3, W4, WC, WS). As an expression of our gratitude for this healing, the Taizé ostinato piece "In the Lord I'll Be Ever Thankful" (G3, SS, W4) would work well during Communion with cantor or choir singing the verses. Additional verses, instrumental parts, and a bilingual refrain can be found in *Taizé: Songs for Prayer* (GIA).

This Sunday might be a good day to sing a hymn of praise and thanksgiving after Communion. "Thanks Be to God" (BB, JS3) with its refrain, "*Deo gratias, Deo gratias,* Thanks be to God most high" would be particularly appropriate, as would "I Will Bless the Lord" (LMGM2) and "Praise Him!" (LMGM2). Finally, examples of appropriate recessional songs include "Praise and Thanksgiving" (G3, SS, W4) and "Now Thank We All Our God" (in most resources).

SPIRITUALITY

GOSPEL ACCLAMATION
Heb 4:12

R̟. Alleluia, alleluia.
The word of God is living and effective,
discerning reflections and thoughts of
    the heart.
R̟. Alleluia, alleluia.

Gospel   Luke 18:1-8; L147C
Jesus told his disciples a
    parable
about the necessity for
        them to pray always
        without becoming
        weary.
He said, "There was a judge
    in a certain town
who neither feared God nor
    respected any human
    being.
And a widow in that town used
    to come to him and say,
    'Render a just decision for me against
        my adversary.'
For a long time the judge was unwilling,
    but eventually he thought,
    'While it is true that I neither fear God
        nor respect any human being,
    because this widow keeps bothering me
    I shall deliver a just decision for her
    lest she finally come and strike me.'"
The Lord said, "Pay attention to what the
    dishonest judge says.
Will not God then secure the rights of his
    chosen ones
    who call out to him day and night?
Will he be slow to answer them?
I tell you, he will see to it that justice is
    done for them speedily.
But when the Son of Man comes, will he
    find faith on earth?"

Reflecting on the Gospel

In this gospel, every character mentioned is seeking justice. Justice as jurisprudence seeks to uphold the rights of all, to balance out differences, to apply uniformly principles of behavior and treatment. In our nation's justice system, the widow of the gospel would probably be held in contempt of court for pestering the judge. The judge would probably be tried for corruption because of his dishonest ways of dealing with people. The widow seeks justice out of need; the judge renders justice out of exasperation. The widow's persistence finally breaks down the judge. She has her day in court. She wins. And that seems to be the end of the story. We do not know what happens to the widow after she wins her case. But this is not the end of the gospel story. If, as humans, we seek to balance fairness, then how much more might we expect from God! God bestows justice out of love for God's "chosen ones / who call out to him day and night." The widow had a legal relationship with the judge that ended the moment he rendered a decision. Our persistence in prayer brings far more than some transitory alleviation of a wrong. We have a personal relationship with God that continually deepens as we "pray always." God renders divine justice—divine-human relationship—out of the nature of who God is. God is relational, resting in the dynamic communion of the Three Persons of the Holy Trinity. Jesus is teaching us that while our prayer tends to be about immediate needs, our life is about ultimate justice, permanent relationship, life-giving communion. Our persistence in prayer really is about a faith relationship with God that reveals we are God's "chosen ones" who are in right relationship with God. This righteousness leads to eternal Life.

The gospel's legal language of judge, judgment, and justice bring to mind the final judgment Jesus renders at his Second Coming. One way to prepare for this Second Coming and alleviate any fears we might have is to be persistent in faith-filled prayer. Our faith grows through persistence in prayer because through this kind of prayer we build a stronger relationship with God. When Jesus comes again, "will he find faith on earth?" Yes, if we are persistent in praying "always without becoming weary." It seems persistence in prayer is a small price to pay for salvation and everlasting glory!

God faithfully hears and answers our prayer, "secur[ing] the rights of his chosen ones." What are these rights? To be heard by God. To be answered by God. To be loved by God into the fullness of divine-human relationship. Persistence in prayer is such a small price to pay for the most Life-giving relationship we can have!

Living the Paschal Mystery

For many setting aside any definite time for prayer during the day may seem all but impossible, especially if we are talking about ten or fifteen uninterrupted minutes. Persistence in praying always might need to take the form in our lives of developing the habit of being aware of God's abiding Presence and blessings even in our busyness. It might mean that we learn to catch little moments for prayer (like we sometimes are able to catch moments for catnaps)—while driving to pick up the youngsters or waiting in a checkout line. The place and manner of prayer aren't nearly so important as the fact that we pray—always and without ceasing. This prayer sustains our relationship with a God who loves beyond measure.

Focusing the Gospel

Key words and phrases: pray always, Render a just decision, judge was unwilling, widow keeps bothering me, secure the rights of his chosen ones, call out . . . day and night

To the point: In this gospel, the widow seeks justice out of need; the judge renders justice out of exasperation; God bestows justice out of love for God's "chosen ones / who call out to him day and night." The widow had a legal relationship with the judge that ended the moment he rendered a decision. We, however, have a personal relationship with God that continually deepens as we "pray always." God faithfully hears and answers our prayer, "secur[ing] the rights of his chosen ones." What are these rights? To be heard by God. To be answered by God. To be loved by God into the fullness of divine-human relationship.

Connecting the Gospel

to the first reading: Moses was as persistent in prayer as the widow in the gospel. So long as Moses sustained his prayer to God, the Israelites were successful against Amalek. Because the widow was persistent with her petition to the judge, she was successful in receiving a just judgment.

to experience: We sometimes limit our practice of prayer to the words we say and texts we recite. In fact, prayer is any turning toward God that deepens our relationship with the Divine One.

Connecting the Responsorial Psalm

to the readings: Psalm 121, used in its entirety this Sunday, is a pilgrimage song. Having journeyed to Jerusalem for festival, the Israelites must now travel home. They see the dark mountains which surround them as a threat, the hideout of thieves and enemies, the home of wild animals. The psalm is a prayer of confidence in God's protection, perhaps said in blessing over them by the temple priest as the pilgrims begin their journey home. What motivates the prayer is surety about God. The Israelites know that God answers the prayer of those who are faithful to the covenant. Moses had such confidence (first reading) as did Jesus (gospel), as do we when we sing this psalm. May our singing reveal the "faith on earth" the Son of Man longs to find when he returns (gospel).

to psalmist preparation: When you sing this responsorial psalm, you are like the temple priest blessing the people as they begin their journey homeward. The people are the Body of Christ, the journey that of faithful discipleship, the homeland God's kingdom. How will your singing assure the assembly of God's Presence and protection on the way?

ASSEMBLY & FAITH-SHARING GROUPS
- I "pray always" because . . .
- My prayer deepens my relationship with God when I . . . when God . . .
- When I pray, God hears . . . When God answers, I hear . . .

PRESIDERS
When I am truly praying as I preside, the assembly hears . . . I hear in the assembly . . .

DEACONS
My ministry answers others' cry for justice when . . . The way my ministry "secures the rights of [God's] chosen ones" is . . .

HOSPITALITY MINISTERS
Like Aaron and Hur (first reading), my ministry of hospitality upholds and enables the prayer of others by . . .

MUSIC MINISTERS
My music ministry becomes a way to "pray always" when I . . . My music ministry helps the assembly enter more deeply into prayer when I . . .

ALTAR MINISTERS
When I truly pray while serving the needs of the liturgy, my manner is . . .

LECTORS
When prayer is part of my preparation for ministry, my proclamation itself becomes a prayer because . . .

EXTRAORDINARY MINISTERS OF HOLY COMMUNION
My distributing Holy Communion is a continuation of my eucharistic praying when . . .

Model Penitential Act

Presider: In today's gospel Jesus teaches his disciples about the necessity to "pray always." As we prepare to pray during this liturgy, let us ask God's mercy for the times we have neglected to be present to God in prayer . . . [pause]

Lord Jesus, you teach us to pray always: Lord . . .

Christ Jesus, you will come to gather your chosen ones into glory: Christ . . .

Lord Jesus, you hear and answer our prayers: Lord . . .

Homily Points

• Some relationships are meant to be limited such as those among coworkers on a contract job, companions on a business trip, jurors at a trial. Other relationships are more lasting such as ties with family, fraternities or sororities, professional organizations. Most permanent of all is our relationship with God, sustained by prayer.

• Prayer is conversation with God, encounter with God, basking in God's Presence. This we can do always because the God to whom we are relating is always responding. Prayer cannot be an occasional practice because our relationship with God is not occasional. It is permanent, pervasive, and persistent.

• All ways of praying sustain and deepen our relationship with God because praying is surrender of ourselves into God's hands. Giving ourselves over to God binds us to the Almighty in a manner that deepens our divine-human relationship. We must "pray always" because that is the way to the fullness of the only relationship that is ultimately most satisfying, most trustworthy, eternally Life-giving.

Model Universal Prayer (Prayer of the Faithful)

Presider: We make known our needs to a God who faithfully hears and answers our prayers.

Response:

Lord, hear our prayer.

Cantor:

we pray to the Lord,

That all members of the church "pray always" and come to the fullness of relationship with God . . . [pause]

That all peoples of the world turn toward God and come to salvation . . . [pause]

That those in any need encounter the God who hears and answers all prayer . . . [pause]

That each of us here gathered learn through persistence in prayer that we are God's chosen ones . . . [pause]

Presider: Loving God, you hear and answer the prayers of those who cry out to you. Grant our prayers and bring us to the fullness of Life. We ask this through Christ our Lord. **Amen**.

COLLECT

Let us pray.

Pause for silent prayer

Almighty ever-living God,
grant that we may always conform our
    will to yours
and serve your majesty in sincerity of
    heart.
Through our Lord Jesus Christ, your Son,
who lives and reigns with you in the unity
    of the Holy Spirit,
one God, for ever and ever. **Amen.**

FIRST READING
Exod 17:8-13

In those days, Amalek came and waged
    war against Israel.
Moses, therefore, said to Joshua,
    "Pick out certain men,
    and tomorrow go out and engage
        Amalek in battle.
I will be standing on top of the hill
    with the staff of God in my hand."
So Joshua did as Moses told him:
    he engaged Amalek in battle
    after Moses had climbed to the top of
        the hill with Aaron and Hur.
As long as Moses kept his hands raised
    up,
    Israel had the better of the fight,
    but when he let his hands rest,
    Amalek had the better of the fight.
Moses' hands, however, grew tired;
    so they put a rock in place for him to
        sit on.
Meanwhile Aaron and Hur supported his
    hands,
    one on one side and one on the other,
    so that his hands remained steady till
        sunset.
And Joshua mowed down Amalek and his
    people
    with the edge of the sword.

RESPONSORIAL PSALM
Ps 121:1-2, 3-4, 5-6, 7-8

℟. (cf. 2) Our help is from the Lord, who
made heaven and earth.

I lift up my eyes toward the mountains;
    whence shall help come to me?
My help is from the LORD,
    who made heaven and earth.

℟. Our help is from the Lord, who made
heaven and earth.

May he not suffer your foot to slip;
    may he slumber not who guards you:
indeed he neither slumbers nor sleeps,
    the guardian of Israel.

R℣. Our help is from the Lord, who made
heaven and earth.

The LORD is your guardian; the LORD is
    your shade;
    he is beside you at your right hand.
The sun shall not harm you by day,
    nor the moon by night.

R℣. Our help is from the Lord, who made
heaven and earth.

The LORD will guard you from all evil;
    he will guard your life.
The LORD will guard your coming and
    your going,
    both now and forever.

R℣. Our help is from the Lord, who made
heaven and earth.

SECOND READING
2 Tim 3:14—4:2

Beloved:
Remain faithful to what you have learned
    and believed,
    because you know from whom you
        learned it,
    and that from infancy you have known
        the sacred Scriptures,
    which are capable of giving you
        wisdom for salvation
    through faith in Christ Jesus.
All Scripture is inspired by God
    and is useful for teaching, for refutation,
        for correction,
    and for training in righteousness,
    so that one who belongs to God may be
        competent,
    equipped for every good work.

I charge you in the presence of God and of
    Christ Jesus,
    who will judge the living and the dead,
    and by his appearing and his kingly
        power:
proclaim the word;
be persistent whether it is convenient or
    inconvenient;
convince, reprimand, encourage through
    all patience and teaching.

About Liturgy

Liturgy as prayer: Of course we all understand that liturgy is prayer. There are a number of indicators within the liturgy itself. For example, before the collect and at the post-Communion prayer the presider specifically invites us to pray: "Let us *pray*." The heart of the Liturgy of the Eucharist is called the eucharistic *prayer*. The universal *prayer* (*prayer* of the faithful) concludes the Liturgy of the Word. We *pray* together the Our Father, probably one of the first prayers we learned as children. How is it, though, that liturgy is more than just a stringing together of prayers? How is the liturgy itself a single, seamless *prayer*?

In the liturgy we pray as *one body*, the Body of Christ. By praying with one voice, we lift up a single prayer to God. Because we are this community, the liturgical prayer doesn't depend on any one individual's ability to pray or not during a particular liturgy. It is as though we are holding each other up and enabling one another to remain strong and persistent in prayer. The constant repetition of liturgy throughout the world is a constant reminder of the persistence of the prayer of the Body of Christ.

Another consideration for understanding liturgy as a single, seamless prayer is that the liturgy has an invariable structure. Individual elements may change and vary somewhat from liturgy to liturgy, but the essential structure is the same. This invariability enables us to surrender to the action and in that surrender both encounter with God and the visibility of the church as the Body of Christ become possible.

Finally, and perhaps most importantly, the overall sentiments of liturgy are praise and thanksgiving. With these attitudes we glorify God and offer our worship, and thus strengthen our relationship with God and each other. All the individual prayer—yes, even the petitionary prayer—redounds to praise and thanksgiving. All prayer converges on our acknowledging God's splendor and being grateful for the gift of divine Presence and loving divine-human relationship.

About Liturgical Music

Music suggestions: Two hymns which ask God to teach us how to pray are "Lord, Teach Us How to Pray" and "Eternal Spirit of the Living Christ" (both found in HG). Either would be appropriate during the preparation of the gifts. Quiet repetitions of the Taizé piece "O Lord, Hear My Prayer" (G3, SS, W4) would be an appropriate choral prelude, with choir and assembly singing together. In the verses of Eugene Englert's "Ask and You Shall Receive" (OF), we beg God to listen to our "sighing," our "pleading," our "cry." In the verses we repeat for one another Jesus' promise that what we ask for we will receive. This simple song would work well during the preparation of the gifts.

The value of familiar, repeated music: There is a great deal of repetition built into the liturgy. One of the purposes of this repetition is to help us persist in prayer. The same is true for liturgical music. It is not how many new songs or new settings of the Mass we sing which transforms us, but how well we pray liturgically when we sing. For this to happen, the music needs to be familiar and repeated. Too much or too frequent changing of the music can keep us on the surface of the liturgy. The constant changing may be interesting, stimulating, and entertaining, but it makes liturgy a kind of musical superhighway with so many distracting billboards we lose track of what road we are on and where we are going. The real role of music, however, is to help us stay focused on where we are going—into the heart of the paschal mystery—and help us persist in the prayer needed to go there.

✚ SPIRITUALITY

GOSPEL ACCLAMATION
2 Cor 5:19

℟. Alleluia, alleluia.
God was reconciling the world to himself in
    Christ,
and entrusting to us the message of salvation.
℟. Alleluia, alleluia.

Gospel   Luke 18:9-14; L150C

Jesus addressed this parable
    to those who were convinced of their
        own righteousness
    and despised everyone else.
"Two people went up to the temple area
        to pray;
    one was a Pharisee and the other was a
        tax collector.
The Pharisee took up his position and
        spoke this prayer to himself,
    'O God, I thank you that I am not like
        the rest of humanity—
        greedy, dishonest, adulterous—or
            even like this tax collector.
I fast twice a week, and I pay tithes on
        my whole income.'
But the tax collector stood off at a
        distance
    and would not even raise his eyes to
        heaven
    but beat his breast and prayed,
    'O God, be merciful to me a sinner.'
I tell you, the latter went home justified,
        not the former;
    for whoever exalts himself will be
        humbled,
    and the one who humbles himself will
        be exalted."

Reflecting on the Gospel

We might chuckle at five-year-old Noah's boast that he will grow up to be stronger than Daddy. Or cringe at sixteen-year-old Hannah's bluster that she can text and drive with no problem. Or wonder at coworkers who brag about how deserving they are of a huge raise because they produce more than anyone else.

Only time will tell if Noah, Hannah, or the coworkers actually reach what they tout. In any case, at the time of the self-praise what tends to run through our minds is that these people don't know themselves very well. Life is about growing in self-knowledge. Prayer is the ingredient that brings honesty and accuracy to our self-knowledge.

Both the Pharisee and tax collector addressed God in prayer. The content of their prayer, however, differed greatly. The Pharisee's prayer was about himself and was turned toward self; his prayer was about justifying himself. The tax collector's prayer, by contrast, was turned toward God in the true self-knowledge of who he was. Jesus declared the tax collector justified, not the Pharisee. Jesus tells us that we are "justified" when we know who we are before God and open ourselves in humility to receive God's mercy. Justification—right relationship with God—comes only from knowing ourselves as God knows us. The message Jesus teaches in this gospel is that justification comes not to those who consider themselves righteous, but to those who humbly acknowledge their need for God's mercy.

Paradoxically, true humility is exaltation. Exaltation is the gift received while being one's true self before God and others. In this there's great hope in this gospel for all of us, for we are all sinners. The tax collector (generally hated for their practice of extortion) "stood off at a distance / and would not even raise his eyes to heaven," a posture indicating he recognized his sinfulness and unworthiness before God. His prayer says something true about God (who is merciful) and himself (who is a sinner). The tax collector's prayer allows God to be God and show mercy. The tax collector's prayer reveals both an understanding of God and the desire to be in right relation with God. The tax collector stands far off, but his prayer draws him near to God. This is exaltation—being near to God.

Justification is knowing who God is and what our relationship to God is. It is addressing God as God and letting God be God. It is acknowledging humbly who we are before God: sinners in need of mercy. The exaltation at the end of time is determined by whether we are justified, that is, humble and in right relationship to God. Good works alone don't justify us—it is right relationship with God. This is our exaltation—humbly seeking and standing before our God.

Living the Paschal Mystery

In practice, probably most of us are totally like neither the Pharisee nor the tax collector. So both can teach us something. The Pharisee can teach us that religious practices are important, but not enough. They must always be performed with humility and with the goal of deepening our relationship with God. The tax collector can teach us that God doesn't offer salvation to the perfect, but to those who acknowledge their sinfulness and cry out for God's mercy. Like the tax collector, we must let God be God and receive the mercy offered. Though sinners, God exalts those who are in right relationship. Rather than focus unduly on our own sinfulness, we need to turn to God and ask for mercy.

Focusing the Gospel

Key words and phrases: convinced of their own righteousness, I thank you that I am not like, me a sinner, justified, humbled, exalted

To the point: Both the Pharisee and tax collector addressed God in prayer. The content of their prayer, however, differed greatly. The Pharisee's prayer was about himself and was turned toward self. The tax collector's prayer, by contrast, was turned toward God in the true self-knowledge of who he was. Jesus declared the tax collector justified, not the Pharisee. Justification—right relationship with God—comes only from knowing ourselves as God knows us. Paradoxically, true humility is exaltation. Exaltation is the gift received while being one's true self before God and others.

Connecting the Gospel

to the first reading: The first reading instills great hope: God hears the prayer of the lowly, affirms them in their prayer, and does not delay in bringing them justice.

to experience: The message Jesus teaches in this gospel is that justification comes not to those who consider themselves righteous, but to those who acknowledge their need for God's mercy.

Connecting the Responsorial Psalm

to the readings: It is not the self-righteous whom God hears in prayer (gospel), but those "crushed in spirit" (responsorial psalm). God is not close-minded to the rich; indeed, God "knows no favorites" (first reading). Rather, it is that the self-satisfied are closed to God. Only those who recognize their need for mercy can see and receive the action of God on their behalf. In this Sunday's responsorial psalm we identify ourselves with the poor, the brokenhearted, the lowly. We acknowledge our right relationship with God—that of dependency, of humility, and of a need for mercy. Out of this attitude we pray, and God hears us.

to psalmist preparation: The words of the responsorial psalm parallel the message Jesus tells in his parable of the Pharisee and the tax collector (gospel). When you sing these words, then, you know what Jesus knew, and you tell it. What was it that Jesus knew?

ASSEMBLY & FAITH-SHARING GROUPS
- When I am "convinced of [my] own righteousness," what ends up humbling me is . . .
- The position I take up before God is . . . before others is . . .
- My prayer focuses on . . . when . . . because . . .

PRESIDERS
In my ministry, what brings me to the truest self-knowledge is . . . This affects the manner of my presiding in that . . . of my relating to my parishioners in that . . .

DEACONS
When serving others, I act like the Pharisee when . . . like the tax collector when . . . like Jesus when . . .

HOSPITALITY MINISTERS
The manner of my greeting helps those gathering for liturgy take up a right position before God when . . .

MUSIC MINISTERS
My music ministry tempts me to exalt myself when . . . What refocuses me in humility on God and the assembly is . . .

ALTAR MINISTERS
What is humbling about serving the liturgy is . . . My serving brings exaltation when . . .

LECTORS
Taking my position at the ambo, I . . .

EXTRAORDINARY MINISTERS OF HOLY COMMUNION
When I am my true self before God, I look upon those receiving Holy Communion as . . .

CELEBRATION

Model Penitential Act

Presider: In today's gospel Jesus contrasts the prayer of the proud Pharisee with that of the humble tax collector. We prepare ourselves to celebrate this liturgy by humbly opening our hearts to God's mercy . . . [pause]

Lord Jesus, you exalt the humble: Lord . . .

Christ Jesus, you are exalted at the right hand of the Father: Christ . . .

Lord Jesus, you exalt those who are honest in prayer: Lord . . .

Homily Points

• We are naturally repelled by arrogant, self-righteous people. Their self-centered behavior subtly degrades "the rest of humanity." Nor do we respond positively to self-deprecating people. Their seeming humility often subtly begs for exaltation. Both groups of people lack true self-knowledge. They are not in right relationship with God, self, or others.

• In this gospel the Pharisee arrogantly takes his position front and center in "the temple area." The tax collector humbly takes his position at a distance. Jesus teaches that authentic prayer and justification before God and others come only from true self-knowledge.

• Let's be honest: Sometimes when we pray we are like the Pharisee, and at other times we are like the tax collector. We are like the Pharisee when we presume we are in right relation with God and others and refuse to acknowledge truthfully our own failings and weaknesses. We are like the tax collector when we acknowledge who we really are and recognize our need for God's mercy. Justification—right relationship with God—comes only from knowing ourselves as God knows us. And praying accordingly.

Model Universal Prayer (Prayer of the Faithful)

Presider: Let us humbly stand before our God and pray for our needs.

Response:

Lord, hear our prayer.

Cantor:

we pray to the Lord,

That all members of the church be honest about themselves before God and be authentic in their prayer . . . [pause]

That all peoples of the world come to salvation by being in right relationship with God and each other . . . [pause]

That the proud be humbled and the humble be exalted . . . [pause]

That each of us admit our sinfulness and in prayer beg for God's mercy . . . [pause]

Presider: Merciful God, you hear the cry of those who humble themselves before your majesty. Hear these our prayers that one day we might be exalted with you forever. We ask this through Christ our Lord. **Amen.**

Let us pray.

Pause for silent prayer

Almighty ever-living God,
increase our faith, hope and charity,
and make us love what you command,
so that we may merit what you promise.
Through our Lord Jesus Christ, your Son,
who lives and reigns with you in the unity
    of the Holy Spirit,
one God, for ever and ever. **Amen.**

FIRST READING
Sir 35:12-14, 16-18

The LORD is a God of justice,
  who knows no favorites.
Though not unduly partial toward the
    weak,
  yet he hears the cry of the oppressed.
The LORD is not deaf to the wail of the
    orphan,
  nor to the widow when she pours out
      her complaint.
The one who serves God willingly is
    heard;
  his petition reaches the heavens.
The prayer of the lowly pierces the clouds;
  it does not rest till it reaches its goal,
nor will it withdraw till the Most High
    responds,
  judges justly and affirms the right,
and the LORD will not delay.

CATECHESIS

RESPONSORIAL PSALM
Ps 34:2-3, 17-18, 19, 23

R⃗. (7a) The Lord hears the cry of the poor.

I will bless the LORD at all times;
   his praise shall be ever in my mouth.
Let my soul glory in the LORD;
   the lowly will hear me and be glad.

R⃗. The Lord hears the cry of the poor.

The LORD confronts the evildoers,
   to destroy remembrance of them from
      the earth.
When the just cry out, the LORD hears
    them,
   and from all their distress he rescues
    them.

R⃗. The Lord hears the cry of the poor.

The LORD is close to the brokenhearted;
   and those who are crushed in spirit he
    saves.
The LORD redeems the lives of his
   servants;
   no one incurs guilt who takes refuge in
    him.

R⃗. The Lord hears the cry of the poor.

SECOND READING
2 Tim 4:6-8, 16-18

Beloved:
I am already being poured out like a
   libation,
   and the time of my departure is at
    hand.
I have competed well; I have finished the
   race;
   I have kept the faith.
From now on the crown of righteousness
   awaits me,
   which the Lord, the just judge,
   will award to me on that day, and not
    only to me,
   but to all who have longed for his
    appearance.

At my first defense no one appeared on
   my behalf,
   but everyone deserted me.
May it not be held against them!
But the Lord stood by me and gave me
   strength,
   so that through me the proclamation
    might be completed
   and all the Gentiles might hear it.
And I was rescued from the lion's mouth.
The Lord will rescue me from every evil
   threat
   and will bring me safe to his heavenly
    kingdom.
To him be glory forever and ever. Amen.

About Liturgy

Humility and liturgy: We have inherited a spirituality from the past that has not always portrayed humility in the best light. When we hear in this Sunday's gospel Jesus admonish us to humble ourselves, we can hear that as putting ourselves down, degrading ourselves, not acknowledging our gifts and talents. This is really a false humility.

Humility comes from the Latin word *humus*, which means ground or soil. It reminds us of the second creation account in which God forms the first human beings from the dust of the ground and breathes life into them (see Gen 2:7). The implication is that true humility is an admission of who we are: formed by God who breathes life into us. Humility is the down-to-earth recognition that God desires to be in relationship with us, loves us, and gives us all good gifts. Humility is rejoicing in who God has called us to be. Humility also leads us to readily acknowledge our weaknesses and failures and ask for God's mercy, as does the tax collector in this Sunday's gospel.

Celebrating liturgy well requires of us a good dose of humility. Liturgy is an awesome gift—God desires to nourish us on word and sacrament, comes to us, transforms us to be more faithful members of the Body of Christ. None of this we deserve. Yet God gives us these good gifts simply out of divine love. Our stance in liturgy, then, ought to be one of openness and acceptance of what God offers us, surrender to God's action, and joy in who God makes us to be. True humility, as this gospel tells us, leads to exaltation—not by us, but by the God who created us, saves us, and loves us.

About Liturgical Music

Music suggestions: When consecutive gospel readings are as clearly interrelated as are the ones for this Sunday and last Sunday, repeating a hymn helps us see the connection. Repeating either "Lord, Teach Us How to Pray" or "Eternal Spirit of the Living Christ" (both found in HG) during the preparation of the gifts would be appropriate. Likewise, repeating quiet repetitions of the Taizé "O Lord, Hear My Prayer" (G3, SS, W4) as a choral prelude, with choir and assembly singing together, would be good. Songs expressing humility before God and one another include Lucien Deiss's setting of Psalm 131, "My Soul Is Longing" (OF, WC, WS), which would be an excellent Communion song; the spiritual "Give Me a Clean Heart" (LMGM2), which would also be a good Communion song; and the Shaker hymn "'Tis the Gift to Be Simple" (G3 provides only the original verse; JS3, WC, WS include the additional verses by Joyce Merman), which would be appropriate during the preparation of the gifts. Adam M. L. Tice's "Two People Came to Church to Pray" (W4) relates the story of this Sunday's gospel. The final verse turns us toward examining how we pray and what we say to God. This hymn would be appropriate during the preparation of the gifts.

OCTOBER 23, 2016
THIRTIETH SUNDAY IN ORDINARY TIME

SPIRITUALITY

R̸. Alleluia, alleluia.
God so loved the world that he gave his only Son,
so that everyone who believes in him might
    have eternal life.
R̸. Alleluia, alleluia.

Gospel   Luke 19:1-10; L153C

At that time, Jesus came to
    Jericho and intended to
    pass through the town.
Now a man there named
    Zacchaeus,
    who was a chief tax collector
        and also a wealthy man,
    was seeking to see who Jesus
        was;
    but he could not see him
        because of the crowd,
    for he was short in stature.
So he ran ahead and climbed a
    sycamore tree in order to see
    Jesus,
    who was about to pass that way.
When he reached the place, Jesus looked
    up and said,
    "Zacchaeus, come down quickly,
    for today I must stay at your house."
And he came down quickly and received
    him with joy.
When they all saw this, they began to
    grumble, saying,
    "He has gone to stay at the house of a
        sinner."
But Zacchaeus stood there and said to the
    Lord,
    "Behold, half of my possessions, Lord,
        I shall give to the poor,
    and if I have extorted anything from
        anyone
    I shall repay it four times over."
And Jesus said to him,
    "Today salvation has come to this
        house
    because this man too is a descendant
        of Abraham.
For the Son of Man has come to seek
    and to save what was lost."

Reflecting on the Gospel

When do we find ourselves up a tree? When we are in a difficult situation and can't seem to find a way out. The idea is to climb down, to find a solution. In this gospel story, Zacchaeus does the opposite. He goes up a tree to solve his problem. What's not to like about this Zacchaeus story? All kinds of things feed our imagination. A "wealthy man" throws aside social propriety and does what an enthusiastic little kid would do—he climbs a tree! And he doesn't pick an easy tree—he climbs a sycamore tree, a very tall tree, one without branches close to the ground. He chooses a very difficult way to get what he wants: "to see who Jesus was." And he gets more than he climbed for—Jesus tells him, "Today salvation has come to this house." Zacchaeus's short stature kept him from seeing Jesus with his physical eyes. His ardent desire to encounter Jesus, however, indicates that he had already seen him with the eyes of his heart. Encountering Jesus does not depend upon the goodness of one's life, but encountering him can bring about conversion of life. Zacchaeus chooses to put his life in right order. For this does Zacchaeus come to salvation. Encountering Jesus and choosing to put our own life in right order brings us to the same salvation. We only need to see Jesus with the eyes of our hearts wide open.

All of us are *invited* to salvation. Those are saved who seek Jesus (Zacchaeus made the first step when he climbed the sycamore tree to see Jesus) and are open to being sought by him (Jesus stayed at his house). Those are saved who change their lives when they encounter Jesus. Seeing Jesus isn't enough. Encounter must lead to a faith relationship that makes a difference in our lives. Moreover, since Jesus continues his saving mission through us his followers, we must be equally responsive to others. We must put our own affairs in order and care for those in any need. We must also live in such a way that when others encounter us, they encounter Jesus.

Zacchaeus is the last person Luke's gospel mentions before Jesus enters Jerusalem—it is as though Luke chooses to end his gospel account with a memorable story about why Jesus came: "For the Son of Man has come to seek / and to save what was lost." If "salvation has come" even for this short tax collector, then who would ever be excluded?

Living the Paschal Mystery

Most of us don't have to be so creative or go to the extreme of climbing a tree to encounter Jesus. However, this gospel forewarns us that we ought to not be complacent about our spiritual lives. Zacchaeus reminds us that we must also always be willing to change and grow and be vigilant about our relationships with others, for these are barometers of our relationship with God. Creativity in seeking Jesus might mean that we are innovative in our personal prayer life rather than continually reciting the prayers we might have learned long ago. What prayers might better meet our spiritual needs now so that we can grow in our relationships? It might mean that we keep certain days of the year (perhaps the days of the Triduum or some days during Advent) as a "mini retreat" in order to diligently seek Jesus and a better relationship with him. It might mean that we don't wait for people to come to us and ask for help but that we notice others' needs and offer to help before they ask. In these and countless other ways we encounter Jesus—and salvation comes to our house.

Focusing the Gospel

Key words and phrases: seeking to see . . . Jesus, give to the poor . . . repay it, salvation has come

To the point: Zacchaeus's short stature kept him from seeing Jesus with his physical eyes. His ardent desire to encounter Jesus, however, indicates that he had already seen him with the eyes of his heart. Encountering Jesus does not depend upon the goodness of one's life, but encountering him can bring about conversion of life. Zacchaeus chooses to put his life in right order. For this does Zacchaeus come to salvation. Encountering Jesus and choosing to put our own life in right order brings us to the same salvation. We only need to see Jesus with the eyes of our hearts wide open.

Connecting the Gospel

to the first reading: In his encounter with Zacchaeus Jesus embodies exactly what Wisdom reveals about God who shows mercy to all and willingly overlooks sins.

to experience: Zacchaeus shimmied up a sycamore tree to see Jesus. To what heights are we willing to go to see Jesus?

Connecting the Responsorial Psalm

to the readings: Psalm 145 is an acrostic hymn, meaning that each verse begins with a successive letter of the Hebrew alphabet. Consequently, the psalm does not develop any theme in depth but simply offers God general praise. The verses chosen for this Sunday praise God for showing mercy and compassion rather than anger, and for lifting up those who have fallen. The reading from Wisdom confirms this attitude of God when it proclaims that the Lord "overlooks people's sins" and gently coaxes offenders back to right living. Clearly God prefers reconciliation to condemnation.

In his encounter with Zacchaeus Jesus is the living embodiment of this orientation of God. Jesus "has come to seek / and to save what was lost" (gospel). In singing this psalm we are the living embodiment of Zacchaeus's response. We recognize ourselves as sinners and shout praise to the One who comes to save us.

to psalmist preparation: Psalm 145 praises God for all that God does, but in the context of the first reading and gospel the praise is particularly for God's mercy to sinners. For what have you been shown this mercy? How have you praised God for it?

**ASSEMBLY &
FAITH-SHARING GROUPS**

- Like Zacchaeus, the heights to which I would go to see Jesus are . . .
- What opens my heart wide to see Jesus is . . .
- A change in me that encountering Jesus needs to bring about is . . .

PRESIDERS

My ministry brings people to encounter Jesus and choose conversion of life when I . . .

DEACONS

In my encounter with others while serving them, I change them by . . . I am changed by . . .

HOSPITALITY MINISTERS

My hospitality ministry is about helping others see Jesus with their hearts and encounter him because . . .

MUSIC MINISTERS

In my music ministry I seek to see who Jesus is by . . . Having seen him, I have chosen to change by . . .

ALTAR MINISTERS

Serving at the liturgy helps me put my life in order for Jesus when I . . .

LECTORS

Like Zacchaeus's encounter with Jesus, my encounter with God's word calls me to change my life by . . . The effect this has on my proclamation is . . .

**EXTRAORDINARY MINISTERS
OF HOLY COMMUNION**

As I distribute Holy Communion, I see others encounter Jesus and this changes me in that . . .

Model Penitential Act

Presider: In today's gospel episode Zacchaeus climbs a sycamore tree in order to see Jesus. Let us open our hearts to encounter Jesus in this celebration and be changed by his Presence . . . [pause]

Lord Jesus, you seek and save the lost: Lord . . .

Christ Jesus, you invite us to stay with you forever: Christ . . .

Lord Jesus, you call us to conversion of life: Lord . . .

Homily Points

• How popular is the Empire State Building! It is tall—very tall! Its observation deck provides quite a panorama of New York City. People come from all over the world to ascend its height and see its view. How popular was Jesus! Zacchaeus, a "tax collector and also a wealthy man," had social stature. But he was short—very short!

• Desiring only to see Jesus, Zacchaeus climbs a sycamore tree—a very tall tree! Jesus wants more, however, than just for Zacchaeus to see him—he initiates a personal encounter with Zacchaeus. Does our desire to see Jesus lift us to such heights as Zacchaeus in the sycamore tree? And even more, when Jesus initiates a personal encounter with us, are we as willing as Zacchaeus to hear Jesus say to us, "salvation has come"? Are we willing to put our feet on the ground and change our lives?

• We deepen our desire to see Jesus when we chat with someone who already knows him very well, when we experience a need for his Presence, when we feel empty and alone. During all our life, Jesus has an even stronger desire to encounter us in prayer, in good works, in community. Our response to Jesus' coming to us is concretely shown by rooting out of our lives anything that keeps us from doing the hard work of becoming who he wants us to be: the lost who are saved. In this conversion process we grow tall—very tall!

Model Universal Prayer (Prayer of the Faithful)

Presider: Let us make our needs known to the God who seeks us and saves us.

Response:

Lord, hear our prayer.

Cantor:

we pray to the Lord,

That all members of the church continually open themselves to encounters with Jesus and his transforming love . . . [pause]

That each person of the world seek conversion to come to a deeper relationship with God . . . [pause]

That the lost be found and those who seek God encounter the richness and grace of divine Presence . . . [pause]

That each of us here more clearly see Jesus in the persons and events around us and respond with joy . . . [pause]

Presider: Saving God, you sent your divine Son to seek and save the lost. Hear these our prayers that one day we might enter into the joy of everlasting Life with you. We ask this through Christ our Lord. **Amen.**

COLLECT
Let us pray.

Pause for silent prayer

Almighty and merciful God,
by whose gift your faithful offer you
right and praiseworthy service,
grant, we pray,
that we may hasten without stumbling
to receive the things you have promised.
Through our Lord Jesus Christ, your Son,
who lives and reigns with you in the unity
    of the Holy Spirit,
one God, for ever and ever. **Amen.**

FIRST READING
Wis 11:22–12:2

Before the LORD the whole universe is as a
        grain from a balance
    or a drop of morning dew come down
        upon the earth.
But you have mercy on all, because you
        can do all things;
    and you overlook people's sins that they
        may repent.
For you love all things that are
    and loathe nothing that you have made;
    for what you hated, you would not have
        fashioned.
And how could a thing remain, unless you
        willed it;
    or be preserved, had it not been called
        forth by you?
But you spare all things, because they are
        yours,
    O LORD and lover of souls,
    for your imperishable spirit is in all
        things!
Therefore you rebuke offenders little by
        little,
    warn them and remind them of the sins
        they are committing,
    that they may abandon their wickedness
        and believe in you, O LORD!

RESPONSORIAL PSALM
Ps 145:1-2, 8-9, 10-11, 13, 14

℟. (cf. 1) I will praise your name forever,
my king and my God.

I will extol you, O my God and King,
    and I will bless your name forever and
        ever.
Every day will I bless you,
    and I will praise your name forever and
        ever.

℟. I will praise your name forever, my
king and my God.

The Lord is gracious and merciful,
   slow to anger and of great kindness.
The Lord is good to all
   and compassionate toward all his
      works.

R̰. I will praise your name forever, my
king and my God.

Let all your works give you thanks, O
      Lord,
   and let your faithful ones bless you.
Let them discourse of the glory of your
      kingdom
   and speak of your might.

R̰. I will praise your name forever, my
king and my God.

The Lord is faithful in all his words
   and holy in all his works.
The Lord lifts up all who are falling
   and raises up all who are bowed down.

R̰. I will praise your name forever, my
king and my God.

SECOND READING
2 Thess 1:11—2:2

Brothers and sisters:
We always pray for you,
   that our God may make you worthy of
      his calling
   and powerfully bring to fulfillment
      every good purpose
   and every effort of faith,
   that the name of our Lord Jesus may be
      glorified in you,
   and you in him,
   in accord with the grace of our God and
      Lord Jesus Christ.

We ask you, brothers and sisters,
   with regard to the coming of our Lord
      Jesus Christ
   and our assembling with him,
   not to be shaken out of your minds
      suddenly, or to be alarmed
   either by a "spirit," or by an oral
      statement,
   or by a letter allegedly from us
   to the effect that the day of the Lord is
      at hand.

About Liturgy

Change and liturgy: Change is generally a good thing—it indicates growth and desire for new directions and accomplishments. Even change in liturgy is good because the need for change is a witness that the liturgical assembly has grown deeper in their relationship with God and each other. Change is a fact of life and of liturgy! Change is good and necessary. But too much change too often in liturgy can actually work against fruitful liturgy.

After a change (especially something rather major), we must give ourselves time to "settle in" and make the change a natural part of the rhythm of our ritual celebrations. If we are always adjusting to something new during liturgy it is very difficult to internalize the fruits of liturgy. We must give ourselves time to "settle in," not in the sense of becoming complacent or resting easy (liturgy is always hard work) or getting sloppy, but in the sense of having the luxury of fine-tuning what changes we have introduced. As we grow in familiarity with our rituals we are free to enter more deeply into the liturgical mystery itself.

While change is necessary and good for the rhythm of our liturgies, novelty and innovation (especially for their own sakes or just to hold people's interest) generally work against good liturgy. We must always remember that liturgy is given an essential ritual structure that has been tested through the centuries of tradition and this structure must be respected. It ensures that we are maximizing liturgy's purpose to make present the paschal mystery and that we are celebrating with the whole church.

About Liturgical Music

Change and liturgical music: The same principles given above about the pace of change in liturgical ritual apply to changes in liturgical music, but with some further comments that are specifically musical. First, we must always remember that music stands in a secondary, supporting role. Its purpose is to enable the assembly to surrender to the liturgical ritual. When we change the music too much or too often, we divert the assembly's energies from the ritual demands. We sidetrack the liturgy. When we change the music for its own sake, we give it a position that doesn't belong to it by making it primary. Again, we sidetrack the liturgy.

Second, the demands of the ritual are intense, and repetition and consistency in the music are meant to facilitate surrendering to these demands. For the average assembly this means introducing two or three new songs a year is enough. In a year when a new setting of the Mass is being introduced, that alone may be sufficient. Any change in service music or introduction of a new song must be related to the goal of enabling deeper participation in the rite, not to the mistaken goal of keeping people "entertained."

Honoring these principles takes discipline. New music should be introduced to support the assembly's liturgical and musical growth. But it is their growth (and the demands of the rite) which must dictate the changes, not the desire for novelty.

Music suggestion: Herman Stuempfle's "When Jesus Passed through Jericho" (HG) turns the story of Zacchaeus into our story. The text needs to be sung in a light storytelling fashion. The tune, the American folk melody DOVE OF PEACE, will probably be unfamiliar to most members of the assembly. Let alternating cantors sing verses 1-4, telling the story of Zacchaeus, then have the assembly join in for verses 5-6 when the story becomes theirs. The hymn would be very suitable either as a prelude or during the preparation of the gifts.

SPIRITUALITY

GOSPEL ACCLAMATION
Matt 11:28

℟. Alleluia, alleluia.
Come to me, all you who labor and are burdened,
and I will give you rest, says the Lord.
℟. Alleluia, alleluia.

Gospel

Matt 5:1-12a; L667

When Jesus saw
   the crowds, he
   went up the
   mountain,
and after he had
   sat down, his
   disciples came
   to him.
He began to teach
   them, saying:
"Blessed are the
    poor in spirit,
  for theirs is the King-
    dom of heaven.
Blessed are they who mourn,
  for they will be comforted.
Blessed are the meek,
  for they will inherit the land.
Blessed are they who hunger and thirst
   for righteousness,
  for they will be satisfied.
Blessed are the merciful,
  for they will be shown mercy.
Blessed are the clean of heart,
  for they will see God.
Blessed are the peacemakers,
  for they will be called children of God.
Blessed are they who are persecuted
   for the sake of righteousness,
  for theirs is the Kingdom of heaven.
Blessed are you when they insult you
   and persecute you
  and utter every kind of evil against
    you falsely because of me.
Rejoice and be glad,
  for your reward will be great in
    heaven."

See Appendix A, p. 312, for the other readings.

Reflecting on the Gospel

Few of us are satisfied with things the way they are. We want a better job with more income, a bigger house with lots of bathrooms (especially when the children hit the teens), more security about health care. And this is a good thing. Ambition, future-looking, desiring a better life spur us on, keep us from settling into the status quo, help us achieve more than just what is necessary. The Beatitudes can be a kind of wish list, a challenge to move us out of our spiritual status quo and a help for making not only a better life for ourselves, but also for others in our family, neighborhood, world. When we live the Beatitudes, we hasten a reversal of plight (for example, those "who mourn . . . will be comforted") and therefore are personally active in changing things, in helping others have what we have, in reaching for the kind of life Jesus taught. But moving forward is not easy. Not everyone will like our choices, our challenges, our upsetting the status quo. So, like Jesus we also will face insult and persecution that comes from having another vision for the way things can be.

Jesus "*began* to teach" his disciples the Beatitudes; "*began*" implies not over and finished, but an ongoing way of living for his followers. The Beatitudes are not an easily learned way of life, nor easily lived. Disciples' learning is not only in the hearing, but even more importantly in the daily living. Throughout their lives the saints faithfully opened themselves to the transforming action of Christ within them. This transforming action strengthened their identity as God's children (see second reading and gospel) and enabled them to embody the Beatitudes as their way of living. For us who share this same identity and way of living, our reward will not only be with the saints in heaven, but is already on earth: we are even now the blessed of God bathed in comfort, mercy, and peace. The paradox of the Beatitudes is that we already *are* what we try to live: those blessed by God.

The most telling mark of being children of God is that we are "blessed." This is *who* we are—those who belong to God, are loved by God, are raised up by God. The Beatitudes describe a way to live consistent with our identity as God's children immersed in Christ. In Christ, who we are and how we live come together as one. The saints we honor today are those who took Jesus' Beatitudes to heart and lived them well. They now dwell in the land of inheritance—"the Kingdom of heaven" where they "see God" and know the fullness of what it means to be called "blessed." Let us "Rejoice and be glad" with them on this, their feast day.

The saints stand out as models who give us courage and strength that we, too, can be faithful to the demands of the way of living the Beatitudes lay out for us. We know some saints by name (those who have been canonized). There are countless others (our deceased relatives and friends) whom we know by name in a different way. This multitude of faithful followers of Christ beckons us to hear what Jesus teaches in this gospel: "Blessed are [you] . . . your reward will be great in heaven."

Living the Paschal Mystery

At first glance the Beatitudes seem an impossible blueprint for Christian living; most of us aren't near at all to the ideal that they express. But nine times is the word "blessed" addressed to us. When our blessedness is our focus, then fidelity to our Gospel way of life is no ideal, but becomes a way of expressing who we are in Christ—blessed. The Beatitudes help us reach by our daily living beyond what is now to the eternal Life that is to come.

Focusing the Gospel

Key words and phrases: his disciples came to him, began to teach, Blessed are . . . , Kingdom of heaven, Rejoice and be glad

To the point: Jesus "*began* to teach" his disciples the Beatitudes, an ongoing way of living for his followers. Disciples' learning is not only in the hearing, but even more importantly in the daily living. The saints we honor today are those who took Jesus' Beatitudes to heart and lived them well. They now dwell in the land of inheritance—"the Kingdom of heaven" where they "see God" and know the fullness of what it means to be called "blessed." Let us "Rejoice and be glad" with them on this, their feast day.

Model Rite for the Blessing and Sprinkling of Water

Presider: Dear friends, this water reminds us of our baptism when we were blessed by God and made children of God. May we remain faithful to our baptismal promises as were the saints whom we honor today . . . [pause]

[*continue with* The Roman Missal, *Appendix II*]

Model Universal Prayer (Prayer of the Faithful)

Presider: Let us make known our needs to God who bestows blessedness upon us.

Response:

Cantor:

That all members of the church faithfully learn and live Jesus' way of life . . . [pause]

That all peoples respond to God's call to blessedness and express it in loving service to others . . . [pause]

That those who are poor be cared for, those who are mourning be comforted, those who are hungry be filled . . . [pause]

That each of us here rejoice with the saints in heaven and, like them, come to the fullness of blessedness . . . [pause]

Presider: Loving God, you receive the praise of the angels and saints who dwell with you in eternal glory. Through their intercession hear these our prayers that one day we might share in the fullness of everlasting blessedness. We pray through Jesus Christ our Lord. **Amen.**

FOR REFLECTION

- To be taught the Beatitudes as an ongoing way of living challenges me to . . . comforts me in that . . .

- I see God even now in . . . through . . . by . . . To be called "blessed" means to me . . .

- The impact the saints have on my daily living the Beatitudes is . . .

Homily Points

- Self-discovery and self-knowledge are lifelong processes of growth. When the Beatitudes are central to our self-understanding, our life and learning unfold in a particular way—living as Jesus did, seeing as Jesus did, coming to the fullness of Life as Jesus did. The saints we honor this day embraced well this process of living and learning.

- The saints were ordinary people like us who took Jesus' teaching to heart and lived it with fidelity. Now they dwell in the land of inheritance—"the Kingdom of heaven." Now they continue their living the Beatitudes by witnessing for us the blessedness God bestows. Now they intercede for us, that we might imitate their lives of holiness. Now they are beacons of hope for us still on the journey of living and learning the Beatitudes. Now we rejoice and are glad in them.

SPIRITUALITY

This is the will of my Father, says the Lord,
that everyone who sees the Son and believes in
  him
may have eternal life.

Gospel

John 6:37-40; L668

Jesus said to the crowds:
  "Everything that the Father gives me
    will come to me,
  and I will not reject anyone who
    comes to me,
  because I came down from heaven
    not to do my own will
  but the will of the one who sent me.
And this is the will of the one who sent
    me,
  that I should not lose anything of
    what he gave me,
  but that I should raise it on the last
    day.
For this is the will of my Father,
  that everyone who sees the Son and
    believes in him
  may have eternal life,
  and I shall raise him on the last day."

See Appendix A, p. 313, for the other readings.

*Other readings in L668 may be chosen or those
given in the Masses for the Dead, L1011–1016.*

Reflecting on the Gospel

Jesus' comforting words in this gospel capture well the meaning of what we celebrate this day: "that I should not lose anything of what [the Father] gave me, / but that I should raise it on the last day." The souls in purgatory are not lost; they lived their lives believing in Jesus, though imperfectly. They await what is already granted them: "eternal life." Our prayers hasten for them "the last day." Our prayers also help us to stay in a kind of direct contact with our beloved departed. They help us not forget. They help us remember why we love them. Why they inspired us. What they taught us. What they learned from us. How they encouraged us. How they challenged us. Who they are for us. Who they are now as they rest in God.

This festival commemorating the faithful departed is a popular one among many people. It is also comforting, reassuring, and hope-filled. It is comforting in that Jesus rejects no one the Father has given to him (see gospel) and raises to new life those who have been buried with him in baptism (see second reading). It is reassuring in that "the just are in the hand of God" (first reading). It is hope-filled because it "is the will of [the] Father" that anyone who believes in Jesus will "have eternal life" (gospel). We celebrate this festival confident of the Good News that our beloved faithful departed are within the embrace of God.

These souls that we commemorate today are not damned in hell; they have remained faithful to their baptismal promises and so also have the promise of eternal glory. No doubt our scriptural image of purifying fires (how we have come to image the soul's time in purgatory) has roused our piety and prompted us to pray for the poor souls. In addition to the purifying benefits of such prayers for the faithful departed, there may be benefits for ourselves as well. Certainly, remembering our departed loved ones in our prayers is an admirable way for us to keep them close to us. We might even suggest that praying for the dead (and to the dead) is an important part of the grieving process—just as we grew in our relationships with our loved ones during their lifetime, so do we continue to deepen our love for them as we remember them in prayer after their death. Praying for the dead reminds us that death isn't an end but a beginning of a new Life. Our prayers can be a concrete expression of our belief in everlasting life.

The only thing that can separate anyone from Christ and sharing in everlasting Life is to refuse to follow Jesus into his death. Our deceased loved ones are awaiting the fullness of Life with Jesus. This festival reminds us to be faithful in our own call to follow Jesus so that one day we will share in his fullness of Life. It's not death that is the worst of things; it's being separated from Jesus that is the worst thing.

Living the Paschal Mystery

Following Jesus means being willing to enter into his death; this is the only way to share in Jesus' eternal glory. Although November 2 and all of the month of November have been the church's time for commemorating the faithful departed, we would do well to remember the deceased throughout the year because they are constant reminders that death leads to life. It might be good practice in our gospel living to keep Fridays not only as days of penance, but also regularly to pray on this day for the faithful departed. This is a kind of Gospel ministry—that we never forget those who have touched our lives and whom we have loved and who have loved us.

Focusing the Gospel

Key words and phrases: Father gives me, I should not lose, raise it on the last day, eternal life

To the point: Jesus' comforting words in this gospel capture well the meaning of what we celebrate this day: "that I should not lose anything of what [the Father] gave me, / but that I should raise it on the last day." The souls in purgatory are not lost; they lived their lives believing in Jesus, though imperfectly. They await what is already granted them: "eternal life." Our prayers hasten for them "the last day."

Model Penitential Act

Presider: We gather today to pray for the faithful departed. Let us open ourselves to the Good News that Jesus who has conquered death will raise up on the last day those who are faithful . . . [pause]

Lord Jesus, you overcome death by your death on the cross: Lord . . .

Christ Jesus, you are raised to new Life with your Father: Christ . . .

Lord Jesus, you reject no one who comes to you: Lord . . .

Model Universal Prayer (Prayer of the Faithful)

Presider: Through our prayer and intercession let us ask God to be merciful to the faithful departed.

Response:

Lord, hear our prayer.

Cantor:

we pray to the Lord,

For all members of the church, that they may find comfort in Jesus' promise of fullness of Life for the faithful departed . . . [pause]

For all people of the world, that they may come to salvation in God . . . [pause]

For those who have died and have no one to pray for them . . . [pause]

For each of us here gathered, that our prayers for the faithful departed bring us to greater belief and hope . . . [pause]

Presider: Merciful God, you lead us from death to eternal Life. Grant our prayers that the faithful departed might have eternal rest and we might one day rejoice with them in the fullness of Life. We ask this through Christ our Lord. **Amen.**

Let us pray.

Pause for silent prayer

Listen kindly to our prayers, O Lord,
and, as our faith in your Son,
raised from the dead, is deepened,
so may our hope of resurrection for your
    departed servants
also find new strength.
Through our Lord Jesus Christ, your Son,
who lives and reigns with you in the unity
    of the Holy Spirit,
one God, for ever and ever. **Amen.**

FOR REFLECTION

• I pray for the dead because . . . What is comforting for me about praying for the dead is . . .

• Believing in Jesus is lived by . . .

• What gives me hope that one day I will be with Jesus forever in "eternal life" is . . .

Homily Points

• Cemeteries are places of quiet, reflection, and peace. We have great respect for the dead. While their earthly remains are here, our visits and prayers include the hope that they are alive with God. The gospel teaches that this is the will of the Father: that Jesus "not lose anything of what he gave me, / but that I should raise it on the last day."

• The will of the Father for us in this life is to see the Son and believe in him. We do so by the goodness of our lives. It is also the will of the Father that we "have eternal life" and be raised up "on the last day." The will of the Father is the total restoration of life, returning us to the goodness at the beginning of creation. Thus the end is, in fact, a return to the beginning. The souls in purgatory have completed their life on this earth; they are preparing for their return to the beginning, their return to the fullness of goodness, their return to being perfect images of God in whom they were created.

SPIRITUALITY

℟. Alleluia, alleluia.
Jesus Christ is the firstborn of the dead;
to him be glory and power, forever and ever.
℟. Alleluia, alleluia.

Gospel
Luke 20:27-38; L156C

Some Sadducees, those who deny
    that there is a resurrection,
came forward and put this
        question to Jesus, saying,
"Teacher, Moses wrote for us,
*If someone's brother dies leaving a
    wife but no child,*
his brother must take the wife
and raise up descendants for his brother.
Now there were seven brothers;
    the first married a woman but
        died childless.
Then the second and the third married
    her,
and likewise all the seven died childless.
Finally the woman also died.
Now at the resurrection whose wife will
    that woman be?
For all seven had been married to her."
Jesus said to them,
    "The children of this age marry and
        remarry;
    but those who are deemed worthy to
        attain to the coming age
    and to the resurrection of the dead
    neither marry nor are given in marriage.
They can no longer die,
    for they are like angels;
    and they are the children of God
    because they are the ones who will rise.
That the dead will rise
    even Moses made known in the passage
        about the bush,
    when he called out 'Lord,'
    the God of Abraham, the God of Isaac,
        and the God of Jacob;
    and he is not God of the dead, but of the
        living,
    for to him all are alive."

or Luke 20:27, 34-38 in Appendix A, p. 314.

Reflecting on the Gospel
How ridiculous we can be sometimes when we argue an untenable position! Children might argue that ice cream makes them strong. Teens might argue that drugs help them feel alive. Adults might argue that cheating on their tax return is just keeping Uncle Sam from wasting their money. Taken to extremes, this way of persuasion is *reductio ad absurdum*—arguments showing a position cannot be true by showing its implications are not tenable. In this gospel Luke presents us with an altercation between Jesus and the Sadducees about life after death. This is an interesting *reductio ad absurdum*. By having seven brothers all marry the same woman and die in succession, the Sadducees are trying to show that the very concept of life after death is absurd. How wrong they are!

Jesus has arrived in Jerusalem, facing his own imminent death and resurrection. Already in Luke's gospel Jesus has predicted his death and resurrection (Luke 9:22; 9:44; 18:32-33). Resurrection is not simply coming back to this life; it is the eternal fullness of Life. For the Sadducees, one's immortality was contingent on having progeny (see, for example, Deut 25:5-6; Gen 38:8), the tradition and context of their argument about marrying and remarrying taken to extremes. Jesus answers them by asserting that there is no marriage and remarriage in heaven because there is no dying in heaven. In heaven, "all are alive," in perfect union with God. The proof of Jesus' truth is his own resurrection, his own perfect union with his Father. The promise of Jesus' truth is our resurrection, our perfect union with God, our eternal fullness of Life.

Belief in the resurrection brings us to encounter the God "of the living," for whom "all are alive." We cannot argue eternal Life because it is beyond our experience. We cannot argue eternal Life because it is mystery, promise, gift. The basis for this belief is *hope*. Although hope always has a future orientation about it, when we have confidence in God's grace to bring about change in us, when we have patience with ourselves while that change comes about, we already have something of the future in the present—we already are living this new, risen Life which is characterized by faithful relationship with God, union with God. The union enabled by risen Life is that of being "children of God" in an everlasting relationship with the living God. This is the core of our hope, borne out by the daily choices we make to be faithful followers of Jesus.

Living the Paschal Mystery
Paschal mystery living means that we live this life in a way that infuses it with the Life that is to come. The dying part of the mystery always reminds us that suffering and death pale in comparison to the categorically new Life that God offers us in Christ.

When we faithfully live our Christian life, like the brothers in the first reading we will meet with controversy. In fact, controversy may be a sign of integrity since truly living the Gospel always precipitates conflict, because Gospel values are so contrary to human selfishness and pride. This doesn't mean that we go out looking for controversy; it does mean that when controversy happens because of the authenticity of our Christian living, we see through the controversy with hope for eternal Life. This hope is what gives us the courage of our convictions and helps us remain steadfast even to death. And through death to resurrection.

Focusing the Gospel

Key words and phrases: Sadducees . . . deny . . . resurrection, attain . . . the resurrection of the dead, neither marry nor are given in marriage, can no longer die, all are alive

To the point: In this gospel Luke presents us with an altercation between Jesus and the Sadducees about life after death. Jesus has arrived in Jerusalem, facing his own imminent death and resurrection. For the Sadducees, one's immortality was contingent on having progeny, the tradition and context of their argument about marrying and remarrying taken to extremes. Jesus answers them by asserting that there is no marriage and remarriage in heaven because there is no dying in heaven. In heaven, "all are alive," in perfect union with God. The proof of Jesus' truth is his own resurrection, his own perfect union with his Father. The promise of Jesus' truth is our resurrection, our perfect union with God.

Connecting the Gospel

to the first reading: In the first reading the seventh son before he dies proclaims his belief and hope that God will raise him from death to life. Jesus proclaims in the gospel that those "deemed worthy" will "attain to the coming age / and to the resurrection of the dead."

to experience: The death of a loved one is an occasion when our thoughts consciously turn to the hope of life after death. The readings this Sunday reassure us that this hope in new life after death stands on the word of Jesus who is the first One risen from the dead.

Connecting the Responsorial Psalm

to the readings: On this Sunday when the church begins to focus on the end times and the Second Coming of Christ, both the first reading and the gospel speak directly of God's promise to raise the just to new Life after death. The martyred brothers in the first reading remain faithful to the covenant even to death, for they believe that the Giver of life and limb will never take back what has been bestowed. Jesus in the gospel asserts "the dead will rise," for God is God "of the living."

Like the brothers, Jesus knows that he will be put to death for remaining faithful to the call of God. In the responsorial psalm we align ourselves with these brothers and with Jesus. We state our hope that on "waking" from death we shall find ourselves in the Presence of God. And we make our commitment that we will remain "steadfast in [the] paths" of discipleship. As we celebrate this Eucharist and sing this psalm, we look to the glory of Christ to come and know that we shall share in that glory just as we have shared in its price.

to psalmist preparation: In this responsorial psalm you proclaim your faith in God's promise of eternal Life and your choice to remain faithful to discipleship no matter what it costs. This is no small thing considering the cost will be your life. What conversation might you have with Christ this week to give you courage and strengthen your hope?

ASSEMBLY & FAITH-SHARING GROUPS

- I am confident in Jesus' promise of Life after death when . . . I struggle with belief in everlasting Life when . . .
- I am most alive and in union with God when I . . .
- My belief in being raised from the dead makes a difference in my daily living in that . . .

PRESIDERS

I am inspired to preach about the resurrection when . . . This preaching helps my assembly to . . .

DEACONS

In my serving others, my belief in eternal Life gives them hope in that . . .

HOSPITALITY MINISTERS

My belief in God's promise of risen Life shapes my hospitality ministry when I . . .

MUSIC MINISTERS

My music ministry is a foretaste of risen Life when . . .

ALTAR MINISTERS

My faithful service expresses my belief in God's promise of everlasting Life in that . . .

LECTORS

The radical fidelity of the brothers in the first reading challenges me to . . .

EXTRAORDINARY MINISTERS OF HOLY COMMUNION

The manner of my distributing Holy Communion helps others realize that they are participating in the new Life Jesus brings when . . .

Model Penitential Act

Presider: In today's gospel Jesus reveals his Father to be the God of the living who leads us through death to risen Life. As we prepare to celebrate this liturgy, let us ask God's mercy for the times we have failed to trust where God is leading us . . . [pause]

Lord Jesus, you are the God of the living: Lord . . .

Christ Jesus, you proclaim hope in eternal Life: Christ . . .

Lord Jesus, you promise your faithful ones a share in your risen Life: Lord . . .

Homily Points

• The trauma and loss after a beloved one dies is palpable. Time eases the pain, and helps us come to a new sense of presence of our beloved one. This sense of presence—not only of our beloved dead but also of the risen Jesus himself—is our certain assurance that Jesus' words of promise of a share in his risen Life are not mere words, but divine truth.

• This gospel teaches that there is life after death. By sharing in Jesus' death and resurrection, we will one day share in perfect union with God. In "this age" marriage is a process of moving toward perfect union. It is a commitment to a life of human fidelity. In "the coming age" risen Life is entrance into perfect union with God and all the angels and saints in heaven. It is a fulfillment of divine fidelity.

• Most of us do not think very often about rising from the dead—it is challenging enough each morning to rise from bed! Yet, even rising from bed every morning out of fidelity to living Jesus' Good News is an act of faith in the resurrection. This, because fidelity in our everyday tasks and relationships is how we are true followers of Jesus seeking union with God. The union we have with God in "this age" leads to our perfect union with God in "the coming age."

Model Universal Prayer (Prayer of the Faithful)

Presider: Let us make our needs known to God who faithfully hears us and answers our prayers.

Response:

Lord, hear our prayer.

Cantor:

we pray to the Lord,

That all members of the church show by their manner of living that they are seeking perfect union with God . . . [pause]

That all people of the world come to peaceful union with one another and perfect union with God . . . [pause]

That those who live without hope in this life find solace in Jesus' words of eternal Life . . . [pause]

That each of us faithfully follow Jesus' lead through death to eternal Life . . . [pause]

Presider: Saving God, your Son Jesus taught us to believe and hope in the resurrection of the dead. Hear these our prayers that one day we might enjoy perfect union with you in everlasting Life. We ask this through Christ our Lord. **Amen.**

Let us pray.

Pause for silent prayer

Almighty and merciful God,
graciously keep from us all adversity,
so that, unhindered in mind and body alike,
we may pursue in freedom of heart
the things that are yours.
Through our Lord Jesus Christ, your Son,
who lives and reigns with you in the unity of the Holy Spirit,
one God, for ever and ever. **Amen.**

FIRST READING 2 Macc 7:1-2, 9-14

It happened that seven brothers with their mother were arrested
and tortured with whips and scourges by the king,
to force them to eat pork in violation of God's law.
One of the brothers, speaking for the others, said:
"What do you expect to achieve by questioning us?
We are ready to die rather than transgress the laws of our ancestors."

At the point of death he said:
"You accursed fiend, you are depriving us of this present life,
but the King of the world will raise us up to live again forever.
It is for his laws that we are dying."

After him the third suffered their cruel sport.
He put out his tongue at once when told to do so,
and bravely held out his hands, as he spoke these noble words:
"It was from Heaven that I received these;
for the sake of his laws I disdain them;
from him I hope to receive them again."
Even the king and his attendants marveled at the young man's courage,
because he regarded his sufferings as nothing.

After he had died,
they tortured and maltreated the fourth brother in the same way.
When he was near death, he said,
"It is my choice to die at the hands of men
with the hope God gives of being raised up by him;
but for you, there will be no resurrection to life."

RESPONSORIAL PSALM
Ps 17:1, 5-6, 8, 15

R̸. (15b) Lord, when your glory appears,
my joy will be full.

Hear, O LORD, a just suit;
    attend to my outcry;
    hearken to my prayer from lips without
        deceit.

R̸. Lord, when your glory appears, my joy
will be full.

My steps have been steadfast in your
        paths,
    my feet have not faltered.
I call upon you, for you will answer me,
        O God;
    incline your ear to me; hear my word.

R̸. Lord, when your glory appears, my joy
will be full.

Keep me as the apple of your eye,
    hide me in the shadow of your wings.
But I in justice shall behold your face;
    on waking I shall be content in your
        presence.

R̸. Lord, when your glory appears, my joy
will be full.

SECOND READING
2 Thess 2:16–3:5

Brothers and sisters:
May our Lord Jesus Christ himself and
        God our Father,
    who has loved us and given us
        everlasting encouragement
    and good hope through his grace,
    encourage your hearts and strengthen
        them in every good deed and word.

Finally, brothers and sisters, pray for us,
    so that the word of the Lord may speed
        forward and be glorified,
    as it did among you,
    and that we may be delivered from
        perverse and wicked people,
    for not all have faith.
But the Lord is faithful;
    he will strengthen you and guard you
        from the evil one.
We are confident of you in the Lord that
    what we instruct you,
    you are doing and will continue to do.
May the Lord direct your hearts to the love
    of God
    and to the endurance of Christ.

About Liturgy

Resurrection of the dead: Easter, of course, is the prime time of the year when we think about Jesus' resurrection from the dead. The end of the liturgical year, when the liturgy invites us to look to the *Parousia* or Christ's Second Coming, is another time when we think of resurrection and this time as it also applies to ourselves. Our own hope in resurrection, naturally, is based on Jesus' being raised from the dead to risen Life. To put this another way (and perhaps make it a bit more concrete and easy to grasp): in his resurrection Jesus was taken into eternity by his Father. Resurrection, then, is less a mystery and more a statement of belief that what happened to Jesus will happen to his faithful disciples as well—we will one day be with God in eternal glory.

Each time we recite a creed we include a statement of our belief in the resurrection from the dead. This is a doctrine that we Christians have held since apostolic times. Moreover, it is more than belief that the soul will live forever; we also believe that at the general resurrection at Christ's Second Coming somehow our bodies will also be united with our souls. Just as Jesus' glorified body was different from his body before the resurrection (he could go through doors, was not immediately recognized, etc.), so will our glorified bodies be different from these, our earthly bodies.

Resurrection and cremation: In the past the church disallowed cremation in view of the resurrection of the body. Now the church allows cremation so long as it isn't chosen out of disbelief in the resurrection of the body. Under all circumstances the church wants to preserve dignity for our earthly bodies since they have been created by God and are holy. Similar to Mary, our bodies have been temples of the Holy Spirit.

About Liturgical Music

Music suggestions: The readings and psalm this Sunday speak of hope in the resurrection, but also of the challenge to be faithful to the demands of discipleship. Both Jeremy Young's "We Shall Rise Again" (G3, LMGM2) and David Haas's "We Will Rise Again" (BB, JS3) speak of the dangers and weariness of faithful discipleship and God's promise of resurrection. These verse-refrain songs would work well during the Communion procession. Another excellent choice for Communion would be Steven Warner's "Come, All You Blessed Ones" (OF, WC, WS) which combines a refrain about the promise of eternal joy with verses based on Psalm 23 and Psalm 34. "Swing Low, Sweet Chariot" (LMGM2) would be a good choice during the preparation of the gifts. "Good News! [the chariot's coming]" (LMGM2) would make an excellent prelude or a rousing recessional. Another rousing recessional would be Janet Vogt's "Rise Up with Him" (BB).

SPIRITUALITY

GOSPEL ACCLAMATION
Luke 21:28

R⁊. Alleluia, alleluia.
Stand erect and raise your heads
because your redemption is at hand.
R⁊. Alleluia, alleluia.

Gospel
Luke 21:5-19; L159C

While some people were
    speaking about
    how the temple was
        adorned with
        costly stones and
        votive offerings,
Jesus said, "All that you see
        here—
    the days will come when there
        will not be left
    a stone upon another stone that
        will not be thrown down."

Then they asked him,
    "Teacher, when will this happen?
And what sign will there be when all
    these things are about to happen?"
He answered,
"See that you not be deceived,
    for many will come in my name,
        saying,
    'I am he,' and 'The time has come.'
Do not follow them!
When you hear of wars and
    insurrections,
    do not be terrified; for such things
        must happen first,
    but it will not immediately be the
        end."
Then he said to them,
    "Nation will rise against nation, and
        kingdom against kingdom.
There will be powerful earthquakes,
    famines, and plagues
    from place to place;
    and awesome sights and mighty signs
        will come from the sky.

Continued in Appendix A, p. 314.

Reflecting on the Gospel

Before time existed, there was no beginning. "[T]he earth was without form or shape, with darkness over the abyss" (Gen 1:2). There was nothing. Except God. God was all. Then there was a beginning. There was creation. And it was "very good" (Gen 1:31). From the beginning of creation God desired an intimate, loving relationship with humanity and all of creation. God would walk "in the garden at the breezy time of the day" (Gen 3:8). Yet, humankind chose and continues to choose to be unfaithful, thwarting the beauty and dignity of what God intended for creation. "Nation will rise against nation," evil people will "seize and persecute" the faithful, some will be put "to death" and "hated." We choose infidelity, chaos, violence, evil, hatred. Because of our sinful choices, all creation has been marred. All creation has become something less than God intended at the beginning of creation.

At the end of time, all creation as we know it will cease to be. But instead of returning to a dark void, those who are faithful will rise to eternal Light and will secure their eternal Life. What happens at the end of time will be a reversal of what took place at the beginning of time. Then, all things were created. At the end of time, all things cease to be. Except God. And those who are faithful who will be united with God.

We might ask, then, what will be so different at the end times? In one sense every day is already the beginning of the end time. Every choice we make has to do with how we will be at the end of time. The signs we observe of human calamities bid us to testify to all that Jesus taught us— that there is more to life than we can see. We must live faithfully *now*. By our perseverance as faithful followers testifying to Jesus' name we secure everlasting Life. Every day is an opportunity to live discipleship fully and confidently. Every day is an opportunity to grow in our relationship with Jesus, the One who promises Life to his faithful ones.

In the beginning, all things came to be. At the end, things as we know them will cease to be. Does anything really last forever? Certainly not temples, not nations, not even the foundations of the earth. So, what does last forever? God, the wisdom of Jesus, divine Life. And, yes, the lives of those who persevere in fidelity to the name and mission of Jesus and who "will secure" a share in divine Life. At the end . . . a new beginning.

Living the Paschal Mystery

The signs of the end of time alert us to the fact that our striving to be faithful disciples has *cosmic* proportions. Living the paschal mystery doesn't just have consequences for ourselves, but also for all others. When we break out of a chronological understanding of time (that is, time as duration with past, present, and future) and break into God's eternal time (time without duration in which everything just *is*), we can begin to understand how even the little acts of kindness and self-sacrifice we perform each day affect all that is. Our unity with Jesus is deepened by striving to care for others, help others, shower others with dignity and respect.

Here is a sobering thought: the way we care for the children, are honest at the workplace, take leisure time to care for ourselves affects our whole world and everyone in it. This is the privilege of discipleship: we can make a difference! This is the effect of faithful discipleship: the world is a better place—we have readied it for Christ's Second Coming at the end of time by our faithful and grace-filled living *now*.

Focusing the Gospel

Key words and phrases: not be left / a stone upon another stone, Nation will rise against nation, powerful earthquakes, my name, I shall give you a wisdom, perseverance, secure your lives

To the point: In the beginning, all things came to be. At the end, things as we know them will cease to be. Does anything really last forever? Certainly not temples, not nations, not even the foundations of the earth. So, what does last forever? God, the wisdom of Jesus, divine Life. And, yes, the lives of those who persevere in fidelity to the name and mission of Jesus and who "will secure" a share in divine Life. At the end . . . a new beginning.

Connecting the Gospel

to the first reading: The end of all things as described in both the gospel and first reading includes the destruction of evil by "the sun of justice." Truly the end is a new beginning for those who "fear my name."

to experience: There are certain things we wish would last forever: a first kiss, a riveting book, a memorable vacation. What God promises is far greater than any of these fetching but fleeting experiences: a share in divine Life for those who are faithful.

Connecting the Responsorial Psalm

to the readings: In the context of this Sunday's first reading and gospel, Psalm 98 is a statement of absolute certainty that the power of Christ will prevail over the forces of evil. We need not lose heart when wars, insurrections, earthquakes, famines arise. We need not be surprised when fidelity to discipleship brings persecution. Even amidst the direst evil, the vision we maintain is of Christ's final coming and victory. And so we sing, blow trumpets, clap hands, and shout for joy, for we know the Lord is coming to rule with justice.

to psalmist preparation: When you sing this responsorial psalm, you stand before the assembly testifying to a vision of the future in which God reigns with justice. Do you believe in this future? Are you looking for it? Will you stake your life on it?

ASSEMBLY & FAITH-SHARING GROUPS

- My most important beginning has been . . . My most important ending has been . . .
- To "secure" my life, I think I must . . . Jesus tells me I must . . .
- What gives me the strength to persevere in fidelity to Jesus' name is . . .

PRESIDERS

When I call on the wisdom of Jesus, my preaching becomes . . .

DEACONS

To those troubled and burdened, my ministry embodies "the sun of justice with its healing rays" (first reading) when I . . .

HOSPITALITY MINISTERS

The manner of my greeting helps those gathering for liturgy to renew their fidelity to the mission of Jesus when I . . .

MUSIC MINISTERS

My music ministry calls me to persevere in discipleship by . . . This makes a difference in my ministry in that . . .

ALTAR MINISTERS

My serving the liturgy strengthens my perseverance in fidelity when . . .

LECTORS

That Jesus promised "a wisdom in speaking" to those who are faithful, makes my proclamation . . .

EXTRAORDINARY MINISTERS OF HOLY COMMUNION

Holy Communion is a foretaste of the time to come in that . . .

Model Penitential Act

Presider: In today's gospel Jesus calls us to turn our attention from the things of this world that will end to the fidelity to his name that secures for us eternal Life. Let us beg God's mercy for the times we have been unfaithful . . . [pause]

Lord Jesus, you come to rule the world with justice: Lord . . .

Christ Jesus, you give us your wisdom and strength: Christ . . .

Lord Jesus, you secure for us eternal Life: Lord . . .

Homily Points

• We tend in everyday living to become mired in what is immediate, tangible, satisfies our present needs. The gospel challenges us to think beyond the present to what really is critical for us: the end of time and the life we do or do not secure for ourselves. Our whole life is a choice about end times.

• This Sunday is a reminder that we secure our Life at the end of time through fidelity to Jesus' name in the present time. Only the irrefutable and irresistible wisdom of Jesus gives us the strength and courage to be faithful to the end. Through our perseverance we discover that what we thought was the end is really a new beginning: God's gift of eternal Life to those who are faithful.

• *Every* choice we make now bears import for our eternal future. Each choice to be faithful to Jesus' name is a new beginning—a deepening of discipleship, a growth in wisdom, a strengthening of unselfish love, a fuller bonding in the Body of Christ, a realization of Jesus' saving mission. Each choice to be faithful stretches us toward the final new beginning: fullness of Life in God.

Model Universal Prayer (Prayer of the Faithful)

Presider: Let us pray for strength and perseverance to be faithful followers of Jesus to the end of time.

Response:

Lord, hear our prayer.

Cantor:

we pray to the Lord,

That all members of the church may grow in the wisdom of Jesus and persevere in fidelity to his name . . . [pause]

That all peoples of the world secure their salvation through fidelity to God's plan for them . . . [pause]

That those who now live in need have the faith to look to the end time when all needs will be fulfilled by God . . . [pause]

That all of us here embrace each day as a new beginning, making choices that will secure for us eternal Life . . . [pause]

Presider: God of the beginning and the end, you will fulfill your promise of the fullness of Life to those who remain faithful. Hear these our prayers and strengthen us to persevere as your Son's followers so that one day we might live forever with you. Through Christ our Lord. **Amen.**

COLLECT

Let us pray.

Pause for silent prayer

Grant us, we pray, O Lord our God,
the constant gladness of being devoted
    to you,
for it is full and lasting happiness
to serve with constancy
the author of all that is good.
Through our Lord Jesus Christ, your Son,
who lives and reigns with you in the unity
    of the Holy Spirit,
one God, for ever and ever. **Amen.**

FIRST READING
Mal 3:19-20a

Lo, the day is coming, blazing like an oven,
    when all the proud and all evildoers will
        be stubble,
and the day that is coming will set them
    on fire,
    leaving them neither root nor branch,
    says the LORD of hosts.
But for you who fear my name, there will
    arise
    the sun of justice with its healing rays.

RESPONSORIAL PSALM
Ps 98:5-6, 7-8, 9

℟. (cf. 9) The Lord comes to rule the earth with justice.

Sing praise to the LORD with the harp,
   with the harp and melodious song.
With trumpets and the sound of the horn
   sing joyfully before the King, the LORD.

℟. The Lord comes to rule the earth with justice.

Let the sea and what fills it resound,
   the world and those who dwell in it;
let the rivers clap their hands,
   the mountains shout with them for joy.

℟. The Lord comes to rule the earth with justice.

Before the LORD, for he comes,
   for he comes to rule the earth;
he will rule the world with justice
   and the peoples with equity.

℟. The Lord comes to rule the earth with justice.

SECOND READING
2 Thess 3:7-12

Brothers and sisters:
You know how one must imitate us.
For we did not act in a disorderly way
   among you,
   nor did we eat food received free from
      anyone.
On the contrary, in toil and drudgery,
   night and day
   we worked, so as not to burden any of
      you.
Not that we do not have the right.
Rather, we wanted to present ourselves as
   a model for you,
   so that you might imitate us.
In fact, when we were with you,
   we instructed you that if anyone was
      unwilling to work,
   neither should that one eat.
We hear that some are conducting
   themselves among you in a disorderly
   way,
   by not keeping busy but minding the
      business of others.
Such people we instruct and urge in the
   Lord Jesus Christ to work quietly
   and to eat their own food.

About Liturgy

Ministry of the assembly: When we speak about cosmic dimensions of our discipleship (as in the spirituality focus, Living the Paschal Mystery), it seems a bit too much for us to grasp. A reflection on the ministry of the assembly might help us make this more concrete.

When we think of "liturgical ministries" we usually think of the visible ministries, for example, hospitality ministers, lectors, altar ministers, and so on. We can easily lose sight of an important ministry that has no "assignment sheet": the ministry of the assembly, a ministry we all share each time we gather. The basic ministry of the assembly is to make visible the church, members united with our Head. This is how we can begin to grasp the cosmic dimension of our discipleship: we are never acting alone, but always as *church*.

Jesus promised that where two or three are gathered *in his name*, he is present. What is key here is not just the gathering, but the gathering *in his name*. When we gather as liturgical assembly, we unite the various members of Christ's Body with the Head. The very idea of gathering, then, is an expression of who we are: the Body of Christ. All ministry is from the body to the Body.

When we absent ourselves from the assembly without good reason, we make a difference in how the Body is manifested. In other words, coming together for liturgical prayer is far more than fulfilling an obligation. The liturgical assembly bids us to surrender ourselves to the transforming action of the liturgy. This generous self-giving is the first step in faithful discipleship and is what church is really all about. It is necessary in order for church to be concretely and most assuredly visible. It is necessary if the Body of Christ is to be built up, to come to full stature. Our presence in and to the assembly is indispensable, for we are all members of the church, the one Body. When the membership of the liturgical assembly is diminished, the Body is diminished. Our presence makes a difference. It is the first expression of faithful discipleship. It is a concrete expression of the cosmic dimension of faithful discipleship—Jesus' kingdom is present through the whole world throughout all times because we (all of us) gather.

About Liturgical Music

Music suggestions: In "How Can I Keep from Singing" (found in most resources) we sing of the "new creation" to come at the end of time, and proclaim that no tempests or tumults can "shake" the "inmost calm" we feel because "Love is Lord of heaven and earth." This song would make an appropriate response to the gospel during the preparation of the gifts. In "Only This I Want" (BB, G3, JS3) we sing our choice to persevere in discipleship that we may "win the prize of the kingdom of my Lord," and "shine like stars in the darkness of the night." This song would also make a reflective response to the gospel during the preparation of the gifts. In "God Is Working His Purpose Out" (W4) we proclaim that God is working in human history and that one day "the earth shall be filled with the glory of God As the waters cover the sea." The canonic repetition of the melody in the bass line intensifies this hymn's forward movement and the chromatic rise in the final phrase captures our hope about the future God has in store for us. This would work well as a recessional hymn. In "Let Heaven Rejoice" (BB, JS3) we call heaven, earth, and all creation to sing and dance before the Lord who has risen from the dead and will one day come in glory. This song would also make a fitting recessional.

✠ SPIRITUALITY

GOSPEL ACCLAMATION
Mark 11:9, 10

R/. Alleluia, alleluia.
Blessed is he who comes in the name
of the Lord!
Blessed is the kingdom of our father
David that is to come!
R/. Alleluia, alleluia.

Gospel

Luke 23:35-43; L162C

The rulers sneered at Jesus and
said,
"He saved others, let him save
himself
if he is the chosen one, the
Christ of God."
Even the soldiers jeered at him.
As they approached to offer him
wine they called out,
"If you are King of the Jews, save
yourself."
Above him there was an inscription
that read,
"This is the King of the Jews."

Now one of the criminals hanging there
reviled Jesus, saying,
"Are you not the Christ?
Save yourself and us."
The other, however, rebuking him, said
in reply,
"Have you no fear of God,
for you are subject to the same
condemnation?
And indeed, we have been condemned
justly,
for the sentence we received
corresponds to our crimes,
but this man has done nothing
criminal."
Then he said,
"Jesus, remember me when you come
into your kingdom."
He replied to him,
"Amen, I say to you,
today you will be with me in
Paradise."

Reflecting on the Gospel

Illness tends to make people grumpy. When we don't feel good, we naturally turn inward upon ourselves. We want this to be over. We want to feel good again and get on with the tasks and challenges at hand. Prolonged illness keeps some people grumpy all the time, while a surprising number of other people seem to be able to rise above their pain and distress and, sometimes even because of it, reach out to others. Jesus, in this Sunday's gospel, is hanging on a cross. He is in much pain and distress. He's being "sneered at." He's being "jeered." He's being "reviled." Was Jesus grumpy and turned inward upon himself? No!

Three hang on crosses, suffering and dying. One reviles, one begs for salvation, One promises Paradise. Indeed, only One *can* promise Paradise. Who but "the Christ of God" could make such a promise? Who but a divine King could reach beyond his own suffering and dying to bestow Life on another? Who but One totally innocent of evil could draw goodness out of one who is "condemned justly"? Three hang on crosses. One remains condemned. One is redeemed. One will rise from the dead, King of the universe.

Although Jesus' kingdom is established from the very beginning of creation (see second reading) and through the Davidic kingship (see the first reading), his reign is not one of power but of mercy, not one of self-service but of self-giving, not one of material wealth but of eternal salvation. His throne is a cross. Such a King the world has never seen. Through his suffering and death this King brings Life to all who are open to receive it. This King offers Paradise to all those who come to him, accept his reign, and remain faithful to the will of his Father. This King remembers each of us and bids us to come into his kingdom, into the eternal Life he won for us.

The cross is where we least expect a king to be. Yet this is where we find Jesus. The cross is where we ourselves least want to be. Yet this is how God's kingdom is established and where our discipleship begins: allowing ourselves to be crucified on the cross of self-giving. Jesus demonstrates his kingship not by saving himself but by saving others. Not by turning in on himself but by turning out toward others. Jesus demonstrates his kingship not by power but by loving reassurance that Paradise awaits faithful disciples. Only by beginning here, on the cross, can our discipleship end like the Good Thief's, hearing Jesus say to us, "Amen, I say to you, / today you will be with me in Paradise."

Living the Paschal Mystery

The Good Thief said, "Jesus, remember me when you come into your kingdom." This solemnity celebrates Christ as King. His kingdom has come. *We* are living in God's kingdom *now*. We are called, however, not to simply pay homage to our exalted King, but to do as he did. This means that each day we must live in a self-giving way because only through goodness expressed in reaching out to others is God's reign at hand. Living the paschal mystery means living the daily dying the cross demands. Just as the cross was the means to Jesus' exaltation, so is the cross our only way into Paradise. When self-giving seems to swallow us up and we are tempted to choose a self-serving attitude, all we need to do is remember that the cross is the door to Paradise. This only way—the cross—is the way out of this life, crossing into eternal Life. The only way.

Focusing the Gospel

Key words and phrases: the Christ of God, King, reviled Jesus, condemned justly, remember me, today you will be with me in Paradise

To the point: Three hang on crosses, suffering and dying. One reviles, one begs for salvation, One promises Paradise. Indeed, only One *can* promise Paradise. Who but "the Christ of God" could make such a promise? Who but a divine King could reach beyond his own suffering and dying to bestow Life on another? Who but One totally innocent of evil could draw goodness out of one who is "condemned justly"? Three hang on crosses. One remains condemned. One is redeemed. One will rise from the dead, King of the universe.

Connecting the Gospel

to the other readings: Jesus is a King who "shepherds [his] people" (first reading), delivers them, and bestows an unimaginable inheritance on them (see second reading).

to experience: In the political world of ancient times, a king was wealthy, powerful, the center of attention and adulation. Jesus, by contrast, is a divine King who does not claim wealth and power. Instead, even at the moment of his own death, this King turns his attention outward to another who begs for salvation, the very reason he came.

Connecting the Responsorial Psalm

to the readings: Israelites arriving at the gates of Jerusalem for annual worship sang Psalm 122. It was a song of great joy, for entering Jerusalem meant encountering God. It meant celebrating membership in God's people. It meant reaffirming who they were and who God was for them. On this Solemnity of Our Lord Jesus Christ, King of the Universe we, too, celebrate who we are and who God is for us. We are the people forgiven by God through Christ's redeeming death (second reading). We are the very "bone" and "flesh" (first reading) of Christ, members of the Body of which he is the Head (second reading). We are the ones remembered by Christ and called by him into Paradise (gospel). Let us enter with rejoicing!

to psalmist preparation: In singing this responsorial psalm you invite the assembly to enter the kingdom of God. They have journeyed through all of Ordinary Time. They have struggled, they have been faithful. Bring them in with joy!

**ASSEMBLY &
FAITH-SHARING GROUPS**

- What this gospel teaches me about Jesus as King is . . .
- The goodness Christ the King draws out of me is . . . I share this goodness with others by . . .
- I experience the fullness of Life in Christ's kingdom when . . .

PRESIDERS
Over the past liturgical year my ministry has helped the assembly to . . .

DEACONS
My service witnesses to my self-emptying when . . . Its effect on others is . . .

HOSPITALITY MINISTERS
The manner of my greeting enables those gathering to encounter Christ the King who . . .

MUSIC MINISTERS
My music ministry turns me from myself to the service of others when . . .

ALTAR MINISTERS
My ministry truly serves Christ my King through serving others when . . .

LECTORS
When I live in a way that proclaims Christ is truly my King, my proclamation sounds like . . .

**EXTRAORDINARY MINISTERS
OF HOLY COMMUNION**
My ministry is a reminder of Jesus' promise of Paradise to all when I . . .

CELEBRATION

Model Penitential Act

Presider: Today we celebrate the victory of Christ the King over sin and death. As we prepare ourselves to celebrate this liturgy, let us seek his mercy that we might strengthen our resolve to overcome sin . . . [pause]

Lord Jesus, you are the King of all the universe: Lord . . .

Christ Jesus, you are the King whose throne is everlasting: Christ . . .

Lord Jesus, you are the King who promises us Paradise: Lord . . .

Homily Points

• Promises! Promises! Promises! We've all suffered from broken promises. We've all gained from kept promises. In all the universe, there has never been a promise like the one Jesus made on the cross. He promised the repentant criminal who begged to be remembered, "today you will be with me in Paradise." This promise is also made to us.

• Are you "the King of the Jews"? I am. "Are you not the Christ?" I am. "Save yourself and us." I am. Jesus is the eternal King, the great I AM, who saves us by the very action of his self-surrender, his sacrifice of himself on the altar of the cross. What looked like defeat was actually victory over sin and death and a sure promise of a share in Paradise. Jesus "the Christ" rose from the dead, King of the universe.

• Jesus has promised Paradise. Like the repentant criminal on the cross, we must look to Jesus and ask to be remembered. We ask not only by the words of prayer, but also by the deeds of faithful discipleship. We ask for a share in Paradise, for example, when we love those who are difficult, when we show mercy to those who do wrong, when we give hope to those who are burdened with the cares of life. Jesus Christ our King keeps his promises. One day we, his faithful disciples, will be with him in Paradise.

Model Universal Prayer (Prayer of the Faithful)

Presider: Let us confidently make known our needs to Christ our King who promises those who are faithful the fullness of Life.

Response:

Cantor:

That all members of the church faithfully follow Christ the King by reaching out to those in need . . . [pause]

That all peoples of the world come to salvation in God's kingdom . . . [pause]

That those who are suffering and dying be comforted by Christ the King's promise of fullness of Life . . . [pause]

That each one of us remember what we have learned during this liturgical year and resolve to enter more deeply into the paschal mystery during the coming year . . . [pause]

Presider: God of goodness and holiness, you offer us fullness of Life in the kingdom of your Son. Hear these our prayers that one day we might share in the joy of Life everlasting. We ask this through our Lord Jesus Christ our King for ever and ever. **Amen.**

COLLECT
Let us pray.

Pause for silent prayer

Almighty ever-living God,
whose will is to restore all things
in your beloved Son, the King of the
    universe,
grant, we pray,
that the whole creation, set free from
    slavery,
may render your majesty service
and ceaselessly proclaim your praise.
Through our Lord Jesus Christ, your Son,
who lives and reigns with you in the unity
    of the Holy Spirit,
one God, for ever and ever. **Amen.**

FIRST READING
2 Sam 5:1-3

In those days, all the tribes of Israel came
    to David in Hebron and said:
    "Here we are, your bone and your flesh.
In days past, when Saul was our king,
    it was you who led the Israelites out and
        brought them back.
And the LORD said to you,
    'You shall shepherd my people Israel
    and shall be commander of Israel.'"
When all the elders of Israel came to
    David in Hebron,
    King David made an agreement with
        them there before the LORD,
    and they anointed him king of Israel.

RESPONSORIAL PSALM
Ps 122:1-2, 3-4, 4-5

R̸. (cf. 1) Let us go rejoicing to the house
of the Lord.

I rejoiced because they said to me,
    "We will go up to the house of the
        LORD."
And now we have set foot
    within your gates, O Jerusalem.

R̸. Let us go rejoicing to the house of the
Lord.

Jerusalem, built as a city
 with compact unity.
To it the tribes go up,
 the tribes of the Lord.

R̸. Let us go rejoicing to the house of the
Lord.

According to the decree for Israel,
 to give thanks to the name of the Lord.
In it are set up judgment seats,
 seats for the house of David.

R̸. Let us go rejoicing to the house of the
Lord.

SECOND READING
Col 1:12-20

Brothers and sisters:
Let us give thanks to the Father,
 who has made you fit to share
 in the inheritance of the holy ones in
  light.
He delivered us from the power of
 darkness
 and transferred us to the kingdom of
  his beloved Son,
 in whom we have redemption, the
  forgiveness of sins.

He is the image of the invisible God,
 the firstborn of all creation.
For in him were created all things in
  heaven and on earth,
 the visible and the invisible,
 whether thrones or dominions or
  principalities or powers;
 all things were created through
  him and for him.
He is before all things,
 and in him all things hold together.
He is the head of the body, the
 church.
He is the beginning, the firstborn
  from the dead,
 that in all things he himself might
  be preeminent.
For in him all the fullness was
  pleased to dwell,
 and through him to reconcile all
  things for him,
 making peace by the blood of his
  cross
 through him, whether those on
  earth or those in heaven.

About Liturgy

Discipleship and victory: For months now we have been traveling with Jesus through the proclamation of Luke's gospel. This festival of Christ the King is the last Sunday and culmination of the whole liturgical year. Next Sunday we begin Advent and thus begin again yet another paschal mystery journey through a liturgical year. This annual celebration reminds us that the difficulties of discipleship are always rewarded by the joy of victory. The cross leads to risen life. As we embrace the cross in our own journey of discipleship each day, we are spurred on to faithfulness by remembering that it all culminates in this victory.

Each year we begin and end the same journey. What keeps this cyclic pattern of our liturgical celebrations from becoming tedious? The answer lies in our taking the time to recognize our own growth in discipleship and our personal relationship with Jesus our King during this past year. Since judgment is one of the themes of the end times, it might be good to take some time this week to judge our own growth and preparedness to enter Paradise with Jesus. Without such self-reflection we run the risk of every liturgical year simply being like all others for us. Endings and beginnings always give us an opportunity to assess growth and recommit ourselves to faithful discipleship. True, the cross is not something we would naturally choose for ourselves. But the end of this liturgical year and the beginning of the new one when we encounter our victorious Christ is exactly what we need in order to be faithful to the disciple's life of self-giving for the good of others.

About Liturgical Music

Liturgical music and growth in discipleship: The Solemnity of Our Lord Jesus Christ, King of the Universe—the last Sunday of the liturgical year—is a good time to assess how we have grown this past year in and through liturgical music. How through our music have we more clearly become the Body of Christ given for the redemption of the world?

For assembly members: How have we grown in singing well together, with willing hearts and full voices? How have we grown in listening to each other as we sing, in becoming one Body rather than individuals singing "our own thing"?

For cantors and choir: How have we grown in focusing on Christ rather than making ourselves the "star" of the liturgy? How have we grown in treating each other as members of the one Body of Christ? How have we grown in unselfishness because of the disciplines required for our ministry?

For music director: How have I grown in my understanding of the role of music in liturgy? How have I stayed faithful to keeping liturgy central and music secondary and supporting? How have I grown through this ministry in my relationship with Christ and in my ability to see the assembly as Body of Christ? How have I helped the cantors and the choir grow in these ways?

✝ SPIRITUALITY

GOSPEL ACCLAMATION
1 Thess 5:18

℞. Alleluia, alleluia.
In all circumstances, give thanks,
for this is the will of God for you in Christ Jesus.
℞. Alleluia, alleluia.

Gospel

Luke 17:11-19; L947.6

As Jesus continued his journey to
      Jerusalem,
   he traveled through Samaria and
      Galilee.
As he was entering a village, ten
      lepers met him.
They stood at a distance from
      him and raised their voices,
      saying,
   "Jesus, Master! Have pity on
      us!"
And when he saw them, he said,
   "Go show yourselves to the
      priests."
As they were going they were cleansed.
And one of them, realizing he had been
      healed,
   returned, glorifying God in a loud voice;
   and he fell at the feet of Jesus and
      thanked him.
He was a Samaritan.
Jesus said in reply,
   "Ten were cleansed, were they not?
Where are the other nine?
Has none but this foreigner returned to
      give thanks to God?"
Then he said to him, "Stand up and go;
   your faith has saved you."

See Appendix A, p. 314, for the other readings.

Reflecting on the Gospel

Although not true in all marriages, there is still much banter about a husband invariably forgetting his wife's birthday and anniversary. Underneath the banter lies an important issue. Rather than missing out on a gift or romantic dinner, a wife is hurt by this forgetfulness because it is a forgetfulness of her. It brings into question how much the husband thinks about the wife, loves her, cares about her. The wife simply wants the husband to turn to her and show that he cherishes her. She wants personal encounter. Healthy relationships are about personal encounter. Thankfulness is one way we grow in our personal encounters.

In the gospel story the one leper who returns to give thanks to Jesus for being healed encounters him in a new way. Giving thanks turns us from the gift received to encountering the gift-giver. No matter how wonderful a gift is—being healed from a terrible disease as was the leper or delighting in the abundant crops, natural resources, and civil liberties which we celebrate this day as a nation—the full value of a gift is realized only when it turns us to the giver. Especially so, when the giver is God. In fact, every gift is from God.

The act of thanksgiving by the Samaritan leper in the gospel expresses the frame of heart and mind we bring to the liturgical celebration on Thanksgiving Day. The civil observance of Thanksgiving Day calls us to gratitude for the abundant blessings we enjoy as a nation. Our liturgical observance of this day calls us to turn to God as the origin of all our blessings. Jesus announced that the Samaritan leper received salvation. This salvation is not simply the human wholeness that comes from his being healed. Gathering to offer God thanks acknowledges our dependency upon God for the fullness of Life given to us through Christ Jesus. The fullness of Life salvation brings is the divine Presence and our attentiveness to it.

An attitude of thanksgiving reorients us from focusing on a gift received to encountering the gift-giver. An act of giving thanks, then, is always a kind of conversion. Thanksgiving draws us out of ourselves and toward another. Thanksgiving helps us forget self and think of the other. Thanksgiving changes us from self-absorption to other-centeredness. Thanksgiving turns us toward God who bestows all gifts and blessings.

Living the Paschal Mystery

Thanksgiving comes once a year. We ought to not wait until the fourth Thursday of November, however, to give thanks for all God has given us. The very life of Christians is one of putting on the habit of thankfulness, because this habit of thankfulness orients us to God as the One who bestows on us abundant blessings.

God forbid that Jesus would ever address to us, "Where are the other nine?" As we die to ourselves and come to new life in living daily the paschal mystery, we want to grow in a stance of gratitude before our God. Even if our own personal circumstances don't seem to leave much room for thankfulness (hurt or broken relationships, economic hard times, sickness and death, etc.), today and every day we are called to acknowledge all God has given us. Our very life is a gift. Our health, such as it may be, is a gift. Our loved ones and friends are gifts. Even our ability to encounter God and recognize the divine blessings in our lives is a gift.

Each day we ought to pause and recognize the gifts given to us. And let each blessing orient us to God with hearts filled with love and gratitude.

Focusing the Gospel

Key words and phrases: realizing he had been healed, returned, fell at the feet of Jesus, thanked him

To the point: In the gospel story the one leper who returns to give thanks to Jesus for being healed encounters him in a new way. Giving thanks turns us from the gift received to encountering the gift-giver. No matter how wonderful a gift is—being healed from a terrible disease as was the leper or delighting in the abundant crops, natural resources, and civil liberties which we celebrate this day as a nation—the full value of a gift is realized only when it turns us to the giver. Especially so, when the giver is God. In fact, every gift is from God.

Model Penitential Act

Presider: We come together today to celebrate God's many blessings and gifts to us. Let us pause at the beginning of this liturgy to open our hearts in gratitude to God, and beg mercy for the times we have not been thankful . . . [pause]

Lord Jesus, you are God's gift who heals us: Lord . . .

Christ Jesus, you are God's gift who saves us: Christ . . .

Lord Jesus, you are God's gift who strengthens us: Lord . . .

Model Universal Prayer (Prayer of the Faithful)

Presider: God has blessed us with an abundance of gifts. We are confident that God will hear our prayers and continue to bless us with all we need.

Response:

Lord, hear our prayer.

Cantor:

we pray to the Lord,

That all members of the church raise grateful hearts always and everywhere for God's abundant blessings . . . [pause]

That all peoples of the world share equitably in the abundant fruits of this earth . . . [pause]

That the poor be raised up, the hungry be fed, and those deprived of liberty be freed . . . [pause]

That each of us gathered here turn our hearts more fully to God who has bestowed on us life, liberty, and salvation . . . [pause]

Presider: Gracious God, you give us abundant gifts and most especially your own Son, Jesus Christ. Grant these our prayers and turn our hearts more perfectly toward you that all might share in your goodness and come to everlasting Life. We ask this through that same Son, Jesus Christ our Lord. **Amen.**

FOR REFLECTION

- I can foster a greater habit of thankfulness in my daily living by . . .

- Of the gifts I've been given, the ones that have brought me to a deeper encounter with God are . . .

- What helps me realize the full value of the gifts in my life is . . .

Homily Points

- Etiquette columnists regularly reiterate that handwriting a personal thank you is still the preferred way of expressing gratitude for a gift. When children, for example, are not taught to do this, we are not helping them turn their attention from gift to gift-giver.

- In the gospel, all ten lepers were healed. Only one returned to Jesus to give thanks for the gift of health and restoration. Only one returned to encounter Jesus in a new way. Only this one leper turned his attention from the gift received to the Gift-giver. On this Thanksgiving Day, we gather for Eucharist (thanksgiving), not only to give thanks for the gifts we have received, but to turn our attention to the divine Gift-giver who has given us all good things—life, liberty, salvation.

Readings *(continued)*

The Immaculate Conception of the Blessed Virgin Mary, *December 8, 2015*

Gospel (cont.)
Luke 1:26-38; L689

But Mary said to the angel,
  "How can this be,
  since I have no relations with a man?"
And the angel said to her in reply,
  "The Holy Spirit will come upon you,
  and the power of the Most High will overshadow you.
Therefore the child to be born
  will be called holy, the Son of God.
And behold, Elizabeth, your relative,
  has also conceived a son in her old age,
  and this is the sixth month for her who was called barren;
  for nothing will be impossible for God."
Mary said, "Behold, I am the handmaid of the Lord.
May it be done to me according to your word."
Then the angel departed from her.

FIRST READING
Gen 3:9-15, 20

After the man, Adam, had eaten of the tree,
  the LORD God called to the man and asked
    him, "Where are you?"
He answered, "I heard you in the garden;
  but I was afraid, because I was naked,
  so I hid myself."
Then he asked, "Who told you that you were
    naked?
You have eaten, then,
  from the tree of which I had forbidden you
    to eat!"
The man replied, "The woman whom you put
    here with me—
  she gave me fruit from the tree, and so I
    ate it."
The LORD God then asked the woman,
  "Why did you do such a thing?"
The woman answered, "The serpent tricked
  me into it, so I ate it."

Then the LORD God said to the serpent:
  "Because you have done this, you shall be
    banned
    from all the animals
    and from all the wild creatures;
  on your belly shall you crawl,
    and dirt shall you eat
    all the days of your life.
  I will put enmity between you and the
    woman,
    and between your offspring and hers;
  he will strike at your head,
    while you strike at his heel."

The man called his wife Eve,
  because she became the mother of all the
    living.

RESPONSORIAL PSALM
Ps 98:1, 2-3, 3-4

℟. (1a) Sing to the Lord a new song, for he has
done marvelous deeds.

Sing to the LORD a new song,
  for he has done wondrous deeds;
His right hand has won victory for him,
  his holy arm.

℟. Sing to the Lord a new song, for he has
done marvelous deeds.

The LORD has made his salvation known:
  in the sight of the nations he has revealed
    his justice.
He has remembered his kindness and his
    faithfulness
  toward the house of Israel.

℟. Sing to the Lord a new song, for he has
done marvelous deeds.

All the ends of the earth have seen
  the salvation by our God.
Sing joyfully to the LORD, all you lands;
  break into song; sing praise.

℟. Sing to the Lord a new song, for he has
done marvelous deeds.

SECOND READING
Eph 1:3-6, 11-12

Brothers and sisters:
Blessed be the God and Father of our Lord
    Jesus Christ,
  who has blessed us in Christ
  with every spiritual blessing in the
    heavens,
  as he chose us in him, before the foundation
    of the world,
  to be holy and without blemish before him.
In love he destined us for adoption to himself
    through Jesus Christ,
  in accord with the favor of his will,
  for the praise of the glory of his grace
  that he granted us in the beloved.

In him we were also chosen,
  destined in accord with the purpose of the
    One
  who accomplishes all things according to
    the intention of his will,
  so that we might exist for the praise of his
    glory,
  we who first hoped in Christ.

Gospel (cont.)
Matt 1:1-25; L13ABC

David became the father of Solomon,
  whose mother had been the wife of Uriah.
Solomon became the father of Rehoboam,
  Rehoboam the father of Abijah,
  Abijah the father of Asaph.
Asaph became the father of Jehoshaphat,
  Jehoshaphat the father of Joram,
  Joram the father of Uzziah.
Uzziah became the father of Jotham,
  Jotham the father of Ahaz,
  Ahaz the father of Hezekiah.
Hezekiah became the father of Manasseh,
  Manasseh the father of Amos,
  Amos the father of Josiah.
Josiah became the father of Jechoniah and his brothers
  at the time of the Babylonian exile.

After the Babylonian exile,
  Jechoniah became the father of Shealtiel,
  Shealtiel the father of Zerubbabel,
  Zerubbabel the father of Abiud.
Abiud became the father of Eliakim,
  Eliakim the father of Azor,
  Azor the father of Zadok.
Zadok became the father of Achim,
  Achim the father of Eliud,
  Eliud the father of Eleazar.
Eleazar became the father of Matthan,
  Matthan the father of Jacob,
  Jacob the father of Joseph, the husband of Mary.
Of her was born Jesus who is called the Christ.

Thus the total number of generations
  from Abraham to David
  is fourteen generations;
  from David to the Babylonian exile,
  fourteen generations;
  from the Babylonian exile to the Christ,
  fourteen generations.

Now this is how the birth of Jesus Christ came about.
When his mother Mary was betrothed to Joseph,
  but before they lived together,
  she was found with child through the Holy Spirit.
Joseph her husband, since he was a righteous man,
  yet unwilling to expose her to shame,
  decided to divorce her quietly.

Such was his intention when, behold,
  the angel of the Lord appeared to him in a dream and said,
  "Joseph, son of David,
  do not be afraid to take Mary your wife into your home.
For it is through the Holy Spirit
  that this child has been conceived in her.
She will bear a son and you are to name him Jesus,
  because he will save his people from their sins."
All this took place to fulfill
  what the Lord had said through the prophet:
    Behold, the virgin shall conceive and bear a son,
      and they shall name him Emmanuel,
    which means "God is with us."
When Joseph awoke,
  he did as the angel of the Lord had commanded him
  and took his wife into his home.
He had no relations with her until she bore a son,
  and he named him Jesus.

or Matt 1:18-25

This is how the birth of Jesus Christ came about.
When his mother Mary was betrothed to Joseph,
  but before they lived together,
  she was found with child through the Holy Spirit.
Joseph her husband, since he was a righteous man,
  yet unwilling to expose her to shame,
  decided to divorce her quietly.
Such was his intention when, behold,
  the angel of the Lord appeared to him in a dream and said,
  "Joseph, son of David,
  do not be afraid to take Mary your wife into your home.
For it is through the Holy Spirit
  that this child has been conceived in her.
She will bear a son and you are to name him Jesus,
  because he will save his people from their sins."
All this took place to fulfill
  what the Lord had said through the prophet:
    Behold, the virgin shall conceive and bear a son,
      and they shall name him Emmanuel,
    which means "God is with us."
When Joseph awoke,
  he did as the angel of the Lord had commanded him
  and took his wife into his home.
He had no relations with her until she bore a son,
  and he named him Jesus.

The Nativity of the Lord, *December 25, 2015 (The Vigil Mass)*

FIRST READING
Isa 62:1-5

For Zion's sake I will not be silent,
    for Jerusalem's sake I will not be quiet,
until her vindication shines forth like the dawn
    and her victory like a burning torch.

Nations shall behold your vindication,
    and all the kings your glory;
you shall be called by a new name
    pronounced by the mouth of the LORD.
You shall be a glorious crown in the hand of
    the LORD,
    a royal diadem held by your God.
No more shall people call you "Forsaken,"
    or your land "Desolate,"
but you shall be called "My Delight,"
    and your land "Espoused."
For the LORD delights in you
    and makes your land his spouse.
As a young man marries a virgin,
    your Builder shall marry you;
and as a bridegroom rejoices in his bride
    so shall your God rejoice in you.

RESPONSORIAL PSALM
Ps 89:4-5, 16-17, 27, 29

℟. (2a) Forever I will sing the goodness of the Lord.

I have made a covenant with my chosen one,
    I have sworn to David my servant:
forever will I confirm your posterity
    and establish your throne for all
        generations.

℟. Forever I will sing the goodness of the Lord.

Blessed the people who know the joyful shout;
    in the light of your countenance, O LORD,
        they walk.
At your name they rejoice all the day,
    and through your justice they are exalted.

℟. Forever I will sing the goodness of the Lord.

He shall say of me, "You are my father,
    my God, the Rock, my savior."
Forever I will maintain my kindness toward
    him,
    and my covenant with him stands firm.

℟. Forever I will sing the goodness of the Lord.

SECOND READING
Acts 13:16-17, 22-25

When Paul reached Antioch in Pisidia and
    entered the synagogue,
    he stood up, motioned with his hand, and
        said,
    "Fellow Israelites and you others who are
        God-fearing, listen.
The God of this people Israel chose our
    ancestors
    and exalted the people during their sojourn
        in the land of Egypt.
With uplifted arm he led them out of it.
Then he removed Saul and raised up David
    as king;
    of him he testified,
    'I have found David, son of Jesse, a man
        after my own heart;
    he will carry out my every wish.'
From this man's descendants God, according
    to his promise,
    has brought to Israel a savior, Jesus.
John heralded his coming by proclaiming a
    baptism of repentance
    to all the people of Israel;
    and as John was completing his course, he
        would say,
    'What do you suppose that I am? I am not he.
Behold, one is coming after me;
    I am not worthy to unfasten the sandals of
        his feet.'"

The Nativity of the Lord, *December 25, 2015 (Mass at Midnight)*

Gospel (cont.)
Luke 2:1-14; L14ABC

Now there were shepherds in that region living in the fields
    and keeping the night watch over their flock.
The angel of the Lord appeared to them
    and the glory of the Lord shone around them,
    and they were struck with great fear.
The angel said to them,
    "Do not be afraid;
    for behold, I proclaim to you good news of great joy
    that will be for all the people.
For today in the city of David
    a savior has been born for you who is Christ and Lord.
And this will be a sign for you:
    you will find an infant wrapped in swaddling clothes
    and lying in a manger."
And suddenly there was a multitude of the heavenly host with the
    angel,
    praising God and saying:
        "Glory to God in the highest
            and on earth peace to those on whom his favor rests."

The Nativity of the Lord, *December 25, 2015 (Mass at Midnight)*

FIRST READING
Isa 9:1-6

The people who walked in darkness
    have seen a great light;
upon those who dwelt in the land of gloom
    a light has shone.
You have brought them abundant joy
    and great rejoicing,
as they rejoice before you as at the harvest,
    as people make merry when dividing
        spoils.
For the yoke that burdened them,
    the pole on their shoulder,
and the rod of their taskmaster
    you have smashed, as on the day of Midian.
For every boot that tramped in battle,
    every cloak rolled in blood,
    will be burned as fuel for flames.
For a child is born to us, a son is given us;
    upon his shoulder dominion rests.
They name him Wonder-Counselor, God-Hero,
    Father-Forever, Prince of Peace.
His dominion is vast
    and forever peaceful,
from David's throne, and over his kingdom,
    which he confirms and sustains
by judgment and justice,
    both now and forever.
The zeal of the LORD of hosts will do this!

RESPONSORIAL PSALM
Ps 96:1-2, 2-3, 11-12, 13

R̲̅. (Luke 2:11) Today is born our Savior,
Christ the Lord.

Sing to the LORD a new song;
    sing to the LORD, all you lands.
Sing to the LORD; bless his name.

R̲̅. Today is born our Savior, Christ the Lord.

Announce his salvation, day after day.
    Tell his glory among the nations;
    among all peoples, his wondrous deeds.

R̲̅. Today is born our Savior, Christ the Lord.

Let the heavens be glad and the earth rejoice;
    let the sea and what fills it resound;
    let the plains be joyful and all that is in
        them!
Then shall all the trees of the forest exult.

R̲̅. Today is born our Savior, Christ the Lord.

They shall exult before the LORD, for he
        comes;
    for he comes to rule the earth.
He shall rule the world with justice
    and the peoples with his constancy.

R̲̅. Today is born our Savior, Christ the Lord.

SECOND READING
Titus 2:11-14

Beloved:
The grace of God has appeared, saving all
    and training us to reject godless ways and
        worldly desires
    and to live temperately, justly, and devoutly
        in this age,
    as we await the blessed hope,
    the appearance of the glory of our great
        God
    and savior Jesus Christ,
    who gave himself for us to deliver us from
        all lawlessness
    and to cleanse for himself a people as his
        own,
    eager to do what is good.

The Nativity of the Lord, *December 25, 2015 (Mass at Dawn)*

FIRST READING
Isa 62:11-12

See, the LORD proclaims
    to the ends of the earth:
say to daughter Zion,
    your savior comes!
Here is his reward with him,
    his recompense before him.
They shall be called the holy people,
    the redeemed of the LORD,
and you shall be called "Frequented,"
    a city that is not forsaken.

RESPONSORIAL PSALM
Ps 97:1, 6, 11-12

R̲̅. A light will shine on us this day: the Lord
is born for us.

The LORD is king; let the earth rejoice;
    let the many isles be glad.
The heavens proclaim his justice,
    and all peoples see his glory.

R̲̅. A light will shine on us this day: the Lord
is born for us.

Light dawns for the just;
    and gladness, for the upright of heart.
Be glad in the LORD, you just,
    and give thanks to his holy name.

R̲̅. A light will shine on us this day: the Lord
is born for us.

SECOND READING
Titus 3:4-7

Beloved:
When the kindness and generous love
    of God our savior appeared,
not because of any righteous deeds we had
        done
    but because of his mercy,
he saved us through the bath of rebirth
    and renewal by the Holy Spirit,
whom he richly poured out on us
    through Jesus Christ our savior,
so that we might be justified by his grace
    and become heirs in hope of eternal life.

Gospel (cont.)
John 1:1-18; L16ABC

The true light, which enlightens everyone,
was coming into the world.

He was in the world,
and the world came to be through him,
but the world did not know him.
He came to what was his own,
but his own people did not accept him.

But to those who did accept him
he gave power to become children of God,
to those who believe in his name,
who were born not by natural generation
nor by human choice nor by a man's decision
but of God.

And the Word became flesh
and made his dwelling among us,
and we saw his glory,
the glory as of the Father's only Son,
full of grace and truth.
John testified to him and cried out, saying,
"This was he of whom I said,
'The one who is coming after me ranks ahead of me
because he existed before me.'"
From his fullness we have all received,
grace in place of grace,
because while the law was given through Moses,
grace and truth came through Jesus Christ.
No one has ever seen God.
The only Son, God, who is at the Father's side,
has revealed him.

or John 1:1-5, 9-14

In the beginning was the Word,
and the Word was with God,
and the Word was God.
He was in the beginning with God.
All things came to be through him,
and without him nothing came to be.
What came to be through him was life,
and this life was the light of the human race;
the light shines in the darkness,
and the darkness has not overcome it.
The true light, which enlightens everyone,
was coming into the world.

He was in the world,
and the world came to be through him,
but the world did not know him.
He came to what was his own,
but his own people did not accept him.

But to those who did accept him
he gave power to become children of God,
to those who believe in his name,
who were born not by natural generation
nor by human choice nor by a man's decision
but of God.

And the Word became flesh
and made his dwelling among us,
and we saw his glory,
the glory as of the Father's only Son,
full of grace and truth.

FIRST READING
Isa 52:7-10

How beautiful upon the mountains
are the feet of him who brings glad tidings,
announcing peace, bearing good news,
announcing salvation, and saying to Zion,
"Your God is King!"

Hark! Your sentinels raise a cry,
together they shout for joy,
for they see directly, before their eyes,
the LORD restoring Zion.
Break out together in song,
O ruins of Jerusalem!
For the LORD comforts his people,
he redeems Jerusalem.
The LORD has bared his holy arm
in the sight of all the nations;
all the ends of the earth will behold
the salvation of our God.

RESPONSORIAL PSALM
Ps 98:1, 2-3, 3-4, 5-6

R̸. (3c) All the ends of the earth have seen the saving power of God.

Sing to the LORD a new song,
for he has done wondrous deeds;
his right hand has won victory for him,
his holy arm.

R̸. All the ends of the earth have seen the saving power of God.

The LORD has made his salvation known:
in the sight of the nations he has revealed
his justice.
He has remembered his kindness and his
faithfulness
toward the house of Israel.

R̸. All the ends of the earth have seen the saving power of God.

All the ends of the earth have seen
the salvation by our God.
Sing joyfully to the LORD, all you lands;
break into song; sing praise.

R̸. All the ends of the earth have seen the saving power of God.

Sing praise to the LORD with the harp,
with the harp and melodious song.
With trumpets and the sound of the horn
sing joyfully before the King, the LORD.

R̸. All the ends of the earth have seen the saving power of God.

The Nativity of the Lord, *December 25, 2015 (Mass during the Day)*

SECOND READING
Heb 1:1-6

Brothers and sisters:
In times past, God spoke in partial and
  various ways
  to our ancestors through the prophets;
  in these last days, he has spoken to us
    through the Son,
  whom he made heir of all things
  and through whom he created the universe,
  who is the refulgence of his glory, the very
    imprint of his being,
    and who sustains all things by his
      mighty word.
  When he had accomplished purification
    from sins,

he took his seat at the right hand of the
  Majesty on high,
  as far superior to the angels
    as the name he has inherited is more
      excellent than theirs.

For to which of the angels did God ever say:
  *You are my son; this day I have begotten
    you?*
Or again:
  *I will be a father to him, and he shall be a
    son to me?*
And again, when he leads the firstborn into
  the world, he says:
  Let all the angels of God worship him.

The Holy Family of Jesus, Mary, and Joseph, *December 27, 2015*

Gospel (cont.)
Luke 2:41-52; L17C

When his parents saw him,
  they were astonished,
  and his mother said to him,
  "Son, why have you done this to us?
Your father and I have been looking for you
  with great anxiety."
And he said to them,
  "Why were you looking for me?
Did you not know that I must be in my
  Father's house?"
But they did not understand what he said to
  them.
He went down with them and came to
  Nazareth,
  and was obedient to them;
  and his mother kept all these things in her
    heart.
And Jesus advanced in wisdom and age and
  favor
  before God and man.

FIRST READING
Sir 3:2-6, 12-14

God sets a father in honor over his children;
  a mother's authority he confirms over her
    sons.
Whoever honors his father atones for sins,
  and preserves himself from them.
When he prays, he is heard;
  he stores up riches who reveres his mother.
Whoever honors his father is gladdened by
    children,
  and, when he prays, is heard.
Whoever reveres his father will live a long life;
  he who obeys his father brings comfort to
    his mother.

My son, take care of your father when he is old;
  grieve him not as long as he lives.
Even if his mind fail, be considerate of him;
  revile him not all the days of his life;
kindness to a father will not be forgotten,
  firmly planted against the debt of your sins
  —a house raised in justice to you.

RESPONSORIAL PSALM
Ps 128:1-2, 3, 4-5

R℣. (cf. 1) Blessed are those who fear the Lord
and walk in his ways.

Blessed is everyone who fears the LORD,
  who walks in his ways!
For you shall eat the fruit of your handiwork;
  blessed shall you be, and favored.

R℣. Blessed are those who fear the Lord and
walk in his ways.

Your wife shall be like a fruitful vine
  in the recesses of your home;
your children like olive plants
  around your table.

R℣. Blessed are those who fear the Lord and
walk in his ways.

Behold, thus is the man blessed
  who fears the LORD.
The LORD bless you from Zion:
  may you see the prosperity of Jerusalem
  all the days of your life.

R℣. Blessed are those who fear the Lord and
walk in his ways.

The Holy Family of Jesus, Mary, and Joseph, *December 27, 2015*

SECOND READING
Col 3:12-21

Brothers and sisters:
Put on, as God's chosen ones, holy and beloved,
   heartfelt compassion, kindness, humility,
      gentleness, and patience,
   bearing with one another and forgiving one
      another,
   if one has a grievance against another;
   as the Lord has forgiven you, so must you
      also do.
And over all these put on love,
   that is, the bond of perfection.
And let the peace of Christ control your hearts,
   the peace into which you were also called in
      one body.
And be thankful.
Let the word of Christ dwell in you richly,
   as in all wisdom you teach and admonish
      one another,
singing psalms, hymns, and spiritual songs
   with gratitude in your hearts to God.
And whatever you do, in word or in deed,
   do everything in the name of the Lord Jesus,
   giving thanks to God the Father through him.

Wives, be subordinate to your husbands,
   as is proper in the Lord.
Husbands, love your wives,
   and avoid any bitterness toward them.
Children, obey your parents in everything,
   for this is pleasing to the Lord.
Fathers, do not provoke your children,
   so they may not become discouraged.

or

Col 3:12-17

Brothers and sisters:
Put on, as God's chosen ones, holy and beloved,
   heartfelt compassion, kindness, humility,
      gentleness, and patience,
   bearing with one another and forgiving one
      another,
   if one has a grievance against another;
   as the Lord has forgiven you, so must you
      also do.
And over all these put on love,
   that is, the bond of perfection.
And let the peace of Christ control your hearts,
   the peace into which you were also called in
      one body.
And be thankful.
Let the word of Christ dwell in you richly,
   as in all wisdom you teach and admonish
      one another,
   singing psalms, hymns, and spiritual songs
   with gratitude in your hearts to God.
And whatever you do, in word or in deed,
   do everything in the name of the Lord Jesus,
   giving thanks to God the Father through him.

Solemnity of Mary, the Holy Mother of God, *January 1, 2016*

FIRST READING
Num 6:22-27

The LORD said to Moses:
   "Speak to Aaron and his sons and tell them:
   This is how you shall bless the Israelites.
Say to them:
   The LORD bless you and keep you!
   The LORD let his face shine upon
      you, and be gracious to you!
   The LORD look upon you kindly and
      give you peace!
So shall they invoke my name upon the
      Israelites,
   and I will bless them."

RESPONSORIAL PSALM
Ps 67:2-3, 5, 6, 8

R̸. (2a) May God bless us in his mercy.

May God have pity on us and bless us;
   may he let his face shine upon us.
So may your way be known upon earth;
   among all nations, your salvation.

R̸. May God bless us in his mercy.

May the nations be glad and exult
   because you rule the peoples in equity;
   the nations on the earth you guide.

R̸. May God bless us in his mercy.

May the peoples praise you, O God;
   may all the peoples praise you!
May God bless us,
   and may all the ends of the earth fear him!

R̸. May God bless us in his mercy.

SECOND READING
Gal 4:4-7

Brothers and sisters:
When the fullness of time had come, God sent
   his Son,
   born of a woman, born under the law,
   to ransom those under the law,
   so that we might receive adoption as sons.
As proof that you are sons,
   God sent the Spirit of his Son into our
      hearts,
   crying out, "Abba, Father!"
So you are no longer a slave but a son,
   and if a son then also an heir, through God.

The Epiphany of the Lord, *January 3, 2016*

Gospel (cont.)
Matt 2:1-12; L20ABC

And behold, the star that they had seen at its rising preceded them,
   until it came and stopped over the place where the child was.
They were overjoyed at seeing the star,
   and on entering the house
   they saw the child with Mary his mother.

They prostrated themselves and did him homage.
Then they opened their treasures
   and offered him gifts of gold, frankincense, and myrrh.
And having been warned in a dream not to return to Herod,
   they departed for their country by another way.

The Baptism of the Lord, *January 10, 2016*

SECOND READING (cont.)
Titus 2:11-14; 3:4-7

When the kindness and generous love
  of God our savior appeared,
not because of any righteous deeds we had
    done
  but because of his mercy,
he saved us through the bath of rebirth
  and renewal by the Holy Spirit,
whom he richly poured out on us
  through Jesus Christ our savior,
so that we might be justified by his grace
  and become heirs in hope of eternal life.

or

FIRST READING
Isa 42:1-4, 6-7

Thus says the LORD:
Here is my servant whom I uphold,
  my chosen one with whom I am pleased,
upon whom I have put my spirit;
  he shall bring forth justice to the nations,
not crying out, not shouting,
  not making his voice heard in the street.
A bruised reed he shall not break,
  and a smoldering wick he shall not quench,
until he establishes justice on the earth;
  the coastlands will wait for his teaching.

I, the LORD, have called you for the victory of
    justice,
  I have grasped you by the hand;

I formed you, and set you
  as a covenant of the people,
  a light for the nations,
to open the eyes of the blind,
  to bring out prisoners from confinement,
  and from the dungeon, those who live in
    darkness.

RESPONSORIAL PSALM
Ps 29:1-2, 3-4, 3, 9-10

R̸. (11b) The Lord will bless his people with peace.

Give to the LORD, you sons of God,
  give to the LORD glory and praise,
give to the LORD the glory due his name;
  adore the LORD in holy attire.

R̸. The Lord will bless his people with peace.

The voice of the LORD is over the waters,
  the LORD, over vast waters.
The voice of the LORD is mighty;
  the voice of the LORD is majestic.

R̸. The Lord will bless his people with peace.

The God of glory thunders,
  and in his temple all say, "Glory!"
The LORD is enthroned above the flood;
  the LORD is enthroned as king forever.

R̸. The Lord will bless his people with peace.

SECOND READING
Acts 10:34-38

Peter proceeded to speak to those gathered
  in the house of Cornelius, saying:
  "In truth, I see that God shows no
    partiality.
Rather, in every nation whoever fears him and
    acts uprightly
  is acceptable to him.
You know the word that he sent to the
    Israelites
  as he proclaimed peace through Jesus
    Christ, who is Lord of all,
what has happened all over Judea,
  beginning in Galilee after the baptism
  that John preached,
  how God anointed Jesus of Nazareth
  with the Holy Spirit and power.
He went about doing good
  and healing all those oppressed by the
    devil,
  for God was with him."

Third Sunday in Ordinary Time, *January 24, 2016*

Gospel (cont.)
Luke 1:1-4; 4:14-21; L69C

He has sent me to proclaim liberty to captives
  and recovery of sight to the blind,
  to let the oppressed go free,
  and to proclaim a year acceptable to the Lord.
Rolling up the scroll, he handed it back to the attendant and sat down,
  and the eyes of all in the synagogue looked intently at him.
He said to them,
  "Today this Scripture passage is fulfilled in your hearing."

Third Sunday in Ordinary Time, *January 24, 2016*

SECOND READING
1 Cor 12:12-30

Brothers and sisters:
As a body is one though it has many parts,
    and all the parts of the body, though many,
        are one body,
    so also Christ.
For in one Spirit we were all baptized into one
    body,
    whether Jews or Greeks, slaves or free
        persons,
    and we were all given to drink of one
        Spirit.

Now the body is not a single part, but many.
If a foot should say,
    "Because I am not a hand I do not belong to
        the body,"
    it does not for this reason belong any less
        to the body.
Or if an ear should say,
    "Because I am not an eye I do not belong to
        the body,"
    it does not for this reason belong any less
        to the body.
If the whole body were an eye, where would
the hearing be?
If the whole body were hearing, where would
    the sense of smell be?
But as it is, God placed the parts,
    each one of them, in the body as he
        intended.
If they were all one part, where would the
    body be?
But as it is, there are many parts, yet one
    body.
The eye cannot say to the hand, "I do not need
    you,"
    nor again the head to the feet, "I do not
        need you."
Indeed, the parts of the body that seem to be
    weaker
    are all the more necessary,
    and those parts of the body that we
        consider less honorable
    we surround with greater honor,
    and our less presentable parts are treated
        with greater propriety,
    whereas our more presentable parts do not
        need this.
But God has so constructed the body
    as to give greater honor to a part that is
without it,
    so that there may be no division in the
        body,
    but that the parts may have the same
        concern for one another.
If one part suffers, all the parts suffer with it;
    if one part is honored, all the parts share
        its joy.

Now you are Christ's body, and individually
    parts of it.
Some people God has designated in the
    church
    to be, first, apostles; second, prophets;
        third, teachers;
    then, mighty deeds;
    then gifts of healing, assistance,
        administration,
    and varieties of tongues.
Are all apostles? Are all prophets? Are all
    teachers?
Do all work mighty deeds? Do all have gifts
    of healing?
Do all speak in tongues? Do all interpret?

Fourth Sunday in Ordinary Time, *January 31, 2016*

SECOND READING
1 Cor 12:31–13:13

Brothers and sisters:
Strive eagerly for the greatest spiritual gifts.
But I shall show you a still more excellent way.

If I speak in human and angelic tongues,
    but do not have love,
    I am a resounding gong or a clashing cymbal.
And if I have the gift of prophecy,
    and comprehend all mysteries and all
        knowledge;
    if I have all faith so as to move mountains,
    but do not have love, I am nothing.
If I give away everything I own,
    and if I hand my body over so that I may
        boast,
    but do not have love, I gain nothing.

Love is patient, love is kind.
It is not jealous, it is not pompous,
    it is not inflated, it is not rude,
    it does not seek its own interests,
    it is not quick-tempered, it does not brood
        over injury,
    it does not rejoice over wrongdoing
    but rejoices with the truth.
It bears all things, believes all things,
    hopes all things, endures all things.

Love never fails.
If there are prophecies, they will be brought
    to nothing;
    if tongues, they will cease;
    if knowledge, it will be brought to
        nothing.
For we know partially and we prophesy
    partially,
but when the perfect comes, the partial will
    pass away.
When I was a child, I used to talk as a child,
    think as a child, reason as a child;
    when I became a man, I put aside childish
        things.
At present we see indistinctly, as in a mirror,
    but then face to face.
At present I know partially;
    then I shall know fully, as I am fully known.
So faith, hope, love remain, these three;
    but the greatest of these is love.

Gospel (cont.)
Luke 5:1-11; L75C

When Simon Peter saw this, he fell at the knees of Jesus and said,
    "Depart from me, Lord, for I am a sinful man."
For astonishment at the catch of fish they had made seized him
    and all those with him,
        and likewise James and John, the sons of Zebedee,
        who were partners of Simon.
Jesus said to Simon, "Do not be afraid;
    from now on you will be catching men."
When they brought their boats to the shore,
    they left everything and followed him.

SECOND READING
1 Cor 15:1-11

I am reminding you, brothers and sisters,
    of the gospel I preached to you,
    which you indeed received and in which
        you also stand.
Through it you are also being saved,
    if you hold fast to the word I preached to
        you,
    unless you believed in vain.
For I handed on to you as of first importance
    what I also received:
    that Christ died for our sins
        in accordance with the Scriptures;
    that he was buried;
    that he was raised on the third day
        in accordance with the Scriptures;
    that he appeared to Cephas, then to the
        Twelve.

After that, he appeared to more
    than five hundred brothers at once,
    most of whom are still living,
    though some have fallen asleep.
After that he appeared to James,
    then to all the apostles.
Last of all, as to one born abnormally,
    he appeared to me.
For I am the least of the apostles,
    not fit to be called an apostle,
    because I persecuted the church of God.
But by the grace of God I am what I am,
    and his grace to me has not been
        ineffective.
Indeed, I have toiled harder than all of them;
    not I, however, but the grace of God that is
        with me.
Therefore, whether it be I or they,
    so we preach and so you believed.

Ash Wednesday, *February 10, 2016*

FIRST READING
Joel 2:12-18

Even now, says the LORD,
    return to me with your whole heart,
    with fasting, and weeping, and mourning;
Rend your hearts, not your garments,
    and return to the LORD, your God.
For gracious and merciful is he,
    slow to anger, rich in kindness,
    and relenting in punishment.
Perhaps he will again relent
    and leave behind him a blessing,
Offerings and libations
    for the LORD, your God.

Blow the trumpet in Zion!
    proclaim a fast,
    call an assembly;
Gather the people,
    notify the congregation;
Assemble the elders,
    gather the children
    and the infants at the breast;
Let the bridegroom quit his room
    and the bride her chamber.
Between the porch and the altar
    let the priests, the ministers of the LORD,
        weep,
And say, "Spare, O LORD, your people,
    and make not your heritage a reproach,
    with the nations ruling over them!
Why should they say among the peoples,
    'Where is their God?'"

Then the LORD was stirred to concern for his
    land
    and took pity on his people.

RESPONSORIAL PSALM
Ps 51:3-4, 5-6ab, 12-13, 14, and 17

R℣. (see 3a) Be merciful, O Lord, for we have
sinned.

Have mercy on me, O God, in your goodness;
    in the greatness of your compassion wipe
        out my offense.
Thoroughly wash me from my guilt
    and of my sin cleanse me.

R℣. Be merciful, O Lord, for we have sinned.

For I acknowledge my offense,
    and my sin is before me always:
"Against you only have I sinned,
    and done what is evil in your sight."

R℣. Be merciful, O Lord, for we have sinned.

A clean heart create for me, O God,
    and a steadfast spirit renew within me.
Cast me not out from your presence,
    and your Holy Spirit take not from me.

R℣. Be merciful, O Lord, for we have sinned.

Give me back the joy of your salvation,
    and a willing spirit sustain in me.
O Lord, open my lips,
    and my mouth shall proclaim your praise.

R℣. Be merciful, O Lord, for we have sinned.

SECOND READING
2 Cor 5:20–6:2

Brothers and sisters:
We are ambassadors for Christ,
    as if God were appealing through us.
We implore you on behalf of Christ,
    be reconciled to God.
For our sake he made him to be sin who did
    not know sin,
    so that we might become the righteousness
    of God in him.

Working together, then,
    we appeal to you not to receive the grace of
    God in vain.
For he says:

In an acceptable time I heard you,
    and on the day of salvation I helped you.

Behold, now is a very acceptable time;
    behold, now is the day of salvation.

First Sunday of Lent, *February 14, 2016*

SECOND READING
Rom 10:8-13

Brothers and sisters:
What does Scripture say?
The word is near you,
    in your mouth and in your heart
—that is, the word of faith that we preach—,
    for, if you confess with your mouth that Jesus is Lord
    and believe in your heart that God raised him from the dead,
    you will be saved.
For one believes with the heart and so is justified,
    and one confesses with the mouth and so is saved.
For the Scripture says,
No one who believes in him will be put to shame.
For there is no distinction between Jew and Greek;
    the same Lord is Lord of all,
    enriching all who call upon him.
For "everyone who calls on the name of the Lord will be saved."

Second Sunday of Lent, *February 21, 2016*

SECOND READING
Phil 3:20–4:1

Brothers and sisters:
Our citizenship is in heaven,
    and from it we also await a savior, the Lord Jesus Christ.
He will change our lowly body
    to conform with his glorified body
    by the power that enables him also
    to bring all things into subjection to himself.

Therefore, my brothers and sisters,
    whom I love and long for, my joy and crown,
    in this way stand firm in the Lord, beloved.

SECOND READING
1 Cor 10:1-6, 10-12

I do not want you to be unaware, brothers and
sisters,
  that our ancestors were all under the cloud
  and all passed through the sea,
  and all of them were baptized into Moses
  in the cloud and in the sea.
All ate the same spiritual food,
  and all drank the same spiritual drink,
  for they drank from a spiritual rock that
    followed them,
  and the rock was the Christ.
Yet God was not pleased with most of them,
  for they were struck down in the desert.

These things happened as examples for us,
  so that we might not desire evil things, as
    they did.
Do not grumble as some of them did,
  and suffered death by the destroyer.
These things happened to them as an
    example,
  and they have been written down as a
    warning to us,
  upon whom the end of the ages has come.
Therefore, whoever thinks he is standing
    secure
  should take care not to fall.

Gospel
John 4:5-15, 19b-26, 39a, 40-42; L28A

Jesus came to a town of Samaria called Sychar,
  near the plot of land that Jacob had given to his son Joseph.
Jacob's well was there.
Jesus, tired from his journey, sat down there at the well.
It was about noon.

A woman of Samaria came to draw water.
Jesus said to her,
  "Give me a drink."
His disciples had gone into the town to buy food.
The Samaritan woman said to him,
  "How can you, a Jew, ask me, a Samaritan woman, for a drink?"
—For Jews use nothing in common with Samaritans.—
Jesus answered and said to her,
  "If you knew the gift of God
  and who is saying to you, 'Give me a drink,'
  you would have asked him
  and he would have given you living water."
The woman said to him,
  "Sir, you do not even have a bucket and the cistern is deep;
  where then can you get this living water?
Are you greater than our father Jacob,
  who gave us this cistern and drank from it himself
  with his children and his flocks?"
Jesus answered and said to her,
  "Everyone who drinks this water will be thirsty again;
  but whoever drinks the water I shall give will never thirst;
  the water I shall give will become in him
  a spring of water welling up to eternal life."
The woman said to him,
  "Sir, give me this water, so that I may not be thirsty
  or have to keep coming here to draw water.

"I can see that you are a prophet.
Our ancestors worshiped on this mountain;
  but you people say that the place to worship is in Jerusalem."
Jesus said to her,
  "Believe me, woman, the hour is coming
  when you will worship the Father
  neither on this mountain nor in Jerusalem.
You people worship what you do not understand;
  we worship what we understand,
  because salvation is from the Jews.
But the hour is coming, and is now here,
  when true worshipers will worship the Father in Spirit and truth;
  and indeed the Father seeks such people to worship him.
God is Spirit, and those who worship him
  must worship in Spirit and truth."
The woman said to him,
  "I know that the Messiah is coming, the one called the Christ;
  when he comes, he will tell us everything."
Jesus said to her,
  "I am he, the one who is speaking with you."

Many of the Samaritans of that town began to believe in him.
When the Samaritans came to him,
  they invited him to stay with them;
  and he stayed there two days.
Many more began to believe in him because of his word,
  and they said to the woman,
  "We no longer believe because of your word;
  for we have heard for ourselves,
  and we know that this is truly the savior of the world."

Gospel

John 4:5-42; L28A

Jesus came to a town of Samaria called Sychar,
    near the plot of land that Jacob had given to his son Joseph.
Jacob's well was there.
Jesus, tired from his journey, sat down there at the well.
It was about noon.

A woman of Samaria came to draw water.
Jesus said to her,
    "Give me a drink."
His disciples had gone into the town to buy food.
The Samaritan woman said to him,
    "How can you, a Jew, ask me, a Samaritan woman, for a drink?"
—For Jews use nothing in common with Samaritans.—
Jesus answered and said to her,
    "If you knew the gift of God
    and who is saying to you, 'Give me a drink,'
    you would have asked him
    and he would have given you living water."
The woman said to him,
    "Sir, you do not even have a bucket and the cistern is deep;
    where then can you get this living water?
Are you greater than our father Jacob,
    who gave us this cistern and drank from it himself
    with his children and his flocks?"
Jesus answered and said to her,
    "Everyone who drinks this water will be thirsty again;
    but whoever drinks the water I shall give will never thirst;
    the water I shall give will become in him
    a spring of water welling up to eternal life."
The woman said to him,
    "Sir, give me this water, so that I may not be thirsty
    or have to keep coming here to draw water."

Jesus said to her,
    "Go call your husband and come back."
The woman answered and said to him,
    "I do not have a husband."
Jesus answered her,
    "You are right in saying, 'I do not have a husband.'
For you have had five husbands,
    and the one you have now is not your husband.
What you have said is true."
The woman said to him,
    "Sir, I can see that you are a prophet.
Our ancestors worshiped on this mountain;
    but you people say that the place to worship is in Jerusalem."
Jesus said to her,
    "Believe me, woman, the hour is coming
    when you will worship the Father
    neither on this mountain nor in Jerusalem.
You people worship what you do not understand;
    we worship what we understand,
    because salvation is from the Jews.

But the hour is coming, and is now here,
    when true worshipers will worship the Father in Spirit and truth;
    and indeed the Father seeks such people to worship him.
God is Spirit, and those who worship him
    must worship in Spirit and truth."
The woman said to him,
    "I know that the Messiah is coming, the one called the Christ;
    when he comes, he will tell us everything."
Jesus said to her,
    "I am he, the one who is speaking with you."

At that moment his disciples returned,
    and were amazed that he was talking with a woman,
    but still no one said, "What are you looking for?"
    or "Why are you talking with her?"
The woman left her water jar
    and went into the town and said to the people,
    "Come see a man who told me everything I have done.
Could he possibly be the Christ?"
They went out of the town and came to him.
Meanwhile, the disciples urged him, "Rabbi, eat."
But he said to them,
    "I have food to eat of which you do not know."
So the disciples said to one another,
    "Could someone have brought him something to eat?"
Jesus said to them,
    "My food is to do the will of the one who sent me
    and to finish his work.
Do you not say, 'In four months the harvest will be here'?
I tell you, look up and see the fields ripe for the harvest.
The reaper is already receiving payment
    and gathering crops for eternal life,
    so that the sower and reaper can rejoice together.
For here the saying is verified that 'One sows and another reaps.'
I sent you to reap what you have not worked for;
    others have done the work,
    and you are sharing the fruits of their work."

Many of the Samaritans of that town began to believe in him
    because of the word of the woman who testified,
    "He told me everything I have done."
When the Samaritans came to him,
    they invited him to stay with them;
    and he stayed there two days.
Many more began to believe in him because of his word,
    and they said to the woman,
    "We no longer believe because of your word;
    for we have heard for ourselves,
    and we know that this is truly the savior of the world."

Third Sunday of Lent, *February 28, 2016*

FIRST READING
Exod 17:3-7

In those days, in their thirst for water,
  the people grumbled against Moses,
  saying, "Why did you ever make us leave
    Egypt?
Was it just to have us die here of thirst
  with our children and our livestock?"
So Moses cried out to the LORD,
  "What shall I do with this people?
A little more and they will stone me!"
The LORD answered Moses,
  "Go over there in front of the people,
  along with some of the elders of Israel,
  holding in your hand, as you go,
  the staff with which you struck the river.
I will be standing there in front of you on the
    rock in Horeb.
Strike the rock, and the water will flow from it
  for the people to drink."
This Moses did, in the presence of the elders
  of Israel.
The place was called Massah and Meribah,
  because the Israelites quarreled there
  and tested the LORD, saying,
  "Is the LORD in our midst or not?"

RESPONSORIAL PSALM
Ps 95:1-2, 6-7, 8-9

R̶/. (8) If today you hear his voice, harden not
your hearts.

Come, let us sing joyfully to the LORD;
  let us acclaim the Rock of our salvation.
Let us come into his presence with
    thanksgiving;
  let us joyfully sing psalms to him.

R̶/. If today you hear his voice, harden not
your hearts.

Come, let us bow down in worship;
  let us kneel before the LORD who made us.
For he is our God,
  and we are the people he shepherds, the
    flock he guides.

R̶/. If today you hear his voice, harden not
your hearts.

Oh, that today you would hear his voice:
  "Harden not your hearts as at Meribah,
  as in the day of Massah in the desert,
where your fathers tempted me;
  they tested me though they had seen my
    works."

R̶/. If today you hear his voice, harden not
your hearts.

SECOND READING
Rom 5:1-2, 5-8

Brothers and sisters:
Since we have been justified by faith,
  we have peace with God through our Lord
    Jesus Christ,
  through whom we have gained access by
    faith
  to this grace in which we stand,
  and we boast in hope of the glory of God.

And hope does not disappoint,
  because the love of God has been poured
    out into our hearts
  through the Holy Spirit who has been given
    to us.
For Christ, while we were still helpless,
  died at the appointed time for the ungodly.
Indeed, only with difficulty does one die for a
    just person,
  though perhaps for a good person one
    might even find courage to die.
But God proves his love for us
  in that while we were still sinners Christ
    died for us.

Fourth Sunday of Lent, *March 6, 2016*

Gospel (cont.)
Luke 15:1-3, 11-32; L33C

I no longer deserve to be called your son;
  treat me as you would treat one of your hired workers.'"
So he got up and went back to his father.
While he was still a long way off,
  his father caught sight of him, and was filled with compassion.
He ran to his son, embraced him and kissed him.
His son said to him,
  'Father, I have sinned against heaven and against you;
  I no longer deserve to be called your son.'
But his father ordered his servants,
  'Quickly bring the finest robe and put it on him;
  put a ring on his finger and sandals on his feet.
Take the fattened calf and slaughter it.
Then let us celebrate with a feast,
  because this son of mine was dead, and has come to life again;
  he was lost, and has been found.'
Then the celebration began.
Now the older son had been out in the field
  and, on his way back, as he neared the house,
  he heard the sound of music and dancing.
He called one of the servants and asked what this might mean.

The servant said to him,
  'Your brother has returned
  and your father has slaughtered the fattened calf
  because he has him back safe and sound.'
He became angry,
  and when he refused to enter the house,
  his father came out and pleaded with him.
He said to his father in reply,
  'Look, all these years I served you
  and not once did I disobey your orders;
  yet you never gave me even a young goat to feast on with
    my friends.
But when your son returns
  who swallowed up your property with prostitutes,
  for him you slaughter the fattened calf.'
He said to him,
  'My son, you are here with me always;
  everything I have is yours.
But now we must celebrate and rejoice,
  because your brother was dead and has come to life again;
  he was lost and has been found.'"

Gospel

John 9:1-41; L31A

As Jesus passed by he saw a man blind from birth.
His disciples asked him,
  "Rabbi, who sinned, this man or his parents,
  that he was born blind?"
Jesus answered,
  "Neither he nor his parents sinned;
  it is so that the works of God might be made visible through him.
We have to do the works of the one who sent me while it is day.
Night is coming when no one can work.
While I am in the world, I am the light of the world."
When he had said this, he spat on the ground
  and made clay with the saliva,
  and smeared the clay on his eyes, and said to him,
  "Go wash in the Pool of Siloam"—which means Sent—.
So he went and washed, and came back able to see.

His neighbors and those who had seen him earlier as a beggar said,
  "Isn't this the one who used to sit and beg?"
Some said, "It is,"
  but others said, "No, he just looks like him."
He said, "I am."
So they said to him, "How were your eyes opened?"
He replied,
  "The man called Jesus made clay and anointed my eyes
  and told me, 'Go to Siloam and wash.'
So I went there and washed and was able to see."
And they said to him, "Where is he?"
He said, "I don't know."

They brought the one who was once blind to the Pharisees.
Now Jesus had made clay and opened his eyes on a sabbath.
So then the Pharisees also asked him how he was able to see.
He said to them,
  "He put clay on my eyes, and I washed, and now I can see."
So some of the Pharisees said,
  "This man is not from God,
  because he does not keep the sabbath."
But others said,
  "How can a sinful man do such signs?"
And there was a division among them.
So they said to the blind man again,
  "What do you have to say about him,
  since he opened your eyes?"
He said, "He is a prophet."

Now the Jews did not believe
  that he had been blind and gained his sight
  until they summoned the parents of the one who had gained his
    sight.
They asked them,
  "Is this your son, who you say was born blind?
How does he now see?"
His parents answered and said,
  "We know that this is our son and that he was born blind.
We do not know how he sees now,
  nor do we know who opened his eyes.
Ask him, he is of age;
  he can speak for himself."

His parents said this because they were afraid of the Jews,
  for the Jews had already agreed
  that if anyone acknowledged him as the Christ,
  he would be expelled from the synagogue.
For this reason his parents said,
  "He is of age; question him."

So a second time they called the man who had been blind
  and said to him, "Give God the praise!
We know that this man is a sinner."
He replied,
  "If he is a sinner, I do not know.
One thing I do know is that I was blind and now I see."
So they said to him,
  "What did he do to you?
How did he open your eyes?"
He answered them,
  "I told you already and you did not listen.
Why do you want to hear it again?
Do you want to become his disciples, too?"
They ridiculed him and said,
  "You are that man's disciple;
  we are disciples of Moses!
We know that God spoke to Moses,
  but we do not know where this one is from."
The man answered and said to them,
  "This is what is so amazing,
  that you do not know where he is from, yet he opened my eyes.
We know that God does not listen to sinners,
  but if one is devout and does his will, he listens to him.
It is unheard of that anyone ever opened the eyes of a person born
    blind.
If this man were not from God,
  he would not be able to do anything."
They answered and said to him,
  "You were born totally in sin,
  and are you trying to teach us?"
Then they threw him out.

When Jesus heard that they had thrown him out,
  he found him and said, "Do you believe in the Son of Man?"
He answered and said,
  "Who is he, sir, that I may believe in him?"
Jesus said to him,
  "You have seen him,
  and the one speaking with you is he."
He said,
  "I do believe, Lord," and he worshiped him.
Then Jesus said,
  "I came into this world for judgment,
  so that those who do not see might see,
  and those who do see might become blind."

Some of the Pharisees who were with him heard this
  and said to him, "Surely we are not also blind, are we?"
Jesus said to them,
  "If you were blind, you would have no sin;
  but now you are saying, 'We see,' so your sin remains."

Gospel

John 9:1, 6-9, 13-17, 34-38; L31A

As Jesus passed by he saw a man blind from birth.
He spat on the ground and made clay with the saliva,
   and smeared the clay on his eyes, and said to him,
   "Go wash in the Pool of Siloam"—which means Sent—.
So he went and washed, and came back able to see.

His neighbors and those who had seen him earlier as a beggar said,
   "Isn't this the one who used to sit and beg?"
Some said, "It is,"
   but others said, "No, he just looks like him."
He said, "I am."

They brought the one who was once blind to the Pharisees.
Now Jesus had made clay and opened his eyes on a sabbath.
So then the Pharisees also asked him how he was able to see.
He said to them,
   "He put clay on my eyes, and I washed, and now I can see."
So some of the Pharisees said,
   "This man is not from God,
   because he does not keep the sabbath."
But others said,
   "How can a sinful man do such signs?"

And there was a division among them.
So they said to the blind man again,
   "What do you have to say about him,
   since he opened your eyes?"
He said, "He is a prophet."

They answered and said to him,
   "You were born totally in sin,
   and are you trying to teach us?"
Then they threw him out.

When Jesus heard that they had thrown him out,
   he found him and said, "Do you believe in the Son of Man?"
He answered and said,
   "Who is he, sir, that I may believe in him?"
Jesus said to him,
   "You have seen him,
   and the one speaking with you is he."
He said,
   "I do believe, Lord," and he worshiped him.

FIRST READING 1 Sam 16:1b, 6-7, 10-13a

The LORD said to Samuel:
   "Fill your horn with oil, and be on your way.
I am sending you to Jesse of Bethlehem,
   for I have chosen my king from among his sons."

As Jesse and his sons came to the sacrifice,
   Samuel looked at Eliab and thought,
   "Surely the LORD's anointed is here before him."
But the LORD said to Samuel:
   "Do not judge from his appearance or from his lofty stature,
   because I have rejected him.
Not as man sees does God see,
   because man sees the appearance
   but the LORD looks into the heart."
In the same way Jesse presented seven sons
      before Samuel,
   but Samuel said to Jesse,
   "The LORD has not chosen any one of these."
Then Samuel asked Jesse,
   "Are these all the sons you have?"
Jesse replied,
   "There is still the youngest, who is tending the sheep."
Samuel said to Jesse,
   "Send for him;
   we will not begin the sacrificial banquet
      until he arrives here."
Jesse sent and had the young man brought to them.
He was ruddy, a youth handsome to behold
   and making a splendid appearance.

The LORD said,
   "There—anoint him, for this is the one!"
Then Samuel, with the horn of oil in hand,
   anointed David in the presence of his brothers;
   and from that day on, the spirit of the LORD
      rushed upon David.

RESPONSORIAL PSALM Ps 23:1-3a, 3b-4, 5, 6

R̸. (1) The Lord is my shepherd; there is nothing I shall want.

The LORD is my shepherd; I shall not want.
   In verdant pastures he gives me repose;
beside restful waters he leads me;
   he refreshes my soul.

R̸. The Lord is my shepherd; there is nothing I shall want.

He guides me in right paths
   for his name's sake.
Even though I walk in the dark valley
   I fear no evil; for you are at my side
with your rod and your staff
   that give me courage.

R̸. The Lord is my shepherd; there is nothing I shall want.

You spread the table before me
   in the sight of my foes;
you anoint my head with oil;
   my cup overflows.

R̸. The Lord is my shepherd; there is nothing I shall want.

Only goodness and kindness follow me
   all the days of my life;
and I shall dwell in the house of the LORD
   for years to come.

R̸. The Lord is my shepherd; there is nothing I shall want.

SECOND READING
Eph 5:8-14

Brothers and sisters:
You were once darkness,
   but now you are light in the Lord.
Live as children of light,
   for light produces every kind of goodness
   and righteousness and truth.
Try to learn what is pleasing to the Lord.
Take no part in the fruitless works of darkness;
   rather expose them, for it is shameful even
      to mention
   the things done by them in secret;
   but everything exposed by the light
      becomes visible,
   for everything that becomes visible is light.
Therefore, it says:
   "Awake, O sleeper,
   and arise from the dead,
   and Christ will give you light."

Gospel

John 11:1-45; L34A

Now a man was ill, Lazarus from Bethany,
    the village of Mary and her sister Martha.
Mary was the one who had anointed the Lord with perfumed oil
    and dried his feet with her hair;
    it was her brother Lazarus who was ill.
So the sisters sent word to Jesus saying,
    "Master, the one you love is ill."
When Jesus heard this he said,
    "This illness is not to end in death,
    but is for the glory of God,
    that the Son of God may be glorified through it."
Now Jesus loved Martha and her sister and Lazarus.
So when he heard that he was ill,
    he remained for two days in the place where he was.
Then after this he said to his disciples,
    "Let us go back to Judea."
The disciples said to him,
    "Rabbi, the Jews were just trying to stone you,
    and you want to go back there?"
Jesus answered,
    "Are there not twelve hours in a day?
If one walks during the day, he does not stumble,
    because he sees the light of this world.
But if one walks at night, he stumbles,
    because the light is not in him."
He said this, and then told them,
    "Our friend Lazarus is asleep,
    but I am going to awaken him."
So the disciples said to him,
    "Master, if he is asleep, he will be saved."
But Jesus was talking about his death,
    while they thought that he meant ordinary sleep.
So then Jesus said to them clearly,
    "Lazarus has died.
And I am glad for you that I was not there,
    that you may believe.
Let us go to him."
So Thomas, called Didymus, said to his fellow disciples,
    "Let us also go to die with him."

When Jesus arrived, he found that Lazarus
    had already been in the tomb for four days.
Now Bethany was near Jerusalem, only about two miles away.
And many of the Jews had come to Martha and Mary
    to comfort them about their brother.
When Martha heard that Jesus was coming,
    she went to meet him;
    but Mary sat at home.
Martha said to Jesus,
    "Lord, if you had been here,
    my brother would not have died.
But even now I know that whatever you ask of God,
    God will give you."
Jesus said to her,
    "Your brother will rise."
Martha said to him,
    "I know he will rise,
    in the resurrection on the last day."
Jesus told her,

    "I am the resurrection and the life;
    whoever believes in me, even if he dies, will live,
    and everyone who lives and believes in me will never die.
Do you believe this?"
She said to him, "Yes, Lord.
I have come to believe that you are the Christ, the Son of God,
    the one who is coming into the world."

When she had said this,
    she went and called her sister Mary secretly, saying,
    "The teacher is here and is asking for you."
As soon as she heard this,
    she rose quickly and went to him.
For Jesus had not yet come into the village,
    but was still where Martha had met him.
So when the Jews who were with her in the house comforting her
    saw Mary get up quickly and go out,
    they followed her,
    presuming that she was going to the tomb to weep there.
When Mary came to where Jesus was and saw him,
    she fell at his feet and said to him,
    "Lord, if you had been here,
    my brother would not have died."
When Jesus saw her weeping and the Jews who had come with her
      weeping,
    he became perturbed and deeply troubled, and said,
    "Where have you laid him?"
They said to him, "Sir, come and see."
And Jesus wept.
So the Jews said, "See how he loved him."
But some of them said,
    "Could not the one who opened the eyes of the blind man
    have done something so that this man would not have died?"

So Jesus, perturbed again, came to the tomb.
It was a cave, and a stone lay across it.
Jesus said, "Take away the stone."
Martha, the dead man's sister, said to him,
    "Lord, by now there will be a stench;
    he has been dead for four days."
Jesus said to her,
    "Did I not tell you that if you believe
    you will see the glory of God?"
So they took away the stone.
And Jesus raised his eyes and said,
    "Father, I thank you for hearing me.
I know that you always hear me;
    but because of the crowd here I have said this,
    that they may believe that you sent me."
And when he had said this,
    he cried out in a loud voice,
    "Lazarus, come out!"
The dead man came out,
    tied hand and foot with burial bands,
    and his face was wrapped in a cloth.
So Jesus said to them,
    "Untie him and let him go."

Now many of the Jews who had come to Mary
    and seen what he had done began to believe in him.

Gospel
John 11:3-7, 17, 20-27, 33b-45; L34A

The sisters of Lazarus sent word to Jesus, saying,
    "Master, the one you love is ill."
When Jesus heard this he said,
    "This illness is not to end in death,
    but is for the glory of God,
    that the Son of God may be glorified through it."
Now Jesus loved Martha and her sister and Lazarus.
So when he heard that he was ill,
    he remained for two days in the place where he was.
Then after this he said to his disciples,
    "Let us go back to Judea."

When Jesus arrived, he found that Lazarus
    had already been in the tomb for four days.
When Martha heard that Jesus was coming,
    she went to meet him;
    but Mary sat at home.
Martha said to Jesus,
    "Lord, if you had been here,
    my brother would not have died.
But even now I know that whatever you ask of God,
    God will give you."
Jesus said to her,
    "Your brother will rise."
Martha said,
    "I know he will rise,
    in the resurrection on the last day."
Jesus told her,
    "I am the resurrection and the life;
    whoever believes in me, even if he dies, will live,
    and everyone who lives and believes in me will never die.
Do you believe this?"
She said to him, "Yes, Lord.
I have come to believe that you are the Christ, the Son of God,
    the one who is coming into the world."

He became perturbed and deeply troubled, and said,
    "Where have you laid him?"
They said to him, "Sir, come and see."
And Jesus wept.
So the Jews said, "See how he loved him."
But some of them said,
    "Could not the one who opened the eyes of the blind man
    have done something so that this man would not have died?"

So Jesus, perturbed again, came to the tomb.
It was a cave, and a stone lay across it.
Jesus said, "Take away the stone."
Martha, the dead man's sister, said to him,
    "Lord, by now there will be a stench;
    he has been dead for four days."
Jesus said to her,
    "Did I not tell you that if you believe
    you will see the glory of God?"
So they took away the stone.
And Jesus raised his eyes and said,
    "Father, I thank you for hearing me.
I know that you always hear me;
    but because of the crowd here I have said this,
    that they may believe that you sent me."
And when he had said this,
    he cried out in a loud voice,
    "Lazarus, come out!"
The dead man came out,
    tied hand and foot with burial bands,
    and his face was wrapped in a cloth.
So Jesus said to them,
    "Untie him and let him go."

Now many of the Jews who had come to Mary
    and seen what he had done began to believe in him.

FIRST READING
Ezek 37:12-14

Thus says the Lord GOD:
   O my people, I will open your graves
   and have you rise from them,
   and bring you back to the land of Israel.
Then you shall know that I am the LORD,
   when I open your graves and have you rise
      from them,
   O my people!
I will put my spirit in you that you may live,
   and I will settle you upon your land;
   thus you shall know that I am the LORD.
I have promised, and I will do it, says the
      LORD.

RESPONSORIAL PSALM
Ps 130:1-2, 3-4, 5-6, 7-8

R⁊. (7) With the Lord there is mercy and fullness of redemption.

Out of the depths I cry to you, O LORD;
   LORD, hear my voice!
Let your ears be attentive
   to my voice in supplication.

R⁊. With the Lord there is mercy and fullness
of redemption.

If you, O LORD, mark iniquities,
   LORD, who can stand?
But with you is forgiveness,
   that you may be revered.

R⁊. With the Lord there is mercy and fullness
of redemption.

I trust in the LORD;
   my soul trusts in his word.
More than sentinels wait for the dawn,
   let Israel wait for the LORD.

R⁊. With the Lord there is mercy and fullness
of redemption.

For with the LORD is kindness
   and with him is plenteous redemption;
and he will redeem Israel
   from all their iniquities.

R⁊. With the Lord there is mercy and fullness
of redemption.

SECOND READING
Rom 8:8-11

Brothers and sisters:
Those who are in the flesh cannot please God.
But you are not in the flesh;
   on the contrary, you are in the spirit,
   if only the Spirit of God dwells in you.
Whoever does not have the Spirit of Christ
      does not belong to him.
But if Christ is in you,
   although the body is dead because of sin,
   the spirit is alive because of righteousness.
If the Spirit of the One who raised Jesus from
      the dead dwells in you,
   the One who raised Christ from the dead
   will give life to your mortal bodies also,
   through his Spirit dwelling in you.

St. Joseph, Spouse of the Blessed Virgin Mary, *March 19, 2016*

Gospel
Matt 1:16, 18-21, 24a; L543

Jacob was the father of Joseph, the husband of Mary.
Of her was born Jesus who is called the Christ.

Now this is how the birth of Jesus Christ came about.
When his mother Mary was betrothed to Joseph,
    but before they lived together,
      she was found with child through the Holy Spirit.
Joseph her husband, since he was a righteous man,
    yet unwilling to expose her to shame,
      decided to divorce her quietly.
Such was his intention when, behold,
    the angel of the Lord appeared to him in a dream and said,
      "Joseph, son of David,
    do not be afraid to take Mary your wife into your home.
For it is through the Holy Spirit
    that this child has been conceived in her.
She will bear a son and you are to name him Jesus,
    because he will save his people from their sins."
When Joseph awoke,
    he did as the angel of the Lord had commanded him
    and took his wife into his home.

FIRST READING
2 Sam 7:4-5a, 12-14a, 16

The LORD spoke to Nathan and said:
"Go, tell my servant David,
    'When your time comes and you rest with
      your ancestors,
    I will raise up your heir after you, sprung
      from your loins,
    and I will make his kingdom firm.
It is he who shall build a house for my name.
And I will make his royal throne firm forever.
I will be a father to him,
    and he shall be a son to me.
Your house and your kingdom shall endure
    forever before me;
    your throne shall stand firm forever.'"

RESPONSORIAL PSALM
Ps 89:2-3, 4-5, 27, and 29

R̃. (37) The son of David will live forever.

The promises of the LORD I will sing forever,
    through all generations my mouth will
      proclaim your faithfulness,
For you have said, "My kindness is
    established forever";
    in heaven you have confirmed your
    faithfulness.

R̃. The son of David will live forever.

"I have made a covenant with my chosen one;
    I have sworn to David my servant:
Forever will I confirm your posterity
    and establish your throne for all
    generations."

R̃. The son of David will live forever.

"He shall say of me, 'You are my father,
    my God, the Rock, my savior!'
Forever I will maintain my kindness toward
    him,
    my covenant with him stands firm."

R̃. The son of David will live forever.

SECOND READING
Rom 4:13, 16-18, 22

Brothers and sisters:
It was not through the law
    that the promise was made to Abraham
      and his descendants
    that he would inherit the world,
    but through the righteousness that comes
      from faith.
For this reason, it depends on faith,
    so that it may be a gift,
    and the promise may be guaranteed to all
      his descendants,
    not to those who only adhere to the law
    but to those who follow the faith of Abraham,
    who is the father of all of us, as it is written,
I have made you father of many nations.
He is our father in the sight of God,
    in whom he believed, who gives life to the
      dead
    and calls into being what does not exist.
He believed, hoping against hope,
    that he would become *the father of many*
      nations,
    according to what was said, *Thus shall*
      your descendants be.
That is why *it was credited to him as*
    righteousness.

Gospel at the Procession with Palms (cont.)
Luke 19:28-40; L37C

They proclaimed:
"Blessed is the king who comes
in the name of the Lord.
Peace in heaven
and glory in the highest."
Some of the Pharisees in the crowd said to him,
"Teacher, rebuke your disciples."
He said in reply,
"I tell you, if they keep silent,
the stones will cry out!"

Gospel at Mass
Luke 22:14–23:56; L38ABC

When the hour came,
Jesus took his place at table with the apostles.
He said to them,
"I have eagerly desired to eat this Passover with you before I suffer,
for, I tell you, I shall not eat it again
until there is fulfillment in the kingdom of God."
Then he took a cup, gave thanks, and said,
"Take this and share it among yourselves;
for I tell you that from this time on
I shall not drink of the fruit of the vine
until the kingdom of God comes."
Then he took the bread, said the blessing,
broke it, and gave it to them, saying,
"This is my body, which will be given for you;
do this in memory of me."
And likewise the cup after they had eaten, saying,
"This cup is the new covenant in my blood,
which will be shed for you.

"And yet behold, the hand of the one who is to betray me
is with me on the table;
for the Son of Man indeed goes as it has been determined;
but woe to that man by whom he is betrayed."
And they began to debate among themselves
who among them would do such a deed.

Then an argument broke out among them
about which of them should be regarded as the greatest.
He said to them,
"The kings of the Gentiles lord it over them
and those in authority over them are addressed as 'Benefactors';
but among you it shall not be so.
Rather, let the greatest among you be as the youngest,
and the leader as the servant.
For who is greater:
the one seated at table or the one who serves?
Is it not the one seated at table?
I am among you as the one who serves.
It is you who have stood by me in my trials;
and I confer a kingdom on you,
just as my Father has conferred one on me,
that you may eat and drink at my table in my kingdom;
and you will sit on thrones
judging the twelve tribes of Israel.

"Simon, Simon, behold Satan has demanded
to sift all of you like wheat,
but I have prayed that your own faith may not fail;
and once you have turned back,
you must strengthen your brothers."
He said to him,
"Lord, I am prepared to go to prison and to die with you."
But he replied,
"I tell you, Peter, before the cock crows this day,
you will deny three times that you know me."

He said to them,
"When I sent you forth without a money bag or a sack or sandals,
were you in need of anything?"
"No, nothing," they replied.
He said to them,
"But now one who has a money bag should take it,
and likewise a sack,
and one who does not have a sword
should sell his cloak and buy one.
For I tell you that this Scripture must be fulfilled in me,
namely, *He was counted among the wicked;*
and indeed what is written about me is coming to fulfillment."
Then they said,
"Lord, look, there are two swords here."
But he replied, "It is enough!"

Then going out, he went, as was his custom, to the Mount of Olives,
and the disciples followed him.
When he arrived at the place he said to them,
"Pray that you may not undergo the test."
After withdrawing about a stone's throw from them and kneeling,
he prayed, saying, "Father, if you are willing,
take this cup away from me;
still, not my will but yours be done."
And to strengthen him an angel from heaven appeared to him.
He was in such agony and he prayed so fervently
that his sweat became like drops of blood
falling on the ground.
When he rose from prayer and returned to his disciples,
he found them sleeping from grief.
He said to them, "Why are you sleeping?
Get up and pray that you may not undergo the test."

While he was still speaking, a crowd approached
and in front was one of the Twelve, a man named Judas.
He went up to Jesus to kiss him.
Jesus said to him,
"Judas, are you betraying the Son of Man with a kiss?"
His disciples realized what was about to happen, and they asked,
"Lord, shall we strike with a sword?"
And one of them struck the high priest's servant
and cut off his right ear.
But Jesus said in reply,
"Stop, no more of this!"
Then he touched the servant's ear and healed him.
And Jesus said to the chief priests and temple guards
and elders who had come for him,
"Have you come out as against a robber, with swords and clubs?
Day after day I was with you in the temple area,
and you did not seize me;
but this is your hour, the time for the power of darkness."

After arresting him they led him away
and took him into the house of the high priest;
Peter was following at a distance.

They lit a fire in the middle of the courtyard and sat around it,
    and Peter sat down with them.
When a maid saw him seated in the light,
    she looked intently at him and said,
    "This man too was with him."
But he denied it saying,
    "Woman, I do not know him."
A short while later someone else saw him and said,
    "You too are one of them";
    but Peter answered, "My friend, I am not."
About an hour later, still another insisted,
    "Assuredly, this man too was with him,
    for he also is a Galilean."
But Peter said,
    "My friend, I do not know what you are talking about."
Just as he was saying this, the cock crowed,
    and the Lord turned and looked at Peter;
    and Peter remembered the word of the Lord,
    how he had said to him,
    "Before the cock crows today, you will deny me three times."
He went out and began to weep bitterly.
The men who held Jesus in custody were ridiculing and beating him.
They blindfolded him and questioned him, saying,
    "Prophesy! Who is it that struck you?"
And they reviled him in saying many other things against him.

When day came the council of elders of the people met,
    both chief priests and scribes,
    and they brought him before their Sanhedrin.
They said, "If you are the Christ, tell us,"
    but he replied to them, "If I tell you, you will not believe,
    and if I question, you will not respond.
But from this time on the Son of Man will be seated
    at the right hand of the power of God."
They all asked, "Are you then the Son of God?"
He replied to them, "You say that I am."
Then they said, "What further need have we for testimony?
We have heard it from his own mouth."

Then the whole assembly of them arose and brought him before Pilate.
They brought charges against him, saying,
    "We found this man misleading our people;
    he opposes the payment of taxes to Caesar
    and maintains that he is the Christ, a king."
Pilate asked him, "Are you the king of the Jews?"
He said to him in reply, "You say so."
Pilate then addressed the chief priests and the crowds,
    "I find this man not guilty."
But they were adamant and said,
    "He is inciting the people with his teaching
        throughout all Judea,
    from Galilee where he began even to here."

On hearing this Pilate asked if the man was a Galilean;
    and upon learning that he was under Herod's jurisdiction,
    he sent him to Herod who was in Jerusalem at that time.
Herod was very glad to see Jesus;
    he had been wanting to see him for a long time,
    for he had heard about him
    and had been hoping to see him perform some sign.
He questioned him at length,
    but he gave him no answer.

The chief priests and scribes, meanwhile,
    stood by accusing him harshly.
Herod and his soldiers treated him contemptuously and mocked him,
    and after clothing him in resplendent garb,
    he sent him back to Pilate.
Herod and Pilate became friends that very day,
    even though they had been enemies formerly.
Pilate then summoned the chief priests, the rulers, and the people
    and said to them, "You brought this man to me
    and accused him of inciting the people to revolt.
I have conducted my investigation in your presence
    and have not found this man guilty
    of the charges you have brought against him,
    nor did Herod, for he sent him back to us.
So no capital crime has been committed by him.
Therefore I shall have him flogged and then release him."

But all together they shouted out,
    "Away with this man!
    Release Barabbas to us."
—Now Barabbas had been imprisoned for a rebellion
    that had taken place in the city and for murder.—
Again Pilate addressed them, still wishing to release Jesus,
    but they continued their shouting,
    "Crucify him! Crucify him!"
Pilate addressed them a third time,
    "What evil has this man done?
    I found him guilty of no capital crime.
Therefore I shall have him flogged and then release him."
With loud shouts, however,
    they persisted in calling for his crucifixion,
    and their voices prevailed.
The verdict of Pilate was that their demand should be granted.
So he released the man who had been imprisoned
    for rebellion and murder, for whom they asked,
    and he handed Jesus over to them to deal with as they wished.

As they led him away
    they took hold of a certain Simon, a Cyrenian,
    who was coming in from the country;
    and after laying the cross on him,
    they made him carry it behind Jesus.
A large crowd of people followed Jesus,
    including many women who mourned and lamented him.
Jesus turned to them and said,
    "Daughters of Jerusalem, do not weep for me;
    weep instead for yourselves and for your children
    for indeed, the days are coming when people will say,
    'Blessed are the barren,
    the wombs that never bore
    and the breasts that never nursed.'
At that time people will say to the mountains,
    'Fall upon us!'
    and to the hills, 'Cover us!'
    for if these things are done when the wood is green
    what will happen when it is dry?"
Now two others, both criminals,
    were led away with him to be executed.

When they came to the place called the Skull,
    they crucified him and the criminals there,
    one on his right, the other on his left.

Then Jesus said,
  "Father, forgive them, they know not what they do."
They divided his garments by casting lots.
The people stood by and watched;
  the rulers, meanwhile, sneered at him and said,
  "He saved others, let him save himself
  if he is the chosen one, the Christ of God."
Even the soldiers jeered at him.
As they approached to offer him wine they called out,
  "If you are King of the Jews, save yourself."
Above him there was an inscription that read,
  "This is the King of the Jews."

Now one of the criminals hanging there reviled Jesus, saying,
  "Are you not the Christ?
  Save yourself and us."
The other, however, rebuking him, said in reply,
  "Have you no fear of God,
  for you are subject to the same condemnation?
And indeed, we have been condemned justly,
  for the sentence we received corresponds to our crimes,
  but this man has done nothing criminal."
Then he said,
  "Jesus, remember me when you come into your kingdom."
He replied to him,
  "Amen, I say to you,
  today you will be with me in Paradise."

It was now about noon and darkness came over the whole land
  until three in the afternoon
  because of an eclipse of the sun.
Then the veil of the temple was torn down the middle.
Jesus cried out in a loud voice,
  "Father, into your hands I commend my spirit";
  and when he had said this he breathed his last.

Here all kneel and pause for a short time.

The centurion who witnessed what had happened glorified God and said,
  "This man was innocent beyond doubt."
When all the people who had gathered for this spectacle
    saw what had happened,
  they returned home beating their breasts;
  but all his acquaintances stood at a distance,
  including the women who had followed him from Galilee
  and saw these events.

Now there was a virtuous and righteous man named Joseph who,
  though he was a member of the council,
  had not consented to their plan of action.
He came from the Jewish town of Arimathea
  and was awaiting the kingdom of God.
He went to Pilate and asked for the body of Jesus.
After he had taken the body down,
  he wrapped it in a linen cloth
  and laid him in a rock-hewn tomb
  in which no one had yet been buried.
It was the day of preparation,
  and the sabbath was about to begin.
The women who had come from Galilee with him followed behind,
  and when they had seen the tomb
  and the way in which his body was laid in it,
  they returned and prepared spices and perfumed oils.
Then they rested on the sabbath according to the commandment.

or Luke 23:1-49

The elders of the people, chief priests and scribes,
  arose and brought Jesus before Pilate.
They brought charges against him, saying,
  "We found this man misleading our people;
  he opposes the payment of taxes to Caesar
  and maintains that he is the Christ, a king."
Pilate asked him, "Are you the king of the Jews?"
He said to him in reply, "You say so."
Pilate then addressed the chief priests and the crowds,
  "I find this man not guilty."
But they were adamant and said,
  "He is inciting the people with his teaching
    throughout all Judea,
  from Galilee where he began even to here."

On hearing this Pilate asked if the man was a Galilean;
  and upon learning that he was under Herod's jurisdiction,
  he sent him to Herod who was in Jerusalem at that time.
Herod was very glad to see Jesus;
  he had been wanting to see him for a long time,
  for he had heard about him
  and had been hoping to see him perform some sign.
He questioned him at length,
  but he gave him no answer.
The chief priests and scribes, meanwhile,
  stood by accusing him harshly.
Herod and his soldiers treated him contemptuously and mocked him,
  and after clothing him in resplendent garb,
  he sent him back to Pilate.
Herod and Pilate became friends that very day,
  even though they had been enemies formerly.
Pilate then summoned the chief priests, the rulers, and the people
  and said to them, "You brought this man to me
  and accused him of inciting the people to revolt.
I have conducted my investigation in your presence
  and have not found this man guilty
  of the charges you have brought against him,
  nor did Herod, for he sent him back to us.
So no capital crime has been committed by him.
Therefore I shall have him flogged and then release him."

But all together they shouted out,
  "Away with this man!
  Release Barabbas to us."
—Now Barabbas had been imprisoned for a rebellion
  that had taken place in the city and for murder.—
Again Pilate addressed them, still wishing to release Jesus,
  but they continued their shouting,
  "Crucify him! Crucify him!"
Pilate addressed them a third time,
  "What evil has this man done?
  I found him guilty of no capital crime.
Therefore I shall have him flogged and then release him."
With loud shouts, however,
  they persisted in calling for his crucifixion,
  and their voices prevailed.
The verdict of Pilate was that their demand should be granted.
So he released the man who had been imprisoned
  for rebellion and murder, for whom they asked,
  and he handed Jesus over to them to deal with as they wished.

Gospel (cont.)
Luke 23:1-49

As they led him away
   they took hold of a certain Simon, a Cyrenian,
   who was coming in from the country;
   and after laying the cross on him,
   they made him carry it behind Jesus.
A large crowd of people followed Jesus,
   including many women who mourned and lamented him.
Jesus turned to them and said,
   "Daughters of Jerusalem, do not weep for me;
   weep instead for yourselves and for your children
   for indeed, the days are coming when people will say,
   'Blessed are the barren,
   the wombs that never bore
   and the breasts that never nursed.'
At that time people will say to the mountains,
   'Fall upon us!'
   and to the hills, 'Cover us!'
   for if these things are done when the wood is green
   what will happen when it is dry?"
Now two others, both criminals,
   were led away with him to be executed.

When they came to the place called the Skull,
   they crucified him and the criminals there,
   one on his right, the other on his left.
Then Jesus said,
   "Father, forgive them, they know not what they do."
They divided his garments by casting lots.
The people stood by and watched;
   the rulers, meanwhile, sneered at him and said,
   "He saved others, let him save himself
   if he is the chosen one, the Christ of God."
Even the soldiers jeered at him.

As they approached to offer him wine they called out,
   "If you are King of the Jews, save yourself."
Above him there was an inscription that read,
   "This is the King of the Jews."

Now one of the criminals hanging there reviled Jesus, saying,
   "Are you not the Christ?
   Save yourself and us."
The other, however, rebuking him, said in reply,
   "Have you no fear of God,
   for you are subject to the same condemnation?
And indeed, we have been condemned justly,
   for the sentence we received corresponds to our crimes,
   but this man has done nothing criminal."
Then he said,
   "Jesus, remember me when you come into your kingdom."
He replied to him,
   "Amen, I say to you,
   today you will be with me in Paradise."

It was now about noon and darkness came over the whole land
   until three in the afternoon
   because of an eclipse of the sun.
Then the veil of the temple was torn down the middle.
Jesus cried out in a loud voice,
   "Father, into your hands I commend my spirit";
   and when he had said this he breathed his last.

Here all kneel and pause for a short time.

The centurion who witnessed what had happened glorified God and said,
   "This man was innocent beyond doubt."
When all the people who had gathered for this spectacle
      saw what had happened,
   they returned home beating their breasts;
   but all his acquaintances stood at a distance,
   including the women who had followed him from Galilee
   and saw these events.

Gospel (cont.)

John 13:1-15; L39ABC

Simon Peter said to him,
  "Master, then not only my feet, but my hands and head as well."
Jesus said to him,
  "Whoever has bathed has no need except to have his feet washed,
    for he is clean all over;
  so you are clean, but not all."
For he knew who would betray him;
  for this reason, he said, "Not all of you are clean."

So when he had washed their feet
  and put his garments back on and reclined at table again,
  he said to them, "Do you realize what I have done for you?
You call me 'teacher' and 'master,' and rightly so, for indeed I am.
If I, therefore, the master and teacher, have washed your feet,
  you ought to wash one another's feet.
I have given you a model to follow,
  so that as I have done for you, you should also do."

FIRST READING

Exod 12:1-8, 11-14

The LORD said to Moses and Aaron in the
    land of Egypt,
  "This month shall stand at the head of
    your calendar;
  you shall reckon it the first month of the
    year.
Tell the whole community of Israel:
  On the tenth of this month every one of
    your families
  must procure for itself a lamb, one apiece
    for each household.
If a family is too small for a whole lamb,
  it shall join the nearest household in
    procuring one
  and shall share in the lamb
  in proportion to the number of persons
    who partake of it.
The lamb must be a year-old male and
    without blemish.
You may take it from either the sheep or the
    goats.
You shall keep it until the fourteenth day of
    this month,
  and then, with the whole assembly of Israel
    present,
  it shall be slaughtered during the evening
    twilight.
They shall take some of its blood
  and apply it to the two doorposts and the
    lintel
  of every house in which they partake of
    the lamb.
That same night they shall eat its roasted
    flesh
  with unleavened bread and bitter herbs.
"This is how you are to eat it:
  with your loins girt, sandals on your feet
    and your staff in hand,
  you shall eat like those who are in flight.

It is the Passover of the LORD.
For on this same night I will go through Egypt,
  striking down every firstborn of the land,
    both man and beast,
  and executing judgment on all the gods of
    Egypt—I, the LORD!
But the blood will mark the houses where you
    are.
Seeing the blood, I will pass over you;
  thus, when I strike the land of Egypt,
  no destructive blow will come upon you.

"This day shall be a memorial feast for you,
  which all your generations shall celebrate
  with pilgrimage to the LORD, as a perpetual
    institution."

RESPONSORIAL PSALM

Ps 116:12-13, 15-16bc, 17-18

℟. (cf. 1 Cor 10:16) Our blessing-cup is a communion with the Blood of Christ.

How shall I make a return to the LORD
  for all the good he has done for me?
The cup of salvation I will take up,
  and I will call upon the name of the LORD.

℟. Our blessing-cup is a communion with the Blood of Christ.

Precious in the eyes of the LORD
  is the death of his faithful ones.
I am your servant, the son of your handmaid;
  you have loosed my bonds.

℟. Our blessing-cup is a communion with the Blood of Christ.

To you will I offer sacrifice of thanksgiving,
  and I will call upon the name of the LORD.
My vows to the LORD I will pay
  in the presence of all his people.

℟. Our blessing-cup is a communion with the Blood of Christ.

SECOND READING

1 Cor 11:23-26

Brothers and sisters:
I received from the Lord what I also handed
    on to you,
  that the Lord Jesus, on the night he was
    handed over,
  took bread, and, after he had given thanks,
  broke it and said, "This is my body that is
    for you.
Do this in remembrance of me."
In the same way also the cup, after supper,
    saying,
  "This cup is the new covenant in my blood.
Do this, as often as you drink it, in
    remembrance of me."
For as often as you eat this bread and drink
    the cup,
  you proclaim the death of the Lord until he
    comes.

Gospel (cont.)
John 18:1–19:42; L40ABC

So the band of soldiers, the tribune, and the Jewish guards seized Jesus,
 bound him, and brought him to Annas first.
He was the father-in-law of Caiaphas,
 who was high priest that year.
It was Caiaphas who had counseled the Jews
 that it was better that one man should die rather than the people.

Simon Peter and another disciple followed Jesus.
Now the other disciple was known to the high priest,
 and he entered the courtyard of the high priest with Jesus.
But Peter stood at the gate outside.
So the other disciple, the acquaintance of the high priest,
 went out and spoke to the gatekeeper and brought Peter in.
Then the maid who was the gatekeeper said to Peter,
 "You are not one of this man's disciples, are you?"
He said, "I am not."
Now the slaves and the guards were standing around a charcoal fire
 that they had made, because it was cold,
 and were warming themselves.
Peter was also standing there keeping warm.

The high priest questioned Jesus
 about his disciples and about his doctrine.
Jesus answered him,
 "I have spoken publicly to the world.
I have always taught in a synagogue
 or in the temple area where all the Jews gather,
 and in secret I have said nothing. Why ask me?
Ask those who heard me what I said to them.
They know what I said."
When he had said this,
 one of the temple guards standing there struck Jesus and said,
 "Is this the way you answer the high priest?"
Jesus answered him,
 "If I have spoken wrongly, testify to the wrong;
 but if I have spoken rightly, why do you strike me?"
Then Annas sent him bound to Caiaphas the high priest.

Now Simon Peter was standing there keeping warm.
And they said to him,
 "You are not one of his disciples, are you?"
He denied it and said,
 "I am not."
One of the slaves of the high priest,
 a relative of the one whose ear Peter had cut off, said,
 "Didn't I see you in the garden with him?"
Again Peter denied it.
And immediately the cock crowed.

Then they brought Jesus from Caiaphas to the praetorium.
It was morning.
And they themselves did not enter the praetorium,
 in order not to be defiled so that they could eat the Passover.
So Pilate came out to them and said,
 "What charge do you bring against this man?"
They answered and said to him,
 "If he were not a criminal,
 we would not have handed him over to you."
At this, Pilate said to them,
 "Take him yourselves, and judge him according to your law."

The Jews answered him,
 "We do not have the right to execute anyone,"
 in order that the word of Jesus might be fulfilled
 that he said indicating the kind of death he would die.
So Pilate went back into the praetorium
 and summoned Jesus and said to him,
 "Are you the King of the Jews?"
Jesus answered,
 "Do you say this on your own
 or have others told you about me?"
Pilate answered,
 "I am not a Jew, am I?
Your own nation and the chief priests handed you over to me.
What have you done?"
Jesus answered,
 "My kingdom does not belong to this world.
If my kingdom did belong to this world,
 my attendants would be fighting
 to keep me from being handed over to the Jews.
But as it is, my kingdom is not here."
So Pilate said to him,
 "Then you are a king?"
Jesus answered,
 "You say I am a king.
For this I was born and for this I came into the world,
 to testify to the truth.
Everyone who belongs to the truth listens to my voice."
Pilate said to him, "What is truth?"

When he had said this,
 he again went out to the Jews and said to them,
 "I find no guilt in him.
But you have a custom that I release one prisoner to you at Passover.
Do you want me to release to you the King of the Jews?"
They cried out again,
 "Not this one but Barabbas!"
Now Barabbas was a revolutionary.

Then Pilate took Jesus and had him scourged.
And the soldiers wove a crown out of thorns and placed it on his head,
 and clothed him in a purple cloak,
 and they came to him and said,
 "Hail, King of the Jews!"
And they struck him repeatedly.
Once more Pilate went out and said to them,
 "Look, I am bringing him out to you,
 so that you may know that I find no guilt in him."
So Jesus came out,
 wearing the crown of thorns and the purple cloak.
And he said to them, "Behold, the man!"
When the chief priests and the guards saw him they cried out,
 "Crucify him, crucify him!"
Pilate said to them,
 "Take him yourselves and crucify him.
I find no guilt in him."
The Jews answered,
 "We have a law, and according to that law he ought to die,
 because he made himself the Son of God."

Now when Pilate heard this statement,
　　he became even more afraid,
　　and went back into the praetorium and said to Jesus,
　　"Where are you from?"
Jesus did not answer him.
So Pilate said to him,
　　"Do you not speak to me?
Do you not know that I have power to release you
　　and I have power to crucify you?"
Jesus answered him,
　　"You would have no power over me
　　if it had not been given to you from above.
For this reason the one who handed me over to you
　　has the greater sin."
Consequently, Pilate tried to release him; but the Jews cried out,
　　"If you release him, you are not a Friend of Caesar.
Everyone who makes himself a king opposes Caesar."

When Pilate heard these words he brought Jesus out
　　and seated him on the judge's bench
　　in the place called Stone Pavement, in Hebrew, Gabbatha.
It was preparation day for Passover, and it was about noon.
And he said to the Jews,
　　"Behold, your king!"
They cried out,
　　"Take him away, take him away! Crucify him!"
Pilate said to them,
　　"Shall I crucify your king?"
The chief priests answered,
　　"We have no king but Caesar."
Then he handed him over to them to be crucified.

So they took Jesus, and, carrying the cross himself,
　　he went out to what is called the Place of the Skull,
　　in Hebrew, Golgotha.
There they crucified him, and with him two others,
　　one on either side, with Jesus in the middle.
Pilate also had an inscription written and put on the cross.
It read,
　　"Jesus the Nazorean, the King of the Jews."
Now many of the Jews read this inscription,
　　because the place where Jesus was crucified was near the city;
　　and it was written in Hebrew, Latin, and Greek.
So the chief priests of the Jews said to Pilate,
　　"Do not write 'The King of the Jews,'
　　but that he said, 'I am the King of the Jews.'"
Pilate answered,
　　"What I have written, I have written."

When the soldiers had crucified Jesus,
　　they took his clothes and divided them into four shares,
　　a share for each soldier.
They also took his tunic, but the tunic was seamless,
　　woven in one piece from the top down.
So they said to one another,
　　"Let's not tear it, but cast lots for it to see whose it will be,"
　　in order that the passage of Scripture might be fulfilled that says:
　　　They divided my garments among them,
　　　and for my vesture they cast lots.

This is what the soldiers did.
Standing by the cross of Jesus were his mother
　　and his mother's sister, Mary the wife of Clopas,
　　and Mary of Magdala.
When Jesus saw his mother and the disciple there whom he loved
　　he said to his mother, "Woman, behold, your son."
Then he said to the disciple,
　　"Behold, your mother."
And from that hour the disciple took her into his home.

After this, aware that everything was now finished,
　　in order that the Scripture might be fulfilled,
　　Jesus said, "I thirst."
There was a vessel filled with common wine.
So they put a sponge soaked in wine on a sprig of hyssop
　　and put it up to his mouth.
When Jesus had taken the wine, he said,
　　"It is finished."
And bowing his head, he handed over the spirit.

Here all kneel and pause for a short time.

Now since it was preparation day,
　　in order that the bodies might not remain
　　　on the cross on the sabbath,
　　for the sabbath day of that week was a solemn one,
　　the Jews asked Pilate that their legs be broken
　　and that they be taken down.
So the soldiers came and broke the legs of the first
　　and then of the other one who was crucified with Jesus.
But when they came to Jesus and saw that he was already dead,
　　they did not break his legs,
　　but one soldier thrust his lance into his side,
　　and immediately blood and water flowed out.
An eyewitness has testified, and his testimony is true;
　　he knows that he is speaking the truth,
　　so that you also may come to believe.
For this happened so that the Scripture passage might be fulfilled:
　　Not a bone of it will be broken.
And again another passage says:
　　They will look upon him whom they have pierced.

After this, Joseph of Arimathea,
　　secretly a disciple of Jesus for fear of the Jews,
　　asked Pilate if he could remove the body of Jesus.
And Pilate permitted it.
So he came and took his body.
Nicodemus, the one who had first come to him at night,
　　also came bringing a mixture of myrrh and aloes
　　weighing about one hundred pounds.
They took the body of Jesus
　　and bound it with burial cloths along with the spices,
　　according to the Jewish burial custom.
Now in the place where he had been crucified there was a garden,
　　and in the garden a new tomb, in which no one had yet been
　　　buried.
So they laid Jesus there because of the Jewish preparation day;
　　for the tomb was close by.

Good Friday of the Passion of the Lord, *March 25, 2016*

FIRST READING
Isa 52:13–53:12

See, my servant shall prosper,
    he shall be raised high and greatly exalted.
Even as many were amazed at him—
    so marred was his look beyond human
        semblance
    and his appearance beyond that of the sons
        of man—
so shall he startle many nations,
    because of him kings shall stand speechless;
for those who have not been told shall see,
    those who have not heard shall ponder it.

Who would believe what we have heard?
    To whom has the arm of the LORD been
        revealed?
He grew up like a sapling before him,
    like a shoot from the parched earth;
there was in him no stately bearing to make
        us look at him,
    nor appearance that would attract us to him.
He was spurned and avoided by people,
    a man of suffering, accustomed to infirmity,
one of those from whom people hide their faces,
    spurned, and we held him in no esteem.

Yet it was our infirmities that he bore,
    our sufferings that he endured,
while we thought of him as stricken,
    as one smitten by God and afflicted.
But he was pierced for our offenses,
    crushed for our sins;
upon him was the chastisement that makes
        us whole,
    by his stripes we were healed.
We had all gone astray like sheep,
    each following his own way;
but the LORD laid upon him
    the guilt of us all.

Though he was harshly treated, he submitted
    and opened not his mouth;
like a lamb led to the slaughter
    or a sheep before the shearers,
    he was silent and opened not his mouth.
Oppressed and condemned, he was taken away,
    and who would have thought any more of
        his destiny?
When he was cut off from the land of the living,
    and smitten for the sin of his people,
a grave was assigned him among the wicked
    and a burial place with evildoers,
though he had done no wrong
    nor spoken any falsehood.
But the LORD was pleased
    to crush him in infirmity.

If he gives his life as an offering for sin,
    he shall see his descendants in a long life,
    and the will of the LORD shall be
        accomplished through him.

Because of his affliction
    he shall see the light
    in fullness of days;
through his suffering, my servant shall justify
        many,
    and their guilt he shall bear.
Therefore I will give him his portion among
        the great,
    and he shall divide the spoils with the
        mighty,
because he surrendered himself to death
    and was counted among the wicked;
and he shall take away the sins of many,
    and win pardon for their offenses.

RESPONSORIAL PSALM
Ps 31:2, 6, 12-13, 15-16, 17, 25

R̸. (Luke 23:46) Father, into your hands I
commend my spirit.

In you, O LORD, I take refuge;
    let me never be put to shame.
In your justice rescue me.
Into your hands I commend my spirit;
    you will redeem me, O LORD, O faithful God.

R̸. Father, into your hands I commend my
spirit.

For all my foes I am an object of reproach,
    a laughingstock to my neighbors, and a
        dread to my friends;
    they who see me abroad flee from me.
I am forgotten like the unremembered dead;
    I am like a dish that is broken.

R̸. Father, into your hands I commend my
spirit.

But my trust is in you, O LORD;
    I say, "You are my God.
In your hands is my destiny; rescue me
    from the clutches of my enemies and my
        persecutors."

R̸. Father, into your hands I commend my
spirit.

Let your face shine upon your servant;
    save me in your kindness.
Take courage and be stouthearted,
    all you who hope in the LORD.

R̸. Father, into your hands I commend my
spirit.

SECOND READING
Heb 4:14-16; 5:7-9

Brothers and sisters:
Since we have a great high priest who has
        passed through the heavens,
    Jesus, the Son of God,
    let us hold fast to our confession.
For we do not have a high priest
    who is unable to sympathize with our
        weaknesses,
    but one who has similarly been tested in
        every way,
    yet without sin.
So let us confidently approach the throne of
        grace
    to receive mercy and to find grace for
        timely help.

In the days when Christ was in the flesh,
    he offered prayers and supplications with
        loud cries and tears
    to the one who was able to save him from
        death,
    and he was heard because of his reverence.
Son though he was, he learned obedience
        from what he suffered;
    and when he was made perfect,
    he became the source of eternal salvation
        for all who obey him.

At the Easter Vigil in the Holy Night of Easter, *March 26, 2016*

FIRST READING
Gen 1:1–2:2

In the beginning, when God created the
heavens and the earth,
the earth was a formless wasteland, and
darkness covered the abyss,
while a mighty wind swept over the waters.

Then God said,
"Let there be light," and there was light.
God saw how good the light was.
God then separated the light from the darkness.
God called the light "day," and the darkness
he called "night."
Thus evening came, and morning followed—
the first day.

Then God said,
"Let there be a dome in the middle of the
waters,
to separate one body of water from the
other."
And so it happened:
God made the dome,
and it separated the water above the dome
from the water below it.
God called the dome "the sky."
Evening came, and morning followed—the
second day.

Then God said,
"Let the water under the sky be gathered
into a single basin,
so that the dry land may appear."
And so it happened:
the water under the sky was gathered into
its basin,
and the dry land appeared.
God called the dry land "the earth,"
and the basin of the water he called "the
sea."
God saw how good it was.
Then God said,
"Let the earth bring forth vegetation:
every kind of plant that bears seed
and every kind of fruit tree on earth
that bears fruit with its seed in it."
And so it happened:
the earth brought forth every kind of plant
that bears seed
and every kind of fruit tree on earth
that bears fruit with its seed in it.
God saw how good it was.
Evening came, and morning followed—the
third day.

Then God said:
"Let there be lights in the dome of the sky,
to separate day from night.
Let them mark the fixed times, the days and
the years,

and serve as luminaries in the dome of the
sky,
to shed light upon the earth."
And so it happened:
God made the two great lights,
the greater one to govern the day,
and the lesser one to govern the night;
and he made the stars.
God set them in the dome of the sky,
to shed light upon the earth,
to govern the day and the night,
and to separate the light from the darkness.
God saw how good it was.
Evening came, and morning followed—the
fourth day.

Then God said,
"Let the water teem with an abundance of
living creatures,
and on the earth let birds fly beneath the
dome of the sky."
And so it happened:
God created the great sea monsters
and all kinds of swimming creatures with
which the water teems,
and all kinds of winged birds.
God saw how good it was, and God blessed
them, saying,
"Be fertile, multiply, and fill the water of
the seas;
and let the birds multiply on the earth."
Evening came, and morning followed—the
fifth day.

Then God said,
"Let the earth bring forth all kinds of
living creatures:
cattle, creeping things, and wild animals of
all kinds."
And so it happened:
God made all kinds of wild animals, all
kinds of cattle,
and all kinds of creeping things of the earth.
God saw how good it was.
Then God said:
"Let us make man in our image, after our
likeness.
Let them have dominion over the fish of the sea,
the birds of the air, and the cattle,
and over all the wild animals
and all the creatures that crawl on the
ground."
God created man in his image;
in the image of God he created him;
male and female he created them.
God blessed them, saying:
"Be fertile and multiply;
fill the earth and subdue it.
Have dominion over the fish of the sea, the
birds of the air,

and all the living things that move on the
earth."
God also said:
"See, I give you every seed-bearing plant all
over the earth
and every tree that has seed-bearing fruit
on it to be your food;
and to all the animals of the land, all the
birds of the air,
and all the living creatures that crawl on
the ground,
I give all the green plants for food."
And so it happened.
God looked at everything he had made, and
he found it very good.
Evening came, and morning followed—the
sixth day.

Thus the heavens and the earth and all their
array were completed.
Since on the seventh day God was finished
with the work he had been doing,
he rested on the seventh day from all the
work he had undertaken.

or

Gen 1:1, 26-31a

In the beginning, when God created the
heavens and the earth,
God said: "Let us make man in our image,
after our likeness.
Let them have dominion over the fish of the sea,
the birds of the air, and the cattle,
and over all the wild animals
and all the creatures that crawl on the
ground."
God created man in his image;
in the image of God he created him;
male and female he created them.
God blessed them, saying:
"Be fertile and multiply;
fill the earth and subdue it.
Have dominion over the fish of the sea, the
birds of the air,
and all the living things that move on the
earth."
God also said:
"See, I give you every seed-bearing plant all
over the earth
and every tree that has seed-bearing fruit
on it to be your food;
and to all the animals of the land, all the
birds of the air,
and all the living creatures that crawl on
the ground,
I give all the green plants for food."
And so it happened.
God looked at everything he had made, and
found it very good.

RESPONSORIAL PSALM

Ps 104:1-2, 5-6, 10, 12, 13-14, 24, 35

R℣. (30) Lord, send out your Spirit, and renew
the face of the earth.

Bless the LORD, O my soul!
  O LORD, my God, you are great indeed!
You are clothed with majesty and glory,
  robed in light as with a cloak.

R℣. Lord, send out your Spirit, and renew the
face of the earth.

You fixed the earth upon its foundation,
  not to be moved forever;
with the ocean, as with a garment, you
    covered it;
  above the mountains the waters stood.

R℣. Lord, send out your Spirit, and renew the
face of the earth.

You send forth springs into the watercourses
  that wind among the mountains.
Beside them the birds of heaven dwell;
  from among the branches they send forth
    their song.

R℣. Lord, send out your Spirit, and renew the
face of the earth.

You water the mountains from your palace;
  the earth is replete with the fruit of your
    works.
You raise grass for the cattle,
  and vegetation for man's use,
producing bread from the earth.

R℣. Lord, send out your Spirit, and renew the
face of the earth.

How manifold are your works, O LORD!
  In wisdom you have wrought them all—
  the earth is full of your creatures.
Bless the LORD, O my soul!

R℣. Lord, send out your Spirit, and renew the
face of the earth.

or

Ps 33:4-5, 6-7, 12-13, 20 and 22

R℣. (5b) The earth is full of the goodness of
the Lord.

Upright is the word of the LORD,
  and all his works are trustworthy.
He loves justice and right;
  of the kindness of the LORD the earth is full.

R℣. The earth is full of the goodness of the Lord.

By the word of the LORD the heavens were
    made;
  by the breath of his mouth all their host.
He gathers the waters of the sea as in a
    flask;
  in cellars he confines the deep.

R℣. The earth is full of the goodness of the Lord.

Blessed the nation whose God is the LORD,
  the people he has chosen for his own
    inheritance.
From heaven the LORD looks down;
  he sees all mankind.

R℣. The earth is full of the goodness of the Lord.

Our soul waits for the LORD,
  who is our help and our shield.
May your kindness, O LORD, be upon us
  who have put our hope in you.

R℣. The earth is full of the goodness of the Lord.

SECOND READING

Gen 22:1-18

God put Abraham to the test.
He called to him, "Abraham!"
"Here I am," he replied.
Then God said:
  "Take your son Isaac, your only one, whom
    you love,
  and go to the land of Moriah.
There you shall offer him up as a holocaust
  on a height that I will point out to you."
Early the next morning Abraham saddled his
    donkey,
  took with him his son Isaac and two of his
    servants as well,
  and with the wood that he had cut for the
    holocaust,
  set out for the place of which God had told
    him.

On the third day Abraham got sight of the
    place from afar.
Then he said to his servants:
  "Both of you stay here with the donkey,
  while the boy and I go on over yonder.
We will worship and then come back to you."
Thereupon Abraham took the wood for the
    holocaust
  and laid it on his son Isaac's shoulders,
  while he himself carried the fire and the
    knife.
As the two walked on together, Isaac spoke to
    his father Abraham:
  "Father!" Isaac said.
"Yes, son," he replied.
Isaac continued, "Here are the fire and the
    wood,
  but where is the sheep for the holocaust?"
"Son," Abraham answered,
  "God himself will provide the sheep for the
    holocaust."
Then the two continued going forward.

When they came to the place of which God
    had told him,

Abraham built an altar there and arranged
    the wood on it.
Next he tied up his son Isaac,
  and put him on top of the wood on the altar.
Then he reached out and took the knife to
    slaughter his son.
But the LORD's messenger called to him from
    heaven,
  "Abraham, Abraham!"
"Here I am," he answered.
"Do not lay your hand on the boy," said the
    messenger.
"Do not do the least thing to him.
I know now how devoted you are to God,
  since you did not withhold from me your
    own beloved son."
As Abraham looked about,
  he spied a ram caught by its horns in the
    thicket.
So he went and took the ram
  and offered it up as a holocaust in place of
    his son.
Abraham named the site Yahweh-yireh;
  hence people now say, "On the mountain
    the LORD will see."

Again the LORD's messenger called to
    Abraham from heaven and said:
  "I swear by myself, declares the LORD,
  that because you acted as you did
  in not withholding from me your beloved
    son,
  I will bless you abundantly
  and make your descendants as countless
  as the stars of the sky and the sands of the
    seashore;
  your descendants shall take possession
  of the gates of their enemies,
  and in your descendants all the nations of
    the earth
    shall find blessing—
  all this because you obeyed my
    command."

or

Gen 22:1-2, 9a, 10-13, 15-18

God put Abraham to the test.
He called to him, "Abraham!"
"Here I am," he replied.
Then God said:
  "Take your son Isaac, your only one, whom
    you love,
  and go to the land of Moriah.
There you shall offer him up as a holocaust
  on a height that I will point out to you."

When they came to the place of which God
    had told him,
  Abraham built an altar there and arranged
    the wood on it.

Then he reached out and took the knife to
 slaughter his son.
But the LORD's messenger called to him from
 heaven,
 "Abraham, Abraham!"
"Here I am," he answered.
"Do not lay your hand on the boy," said the
 messenger.
"Do not do the least thing to him.
I know now how devoted you are to God,
 since you did not withhold from me your
 own beloved son."
As Abraham looked about,
 he spied a ram caught by its horns in the
 thicket.
So he went and took the ram
 and offered it up as a holocaust in place of
 his son.

Again the LORD's messenger called to
 Abraham from heaven and said:
 "I swear by myself, declares the LORD,
 that because you acted as you did
 in not withholding from me your beloved son,
I will bless you abundantly
 and make your descendants as countless
 as the stars of the sky and the sands of the
 seashore;
 your descendants shall take possession
 of the gates of their enemies,
 and in your descendants all the nations of
 the earth
 shall find blessing—
 all this because you obeyed my command."

RESPONSORIAL PSALM

Ps 16:5, 8, 9-10, 11

R̸. (1) You are my inheritance, O Lord.

O LORD, my allotted portion and my cup,
 you it is who hold fast my lot.
I set the LORD ever before me;
 with him at my right hand I shall not be
 disturbed.

R̸. You are my inheritance, O Lord.

Therefore my heart is glad and my soul rejoices,
 my body, too, abides in confidence;
because you will not abandon my soul to the
 netherworld,
 nor will you suffer your faithful one to
 undergo corruption.

R̸. You are my inheritance, O Lord.

You will show me the path to life,
 fullness of joys in your presence,
 the delights at your right hand forever.

R̸. You are my inheritance, O Lord.

THIRD READING

Exod 14:15–15:1

The LORD said to Moses, "Why are you crying
 out to me?
Tell the Israelites to go forward.
And you, lift up your staff and, with hand
 outstretched over the sea,
 split the sea in two,
 that the Israelites may pass through it on
 dry land.
But I will make the Egyptians so obstinate
 that they will go in after them.
Then I will receive glory through Pharaoh
 and all his army,
 his chariots and charioteers.
The Egyptians shall know that I am the LORD,
 when I receive glory through Pharaoh
 and his chariots and charioteers."

The angel of God, who had been leading
 Israel's camp,
 now moved and went around behind them.
The column of cloud also, leaving the front,
 took up its place behind them,
 so that it came between the camp of the
 Egyptians
 and that of Israel.
But the cloud now became dark, and thus the
 night passed
 without the rival camps coming any closer
 together all night long.
Then Moses stretched out his hand over the
 sea,
 and the LORD swept the sea
 with a strong east wind throughout the night
 and so turned it into dry land.
When the water was thus divided,
 the Israelites marched into the midst of the
 sea on dry land,
 with the water like a wall to their right and
 to their left.

The Egyptians followed in pursuit;
 all Pharaoh's horses and chariots and
 charioteers went after them
 right into the midst of the sea.
In the night watch just before dawn
 the LORD cast through the column of the
 fiery cloud
 upon the Egyptian force a glance that
 threw it into a panic;
 and he so clogged their chariot wheels
 that they could hardly drive.
With that the Egyptians sounded the retreat
 before Israel,
 because the LORD was fighting for them
 against the Egyptians.

Then the LORD told Moses, "Stretch out your
 hand over the sea,
 that the water may flow back upon the
 Egyptians,
 upon their chariots and their charioteers."
So Moses stretched out his hand over the sea,
 and at dawn the sea flowed back to its
 normal depth.
The Egyptians were fleeing head on toward
 the sea,
 when the LORD hurled them into its midst.
As the water flowed back,
 it covered the chariots and the charioteers
 of Pharaoh's whole army
 which had followed the Israelites into the sea.
Not a single one of them escaped.
But the Israelites had marched on dry land
 through the midst of the sea,
 with the water like a wall to their right and
 to their left.
Thus the LORD saved Israel on that day
 from the power of the Egyptians.
When Israel saw the Egyptians lying dead on
 the seashore
 and beheld the great power that the LORD
 had shown against the Egyptians,
 they feared the LORD and believed in him
 and in his servant Moses.

Then Moses and the Israelites sang this song
 to the LORD:
 I will sing to the LORD, for he is gloriously
 triumphant;
 horse and chariot he has cast into the sea.

RESPONSORIAL PSALM

Exod 15:1-2, 3-4, 5-6, 17-18

R̸. (1b) Let us sing to the Lord; he has covered
himself in glory.

I will sing to the LORD, for he is gloriously
 triumphant;
 horse and chariot he has cast into the sea.
My strength and my courage is the LORD,
 and he has been my savior.
He is my God, I praise him;
 the God of my father, I extol him.

R̸. Let us sing to the Lord; he has covered
himself in glory.

The LORD is a warrior,
 LORD is his name!
Pharaoh's chariots and army he hurled into
 the sea;
 the elite of his officers were submerged in
 the Red Sea.

R̸. Let us sing to the Lord; he has covered
himself in glory.

The flood waters covered them,
  they sank into the depths like a stone.
Your right hand, O Lord, magnificent in
    power,
  your right hand, O Lord, has shattered the
    enemy.

R̂. Let us sing to the Lord; he has covered
himself in glory.

You brought in the people you redeemed
  and planted them on the mountain of your
    inheritance—
the place where you made your seat, O Lord,
  the sanctuary, Lord, which your hands
    established.
The Lord shall reign forever and ever.

R̂. Let us sing to the Lord; he has covered
himself in glory.

FOURTH READING
Isa 54:5-14

The One who has become your husband is
    your Maker;
  his name is the Lord of hosts;
your redeemer is the Holy One of Israel,
  called God of all the earth.
The Lord calls you back,
  like a wife forsaken and grieved in spirit,
  a wife married in youth and then cast off,
  says your God.
For a brief moment I abandoned you,
  but with great tenderness I will take you
    back.
In an outburst of wrath, for a moment
  I hid my face from you;
but with enduring love I take pity on you,
  says the Lord, your redeemer.
This is for me like the days of Noah,
  when I swore that the waters of Noah
  should never again deluge the earth;
so I have sworn not to be angry with you,
  or to rebuke you.
Though the mountains leave their place
  and the hills be shaken,
my love shall never leave you
  nor my covenant of peace be shaken,
  says the Lord, who has mercy on you.
O afflicted one, storm-battered and unconsoled,
  I lay your pavements in carnelians,
  and your foundations in sapphires;
I will make your battlements of rubies,
  your gates of carbuncles,
  and all your walls of precious stones.
All your children shall be taught by the Lord,
  and great shall be the peace of your children.
In justice shall you be established,

far from the fear of oppression,
  where destruction cannot come near you.

RESPONSORIAL PSALM
Ps 30:2, 4, 5-6, 11-12, 13

R̂. (2a) I will praise you, Lord, for you have
rescued me.

I will extol you, O Lord, for you drew me clear
  and did not let my enemies rejoice over me.
O Lord, you brought me up from the
    netherworld;
  you preserved me from among those going
    down into the pit.

R̂. I will praise you, Lord, for you have
rescued me.

Sing praise to the Lord, you his faithful ones,
  and give thanks to his holy name.
For his anger lasts but a moment;
  a lifetime, his good will.
At nightfall, weeping enters in,
  but with the dawn, rejoicing.

R̂. I will praise you, Lord, for you have
rescued me.

Hear, O Lord, and have pity on me;
  O Lord, be my helper.
You changed my mourning into dancing;
  O Lord, my God, forever will I give you
    thanks.

R̂. I will praise you, Lord, for you have
rescued me.

FIFTH READING
Isa 55:1-11

Thus says the Lord:
All you who are thirsty,
  come to the water!
You who have no money,
  come, receive grain and eat;
come, without paying and without cost,
  drink wine and milk!
Why spend your money for what is not bread,
  your wages for what fails to satisfy?
Heed me, and you shall eat well,
  you shall delight in rich fare.
Come to me heedfully,
  listen, that you may have life.
I will renew with you the everlasting
    covenant,
  the benefits assured to David.
As I made him a witness to the peoples,
  a leader and commander of nations,
so shall you summon a nation you knew not,
  and nations that knew you not shall run
    to you,

because of the Lord, your God,
  the Holy One of Israel, who has glorified you.

Seek the Lord while he may be found,
  call him while he is near.
Let the scoundrel forsake his way,
  and the wicked man his thoughts;
let him turn to the Lord for mercy;
  to our God, who is generous in forgiving.
For my thoughts are not your thoughts,
  nor are your ways my ways, says the Lord.
As high as the heavens are above the earth,
  so high are my ways above your ways
  and my thoughts above your thoughts.

For just as from the heavens
  the rain and snow come down
and do not return there
  till they have watered the earth,
  making it fertile and fruitful,
giving seed to the one who sows
  and bread to the one who eats,
so shall my word be
  that goes forth from my mouth;
my word shall not return to me void,
  but shall do my will,
  achieving the end for which I sent it.

RESPONSORIAL PSALM
Isa 12:2-3, 4, 5-6

R̂. (3) You will draw water joyfully from the
springs of salvation.

God indeed is my savior;
  I am confident and unafraid.
My strength and my courage is the Lord,
  and he has been my savior.
With joy you will draw water
  at the fountain of salvation.

R̂. You will draw water joyfully from the
springs of salvation.

Give thanks to the Lord, acclaim his name;
  among the nations make known his deeds,
  proclaim how exalted is his name.

R̂. You will draw water joyfully from the
springs of salvation.

Sing praise to the Lord for his glorious
    achievement;
  let this be known throughout all the earth.
Shout with exultation, O city of Zion,
  for great in your midst
  is the Holy One of Israel!

R̂. You will draw water joyfully from the
springs of salvation.

SIXTH READING
Bar 3:9-15, 32–4:4

Hear, O Israel, the commandments of life:
    listen, and know prudence!
How is it, Israel,
    that you are in the land of your foes,
    grown old in a foreign land,
defiled with the dead,
    accounted with those destined for the
        netherworld?
You have forsaken the fountain of wisdom!
    Had you walked in the way of God,
    you would have dwelt in enduring peace.
Learn where prudence is,
    where strength, where understanding;
that you may know also
    where are length of days, and life,
    where light of the eyes, and peace.
Who has found the place of wisdom,
    who has entered into her treasuries?

The One who knows all things knows her;
    he has probed her by his knowledge—
the One who established the earth for all
        time,
    and filled it with four-footed beasts;
he who dismisses the light, and it departs,
    calls it, and it obeys him trembling;
before whom the stars at their posts
    shine and rejoice;
when he calls them, they answer, "Here we
    are!"
shining with joy for their Maker.
Such is our God;
    no other is to be compared to him:
he has traced out the whole way of
        understanding,
    and has given her to Jacob, his servant,
    to Israel, his beloved son.

Since then she has appeared on earth,
    and moved among people.
She is the book of the precepts of God,
    the law that endures forever;
all who cling to her will live,
    but those will die who forsake her.
Turn, O Jacob, and receive her:
    walk by her light toward splendor.
Give not your glory to another,
    your privileges to an alien race.
Blessed are we, O Israel;
    for what pleases God is known to us!

RESPONSORIAL PSALM
Ps 19:8, 9, 10, 11

R︤. (John 6:68c) Lord, you have the words of
everlasting life.

The law of the LORD is perfect,
    refreshing the soul;
the decree of the LORD is trustworthy,
    giving wisdom to the simple.

R︤. Lord, you have the words of everlasting life.

The precepts of the LORD are right,
    rejoicing the heart;
the command of the LORD is clear,
    enlightening the eye.

R︤. Lord, you have the words of everlasting life.

The fear of the LORD is pure,
    enduring forever;
the ordinances of the LORD are true,
    all of them just.

R︤. Lord, you have the words of everlasting life.

They are more precious than gold,
    than a heap of purest gold;
sweeter also than syrup
    or honey from the comb.

R︤. Lord, you have the words of everlasting life.

SEVENTH READING
Ezek 36:16-17a, 18-28

The word of the LORD came to me, saying:
    Son of man, when the house of Israel lived
        in their land,
    they defiled it by their conduct and deeds.
Therefore I poured out my fury upon them
    because of the blood that they poured out
        on the ground,
    and because they defiled it with idols.
I scattered them among the nations,
    dispersing them over foreign lands;
    according to their conduct and deeds I
        judged them.
But when they came among the nations
        wherever they came,
    they served to profane my holy name,
    because it was said of them: "These are the
        people of the LORD,
    yet they had to leave their land."
So I have relented because of my holy name
    which the house of Israel profaned
    among the nations where they came.
Therefore say to the house of Israel: Thus
        says the Lord GOD:
    Not for your sakes do I act, house of Israel,
    but for the sake of my holy name,
    which you profaned among the nations to
        which you came.
I will prove the holiness of my great name,
    profaned among the nations,
    in whose midst you have profaned it.
Thus the nations shall know that I am the
    LORD, says the Lord GOD,
    when in their sight I prove my holiness
        through you.
For I will take you away from among the
    nations,

gather you from all the foreign lands,
    and bring you back to your own land.
I will sprinkle clean water upon you
    to cleanse you from all your impurities,
    and from all your idols I will cleanse you.
I will give you a new heart and place a new
        spirit within you,
    taking from your bodies your stony hearts
    and giving you natural hearts.
I will put my spirit within you and make you
        live by my statutes,
    careful to observe my decrees.
You shall live in the land I gave your fathers;
    you shall be my people, and I will be your
        God.

RESPONSORIAL PSALM
Ps 42:3, 5; 43:3, 4

R︤. (42:2) Like a deer that longs for running
streams, my soul longs for you, my God.

Athirst is my soul for God, the living God.
    When shall I go and behold the face of God?

R︤. Like a deer that longs for running streams,
my soul longs for you, my God.

I went with the throng
    and led them in procession to the house of
        God,
amid loud cries of joy and thanksgiving,
    with the multitude keeping festival.

R︤. Like a deer that longs for running streams,
my soul longs for you, my God.

Send forth your light and your fidelity;
    they shall lead me on
and bring me to your holy mountain,
    to your dwelling-place.

R︤. Like a deer that longs for running streams,
my soul longs for you, my God.

Then will I go in to the altar of God,
    the God of my gladness and joy;
then will I give you thanks upon the harp,
    O God, my God!

R︤. Like a deer that longs for running streams,
my soul longs for you, my God.

or

Isa 12:2-3, 4bcd, 5-6

R︤. (3) You will draw water joyfully from the
springs of salvation.

God indeed is my savior;
    I am confident and unafraid.
My strength and my courage is the LORD,
    and he has been my savior.
With joy you will draw water
    at the fountain of salvation.

R︤. You will draw water joyfully from the
springs of salvation.

Give thanks to the LORD, acclaim his name;
    among the nations make known his deeds,
    proclaim how exalted is his name.

R̶7. You will draw water joyfully from the springs of salvation.

Sing praise to the LORD for his glorious
        achievement;
    let this be known throughout all the earth.
Shout with exultation, O city of Zion,
    for great in your midst
    is the Holy One of Israel!

R̶7. You will draw water joyfully from the springs of salvation.

or

Ps 51:12-13, 14-15, 18-19

R̶7. (12a) Create a clean heart in me, O God.

A clean heart create for me, O God,
    and a steadfast spirit renew within me.
Cast me not out from your presence,
    and your Holy Spirit take not from me.

R̶7. Create a clean heart in me, O God.

Give me back the joy of your salvation,
    and a willing spirit sustain in me.
I will teach transgressors your ways,
    and sinners shall return to you.

R̶7. Create a clean heart in me, O God.

For you are not pleased with sacrifices;
    should I offer a holocaust, you would not
        accept it.
My sacrifice, O God, is a contrite spirit;
    a heart contrite and humbled, O God, you
        will not spurn.

R̶7. Create a clean heart in me, O God.

EPISTLE
Rom 6:3-11

Brothers and sisters:
Are you unaware that we who were baptized
        into Christ Jesus
    were baptized into his death?
We were indeed buried with him through
        baptism into death,
    so that, just as Christ was raised from the
        dead
    by the glory of the Father,
    we too might live in newness of life.

For if we have grown into union with him
        through a death like his,
    we shall also be united with him in the
        resurrection.
We know that our old self was crucified with
        him,
    so that our sinful body might be done away
        with,
    that we might no longer be in slavery to sin.
For a dead person has been absolved from
        sin.
If, then, we have died with Christ,
    we believe that we shall also live with
        him.
We know that Christ, raised from the dead,
        dies no more;
    death no longer has power over him.
As to his death, he died to sin once and for
        all;
    as to his life, he lives for God.
Consequently, you too must think of
        yourselves as being dead to sin
    and living for God in Christ Jesus.

RESPONSORIAL PSALM
Ps 118:1-2, 16-17, 22-23

R̶7. Alleluia, alleluia, alleluia.

Give thanks to the LORD, for he is good,
    for his mercy endures forever.
Let the house of Israel say,
    "His mercy endures forever."

R̶7. Alleluia, alleluia, alleluia.

"The right hand of the LORD has struck with
        power;
    the right hand of the LORD is exalted.
I shall not die, but live,
    and declare the works of the LORD."

R̶7. Alleluia, alleluia, alleluia.

The stone which the builders rejected
    has become the cornerstone.
By the LORD has this been done;
    it is wonderful in our eyes.

R̶7. Alleluia, alleluia, alleluia.

Gospel

Luke 24:1-12; L41C

At daybreak on the first day of the week
  the women who had come from Galilee with Jesus
  took the spices they had prepared
  and went to the tomb.
They found the stone rolled away from the tomb;
  but when they entered,
  they did not find the body of the Lord Jesus.
While they were puzzling over this, behold,
  two men in dazzling garments appeared to them.
They were terrified and bowed their faces to the ground.
They said to them,
  "Why do you seek the living one among the dead?
He is not here, but he has been raised.
Remember what he said to you while he was still in Galilee,

that the Son of Man must be handed over to sinners
  and be crucified, and rise on the third day."
And they remembered his words.
Then they returned from the tomb
  and announced all these things to the eleven
  and to all the others.
The women were Mary Magdalene, Joanna, and Mary the mother of
    James;
  the others who accompanied them also told this to the apostles,
  but their story seemed like nonsense
  and they did not believe them.
But Peter got up and ran to the tomb,
  bent down, and saw the burial cloths alone;
  then he went home amazed at what had happened.

or, at an afternoon or evening Mass

Gospel

Luke 24:13-35; L46

That very day, the first day of the week,
  two of Jesus' disciples were going
  to a village seven miles from Jerusalem called Emmaus,
  and they were conversing about all the things that had occurred.
And it happened that while they were conversing and debating,
  Jesus himself drew near and walked with them,
  but their eyes were prevented from recognizing him.
He asked them,
  "What are you discussing as you walk along?"
They stopped, looking downcast.
One of them, named Cleopas, said to him in reply,
  "Are you the only visitor to Jerusalem
  who does not know of the things
  that have taken place there in these days?"
And he replied to them, "What sort of things?"
They said to him,
  "The things that happened to Jesus the Nazarene,
  who was a prophet mighty in deed and word
  before God and all the people,
  how our chief priests and rulers both handed him over
  to a sentence of death and crucified him.
But we were hoping that he would be the one to redeem Israel;
  and besides all this,
  it is now the third day since this took place.
Some women from our group, however, have astounded us:
  they were at the tomb early in the morning
  and did not find his body;
  they came back and reported
  that they had indeed seen a vision of angels
  who announced that he was alive.
Then some of those with us went to the tomb
  and found things just as the women had described,
  but him they did not see."

And he said to them, "Oh, how foolish you are!
How slow of heart to believe all that the prophets spoke!
Was it not necessary that the Christ should suffer these things
  and enter into his glory?"
Then beginning with Moses and all the prophets,
  he interpreted to them what referred to him
  in all the Scriptures.
As they approached the village to which they were going,
  he gave the impression that he was going on farther.
But they urged him, "Stay with us,
  for it is nearly evening and the day is almost over."
So he went in to stay with them.
And it happened that, while he was with them at table,
  he took bread, said the blessing,
  broke it, and gave it to them.
With that their eyes were opened and they recognized him,
  but he vanished from their sight.
Then they said to each other,
  "Were not our hearts burning within us
  while he spoke to us on the way and opened the Scriptures to us?"
So they set out at once and returned to Jerusalem
  where they found gathered together
  the eleven and those with them who were saying,
  "The Lord has truly been raised and has appeared to Simon!"
Then the two recounted
  what had taken place on the way
  and how he was made known to them in the breaking of the bread.

Easter Sunday, *March 27, 2016*

FIRST READING
Acts 10:34a, 37-43

Peter proceeded to speak and said:
    "You know what has happened all over
        Judea,
    beginning in Galilee after the baptism
    that John preached,
    how God anointed Jesus of Nazareth
    with the Holy Spirit and power.
He went about doing good
    and healing all those oppressed by the devil,
    for God was with him.
We are witnesses of all that he did
    both in the country of the Jews and in
        Jerusalem.
They put him to death by hanging him on a
        tree.
This man God raised on the third day and
        granted that he be visible,
    not to all the people, but to us,
    the witnesses chosen by God in advance,
    who ate and drank with him after he rose
        from the dead.
He commissioned us to preach to the people
    and testify that he is the one appointed by
        God
    as judge of the living and the dead.
To him all the prophets bear witness,
    that everyone who believes in him
    will receive forgiveness of sins through his
        name."

RESPONSORIAL PSALM
Ps 118:1-2, 16-17, 22-23

R⁊. (24) This is the day the Lord has made; let
us rejoice and be glad.
    or
R⁊. Alleluia.

Give thanks to the LORD, for he is good,
    for his mercy endures forever.
Let the house of Israel say,
    "His mercy endures forever."

R⁊. This is the day the Lord has made; let us
rejoice and be glad.
    or
R⁊. Alleluia.

"The right hand of the LORD has struck with
        power;
    the right hand of the LORD is exalted.
I shall not die, but live,
    and declare the works of the LORD."

R⁊. This is the day the Lord has made; let us
rejoice and be glad.
    or
R⁊. Alleluia.

The stone which the builders rejected
    has become the cornerstone.
By the LORD has this been done;
    it is wonderful in our eyes.

R⁊. This is the day the Lord has made; let us
rejoice and be glad.
    or
R⁊. Alleluia.

SECOND READING
1 Cor 5:6b-8

Brothers and sisters:
Do you not know that a little yeast leavens all
        the dough?
Clear out the old yeast,
    so that you may become a fresh batch of
        dough,
    inasmuch as you are unleavened.
For our paschal lamb, Christ, has been
        sacrificed.

Therefore, let us celebrate the feast,
    not with the old yeast, the yeast of malice
        and wickedness,
    but with the unleavened bread of sincerity
        and truth.

or Col 3:1-4

Brothers and sisters:
If then you were raised with Christ, seek what
    is above,
    where Christ is seated at the right hand of
        God.
Think of what is above, not of what is on earth.
For you have died, and your life is hidden
        with Christ in God.
When Christ your life appears,
    then you too will appear with him in glory.

SEQUENCE *Victimae paschali laudes*

Christians, to the Paschal Victim
    Offer your thankful praises!
A Lamb the sheep redeems;
    Christ, who only is sinless,
    Reconciles sinners to the Father.
Death and life have contended in that combat
        stupendous:
    The Prince of life, who died, reigns immortal.
Speak, Mary, declaring
    What you saw, wayfaring.
"The tomb of Christ, who is living,
    The glory of Jesus' resurrection;
Bright angels attesting,
    The shroud and napkin resting.
Yes, Christ my hope is arisen;
    To Galilee he goes before you."
Christ indeed from death is risen, our new life
        obtaining.
    Have mercy, victor King, ever reigning!
    Amen. Alleluia.

Second Sunday of Easter (or Divine Mercy Sunday), *April 3, 2016*

Gospel (cont.)
John 20:19-31; L45C

Then he said to Thomas, "Put your finger here and see my hands,
    and bring your hand and put it into my side,
    and do not be unbelieving, but believe."
Thomas answered and said to him, "My Lord and my God!"
Jesus said to him, "Have you come to believe because you have seen
        me?
Blessed are those who have not seen and have believed."

Now Jesus did many other signs in the presence of his disciples
    that are not written in this book.
But these are written that you may come to believe
    that Jesus is the Christ, the Son of God,
    and that through this belief you may have life in his name.

The Annunication of the Lord, *April 4, 2016*

FIRST READING
Isa 7:10-14; 8:10

The LORD spoke to Ahaz, saying:
Ask for a sign from the LORD, your God;
    let it be deep as the netherworld, or high as
        the sky!
But Ahaz answered,
    "I will not ask! I will not tempt the LORD!"
Then Isaiah said:
    Listen, O house of David!
Is it not enough for you to weary people,
    must you also weary my God?
Therefore the Lord himself will give you this
    sign:
    the virgin shall conceive, and bear a son,
    and shall name him Emmanuel,
    which means "God is with us!"

RESPONSORIAL PSALM
Ps 40:7-8a, 8b-9, 10, 11

R℣. (8a and 9a) Here am I, Lord; I come to do
your will.

Sacrifice or offering you wished not,
    but ears open to obedience you gave me.
Holocausts and sin-offerings you sought not;
    then said I, "Behold, I come";

R℣. Here am I, Lord; I come to do your will.

"In the written scroll it is prescribed for me.
To do your will, O God, is my delight,
    and your law is within my heart!"

R℣. Here am I, Lord; I come to do your will.

I announced your justice in the vast assembly;
    I did not restrain my lips, as you, O LORD,
        know.

R℣. Here am I, Lord; I come to do your will.

Your justice I kept not hid within my heart;
    your faithfulness and your salvation I have
        spoken of;
I have made no secret of your kindness and
    your truth
    in the vast assembly.

R℣. Here am I, Lord; I come to do your will.

SECOND READING
Heb 10:4-10

Brothers and sisters:
It is impossible that the blood of bulls and
    goats
    takes away sins.
For this reason, when Christ came into the
    world, he said:
    "Sacrifice and offering you did not desire,
        but a body you prepared for me;
    in holocausts and sin offerings you took no
        delight.
    Then I said, 'As is written of me in the scroll,
    behold, I come to do your will, O God.'"

First he says, "Sacrifices and offerings,
    holocausts and sin offerings,
    you neither desired nor delighted in."
These are offered according to the law.
Then he says, "Behold, I come to do your will."
He takes away the first to establish the
    second.
By this "will," we have been consecrated
    through the offering of the Body of Jesus
    Christ once for all.

Third Sunday of Easter, *April 10, 2016*

Gospel (cont.)
John 21:1-19; L48C

When they climbed out on shore,
    they saw a charcoal fire with fish on it and bread.
Jesus said to them, "Bring some of the fish you just caught."
So Simon Peter went over and dragged the net ashore
    full of one hundred fifty-three large fish.
Even though there were so many, the net was not torn.
Jesus said to them, "Come, have breakfast."
And none of the disciples dared to ask him, "Who are you?"
    because they realized it was the Lord.
Jesus came over and took the bread and gave it to them,
    and in like manner the fish.
This was now the third time Jesus was revealed to his disciples
    after being raised from the dead.

When they had finished breakfast, Jesus said to Simon Peter,
    "Simon, son of John, do you love me more than these?"
Simon Peter answered him, "Yes, Lord, you know that I love you."
Jesus said to him, "Feed my lambs."

He then said to Simon Peter a second time,
    "Simon, son of John, do you love me?"
Simon Peter answered him, "Yes, Lord, you know that I love you."
Jesus said to him, "Tend my sheep."
Jesus said to him the third time,
    "Simon, son of John, do you love me?"
Peter was distressed that Jesus had said to him a third time,
    "Do you love me?" and he said to him,
    "Lord, you know everything; you know that I love you."
Jesus said to him, "Feed my sheep.
Amen, amen, I say to you, when you were younger,
    you used to dress yourself and go where you wanted;
    but when you grow old, you will stretch out your hands,
    and someone else will dress you
    and lead you where you do not want to go."
He said this signifying by what kind of death he would glorify God.
And when he had said this, he said to him, "Follow me."

Third Sunday of Easter, *April 10, 2016*

Gospel
or John 21:1-14; L48C

At that time, Jesus revealed himself again to his disciples at the Sea of
    Tiberias.
He revealed himself in this way.
Together were Simon Peter, Thomas called Didymus,
    Nathanael from Cana in Galilee,
    Zebedee's sons, and two others of his disciples.
Simon Peter said to them, "I am going fishing."
They said to him, "We also will come with you."
So they went out and got into the boat,
    but that night they caught nothing.
When it was already dawn, Jesus was standing on the shore;
    but the disciples did not realize that it was Jesus.
Jesus said to them, "Children, have you caught anything to eat?"
They answered him, "No."
So he said to them, "Cast the net over the right side of the boat
    and you will find something."
So they cast it, and were not able to pull it in
    because of the number of fish.
So the disciple whom Jesus loved said to Peter, "It is the Lord."

When Simon Peter heard that it was the Lord,
    he tucked in his garment, for he was lightly clad,
    and jumped into the sea.
The other disciples came in the boat,
    for they were not far from shore, only about a hundred yards,
    dragging the net with the fish.
When they climbed out on shore,
    they saw a charcoal fire with fish on it and bread.
Jesus said to them, "Bring some of the fish you just caught."
So Simon Peter went over and dragged the net ashore
    full of one hundred fifty-three large fish.
Even though there were so many, the net was not torn.
Jesus said to them, "Come, have breakfast."
And none of the disciples dared to ask him, "Who are you?"
    because they realized it was the Lord.
Jesus came over and took the bread and gave it to them,
    and in like manner the fish.
This was now the third time Jesus was revealed to his disciples
    after being raised from the dead.

Fourth Sunday of Easter, *April 17, 2016*

SECOND READING
Rev 7:9, 14b-17

I, John, had a vision of a great multitude,
    which no one could count,
    from every nation, race, people, and tongue.
They stood before the throne and before the
    Lamb,
    wearing white robes and holding palm
        branches in their hands.

Then one of the elders said to me,
    "These are the ones who have survived the
        time of great distress;

they have washed their robes
and made them white in the blood of the
    Lamb.

    "For this reason they stand before God's
        throne
    and worship him day and night in his
        temple.
The one who sits on the throne will
    shelter them.
They will not hunger or thirst anymore,
    nor will the sun or any heat strike
        them.

For the Lamb who is in the center of the
    throne
    will shepherd them
    and lead them to springs of life-giving
        water,
    and God will wipe away every tear
        from their eyes."

Sixth Sunday of Easter, *May 1, 2016*

SECOND READING
Rev 21:10-14, 22-23

The angel took me in spirit to a great, high
    mountain
    and showed me the holy city Jerusalem
    coming down out of heaven from God.
It gleamed with the splendor of God.
Its radiance was like that of a precious stone,
    like jasper, clear as crystal.
It had a massive, high wall,
    with twelve gates where twelve angels were
        stationed

and on which names were inscribed,
    the names of the twelve tribes of the
        Israelites.
There were three gates facing east,
    three north, three south, and three west.
The wall of the city had twelve courses of
        stones as its foundation,
    on which were inscribed the twelve names
    of the twelve apostles of the Lamb.

I saw no temple in the city
    for its temple is the Lord God almighty and
        the Lamb.

The city had no need of sun or moon to shine
    on it,
    for the glory of God gave it light,
    and its lamp was the Lamb.

The Ascension of the Lord, *May 5, 2016 (Thursday) or May 8, 2016*

SECOND READING
Eph 1:17-23

Brothers and sisters:
May the God of our Lord Jesus Christ, the
    Father of glory,
  give you a Spirit of wisdom and revelation
  resulting in knowledge of him.
May the eyes of your hearts be enlightened,
  that you may know what is the hope that
        belongs to his call,
  what are the riches of glory
  in his inheritance among the holy ones,
  and what is the surpassing greatness of
        his power
  for us who believe,
  in accord with the exercise of his great
        might,
  which he worked in Christ,
  raising him from the dead
  and seating him at his right hand in the
        heavens,
  far above every principality, authority,
        power, and dominion,
  and every name that is named
  not only in this age but also in the one to
        come.

And he put all things beneath his feet
  and gave him as head over all things to the
        church,
  which is his body,
  the fullness of the one who fills all things
        in every way.

or

Heb 9:24-28; 10:19-23

Christ did not enter into a sanctuary made by
        hands,
  a copy of the true one, but heaven itself,
  that he might now appear before God on
        our behalf.
Not that he might offer himself repeatedly,
  as the high priest enters each year into the
        sanctuary
  with blood that is not his own;
  if that were so, he would have had to suffer
        repeatedly
  from the foundation of the world.
But now once for all he has appeared at the
        end of the ages
  to take away sin by his sacrifice.
Just as it is appointed that men and women
        die once,

and after this the judgment, so also Christ,
  offered once to take away the sins of many,
  will appear a second time, not to take away
        sin
  but to bring salvation to those who eagerly
        await him.

Therefore, brothers and sisters, since through
        the blood of Jesus
  we have confidence of entrance into the
        sanctuary
  by the new and living way he opened for us
        through the veil,
  that is, his flesh,
  and since we have "a great priest over the
        house of God,"
  let us approach with a sincere heart and in
        absolute trust,
  with our hearts sprinkled clean from an
        evil conscience
  and our bodies washed in pure water.
Let us hold unwaveringly to our confession
        that gives us hope,
  for he who made the promise is
        trustworthy.

Pentecost Sunday At the Mass during the Day, *May 15, 2016*

SECOND READING
Rom 8:8-17

Brothers and sisters:
Those who are in the flesh cannot please
        God.
But you are not in the flesh;
  on the contrary, you are in the spirit,
  if only the Spirit of God dwells in you.
Whoever does not have the Spirit of Christ
        does not belong to him.
But if Christ is in you,
  although the body is dead because of sin,
  the spirit is alive because of righteousness.
If the Spirit of the one who raised Jesus from
        the dead dwells in you,
  the one who raised Christ from the dead
  will give life to your mortal bodies also,
  through his Spirit that dwells in you.
Consequently, brothers and sisters,
  we are not debtors to the flesh,
  to live according to the flesh.
For if you live according to the flesh, you
        will die,
  but if by the Spirit you put to death the
        deeds of the body,
  you will live.

For those who are led by the Spirit of God are
        sons of God.
For you did not receive a spirit of slavery to
        fall back into fear,
  but you received a Spirit of adoption,
  through whom we cry, "Abba, Father!"
The Spirit himself bears witness with our
        spirit
  that we are children of God,
  and if children, then heirs,
  heirs of God and joint heirs with Christ,
  if only we suffer with him
  so that we may also be glorified with him.

or

1 Cor 12:3b-7, 12-13

Brothers and sisters:
No one can say, "Jesus is Lord," except by the
        Holy Spirit.
There are different kinds of spiritual gifts but
        the same Spirit;
  there are different forms of service but the
        same Lord;
  there are different workings but the same God
  who produces all of them in everyone.

To each individual the manifestation of the
        Spirit
  is given for some benefit.

As a body is one though it has many parts,
  and all the parts of the body, though many,
        are one body,
  so also Christ.
For in one Spirit we were all baptized into one
        body,
  whether Jews or Greeks, slaves or free
        persons,
  and we were all given to drink of one Spirit.

Pentecost Sunday At the Mass during the Day, *May 15, 2016*

SEQUENCE

Veni, Sancte Spiritus

Come, Holy Spirit, come!
And from your celestial home
    Shed a ray of light divine!
Come, Father of the poor!
Come, source of all our store!
    Come, within our bosoms shine.
You, of comforters the best;
You, the soul's most welcome guest;
    Sweet refreshment here below;
In our labor, rest most sweet;
Grateful coolness in the heat;
    Solace in the midst of woe.
O most blessed Light divine,
Shine within these hearts of yours,
    And our inmost being fill!

Where you are not, we have naught,
Nothing good in deed or thought,
    Nothing free from taint of ill.
Heal our wounds, our strength renew;
On our dryness pour your dew;
    Wash the stains of guilt away:
Bend the stubborn heart and will;
Melt the frozen, warm the chill;
    Guide the steps that go astray.
On the faithful, who adore
And confess you, evermore
    In your sevenfold gift descend;
Give them virtue's sure reward;
Give them your salvation, Lord;
    Give them joys that never end. Amen.
    Alleluia.

The Solemnity of the Most Holy Body and Blood of Christ, *May 29, 2016*

OPTIONAL SEQUENCE

Lauda Sion

Laud, O Zion, your salvation,
Laud with hymns of exultation,
    Christ, your king and shepherd true:

Bring him all the praise you know,
He is more than you bestow.
    Never can you reach his due.

Special theme for glad thanksgiving
Is the quick'ning and the living
    Bread today before you set:

From his hands of old partaken,
As we know, by faith unshaken,
    Where the Twelve at supper met.

Full and clear ring out your chanting,
Joy nor sweetest grace be wanting,
    From your heart let praises burst:

For today the feast is holden,
When the institution olden
    Of that supper was rehearsed.

Here the new law's new oblation,
By the new king's revelation,
    Ends the form of ancient rite:

Now the new the old effaces,
Truth away the shadow chases,
    Light dispels the gloom of night.

What he did at supper seated,
Christ ordained to be repeated,
    His memorial ne'er to cease:

And his rule for guidance taking,
Bread and wine we hallow, making
    Thus our sacrifice of peace.

This the truth each Christian learns,
Bread into his flesh he turns,
    To his precious blood the wine:

Sight has fail'd, nor thought conceives,
But a dauntless faith believes,
    Resting on a pow'r divine.

Here beneath these signs are hidden
Priceless things to sense forbidden;
    Signs, not things are all we see:

Blood is poured and flesh is broken,
Yet in either wondrous token
    Christ entire we know to be.

Whoso of this food partakes,
Does not rend the Lord nor breaks;
    Christ is whole to all that taste:

Thousands are, as one, receivers,
One, as thousands of believers,
    Eats of him who cannot waste.

Bad and good the feast are sharing,
Of what divers dooms preparing,
    Endless death, or endless life.

Life to these, to those damnation,
See how like participation
    Is with unlike issues rife.

When the sacrament is broken,
Doubt not, but believe 'tis spoken,

That each sever'd outward token
    Doth the very whole contain.

Nought the precious gift divides,
Breaking but the sign betides
    Jesus still the same abides,
    Still unbroken does remain.

The shorter form of the sequence begins here.

Lo! the angel's food is given
To the pilgrim who has striven;
    See the children's bread from heaven,
        Which on dogs may not be spent.

Truth the ancient types fulfilling,
Isaac bound, a victim willing,
    Paschal lamb, its lifeblood spilling,
        Manna to the fathers sent.

Very bread, good shepherd, tend us,
Jesu, of your love befriend us,
    You refresh us, you defend us,
    Your eternal goodness send us
In the land of life to see.

You who all things can and know,
Who on earth such food bestow,
    Grant us with your saints, though lowest,
    Where the heav'nly feast you show,
Fellow heirs and guests to be. Amen. Alleluia.

The Solemnity of the Most Sacred Heart of Jesus, *June 3, 2016*

FIRST READING
Ezek 34:11-16

Thus says the Lord GOD:
    I myself will look after and tend my sheep.
As a shepherd tends his flock
    when he finds himself among his scattered
      sheep,
    so will I tend my sheep.
I will rescue them from every place where
      they were scattered
    when it was cloudy and dark.
I will lead them out from among the peoples
    and gather them from the foreign lands;
    I will bring them back to their own country
    and pasture them upon the mountains of
      Israel
    in the land's ravines and all its inhabited
      places.
In good pastures will I pasture them,
    and on the mountain heights of Israel
    shall be their grazing ground.
There they shall lie down on good grazing
      ground,
    and in rich pastures shall they be pastured
    on the mountains of Israel.
I myself will pasture my sheep;
    I myself will give them rest, says the Lord
      GOD.
The lost I will seek out,
    the strayed I will bring back,
    the injured I will bind up,
    the sick I will heal,
    but the sleek and the strong I will destroy,
    shepherding them rightly.

RESPONSORIAL PSALM
Ps 23:1-3a, 3b-4, 5, 6

R̷. (1) The Lord is my shepherd; there is nothing I shall want.

The LORD is my shepherd; I shall not want.
    In verdant pastures he gives me repose;
beside restful waters he leads me;
    he refreshes my soul.

R̷. The Lord is my shepherd; there is nothing I shall want.

He guides me in right paths
    for his name's sake.
Even though I walk in the dark valley
    I fear no evil; for you are at my side
with your rod and your staff
    that give me courage.

R̷. The Lord is my shepherd; there is nothing I shall want.

You spread the table before me
    in the sight of my foes;
you anoint my head with oil;
    my cup overflows.

R̷. The Lord is my shepherd; there is nothing I shall want.

Only goodness and kindness follow me
    all the days of my life;
and I shall dwell in the house of the LORD
    for years to come.

R̷. The Lord is my shepherd; there is nothing I shall want.

SECOND READING
Rom 5:5b-11

Brothers and sisters:
The love of God has been poured out into our
      hearts
    through the Holy Spirit that has been given
      to us.
For Christ, while we were still helpless,
    died at the appointed time for the ungodly.
Indeed, only with difficulty does one die for a
      just person,
    though perhaps for a good person
    one might even find courage to die.
But God proves his love for us
    in that while we were still sinners Christ
      died for us.
How much more then, since we are now
      justified by his blood,
    will we be saved through him from the
      wrath.
Indeed, if, while we were enemies,
    we were reconciled to God through the
      death of his Son,
    how much more, once reconciled,
    will we be saved by his life.
Not only that,
    but we also boast of God through our Lord
      Jesus Christ,
    through whom we have now received
      reconciliation.

Tenth Sunday in Ordinary Time, *June 5, 2016*

SECOND READING *(cont.)*
Gal 1:11-19

But when God, who from my mother's womb
      had set me apart
    and called me through his grace,
    was pleased to reveal his Son to me,
    so that I might proclaim him to the
      Gentiles,
    I did not immediately consult flesh and
      blood,
    nor did I go up to Jerusalem
    to those who were apostles before me;
    rather, I went into Arabia and then
      returned to Damascus.

Then after three years I went up to
      Jerusalem
    to confer with Cephas and remained with
      him for fifteen days.
But I did not see any other of the apostles,
    only James the brother of the Lord.

Gospel (cont.)

Luke 7:36–8:3; L93C

Simon said in reply,
  "The one, I suppose, whose larger debt was forgiven."
He said to him, "You have judged rightly."

Then he turned to the woman and said to Simon,
  "Do you see this woman?
When I entered your house, you did not give me water for my feet,
  but she has bathed them with her tears
  and wiped them with her hair.
You did not give me a kiss,
  but she has not ceased kissing my feet since the time I entered.
You did not anoint my head with oil,
  but she anointed my feet with ointment.
So I tell you, her many sins have been forgiven
  because she has shown great love.
But the one to whom little is forgiven, loves little."
He said to her, "Your sins are forgiven."
The others at table said to themselves,
  "Who is this who even forgives sins?"
But he said to the woman,
  "Your faith has saved you; go in peace."

Afterward he journeyed from one town and village to another,
  preaching and proclaiming the good news of the kingdom of God.
Accompanying him were the Twelve
  and some women who had been cured of evil spirits and infirmities,
  Mary, called Magdalene, from whom seven demons had gone out,
  Joanna, the wife of Herod's steward Chuza,
  Susanna, and many others who provided for them out of their
    resources.

or Luke 7:36-50

A Pharisee invited Jesus to dine with him,
  and he entered the Pharisee's house and reclined at table.
Now there was a sinful woman in the city
  who learned that he was at table in the house of the Pharisee.

Bringing an alabaster flask of ointment,
  she stood behind him at his feet weeping
  and began to bathe his feet with her tears.
Then she wiped them with her hair,
  kissed them, and anointed them with the ointment.
When the Pharisee who had invited him saw this he said to himself,
  "If this man were a prophet,
  he would know who and what sort of woman this is who is
    touching him,
  that she is a sinner."
Jesus said to him in reply,
  "Simon, I have something to say to you."
"Tell me, teacher," he said.
"Two people were in debt to a certain creditor;
  one owed five hundred day's wages and the other owed fifty.
Since they were unable to repay the debt, he forgave it for both.
Which of them will love him more?"
Simon said in reply,
  "The one, I suppose, whose larger debt was forgiven."
He said to him, "You have judged rightly."

Then he turned to the woman and said to Simon,
  "Do you see this woman?
When I entered your house, you did not give me water for my feet,
  but she has bathed them with her tears
  and wiped them with her hair.
You did not give me a kiss,
  but she has not ceased kissing my feet since the time I entered.
You did not anoint my head with oil,
  but she anointed my feet with ointment.
So I tell you, her many sins have been forgiven
  because she has shown great love.
But the one to whom little is forgiven, loves little."
He said to her, "Your sins are forgiven."
The others at table said to themselves,
  "Who is this who even forgives sins?"
But he said to the woman,
  "Your faith has saved you; go in peace."

The Nativity of St. John the Baptist, June 24, 2016

FIRST READING

Isa 49:1-6

Hear me, O coastlands,
  listen, O distant peoples.
The LORD called me from birth,
  from my mother's womb he gave me my
    name.
He made of me a sharp-edged sword
  and concealed me in the shadow of his arm.
He made me a polished arrow,
  in his quiver he hid me.
You are my servant, he said to me,
  Israel, through whom I show my glory.

Though I thought I had toiled in vain,
  and for nothing, uselessly, spent my strength,

yet my reward is with the LORD,
  my recompense is with my God.
For now the LORD has spoken
  who formed me as his servant from the
    womb,
that Jacob may be brought back to him
  and Israel gathered to him;
and I am made glorious in the sight of the
  LORD,
  and my God is now my strength!
It is too little, he says, for you to be my servant,
  to raise up the tribes of Jacob,
  and restore the survivors of Israel;
I will make you a light to the nations,
  that my salvation may reach to the ends of
    the earth.

The Nativity of St. John the Baptist, June 24, 2016

RESPONSORIAL PSALM
Ps 139:1b-3, 13-14ab, 14c-15

R̶. (14a) I praise you, for I am wonderfully made.

O LORD, you have probed me, you know me;
 you know when I sit and when I stand;
 you understand my thoughts from afar.
My journeys and my rest you scrutinize,
 with all my ways you are familiar.

R̶. I praise you, for I am wonderfully made.

Truly you have formed my inmost being;
 you knit me in my mother's womb.
I give you thanks that I am fearfully,
 wonderfully made;
 wonderful are your works.

R̶. I praise you, for I am wonderfully made.

My soul also you knew full well;
 nor was my frame unknown to you
When I was made in secret,
 when I was fashioned in the depths of the
 earth.

R̶. I praise you, for I am wonderfully made.

SECOND READING
Acts 13:22-26

In those days, Paul said:
 "God raised up David as their king;
 of him God testified,
 'I have found David, son of Jesse, a man
 after my own heart;
 he will carry out my every wish.'
From this man's descendants God, according to
 his promise,
has brought to Israel a savior, Jesus.
John heralded his coming by proclaiming a
 baptism of repentance
to all the people of Israel;
 and as John was completing his course, he
 would say,
 'What do you suppose that I am? I am not he.
Behold, one is coming after me;
 I am not worthy to unfasten the sandals of
 his feet.'

"My brothers, sons of the family of Abraham,
 and those others among you who are God-
 fearing,
 to us this word of salvation has been sent."

SS. Peter and Paul, Apostles, June 29, 2016

FIRST READING
Acts 12:1-11

In those days, King Herod laid hands upon
 some members of the church to harm
 them.
He had James, the brother of John, killed by
 the sword,
 and when he saw that this was pleasing to
 the Jews
 he proceeded to arrest Peter also.
—It was the feast of Unleavened Bread.—
He had him taken into custody and put in
 prison
 under the guard of four squads of four
 soldiers each.
He intended to bring him before the people
 after Passover.
Peter thus was being kept in prison,
 but prayer by the church was fervently
 being made
 to God on his behalf.

On the very night before Herod was to bring
 him to trial,
 Peter, secured by double chains,
 was sleeping between two soldiers,
 while outside the door guards kept watch
 on the prison.
Suddenly the angel of the Lord stood by him
 and a light shone in the cell.
He tapped Peter on the side and awakened
 him, saying,
 "Get up quickly."
The chains fell from his wrists.

The angel said to him, "Put on your belt and
 your sandals."
He did so.
Then he said to him, "Put on your cloak and
 follow me."
So he followed him out,
 not realizing that what was happening
 through the angel was real;
 he thought he was seeing a vision.
They passed the first guard, then the second,
 and came to the iron gate leading out to
 the city,
 which opened for them by itself.
They emerged and made their way down an
 alley,
 and suddenly the angel left him.
Then Peter recovered his senses and said,
 "Now I know for certain
 that the Lord sent his angel
 and rescued me from the hand of Herod
 and from all that the Jewish people had
 been expecting."

RESPONSORIAL PSALM
Ps 34:2-3, 4-5, 6-7, 8-9

R̶. (8) The angel of the Lord will rescue those
who fear him.

I will bless the LORD at all times;
 his praise shall be ever in my mouth.
Let my soul glory in the LORD;
 the lowly will hear me and be glad.

R̶. The angel of the Lord will rescue those
who fear him.

Glorify the LORD with me,
 let us together extol his name.
I sought the LORD, and he answered me
 and delivered me from all my fears.

R̶. The angel of the Lord will rescue those
who fear him.

Look to him that you may be radiant with joy,
 and your faces may not blush with shame.
When the poor one called out, the LORD heard,
 and from all his distress he saved him.

R̶. The angel of the Lord will rescue those
who fear him.

The angel of the LORD encamps
 around those who fear him, and delivers
 them.
Taste and see how good the LORD is;
 blessed the man who takes refuge in him.

R̶. The angel of the Lord will rescue those
who fear him.

SS. Peter and Paul, Apostles, *June 29, 2016*

SECOND READING
2 Tim 4:6-8, 17-18

I, Paul, am already being poured out like a libation,
  and the time of my departure is at hand.
I have competed well; I have finished the race;
  I have kept the faith.
From now on the crown of righteousness awaits me,
  which the Lord, the just judge,
  will award to me on that day, and not only to me,
  but to all who have longed for his appearance.

The Lord stood by me and gave me strength,
  so that through me the proclamation might be completed
  and all the Gentiles might hear it.
And I was rescued from the lion's mouth.
The Lord will rescue me from every evil threat
  and will bring me safe to his heavenly kingdom.
To him be glory forever and ever. Amen.

Fourteenth Sunday in Ordinary Time, *July 3, 2016*

Gospel (cont.)
Luke 10:1-12, 17-20; L102C

Yet know this: the kingdom of God is at hand.
I tell you,
  it will be more tolerable for Sodom on that day than for that town."

The seventy-two returned rejoicing, and said,
  "Lord, even the demons are subject to us because of your name."
Jesus said, "I have observed Satan fall like lightning from the sky.
Behold, I have given you the power to 'tread upon serpents' and
    scorpions
  and upon the full force of the enemy and nothing will harm you.
Nevertheless, do not rejoice because the spirits are subject to you,
  but rejoice because your names are written in heaven."

or Luke 10:1-9; L102C

At that time the Lord appointed seventy-two others
  whom he sent ahead of him in pairs
  to every town and place he intended to visit.

He said to them,
  "The harvest is abundant but the laborers are few;
  so ask the master of the harvest
  to send out laborers for his harvest.
Go on your way;
  behold, I am sending you like lambs among wolves.
Carry no money bag, no sack, no sandals;
  and greet no one along the way.
Into whatever house you enter, first say,
  'Peace to this household.'
If a peaceful person lives there,
  your peace will rest on him;
  but if not, it will return to you.
Stay in the same house and eat and drink what is offered to you,
  for the laborer deserves his payment.
Do not move about from one house to another.
Whatever town you enter and they welcome you,
  eat what is set before you,
  cure the sick in it and say to them,
  'The kingdom of God is at hand for you.'"

Fifteenth Sunday in Ordinary Time, *July 10, 2016*

Gospel (cont.)
Luke 10:25-37; L105C

But a Samaritan traveler who came upon him
  was moved with compassion at the sight.
He approached the victim,
  poured oil and wine over his wounds and
    bandaged them.
Then he lifted him up on his own animal,
  took him to an inn, and cared for him.
The next day he took out two silver coins
  and gave them to the innkeeper with the
    instruction,
  'Take care of him.
If you spend more than what I have given you,
  I shall repay you on my way back.'
Which of these three, in your opinion,
  was neighbor to the robbers' victim?"

He answered, "The one who treated him with
    mercy."
Jesus said to him, "Go and do likewise."

RESPONSORIAL PSALM
Ps 19:8, 9, 10, 11

℟. (9a) Your words, Lord, are Spirit and life.

The law of the LORD is perfect,
  refreshing the soul;
the decree of the LORD is trustworthy,
  giving wisdom to the simple.

℟. Your words, Lord, are Spirit and life.

The precepts of the LORD are right,
  rejoicing the heart;
the command of the LORD is clear,
  enlightening the eye.

℟. Your words, Lord, are Spirit and life.

The fear of the LORD is pure,
  enduring forever;
the ordinances of the LORD are true,
  all of them just.

℟. Your words, Lord, are Spirit and life.

They are more precious than gold,
  than a heap of purest gold;
sweeter also than syrup
  or honey from the comb.

℟. Your words, Lord, are Spirit and life.

Seventeenth Sunday in Ordinary Time, July 24, 2016

Gospel (cont.)
Luke 11:1-13; L111C

"And I tell you, ask and you will receive;
  seek and you will find;
  knock and the door will be opened to you.
For everyone who asks, receives;
  and the one who seeks, finds;
  and to the one who knocks, the door will be opened.
What father among you would hand his son a snake
  when he asks for a fish?
Or hand him a scorpion when he asks for an egg?
If you then, who are wicked,
  know how to give good gifts to your children,
  how much more will the Father in heaven
  give the Holy Spirit to those who ask him?"

SECOND READING
Col 2:12-14

Brothers and sisters:
You were buried with him in baptism,
  in which you were also raised with him
  through faith in the power of God,
  who raised him from the dead.
And even when you were dead
  in transgressions and the uncircumcision of your flesh,
  he brought you to life along with him,
  having forgiven us all our transgressions;
obliterating the bond against us, with its legal claims,
  which was opposed to us,
  he also removed it from our midst, nailing it to the cross.

Nineteenth Sunday in Ordinary Time, August 7, 2016

Gospel (cont.)
Luke 12:32-48; L117C

You also must be prepared, for at an hour you do not expect,
  the Son of Man will come."

Then Peter said,
  "Lord, is this parable meant for us or for everyone?"
And the Lord replied,
  "Who, then, is the faithful and prudent steward
  whom the master will put in charge of his servants
  to distribute the food allowance at the proper time?
Blessed is that servant whom his master on arrival finds doing so.
Truly, I say to you, the master will put the servant
  in charge of all his property.
But if that servant says to himself,
  'My master is delayed in coming,'
  and begins to beat the menservants and the maidservants,
  to eat and drink and get drunk,
  then that servant's master will come
  on an unexpected day and at an unknown hour
  and will punish the servant severely
  and assign him a place with the unfaithful.
That servant who knew his master's will
  but did not make preparations nor act in accord with his will
  shall be beaten severely;
  and the servant who was ignorant of his master's will
  but acted in a way deserving of a severe beating
  shall be beaten only lightly.
Much will be required of the person entrusted with much,
  and still more will be demanded of the person entrusted with more."

or Luke 12:35-40

Jesus said to his disciples:
"Gird your loins and light your lamps
and be like servants who await their master's return from a wedding,
ready to open immediately when he comes and knocks.
Blessed are those servants
  whom the master finds vigilant on his arrival.
Amen, I say to you, he will gird himself,
  have them recline at table, and proceed to wait on them.
And should he come in the second or third watch
  and find them prepared in this way,
  blessed are those servants.
Be sure of this:
  if the master of the house had known the hour
  when the thief was coming,
  he would not have let his house be broken into.
You also must be prepared, for at an hour you do not expect,
  the Son of Man will come."

Nineteenth Sunday in Ordinary Time, *August 7, 2016*

So it was that there came forth from one man,
   himself as good as dead,
      descendants as numerous as the stars in
         the sky
      and as countless as the sands on the
         seashore.

All these died in faith.
They did not receive what had been promised
   but saw it and greeted it from afar
   and acknowledged themselves to be
      strangers and aliens on earth,
      for those who speak thus show that they
         are seeking a homeland.
If they had been thinking of the land from
   which they had come,
   they would have had opportunity to return.
But now they desire a better homeland, a
   heavenly one.
Therefore, God is not ashamed to be called
   their God,
   for he has prepared a city for them.

By faith Abraham, when put to the test,
   offered up Isaac,
   and he who had received the promises was
      ready to offer his only son,
   of whom it was said,
   "Through Isaac descendants shall bear
      your name."
He reasoned that God was able to raise even
   from the dead,
   and he received Isaac back as a symbol.

or Heb 11:1-2, 8-12

Brothers and sisters:
Faith is the realization of what is hoped for
   and evidence of things not seen.
Because of it the ancients were well attested.

By faith Abraham obeyed when he was called
   to go out to a place
   that he was to receive as an inheritance;
   he went out, not knowing where he was to
      go.
By faith he sojourned in the promised land as
   in a foreign country,
   dwelling in tents with Isaac and Jacob,
      heirs of the same promise;
   for he was looking forward to the city with
      foundations,
   whose architect and maker is God.
By faith he received power to generate,
   even though he was past the normal age
   —and Sarah herself was sterile—
   for he thought that the one who had made
      the promise was trustworthy.
So it was that there came forth from one man,
   himself as good as dead,
      descendants as numerous as the stars in
         the sky
      and as countless as the sands on the
         seashore.

The Assumption of the Blessed Virgin Mary, *August 15, 2016*

Gospel (cont.)
Luke 1:39-56; L622

He has shown the strength of his arm,
   and has scattered the proud in their conceit.
He has cast down the mighty from their thrones,
   and has lifted up the lowly.
He has filled the hungry with good things,
   and the rich he has sent away empty.
He has come to the help of his servant Israel
   for he has remembered his promise of mercy,
   the promise he made to our fathers,
   to Abraham and his children forever."

Mary remained with her about three months
   and then returned to her home.

The Assumption of the Blessed Virgin Mary, *August 15, 2016*

FIRST READING
Rev 11:19a; 12:1-6a, 10ab

God's temple in heaven was opened,
and the ark of his covenant could be seen
in the temple.

A great sign appeared in the sky, a woman
clothed with the sun,
with the moon under her feet,
and on her head a crown of twelve stars.
She was with child and wailed aloud in pain
as she labored to give birth.
Then another sign appeared in the sky;
it was a huge red dragon, with seven heads
and ten horns,
and on its heads were seven diadems.
Its tail swept away a third of the stars in the
sky
and hurled them down to the earth.
Then the dragon stood before the woman
about to give birth,
to devour her child when she gave birth.
She gave birth to a son, a male child,
destined to rule all the nations with an iron
rod.
Her child was caught up to God and his
throne.
The woman herself fled into the desert
where she had a place prepared by God.

Then I heard a loud voice in heaven say:
"Now have salvation and power come,
and the Kingdom of our God
and the authority of his Anointed One."

RESPONSORIAL PSALM
Ps 45:10, 11, 12, 16

R︎. (10bc) The queen stands at your right
hand, arrayed in gold.

The queen takes her place at your right hand
in gold of Ophir.

R︎. The queen stands at your right hand,
arrayed in gold.

Hear, O daughter, and see; turn your ear,
forget your people and your father's house.

R︎. The queen stands at your right hand,
arrayed in gold.

So shall the king desire your beauty;
for he is your lord.

R︎. The queen stands at your right hand,
arrayed in gold.

They are borne in with gladness and joy;
they enter the palace of the king.

R︎. The queen stands at your right hand,
arrayed in gold.

SECOND READING
1 Cor 15:20-27

Brothers and sisters:
Christ has been raised from the dead,
the firstfruits of those who have fallen
asleep.
For since death came through man,
the resurrection of the dead came also
through man.
For just as in Adam all die,
so too in Christ shall all be brought to life,
but each one in proper order:
Christ the firstfruits;
then, at his coming, those who belong to
Christ;
then comes the end,
when he hands over the Kingdom to his
God and Father,
when he has destroyed every sovereignty
and every authority and power.
For he must reign until he has put all his
enemies under his feet.
The last enemy to be destroyed is death,
for "he subjected everything under his feet."

Twenty-Second Sunday in Ordinary Time, *August 28, 2016*

Gospel (cont.)
Luke 14:1, 7-14; L126C

Then he said to the host who invited him,
"When you hold a lunch or a dinner,
do not invite your friends or your brothers
or your relatives or your wealthy neighbors,
in case they may invite you back and you have repayment.
Rather, when you hold a banquet,
invite the poor, the crippled, the lame, the blind;
blessed indeed will you be because of their inability to repay you.
For you will be repaid at the resurrection of the righteous."

Gospel (cont.)
Luke 15:1-32; L132C

And when she does find it,
   she calls together her friends and neighbors
   and says to them,
   'Rejoice with me because I have found the coin that I lost.'
In just the same way, I tell you,
   there will be rejoicing among the angels of God
   over one sinner who repents."

Then he said,
   "A man had two sons, and the younger son said to his father,
   'Father give me the share of your estate that should come to me.'
So the father divided the property between them.
After a few days, the younger son collected all his belongings
   and set off to a distant country
   where he squandered his inheritance on a life of dissipation.
When he had freely spent everything,
   a severe famine struck that country,
   and he found himself in dire need.
So he hired himself out to one of the local citizens
   who sent him to his farm to tend the swine.
And he longed to eat his fill of the pods on which the swine fed,
   but nobody gave him any.
Coming to his senses he thought,
   'How many of my father's hired workers
   have more than enough food to eat,
   but here am I, dying from hunger.
I shall get up and go to my father and I shall say to him,
   "Father, I have sinned against heaven and against you.
I no longer deserve to be called your son;
   treat me as you would treat one of your hired workers."'
So he got up and went back to his father.
While he was still a long way off,
   his father caught sight of him,
   and was filled with compassion.
He ran to his son, embraced him and kissed him.
His son said to him,
   'Father, I have sinned against heaven and against you;
   I no longer deserve to be called your son.'
But his father ordered his servants,
   'Quickly bring the finest robe and put it on him;
   put a ring on his finger and sandals on his feet.
Take the fattened calf and slaughter it.
Then let us celebrate with a feast,
   because this son of mine was dead, and has come to life again;
   he was lost, and has been found.'
Then the celebration began.
Now the older son had been out in the field
   and, on his way back, as he neared the house,
   he heard the sound of music and dancing.
He called one of the servants and asked what this might mean.

The servant said to him,
   'Your brother has returned
   and your father has slaughtered the fattened calf
   because he has him back safe and sound.'
He became angry,
   and when he refused to enter the house,
   his father came out and pleaded with him.
He said to his father in reply,
   'Look, all these years I served you
   and not once did I disobey your orders;
   yet you never gave me even a young goat to feast on with my
      friends. But when your son returns,
   who swallowed up your property with prostitutes,
   for him you slaughter the fattened calf.'
He said to him,
   'My son, you are here with me always;
   everything I have is yours.
But now we must celebrate and rejoice,
   because your brother was dead and has come to life again;
   he was lost and has been found.'"

or Luke 15:1-10

Tax collectors and sinners were all drawing near to listen to Jesus,
   but the Pharisees and scribes began to complain, saying,
   "This man welcomes sinners and eats with them."
So to them he addressed this parable.
"What man among you having a hundred sheep and losing one of them
   would not leave the ninety-nine in the desert
   and go after the lost one until he finds it?
And when he does find it,
   he sets it on his shoulders with great joy
   and, upon his arrival home,
   he calls together his friends and neighbors and says to them,
   'Rejoice with me because I have found my lost sheep.'
I tell you, in just the same way
   there will be more joy in heaven over one sinner who repents
   than over ninety-nine righteous people
   who have no need of repentance.

"Or what woman having ten coins and losing one
   would not light a lamp and sweep the house,
   searching carefully until she finds it?
And when she does find it,
   she calls together her friends and neighbors
   and says to them,
   'Rejoice with me because I have found the coin that I lost.'
In just the same way, I tell you,
   there will be rejoicing among the angels of God
   over one sinner who repents."

Twenty-Fifth Sunday in Ordinary Time, *September 18, 2016*

Gospel (cont.)
Luke 16:1-13; L135C

The steward said to him, 'Here is your promissory note;
   write one for eighty.'
And the master commended that dishonest steward for acting
   prudently.

"For the children of this world
   are more prudent in dealing with their own generation
   than are the children of light.
I tell you, make friends for yourselves with dishonest wealth,
   so that when it fails, you will be welcomed into eternal dwellings.
The person who is trustworthy in very small matters
   is also trustworthy in great ones;
   and the person who is dishonest in very small matters
   is also dishonest in great ones.
If, therefore, you are not trustworthy with dishonest wealth,
   who will trust you with true wealth?
If you are not trustworthy with what belongs to another,
   who will give you what is yours?
No servant can serve two masters.
He will either hate one and love the other,
   or be devoted to one and despise the other.
You cannot serve both God and mammon."

or Luke 16:10-13

Jesus said to his disciples,
   "The person who is trustworthy in very small matters
   is also trustworthy in great ones;
   and the person who is dishonest in very small matters
   is also dishonest in great ones.
If, therefore, you are not trustworthy with dishonest wealth,
   who will trust you with true wealth?
If you are not trustworthy with what belongs to another,
   who will give you what is yours?
No servant can serve two masters.
He will either hate one and love the other,
   or be devoted to one and despise the other.
You cannot serve both God and mammon."

Twenty-Sixth Sunday in Ordinary Time, *September 25, 2016*

Gospel (cont.)
Luke 16:19-31; L138C

Moreover, between us and you a great chasm is established
   to prevent anyone from crossing who might wish to go
   from our side to yours or from your side to ours.'
He said, 'Then I beg you, father,
   send him to my father's house, for I have five brothers,
   so that he may warn them,
   lest they too come to this place of torment.'
But Abraham replied, 'They have Moses and the prophets.
Let them listen to them.'
He said, 'Oh no, father Abraham,
   but if someone from the dead goes to them, they will repent.'
Then Abraham said, 'If they will not listen to Moses and the prophets,
   neither will they be persuaded if someone should rise from the dead.'"

FIRST READING
Rev 7:2-4, 9-14

I, John, saw another angel come up from the
East,
    holding the seal of the living God.
He cried out in a loud voice to the four angels
    who were given power to damage the land
        and the sea,
    "Do not damage the land or the sea or the
        trees
    until we put the seal on the foreheads of
        the servants of our God."
I heard the number of those who had been
    marked with the seal,
    one hundred and forty-four thousand
        marked
    from every tribe of the children of Israel.

After this I had a vision of a great multitude,
    which no one could count,
    from every nation, race, people, and tongue.
They stood before the throne and before the
    Lamb,
    wearing white robes and holding palm
        branches in their hands.
They cried out in a loud voice:
    "Salvation comes from our God,
        who is seated on the throne,
    and from the Lamb."

All the angels stood around the throne
    and around the elders and the four living
        creatures.
They prostrated themselves before the throne,
    worshiped God, and exclaimed:

    "Amen. Blessing and glory, wisdom and
        thanksgiving,
        honor, power, and might
    be to our God forever and ever. Amen."

Then one of the elders spoke up and said to
    me,
    "Who are these wearing white robes, and
        where did they come from?"
I said to him, "My lord, you are the one who
    knows."
He said to me,
    "These are the ones who have survived the
        time of great distress;
    they have washed their robes
    and made them white in the Blood of the
        Lamb."

RESPONSORIAL PSALM
Ps 24:1-2, 3-4, 5-6

R̦. (cf. 6) Lord, this is the people that longs to
see your face.

The LORD's are the earth and its fullness;
    the world and those who dwell in it.
For he founded it upon the seas
    and established it upon the rivers.

R̦. Lord, this is the people that longs to see
your face.

Who can ascend the mountain of the LORD?
    or who may stand in his holy place?
One whose hands are sinless, whose heart is
    clean,
    who desires not what is vain.

R̦. Lord, this is the people that longs to see
your face.

He shall receive a blessing from the LORD,
    a reward from God his savior.
Such is the race that seeks him,
    that seeks the face of the God of Jacob.

R̦. Lord, this is the people that longs to see
your face.

SECOND READING
1 John 3:1-3

Beloved:
See what love the Father has bestowed on us
    that we may be called the children of God.
Yet so we are.
The reason the world does not know us
    is that it did not know him.
Beloved, we are God's children now;
    what we shall be has not yet been revealed.
We do know that when it is revealed we shall
    be like him,
    for we shall see him as he is.
Everyone who has this hope based on him
    makes himself pure,
    as he is pure.

All Souls, *November 2, 2016*

(Other options can be found in the Lectionary for Mass, L668.)

FIRST READING
Wis 3:1-9

The souls of the just are in the hand of God,
  and no torment shall touch them.
They seemed, in the view of the foolish, to be
    dead;
  and their passing away was thought an
      affliction
  and their going forth from us, utter
      destruction.
But they are in peace.
For if before men, indeed they be punished,
  yet is their hope full of immortality;
chastised a little, they shall be greatly
      blessed,
  because God tried them
  and found them worthy of himself.
As gold in the furnace, he proved them,
  and as sacrificial offerings he took them to
      himself.
In the time of their visitation they shall shine,
  and shall dart about as sparks through
      stubble;
they shall judge nations and rule over
      peoples,
  and the LORD shall be their King forever.
Those who trust in him shall understand
      truth,
  and the faithful shall abide with him in
      love:
because grace and mercy are with his holy
      ones,
  and his care is with his elect.

RESPONSORIAL PSALM
Ps 23:1-3a, 3b-4, 5, 6

R̸. (1) The Lord is my shepherd; there is
nothing I shall want.
  or:
R̸. (4ab) Though I walk in the valley of
darkness, I fear no evil, for you are with me.

The LORD is my shepherd; I shall not want.
  In verdant pastures he gives me repose;
beside restful waters he leads me;
  he refreshes my soul.

R̸. The Lord is my shepherd; there is nothing
I shall want.
  or:
R̸. Though I walk in the valley of darkness, I
fear no evil, for you are with me.

He guides me in right paths
  for his name's sake.
Even though I walk in the dark valley
  I fear no evil; for you are at my side
with your rod and your staff
  that give me courage.

R̸. The Lord is my shepherd; there is nothing
I shall want.
  or:
R̸. Though I walk in the valley of darkness, I
fear no evil, for you are with me.

You spread the table before me
  in the sight of my foes;
You anoint my head with oil;
  my cup overflows.

R̸. The Lord is my shepherd; there is nothing
I shall want.
  or:
R̸. Though I walk in the valley of darkness, I
fear no evil, for you are with me.

Only goodness and kindness follow me
  all the days of my life;
and I shall dwell in the house of the LORD
  for years to come.

R̸. The Lord is my shepherd; there is nothing
I shall want.
  or:
R̸. Though I walk in the valley of darkness, I
fear no evil, for you are with me.

SECOND READING
Rom 6:3-9; L1014.3

Brothers and sisters:
Are you unaware that we who were baptized
      into Christ Jesus
  were baptized into his death?
We were indeed buried with him through
      baptism into death,
  so that, just as Christ was raised from the
      dead
  by the glory of the Father,
  we too might live in newness of life.

For if we have grown into union with him
      through a death like his,
  we shall also be united with him in the
      resurrection.
We know that our old self was crucified with
      him,
  so that our sinful body might be done away
      with,
  that we might no longer be in slavery to sin.
For a dead person has been absolved from sin.
If, then, we have died with Christ,
  we believe that we shall also live with him.
We know that Christ, raised from the dead,
      dies no more;
  death no longer has power over him.

313

Thirty-Second Sunday in Ordinary Time,
November 6, 2016

Gospel
Luke 20:27, 34-38; L156C

Some Sadducees, those who deny that there is a resurrection,
  came forward.

Jesus said to them,
  "The children of this age marry and remarry;
  but those who are deemed worthy to attain to the coming age
  and to the resurrection of the dead
  neither marry nor are given in marriage.
They can no longer die,
  for they are like angels;
  and they are the children of God
  because they are the ones who will rise.
That the dead will rise
  even Moses made known in the passage about the bush,
  when he called out 'Lord,'
  the God of Abraham, the God of Isaac, and the God of Jacob;
  and he is not God of the dead, but of the living,
  for to him all are alive."

Thirty-Third Sunday in Ordinary Time,
November 13, 2016

Gospel (cont.)
Luke 21:5-19; L159C

"Before all this happens, however,
  they will seize and persecute you,
  they will hand you over to the synagogues and to prisons,
  and they will have you led before kings and governors
  because of my name.
It will lead to your giving testimony.
Remember, you are not to prepare your defense beforehand,
  for I myself shall give you a wisdom in speaking
  that all your adversaries will be powerless to resist or refute.
You will even be handed over by parents, brothers, relatives, and
    friends,
  and they will put some of you to death.
You will be hated by all because of my name,
  but not a hair on your head will be destroyed.
By your perseverance you will secure your lives."

Thanksgiving Day, *November 24, 2016*
(Other options can be found in the Lectionary for Mass, L943–947.)

FIRST READING
Sir 50:22-24; L943.2

And now, bless the God of all,
  who has done wondrous things on earth;
Who fosters people's growth from their
    mother's womb,
  and fashions them according to his will!
May he grant you joy of heart
  and may peace abide among you;
May his goodness toward us endure in Israel
  to deliver us in our days.

RESPONSORIAL PSALM
Ps 138:1-2a, 2bc-3, 4-5; L945.3

℟. (2bc) Lord, I thank you for your
faithfulness and love.

I will give thanks to you, O LORD, with all of
    my heart,
  for you have heard the words of my mouth;
  in the presence of the angels I will sing
    your praise;
I will worship at your holy temple.

℟. Lord, I thank you for your faithfulness and
love.

I will give thanks to your name,
Because of your kindness and your truth.
When I called, you answered me;
  you built up strength within me.

℟. Lord, I thank you for your faithfulness and
love.

All the kings of the earth shall give thanks to
    you, O LORD,
  when they hear the words of your mouth;
And they shall sing of the ways of the LORD:
  "Great is the glory of the LORD."

℟. Lord, I thank you for your faithfulness and
love.

SECOND READING
1 Cor 1:3-9; L944.1

Brothers and sisters:
Grace to you and peace from God our Father
  and the Lord Jesus Christ.

I give thanks to my God always on your
    account
  for the grace of God bestowed on you in
    Christ Jesus,
  that in him you were enriched in every way,
  with all discourse and all knowledge,
  as the testimony to Christ was confirmed
    among you,
  so that you are not lacking in any spiritual
    gift
  as you wait for the revelation of our Lord
    Jesus Christ.
He will keep you firm to the end,
  irreproachable on the day of our Lord Jesus
    Christ.
God is faithful,
  and by him you were called to fellowship
    with his Son, Jesus Christ our Lord.

APPENDIX B

Choral Settings for the Universal Prayer (Prayer of the Faithful)

Purchasers of this volume may reproduce these choral arrangements for use in their parish or community. The music must be reproduced as given below, with composer's name and copyright line.

ORDINARY TIME, WEEKS 2-5

Cantor:

ORDINARY TIME, WEEKS 10-20

Cantor:

ORDINARY TIME, WEEKS 21-33

Cantor:

Lectionary Pronunciation Guide

Lectionary Word	Pronunciation
Aaron	EHR-uhn
Abana	AB-uh-nuh
Abednego	uh-BEHD-nee-go
Abel-Keramin	AY-b'l-KEHR-uh-mihn
Abel-meholah	AY-b'l-mee-HO-lah
Abiathar	uh-BAI-uh-ther
Abiel	AY-bee-ehl
Abiezrite	ay-bai-EHZ-rait
Abijah	uh-BAI-dzhuh
Abilene	ab-uh-LEE-neh
Abishai	uh-BIHSH-ay-ai
Abiud	uh-BAI-uhd
Abner	AHB-ner
Abraham	AY-bruh-ham
Abram	AY-br'm
Achaia	uh-KAY-yuh
Achim	AY-kihm
Aeneas	uh-NEE-uhs
Aenon	AY-nuhn
Agrippa	uh-GRIH-puh
Ahaz	AY-haz
Ahijah	uh-HAI-dzhuh
Ai	AY-ee
Alexandria	al-ehg-ZAN-dree-uh
Alexandrian	al-ehg-ZAN-dree-uhn
Alpha	AHL-fuh
Alphaeus	AL-fee-uhs
Amalek	AM-uh-lehk
Amaziah	am-uh-ZAI-uh
Amminadab	ah-MIHN-uh-dab
Ammonites	AM-uh-naitz
Amorites	AM-uh-raits
Amos	AY-muhs
Amoz	AY-muhz
Ampliatus	am-plee-AY-tuhs
Ananias	an-uh-NAI-uhs
Andronicus	an-draw-NAI-kuhs
Annas	AN-uhs
Antioch	AN-tih-ahk
Antiochus	an-TAI-uh-kuhs
Aphiah	uh-FAI-uh
Apollos	uh-PAH-luhs
Appius	AP-ee-uhs
Aquila	uh-KWIHL-uh
Arabah	EHR-uh-buh
Aram	AY-ram
Arameans	ehr-uh-MEE-uhnz
Areopagus	ehr-ee-AH-puh-guhs
Arimathea	ehr-uh-muh-THEE-uh
Aroer	uh-RO-er

Lectionary Word	Pronunciation
Asaph	AY-saf
Asher	ASH-er
Ashpenaz	ASH-pee-naz
Assyria	a-SIHR-ee-uh
Astarte	as-TAHR-tee
Attalia	at-TAH-lee-uh
Augustus	uh-GUHS-tuhs
Azariah	az-uh-RAI-uh
Azor	AY-sawr
Azotus	uh-ZO-tus
Baal-shalishah	BAY-uhl-shuh-LAI-shuh
Baal-Zephon	BAY-uhl-ZEE-fuhn
Babel	BAY-bl
Babylon	BAB-ih-luhn
Babylonian	bab-ih-LO-nih-uhn
Balaam	BAY-lm
Barabbas	beh-REH-buhs
Barak	BEHR-ak
Barnabas	BAHR-nuh-buhs
Barsabbas	BAHR-suh-buhs
Bartholomew	bar-THAHL-uh-myoo
Bartimaeus	bar-tih-MEE-uhs
Baruch	BEHR-ook
Bashan	BAY-shan
Becorath	bee-KO-rath
Beelzebul	bee-EHL-zee-buhl
Beer-sheba	BEE-er-SHEE-buh
Belshazzar	behl-SHAZ-er
Benjamin	BEHN-dzhuh-mihn
Beor	BEE-awr
Bethany	BEHTH-uh-nee
Bethel	BETH-el
Bethesda	beh-THEHZ-duh
Bethlehem	BEHTH-leh-hehm
Bethphage	BEHTH-fuh-dzhee
Bethsaida	behth-SAY-ih-duh
Beth-zur	behth-ZER
Bildad	BIHL-dad
Bithynia	bih-THIHN-ih-uh
Boanerges	bo-uh-NER-dzheez
Boaz	BO-az
Caesar	SEE-zer
Caesarea	zeh-suh-REE-uh
Caiaphas	KAY-uh-fuhs
Cain	kayn
Cana	KAY-nuh
Canaan	KAY-nuhn
Canaanite	KAY-nuh-nait
Canaanites	KAY-nuh-naits

Lectionary Word	Pronunciation
Candace	kan-DAY-see
Capernaum	kuh-PERR-nay-uhm
Cappadocia	kap-ih-DO-shee-u
Carmel	KAHR-muhl
carnelians	kahr-NEEL-yuhnz
Cenchreae	SEHN-kree-ay
Cephas	SEE-fuhs
Chaldeans	kal-DEE-uhnz
Chemosh	KEE-mahsh
Cherubim	TSHEHR-oo-bihm
Chislev	KIHS-lehv
Chloe	KLO-ee
Chorazin	kor-AY-sihn
Cilicia	sih-LIHSH-ee-uh
Cleopas	KLEE-o-pas
Clopas	KLO-pas
Corinth	KAWR-ihnth
Corinthians	kawr-IHN-thee-uhnz
Cornelius	kawr-NEE-lee-uhs
Crete	kreet
Crispus	KRIHS-puhs
Cushite	CUHSH-ait
Cypriot	SIH-pree-at
Cyrene	sai-REE-nee
Cyreneans	sai-REE-nih-uhnz
Cyrenian	sai-REE-nih-uhn
Cyrenians	sai-REE-nih-uhnz
Cyrus	SAI-ruhs
Damaris	DAM-uh-rihs
Damascus	duh-MAS-kuhs
Danites	DAN-aits
Decapolis	duh-KAP-o-lis
Derbe	DER-bee
Deuteronomy	dyoo-ter-AH-num-mee
Didymus	DID-I-mus
Dionysius	dai-o-NIHSH-ih-uhs
Dioscuri	dai-O-sky-ri
Dorcas	DAWR-kuhs
Dothan	DO-thuhn
dromedaries	DRAH-muh-dher-eez
Ebed-melech	EE-behd-MEE-lehk
Eden	EE-dn
Edom	EE-duhm
Elamites	EE-luh-maitz
Eldad	EHL-dad
Eleazar	ehl-ee-AY-zer
Eli	EE-lai
Eli Eli Lema Sabachthani	AY-lee AY-lee luh-MAH sah-BAHK-tah-nee

Lectionary Word	Pronunciation	Lectionary Word	Pronunciation	Lectionary Word	Pronunciation
Eliab	ee-LAI-ab	Gilead	GIHL-ee-uhd	Joppa	DZHAH-puh
Eliakim	ee-LAI-uh-kihm	Gilgal	GIHL-gal	Joram	DZHO-ram
Eliezer	ehl-ih-EE-zer	Golgotha	GAHL-guh-thuh	Jordan	DZHAWR-dn
Elihu	ee-LAI-hyoo	Gomorrah	guh-MAWR-uh	Joseph	DZHO-zf
Elijah	ee-LAI-dzhuh	Goshen	GO-shuhn	Joses	DZHO-seez
Elim	EE-lihm	Habakkuk	huh-BAK-uhk	Joshua	DZHAH-shou-ah
Elimelech	ee-LIHM-eh-lehk	Hadadrimmon	hay-dad-RIHM-uhn	Josiah	dzho-SAI-uh
Elisha	ee-LAI-shuh	Hades	HAY-deez	Jotham	DZHO-thuhm
Eliud	ee-LAI-uhd	Hagar	HAH-gar	Judah	DZHOU-duh
Elizabeth	ee-LIHZ-uh-bth	Hananiah	han-uh-NAI-uh	Judas	DZHOU-duhs
Elkanah	el-KAY-nuh	Hannah	HAN-uh	Judea	dzhou-DEE-uh
Eloi Eloi Lama	AY-lo-ee AY-lo-ee	Haran	HAY-ruhn	Judean	dzhou-DEE-uhn
Sabechthani	LAH-mah sah-	Hebron	HEE-bruhn	Junia	dzhou-nih-uh
	BAHK-tah-nee	Hermes	HER-meez	Justus	DZHUHS-tuhs
Elymais	ehl-ih-MAY-ihs	Herod	HEHR-uhd	Kephas	KEF-uhs
Emmanuel	eh-MAN-yoo-ehl	Herodians	hehr-O-dee-uhnz	Kidron	KIHD-ruhn
Emmaus	eh-MAY-uhs	Herodias	hehr-O-dee-uhs	Kiriatharba	kihr-ee-ath-AHR-buh
Epaenetus	ee-PEE-nee-tuhs	Hezekiah	heh-zeh-KAI-uh	Kish	kihsh
Epaphras	EH-puh-fras	Hezron	HEHZ-ruhn	Laodicea	lay-o-dih-SEE-uh
ephah	EE-fuh	Hilkiah	hihl-KAI-uh	Lateran	LAT-er-uhn
Ephah	EE-fuh	Hittite	HIH-tait	Lazarus	LAZ-er-uhs
Ephesians	eh-FEE-zhuhnz	Hivites	HAI-vaitz	Leah	LEE-uh
Ephesus	EH-fuh-suhs	Hophni	HAHF-nai	Lebanon	LEH-buh-nuhn
Ephphatha	EHF-uh-thuh	Hor	HAWR	Levi	LEE-vai
Ephraim	EE-fray-ihm	Horeb	HAWR-ehb	Levite	LEE-vait
Ephrathah	EHF-ruh-thuh	Hosea	ho-ZEE-uh	Levites	LEE-vaits
Ephron	EE-frawn	Hur	her	Leviticus	leh-VIH-tih-kous
Epiphanes	eh-PIHF-uh-neez	hyssop	HIH-suhp	Lucius	LOO-shih-uhs
Erastus	ee-RAS-tuhs	Iconium	ai-KO-nih-uhm	Lud	luhd
Esau	EE-saw	Isaac	AI-zuhk	Luke	look
Esther	EHS-ter	Isaiah	ai-ZAY-uh	Luz	luhz
Ethanim	EHTH-uh-nihm	Iscariot	ihs-KEHR-ee-uht	Lycaonian	lihk-ay-O-nih-uhn
Ethiopian	ee-thee-O-pee-uhn	Ishmael	ISH-may-ehl	Lydda	LIH-duh
Euphrates	yoo-FRAY-teez	Ishmaelites	ISH-mayehl-aits	Lydia	LIH-dih-uh
Exodus	EHK-so-duhs	Israel	IHZ-ray-ehl	Lysanias	lai-SAY-nih-uhs
Ezekiel	eh-ZEE-kee-uhl	Ituraea	ih-TSHOOR-ree-uh	Lystra	LIHS-truh
Ezra	EHZ-ruh	Jaar	DZHAY-ahr	Maccabees	MAK-uh-beez
frankincense	FRANGK-ihn-sehns	Jabbok	DZHAB-uhk	Macedonia	mas-eh-DO-nih-uh
Gabbatha	GAB-uh-thuh	Jacob	DZHAY-kuhb	Macedonian	mas-eh-DO-nih-uhn
Gabriel	GAY-bree-ul	Jairus	DZH-hr-uhs	Machir	MAY-kih
Gadarenes	GAD-uh-reenz	Javan	DZHAY-van	Machpelah	mak-PEE-luh
Galatian	guh-LAY-shih-uhn	Jebusites	DZHEHB-oo-zaits	Magdala	MAG-duh-luh
Galatians	guh-LAY-shih-uhnz	Jechoniah	dzhehk-o-NAI-uh	Magdalene	MAG-duh-lehn
Galilee	GAL-ih-lee	Jehoiakim	dzhee-HOI-uh-kihm	magi	MAY-dzhai
Gallio	GAL-ih-o	Jehoshaphat	dzhee-HAHSH-uh-fat	Malachi	MAL-uh-kai
Gamaliel	guh-MAY-lih-ehl	Jephthah	DZHEHF-thuh	Malchiah	mal-KAI-uh
Gaza	GAH-zuh	Jeremiah	dzhehr-eh-MAI-uh	Malchus	MAL-kuhz
Gehazi	gee-HAY-zai	Jericho	DZHEHR-ih-ko	Mamre	MAM-ree
Gehenna	geh-HEHN-uh	Jeroham	dzhehr-RO-ham	Manaen	MAN-uh-ehn
Genesis	DZHEHN-uh-sihs	Jerusalem	dzheh-ROU-suh-lehm	Manasseh	man-AS-eh
Gennesaret	gehn-NEHS-uh-reht	Jesse	DZHEH-see	Manoah	muh-NO-uh
Gentiles	DZHEHN-tailz	Jethro	DZHEHTH-ro	Mark	mahrk
Gerasenes	DZHEHR-uh-seenz	Joakim	DZHO-uh-kihm	Mary	MEHR-ee
Gethsemane	gehth-SEHM-uh-ne	Job	DZHOB	Massah	MAH-suh
Gideon	GIHD-ee-uhn	Jonah	DZHO-nuh	Mattathias	mat-uh-THAI-uhs

Lectionary Word	Pronunciation	Lectionary Word	Pronunciation	Lectionary Word	Pronunciation
Matthan	MAT-than	Parmenas	PAHR-mee-nas	Sabbath	SAB-uhth
Matthew	MATH-yoo	Parthians	PAHR-thee-uhnz	Sadducees	SAD-dzhoo-seez
Matthias	muh-THAI-uhs	Patmos	PAT-mos	Salem	SAY-lehm
Medad	MEE-dad	Peninnah	pee-NIHN-uh	Salim	SAY-lim
Mede	meed	Pentecost	PEHN-tee-kawst	Salmon	SAL-muhn
Medes	meedz	Penuel	pee-NYOO-ehl	Salome	suh-LO-mee
Megiddo	mee-GIH-do	Perez	PEE-rehz	Salu	SAYL-yoo
Melchizedek	mehl-KIHZ-eh-dehk	Perga	PER-guh	Samaria	suh-MEHR-ih-uh
Mene	MEE-nee	Perizzites	PEHR-ih-zaits	Samaritan	suh-MEHR-ih-tuhn
Meribah	MEHR-ih-bah	Persia	PER-zhuh	Samothrace	SAM-o-thrays
Meshach	MEE-shak	Peter	PEE-ter	Samson	SAM-s'n
Mespotamia	mehs-o-po-TAY-mih-uh	Phanuel	FAN-yoo-ehl	Samuel	SAM-yoo-uhl
		Pharaoh	FEHR-o	Sanhedrin	san-HEE-drihn
Micah	MAI-kuh	Pharisees	FEHR-ih-seez	Sarah	SEHR-uh
Midian	MIH-dih-uhn	Pharpar	FAHR-pahr	Sarai	SAY-rai
Milcom	MIHL-kahm	Philemon	fih-LEE-muhn	saraph	SAY-raf
Miletus	mai-LEE-tuhs	Philippi	fil-LIH-pai	Sardis	SAHR-dihs
Minnith	MIHN-ihth	Philippians	fih-LIHP-ih-uhnz	Saul	sawl
Mishael	MIHSH-ay-ehl	Philistines	fih-LIHS-tihnz	Scythian	SIH-thee-uihn
Mizpah	MIHZ-puh	Phinehas	FEHN-ee-uhs	Seba	SEE-buh
Moreh	MO-reh	Phoenicia	fee-NIHSH-ih-uh	Seth	sehth
Moriah	maw-RAI-uh	Phrygia	FRIH-dzhih-uh	Shaalim	SHAY-uh-lihm
Mosoch	MAH-sahk	Phrygian	FRIH-dzhih-uhn	Shadrach	SHAY-drak
myrrh	mer	phylacteries	fih-LAK-ter-eez	Shalishah	shuh-LEE-shuh
Mysia	MIH-shih-uh	Pi-Hahiroth	pai-huh-HAI-rahth	Shaphat	Shay-fat
Naaman	NAY-uh-muhn	Pilate	PAI-luht	Sharon	SHEHR-uhn
Nahshon	NAY-shuhn	Pisidia	pih-SIH-dih-uh	Shealtiel	shee-AL-tih-ehl
Naomi	NAY-o-mai	Pithom	PAI-thahm	Sheba	SHEE-buh
Naphtali	NAF-tuh-lai	Pontius	PAHN-shus	Shebna	SHEB-nuh
Nathan	NAY-thuhn	Pontus	PAHN-tus	Shechem	SHEE-kehm
Nathanael	nuh-THAN-ay-ehl	Praetorium	pray-TAWR-ih-uhm	shekel	SHEHK-uhl
Nazarene	NAZ-awr-een	Priscilla	PRIHS-kill-uh	Shiloh	SHAI-lo
Nazareth	NAZ-uh-rehth	Prochorus	PRAH-kaw-ruhs	Shinar	SHAI-nahr
nazirite	NAZ-uh-rait	Psalm	Sahm	Shittim	sheh-TEEM
Nazorean	naz-aw-REE-uhn	Put	puht	Shuhite	SHOO-ait
Neapolis	nee-AP-o-lihs	Puteoli	pyoo-TEE-o-lai	Shunammite	SHOO-nam-ait
Nebuchadnezzar	neh-byoo-kuhd-NEHZ-er	Qoheleth	ko-HEHL-ehth	Shunem	SHOO-nehm
		qorban	KAWR-bahn	Sidon	SAI-duhn
Negeb	NEH-gehb	Quartus	KWAR-tuhs	Silas	SAI-luhs
Nehemiah	nee-hee-MAI-uh	Quirinius	kwai-RIHN-ih-uhs	Siloam	sih-LO-uhm
Ner	ner	Raamses	ray-AM-seez	Silvanus	sihl-VAY-nuhs
Nicanor	nai-KAY-nawr	Rabbi	RAB-ai	Simeon	SIHM-ee-uhn
Nicodemus	nih-ko-DEE-muhs	Rabbouni	ra-BO-nai	Simon	SAI-muhn
Niger	NAI-dzher	Rahab	RAY-hab	Sin *(desert)*	sihn
Nineveh	NIHN-eh-veh	Ram	ram	Sinai	SAI-nai
Noah	NO-uh	Ramah	RAY-muh	Sirach	SAI-rak
Nun	nuhn	Ramathaim	ray-muh-THAY-ihm	Sodom	SAH-duhm
Obed	O-behd	Raqa	RA-kuh	Solomon	SAH-lo-muhn
Olivet	AH-lih-veht	Rebekah	ree-BEHK-uh	Sosthenes	SAHS-thee-neez
Omega	o-MEE-guh	Rehoboam	ree-ho-BO-am	Stachys	STAY-kihs
Onesimus	o-NEH-sih-muhs	Rephidim	REHF-ih-dihm	Succoth	SUHK-ahth
Ophir	O-fer	Reuben	ROO-b'n	Sychar	SI-kar
Orpah	AWR-puh	Revelation	reh-veh-LAY-shuhn	Syene	sai-EE-nee
Pamphylia	pam-FIHL-ih-uh	Rhegium	REE-dzhee-uhm	Symeon	SIHM-ee-uhn
Paphos	PAY-fuhs	Rufus	ROO-fuhs	synagogues	SIHN-uh-gahgz